Map-making, Landscapes and Memory

CRITICAL CONDITIONS: FIELD DAY ESSAYS AND MONOGRAPHS

Edited by Seamus Deane

Critical Conditions: Field Day Monographs

Map-making, Landscapes and Memory

A Geography of Colonial and Early Modern Ireland c.1530–1750

William J. Smyth

CORK UNIVERSITY PRESS
in association with
FIELD DAY

First published in 2006 by
Cork University Press
Youngline Industrial Estate
Pouladuff Road, Togher
Cork
Ireland

Reprinted 2006

© William J. Smyth 2006

British Library Cataloguing in Publication Data
A CIP catalogue record for this book is available
from the British Library

ISBN 1–85918–397–2
978–1–85918–397–7
Typeset by Tower Books, Ballincollig, Co. Cork
Printed by Inspire Design and Print, Skibbereen, Co. Cork

www.corkuniversitypress.com

CONTENTS

ILLUSTRATIONS

Acknowledgements

My thanks to University College Cork and presidents Michael P. Mortell and Gerard W. Wrixon for their support for this project. In particular, my thanks to Professor Wrixon for granting me a year's research leave in 2002–3 to commence the writing up of this material. The dean of the Faculty of Arts, Professor David Cox, has also been most generous in providing financial support from the Arts Faculty Fund, as has the National University of Ireland via its Publication Fund.

I would like to thank all the members of the Department of Geography, UCC for their support. I especially wish to thank Patrick O'Flanagan who took over from me as head in April 2002 and has since led the department with skill and energy. My special thanks to Denis Linehan for his suggestions regarding some key readings and the ongoing intellectual stimulus; likewise that of Darius Bartlett, Barry Brunt, Robert Devoy, Jim McLaughlin, Ray O'Connor and John Tyrrell, who all provided useful insights along the journey. To John Crowley, my particular appreciation for his meticulous work in abstracting and locating a specific list of activities from the 1641 Depositions. My heartfelt thanks, too, to my former research assistant Millie Glennon for her careful work on both the 1641 Depositions and the '1659 Census'; and to Maeve Bent for her assistance with the '1659 Census'. My thanks also to Charlie Roche for digitising the civil parish map.

Three colleagues have been central to the realization of this project. One of my greatest debts is to departmental cartographer Michael Murphy, who with great patience and skill drew all my maps in this volume and at a time when he was under great pressure on other departmental publishing fronts. Likewise, I am eternally indebted to Orla O'Sullivan, who translated my script into typewritten form and processed draft after draft with such ability and good humour. My third major debt is to departmental operative Brendan Dockery. Brendan not only xeroxed many relevant materials and facilitated so many interlibrary loans but towards the end acted as my virtual research assistant on a whole series of missions.

My thanks to all the secretarial staff in the department – Sheila Hyde, Noreen McDowell and Suzanne O'Sullivan – for all their ongoing help and GIS Officer Helen Bradley for her computer expertise. Particular thanks to Rose Walsh for her assistance on so many fronts. And to Joan Walsh for all her hospitality.

Former graduate students provided much stimulus and support. My very particular thanks to Pat Nugent and David Butler for the many challenging discussions and for particular works of assistance. Special thanks too to Liam Coakley, who helped in many ways, most especially in the drafting of Figs. 3.2, 3.15, 11.1 and 11.6. Almar Barry, Michael Costelloe, Elaine Cullinane, Kathleen Curtin, John Keane, Mary Kelly, Catherine Ketch, Jean Lucy, Joanne McCarthy, Mark McCarthy, Ade Mulligan, David Nally and John O'Shea all provided further inspiration.

Colleagues in other departments at UCC have also been especially helpful. Both Neil Buttimer and Brendán Ó Conchúir have had to put up with my numerous queries about Irish poetry and related matters. Both were most generous in their assistance, as were John Carey and Seán Ó Duinnsléibhe. Members of the History Department were equally helpful, most particularly that doyen of the sixteenth century, Kenneth Nicholls; Andy Bielenberg, David Edwards, Hiram Morgan and Alf O'Brien were also obliging, as was Joe Ruane (Social Theory and Institutions), Gearóid Ó Crualaioch (Folklore) and Patricia Coughlan (English).

On the wider academic front, my greatest debt is to my own research supervisor and mentor, Tom Jones Hughes at University College Dublin. He inspired my interest in the historical and social geography of Ireland and has remained a very good friend to this day. John Andrews at Trinity College Dublin and the late Estyn Evans at Queen's University Belfast also provided much inspiration and insight, as has economic (and cultural) historian Louis Cullen. At Syracuse University both Don Meinig and the late David Sopher offered many new insights and perspectives, each in their own particular way. The late Pierre Flatrès (Lille and Paris IV) also provided me with different ways of researching and seeing things. Robin Butlin (Loughborough and Leeds), Jimmy Caird (Glasgow and Dundee) and Bob Dodgshon (Aberyswyth) have been both good friends and mentors over the years.

Other academics who assisted the project at various points include, most particularly, Nicholas Canny, Paddy Duffy and Anngret Simms, as well as Fred Aalen, Terry Barry, Jonathan Bell, Ciaran Brady, Ronnie Buchanan, Jack Burtchaell, Anne Buttimer, Harold Carter, Trevor Cartleton, Sam Clark, Paul Claval, Bill Crawford, Patrick Crotty, David Dickson, David Doyle, Raymond Gillespie, Philip Gulliver, Arnold Horner, Stephen Jackson, Gerry Kearns, Fergus Kelly, Ullrich Kockel, David Livingstone, John Mannion, Bill McAffee, Des McCourt, Thomas McErlean, Máiréad NicCraith, Tony Parker, Richard Preston, Denis Pringle, Philip Robinson, Liam Ryan, Marilyn Silverman, Matthew Stout, Fran Walsh and Kevin Whelan.

Librarians and archivists have equally been most helpful. My thanks to John Fitzgerald, Librarian at UCC, and his staff for all their help and, most particularly, Helen Davis, Peadar Cranitch and Anne Cronin (and remembering Pat Connolly) in the Q-1 Archives section. My thanks also to Mary Clapinson (Bodleian Library), Sheila Edwards (the Royal Society), Kate Fielden (Bowood House), Frances Harris (British Library), Gerry Lyne (National Library of Ireland), Muriel McCarthy (Marsh's Library), Trevor Parkhill (Public Record Office of Northern Ireland) and Stuart Ó Seanóir (Trinity College).

Likewise, Emma Buttlerfield (National Portrait Gallery, London), Paul Ferguson (Trinity College Map Library), Elizabeth Kirwan (National Library of Ireland), Paul Johnson (Public Record Office, London), Brian Thynne (National Maritime

Museum, Greenwich) and Thomás Tyner (UCC) have been most helpful about reproductions.

I asked a number of people to read some of the early chapters of the book. I am most grateful to Paddy Corish, Brian Graham, Máirín Ní Dhonnchada and Willie Nolan for patiently wading through these penultimate drafts, for their helpful comments, and for suggested additional readings. All sins of inclusion and/or omission remain mine alone.

It was Sara Wilbourne, then at the Cork University Press, who encouraged and commissioned me to write this book. In its initial stages she could not have been more supportive. Critical Conditions series editor Seamus Deane has at all stages provided strong critical support. The current staff at Cork University Press could not be more helpful. Managing editor Tom Dunne has been a discerning guide and Caroline Somers, Mike Collins, Mary White-Fitzpatrick and Colette Darcy have all done sterling work in the production of this book. Hilary Bell was a wonderful copy editor and a pleasure to work with. My thanks also to Pat Deasy of Tower Books. I also wish to thank the two Cork UP Readers for their careful assessment of the book in draft form. I trust that their critical suggestions have been adequately addressed.

I thank Karin Smyth for her help and support over many years. I also wish to thank Mary and Éamon Ó Carragáin, Hilary O'Kelly and William Gallagher, Daphne Pochin-Mould, Nuala Fenton and Michael and Marion Burke.

My thanks to all the Smyths for their support: to Mick, Mary and all the family in Donnybrook for their hospitality; to my sisters Breeda and Kathleen and families in Kilsheelan and Clonmel; and, most particularly, to my sister Grace, John and Billy Kennedy for their welcome at Loran Park and for the loan of the Lodge where some parts of the book were written.

Thanks to Lucy Trench and Robert Collingwood (and Elizabeth and Patrick) for their hospitality and generosity while I was researching in London; and to Ro and Shay Deering in Terenure and the Ryans of Ranelagh and Rathdowney for providing other havens for writing, research and reflection.

Thanks to Cormac, Peigín and Neil for commenting on some parts of the text, for enduring the long years of my ráiméising on the subject and above all for their love and support. Likewise, thanks to Tom O'Byrne for his enduring interest.

It is doubtful if this book would have been completed but for the wholehearted support of Vera Ryan and Brendan O'Mahony. They critiqued chapter after chapter and debated many issues. In addition to editorial insights, Vera provided invaluable and irreverent advice, as well as much affection and care. Apart from providing moral support, Brendan used his red pen to great effect in seeking to realign my wayward paragraphs and sentences. The dedication reflects my appreciation of that deep-felt support, as well as that of my three 'children'.

William J. Smyth
July 4, 2005

Cork University Press wish to thank the following for permission to reproduce maps or other images: 'The Board of Trinity College Library' for figures 2.11, 4.1, 4.5, 12.3(a), 12.3(b), and 12. 3(c); the British Library for Figures 2.2, 2.8 and 3.14; author Patrick J Duffy for figures 13.6(a) and 13.6(b); author John Reps for figures 12.4(a), 12.4(b) and 12.7; The National Portrait Gallery London for figure 5.1; The National Maritime Museum, Greenwich for figures 2.12, 2.14(a) and 2.14(b); The National Library Dublin for figures 2.16, 2.17 and 2.18; The National Gallery Dublin for figure 8.8; The Ordnance Survey Ireland for figures 10.3 and 10.7; The Public Record Office, London for figures 2.3, 2.6, 2.7, 2.10, 2.15, 2.19, 2.20, 3.4, 3.7 and 3.8; *Atlas of the Irish Rural Landscape* editors F.H.A. Aalen, Kevin Whelan and Matthew Stout with regard to figures 6.6, 6.7 and 10.11; the US Geological Survey and US Census for figure 12.1 and the owners of private collections for figure 12.8(a) and figure 12.8(b).

For permission to adapt maps and other illustrative material, Cork University Press wish to thank Oxford University Press with regard to figures 3.1, 3.5, 3.11, 3.13, 5.2, 10.2 and 12.7; J.H. Andrews for figure 2.9 and the same author and K.M Davies for permission to reproduce figure 12.7(b); McGill–Queens University Press for figures 4.2 and 4.3. Thanks to Michael Perceval-Maxwell for his assistance; and author Donald W. Meinig for his help with figures 2.4, 12.2, 12.5 and 12.6. Every effort has been made to trace the copyright holder of materials used herein. If there are any omissions Cork University Press will correct them in reprints and future editions of this book.

Earlier versions of chapters 6–10 and chapter 12 appeared in William J. Smyth and Kevin Whelan (eds.), *Common Ground: Essays on the Historical Geography of Ireland* (Cork: Cork University Press, 1998) pp. 55–83; F.H.A. Aalen and Kevin Whelan (eds.), *Dublin City and County: from Prehistory ot Present* (Dublin: Geography Publications, 1992), pp. 121-179; William Nolan and Kevin Whelan (eds.), *Kilkenny: History and Society* (Dublin: Geography Publications, 1990), pp. 127–160 and William Nolan and Thomas G. McGrath (eds.), *Tipperary: History and Society* (Dublin: Geography Publications, 1985), pp. 104–138; in Terry Barry (ed.), *A History of Settlement in Ireland* (London and New York: Routledge, 2000), pp. 158–186 and in *Irish Geography*, xi, 1978, pp. 1–22.

For Vera, Brendan, Cormac, Peigín and Neil

Introduction

They, like all creatures, being made
For the shovel and worm,
Ransacked their perishable minds and found
Pattern and form
And with their own hands quarried from hard words
A figure in which secret things confide.

                                   Eavan Boland[1]

The New English colonization of Ireland from the 1530s onwards may be seen as the equivalent of a major continental invasion that transformed the island from Malin Head to Rosslare and from Fair Head to Cape Clear.

Since the task of the historical geographer is to track, map and interpret patterns and processes of geographical change, a central concern of this study involves the geographical reconstruction of Ireland, its societies and regions before New English plantation and colonization, and a geographic exploration of the nature and varying effects of such intrusive processes on existing Irish societies and landscapes. Attempts to bring some order to questions of continuity and change in geographic patterns and processes are made by examining three interconnected levels – the material, social and ideological.

One can examine the radical transformation in the environments and material worlds of the peoples dwelling in Ireland as old ways of understanding and using such environments were eroded. How woodlands, wetlands and cultivated lands were transformed and used; how rural settlement patterns and urban hierarchies survived, were disrupted, reconstituted and expanded; how new fields and fences, roads and bridges, iron forges and industries impacted on landscapes and lifestyles; how parish churches were neglected, destroyed, rebuilt and relocated – all these questions are of concern. I seek to recognize the freshness and originality of many new urban and village creations, as well as understanding the dramatic transformations in the size, morphology, social complexities and functions of the key county towns and port-cities.

The changing social geography in early modern Ireland is a central concern. In particular, the reconstruction of patterns of landownership, occupation and use will be detailed so as to establish the levels of transformation that followed from a long series of plantations, as well as from wider economic, legal and political processes.

The consequences of geographic battles for continuity or change, between the old or the new and between conserving *vis-à-vis* innovative forces, need to be kept in focus. The impact of new settler ethnic groups on existing social geographies will be explored. The tensions, conflicts, disruptions and accommodations that arose along the geographic 'frontier' or 'contact zone' between different peoples and class groups as the competition for scarce resources and particularly the right to own, lease and work land will also be examined. All of this impinges on questions of individual and group identity, ethnicity and nationality. I seek to explore in this fluid, turbulent world how contrasting symbols and rituals of community identity are abstracted and perpetuated by competing national/ethnic groups. Middle-ground spaces, meeting-places, and actors – the 'brokers' of relationships across 'the frontier' – need to be kept in mind.

This brings us to the third related level – the ideological geographies – and how colonizer and colonized represented and justified their positions, actions and reactions, their different strategies for survival and the geographic consequences of particular forms of conquest, resistance or accommodation. Between 1540 and 1750 Irish places were being mapped and refigured by the new ruling landowning elites and their agents, by the governors, their military commanders, by the engineers, secretaries, map-makers and government officers. Their concepts of territory and 'proper' territorial organization are compared with Irish ways of remembering, narrating, understanding and using landscape and territory to define, defend and use their patrimonies.

An enduring concern is to try to get behind and beyond the more richly documented worlds of the ruling elites (old and new), to penetrate and excavate the whole society, so as to provide some glimpses of the forces, beliefs, experiences and events that shaped the lives and localities of the ordinary men and women who lived during this revolutionary and tumultuous era.

What follows provides both an overview of the structure and layout of the book and some rationale for the whole project.

The first chapter seeks to define the concepts of 'forging', 'colonial' and 'early modern', as applied in the Irish context. It also summaries the main methods of analysis. The remainder of the book comprises four sections: I 'Making the Documents of Conquest Speak'; II 'Regional Case-Studies'; III 'A World Turned Upside Down'; IV 'A Global Context'; followed by a concluding chapter.

The five chapters of section I include a study of the manuscript maps, either of regions within Ireland or of the island as a whole, dating from the 1520s to the early 1700s; the written records from some of the early plantations; and the complex of documented materials dealing with the Irish wars of 1641 to 1653, particularly the evidence emerging from the so-called 1641 Depositions and later Cromwellian 'examinations'.

The reconstruction of mid-seventeenth-century Ireland and especially the impact of the Cromwellian plantation and settlement depends heavily on the Civil Survey (1654–6) and the Down Survey (1654–9), on William Petty's recollections of the makings of the latter and on his brilliantly engineered '1659 Census', which is based on poll-tax returns. It is a pleasure to have such meticulous accounts available of the intimate territorial units and of local populations as they existed in the mid-seventeenth century – although we have to recognize how difficult and intractable is the interpretation of some of these materials. Here in section I, I carry out two strategies of investigation – first, I take these documents of conquest at face value to explain as fully as possible the construction of new Irelands as revealed in these sources. My second strategy is to subvert these documents – such as the great Cromwellian ledgerbooks and maps – to try to reveal the variety and richness of the Irish worlds that lie buried and hidden 'beneath' these texts.

I should stress that I am not writing a history of events. These five chapters are not arranged in a strictly linear/chronological order but are designed to address particular themes in a more interfoliated way. There is a concern to illustrate both the ongoing geographic battles for military and administrative control and the patterns of political, economic and social transformation. But equally, the stories, as told, oscillate over time to allow for my central concerns with unravelling particular ways of both understanding and narrating the nature and memory of Irish territories, places and peoples. A parallel concern is to reveal the reshaping of such Irish realities, as the settlers and the original inhabitants engaged with one another in a context of intrusion, conquest and colonization. The focus is on how and where the prior Irish inhabitants were displaced from both the resources and positions of power, as subsequent economic, political and cultural control is exercised over this population by the New English and Scottish and their descendants, acting both for themselves and in the interest of the metropolitan 'mother-country', England.

Having thus provided a series of insights into the geography of conquest, resistance and settlement, there follows in section II three regional case-studies (chapters 7, 8 and 9). These case-studies take us from the early anglicized county of Dublin and the Pale region generally, through to the hybrid, if feudalized, county of Kilkenny, and on to the Gaelic world of north Tipperary.

County Dublin is the focus of the first case-study (chapter 7). In Dublin we find both long-established city and county subcultures, which were exposed from the very beginning of this era to impulses, actions and actors coming directly from 'modernizing' England. How this Dublin/Pale region, and particularly its exceptionally well-documented local communities, mediated these deep-seated changes is the subject of this chapter.

The second regional case-study is of Co. Kilkenny (chapter 8) – the centre of the powerful Ormond Butler lordship, whose ruling family, for the most part, remained loyal to the English crown. This is emphatically an Old English-controlled world and its city the home of the capital of the Catholic Confederate government between 1642 and 1647. Its landscapes and societies reflect the depth and richness of an enduring, deeply feudalized, if hybrid cultural world. This chapter seeks to reconstruct in detail pre-Cromwellian Co. Kilkenny and then examines the levels of continuity and change that characterized this key Leinster county after the Cromwellian settlement.

I end with the Munster county of Tipperary, which occupies a critical central location in the historical geography of Ireland. Its northwestern baronies belonged to a Gaelic/gaelicized world, which compare closely with the adjacent county of Clare and parts of Connacht. An understanding of this Gaelic region links the reader with the emphasis placed in the first three chapters of section I on the reconstruction of the Gaelic regions of Ulster, the Midlands and parts of Leinster. Mid-Tipperary is a transitional zone between the Gaelic northwest and the more heavily feudalized Old English-dominated world of the southeast of the county. The Tipperary case-study thus provides insights into the landscapes, settlements and experiences of three different cultural regions in Ireland. If readers find the regional case-studies rather too specific or too detailed, they may prefer to move on directly to the following chapters.

Section III goes on to provide an overview of the processes and patterns of transformation across Ireland as a whole, from the mid-sixteenth century to the mid-eighteenth century. Chapter 10 examines the revolution in systems of territorial control, as the state, the cities, the county towns, the Anglican dioceses and parishes, as well as the landlord estate system, are remodelled in the image of the New English elite and reorganized to serve the needs of an expanding empire. In this difficult context, both the Catholic and Presbyterian Churches had to carve out new territories and build new chapels to serve their communities.

By way of contrast, chapter 11 explores the geographical transformations in modes of exchange, address and communication as an early capitalist economy is painfully and unevenly constructed across the island. In this wider process, place-names, family and personal names and indeed the whole symbolic universe of the Irish – best epitomized in Irish language and literature – are either reformed or eroded in the face of an expanding English economic, political and linguistic hegemony. The consequent hybridites that emerged in the interface between the two cultures are examined, while beneath the colonial superstructure, close-knit kinship networks and embryonic agrarian resistance movements are revealed.

The final section (chapter 12) opens the lenses further to provide a global context for Ireland's experiences. It examines the similarities and differences in the processes and patterns of colonization in early colonial Ireland and America. This chapter demonstrates the growing integration of Ireland into a wider Atlantic culture and economy, which saw massive emigration to, firstly, colonial America and then more particularly to the burgeoning United States. It concludes by comparing the mature colonial societies and landscapes of the two countries by the end of the eighteenth century. As with most comparisons, it is the differences that turn out to be most significant. Seventeenth- and eighteenth-century Ireland's strange position and status in the Atlantic is confirmed: a country that is deeply European is subject to one form of European imperialism and becomes a conquered 'colonial' society, yet also becomes an active participant in the expansion of an Anglo-American English-speaking world.

The Conclusion summarizes the major findings of the work. It compares the Ireland of the 1530s with that of the 1770s. In particular, the revolutionary transformations, the evolutionary changes, and the deep-seated continuities that characterized its cultures and systems of territorial organization are examined from a geographer's perspective.

A study of the historical geography of 'colonial'/'early modern' Ireland reveals a revolutionary transformation in the nature of Irish societies and landscapes from the mid-sixteenth century onwards. That transformation resulted from a violent collision between the peoples of these islands. This work endeavours to explore the geographical dimensions and consequences of these encounters. Ongoing research across a range of disciplines is providing new insights and vistas into and under-standings of Ireland's complex and contested heritage. Geography, as a discipline, has its part to play in broadening that vista and enlarging that understanding.[2]

A word on the making of the maps and their relationship to the writing of the narrative. The making of maps involves abstracting, reducing, simplifying and representing aspects of a complex reality into an accessible, visual format. I have interpreted the mainly manuscript maps produced during the sixteenth and seven-teenth centuries as representing part of the New English administrations' way of visualizing, knowing and ruling Ireland. The maps that I have drawn myself are very different. Here I am both map-maker and interpreter. These maps are, for the most part, based on an immersion in, and labour-intensive analysis of, the rich corpus of documents produced between the late sixteenth century and the mid-eighteenth century by the New English administrations, documents which itemize in great geographical detail conditions on the ground in Ireland. Nevertheless, the specific selection, particular forms of representation and interpretation of these maps are my responsibility. As is the case with narrative accounts, other geog-raphers or historians might have – would have – made different selections and used different modes of representation and interpretation. In short, this book represents the work of one geographer engaged with, and seeking further understanding of, an island world in which he was born and now lives. I wish the reader – hopefully fortified with plenty of stamina – a fruitful journey through these pages.

1

Marking Out the
Terrain

We marked the pitch: four jackets for four goalposts,
That was all. The corners and the squares
Were there like longitude and latitude
Under the bumpy thistly ground, to be
Agreed about or disagreed about
When the time came.
And then we picked the teams
And crossed the line our called names drew between us.

Seamus Heaney[1]

This is one story of the conquest and transformation of Ireland in the early modern era (1530–1750) as understood by a historical geographer. In one sense, the telling of this story represents a continuation of the *Lebar Gabála Érenn* – The Book of the Taking of Ireland,[2] which tells the story of the colonization of Ireland from its early mythic beginnings to the arrival, conquest and settlement of the *Gaedhil*. Seathrún Céitinn (Geoffrey Keating), who wrote *Foras Feasa ar Éirinn* (The History of Ireland),[3] carries the story of Ireland's conquests to the Norman invasion and Norman rule.[4] The central concern of this book is to carry out a geographical analysis of the conquest and settlement of Ireland by the New English (and Scottish) from the 1530s onwards and the consequences of this often violent and deep-seated intrusion on the lives, properties, settlements and landscapes of pre-existing Irish societies.

The functions of this chapter are, first, to provide some explanation for the concepts of 'forging', 'colonial' and 'early modern', and second, to explore ways in which the historical and cultural geographer approaches and interprets his/her source materials.

The Forging of Ireland

Ireland is a very old land. Its civilizations were deeply rooted long before the sixteenth century. The forging of the physical geography of Ireland is a story that involves millions of years of earth formation, mountain-building, the evolution of extensive sedimentary limestone plains, the later gouging and shaping of the land by great glaciers with their extensive boulder-clay, morainic and drumlin deposits;

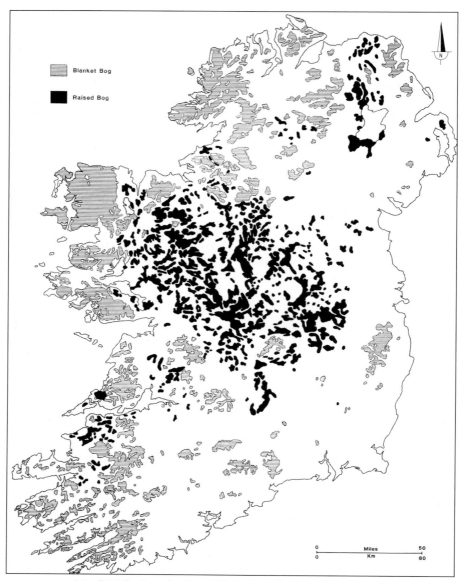

1.1   Distribution of upland (blanket) and lowland (raised) bogs

and the subsequent colonization of the island by a rich variety of trees and shrubs, headed by the oak and ash.[5] Great potential for the development of both grass-lands and oats cultivation characterized Ireland. However, its Atlantic climate placed the island on the margins of successful wheat production so central to the manorial village cultures of southern England and northern France.[6] Cattle and cows were far more central to Ireland's economy, settlement patterns and mytholo-gies. The seemingly eternal rain also meant the extensive development of both upland and lowland bogs (see Fig. 1.1) and, where good drainage systems were absent, the evolution of significant expanses of difficult, wet gley soils.

Ireland has a very complicated interweaving of upland and lowland zones, which facilitated the evolution and crystallization of many highly self-conscious local and regional subcultures.[7] Comprising 32,000 square miles (c. 83,000 square kilometres), Ireland is an island of impressive size, difficult to conquer, even more difficult to hold. In understanding Ireland, therefore, we need to recognize the stubborn realities of its island nature, its particular size, varied topography and ecology and the deep prehistoric bases for its cultural formations.

The minute naming of Ireland's landscape features, its settlements and peoples, and indeed the forging of many and meaningful stories about these landscape features and their numerous placenames, is a function of a long-running narrative, fabricated, transformed, told and retold by the generations of dwellers-cum-story-tellers who have occupied this island over the millennia. Both the *Lebar Gabála* and the *Dindshenchas* (The Book of Placelore)[8] construct their own theories of the *human* creation of Ireland's mountains, rivers, lakes and plains, which bear little resemblance to the interpretations of the modern 'scientific' physical geographer.[9] These stories of Irish places and peoples were deeply embedded in the world view of the Irish before the New English conquest and colonization. The ideology and, indeed, central values of the culture were wrapped up in the landscape – its occupation, its use, its names, stories and legends.[10] Likewise, long-established traditions in family naming patterns – both of first names and surnames – were incorporated into the rich genealogical histories of the different lordships, localities and parishes of the island,[11] which knitted landscapes (including vegetation and animals), peoples and stories into a complex web that enveloped most of the island, say, by 1500.

The historical geographer's concerns with the forging of Ireland after 1530 must acknowledge these given realities of both enduring regional landscape types and resource-bases, as well as the complex, varied and often highly successful solutions reached by earlier dwellers to the business of colonizing, settling and cultivating this diverse island. The Irish land mass has a very uneven and indented coastline that stretches to close on 7,500 kilometres. Its surviving four provinces speak to very different regional histories and linkages with outside worlds, stretching from Norway and the Orkneys in the north to Galicia and Portugal in the south, as well as embracing the peninsulas, bays and inner seas that stretch from Bordeaux and the Irish Sea, Celtic Sea and North Sea on to the Baltic.[12] In the early modern era, two different and conflicting continental European worlds – a Protestant north and a Catholic south[13] – clashed in this far western island, fracturing it, and contributing to wars of conquest and resistance that lasted, with intermittent breaks, from the 1530s to the 1690s.

The forging of Ireland in the early modern era involves a number of meanings and considerations. 'Forging' means the use of fire, iron, timber, water, wind and muscle-power in the transformation of Ireland's material culture and landscapes. A central theme here is the radical transformation of Ireland's physical and biotic environments – via ploughshares and spades, axes and swords – consequent on New English colonization and the imposition of a new economic system that we now recognize as early capitalist in form. For example, the numerous iron forges developed by the New English, which spread across the Irish landscape between 1580 and 1760, played a key role in the denudation of an island that – with the exception of the Pale and a few other lowland regions – was characterized by extensive strands of woodland.[14] The material culture and landscape was also dramatically transformed by the erection of new fortresses, towns, villages, and eventually great mansion houses, enclosures and gardens in countryside and city.

This forging of the material world entailed a series of social changes – in forms and rhythms of work, in levels and networks of economic exploitation, in exposure to monetary and market forces, in learning New English words and technical skills. In short, in modes of living as a whole. Many of the formerly relatively self-sufficient communities and localities were drawn into a market and urban orbit, if only to find ways of paying the new rents to a mainly intrusive landlord class.[15] These local circuits were connected by a series of strands and webs to the metropolitan cores in both Dublin and London – the two great gainers in the transfer of surpluses from both the Irish countryside and the towns.

This forging involved the deformation of many older regional societies. The cumulative consequences of the continued intensification of the English/British conquest, plantation and colonization was the stripping of regional lordships of many key institutions and leadership positions. Irish systems of landownership and occupation were itemized, ridiculed and eroded; the old landowning elites were often displaced and the ideological and literate defenders of Irish ways of living – the poets, the brehons, the genealogists and the keepers of the *seanchas* – saw their ancient and highly esteemed functions marginalized; they were either made redundant or were assimilated to the new economic and political order.

The landscape itself bore witness to this devastation. Lordship capitals were often turned into new county towns, while the old prestigious inauguration sites of the regional lords were deserted and/or destroyed. The ruins of so many abbeys, convents and monasteries, or their conversion into refurbished colonial fortresses and mansions, spoke to the cumulative impact of the Henrician dissolution and the continued persecution of Catholicism, whose priests often came to assume a heroic role in the battle to sustain religious and cultural continuities. According as every ancient ecclesiastical site and indeed the whole territorial and resource capacity of the late medieval parish and diocesan system were put in the hands of an intrusive if legally established Reformation Church, many old churches fell into ruin during the sixteenth and seventeenth centuries and very few new churches were built.[16] The other bulwarks of village life and culture – the tower-houses – were often left in ruins, reflecting the breaking up of both local communities and the power of the old landowning elites. Settlement patterns were therefore often radically changed, according as many old villages, parish centres, and hamlets were left either deserted or shrunken in form – contrasting sharply with the freshness and vitality of the many new plantation and estate villages and towns that sprang up across 'colonial' Ireland. Louis Cullen paints the picture:

> When the slanting sunlight of evening falls on the countryside, it frequently reveals
> a haunting profusion of overlapping layers of indigenous and external settlement
> imposed within a handful of generations. . . . Differences in the landscape parallel
> differences in thought and behaviour.[17]

The notion of forging also involves the creation of new local, regional and
national societies. The breaking of the power of the old autonomous lordships –
it is said that there were ninety of these across the island c.1530[18] – saw the slow
but certain construction of a centralized, island-wide state system centred on
Dublin and the putting in place of a new island-wide ruling elite. Parallel to these
processes, a single economic system was gradually and literally put in place,
road networks were enhanced, more fairs and markets established, and older
modes of production were either assimilated or destroyed. Resistance to such
centralizing political and economic controls gave rise to a wide variety of military alliances, accommodations, coalitions and oppositions; but the eventual
outcome was the emergence of a single monolithic social system we now call
landlordism.[19]

The New English conquest of Ireland is a story, on the one hand, of the violent
breaking down of the power of those regional lordships that ultimately set their
faces against and actively opposed the centralizing drive of the absolutist English
state to establish full military and political control over all the island. The Kildare
Fitzgeralds, most of the Gaelic lordships of Leinster and elsewhere, the Desmond
lordship in Munster, that of the O'Neills and O'Donnells of Ulster and of the
Burkes and O'Connors of north Connacht all felt at various times the iron glove of
expanding English military power, as did a whole variety of lesser Gaelic, gaelicized and Old English (or 'English-Irish') magnates and their territories. The end
result of their opposition was almost invariably formal state plantations, the two
greatest being established in Munster and Ulster, thus leading to the creation of
two new regional colonial societies in the heart of both these provinces.[20]

On the other hand, those lordships which accommodated themselves more
adroitly to the changed political circumstances – such as the extensive territories
of the Butler Ormonds centred on counties Tipperary and Kilkenny, and of the
'Lords of the Pale' (northeast Leinster), the lordships of the Clanricard Burkes in
east Galway, of the Thomond O'Briens of Clare, the Barry lordships in south Cork
and of lesser lordships such as that of the Fitzpatricks of Upper Ossory (Queen's
County)[21] – saw the evolution of rather different regional societies. The assimilation of these regional powers, at least at the elite levels, to the norms and goals of
the imperial power meant that these societies were shielded for perhaps a century
from the excesses of conquest (until Cromwell's), and were, therefore, better able
to negotiate and moderate the cumulative forces of change. The longer-term social
and cultural geographies of the latter regions reveal greater continuities, stabilities
and flexibilities.

The notion of forging also involves the construction of new stories of the land,
its territories and peoples. Here the battle for hegemony was long, hard, deep and,
it seems, never-ending. A key instrument of forging in this context is the pen. The
conqueror always validates the conquest by writing, telling and repeating his

story, thereby justifying the modes and consequences of conquest. One of the central concerns of this book is to elucidate the New English construction, by a wide variety of modes of representations, of a discourse that validated its conquest of and hegemony in Ireland, a construction that would provide a useful prototype for legitimizing British imperial drives elsewhere.

In Ireland, the construction of this colonial discourse involved a cumulative interweaving of a variety of texts and related geographical practices. The texts include maps, books, pamphlets, government edicts, travellers' descriptions, advertisements, commentaries and letters. Justified by borrowings from the large stream of Renaissance writing and thought, English colonial theory built upon medieval writings, most notably the *Topographica Hibernica* and the *Expugnatio Hibernica* by Giraldus Cambrensis (Gerald of Wales), which were the foundational texts for Elizabethan 'colonial' commentaries. However, the thematics of space in *Topographica* are based around a centre-periphery opposition within Europe. In the centre of the feudalized realms of twelfth-century Europe, the concept of core and periphery was a reality in the minds of people who saw themselves as heirs to the civilization of Latin Christendom.[22] In these core European cultures this consciousness of superiority was one of the driving forces of medieval colonization. The Anglo-Norman colonization of Ireland can be located in this wider European framework – Ireland at the western edge shares similar colonial experiences to those of the Slavic peoples at the eastern periphery of the medieval core area of Europe. But the development of New English colonial theories from the second half of the sixteenth century onwards now also embraced the globalizing concepts of 'modernity' and 'backwardness'.

The forging of this colonial world view pivoted around a binary opposition between 'civility' and 'barbarity'. Its subordinate polar oppositions included: humanity versus brutality; knowledge versus ignorance; reason versus unreason; health versus disease; sexual correctness versus sexual transgression; urban versus rural; arable versus pastoral; industry versus indolence; the lawful versus the illicit; the agency of God's will versus the locus of his displeasure; order versus disorder; and the most geographical of these oppositional categories – form versus formlessness.[23] 'Civility' and all its attributes of superior knowledge, order and form is represented by the New English colonizer: the 'othered' Irish are constructed as the inversion of the colonist and all his values – inferior, savage/barbaric, ignorant, nomadically pastoral, careless of a land flowing with milk and honey, agents of a disordered and formless Irish landscape in need of reformation and renewal.

The dream of forging a new beginning is a recurring feature of the artist's endeavour; and never more so than in the life and work of an artist-colonist like Edmund Spenser. We cannot easily imagine of Ireland in the sixteenth and seventeenth centuries as an 'empty space'. Yet when we examine English colonial discourse, ideology and fantasy, we note that Ireland could become emptied space, emptied of its people – conceived of as a *tabula rasa*, or, as Petty called it, 'a white paper', ready for new printing, or in Spenser's famous phrase, made ready for 'a new framing as it were a forge'.[24]

At the time of Spenser's writing *A View of the State of Ireland* (1596–7), Irish culture was in reality fractured and factional. First, there was a growing number of New English colonists, administrators, soldiers, and churchmen; an embryonic Protestant planter class, speaking, writing and printing in the Queen's 'New English', shaped by such new sciences as cartography and the 'tough' sensibilities of Renaissance England and thoroughly convinced of England's right to rule Ireland and civilize the Irish. Second, there were the old 'colonials' of the Pale and port-regions – the descendants of the Anglo-Normans, ancient enemies and shielders of the medieval frontier against the Gaelic Irish. They were headed by the powerful feudal magnates, speaking an older form of English and usually bilingual, potentially Protestant but increasingly alienated as they were pushed out of positions of power in law and government and actively became powerful patrons of Counter-Reformation Catholicism. But not all of this group diverged; some conformed to the New English Protestant model – none more significantly than the Butler earls of Ormond. Third, further away from the Dublin Pale and the old port-cities, and now culturally part of a mainly Irish-speaking Catholic world, was a gaelicized, hybrid 'middle nation' of lordships, inland towns, tower-houses and the ancient field game of hurling – in varying states of allegiance or disobedience to the Dublin administration and the crown. Fourth, over the southwest, the northwest and the north was a still resurgent Gaelic culture, Irish-speaking and characterized by a more traditional Franciscan-led Catholicism, while also using Latin as an elite language; clan-based societies with their own lordships, old elaborate laws, systems of territorial organization, costumes, and settlement structures. Fifth, infiltrating into the northeast and feared by the New English ruling class (including Spenser) were frontier Scottish settlers – both from the Highlands and islands as well as the adjacent western coastal lowlands. (With the accession of James I to the English throne, Reformation Scotland became a major player in Ireland, the Ulster plantation follows, as King James blunts the longstanding political and cultural alliances between Gaelic Scotland and Gaelic Ireland.)

Ireland's cultural geography was, therefore, plural. But its political geography was increasingly represented and simplified as a battle for hegemony between an expansive English national culture, and a defensive but resistant Gaelic/Irish world, seeking its own legislative and cultural autonomy. Caught in the middle were the Old English – neither 'metropolitan' nor 'marginalized other'. By the late 1500s, they were becoming surplus to the needs of the expanding English state. This was certainly Spenser's view.

Spenser was a beneficiary of the Munster plantation in 1586–7. This followed on from the putting down of the Desmond rising/rebellion with a ferocity by the state and its military officers never seen before. A scorched-earth policy – a policy of deliberate starvation of the Irish-cum-Old English enemy – was implemented. The consequence was severe depopulation in the heartland of Munster – the emptying of the land for plantation and civilizing.[25] The new colonial policy was now justified, since the lands in question lay 'vacant'. Its former inhabitants were 'not thrifty, civil and human creatures but heathen or rather savage and brute beasts'.[26] People, if defined as subhuman, are thus made invisible in the land-scape.

We may stay with the paradigmatic figure of Edmund Spenser a little longer to elucidate the central idea that the forging of a colonial ideology hinges on a congruence 'between levels of practice and of legitimising narrative'.[27] Spenser in Ireland is a classic borderland figure – an exile and homemaker. Always anxious about defending his Englishness on the margins and very much on edge, he appro-priates a Desmond castle at Kilcolman for his new planter-mansion and estate, which he prophetically called Hap Hazard.[28] (He was burnt out of his house in the rising/rebellion of 1598 and died in London in 1599 'for lack of bread'.[29]) Cambridge-educated, a widely read, classical scholar, this poet is aware of the qualities and craft of the now outlawed Irish bard-poets and familiar with the Munster landscape of mountains, rivers and streams.[30] In Spenser, who wrote part of the *Faerie Queene* at Hap Hazard, we see a love-hate relationship with Ireland – loving the land and fearing hibernicization, seeking to maintain a purified Englishness on the insidious yet seductive Irish frontier. He is already convinced of the 'moral imperative' of uprooting and, if necessary, eradicating the 'wild Irish' and their culture from this 'sweet good land'.[31] Spenser was convinced that the corollary of maintaining a strong English identity in Ireland was the oblitera-tion of Irish identity. And Spenser perceived the Old English as providing a fatal bridge to hibernicization – they were far too prone to assimilation to the 'mere Irish' – so they too were constituted as 'the enemy'.

At the end of the first section of *A View of the State of Ireland*,[32] court-based Eudoxus is finally convinced by Irenius, the English colonist in Ireland, that only ruthless violence – that is, the exercise of the sword – will effect change in Ireland. The imposition of English law has not and will not work on its own. To quote Andrew Hadfield and Willy Maley: 'the case is that in order to protect civilized values from the attacks of horrible savages, savage methods will have to be used'.[33] These methods were seen by Spenser to be successful in putting down the Munster rising/rebellion in the early 1580s, and are now recommended in the middle of the Nine Years War of the 1590s to be applied to both Ulster and rebel-lious Ireland as a whole. In the *View*, he thus sets the scene and lays down the strategic parameters for the intensification of the battle for hegemony between the English and Irish forces.

In this context it is worth noting that Spenser's *View* was sent to be printed in 1598 but was not published for another thirty-five years. Nevertheless, it circulated widely at an elite level in manuscript form, read by, amongst others, the secretary to Lord Mountjoy, travel-writer Fynes Moryson, poet and legal imperialist, Sir John Davies, and later by the poet and Cromwellian intellectual John Milton. It is uncanny how so many of the key recommendations of this 'dreamy conservative', as outlined in the *View*, were brought into effect over the following fifty years. Spenser recommended the location of key new garrisons to encircle O'Neill's Ulster and the carrying-on of military campaigns against the Irish and their food supply in winter, so as to more quickly starve them out. Mountjoy successfully implemented these strategies. The planting of many Protestant borough towns, the importance attached to establishing civil settlements for disbanded soldiers, down to the use of widespread land confiscations and the break-up of Irish clans, were also part of Spenser's agenda.

Between the 1580s and 1650s much of the natural and institutional resources of Ireland had been taken over by a new elite and its supporting classes. Ireland had been newly framed in the forge or, should one say, the furnace of Cromwellian conquest.

'Colonialism' and Ireland

Thus, uniquely in western Europe, Ireland becomes a colonized rather than a colonizing/imperial country. This is not to deny that some Irish at home and most Irish emigrating abroad participated in, and benefited from, the expansion of the British Empire, and indeed other imperial worlds. But this latter participation should not be advanced to simply obscure the long-drawn-out wars for supremacy between the Irish peoples and the New English officials and colonizers, the particular colonial structures imposed on the island of Ireland and the consequential and often shameful exploitation of the declassed Irish who stayed at home.

'Colonialism' is defined as a process that involves the intrusion into and conquest of an inhabited territory by representatives of an external power,[34] or as geographer Donald Meinig notes, 'the aggressive encroachment of one people upon the territory of another, resulting in the subjugation of the latter people to alien rule'.[35] It is the exercise of ultimate political authority by the invader over the invaded.[36] Such subordination, in order to be sustained, requires the putting in place of a hierarchy of colonial agents and agencies, headed by a governor – in Ireland by the lord lieutenant or viceroy – who are supported by the coercive power of the military and local settler militias, as extensions of the central instruments of the imperial/colonial state. One of my concerns is to explore and interpret, as a geographer, the cumulative expansion and positioning of such agents at strategic points within the island so as to acquire and maintain full territorial and political control.

The exercise of colonial political authority necessitates direct contact between the agents of the colony and the representatives of the subjected population.[37] Given the inequality of political power relationships, such interaction imposes an inequality in social relationships in order to create both a new social and psychological stratification. Hence, the representatives of the conqueror assume a dominant position and come to constitute a new ethnic aristocracy – in Ireland this became known as the Anglo-Irish or Protestant Ascendancy.[38] Sustained colonialism – such as was the case in Ireland – inevitably leads to a widening of the forms of contact between the two peoples and the creation of new kinds of intermediaries, social relations, and hierarchies involving such people as servants, lawyers, teachers, priests, parsons, middlemen, midwives, cattle dealers, prostitutes and 'going' women, moneylenders and bankers, merchants and shopkeepers, carmen, artisans, stewards, tenants, estate officials and millers. At the territorial level, even though we know the segregation of residential quarters became the norm in most colonial towns – whence the emergence of so many 'Irishtowns'[39] – clearly one of the great meeting-places was the main street and the market square, the nexus of so many transactions and interactions. All of this concern requires an elucidation of how new social geographies were created, with bi- or tri-cultural localities often emerging,[40] separate residential zones constructed, and a sustained separation in the social geography or social/gossiping fields of the two groups. I will seek to explore the geography of such contacts, interactions and divisions within colonial Ireland.

Significant cultural change between the colonial and colonized groups is an inevitable outcome of such sustained contacts between the two populations; and it is invariably assymetrical. The resulting processes of acculturation are selective in content, uneven in their geographic spread and penetration and inevitably imbalanced in their effects on the two peoples.[41] The greatest pressure for change in culture is on the colonized peoples. The imperial powers can apply explicit cultural pressures towards conformity in certain key institutions. These include the colonial Churches. In the Irish context, successive Tudor and Stuart administrations sought to enforce conformity to the Anglican Church amongst the majority population.[42] Likewise, the county administrations and the law courts became pivotal instruments in the application and expansion of the English common law. Schools may have been less effective instruments of acculturation in Ireland, particularly as the cumulative effects of legal restrictions culminating in the infamous penal laws denied the majority population formal access to schooling.[43] The 'underground' Catholic 'hedge schools' can therefore be seen as sites of both acculturation and resistance.[44]

Most cultural exchanges arise from the mundane routines of everyday life. The geographer seeks to elucidate which are the points or sites of most intensive cultural interaction; how such cultural change expands geographically and which classes are most susceptible to assimilation in such a bi-cultural society. In this context, the study of the geography of language contact and change can be explored, as can an unevenness in the acceptance of new forms of naming and address, in levels of intermarriage, as well as a whole complex of subtle steps from traditional to new activities and modes of behaviour.[45] The emergence of hybrid musical and dance forms may be critical diagnostic features here. The geographer needs to explore the distribution of such elements that are indicative of either imperial pressure and impact or hybrid constructions and behaviours at the interface between the two communities.

Imperial/colonial expansion is fundamentally predatory. The agents of the imperial power will endeavour to extract as much wealth and gain as they can from the conquered territory and peoples, creating new economic relationships and impositions. The most obvious change is in the form of direct taxation. In the Irish context, the imposition of subsidies, cesses and, particularly, poll-taxes and hearth-taxes provides us with some of the comprehensive, detailed and intimate pictures of the distribution, composition and relative wealth of the different populations.[46] Economic intrusions also involve the confiscation by colonial agents of key facilities and resources, particularly urban properties.[47] Most particularly – as in Ireland – such economic imperialism involves the manipulation of regulations so as to alter both import/export patterns and capital flows in favour of the metropolitan power. A whole series of early seventeenth-century customs regulations, as well as the later mercantilist cattle and woollen Acts imposed on Irish trade, reflect this economic ideology.[48]

But above all, colonial economic control involves a reinterpretation of property terms and tenurial relationships. It was a long and winding road between the astute Tudor Irish policy of 'Surrender and Regrant'[49] (which from an English government point of view feudalized all Ireland's landowning systems) and the totality of property confiscations that followed on from the many plantations and from the Cromwellian and Williamite conquests and confiscations. But the end result is the emphatic confirmation of Ireland's status as a fully fledged colony. 'Surrender and Regrant' can actually be interpreted to mean the 'surrender' not only of Irish property rights but Irish ways of living as a whole and the (attempted) 'regranting' and imposition of the totality of English property, economic, political and cultural norms in their place – that is, a policy of the full anglicization of Irish culture.[50]

Economic imperialism is not only a business of one-way flows: the imperial power must also invest heavily not only in its conquering armies and navies and its other instruments of conquest – artillery, fortresses, walled towns and plantation settlements[51] – but it must also seek to make the conquered area an integral part of the enlarged economic space. This involves investment in the elaboration of roads and all transportation links, as well as a continuous smoothening of the most obvious circuits of trade and economic interaction. Behind all of these strategies and actions, the relentless if more subtle, intricate and indirect networks of economic relations – which bend the labour and products of the colonized to the iron will of the conquering agents – are patiently constructed. A geographic analysis thus seeks to understand where the key economic decisions are made, to identify the role and place of key actors and to map and understand the functions of the key nodes of economic transactions – from the crossroads, the artisan workshop, the market-house, the fair town, the forges, mills and factories, the exchanges, warehouses and shipping facilities on to the key overseas ports, plantations and financial houses.[52]

In order for imperial rulers to continue their domination and minimize costs and troubles, they must attempt to win the allegiance of the conquered people.[53] This means the co-option of key broker groups – the so-called 'comprador' class, led in Ireland by the anglicizing great lords and their families and subsequently by a number of lesser lords and merchants. The assimilation of the conquered to the hegemonic power of the conqueror also means a shift in psychological focus and so involves the manipulation of systems of authority, power and prestige so as to invoke response, fear and/or admiration.

The landscape becomes a key vehicle for the manifestation of such visible symbols of colonial rule. The management and adornment of carefully selected sites such as parliament buildings, fortresses, the official residences of key officials, cathedrals and other church buildings, as well as either the conscious adaptation or destruction of sites of key symbolic significance to the conquered people, are all components of this landscape strategy. The adornment of Dublin as colonial capital – epitomized firstly in the duke of Ormond's inspired Royal Hospital at Kilmainham (1682), and later in the elegance and scale of the Trinity College buildings, the curved façade of the College Green Parliament buildings, the striking old Custom House on Essex Quay and the Royal Exchange facing the Liffey – is part of this story and is well told by others.[54] So is the enhancing of the Custom House and administrative buildings of key port-cities such as Belfast, Cork and Waterford,[55] as well as the public buildings in the county towns epitomized above all by the sessions – and the market-house. Likewise, the elaborate building and specific naming of grand vistas, spaces and squares – as where the architecture and language of authority and power is deliberately developed in the many landlord towns – provides a style and scale of development to cow and control the subject population.[56] The Big House in the countryside, with its gatelodges, high hedges and walls enclosing and protecting the privileged world of the landlord, is one of the great island-wide symbols of such power and authority.[57] Finally, the routinized display of both distinctions in culture and disparities in wealth – via the use of elaborate robes, carriages, and a briskly outfitted army officer corps at public processions and 'colonial' celebration days – also functioned to assert and sustain patterns of stratification and power.[58]

English imperialism/colonialism generated its own ideologies and images of conquest and rule, which its agents put into geographic practice on the ground in Ireland and on the bodies and minds of its peoples. But colonized people are not passive, even if – as in colonial mapping – they lose control of the representation and narration of stories about their own lands and lose their own voice as the language of the map translates Irish landscapes, localities and placenames into English language forms. A central theme in writing about any such conquest must include the strategies used by the colonized people, and especially its leaders, to rid the island of these invaders, must address the long-drawn geographies of war and must explore these forms and sites of resistance as colonial power widens and deepens its grip.[59] It also involves an elucidation of the subtle (and not so subtle) ways that the invaded/colonized people use to defend and protect their housing, properties and patrimony. It is necessary to provide some understanding of how the conquered people negotiated ways of earning a living and sustaining livelihoods and families in the very changed conditions that followed sustained imperial/colonial rule. We need to explore their modes of representation and use of ritual and recreation in forging both their changing identities and forms of resistance,[60] as well as being aware of the fragmentation of the society, as middling leaseholders and other jobholders come to occupy more prestigious status positions in the new society. The latter may act as bilingual cultural brokers in a complex and ever-shifting situation.[61]

I am therefore working on the supposition that Ireland can be regarded as 'colonial' in the sense defined for this era, and that the island must be located within the wider historical and geographic frame of Western colonial capitalism. Ireland is systematically colonized in an early modern context, which saw the expansion of the Spanish and Portuguese, as well as the English, empires. Four dominant types of overseas colonialism can be identified – the 'administrative', 'plantation', 'mixed settlement' and 'pure settlement' colony.[62] In the administrative colony, imperial control is achieved by military, economic and jurisdictional means without mass European settlement. Examples include the colonies of South Asia, much of Africa and the so-called Middle East. In plantation economies, white European rule involved slave- and/or indentured servant-based plantation production systems. In pure settlement colonies, as in the United States, Canada and Australia, an expanding European settlement frontier either exterminated or displaced the broken remnants of the original populations onto marginal reservations as Europeans became the dominant population.

The mixed settlement model is most relevant to Ireland's experience and includes particularly the impressive highland societies of Latin America, where the ancestral populations were not destroyed but where 'Iberian settler culture and social structures nonetheless became the dominant ones'.[63] One of the great differences between Ireland and such Latin American societies was that the latter suffered massive demographic decline in the face of Spanish and Portuguese military conquest, forms of exploitation and lack of immunity to European-derived diseases. In Ireland, in contrast, descendants of the original populations retained significant demographic vitality (despite some serious war-induced famines and plagues) and – outside of the northeast – won out demographically to begin with, and eventually politically. Yet there are striking similarities between Latin America and Irish colonial societies, particularly in the centrality of the 'colonial city and town' and 'the great estate' in both cultures.[64]

However, in the mixed colonial settlements of Latin America, the colonizers' single religious system of Catholicism was to prevail. Combined with a severe male bias in the gender structures of Iberian emigration to the 'New World' and other factors, this meant that a large mixed mestizo buffer class emerged between the Iberian ruling elites and the retreating and reduced Indian societies.[65] Almost uniquely in the colonial world, in Ireland religious affiliation became the key ethnic marker that differentiated the colonizer from the colonized.[66] Once the settler community reached a demographic threshold sufficient for self-perpetuation, there was little intermarriage between the Protestant and Catholic groups. Amongst Irish Protestants, it is true that the Anglican Church population held the establishment upperhand and that the Presbyterian and other dissenting groups suffered a number of civil disabilities. Nevertheless, the latter's status never approached that of the Catholic majority population – seen as an inferior class, unfit to be granted any civil rights, disenfranchised, distrusted and made to feel strangers in their own land. With the notable exception of the later eighteenth-century Enlightenment and United Irishmen movements, from at least the 1580s onwards, and certainly from 1641, the primary ethnic, political and cultural fault-line in Ireland lay along the boundary between the 'Catholic' and 'Protestant' communities.

Ireland, therefore, has to be seen as an anomalous European country in this era.[67] It is the meeting-place of not only continental European and English cultural political forces. Given its colonial status, it shares in and comes to acquire greater understanding of other colonial/'Third World' countries, while in its emigrant experiences (and the reciprocities and impulses that flow from such encounters) it was to become a not insignificant player across the English-speaking archipelago – or sea of islands – that then centred on North America and the Caribbean.

'Early Modernity' and Ireland

Ireland's strangeness thus relates to a deep European inheritance which is profoundly complicated in the early modern period both by its colonial status and by its growing integration into an Atlantic archipelago. From an English point of view, the 'reconquest' of Ireland involved both the reclaiming of perceived 'lost ground', as well as the necessary territorial expansion (and protection) of the New English nation-state.[68] From a complex of geopolitical concerns was generated England's need to conquer, subdue and rule Ireland from the Tudor era onwards. A central and enduring legacy here is that England defines and 'discovers' itself as a nation precisely during that Tudor/Elizabethan era when it is deeply embroiled in the violent conquest of the neighbouring western island and its peoples.[69] Lessons learned and attitudes generated by this lengthy and often brutal encounter with the Irish were both carried to and replicated in other British colonies, beginning with North America.

The ethos underpinning this enormous English energy and outward drive may be summarized as 'early modern'. The Tudor and especially the Elizabethan age saw England open up to a highly innovative European world, born of Renaissance ideas, concepts, techniques and attitudes and the excitement of New World discoveries and opportunities. New ways of seeing, representing, and acting on, the world – whether in art, cartography or science – became paramount in reshaping perspectives and practices as the centre of the European world shifted from the Mediterranean to the North Sea and the Atlantic. These new visibilities were linked to the growth of individualism. This growth in the construction of the 'subject' and in individual identity is epitomized by the growing popularity of secular portrait painting.[70] The printing press and the rapid production and mass circulation of books, prints and atlases had opened up many new worlds, perspectives and debates among a nationalizing literate elite.[71] In this early nation-building phase, history in England, as elsewhere in the 'new Europe', is no longer a chronicle of events but a discipline that seeks via the use of relevant source-materials to explain – and justify – national cultures and policies.[72] Likewise, geography – in tandem with the development of cartographic, mathematical and navigational techniques and measures – becomes a central discipline in support of both nationalizing and imperial agendas. The Renaissance fusion of studies in law, literature, chivalry and the martial arts produces the ideal of the poet-warrior, epitomized by people like Philip Sidney,[73] while the writings of Niccolo Machiavelli in *The Prince*[74] and Thomas More's *Utopia*[75] justify, amongst other things, imperial conquest and colonization.

Reformation is a central theme in early modern England – and not just a religious reformation. The drive is to re-*form*, to give new shape and meaning to old societies, economies and landscapes, which to the 'alien' modernizing eye appear formless and uncouth. Notions of 'progress', 'development', 'improvement' and 'modernity' become part of this new reforming agenda. There is a sense of liberation from the constraints of tradition and custom (yet the modernity of the English nation-state also produced and needed new disciplinary/surveillance powers).[76] A central feature of this 'modernizing' discourse is the distinction drawn between innovative European societies, such as that of the English, and huge areas of the rest of the world whose cultures are now defined as traditional, backward, primitive, uncivilized. Recent literature rightly refers to the problematic impact of European-centred modernity drives *outside* of Europe – the dark side of modernity, which involved 'violent, coercive and insidious cultural practices' against these 'traditional' societies.[77] Given Ireland's experience, this problematic might also be applied *within* Europe as well.

A part of the modernizing drive was the transition in fifteenth- and sixteenth-century England from feudal to capitalistic modes of production and relations of production. This entailed a shift to new forms of wage labour and the consolidation of rural landownership through the enclosure movements in the countryside.[78] An agricultural revolution follows by way of improving of land and stock, including the introduction of new crop rotations and new breeds of cattle and sheep, wetlands are drained and the former communal open field systems are regularized into individually worked, separate, enclosed plots.[79] The modern estate system had been established and the estate surveyor is a key figure in this modernizing process.[80] By the early seventeenth century, a 'modern' English rural landscape – 'newly ordered, productive, capitalised and commodified'[81] – is being created. The common lands are enclosed, class and gender structures radically transformed, the old moral economy is eroded as men and women of commerce assumed leadership roles in town and countryside. All these experiences, transformations and attitudes, and associated technical skills, were to shape New English interventions and interactions in Ireland.

This early modern world involves a whole new way of learning and a range of knowledge strategies, including the ethos of applying new scientific understandings to the practical business of statecraft, shipping, farming and industry. It involves the use of new technologies of production and new forms of transportation and communication in fostering the growth of a permanent bureaucratic organization at the heart of the centralizing absolutist English state.[82] This monarchical state utilizes the modernizing segments in the society to override and subordinate local and regional governments and powers to the goals of the centre. A standardizing legal system is codified, a standing army put in place; naval and mercantile shipping power is greatly enhanced as the society's local, national and international economies are gradually and forcefully integrated.[83] England's oldest universities play a key role here, as do later institutions such as the Royal Society.[84] One of the latter's founding members, William Petty, is the archetypal expression of the 'early modern' in Ireland (see chapters 5 and 6).

The centralizing nation-state, early capitalism, modernization, urbanization and a 'knowledge economy' are, thus, all part of this 'modernizing new world', as is the imperial drive to conquer and exploit New World colonies. This latter process is accompanied by the commodification of land, the disturbance and sometimes destruction of existing complex ecologies, the growth of dangerous and vulnerable forms of monoculture and the promotion of new divisions of labour which greatly damage both natural and human communities.[85] Above all, the 'early modern' is characterized by the accelerated rate of change in the societies and economies affected by its impulses, including the increased interaction between places and peoples at a great variety of scales.[86] Networks of communication, trade and migration now develop on a globalizing scale. Indeed, the loosening of individuals and families from their rooted parent societies and localities and their migration across vast spaces to New World destinations is one of the central and enduring themes of this era of accelerated change.[87]

This is the swirl of contexts from which New English men and women came to create 'early modern' Ireland. These individuals were imbued with notions of progress, improvement, reformation and profit-making, which led to the colonial subjugation of the great majority of the Irish population. Ireland's colonial experience was *not* shared by other west European countries. Rather, like many equivalent peoples in colonized Middle and South America, Ireland then saw much of its ancient ways of living – its language, law codes, systems of land occupation and territorial organization, its settlement, social and artistic structures – either replaced or radically reconfigured by a powerful English-speaking state and its agents and settlers.

Despite a heritage of earlier intrusions into Ireland, this New English conquering mentality could not easily and did not really want to understand existing Irish life and culture, not even that of the Old English. Hence, a deep duality enters Irish life – two dominant cultures emerge, two peoples, generally out of touch and out of sympathy with one another.[88] One might ask, for example, why the 1641 rising/rebellion is perceived by the new ruling elites (and many subsequent commentators) as so sudden, so swift, so unexpected.[89] It suggests that they had little understanding of or insight into the feelings and experiences of the subjugated majority.

In all of this, the power and depth of the English cultural impress has to be recognized. Beginning in the Middle Ages but intensifying dramatically after *c*.1530, the institutional pressures on the Irish language became immense. The relentless expansion of English garrisons, towns, villages, schools, sessions-houses, coach traffic, inns, and a whole host of other agencies and agents created at best a bifurcated linguistic world. As the conquest deepened and widened from the seventeenth century, more and more of the key domains of language became English-speaking or involved literacy in English.[90] In the political domain, the language and literature of government and administration was English-speaking; likewise in the law courts and in the military barracks. The world of communications – that of the press and printed literature – was dominated by English publications and voices. Increasingly the city, the town and the market – that is, the commercial world – sees a bilingual environment lean towards English. And even the 'lessons' of the local hedge school were conducted through English. [11]

Central to all this cultural transformation was the imposition, institutionalization and the geographical expansion of English law in all spheres of Irish life from the 1540s onwards – slowly but surely undermining traditional Irish codes and processes of land management and land transfers.[91] The geographical spread of English common law – via the manor, assize and other courts[92] – carried with it a whole host of English cultural assumptions about property rights and procedures, born of centuries of evolution in the homeland but, outside of the counties of the Pale and parts of the southeast, imposed swiftly and ruthlessly in the very different Irish contexts.[93] One has to be aware of the suddenness and speed of this overall transition and recognize how deeply disturbing and destructive such processes were to the social and psychological well-being of the colonized.[94] When conquerors manage to impose their will on the crucial domains of language and law, they are well on their way to achieving hegemony. But, as with all forms of colonialism, these processes were uneven in their geographical expansion and effects, involved different class groups variously, and generated a host of unintended consequences.

Historical and Cultural Geography

In constructing the story, I have given preference to those documentary sources that offer a comprehensive and detailed view of all or most of Ireland. Manuscript maps of Ireland from the 1530s to Petty's Down Survey maps (1654–9) and his printed Atlas of Ireland (*Hiberniae Delineatio*, 1685), his 'Census of 1659', the Civil Survey (1654–6), the Books of Survey and Distribution (1641–1708), the so-called 1641 Depositions and Cromwellian examinations (1641–54), the Trustees Surveys (1705–06) and the *Report on the State of Popery* (1731), as well as hearth-money records from the mid-seventeenth century to the mid-eighteenth century, are all of a type that facilitate or come close to facilitating island-wide mapping at county, barony, and even more intimately, at the civil parish scale.[95]

The historical geographer is interested in territorial completeness in his/her documentary sources for a great variety of reasons. They help to provide a panoptic view of conditions across the whole island, while also being critical in the delineation of significant regional similarities and differences. Equally significant, many of these source-materials allow for further insights and generalizations to be garnered at the level of the county and, more particularly, at the barony and parish levels. Ability to work at these levels allows for the excavation and mapping of a great variety of communities, localities and settlements and brings us closer to the lives of the common people whose struggles and experiences rarely surface in official governmental records. A large number of such maps in this volume will hopefully help to illuminate many hidden Irelands. The maps are an essential part of the text and looking at, and 'reading' them will greatly facilitate the reader's understanding of the presentation.

Some of the documents also allow us to examine the intimate geographies of townlands, families and households. The unique survey of nearly 600 households in south Co. Dublin for 1650–2 is one such rare source.[96] The 1641 Depositions allows one to explore the very harsh treatment meted out to individuals, bodies and families in this traumatic time. In addition to those of the elites, uniquely we can also listen in these specific returns to the voices and concerns of artisans, farmers and shopkeepers, as well as gaining some insights and understandings into the roles and experiences of a wide spectrum of women, so often written out of the historic record.[97]

Whereas the views of the conqueror have been well documented and articulated in the various state records, the lived experienced worlds of the colonized Irish are more difficult to penetrate and articulate.[98] Here insights and methods from both long-established and 'new' cultural geography are helpful.[99] For beyond the written records the geographer may use a wide variety of other texts and forms of expression to map and penetrate worlds of continuity and change at ground level which have escaped the 'official eye'. The landscape itself, as the poet John Montague reminds us, is a manuscript[100] that geographers have learned the skill to read. Embedded in the landscape and people's localities are place-names, Christian names, family names,[101] and a host of other intangibles such as musical and sporting styles.[102] These can be mapped and analysed. Particularly relevant here is the geography of the transformation of first and second names, which reveals deeply incised and highly divergent surfaces of cultural change, accommodation and resistance in seventeenth- and eighteenth-century Ireland.[103] In addition, Irish language sources – sadly neglected by Irish geographers – need to be explored and examined, whether in the form of the annals, the genealogies or the poetry, so as to provide some insight into how the submerged Irish-speaking community lived and responded to the pressures of the new political and colonial order. There is a huge imbalance between the weight of evidence in the English language sources and what has survived in Irish language sources, which reminds us how much of what happened to peoples and localities in colonial/early modern Ireland is lost, erased or unrecorded.

The writing of this story involves one other kind of forging – it involves a deliberate and slow process of identifying and selecting what the author deems to be the most critical themes, source-materials and readings. These materials are tested, shaped and moulded into a new form to reflect the specific concerns and methods of this geographer. The actual forging of Ireland in the sixteenth and seventeenth centuries involved the hammering out of many new settlements and the erasure of many others. It also resulted in the reshaping of both old and new societies as their members sought to negotiate and mediate the accelerated forces of 'early modernity'. The forging of this story also involves negotiating and mediating between conflicting interpretations and forms of evidence. And in the telling of this story some themes are highlighted, while others are left in the shade.

I

MAKING THE DOCUMENTS OF CONQUEST SPEAK

2

Making Ireland Visible
Maps as Instruments of Conquest

This was a fundamental achievement of the Renaissance;
it shaped ways of seeing for four centuries.

David Harvey[1]

The earliest known English-derived map of Ireland, dating from the late 1520s, has an opaque, shadowy look. A mainly egg-shaped island with some few indentations on its east side emerges from the dark deep blue of the surrounding seas. Apart from a few dominant rivers shown as wide blue rivulets, and square blobs of red which mark the main cities and towns in the eastern half, the rest of the island is a pale, creamy shadow, full of silences and absences. It is an island in embryo – slowly leaving behind the dark shadows of the later Middle Ages to emerge out of the womb of the early modern revolution in art, government, science and technology.

The story of the mapping of Ireland in the sixteenth and seventeenth centuries is the story of the English construction and conquest of Ireland. By the time Sir William Petty publishes his famous Atlas of Ireland – *Hiberniae Delineatio* – in 1685, this view of Ireland has been 'normalized' to almost satellite precision. The old, rounded image of the island has yielded to a sharp modernity, born of the sciences of surveying, navigation, mathematics and cartography. The late medieval shadows have been dispelled and a new 'modern' Ireland, complete with at least 10,000 placenames in the English language, has been made visible and is clearly enframed on the map of Europe and the world.

Figure 2.1 suggests the intellectual, military and political distance that existed between the nature of Ireland's relationship with England in the 1520s as compared with the 1660s. Included in this composite figure is the small, strange, opaque yet brilliant image of Ireland, mapped in the reign of Henry VIII and preserved in Robert Cotton's collection in the British Library.[2] This earlier map is dominated by the very different but equally brilliant map of Ireland, first compiled by William Petty and his chief cartographer Thomas Taylor in 1659 but which was not published until 1685.[3]

Cotton's map of Ireland (see also Fig. 2.2) is a very strange one – it greatly exaggerates the area of the Dublin/English Pale with the islands off Skerries shown around Co. Down and the island of Dalkey drifting southwards towards Wicklow

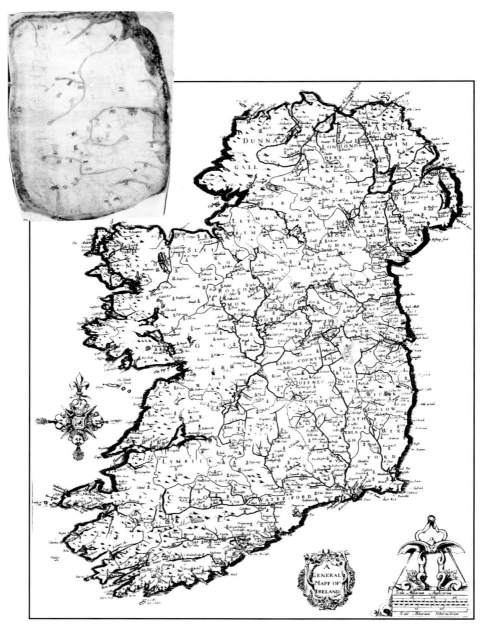

2.1   William Petty's map of Ireland, almost complete by 1659, engraved by the mid-1660s but not published until 1685 (inset: the 'Cotton' map of Ireland *c*.1526: see Fig. 2.2, Pl. 1a)

and Arklow. Likewise, the interior of the map exaggerates the Dublin city hinterland and the lands of the Kildare Fitzgeralds. To the modern eye practised in map- and atlas-reading the southeast coast appears reasonably accurate but the northeast coast is skewed westwards after Drogheda. Similarly, the southwest coast is made to fully accommodate the Shannon estuary and Limerick city. The north

Ulster coast is signalled by only three named entries – the Bann, Aran (island) and Lough Swilly – while the whole west coast from Donegal to Kerry is represented as a single smooth curved line with only one entry – the city of Galway.

The inclusion of Galway as the sole beacon of a distant and unknown west coast is not surprising, given that at this time Galway was probably second to Dublin in Ireland's urban structure. English awareness of Galway was also sharpened by the outreach of the Bristol fisheries through Galway and on across the Atlantic to Newfoundland – known in Irish as *Talamh an Éisc* (the Fish Bank). Galway occupied a crucial position in the now broadening Atlantic, given its links with the expanding empires of Spain and Portugal. And not surprisingly, the early sixteenth-century Iberian maps of northwest Europe and the Atlantic were far more precise and knowledgeable about the west of Ireland and especially the peninsulas and bays of southwest Ireland than the Cotton map suggests for the English. For example, a series of Portuguese maps from the 1500s are not only knowledgeable of the shape of northwest France, the West Country and south Wales, but are knowledgeable and reasonably precise about the shape of southwest Ireland (see Fig. 2.3). The Dingle peninsula is clearly well known and delineated, as is the Shannon estuary into Limerick city. The importance of Galway Bay is mapped; and Clew Bay to the north is given prominence. And those early Portuguese and Spanish maps deliberately show their own great ships – masts and flags flying – dominating the North Atlantic off the coast of southern and western Ireland.[4]

In sharp contrast, the clear focus of the Cotton map is the east coast of Ireland that faces England. In addition to the rather exaggerated Liffey, the river system is also both focused on the east and massively distorted. The Boyne river dominates the northern half of the map and runs north–east. Likewise, the Barrow swallows up much of the southern half of the island and runs from west to east rather than from north to south. Knowledge of the Shannon river basin peters out beyond Limerick. The other river systems of the island are unknown.

While this is a strange map of Ireland, it serves to disclose the level of geographical knowledge – or more correctly, the level of geographical ignorance – which Henry VIII and his administrators in London display about Ireland just a decade or so before the English monarch is declared king rather than simply lord of Ireland. The map, therefore, illustrates the chasm between England's dream of ruling all Ireland in early Tudor times and its current capacity to realize such an objective.

The Cotton map, however, highlights the king's and England's clear potential to expand control westwards, southwards and northwards from the eastern core of English administration. The map is sufficiently strategic to carefully display, with large prestigious symbols, the cities and spaces still under crown control – from the key nerve centre of Dublin, south through Wicklow, Waterford, Dungarvan, Cork and Limerick and northwards from Dublin through Drogheda, Carlingford, Greencastle and Knockfergus (Carrickfergus), the Bann and Lough Swilly. The map highlights the first area of strategic 'colonial' expansion westwards into the lands of the earls of Kildare. The map also notes the strongholds of key allies such as the archbishop of Dublin, the duke of Norfolk, the earl of Shrewsbury and, in

particular, the earl of Ormond. In contrast, shadowing the map on Dublin's southern flanks are the Gaelic lands of the O'Tooles, O'Byrnes and Mac Murrogh
Kavanagh. Likewise, and barely squeezed onto the corner of the map in the almost
totally unknown territories of the west and north, are the names of such key lordships as MacWilliam (Burke), O'Kelly, O'Farrell, O'Reilly, O'Donnell, Maguire,
Magennis, MacMahon, O'Hanlon and, above all, that of O'Neill. These names and
lordships would loom large both on the maps and in the political and military
conquest of the island over the rest of the sixteenth century and beyond.

Figure 2.1 (p. 22) is designed most particularly to illustrate the chasm between
levels of English knowledge and political control c.1526 and 1685 when Petty's
Hiberniae Delineatio was published. With Petty's maps, we are close to the physical
reality, neatly detailed topography and settlement structure of Ireland. On his
maps Ireland appears as a conquered, known, anglicized and tightly administered
land. Complete with this modern map of Ireland as a whole, Petty's Atlas includes
detailed maps of each of the four provinces and each of the now firmly defined
thirty-two counties. Christopher Saxton had published the first of many 'deep-
plotted' county atlases of England as far back as 1579.[5] No possibility existed for
such an accurate mapping of Ireland's counties before the Cromwellian conquest
and settlement. Interim maps that displayed the county boundaries included
Baptiza Boazio's Lythe-dependent map of 1599 and John Speed's and John Norden's maps of the first decades of the seventeenth century. Speed's reasonably
accurate provincial maps (1611) use different colours to demarcate each of the
counties – thus highlighting the distinctive shape of these units which were to
become one of the most enduring and assimilated features of modern Irish culture.[6]

It took the Cromwellian conquest and settlement, and Petty's organizational
genius, to produce the county maps of *Hiberniae Delineatio*, engraved in Amsterdam. Petty's Down Survey – the mapping of Ireland, parish by parish, to facilitate
the allocation of lands from the old Irish and Old English to the New English
elites and completed by 1659 – meant that Ireland became the first European
country to be entirely mapped by a systematic, almost island-wide, *field* survey.[7]
This survey identifies three key points about Ireland's location in the wider
context of European representation. First, it pinpoints Ireland's 'colonial' status,
since such an island-wide field survey, aimed at facilitating massive land appropriation and reallocation, was deemed necessary in the first instance. Second, it
demonstrates the incorporation of Ireland within the mainstream of a European
mapping, scientific and technological revolution that stretched back to the Renaissance and the early Iberian reach across the Atlantic. Third, it illustrates the sharp
learning curve displayed by Tudor and Jacobean England in embracing new continental European ideas and techniques of rule and survey, a learning curve which
began with the radical revolution in Henry VIII's Reformation administration and
the redefinition of England's place in Europe and the world. In 1500, England was
a peripheral and minor actor on the 'Old World' stage – by 1700 it had become the
dominant player in both Europe and the 'New World'.

The great Flemish geographer/cartographer/publisher Abraham Ortelius –
close friend of another painter of reality, Bruegel – described the map as 'the eye

of history'.[8] In the sixteenth and seventeenth centuries, it could also be said that the map became 'the eye of the state', the 'imperial eye' which ranged over land-scapes and peoples as an instrument of both survey and surveillance, and, if necessary, as an instrument of conquest.

The thesis being advanced here is that maps did not simply mirror or reflect the reality of the English conquest of Ireland – rather, maps were crucial instruments in the hands of monarchs, statesmen and soldiers in the business of conquest, coloni-zation and economic exploitation and transformation. Maps are not neutral – they reflect the objectives, agendas and cultural assumptions of their patrons and makers; and, in the early modern period, they were part of the armoury of the state – like guns, forts and ships. And so it happened that between 1530 and 1700 Ireland was gradually made visible, accessible and potentially governable through the agency of, amongst other instruments, a series of English-inspired maps. A new construction of Ireland emerged via these cartographic images. The language of the maps is English and the views of Ireland are almost invariably filtered through English cultural lenses and assumptions. Maps are as much an image of the social order as a measurement of the phenomenal world of objects.[9] And some of these maps did provide images of an intended ideal social and spatial order.

Spatial freedom – to be able to move freely across and between landscapes and territories – is a good indication of power. What this collection of maps of Ireland reveals is the gradual, sometimes very slow and sometimes swift transformation in the levels of spatial freedom achieved by the New English *vis-à-vis* the Irish in Ireland. The endgame for the conquering English was to create as much geograph-ical freedom for themselves as possible, while at the same time constraining, containing and confining the 'subject' Irish to specific spaces and locales.

This chapter focuses on the emergence and evolution of the imperial eye, on maps as instruments of English monarchs, soldiers and statesmen. Chapter 3 will broaden the perspective to explore the dialectic between this kind of mapping (along with its associated spatial strategies) and the Irish way of 'mapping' the landscape – that is, its own 'insider' systems of territorial organization and strate-gies for adapting to, subverting, neutralizing and transcending the imperial eye of the English-inspired map.

The 'Ptolemaic Grid': Enframing Ireland on the World Map

Two of the world's greatest geographers – Ptolemy and Mercator – put Ireland on the world map in two very different imperial eras. It was Ptolemy of Alexandria – with his famous work *Geographia* – who mapped the world as known to the Romans (and Greeks) *c*.AD 150. In the process, he provided the latitudes and longitudes of fifty Irish capes, settlements, estuaries and 'peoples', which allows for the earliest construction of the shape and size of Ireland.[10] Ptolemy's impor-tance for the early modern world and Ireland, however, relates more to the great revival of classical learning that followed on from the Renaissance and which included a critical revolution in the nature and concerns of geography and cartography. Ptolemy's *Geographia* was printed for the first time as early as 1477 and Gerard Mercator was to honour him by reprinting some of his maps as late as 1578.

To the Netherlander Mercator (1512–94), who spent most of his extraordinarily productive life in Duisburg in Germany, to his friend Ortelius and indeed a host of other geographers and cartographers, the real achievement of Ptolemy lay in his conceptualization of the world in geometrical terms. It was Ptolemy who provided the model for describing and embracing the earth within predetermined gridlines of latitude and longitude. As Jeremy Brotton emphasizes, 'the guiding force for this grid system was the principles of abstract geometry rather than those of Christian symbolism'.[11] Medieval Europe's image of the world was dominated by theocentric maps. Muslim and Chinese cartographers were the real innovators throughout the Middle Ages. It was the introduction of the Ptolemaic maps from Alexandria to Florence around 1400 that was to play a crucial role in the Renaissance discovery and use of perspectivism. As David Harvey notes: 'fundamental rules of perspective – rules that broke radically with the practices of medieval art and architecture and which were to dominate until the beginning of the 20th century – were elaborated in mid-fifteenth century Florence. This was a fundamental achievement of the Renaissance; it shaped ways of seeing for four centuries.'[12] Renaissance mapping was to take on 'entirely new qualities of objectivity, practicality and functionality'; the fixed viewpoint of the perspective maps and paintings 'is elevated and distant', generating a 'coldly geometrical and systematic sense of space'.[13]

Harvey, drawing on Samuel Edgerton's work, goes on to note that

> perspectivism conceives of the world, from the standpoint of the 'seeing eye' of the individual. It emphasises the science of optics and the ability of the individual to represent what he or she sees as in some sense 'truthful', compared to the superimposed truths of mythology and religion.[14]

Thus, new forms of mapping, striving for so-called objectivity in the representation of spaces, became valued attributes 'because accuracy of navigation, determination of property rights in land . . . property boundaries, rights of passage and transportation became economically as well as politically imperative'.[15]

And it was Mercator and Ortelius who most successfully seized the opportunities offered by the new technologies of surveying and the new instrument of printing to reshape the image of the world and of Ireland. Ptolemy had provided the mathematical grid where the most distant places could be precisely located in relation to one another by unchanging coordinates 'so that their proportionate distance as well as their directional relationship would be apparent'.[16] But Ptolemy's was an Old World view. It was Mercator who ingeniously devised the new map projection, which not only involved the Old World but also embraced the New. For the first time, navigators and sailors could calculate true distance and orientation over the round earth on the flat surface of Mercator's map-projection. It was thus Mercator – through this projection – who reinforced a Eurocentric ideology and, in effect, shifted the centre of the world to the North Atlantic. And the last major island between the Old European core and the New World was Atlantic Ireland. Ireland's position on the New World map was now both radically rede-

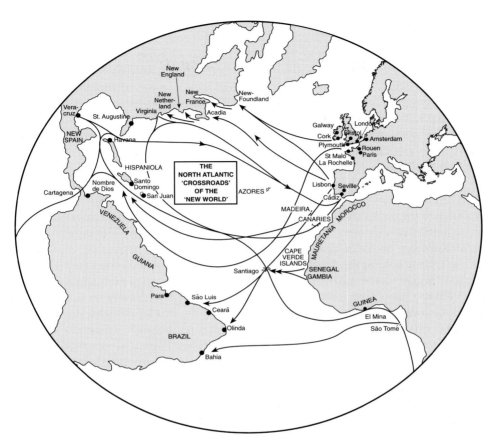

2.4 Ireland's maritime location in the 'new' Atlantic world (*c.* 1630) (adapted from Figure 8 in D.W. Meinig's *Atlantic America 1492–1800*, p. 56; see reference 17)

fined and more precisely located. Donald Meinig's *Atlantic America 1492–1800* demonstrates this transformation as experienced from America (see Fig. 2.4).[17]

Mercator published his new world map-projection in 1569. Five years earlier, he had published a map of Ireland that was 'the first post-medieval representation of Ireland' to make an indelible impression on the map-reading public.[18] As John Andrews notes: 'Mercator is the first and perhaps the last continental scholar since Ptolemy to have published a completely original contribution to the map of Ireland.'[19] This he did with his *Angliae Scotiae et Hiberniae Nova Descriptio*, published at Duisburg in 1564. Mercator never visited Ireland but was a supreme synthesizer. Using the work of other map-makers, he presents a far more 'realistic' view of Ireland than other Irish maps of this era. The south and east are carefully delineated but, as always at this time, both the provinces of Ulster and Connacht appear very problematic to the modern eye. Unlike the manuscript maps, however, such a printed map allowed for the 'exactly repeatable pictorial statement'[20] to be circulated, reproduced and reprinted. Mercator had positioned Ireland on the world map as part of the British Isles.

It was Mercator's enterprising friend, Ortelius, who immortalized Mercator's brilliant synthesis of Ireland's map by publishing it (beside a map of Britain) in that famous world atlas *Theatrum Orbis Terrarum* (1570). Ortelius thus turned the earth into a saleable, portable book and enframed Ireland in an image which emphasized 'the British Isles'. Three years later, Ortelius was to give turbulent, sea-tossed Ireland a page of its own, with a title which, as Andrews notes, 'was even more imperialistic than Mercator's – *Hiberniae Britannicae insulae nova descriptio*'[21] (see Fig. 2.5). Apart from improving the shapes and river system associated with Belfast, Strangford Lough and Lough Neagh (probably derived from Sir Thomas Smith's maps of his intended plantation of this region), Ortelius otherwise still depends on his friend's mapping synthesis. The great difference was that close on 6,000 impressions of this Ireland were printed in successive editions of the *Theatrum*. They found their way into the libraries and offices of the most influential statesmen and scholars of England and elsewhere in Europe. The normalization and standardization of Ireland's image on 'British', European and world maps had begun.

The cartographer John Goghe was one of the first to literally enframe Ireland on the world grid in the mid-1560s.[22] Goghe's beautiful map of Ireland defines and locates the island along specified lines of latitude and longitude (see Fig. 2.6). The lines of longitude are calculated from the Azores. England's and Greenwich's imperial centrality had to wait until the later eighteenth century – the old Mediterranean-derived longitudinal coordinates still ruled. And Goghe recognizes the then current Spanish power and threat by naming the sea off south Munster as 'the Spanish Sea'. Apart from characteristic errors of the still uncharted western coasts, Goghe's map is quite accurate and testifies to important advances in English mapping by the late 1560s: there are significant improvements in representing the interior spaces of the Irish river system, and also a high level of accuracy in locating the key Irish lordships and families. The west and the north still present the greatest obstacles to penetration and understanding – symbolized, amongst other things, both by the continued representation of Lough Erne as a very large but single lake entity and the three warrior figures in north Donegal. But overall, Goghe's, and Lawrence Nowell's, work show that the sharing in a wider circuit of shipping, navigational and cartographic skills that connected southern and northwestern Europe was transforming England's mapping initiatives, and with them the continual filling in of the blank spaces of interior Ireland. For the next hundred years, the cold clinical 'eye' of the god-like Cartographer would gaze down on Ireland, *his* maps used to define and rule, to subjugate and eradicate old social worlds, and to help re-create the island in the image of the colonizing English.

Mapping, the Reform of the Tudor Administration, and Ireland

The Goghe map, the unknown antecedents of Mercator's 1564 map of Ireland, as well as Nowell's map of the same year, are all heirs to the revolution in map-making and map use ushered in under Henry VIII and which continued into the

1550s and 1560s. The emergence of England as a new Protestant state resulted in a radical redefinition of the island's geopolitical position in both Europe and the Atlantic and released an astonishing range of energies – intellectual, political, cultural and infrastructural – to deal with the highly charged new situation. In what was a profoundly defining moment, England met the challenge of its new alienation from Catholic Christendom by redefining its maritime destiny and vigorously engaging the challenges of the emerging world order. The confiscation of its vast monastic lands provided Henry and England with both the freedom and the capacity to modernize and expand coastal defences and military infra-structure on a scale that was not equalled again until the nineteenth century.[23] In a sense, England literally moved seawards.

Henry VIII employed specialists from the Low Countries, France – his chief marine cartographer was French – Italy and Portugal to further develop England's own cartographic, engineering and maritime expertise.[24] A kind of North Sea intellectual and political nexus was emerging and the Low Countries led Europe in the interweaving of the skills and insights born of mapping, making pictures and painting. *Descriptio* is a term that then comes to mean the realistic assemblage of landscape items on a flat surface in either a map or a painting.[25] John Dee, amongst others, demonstrated the practical consequences of new knowledge in navigation, mathematics, astronomy and geography in the search for the New World 'discoveries' and trading ventures. John Cabot was a precursor for all of this with his explorations of the North-West Passage in the 1490s. Earlier still, Prince Henry the Navigator established his school of cosmography and cartography at Sagres at the southwestern end of Portugal and inspired the great Portuguese explorers to leap across the seas.[26] In short, a whole series of intercon-nected forces arising out of the Renaissance, the scientific revolution, and in artistic and political/state arenas made the use of maps far more central to governments. Geography and cartography were seen as central to a new way of seeing, understanding and governing the world; geographic metaphors echo across a host of disciplines and reverberate within the theatre, poetry and litera-ture of Elizabethan England, as evidenced in the works of William Shakespeare, Philip Sidney and later John Donne.

By the late 1540s, maps were becoming fully integrated into the policy-making and administrative machines of the modernizing English state, amongst a gener-ation that had grown up with the excitement of the New World discoveries. The royal palaces reflected these trends, and were furnished with magnificent maps and globes, including the New World map of Cabot and Francis Drake – a map later used to justify English claims to a number of overseas territories.[27] Maps now became a central tool of a government shaped by the new understandings that knowledge could be gained and stored through such pictorial strategies. Hence-forth military mapping, on various scales, became central to both defence and in carrying out war. Maps were also central to the English administration in devel-oping a greater knowledge of the world so as to foster trade, commerce and further 'discoveries'. Training in the subject of geography and better mapping techniques was also seen as important in the education of the ruling elites, in order to further enhance local and national and later imperial administration.[28] The formation of policy now often involved strategies, sketches and scaled maps for planning; and, as Ireland was to discover, maps became imperative in the carving out and planning of colonies.

From the late 1530s and more particularly the early 1540s there was a significant growth in the number of officials and officers imported from England into Ireland. These included very specialist people like the new Master of the Ordnance John Travers. The destinies of map-making and gunnery have long been intertwined, and Ireland was no exception to this rule. Henry VIII was referring to a 'new map of Ireland' not long after a visit from Travers.[29] Travers was responsible for a map of Irish ports and harbours in 1543. It may well be that it is this mapping survey that provided the information for a rather intriguing early map, now in the Public Record Office (see Fig. 2.7), which, apart from indicating the expansion of the Pale westwards and southwards, seems particularly concerned with defining and item- izing the peninsulas and bays all around Ireland.[30] And it is certain that England's fortifying of Ireland's coastlands – already a huge priority in the defences of the English homeland – was to become a central pivot in England's infrastructural investments in Ireland from the mid-sixteenth century. John Rogers, one of the great Tudor military engineers, was employed in making maps and planning forti- fications for Cork, Kinsale and Baltimore in 1551, the precursor to similar work by Robert Lythe, Francis Jobson, and Paul Ivy in later decades.[31]

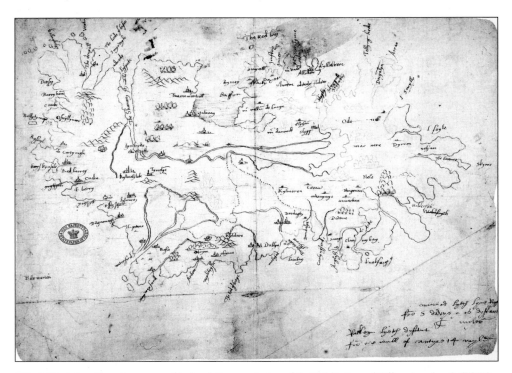

2.7   Mid-sixteenth century map of Ireland. By permission of the Public Record Office, London (MPF 72).

The central figure in all this planning and mapping was Sir William Cecil (later Lord Burghley), who began as secretary of state in 1550 and became Elizabeth's most trusted minister, until she in turn administered to him on his deathbed in 1598. Cecil was at the centre of England's growing administration for half a century and was the dominant figure in defining and monitoring English policy in both Ireland and the 'overseas' world as a whole.

Cecil was an inveterate annotator of maps. He used Goghe's maps to discuss suggested garrison locations in Ireland with Sidney; he corrected the Ortelius/Mercator-derived map of 1564, as well as earlier mid-sixteenth-century maps probably derived from the work of Travers and Sir James Croft, revealing both the extent to which he thought cartographically and the extent to which he saw maps as central to the state's strategy to rule and govern.[32] Cecil had the pioneer's sense of excitement about maps; and it is said of him that he carried Nowell's small atlas of Britain and Ireland around in his pocket for quick reference.[33] Nowell's map brilliantly portrays the cultural and political gap between England and Ireland, as perceived by this distinguished map-maker (see Fig. 2.8). The England portrayed there is that of an ordered realm with clearly defined and long-established county shires illustrated in red and a hierarchy of red dots and lines depicting shire towns, bishops' sees and city-ports. Apart from the Pale area, Ireland is revealed as mainly a green wilderness area of forests and bogs, dominated by an array of lordships and families in various states of disobedience to the crown. The subtext suggests that Ireland must be made to look and behave like England and that the central royal authority must be imposed on these outlying recalcitrant subjects and regions.

The figures at the bottom of this map are probably Cecil and Nowell. Bottom right, the imperious Cecil, arms folded, glares westwards across at Nowell, seemingly requiring and demanding a better mapping of Ireland. He can be seen as symbolizing 'the superior gaze' of an expansionist England. Nowell, as cartographer, surveyor, faces the viewer with an anguished look which speaks of the difficulties – material and psychological – of map-making on the Irish frontier. The baying hound, the scourge of all surveyors – and in Bernhard Klein's view,[34] a metaphor for the wolf-like 'barbaric' Irish as well – accentuates the cartographer's predicament. The text beside Cecil speaks of the hope and desire of capturing and subjugating this mobile country within the fixed frame of the cartographer's lens. The map itself, with the island of Britain curved slightly westwards to encircle and embrace Ireland, speaks to the dream of enclosure and anglicized rule. It also suggests the power of the map to bend space and bend realities to better satisfy the monarch's/statesman's hopes and desires and to specify the dreams and objectives still to be achieved. But the map of Ireland itself remains a rough sketch of a stubborn physical and cultural terrain. It is an unfurnished Ireland and its lack of geographical order – as viewed from England – tells of the incomplete conquest of a still alien island world.

Nevertheless, Cecil continued to make strategic use of this and other maps for pragmatic state purposes. He perceived maps as central to planning both the state's defences and the state's expansion, whether relating to the location of coastal or inland fortifications, the distribution of military supplies or the distribution of military divisions. Cecil constantly used his existing samples of maps to plan the location of garrisons and called for new maps when a greater density of forts and shorter lines of communication were deemed necessary by the military strategists working on the ground in Ireland. Maintenance of supplies to the garrisons was invariably problematic, given the guerrilla tactics of the Irish.

What is most striking is the time, effort and expense that went into the planning, mapping and building of a great number of new fortifications, both along the most vulnerable coastlands and for strategic expansions inland. We can detect a cartographic-cum-military mentality at work when new garrisons are strategically and systematically established to encircle rebellious lordships like that of the O'Byrnes in Wicklow. We know that fortifications and garrisons were reinforced or newly and shrewdly established to create corridors and passes through the Midlands and south Leinster, so little by little to enlarge the Pale.[35] We also know that considerable investments were made in constructing and enlarging the key garrisons of Fort Protector (later Maryborough) and Fort Governor (later Philipstown) to protect the Dublin hinterland to the east and expand the Pale westwards, as well as commanding, surveying and supporting the settlers of the relatively newly colonized territories.[36] So it may well be that in that short but highly innovative period of Edward VI's rule (1547–53) (and Sir Edward Bellingham's and Sir James Croft's administrations in Ireland) that wider strategic considerations were also at play in the investments made at Fort Governor and Fort Protector. The English government was seeking to build critical bridgeheads – clear land corridors, and better lines of communication and supply – to link up with the pivotal western and southwestern port-cities and royal garrisons at Galway and Limerick.

Galway was seen as vitally strategic from the beginning of England's new policy for Ireland after 1534. Clearly, Galway's Iberian links were a major concern. As early as 1538, Lord Deputy Grey sent artillery guns to Galway by sea, thus avoiding the then difficult problems of transporting them overland.[37] So, investment in this midland corridor may have been to further enhance command of the midland access to the west via the vital lynchpin on each side of the Shannon at Athlone. Athlone occupied the most strategic inland position on the island as a whole, not only along an east–west but also along a north–south axis. Control of Athlone guaranteed Dublin its access to drive westwards to Galway; and enabled it to deliver and maintain supplies to the royal garrison at Roscommon. Likewise, Athlone sought to guarantee control of the vital north–south artery of the Shannon and also assisted in frustrating possible north–south Irish military alliances from blossoming. Keeping Clanricard faithful so as to control Portumna and Loughrea may also have been relevant to this overall strategy.

One can therefore see shrewd military planning and geometric, cartographic thinking in this attention to the midland-west corridor. The same may be true of the southwestern land corridor, where again the consistently refurbished Maryborough and the enhanced garrisons at Nenagh and Roscrea helped 'pave the way' to Limerick city. Equally, Leighlin Bridge was to be given special investment to enable its fortifications to command that narrow, funnel-like space along the Barrow. Thus, in conjunction with further military and settler investment in Athy, Carlow, Enniscorthy, New Ross, Ferns and St Mullins, the Dublin corridor southwards – giving access to the Waterford port region – was widened. All of this building, mapping and military planning had meant that these corridors assisted in another function – to separate Irish lordships one from another. This enlarged southern corridor sought to prevent (or at least minimize) major regional alliances from being created or sustained between the Gaelic lords of the Midlands and those of the southeast.

Cecil and his English strategists in Ireland sought also to expand the coastal corridor extending northwards from the Pale, having a key inland pivot at Trim and a vital lynchpin at Newry. Nicholas Bagenal was placed here in 1549 to bolster the defences of Carlingford and Greencastle and to develop the key site of Newry, which Lythe was to map in great detail. Two years later, Bagenal was busy adapting the church buildings at Armagh – blocking their doors and windows – so as to create an English garrison to drive a further wedge northwestwards.[38] And the final anchor along this northern corridor-cum-frontier was the ancient fortress at Carrickfergus – jumping off point and the crucial garrison facing both the O'Neills to the west and the incoming aggressive Scots, more active by far as settlers in northeast Ireland in the later sixteenth century than the English. England rightly and carefully invested in Carrickfergus's defences. The old castle at Belfast was to be garrisoned later but for the sixteenth century Carrickfergus was the crucial base for expeditions by sea to the north, to the Bann mouth or on to Lough Foyle.

When Sir Henry Sidney became lord deputy in 1566, the first large-scale project of plantation in Ulster was attempted – including both private planters and the military and naval forces of Elizabeth I. As part of this project, Colonel Edmund Randolph arrived via Lough Foyle and fortified the church buildings at Derry. However, he lost out to the O'Neills; and, in 1567, the garrison had to be evacuated, following a fire and gun-powder explosion. But this landing at Lough Foyle had emphasized the growing effectiveness of English sea power and its capacity to give vital support to civil plantations.[39] It was from the craggy seafortress at Carrickfergus that Sir Henry Dowcra sailed in May 1600 with his force of 4,000 men, and proceeded to control Lough Foyle and fortified Culmore, Derry, Dunalong (a former O'Neill castle) and later Lifford. This landing at Lough Foyle and the establishment of a vector of control inland was one of the most critical manoeuvres in the Nine Years War (1595–1603).

In one sense, I have advanced the story too far forward. But in another sense I have not, for what the totality of Tudor maps and plans for coastal Ireland shows is the obvious central importance of English sea power – understated, I feel, in the story of the sixteenth-century conquest of Ireland. As Paul Kerrigan has detailed, proposals and plans for both coastal defences and coastal hinterland plantations by loyal English settlers must be understood in part, at least, as Tudor England's response to the threat of continental invasion, especially from Catholic Spain and, to a lesser extent, France.[40] Concern over Scotland's expansionist tendencies in the north was also a key consideration. On the European scale, 'only the central authority of the state or the more wealthy cities . . . could afford to equip and maintain a train of artillery, a development that was to contribute considerably to the consolidation of state power in the early modern period'.[41] The emergence of the square-rigged sailing ship, complete with 'a broadside armament of heavy cannon in the early years of the 16th century emphasised the importance of fortifications equipped with artillery for defending ports and anchorages'.[42] The Italians were the innovators here, followed quickly by the French, the Spanish, the Portuguese, and then the English and the Dutch. Control of the Irish seas, coasts and port-cities was to become a crucial element in the Tudor conquest of Ireland.

The most central – and sometimes overlooked – maritime anchor of English rule in Ireland was Dublin itself. The military fortress of Dublin Castle was the enduring fulcrum of the military administration in Ireland. It was in Dublin Castle that the ammunition and powder from the royal ordnance was stored and distributed. Dublin was also the central depot for victualling the hierarchy of forts and garrisons that stretched out along the Irish frontiers. On the exposed western flank, Galway city, a strongly walled and well-built town, had its military defences upgraded a number of times from 1538 onwards. The vulnerability of the peninsular/insular/bay world of the south coast also called for much naval vigilance. Cork and its great harbour was most strategic to this region. The earliest bastioned work of the Italian style in Ireland – that of Corkbeg – was established at the mouth of the harbour c.1557. This is known on some maps as 'the King's Work' (that of Edward VI) and was to be specifically mapped by Lythe.[43] Corkbeg thus became the great 'bulwarke for the haven mouthe', while the fort built to the east protected 'this harbour-mouth gun battery from attack on the landward side'.[44] Kinsale was also a critical focus for maritime defences. Plans exist of the port's new defences made by John Rogers. From the mid-sixteenth century, Kinsale received periodic upgrading of its military fortifications to match its key naval function. The military needs of the cities of Waterford and Limerick were also well attended to over the second half of the sixteenth century when English and Dutch marine engineers appear on the Irish scene.

Rogers also planned a new fort at Olderfleet at the mouth of the Larne river in the strategic northeast. All along the east coast from Drogheda to Dundalk and particularly at Newry, Carlingford, Strangford, Greencastle and the most strategic of all, Carrickfergus, the Tudor administration endeavoured to map, protect and enhance these coastal defences – however restrictive the financial arrangements. Likewise, in the southeast and southwest, Arklow, Wexford, New Ross, Youghal, Baltimore and Berehaven were seen as important second-level port-towns or harbours. All received periodic reviews; plans were made and sometimes their fortifications were refurbished and upgraded.

Cecil's portfolio of maps came to include numerous plans and profiles of Irish coastal sites, ports and their fortifications. Tudor plans of key fortifications all around the Irish coast stress England's drive to enclose and enframe Ireland within the wider maritime grip of England's naval and military power. 'Enclosure' is a most fashionable word and motive in eighteenth-century Ireland; but 'enclosure' was also a key metaphor for England's conquest of sixteenth-century Ireland. It denoted enclosure and bounding of new fields, roads and properties at the microscale, key enclosures/walls at garrison and urban sites, as well as political/administrative enclosures at the barony and county scale, and enclosures at the provincial scale.[45] It is quite clear that Cecil and the lord deputies of Ireland (from Croft and Sidney through to Sir William Gerrard and Sir John Perrott), while concentrating on specific tactics for different provinces, still kept a strategic overall island view. Whatever the vacillations, whatever the set-backs and short-term changes in tactics, the endgame was to continue to advance the Pale in all directions – and, in particular, push north beyond that crucial divide that stretched from Galway past Loughrea and Lough Ree, through to the southern end of Lough Erne and across to Strangford and Carrickfergus. From the beginning, and central to this strategy, was the defence of and control of Irish seas, coasts and seaports. The concept of the *mare clausum* belongs to this era; and the English strove to ensure that the seas all around Ireland became a 'space of enclosure' under their control.

But maps and port-cities do not only enclose; they also help to open up spaces – new opportunities, new vistas. All of these well-defended port-cities had a double face – they faced outwards to defend England's Ireland from external aggression; and also faced inwards, acting as the axes for controlling and extending their hinterlands and facilitating the free movement of new settlers, their goods and stock inland. The port-cities were also the last strongholds if insurrections should force the settlers back to the fortified ports to escape destruction. Crucially, however, the port-cities were the pivots of internal and external trade. The expansion and protection of land corridors across the main arteries of the island, likewise, albeit slowly, facilitated the exploitation and movement of inland resources for profit to the ports. From the time of the Vikings (at least), Ireland's settlement foci had moved seawards. The Tudor English were to enhance significantly this outward maritime drive according as Ireland was incorporated into the trading, settlement and cultural networks of the wider Atlantic.

Cecil had another important use for maps: to identify the key families of Ireland (and of England) so as to be able to locate the government's friends and enemies. Over time he developed a formidable command of the physical and political geography of Ireland and of intricate Gaelic institutions.[46] To plan a good geographical spread of local government officials and to measure the correct taxation levels per area, maps were also helpful instruments. And for Ireland specifically, maps were critical in meeting the needs for colonial expansion: in illustrating and planning expeditions, battles and sieges; in clarifying tactical topographical features from a military point of view; in locating the regions of political and military resistance; in marshalling the troops and, as we have seen, in planning the location of forts, and most particularly in supervising and controlling the seizure, delimitation and reallocation of land in the plantations proper (as, for example, in Munster). Cecil, 'in his understanding of the geographical facts which govern policy . . . was unsurpassed, and possibly unequalled by any other statesman or administration of his time'.[47]

To Cecil and like-minded administrators, maps were also instrumental in defining many county boundaries in Ireland – examples include early county maps of Mayo, Sligo and Monaghan and Jobson's rather slap-dash version of Co. Cork.[48] The quality of communications between the two islands had also to be established, as well as the best sites for county and postal towns, gaols and court-houses. Maps were instrumental in nurturing economic development through the fostering of trade, ports, mining and industrial ventures. Maps were also important aids to people like Cecil and many other patriotic Elizabethans interested in reconstructing the history of their own burgeoning nation. In a word, maps could be used either to construct or to subvert a nation.

Whereas Cecil had very few maps of Ireland on which to work and plan strategy in 1550, by the end of the sixteenth century, he had put together two books of Irish maps dealing mainly with the expansion of the Tudor frontier in that 'rebellious and troublesome' adjacent island.[49] Cecil, therefore, took seriously the admonition that any secretary of state in England must have 'the book of Ortelius's maps, a book of the maps of England . . . a good description of the realm of Ireland, a note of the Noblemen and surnames English or Irish of their sept, Enraghes, Gallowglasses, Kerns and followers, and if any other plots or maps come to his hands, let them be kept safely'.[50] Cecil certainly did this and more: 'his requests for new maps were a continuing source of trouble for the royal officials in Dublin, who seem seldom to have initiated mapping projects of their own or even to have made a regular practice of keeping duplicates of the maps they sent to London'.[51] Many of the requests were inspired by the latest regional crisis – they pointed up the Tudor administration's lack of detailed knowledge of the Irish domain and highlighted the confusions and anxieties surrounding the Tudor conquest of Ireland.

In short, Cecil was the orchestrator of a prolific, if spasmodic and uneven, mapping enterprise, which played a key role in the Tudor conquest of Ireland.

Mapping the New Frontier: Lythe, Jobson and Bartlett

In the colonization of Ireland Sir Henry Sidney was another key strategist who was passionately interested in maps. He formed a powerful axis with Cecil in developing a strategy for the island's colonization and was part of a wider circle of statesmen and scholars in England who were both interested in and investing in other overseas ventures. Appointed lord deputy to Ireland for the years 1565–71 and 1575–8, Sidney has been rightly ascribed a central role in redefining England's strategy for ruling Ireland.[52] He was a key figure in moving the agenda from one of persuasion to one of coercion. To give this new and radical strategic drive geographical meaning on the ground required more troops in more regions, a greater and more 'thickly-plotted' set of forts and garrisons, more settler colonies and, most particularly, a country that was fully shired, so as to allow a circuit court system and English 'law and order' to be extended over all the island. Thus, in the second half of the sixteenth century, a new pattern of conquest and rule is set in train. And a more comprehensive strategy of mapping is initiated to reduce the uncertainties and anxieties of campaigning in and ruling this still mainly uncharted and 'dangerous' country.

One such territory was ruled by Shane O'Neill in Ulster. In July 1567, Queen Elizabeth wrote to Sidney outlining her specific Irish policies, following on from 'the late death of the troublesome rebelle Shane Oneile'.[53] The second edition of *Holinshed's Chronicles* (1587) records that moment when 'the queens maiestie . . . having all Ulster at hir commandement and disposition, was verie desirous to have a true plot of the whole land, whereby she might in some sort see the same . . .'[54] Lythe was sent over to Ireland to do this job. Klein rightly dramatizes this histori- cal account of one man's exit *vis-à-vis* another man's entrance. The regional lord of Ulster yields to the modern map-maker who, through his surveys, would turn Ireland into a visible space of knowledge and political appropriation.[55] Under Sidney's guidance, Lythe would be instructed to make a 'true plot' and 'perfect description' of Ulster (and Ireland), which land Elizabeth could then 'see', command and rule properly. *Holinshed's Chronicles*, therefore, specify the critical moment prior to the need for the survey – the moment of 'rebellion' and 'corrup- tion' that necessitated what the English saw as the reforming, purifying power of cartographic order and proper rule. Thus, as Klein argues, 'the colonial rhetoric surrounding the representation of Ireland constructs Irish space as the inherently transgressive realm of the savage or rebel where renewal of political control must be preceded by systematic description'.[56] Lythe was the 'magical' map-maker whose acts of surveying introduced 'a mode of representing land which subsumes the social under the geometric and effaces attention to human detail by relying on the levelling impact of cartographic scale'.[57]

Between 1567 and 1571, Sidney, with Cecil's support, 'was the inspiration for and assured the completion of Robert Lythe's surveys in the south coast of Ireland'.[58] This was the first detailed and comprehensive survey of any major region in Ireland. Lythe's cartographic achievements in the very difficult condi- tions of the late 1560s/early 1570s are said to rank beside Petty's mapping achievements for mid-seventeenth-century Ireland. Lythe is the giant of sixteenth- century mapping in Ireland and his image of Ireland was to be perpetuated via Boazio's and Speed's maps until Petty's own masterful survey.[59]

Lythe, like most early map-makers in Ireland, was a stranger to the country. London-born, he had previously served as a young military engineer on England's eastern frontier at Calais. In Ireland he had to work at great speed in a relatively short time, carrying out a kind of rapid frontier surveying that was also to charac- terize map-making in early colonial America. And like other early map-makers, he had to work with inadequate back-up facilities and resources in what was almost invariably 'a hostile and uncomfortable environment'.[60] Most of the places on his maps of the south and east of Ireland are sites of military significance. He carefully distinguishes the key towns from their rural surrounds. Castles-cum-tower-houses and fortified sites generally are most carefully mapped. Churches are also itemized as conspicuous features in the landscape, both as guides to travel and for their potential military use. Strongly built houses and clustered settlements are mapped, as are strategic non-urban coastal/riverside locations. As always with Ireland, exceptionally in a west European mapping but not in the wider imperial context, the names and territories of key families, clans and lordships are clearly identified.

Sidney kept a keen eye on Lythe's progress on the frontier. From July to September 1569 Lythe worked under the protection of Sidney as the latter made one of his characteristic circuits throughout a countryside he hoped to tame and civilize, 'to traverse, chart and subdue', ruthlessly exercising 'over the space of the colony the power to map which imperialism affords'.[61] In his baggage, Sidney carried all the apparatus of colonial rule, including up-to-date maps. He had previously held (and still retained) the function of president of the Council of the Welsh Marches, where he was particularly active in deepening the administrative capacity of local and regional government under the Tudors. In Ireland, he was to be a key architect in the construction of the presidencies of Munster and Connacht – strategic, halfway, military and legal administrations before full state control could be established from London. Dublin, one assumes, amongst its many functions, was to rule Leinster. Likewise, Sidney was a central figure in the extension of the shiring system across the country and especially in the now strategic province of Connacht. It was under Sidney's direction that the Dublin parliament of 1569 gave statutory backing to the process of turning all Ireland into 'shire ground'.[62] It is not surprising, therefore, that under his supervision and direction Lythe was also to pay particular attention to defining county and provincial boundaries.

The detailed accounts of Lythe's expenses over the period 1567 to 1571 show that he was specifically involved in tracking the precise county boundaries of Meath and the relatively new county of Westmeath established in 1542 (see Figs. 2.9 and 10.2). It is also noticeable that for the most part he renders his accounts county by county.[63] Sidney was thus consolidating new systems of administration using both old and new boundaries, mapping and marking them on the ground and so enclosing Ireland within tighter grids of rule at county and subcounty levels. As well as shire reform, mapping and deepening the reality of the new provincial administrations was clearly in Sidney's mind. Indeed, Lythe himself – in a letter to Lord Burghley, dated March 1571 – confirms these mapping objectives:

> That I trust in God I have taken the true bounds and limits of every particular
> province and shire and chief lordships in the same as nigh as I can gather them by
> information of the country and my own knowledge and judgement.[64]

Consequently, Lythe was instructed to draw his famous *A Single Draght of Mounster*, which is the first modern map of the province of Munster[65] (see Fig. 2.10).

Lythe's map of Munster signals the dramatic shift in policy under Sidney if we compare it with John Goghe's island-wide map, drawn only four years earlier. English knowledge and strategy, up to the mid-1560s, was still at the level of the island as a whole and still worked, in part at least, through the great lords and earls, all of whom Goghe places on his map. But Sidney's need for more detailed geographical knowledge and control at the provincial scale signalled his determination to reduce the power of these great lordships and deliberately to release the lesser lords from this form of overlordship so as to bring the latter more closely

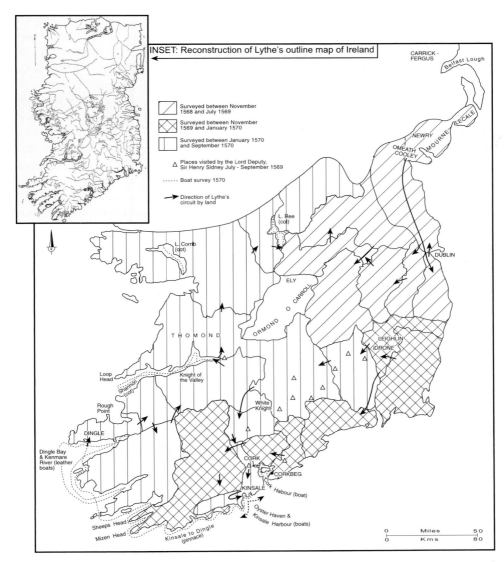

2.9   The 'progress' of Robert Lythe's surveys in Ireland (1567–71) and, inset, a reconstruction of his map of Ireland (adapted from the work of J.H. Andrews on Robert Lythe: see, in particular, reference 63)

under her majesty's administrative and legal control. Sidney wanted to win over the loyalty of these lesser lords to the crown. It is not surprising, therefore, that Lythe's highly original map of Munster provides much detailed and accurate information as to the geography of the lesser lords and their lands. Even in the poorly surveyed north Tipperary, 'O'Kennedy Roe, O'Kennedy Donne and O'Kennedy Fyn' are identified controlling the lands east of Lough Derg, while the territories of 'McBryne Arra, O'Dywer, Burke [of Clanwilliam] and Sr. Tybbot Butler' are also identified. Moving into north Cork, the lands of the 'Whytknyght,

Condam [Condon], Lord Roche, O'Calaghan' and other local lords, like the O'Keefes, Barrymore, and Viscount Buttevant, are detailed. Thus, Sidney and Cecil (for his annotations are on the map) gained a much more comprehensive view of the political and proprietorial geography from Lythe's careful survey.

Lythe's map of Munster is the first of a series of provincial maps executed to further the conquest and control of Ireland at this time. The control of the outlying Gaelic-Irish regions of Leinster still involved an enhanced role for local English seneschals and captains so as to eventually bring such territories within the existing county system. In contrast, for the feudalized regions of Munster and Connacht, provincial presidencies with extensive powers – both military and legal – were the main driving forces.[66] The essentially Gaelic-Irish province of Ulster presented very different challenges.

Lythe's *A Single Draght of Mounster* is part of a wider collection of his maps that originally included 'a "plot" of Ireland eight and a half feet long and five and a half feet wide', which has not survived.[67] Surviving copies of Lythe's own survey work carefully delineates Munster, Leinster and south Connacht but fails to advance into the still unconquered territories of north Connacht. The presidency of Connacht, therefore, demanded detailed mapping, as did the follow-up to the highly innovative and successful Composition Book of Connacht (1585), which established a territorial basis for crown rents down to the 'quarter' and townland scale. John Browne's earlier, precocious map of Co. Mayo, where he held the post of sheriff, points the way, as does a highly impressive map that records the advance, defeat and retreat of Scots mercenaries across north Connacht in August/September 1586. In this latter map, a broad picture is presented of all of north Connacht (including its woodland distribution), beginning on the borders with Donegal and Bellick (and a still very bloated and single Lough Erne) and working westwards to Clew Bay and Killary harbour. This map also presents a foreshortened yet still innovative portrayal of west Galway, Lough Mask, and Lough Corrib, which was recorded as entering the sea near the city of Galway. This map survey can be seen as a kind of precursor to the superb map of Connacht and Thomond surveyed for the government by the same John Browne of Mayo and completed after his untimely death by his namesake and nephew in 1591.[68]

As Andrews notes, 'this map improves on Lythe's treatment of southwest Connacht and was creditably accurate in areas that Lythe was unable to visit'.[69] It is also impressive in the distinctions it makes between wooded and long-settled farming territories, showing for example, extensive woods west and south of Athlone, which contrast sharply with the open, long-settled landscape of east Galway. In this map Browne names not only the new counties but also the new baronies. It can be said to synthesize the success of Sidney's provincial policies in the west (see Fig. 2.11), confirming that 'the sway of the President was extended also into the almost totally Gaelicised northern part of Connacht and these areas were eventually brought to conformity also by forceful persuasion rather than colonisation. As a result of this programme laid down by Sidney, Connacht, not Munster, remained a bastion of the "English-Irish" into the 17th century.'[70]

There are other important lessons to be gained from comparing Lythe's map of

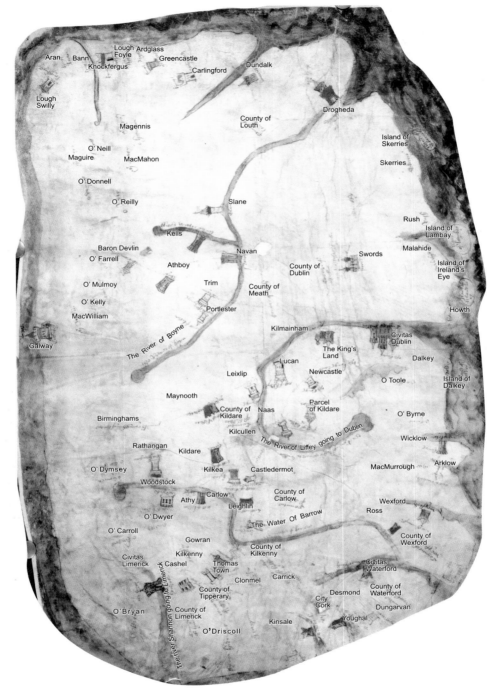

Plate 1a, fig. 2.2 The 'Cotton' 1520s map of Ireland (placename and family name identifications adopted from figure 1.4, *Shapes of Ireland*, p. 12; see reference 2).

Plate 1b, fig. 2.3 Part of the North Atlantic and northwest Europe as mapped by the Portuguese in 1519 (Vol. I, Plate 17 of the Lopo Homem – Reinels atlas in *Portugaliae Monumenta Cartographica:* see reference 4).

Plate 1c, fig. 2.5 Eryn: *Hibernia Britannicae insulae, nova descriptio Irlandt*, Map of Ireland, from Abraham Ortelius's *Theatrum orbis terrarum* (1573).

Plate 1d, fig. 2.6 *Hibernia, insulae non procul ab Anglia vulgare Hirlandia vocata*, John Goghe's map of Ireland (c. 1567). By permission of Public Record

Plate 1e, fig. 2.8 Laurence Nowell's *A General Description of England and Ireland* (1564–5). By permission of the British Library (Add MS 62540).

Plate 1f, fig. 2.10 Robert Lythe's map of Munster (1571). By permission of the Public Record Office, London (MPF/173).

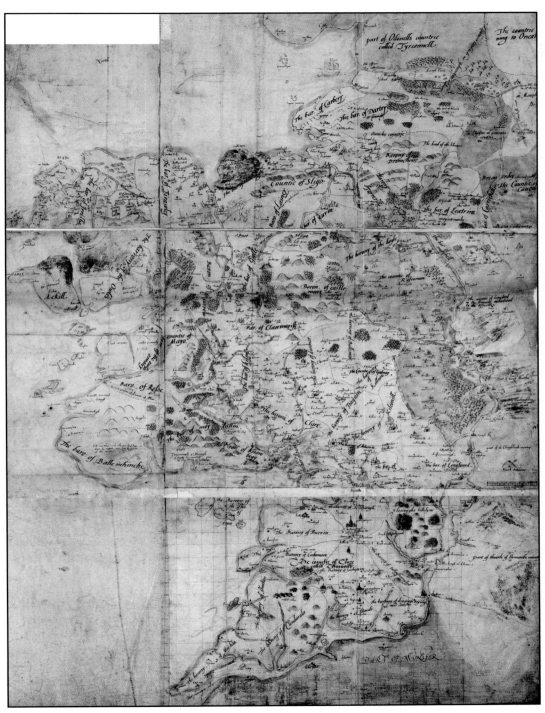

Plate 1g, fig. 2.11 Map of the province of Connacht and Clare (1591) by John Browne I and II. By permission of 'The Board of Trinity College Dublin' (MS 1209/68).

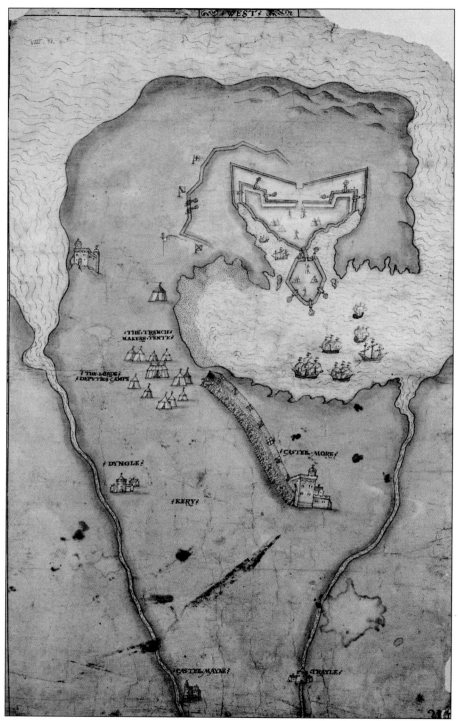

Plate 1h, fig. 2.12 'Cartogram' of Dún an Óir, Smerwick harbour and the Dingle peninsula with the distribution of English forces under Lord Grey de Wilton (1579). By permission of the National Maritime Museum, Greenwich [P/49 (29)].

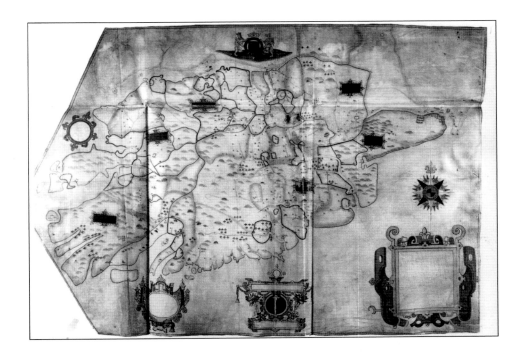

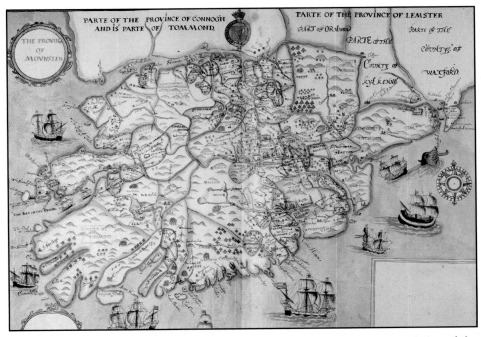

Plate 1i, fig. 2.14 (a) and (b) Francis Jobson's maps of Munster (1589). By permission of the National Maritime Museum [B 8956/L and P/49 (20)].

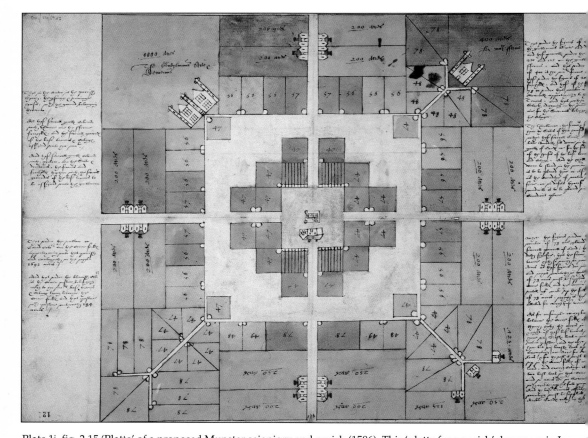

Plate 1j, fig. 2.15 'Platte' of a proposed Munster seigniory and parish (1586). This 'platte for a parish' drawn up in January 1586 shows the proposal for a Munster seigniory of 12,000 acres and depicts farm-boundaries, dwellings and roads. shows the parish church and mill at the centre with its small-holding villagers. The main planter's 'gentleman's demesn of 1000 acres and his 'Big House' are shown to the northwest with an array of tenant farms, ranging from 78 to 400 acre located on each side of this idealised 'manor/parish' as well as other small-holdings (see reference 35). A very simil pattern of manorial settlement planning was intended by Henry Oglethorpe for his plantation in Georgia as late as 171 By permission of the Public Record Office, London (MPF. 305).

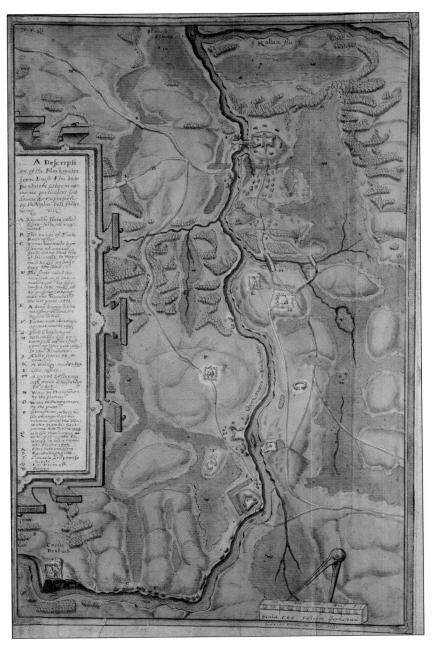

Plate 1k, fig. 2.16 Richard Bartlett's map of the Blackwater valley, southwest of Lough Neagh (1602–3). By permission of the National Library of Ireland, Dublin. This shows that part of the Blackwater Valley that lies between Benburb to the south and the mouth of the River Callan to the north – with the river or Owen More (*Abhainn Mhór*), which here divides counties Tyrone and Armagh – occupying the central areas of the composition. This complex region was the crucial battleground between O'Neill and Mountjoy, then characterised by an advancing series of English forts, including Fort Mullin (marked 'D' on the map) to the south and Charlemont Fort (marked 'G' on the map) as well as the field fortifications built by O'Neill at crucial crossing points. The wider landscape reveals the network of communications and passages, some newly cut-through O'Neill's great woodland fortresses, and so define the 'waie to Dungannon by the plaines'.

Plate 1l, fig. 2.17 Bartlett's 'map' of a ruined Armagh and the new fort of
Mullin. By permission of the National Library of Ireland, Dublin. The upper
part of the composition shows the ruined and desolate city of Armagh. Given
its strategic frontline position, Armagh had suffered badly in all the wars after
1550. Most of its street houses have been burned and beaten flat and its friary,
abbey and other churches are also shown in ruins. The road at the very top of
the picture follows the line of the old road from Armagh to the west and the
mound shown beside it is Navan Fort (*Eamhain Macha*), the ancient capital of
Ulster. The cathedral is at the centre and below it is the Market Street Cross
which marks the meeting-point of the 'trians' or three civic districts of the
ancient city of Armagh. The new fortress of the Mullin (Irish *muileann*: mill) is
shown at the bottom with three bastions and houses of the English style,
single-storied, thatched with gabled roofs and chimneys. A cot or dug-out
canoe – the characteristic Irish boat for lakes and rivers – is shown in the River
Blackwater.

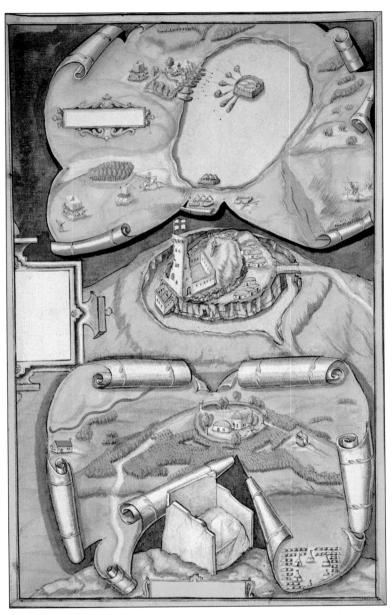

Plate 1m, fig. 2.18 Bartlett's 'map' of Dungannon and Tullyhoge (1602–3). By permission of the National Library of Ireland, Dublin. Here, Richard Bartlett, artist/cartographer of the war with Hugh O'Neill, celebrates the climactic victories of Mountjoy. Occupying the centre of the composition is the triumphant flag of St George – the English flag – flying over the ruined O'Neill capital of Dungannon. Equally significant, the lower part of the composition depicts the ancient inauguration place of the O'Neill at Tullyhoge situated on a commanding hill, and located in the wide countryside north of Dungannon. After a war of attrition which left thousands dying of famine, Mountjoy marked this ultimate defeat of the O'Neill by smashing the inauguration stone-chair (shown as an inset at bottom). The nearby rath shown on the top of the hill is that of the O'Hagan's, hereditary guardians of Tullyhoge, and legal advisers to the O'Neill kings for centuries and chief officers at the inauguration of these kings.

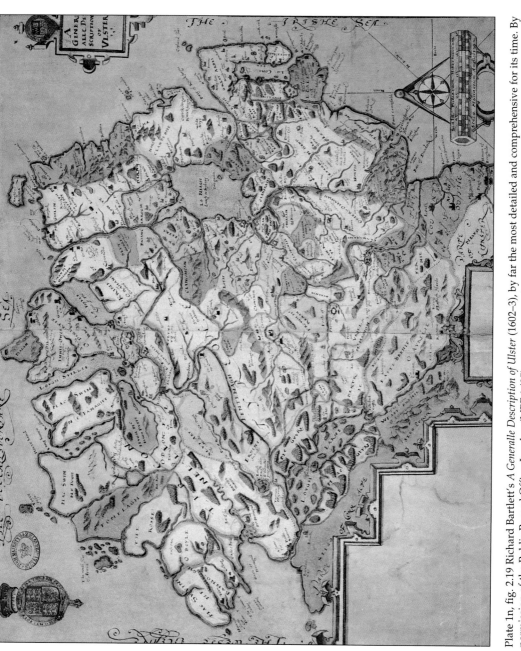

Plate 1n, fig. 2.19 Richard Bartlett's *A Generalle Description of Ulster* (1602–3), by far the most detailed and comprehensive for its time. By permission of the Public Record Office, London (MPF 1/35).

Plate 1o, fig. 2.20 Richard Bartlett's map of south Ulster (1602–3). By permission of the Public Record Office, London (MPF 1/36).

Plate 1p, fig. 2.21 Probable likeness of Hugh O Neill, Earl of Tyrone, from an engraving published in *La Spada d'Orione Stellata nel Ciclo di Marte*, by Primo Damschino, Rome, 1680. Thanks to Dr. Hiram Morgan, History, UCC for providing a copy of this image.

Munster and that of the Brownes' of Connacht. Cecil's hand is to be found on both maps as he probes the strengths and weaknesses of the existing political order, notes additional families and settlements and contemplates the next moves via sketch-plans and memos long since lost. Ironically, this magnificent map of Connacht by the Brownes, while commissioned by the government and used by its most senior officials, disappears from the policy domain in the early seventeenth century when it was acquired by Sir George Carew for his private collection. Equally surprising, Lythe's accurate and detailed map of Munster is also strangely neglected in the planning of the Munster plantation initiated only fifteen years after the production of this map. On the other hand, it could be argued that Lythe's map had done its job: it had identified the locations of the old territorial lords, many of whom were later displaced. Fresh maps would be needed to plan the new proprietorial world of the Munster planters.

So discontinuities and faultlines abound: in what the sixteenth-century maps managed to show of different Irish regions; in the use made of key manuscript maps, which disappear from the official record; between pre-plantation and post-plantation 'views' of the same regions. The meticulous scholarship, not to say fine detective work, of John Andrews on the genealogy of Irish maps allows him to state confidently that more sixteenth-century maps have disappeared than have survived. And of those that did survive, quite a number did not become part of a sustained, cumulative view by the English administrators of Ireland, its provinces and regions. Of Cecil's extensive collection of Irish maps, acquired between 1571 and his death in 1598, 'none owes anything to Lythe'.[71]

Discontinuities, absences, errors and imaginative inventions were also an integral part of the sixteenth-century mapping heritage. Indeed, one could argue that the whole mapping drive over the century and a half between the 1530s and the 1680s was aimed at reducing these ambiguities and geographical anxieties, eliminating the errors and exorcizing the ghosts of long-lost imagined islands and other fantastic landscape features and legends, so as to produce a more rational, 'scientific' view of Ireland, albeit one heavily coloured by anglo-centric lenses and concerns. Ireland's complex river systems – compared by Sean O'Faolain to the intricacies of the Book of Kells – its extensive and numerous bogs, woods and mountains and its very numerous lakes, not to speak of a lengthy coastline whose intricacies and loops could be said to stretch to infinity – all meant that the precise mapping of Ireland and its parts was a Herculean task. This was the diverse and anxious world that Sidney set out to picture, secure and conquer – and no other sixteenth-century cartographer in Ireland was to match Lythe's determination, skill and persistence in helping Sidney's England achieve its goals.

Mapping on the frontier was a dangerous and precarious business. Lythe's accounts demonstrate that he both needed and sought the protection of each of the local lords as he travelled by horseback with his guides and surveyed one territory after another. I suspect Lythe needed Sidney's personal entourage as protection when he attempted to map the county palatinate of Tipperary. There was no love lost between the earl of Ormond – the ruler of the palatinate – and Sidney, who deplored this seemingly anarchic and ancient jurisdiction. Such a separate palatinate administration cut right across Sidney's ambition to establish a single modern administrative system over the whole country.[72] The last thing he wanted was a fractured landscape, full of internal borders and multiple forms of administration.

Lythe's failure to map the northern half of Tipperary may thus relate to restrictions and obstacles imposed by Ormond on Sidney, who, as we have seen, was interested in more than administrative reform. The planting and settling of the most strategic areas of Ireland with loyal settlers was also very much part of his agenda. Consequently, it is not surprising that Sidney was once again at Lythe's shoulder when he made what is a wonderfully accurate map of the barony of Idrone in Co. Carlow. This map provides in colourful detail a most unique vista of the village geography of this important feudalized region.[73] One can also depend on Lythe to guesstimate the acreage of the woodland mapped. For Idrone this comes to around 12 per cent of the total territory mapped, a percentage that supports Eileen McCracken's generalization for Tudor Ireland as a whole c.1600. The real reason for this very particularized Idrone survey rests with Sir Peter Carew of Cornwall. Carew was making ancestral – and very dubious – ownership claims to this Butler-controlled territory with Sidney's (and Cecil's) support. This map was, therefore, staking out another potential settler region. Lythe was never an innocent map-maker – he was a key intelligence officer for the crown and its rulers.[74]

Elizabeth and Sidney, like Henry VIII's and Edward VI's administrations before them, were concerned about the defences of southwest Munster. In June 1567, the queen wrote to Sidney about this strategic yet highly exposed part of Ireland: 'You make mention of the great traffike of the Spaniards unto the sea coast of Munster and Conaugh[t] by which the townes upon ye sea coast do not onley suffre decay but alsy may be in such danger as wer meete to be foreseene.'[75] Sidney was equally anxious to establish and facilitate new private enterprise colonies along the Munster coast west of Cork city. He was also interested in getting a proper cartographic survey of the complicated peninsular/bay structure of a southwest coast greatly valued for its fisheries. Consequently, Lythe was made to pay particular attention to these coastal worlds, closely tracking their contours by land and carrying out a number of detailed, instrument-based, maritime surveys from smaller boats. But for the maritime world that stretched, curved and looped all the way from Kinsale to Dingle, Lythe had the assistance of a warship's pinnace, manned by sixty men. This, therefore, was very serious mapping in a crucial and sensitive terrain. Naval issues were clearly on Lythe's and Sidney's agenda, for the former regularly takes notes on the shape and depth of the many harbours, creeks and havens (see Fig. 2.9, p. 39). It is therefore not surprising to find that of the total investment of Lythe's time and effort in mapping Ireland, one-half was spent on Munster alone.[76]

It is significant how often the early cartographers stress the control of the seas – not only for strategic and military reasons but also for the economic wealth of the Irish fisheries. Apart from providing detailed and very specific information on coasts and harbours, Lythe regularly itemized natural resources and physical features. His very earliest map of the survey (October/November 1567) for the northeast Ulster coast also details the arable, pastoral and wooded proportions, as well as the acreage of different coastal territories.[77] As Andrews sees it, Lythe followed 'his master Sidney in seeing Ireland mainly as a field of economic development'.[78] In fact, the Elizabethans generally saw Ireland as an underutilized economic zone, ripe for exploitation and profit-making. But first military conquest was necessary to achieve full and free economic penetration.

However, like Sidney, Lythe failed to penetrate, map or dominate the north and northwest of the country. Sidney's dream of shiring all of Ireland failed in these difficult-to-conquer northern lands and it is surely both fitting and ironic that on one of the rare occasions when Sidney found himself lost in the Irish countryside, the land in which he was 'dislocated' lay well north of the line of country that Lythe failed to map. North of this country, from Killary harbour to Strangford Lough, Lythe was unable to safely track and map. Indeed, his first foray into Ireland had ended in failure. His original mission in September 1567 was to draw accurate maps of northeast Ulster, so as to assist with a proposed colonial settlement after the collapse of Shane O'Neill's 'rebellion'. But this project came to nought, except for what is likely to be his highly instructive map of Carrickfergus Lough, which still shows very significant woodlands in the vicinity of the castle of Belfast and along the Lagan valley proper.[79]

The artist/painter/cartographer Baptiza Boazio – who is likely to be the Jean Baptiste that painted a number of earlier maps of the west and north of Ireland (including Browne's Mayo) – produced a beautiful and highly decorative coloured map of Ireland in 1599. This striking map has been made even more famous in recent years, as it illuminates the cover of John Andrews's magisterial *Shapes of Ireland*. But as Andrews points out, Boazio's mapping achievement is in reality that of Robert Lythe.[80] Boazio's 1599 map is now seen as an anachronistic failure, which matches the failure of his patron Essex's expedition into Ireland in the same year. With its many ghostly echoes, this map actually dates back to Lythe's final mapping of Ireland as a whole in 1571 (see Fig. 2.9 inset, p. 39). And the sharpest line on both Boazio's map and Lythe's map – the greatest faultline – is a cartographic, environmental, military and cultural boundary between the settled and now shired world south of the Killary–Strangford line and a resistant north. The world shown to the north is still more opaque, vacant and shadowy; placenames and settlements are rather thin on the ground and many green woodlands dominate the region. It is very doubtful if the 1599 map provides a realistic distribution of woodland for the northern province in the late sixteenth century.

Indeed, the woodland extravaganza on Boazio's map may support Klein's argument that 'precise geographical information was not the map's principal objective'.[81] He recognizes the accomplished finish of the map, but sees 'its lavish ornamental flourish, the purely fictional character of some of the map's topographic details and the way Ireland is visibly encased by the decorative frame' as pointing to other discursive objectives.[82] In Klein's view, 'what makes Boazio's map such an important example of how many 16th century Englishmen made spatial sense of the intractable and "barbaric" Irish territory is precisely its value as a decorative image of Ireland fluctuating between fact and fiction'.[83] Both Boazio, the map-maker, and Renold Elstrack, the engraver, are twice represented on the map – in two cartouches bearing their names but also, in what Klein sees as 'a more imaginative but a deeply colonial gesture', their names turned into two toponyms: Baptiste's Rock (off Antrim) and Elstrake's Isle (off the northern Donegal coast).[84] The extravagant display of both the map and its makers is seen as stressing 'Ireland's status as the property of those that give it visual and verbal presence in maps and texts'.[85] This form of appropriation is accentuated by the opulent surrounds of the map, which powerfully express the claims of English domination of Irish land and people: 'St George's flag at the top, two majestic English ships sailing the Irish coastline, a dedicatory address to the Queen in the bottom left-hand corner crowned by the Royal court of arms'.[86] Land and map are both dedicated and handed over to Elizabeth, apparently allowing her to oversee the whole of Ireland from her throne in England. But not quite – a wooded, partly fanciful and bloated Ulster still both fascinates and threatens.

Jonathan Swift was to say that African map-makers covered the unknown empty spaces with wild beasts and strange figures.[87] It is likely that the equivalent cartographic conceit for Ireland was to enclose its lesser-known parts – as Boazio does – with a dense cover of woodland. Where the cartographer, the soldier and the administrator could not go – where the power of the empire had not yet penetrated – additional woodland often came in handy to clothe this 'nakedness'. After Essex and Boazio, it would take a more powerful military leader, Charles Blount, Lord Mountjoy, and the greatest artist/cartographer ever to work in Ireland, Richard Bartlett, to penetrate and make visible for the first time this inhospitable and obstinate world of Ulster – this *terra incognita* – the last military and cartographic frontier of Tudor Ireland.

But that is to anticipate. The Nine Years War constituted one of the bloodiest and most devastating of all Irish wars. Early victories by Hugh O'Neill (as at Clontibret), his careful building up and marshalling of regional and provincial alliances and his astuteness and (partly ancient) skill in waging a food war against the still standing Ulster garrisons had fanned the hopes and spirits of the Irish everywhere. O'Neill's success at the battle of the Yellow Ford (1598), when a whole English army was routed, acted as a further catalyst to light the fires of rebellion all over Ireland, not least in Munster. In *A View of the State of Ireland* Spenser was prescient enough to anticipate his own hasty departure from his planter's house in Munster. An abiding theme in *A View* is the recognition of the fragility of all English conquests in Ireland. As Mary Kelly has argued, a kind of historical geography of the colonial settlement since the Middle Ages is outlined in the *View*.[88] Spenser emphasized how often the Irish, after retreating to the woods, boglands and mountains, remerged from the so-called 'wilderness' areas to attack, erode and drive back the frontiers of English settlement. He was also to articulate eloquently and reiterate the prevailing English racist agenda – which went back to Giraldus Cambrensis – seeing the Irish as an inferior 'barbarous' people who were treacherously interacting with their Catholic allies in Europe to undermine England's 'civilizing' rule. Spenser's knowledge and experience of Irish resistance in Munster and Ireland generally prompted him to stress the critical role of the Irish landscape in facilitating the Irish capacity for mobility, seclusion and counter-attack. To Spenser the 'reformation' of Ireland – and reformation is one of the great ambitious themes of Elizabethan writings on Ireland – required a fortified geography and, above all, the establishment of a visualized landscape, where the 'wild' Irish are forced and flushed out of their woodland/bogland/mountain fastnesses and defeated out in the open plains. With conquest achieved, the subjected landscape and population was to be redesigned in the image and ideals of England. Spenser's use of mapping metaphors throughout the text of the *View* goes so deep as to imagine the process of the reformation of the Irish and Irish landscape as the equivalent of drawing a new map on a blank surface and remodelling the whole terrain, both natural and cultural.[89]

Already in 1570 Sidney was so satisfied with Humphrey Gilbert's savage pacification of Munster that he was moved to use a similar metaphor: 'The iron is now hot, apt to receive what prynt shall be stryken.'[90] In September 1569, in response to the rising/rebellion led by James Fitzmaurice, Sidney appointed Gilbert as colonel and governor of the province. Uninhibited by any administrative constraints and 'empowered to govern by martial law and requisition troops at will', Gilbert smashed the rising with absolute ruthless efficiency.[91] He had taken twenty-three castles in six weeks 'and slaughtered all occupants, men, women and children'.[92] As Colm Lennon puts it, 'His savage methods, such as the killing of non-belligerents and the grisly use of [an avenue of] severed heads to induce abject surrenders, won him notoriety and introduced a new dimension into Irish warfare.'[93]

Fitzmaurice was again centrally involved in the landing of a squadron of mostly Italian and some Spanish soldiers at Dún an Óir at Smerwick harbour (Co. Kerry) in 1579, which sparked off the wider Desmond rising/rebellion (see Fig. 2.12). And Gilbert was also back, this time patrolling the offshore waters with a fleet, so as to secure the coasts from further continental invasion.[94] Atrocities fuelled counter-atrocities. The government reacted with greatest ferocity, 'burning lands and property which were of potential value to the insurgents and also the indiscriminate killing of non-belligerents'.[95] Lord Grey de Wilton, the lord deputy up to the summer of 1582, following on orders to massacre the 600 unarmed soldiers at Dún an Óir, enhanced his dubious reputation for appalling brutality by further accentuating a scorched-earth policy in Munster. The massacre at Dún an Óir was England's way of signalling to Ireland's Catholic allies what lay in store for them if they collaborated in Irish insurrections. Under Grey's and Ormond's directions, this systematic burning of the people's corn, the spoiling of their harvests and the killing and driving of their cattle continued in Munster. Lennon noted: 'by 1582 famine conditions were rife in many parts of the province, coupled with disease brought on by malnutrition'.[96] In that year it was reported that around forty were dying daily in Cork city alone.

The Desmond Wars (1579–83) were one of the most brutal of the early modern period in Ireland. The earl of Ormond (Black Tom) led the crown forces in ruthlessly putting down the rising/rebellion. As many as 16,000–17,000 were killed

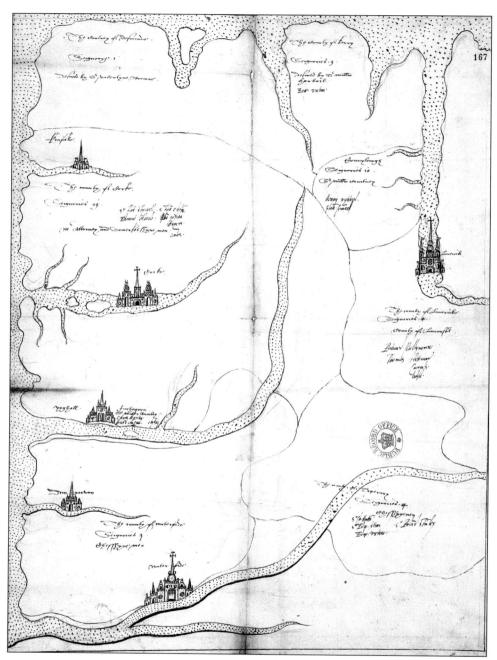

2.13 'Rough' map of Munster (1586) with Burghley's annotations of names of some of the proposed Munster planters. By permission of Public Record Office (MPF 1/273).

during these wars, many of them ordinary civilians. The destruction of the land and the food supply ushered in famine by the summer of 1580, which was to continue for another three years. Overall, it is estimated that there were over 35,000 famine victims. David Edwards has calculated that, in total, as many as 50,000 people died during the wars between 1579 and 1583.[97] Depending on which estimate of the size of the total Irish population is used, the number of deaths in the province could range from one-fifth to one-eighth. Given that Munster's population then constituted about one-third of the island total, overall losses between 1579 and 1583 are likely to be closer to one-eighth of the province's population.

Lord Grey's secretary, Edmund Spenser, famously describes the effects of this campaign: 'Out of every corner of the woods and glens they came creeping forth upon their hands, for their legs could not carry them: they looked like anatomies of death, they spake like ghosts crying out of their graves.' He goes on to add, 'They did eat the dead carrions, happy where they could find them, yes, and one another soon after, in so much as the very carcasses they spared not to scrape out of their graves.'[98] Klein has, however, drawn attention to how this most frequently quoted passage of horror is framed by beginning and concluding statements that provide a very different totalizing cartographic view of an Arcadian Munster. In the beginning of this section of the *View*, Spenser describes Munster as 'a most rich and plentiful country full of corn and cattle'. The end of the passage notes that in a bountiful Munster 'in short space there were none almost left and a most populous and plentiful country suddenly left void of man or beast, yet sure in all that war there perished not many by the sword but all by the extremity of famine which they themselves wroughte'.[99] Thus, an initially peaceful and bountiful province is transformed into an image of death, decay and self-destruction while at the end we are back looking at a view of the whole territory – once populous and plentiful – but 'now transformed into the colonial fantasy of a spatial *tabula rasa*, a land "suddenly left void of man or beast"'.[100]

A different and 'higher' sense and control of space rules in the beginning and end of the passage – and this cartographic view, reinforcing a narrative that stresses self-inflicted depopulation, thus marks and justifies the transfer of the Munster properties from 'a state of savagery to a state of civilisation'.[101] The Irish population's existence is erased in these global totalizing views – just as the horrific details of the putting down of the rising/rebellion by the crown forces is glossed over and ignored completely. Spenser's geographically inspired rhetoric parallels that of the cold ruthless gaze of the geometric map. Both would facilitate the inscribing and forging of 'a "groundless" fiction of a fully anglicised extension of the [English] national sphere, encompassing Irish space and Irish bodies alike'.[102]

Early in 1584, then, much of the province of Munster – its population markedly reduced and its old elites dead or defeated – was opened up to the first great state plantation in Ireland. And Cecil – now Lord Burghley – was a major figure in planning, honing and monitoring this daring state enterprise. Figure 2.13 illustrates an early map of Munster now held in the Public Record Office, London.[103] It is an extraordinary schematic rendering of the province, with only the rivers (greatly exaggerated) and the main cities shown. The map is almost a blank sheet. But the blank spaces on this rough-hewn map, on which Lord Burghley has written the names of the intended key Munster planters, suggest the devastation of Munster. And the blankness and silence of his crude map was echoed on the ground in a landscape of ruptures, bitterness and pain.

Lord Burghley was dissatisfied with this map for other reasons. Despite the proposed seigniorial locations of the new lords of south Munster – such as Sir William Courtenay and Edward Mainwaring, Sir Walter Raleigh and Sir William Herbert, Sir Christopher Hatton and Sir Edmund Fitton – the gap between plantation planning and the geographic realities of this terrain required far more precise mapping. In fact, it required a proper plantation survey to follow from the commissioner's jury-based reports, which estimated that around 580,000 English acres was available to plant people of English birth on the confiscated lands.[104] The story of this mapping, whose main surveyors were Francis Jobson and Arthur Robins, is rather a mirror image of the story of the plantation itself – it is a tale of delays, confusions, disputes, indecisions, changes in methods of surveying, charges of dishonesty and not a little opportunism.[105] For all that, the National Maritime Museum at Greenwich is home to a series of maps that chronicle the reshaping of south and middle Munster via this plantation scheme.

This series by Jobson shows how maps were used to pummel and reorganize space (see Fig. 2.14a and Fig. 2.14b) – literally ground-breaking instruments of conquest. A preliminary sketch-plan shows the clinical dissecting of the plantation arenas, with the new seigniorial boundaries incised into an almost blank surface.[106] His finished maps, dated 1589, not only shows the now clearly named owners of the bounded plantation estates but also displays the urban and rural topographies of Munster, including its mountains, woodlands and rivers. (Jobson was also to make an even more impressive seigniorial map of the county of Limerick.[107]) And out on the high seas off Munster, Jobson displays the English galleons riding the waves. The subtext appears to be that the coastal regions of Munster – now well planted – were safer havens and offered better protection against Spanish and other continental interventions.

A contemporary cartographic record exists of the proposed layout of a Munster seigniory of 12,000 acres, itemizing roads, houses and farm boundaries (see Fig. 2.15). This plan displays an ingenious compromise between dispersion and nucleation in the planning of the colony.[108] Such geometric linear-style planning – so successful in America – was rarely if ever achieved on the ground in either rural Munster or elsewhere in Ireland. We do have some impressive early maps of Raleigh's estates (1598), mapped by Jobson and probably John White, who also mapped and painted Virginia.[109] But overall, compromises abound in the actual Munster settlement, according as Elizabethan dreams of a highly utopian geometric plantation yield to the stiffer realities of deeply rooted boundaries, peoples and ecologies. It is true to say that the Munster plantation witnessed failures in mapping, planning and implementation. Yet I do not think it is correct to see the plantation as a whole as a failure. Looked at in the middle and long term, this plantation was to provide a solid enough infrastructural and institutional framework to allow for later successful replanting, substantial immigration and settlement expansion. By 1641 Munster is by far the most successful and one of the most densely settled of plantation regions.

Ulster is another region of successful plantation by 1641. And this brings us back to Mountjoy and Bartlett. In 1603, at the end of the Nine Years War, Mountjoy was close to achieving England's objectives in Ulster by implementing a scorched-earth policy of burning the crops, killing the cattle and starving out popular support for Hugh O'Neill. English investment in the war reached a new peak as Mountjoy implemented a policy of surrounding Tyrone's now shrinking power-base with a ring of new forts. The strategic plan for the enclosure of Gaelic Ulster within a ring of garrisons goes back to Sir Henry Sidney: it figures in Spenser's *View* and, in a series of maps of Ulster, culminates in Jobson's 1598 map with plans for establishing garrisons at Belfast, Coleraine, Monaghan, Newry, on the Black-water, on Lough Erne and at either Bundoran or Ballyshannon.[110] Mountjoy's military push (1600–02) was from the south, combined with a critical southward drive from Lough Foyle by Dowcra, with Chichester closing in from the east from across Lough Neagh. There is an eerie quality to Bartlett's maps, as he rides beside 'his lordship' and records for posterity the defeat of an Ulster realm never defeated before and the march of a conquering English army where no such army had marched before. His overview of the Blackwater valley (see Fig. 2.16), from Castle Benburb northwards to the junction of the Callan, is stunning.[111] A whole series of new English fortifications – Fort Mount Norris, Fort Mullin, Fort Charlemont, and finally Fort Mountjoy on Lough Neagh itself – mark what on the map looks like the giant footsteps of the invader as pathways are sliced through the woodlands, O'Neill's defences dismantled and new bridges built at crucial crossing points. Well clear of the physical barriers of wood and bogland and with the Irish army in retreat, the top of the map notes 'the way to Dungannon by the plains'. The heartland of Ulster was opening up to the conqueror.

A series of other mapping vignettes detail the precise geometry of these new star- or triangle-shaped forts, down to the last windows and chimneys of the buildings within and without the fortifications. There is one striking illustration of the new fort of Mullin, a beautiful Renaissance-style triangular fort juxtaposi-tioned on the same sheet against the ruined streets and derelict houses and churches of the ancient episcopal capital of Ulster, Armagh (see Fig. 2.17).

Riding on the other side of Mountjoy was his secretary Fynes Moryson, who provides a complementary narrative to Bartlett's sketches and maps. As Mary Kelly has documented, Moryson echoes his master's voice when he notes that 'they [the Irish] would never be faithful to the state until they could not subsist against it'.[112] Like Spenser, Moryson recognized how the natural landscape was so skilfully used by the Irish to create for so long very dangerous and impenetra-ble spaces for the English. But the step-by-step creation of new fortifications across the landscape – like the maps themselves – was to provide key instruments of surveillance, penetration, control, and eventually sites for new 'civilizing' settlements. Following on from Spenser, Moryson wished to see that impenetrable landscape opened up and made visible. And as Mountjoy battles his way north-wards, and with two pincer movements coming south towards Lough Neagh and Dungannon, Bartlett's maps show the actual realization of these objectives – as fort after fort is built into O'Neill's face. No other cartographer in Ireland has mapped, painted and narrated the story of a conquered and subjected landscape and people as eloquently as Bartlett did.

The most powerful and poignant of Bartlett's map-paintings contains four scenes in ascending order of magnification (see Fig. 2.18).[113] The upper part shows the portion of the English army attacking an unidentified *crannóg* – two very different worlds colliding on a northwestern frontier. The middle sketch shows the circular moat and dwellings surrounding O'Neill's now roofless castle-dwelling at Dungannon: the lead roof had been previously stripped to provide ammunition for O'Neill's soldiers. But the castle now flies the triumphant flag of St George. Earlier still, as Mountjoy, Bartlett, Moryson and the English army advanced beyond the Blackwater along 'the way to Dungannon by the plains' via the banks of Lough Neagh – then optimistically called Lough Sidney – they witnessed O'Neill's Dungannon stronghold in flames as O'Neill burnt his home to retreat deep into the wooded fastness of Glenconkein. And it was there that this proud, skilful and subtle leader of the Irish – reduced to a woodkern – agreed to surrender.[114] The third and most dramatic scene sketches the fine Tullyhoge residence of the legal family of the O'Hagans – involved in the inauguration of the O'Neill as kings of Ulster for centuries – and beside the house the stone inauguration throne itself. This scene is further magnified by Bartlett in his fourth inset of the throne, which catches beautifully that poignant moment when the most sacred symbol of the last great lordship of Ireland yields to the hammer of the absolutist, centralizing English state. And just as O'Neill's Ulster has been 'closed down' by Mountjoy's victories, so the inset of the throne can be closed down when covered by the surrounding overlay.

Bartlett's brilliance as an artist and cartographer is further confirmed by his ability to move from the intimate and deeply symbolic bird's-eye sketches to panoramic map-views depicting either the whole of, or major regions within, Ulster. The English military conquest of Ulster is now matched by his precise portrait of the topography of one Old World going down and a New World in embryo. Not surprisingly, the two main cartouches on his superb *A Generalle Description of Ulster* (see Fig. 2.19) are the coat of arms of Queen Elizabeth and of Charles Blount, Lord Mountjoy.[115] English power now reigns supreme across the Ulster landscape.

For the first time in Irish cartographic history, the shape of coastal Ulster as we now know it today faithfully swims into view. And the complicated contours of the northwest – particularly the complex inlets and bays of north and west Donegal – finally emerge in a way never depicted before. Here Bartlett benefits from the representation of the Donegal and northwestern coastline as a whole, as observed and mapped from the warship *Tramontayne* c.1601.[116] Once again the importance of the sea skills and maritime power is emphasized for both the mapping and conquest of Ireland. The numerous wooded and mountainous regions of Ulster are also portrayed in great detail. Bartlett's maps suggest that around 16–18 per cent of Ulster is still in woodland. Also faithfully represented are the ancient territories of the long-established families – great and small – from 'Mac Swin ne Dogh' in north Donegal through 'Macgwyers' country in

Fermanagh to 'O'Awrelie' (O'Reilly) of 'East Brenie' (Breffny) right across to the Old English Savage lands of the southern Ards.

In a related meso-scale map of the southern part of Ulster, Bartlett provides even more telling details of the Gaelic ordering of this landscape (see Fig. 2.20).[117] Southeast of Lough Neagh (or 'Lough Sidney' – complete with an English ship, cannons blazing), Bartlett shows 'Neale Mac Cormock of the Neales of Clande-boie', chief of these woods 'of Kilultogh'; to the southeast of 'Fort Mont-Norris' is shown 'Clankernie – this contrie, the O'Neales have used to give unto the Capts of their Gallyglass' for their maintenance. West of Lough Neagh is shown the O'Hagan world and 'Tullogh-oge – on the hill were four stones in the manner of a chair wherein The O'Neale this manie years has been made the same are now taken away by his Lordship [Mountjoy]'. Further west of O'Hagan's Tullogh-oge is the 'Lotie ['lucht-tighe'] wch is the household or demesne land of the O'Neales', while beyond Donaghmore in middle Tyrone is shown the lands of 'McCahel one of the five farmers of the Lotie'. Bartlett therefore, provides telling and intimate details on the territorial organization of Gaelic society of Ulster as a whole.

But Bartlett, we must remember, is also dealing with a landscape in ruins and the emergence of a new political and settlement order. His maps depict a great series of roads converging on the still almost empty Armagh: ruined churches and abbeys are strewn across the landscape in sharp contradiction to the freshness, originality and power of the many new forts that run on from Monaghan through Mountnorris through to 'Fort Charlemont', 'Fort Mountjoie', as well as the wooden fort of Irishloughon 'taken from Bryan McArte O'Neill'. Looking beyond the map of south Ulster to the detailed map of all of Ulster, we find that it displays the strategic distribution of greater or lesser fortifications now encircling Ulster from Derry, Culmore and Dunalong through Lifford and Monaghan all the way around to the ancient bastion of Carrickfergus. The recency of the conquest is captured by the numerous temporary army stations, complete with tents and flags, which billow across the Ulster landscape. O'Neill had surrendered to Mountjoy and the queen in March 1603 at Mellifont, not knowing that Elizabeth had died a few days previously. Tudor England was coming to an end: so was the aristocratic world of Gaelic Ulster (Fig. 2.21).

A few years later the by now establishment figure of John Speed produced his Jacobean atlas *The Theatre of the Empire of Great Britain*.[118] The atlas title recalls and echoes Ortelius. But unlike the Ortelius version, the 'Kingdom of Ireland' is now *all* shown to be under full English military and administrative control – fully anglicized and integrated into 'the empire'. On Speed's map, Ireland is portrayed as a peaceful, harmonious entity following on from the 'overthrow of all treasons and rebellions', for which he, like all 'true-hearted subjects', had prayed.[119] Ireland is now divided into thirty-two counties – symbolizing the universal application of English law across the whole Irish landscape. 'Reminiscent in colour and texture of Speed's own map of England', as Klein comments, Ireland is now made visible as a homogenized 'perfectly "natural" extension of "Great Britain"'.[120] The island is fully conquered, assimilated and appropriated. There would be no more need for any maps of conquest.

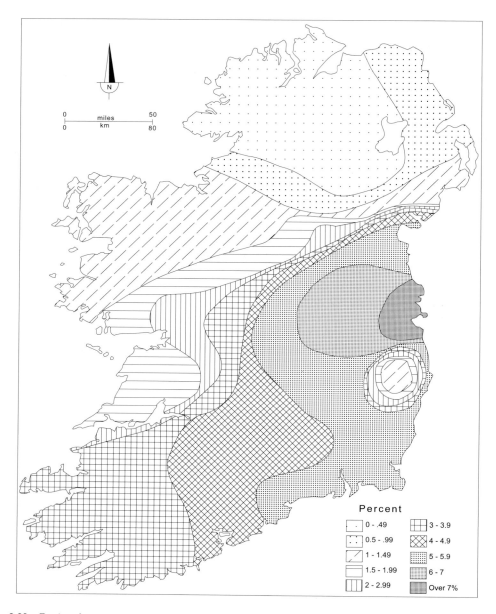

2.22   Regional variations in the cumulative island-wide impact of the Elizabethan civil administration (at city, county and provincial levels) 1558–1603. (Based on *The Irish Fiants of the Tudor
Sovereigns, Vol IV, Queen Elizabeth I*)

   Or so it seemed. Yet the 'wild Irishman' – complete with mantle and spear and
represented amongst the portraits alongside Speed's map of Ireland – suggests
residual unassimilated forces. Figure 2.22 illustrates major regional variations in the
effective reach of English civil administration in Ireland during Elizabeth's reign.
As in the late medieval period, the most forceful impress of English governmental

power was confined to the Dublin/Pale region. A second region of effective local government comprises much of the province of Leinster and Co. Waterford. East and west Munster are clearly being incorporated within this centralizing framework, as is the west Midlands. In contrast, much of Connacht and Co. Clare is still only weakly tied into the orbit of an effective English local government system. And, as is so often the case in sixteenth- and seventeenth-century maps, a sharp frontier emerges between north Leinster and Ulster. As late as 1603, this latter province remains outside the reach of the English civil administration. For the conqueror there would be no end to the mapping; 'the coloniser must always be prepared to define his terrain anew and defend his territories again and again'.[121] Further mapping would be needed, for, as Michel Foucault has so eloquently reminded us all, power is located everywhere.[122] The 'subjected' people on their own ground had their own maps in their heads and knew well how to subvert, redraw and bend the maps of the new imperial power. It was Spenser who intimated that it was a very difficult task indeed to make a good 'plot' for Ireland – and by 'plot' he meant both a plan and a map.[123]

The blueprint and design of these newly painted maps were often destined to be buckled and washed out by insurrections, and 'colonial' adaptations, by different understandings about strategies of territorial organization and by forms of mental mapping that had more to do with narrative memory and poetry than the measured certainties of Cartesian cartography. It is that dialectic which is the subject of the next chapter.

3

Maps versus Memory
Exploring the Hidden Irelands

It's not down in any map; true places never are.
Herman Melville[1]

'For though the country be now quiet and the heads of greatness gone, yet our geographers do not forget what entertainment the Irish of Tyrconnell gave to a map-maker about the end of the late great rebellion: for one Barkeley [Bartlett] being appointed by the late Earl of Devonshire to draw a true and perfect map of the north parts of Ulster (the old maps being false and defective), when he came into Tyrconnell the inhabitants took off his head, because they would not have their country discovered.'[2] Thus wrote Sir John Davies, the Irish attorney-general, to the earl of Salisbury on 29 August 1609, describing the tragic death of that gifted artist/cartographer Richard Bartlett. Before him, Robert Lythe, who began his cartographic mission in east Ulster in September 1567, was obliged for security reasons to withdraw southwards to the more peaceful lands of Munster and Leinster. And Lythe was once again defeated at the end of his second mapping enterprise, for he deemed the territories north of a line from Killary harbour to Strangford Lough as unfit, unsafe for surveying. Francis Jobson – who lasted longer and mapped a greater variety of locales all over Ireland than any other sixteenth-century cartographer – was to observe when mapping Ulster in 1590 that the province was 'inhabited with a most savage and rebellious people from whose cruelty . . . God only by his divine power delivered me being every hour in danger to lose my head'.[3] The first man ever to draw a county map of Mayo in 1584, John Browne, later lost his life in a local war when surveying Connacht.[4]

By 1609 lessons had been learned and the surveyors for the Ulster plantation 'formed part of a strong expeditionary force which the Lord Deputy, Sir Arthur Chichester, led into Ulster in July'.[5] Mapping the plantation counties was an integral part of this expedition, which was involved in 'conducting inquisitions, settling controversies as to which estates were exempted from forfeiture, drawing up cases to prove the King's title to the remaining lands, and holding assizes at a convenient centre in each county'.[6] These surveyors worked under guard, and their field parties kept within range of the lord deputy's power. When William Petty set about making the Down Survey in 1654, his 'army' of 1,000 surveyors and field assistants were backboned by experienced Cromwellian soldiers. Even then, near Timolin in Co. Wicklow 'a reward of £100 was given in 1655 to killers of tories, who after a drum-head courtmartial, had executed eight of Sir William Petty's surveyors engaged in the Down Survey'.[7] Mapping in sixteenth- and seventeenth-century Ireland was neither a safe nor an innocent activity. Bartlett died because the people of Donegal would not have their own ancestral lands known, defined, bounded, controlled; they would not have their lands so well known and so well defined as to lead to their own displacement and dispossession.

The measured scale on these new maps is often depicted as a 'ruler' – that linear piece of wood that marked out the world in inches. The conquest and rule of Ireland meant turning ancient and local assessments of areas into square inches on the map, and into acres and square miles on the ground, according as the planting of the new colonial Ireland progressed. As late as the mid-seventeenth century, Co. Tipperary had seven different measures of land; but all such regional distinctions and variations were now to be reduced to a single measure: the plantation acre.

No one described the objectives of mapping better than Sir John Davies – the classic legal imperialist – when he described the functions of the 1609 plantation survey:

> The use and fruit of this survey and description will not only consist in this, that his majesty shall hereby know what land he hath here, and how to distribute it to undertakers; but in this also, that it will discourage and disable the natives hence-forth to rebel against the crown of England; and be a special means hereafter of preventing and suppressing rebellions in this country. For this country (wherein there were never any cities and towns to draw commerce and trade and wherein the crown of England never appointed magistrates or visitations of justice till within these five years past) was heretofore so obscure and unknown to the English here as the most inland part of Virginia is yet unknown to our English colony there: so as our ignorance of their places of retreat and fastnesses made them confident in their rebellions and it was their only advantage: and made us diffident in our prosecutions and was our only disadvantage, whereas now we know all the passages, have penetrated every thicket and fast place, have taken notice of every notorious tree or bush: all of which will not only remain in our knowledge and memory during this age: but being found by inquisitions of record, and drawn into cards and maps are discovered and laid open to all posterities.[8]

Davies encapsulates the key political and military importance of the mapping project and highlights the contrast between local place knowledge, passed on mainly within an oral/manuscript tradition from one generation to the next, and the new science of map-making, which turns the landscape into a permanent documentary record to be indexed and filed away in cards and maps for the use of future rulers and administrators. Davies is once again stressing the role of the map as a strategic instrument for administering territories and as a key weapon in creating and sustaining state power. For if the map classifies and locates precisely every plot of land, it makes that space amenable to state regulation, allocation, inspection and taxation.

Davies belongs to a new elite of English courtly society. Schooled at the Inns of Court in London and sharing in a lively, competitive and most influential law school environment which also shaped Raleigh, Bacon and (Philip) Sidney, Davies graduated from a world of literature and poetry to gain a rewarding legal career under both Elizabeth I's and James I's patronage. Davies also belonged to a society of geographers, historians and antiquarians, including the great English historian William Camden, who met in the house of Sir Robert Cotton in Westminster from the 1580s onwards to explore and discuss the history of England (and Ireland).[9] Davies's world also overlapped with that of the older Lord Burghley. He therefore belonged to that formative Elizabethan era which had been born of the 'Henrician revolution' in religion and government and which was, in part, shaped by the new sciences and rugged sensibilities of the Renaissance.

The *Annála Rioghachta Éireann: Annals of the Kingdom of Ireland* – the Annals of the Four Masters, as these early seventeenth-century annals have come to be known, take a rather different view of this revolution in the modes of thinking and behaviour in England and their implications for Ireland:

A heresy and a new error [sprang up] in England through pride, vain glory, avarice and lust, and through many strange sciences, so that the men of England went into opposition to the Pope and to Rome. They at the same time adopted various opinions and [among others] the old law of Moses, in imitation of the Jewish people; and they styled the King the Chief Head of the Church of God in his own Kingdom. New laws and statutes were enacted by the King and Council [Parliament] according to their own will. They destroyed the orders to whom worldly possessions were allowed, namely the Monks, Canons, Nuns, Brethren of the Cross, and the four poor orders i.e. the orders of the Minors, Preachers, Carmelites and Augustinians: and the Lordship and livings of all these were taken up for the King. They broke down the monasteries, and sold their roofs and bells so that from Aran of the Saints [Aranmore in Galway Bay] to the Iccian Sea [the English Channel] there was not one monastery that was not broken and shattered, with the exception of a few in Ireland, of which the English took no heed or notice [and which were protected by the power of the local chieftains]. They afterwards burned the images, shrines and relics of the Saints of Ireland and England: they likewise burned the celebrated image of [the Blessed Virgin] Mary at Trim, which used to perform wonders and miracles, which used to heal the blind, the deaf and the crippled and persons affected with all kinds of diseases: and [they also burned] the staff of Jesus, which was in Dublin performing miracles, from the time of St. Patrick down to that time, and had been in the hands of Christ while he was among men. They also appointed Archbishops and sub-bishops for themselves [without any authority from the Pope]; and though great was the persecution of the Roman emperors against the Church, scarcely had there come so great a persecution from [pagan] Rome as this [now set foot in Christian England]: so that it is impossible to narrate or tell its description, unless it should be narrated by one who saw it.[10]

The Four Masters and their Annals belong to a world in which attitude to authority and beliefs differed greatly from the world of the English colonizers. For the former, the notion of 'description' meant a historical narrative and not perspective mapping. These Annals are in a different tradition to all the earlier Irish annals.

First, they are a synthesis of previous annals and other historical sources. Second, they were consciously constructed as the story of the kingdom of Ireland as a whole – they are not the annals of any region, of Ulster, or Connacht or Munster, but of the island of Ireland as a single entity.[11] Written and compiled between 1632 and 1636 by the Four Masters under the leadership of the Franciscan brother Micheál Ó Clérigh, the Annals were, therefore, produced at a particular time when there was a growing consciousness – both at home and abroad – of the Irish as a Catholic nation and at a period when Ireland's leading intellectuals set out to integrate old Gaelic and Old English strands of the culture into a single united corporate entity.

The earliest nuclei of this 'new departure' were in the Irish colleges on the Continent – and in particular Louvain – where emigrants from all Irish regions and traditions lived, worked and debated together (see Fig. 3.1). Micheál Ó Clérigh was

3.1   Distribution of Irish Catholic Colleges on the Continent and Irish writing in Latin in Europe as a whole (c.1550–c.1700)(adapted in part from Maps 19 and 21, p. 564 and p. 616, *A New History of Ireland, III*; see reference 24)

to share in these experiences and it was one of these leaders, Hugh Ward, the head of the Franciscan College in Louvain, who instructed Ó Clérigh to return to Ireland 'to collect Irish manuscripts, and other helps towards this great undertaking'.[12] These Irish scholar-historians on the Continent were sharing in the fruits of new insights born of Renaissance humanism, the Reformation and the Counter-Reformation. It was this era that saw the emergence of the new science of history, with its emphasis on primary sources, on causation and method. Much of this new history was focused on the rediscovery of past national histories. And fundamental differences between the Catholic and Reformation Churches meant that the new historical research often focused on, and competed strongly about, the origins and evolution of the Christian tradition in different European countries.[13] It was in this kind of charged intellectual milieu that the tireless Ó Clérigh and his comrades constructed the Annals.

While sharing in these wider movements in historiography, Davies and his peers were also products of the 'many strange sciences' that had grown up in England. And included amongst these is the new science and art of map-making. It is Davies's view that Bartlett's work in Donegal was to draw 'a true and perfect map' of those parts of northwest Ulster, since the old maps were 'false and defective'. There are, therefore, very different perceptions operating in Ireland about what is true or false, whether we talk of maps or doctrines or religious beliefs.

As the poet Eavan Boland puts it, 'the science of cartography is limited'.[14] It is one of many different cultural grammars for describing, reading and organizing landscapes, territories, places. What this chapter seeks to explore is the dialectic between different ways of reading landscapes, territories and people in sixteenth- and seventeenth-century Ireland. In particular, I am concerned here with the uneven battle between the power to shape and flatten worlds which are defined more by accounting, geometry, mathematics and perspective mapping, on the one hand, and on the other, a gaelicized/Gaelic world, where such maps were either unknown or not formally used and where territories and peoples were ruled and administered mainly by the words and the living images associated with manuscripts, memory, local lore and myth. The genealogies of Irish families and dynasties and the related topographical poems/narratives/dindshenchas constituted central vehicles for 'mapping' territories and peoples, thus defining their respective positions and rights within deeply longitudinal views of space, time and inheritance. In that period, the Irish read off their genealogies like rosaries. And even the narrative flow of the Annals is regularly compelled to slow down to insert and repeat abbreviated yet essential genealogical information about Irish elite figures.

The polarity between map and memory (or folklore, genealogy, tradition) can be overdrawn. There are other ways of scouting the territory, as there are of remembering and ruling. Besides mapping, there are the surveys and documents of sixteenth- and seventeenth-century English administration, including the fiants, inquisitions, compositions, and, particularly, the almost island-wide listing of the old elites and their properties as evidenced in the Civil Survey of the early 1650s. In the Irish language, there are many manuscript charters, chronologies, genealogies, law texts, poems and stories. The contrast in the two forms of civilization are clearly expressed in the very different modes used in comprehending the nature of places.

Conceptual Landmarks

In Chapter 2 the focus was on the 'strange new science' of mapping, according as English cartographers and officials slowly, unevenly yet progressively came to grips with the overall shape, terrain and particular spaces of Ireland. I now want to explore the more complicated story of the dialectic between the two main competing hegemonic forces: the Germanic/British/English world on the one hand and the Celtic/Irish/Gaelic on the other.

On the one side is England's imperial expansionist drive into Ireland, seeing itself in the process as a superior, civilizing force. Key characteristics of this expansionist culture included a centralizing and modernizing state system, headed by a powerful monarch and supported by an elaborate but co-ordinated system of administration and command that included ministers, the judiciary, army and navy officers, local government officials, soldiers, merchants and the 'officers' of the state Church. This culture expressed itself in a rapidly evolving and rich language – English – and, most critically, now wrote itself and its identity into world history via the new print technology.

Maps and atlases are part of this print culture. Pamphlets, books, plays, poems, government reports, proclamations and edicts, travellers' descriptions, the Bible and other religious texts are all part of the construction of the English nation after 1534. The rapid use and spread of the printing press points to an innovative society on the technological side of things, geared to inventions and improvements in the instruments and machines used in surveying, shipping, farming, industrial and mining activities, as well as in warfare. All of these innovations had profound implications for the design and transformation of English (and later Irish) landscapes. This drive to innovate technologically is clearly linked to a new empiricist philosophy advanced by Bacon and like-minded scholars and scientists anxious to link the observational powers of the new sciences to practical, applied purposes. Furthermore, England had by now evolved into a property-owning society, where the traits and obligations of a feudal culture were being shed according as written agreements about *individual* land tenures and leases were backed up by statute and punitive law.[15]

So this writ-governed, early modern England is increasingly geared to developing new knowledge and to furthering its own capacity to transform and expand its resource-base into a wealth-creating 'commonwealth'. In this, England belongs to a wider Reformation culture, powerfully linked with other key Protestant states and cities, especially with those of the Low Countries. The acceptance of Protestantism and the intellectual and political consequences of such a seachange act as a further spur to educational, economic and military development, as well as sharpening an already well-developed pragmatic, materialistic individualism that extended into a number of overseas ventures (see Fig. 3.2).

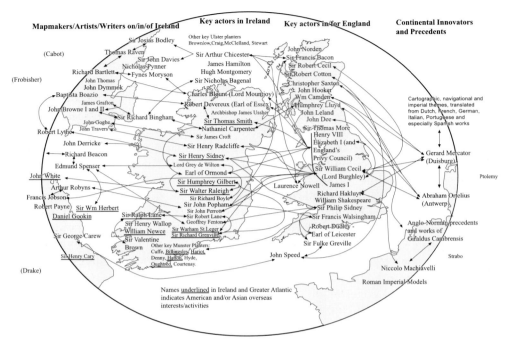

3.2 Key actor networks in the creation and the expansion of an English world-view into Ireland (*c*.1530 – *c*.1620)

In short, as England moves from the Elizabethan to the Jacobean age (and with Scotland now a decisive player as well), it confidently sees itself as having an ever more superior civilization than that of Ireland. And central to the eventual success of the invader is centralized government, a developed patriotism and unified objectives and assumptions. In expanding westwards, seeking to conquer Ireland – and securing their western flank in the new global maritime age – the English set about their colonizing armed with a whole series of key cultural assumptions: first, they see English rule and civilization as distinctly superior to that of the Irish; second, they accept unquestioningly their own right and authority to use their full powers to conquer and subdue Ireland; a third and consequential premise of their ideology is that Ireland and its people will be vastly 'improved' by becoming English – in speech, religious affiliation, landscape design, acceptance of a fixed village life and the fostering of towns, trade and commerce, centralized government and concepts of law and order. A 'civic' life is thus set against 'a life of the woods'.[16]

At the other pole of this hegemonic drive by the English were the Irish – engaged in opposing, deflecting, adapting to or assimilating the English cultural norms. The use of the term 'Irish' here brings its own set of problems. There is an interesting shift in the hundred-year span from the 1530s to 1640 in the use of the more exclusive term 'Gaedhil' as often used in the Annals, and the more inclusive term 'Éireannach'. The term 'Gaedhil' denoted a strong ethnic distinction both between and with the *Sean-Ghaill* (Old English) and the *Nua-Ghaill* (the New

English/Scottish). The gradual emergence of the term 'Éireannach' reflected the growing convergence of Gaelic and Old English into a single Catholic political culture.[17] Yet the country still remained highly fragmented and there were clearly varying and multiple shades of identities. Allegiances and loyalties often did not transcend the boundaries of the local or regional lordship and the person of the lord – whether that of Desmond, O'Donnell, O'Neill or, indeed, Ormond.

This single, political culture was predominantly (but not exclusively) Irish-speaking.[18] The primary modes of discourse were in Irish and Latin: they were oral and manuscript-based, with rich traditions and practitioners of bardic poetry, genealogical, historical and legal scholarship, *dindshenchas* and the keeping of annals. So, Irish culture at this time was complex and sophisticated; but it tended to be more conservative and conserving in both its material and ideological concerns. Estyn Evans has written that such an enduring and subtle society should not be underestimated, and having reasserted itself in the fourteenth century and having continued viably down to the early seventeenth century and beyond, this culture had remained confident and strong over a very long period.[19] Central to this culture was the scattering and dispersal of institutions of power and settlement; it fostered the coexistence of both strong cultural unity and regional diversities, as well as a powerful belief in the place of poetry and the imagination, the spiritual world and 'older' faiths. O'Faolain puts it very well: 'behind the ring of port-towns, behind these [wild] Irish woods and those [dark] Irish bogs with their gleaming pools of water, there was another model of life as valid, as honourable, as cultured, as complex'[20] as that of the English. In the early modern era this was not an expansionist culture; and it found itself on the defensive. Its people had the advantage of knowing intimately the ancestral lands and terrains – from the townland foundations through to the large lordships. It was a society still mainly based on a mosaic of smaller, medium and larger-sized territorial units where the group, the clan, the family counted for more than the individual. Here the governing culture of the lordships and sublordships attained levels of territorial control through 'the obligations of kinship backed up by various forms of partly ritualized violence'.[21]

In this culture, geographical knowledge remained mainly local and regional. Politically, Ireland had not evolved a unified, centralized governmental system and there were often sharp political differences between and within Old English, gaelicized and Gaelic lordships. Quite a number of these lordships – those of Kildare, Ormond, Desmond, that of Clanricard and Tyrone – were powerful political and economic entities and all, with the exception of O'Neill's Tyrone, had access to or control of a major port-city. So in the mid-sixteenth century Ireland consisted of a series of large and small lordships or counties, fragmented and fragmenting, of various strengths and dispositions. This balkanization was both a strength and a weakness: a strength in that each region/province/lordship must be conquered separately; a weakness in so far as the creation of a unified polity was very difficult. The effective waging of war against the English required the creation and maintenance of elaborate regional and local alliances and dependencies, which invariably came under constant strain and tension. And invariably

English policy was to exploit these fissures: an important survey of Irish military strength in or about 1590 systematically sets out to identify and exploit the existing enmities and conflicts between local Irish lords.[22] In Connacht and Thomond alone, this English government document identifies the following factions and the reasons for their conflicts: between the earl of Thomond and Sir Donogh O'Brien and his sons ('for chiefry'); between the MacNamaras and the earl of Thomond ('for exactions'); between the earl of Clanricard and MacWilliam Íochtar ('for greatness'); between the Lord Bermingham and Mac Davy Burke ('for title to lands'); between the earl of Clanricard and Burke of Derrinlaghlin ('for ye Burke will not be commanded by him [the earl] but depended upon her majestie'); between the earl of Clanricard and O'Shaughnessy ('since O'Shaughnessy was privledged from the King of England to be exempted from paying homage'); between O'Connor Sligo and O'Donnell ('because O'Donnell claimeth a rent of 240[l] [pounds] per annum by precedents of 200 years'); and between O'Rourke and O'Farrell (because of a 'frontier warr').

English knowledge and manipulation of such internal conflicts was exercised at every opportunity. For example, the deliberate choice of the earl of Ormond – ancient enemy of the Desmond Fitzgeralds – as the chief military officer of Munster to put down the Desmond rising/rebellion simply ensured the intensification of that revolt. Numerous examples confirm this English policy of exploiting and encouraging enmities both between competing Irish lordships and factions within a single lordship. Yet there is no doubt that these Irish warlords were innovative in terms of war strategy and political intrigues, in developing trading networks and, where resources and opportunities allowed, were equally adept at acquiring new forms of military arsenal.[23]

Possibly Ireland's greatest cultural strength, which eventually acted as a powerful unifying force, was that it progressively identified itself with a Counter-Reformation European culture. It thus constructed a supranational network of links across Catholic Europe that expressed itself not only in its capacity to defend and reinvigorate its Catholicism, to establish an extraordinarily wide continental network of seminaries for the training of clergy, but also led to the enhancement of a wider orbit for the movement and integration of Irish emigrants into mainland Europe's intellectual, military, medical, ecclesiastical and merchant alliances. Figure 3.1 (p. 57) not only illustrates the densities of Irish colleges across the Continent but also highlights other centres where Irish writers continued to publish in Latin. At least 10,000 Irish soldiers served in Spanish Flanders alone between 1585 and 1630.[24] Irish European spaces thus provided useful training grounds for the education of Irish soldier officers in the most modern European systems of warfare, as well as powerful emigrant centres and communities for the elaboration and cultivation of a new nationalist ideology.

In examining the mapping components of this comparison, I am exploring the processes by which English power was created and sustained in Ireland. The long sequence of maps throw into relief the implantation, delimination and demarcation of both English landscape and territorial creations (forts, houses, towns, villages, baronies, counties) and their associated immigrant populations. It is recognized that maps are abstractions, constructions, simplifications of reality. And maps are better understood not as autonomous images of a reality but as 'accents' or 'dialects' within a wider framework of representation and discourse.[25] They, together with pamphlets, reports and other 'descriptions' and 'views of the state of Ireland', involve different but related ways of seeing, representing and understanding the Irish landscape and people. Maps are part of larger, interlocking narratives and practices.

Foucault's concept of 'discursive formation' is helpful here.[26] For Foucault, the formation of a key state policy as, for example, the construction of a serious, reflective, inscribed English discourse on conquering and 'reforming' Ireland must needs be analysed in terms of tactics and strategies of power. Such tactics and strategies are always explained, he argues, through implantations, distributions, demarcations, the control of territories and the distribution of domains.[27] In short, the relationship between English discursive formation on colonizing Ireland and its actual realization in space is best understood as a kind of geopolitics. So an analysis of English mapping strategies in Ireland involves critical geopolitical considerations.

There is a double geometry associated with mapping. There are the geometric understandings about scale, distance, latitude, and orientation that go with the surveying and making of the maps. But there is also the related geometry of the substantive historical geography of how the sites mapped are distributed and often newly created across the landscape. The formation of landscapes, places and spaces are inextricably linked up with the events, peoples, ideas and institutions that swirled and moved about them. From at least the 1530s onwards, the New English made very determined attempts to enlarge their footholds and domains in Ireland – to literally 'gain ground'. This involved the establishment and consolidation of what Joanne Woolway calls 'significant spaces'.[28] These were the new (or revamped) walled towns, the fortified garrisons, the well-guarded bridges and bridge towns, as well as the protected safe pathways and roadways through woodland territories. All the while, the objective is to enlarge these spaces of inclusion, so as to add to the safety for the English settler and administration, while at the same time reducing the spaces of English exclusion where the 'othered' Irish lived.

There is thus a geopolitics of spaces in colonial Ireland from the bed-chamber and study of the officer/administrator, to the sites and shapes of forts, towns, counties and provinces, on through to the whole embryonic English land empire in North America and the West Indies, not to speak of its battle zones around Europe and across the Atlantic seas. The analysis of the maps, therefore, and their associated policy documents helps to establish the connections between what is written, plotted and planned and the 'visibilities' on the ground – the material objects of the landscape. 'Discourse' and 'landscape' are interfoliated and there are regular and mutually conditioned interactions and connections between maps/words/statements and the visible landscape objects on the ground.[29] These interactions and frictions generate new energies, keep things moving, working and probing – and keep shunting people and objects around. Thus, for example, the chessboard of the Irish landscape, complex, deep and subtle – as outlined, for example, in Bartlett's maps of Irish territories and properties – is constantly being rearranged as the conflicts and accommodations between the two hegemonic forces deepen and widen.

On the English side we have the material artefacts of the discourse – the books, pamphlets, reports, scrolls, maps and paintings – that make up one side of the debate on colonization and conquest. We want to explore how this geopolitical discourse is constructed and legitimized, particularly through the creation of various forms of geographic knowledge and specifically by maps. One could argue that there is a complex triangular relationship between knowledge, power, and actions on people and landscapes.[30] At one corner of the triangle is the developing ideology of colonialism and conquest – this is fed by new ideas and knowledge involving advances in mapping, surveying, navigation and systems of territorial control. Another pivot of the triangle involves the significant spaces of rule, inclusion and administration established on the ground in Ireland and grounded even more emphatically in the key significant spaces of England (whether palaces and courts, parliament, naval bases, Inns and colleges), where the central and centralizing political, intellectual and military institutions are located and embedded. Within Ireland, Dublin Castle, the county capitals, the seats of the provincial presidencies and the courts, key fortifications and walled towns are central. Here the holders and wielders of English power reside and act. And the third pivot of the triangle are the consequent actions exerted by the power-wielders of these privileged or significant spaces on the bodies, minds, buildings and landscapes of the people on the ground. Here we are talking about the authority and power of the state to reshape or destroy buildings, roads, towns, woods, people, minds and bodies.

Foucault's concept of 'normalization' is fruitful here.[31] The colonial discourse seeks to normalize a certain view of the 'perfect' or 'correct' society or civilization. Discourse in England – linked with that of the English officials and intelligentsia in Ireland (including Sidney, Spenser, Moryson, Davies, Petty and others) – developed a model of what might be accepted as normal, correct behaviours and civilized landscapes as against what is 'abnormal/incorrect/uncivilized'. And this English colonial ideology was to glorify the emerging features of maturing Elizabethan English culture as the 'civilized norm'. The greater the deviation from the prescribed norm, the greater the lack of civilization. Thus, to English ways of seeing and understanding, Ireland and the Irish presented a cheerless 'wild', 'savage' face – underpeopled, mobile, unruly, underdeveloped, underurbanized and bereft of most symbols of English civilization.[32] Even the earliest maps of Ireland reinforce these enduring stereotypes – providing rare glimpses of the heads of the 'wild Irish' located amongst the hills and woods, in the company of animals, particularly the wolves. Similar images prevail on early colonial American maps, where the frontier is dominated by Indians, animals, demons and the dark dank forest.[33]

But it should not be assumed that this symbiosis of new knowledge, power and capacity to act on bodies and landscapes was a simple process of conquest, submission and assimilation. In reality, this process was infinitely more complex and of a labyrinthine perplexity. As O'Faolain notes,

> that perplexity arose chiefly from the fact that in England's decision to make Ireland her first real colony two civilizations became interlocked that were in spirit utterly divergent. The 16th century wars of conquest there [in Ireland] mingled what was by nature immiscible. . . . It is the same forced juncture of modernity and antiquity that comes with every imperial conquest, whether in the conquest of Mexico by the Spaniards, or the colonisation of India by the Hanoverians, or the plantation of Ireland by the Tudors. . . . In such a clash there is no single story because there is no clear mind. In the final stage of all, nothing remains but the oversimplified story of the victor and the oversimplified memories of the defeated, both of those unfaithful to the always confused and occasionally troubled split-mindedness of the time.[34]

While I would have to challenge his use of the term 'antiquity', O'Faolain's description is otherwise apt. This triad of ideology, power and actions on peoples and landscapes, therefore, involves not only a simple uni-directional flow of energy and pressures: there is conflict between the 'homeland' English themselves as to the definition and elaboration of a colonial/imperial ideology, its recognition and elaboration amongst its Irish-based English stakeholders, and its application to the Irish. There are also powerful forces at work on the ground, as the Irish react, assimilate, and negotiate their 'spaces of freedom' or created alternative strategies of adaptation and resistance. Their use and conception of space, their knowledge of the material landscape, as well as their ability to outflank, neutralize and even to outwit the colonial power, must also be explored and understood.

Through this exploration of Irish conceptions of space, we may be able to construct or define a different tripod of ideology, power, and landscape actions, which may give us a more comprehensive geographical picture of Irish civilization at the time. Questions arise: how are we to map these invisibilities which the English map-maker may have missed? What was deemed to be correct and civilized in this culture? What forms of resistance and adaptation did the threatened hegemony of the English produce? How did the Irish submit to, subvert, and overcome the objectives of the map and plan? 'Map' no longer simply means the sheets of paper on which the 'objective' reality of the landscape was appropriated, but includes the larger 'imperialist' maps the English carried in their heads as a result of the wider discursive formation on colonialism.

For the purposes of this analysis, we are collapsing the complex cultural formation of the Irish – and its various forms of discourse – into the concept of 'memory'. Central here is the importance of a mainly aural and manuscript transmission and understanding of culture – given the absence or weakness of a print technology. We are looking at the centrality of forms of discourse and action that cluster around such key features as annals, genealogies, folklore, landmarks, music, placenames, poems, songs and stories about places and people, and the often wooded or boggy landscape itself. But the central theme being advanced here is the gulf that existed between these two ways of knowing and seeing: the dominance of visual perspectives, views, descriptions, images and maps geared to militarize the conquest and planning of future anglicized landscapes and societies, as opposed to the perspective of the song/poem, the story, local place-knowledge and the defence and elaboration of a distinctive Irish way of loving, knowing and doing.

We can best explore these themes by analysing how the Ulster and other early seventeenth-century plantation strategists and surveyors reconfigure Irish landscapes and territories in ways very different to how the Irish themselves imagined, understood and used such territories.

'Mapping' the Lands of the Ulster and Later Plantation Regions – 'Polls', 'Quarters' and 'Ballybetaghs'

Bartlett's maps document and celebrate the defeat of Gaelic Ulster and, symbolically, all of Gaelic Ireland. A parallel moment is recorded in the Annals of the Four Masters when it seems that Ireland, under Hugh O'Neill's leadership, is poised for total victory. It is the late winter/early spring of 1600 when, after marching south through Ireland – cementing alliances and chastening severely the midland lords like the Dillons and the O'Carrolls, and further south the Barrymores, who were 'always on the side of the Queen' – O'Neill pitches his camp deep in south Munster. Here he further stiffens resistance, meeting with his allies, adjudicating between their disputes and 'reconciling them to each other in the contentions' – in short, behaving like a 'modernizing' high king of Ireland.[35] On the western flanks, his most powerful ally and friend, Hugh O'Donnell, dominates these territories as far south as Thomond. It is a moment full of expectation.

Then, in a freak encounter after a day of spoiling around Kinsale and Kinelea, Maguire, another of O'Neill's most trusted and able allies, engaged and killed Sir Warham St Leger, deputy governor of Munster, in single combat. But he himself is also mortally wounded. The Annals tell us that O'Neill is deflated and depressed by this event and leaves Munster rather earlier than anticipated.[36] Meanwhile the president of Munster, Sir George Carew, and the earl of Thomond succeeded in undermining the loyalty of the earl of Desmond's powerful ally and right-hand lieutenant – Dermot O'Connor – by promising him substantial monies and land. The earl of Desmond is subsequently imprisoned; and, in turn, is rescued by his own people. But O'Connor, along with every Connachtman who was with him and their kerns, had to quit the province.[37] The Munster coalition fragments and dissolves. Earlier still, the fragile coalitions within Gaelic Ulster have withered. The moment is lost. The battle of Kinsale soon follows, as does Mountjoy's final push into the plains of Dungannon. Subsequently, O'Neill and the young Rory O'Donnell – possibly implicated in a further 'plan' against the crown – leave Ireland in the famous flight of the earls from Lough Swilly on 4 September 1607. Ulster was now open to full-blooded plantation. The Annals record what happened with the departure of the earls: 'their principalities, their territories, their estates, their lands, their forts, their fortresses, their fruitful harbours, and their fishful bays, were taken from the Irish of the province of Ulster, and given in their presence to foreign tribes; and they were expelled and banished into other countries, where most of them died'.[38]

The planting of the six 'escheated' counties of Ulster began in 1609 with an unmapped survey of the Gaelic territories, whether large or small and including the extensive Church and monastic lands. The survey also provided information on existing fairs, ferries and markets, with particular attention being paid to the rich fisheries of the province. The only details recovered for the territorial units known as ballybetaghs were their names and areas.[39] But the estimation of area was by traditional local measures, that is, number of 'polls' in Co. Cavan, the number of 'tates' for Co. Fermanagh and of 'balliboes' for counties Tyrone, Coleraine (which, with the addition of the barony of Loughlinsholin, later became known as Co. Londonderry) and Armagh. The ballyboes were each estimated to contain 60 acres by the plantation enumerators, which constituted a significant underestimation of the average size of each ballyboe as well as ignoring the fact that each of these 'townlands' varied greatly in size to begin with.[40] Similar problems of severe underestimation also applied to the polls, tates and other 'local measures'.

All of this meant that the real acreage of the allocated plantation estates was far greater than that estimated by the planners. Apart from the general deficiency which persisted beyond the mapping stage, this first unmapped survey was found to be deficient on other grounds – much of the land had been left out of the equation altogether. In addition, the enumerators had amalgamated the basic 'townland' unit into their respective ballybetagh territories (usually comprising 16 ballyboes or the equivalent) but they had provided no account of the actual layout and relationship of these territories one to another. In the plantation proper, it was planned to divide the county into 'large precincts and then into estates or "proportions" of three different sizes – 2000 acres, 1500 acres and 1000 acres respectively of productive land'.[41] A mapped survey was, therefore, deemed essential not only to get an accurate estimate of the total area available for plantation but more urgently to establish the proper 'grounds' for carving out compact estates that fitted into and bounded one another across the Ulster landscape.

By May 1609, 'mapping was expressly listed among the duties of a commission appointed to complete the arrangements for the plantation'.[42] The actual mapping survey began in late July and was completed by late September. Close on 5,700 square miles had been surveyed in just under ten weeks. As Andrews points out, 'several kinds of work were involved in the operation: they included the interrogating of local inhabitants and the compiling of townland lists; the collecting of geographical information whether by hearsay, sketching or instrumental survey; and the plotting of the results in diagrammatic form'.[43] With Sir Josias Bodley as the key organizer, eight people were involved in one or more of these mapping activities; and the survey came to be known as the Bodley survey. Among the other surveyors, only Thomas Raven was to establish a reputation as a first-class cartographer.

Speed was of the essence in the operation and a fully scientific 'true content' survey was not possible. It would take far too long and would involve a level of surveying manpower that simply was not available. Sir John Davies summarizes the compromise strategy in his description of the surveying of the five baronies of Co. Armagh, the first county attempted. He noted that the five surveyors, each accompanied by key local informants, 'were sent forth into each barony . . . and in their perambulation took notes. . . . These surveyors, being returned to the camp, out of their notes drew up cards or maps wherein every ballibo is named and placed in his proper situation.'[44] Bodley broadly confirms this strategy when he wrote:

> we thought it our readiest course that . . . we should call unto us out of every barony, such persons as by their experience in the country could give us the name and quality of every ballibo, quarter, tate or other common measure in any of the precincts of the same; with special notice how they butted or mered interchangeably the one on the other. By which means and other necessary helps, we *contrived* those maps [my emphasis].[45]

So the survey technique was constructed and contrived. The resultant maps were, therefore, a series of compromises – not done by precise measurement in the field but by the mapping out in diagrammatic form of essentially verbal information, albeit accompanied by a rapid-fire treading out – with the help of local people – of the confines of 'every parish, ballibo or ballybetagh'.[46] There are, then, significant variations in the quality and accuracy of the maps provided for each barony and county. Yet when compared with what, for argument's sake, one can assume to be a 100 per cent accurate one-inch Ordnance Survey (OS) map, an overall level of accuracy of close on 70 per cent is achieved.[47] And if one excludes the really poor level of mapping accuracy achieved for the baronies of Oneilland and Armagh in Co. Armagh and those of Clanawley and Magherastephana / Tir Kennedy combined in Fermanagh, the accuracy of the remainder rises to close on 80 per cent. Lower Strabane (90.2 per cent), Dungannon (90.2 per cent) and Loughlinsholin (90.2 per cent) – all then in Co. Tyrone – and the Cavan baronies of Clankee (90.0 per cent) and Tullygarvey (91.6 per cent) are all very impressive. It appears that Co. Cavan – with little previous mapping record – is the best surveyed county.

These maps are compromised, however, in some crucial details: many townlands are rendered inaccurately both as to their shape and their boundary relationships with adjacent townlands. The greatest difficulties occur – as one would expect – on the edges and borders of the baronies where duplications and omissions are most common. Similarly, many of the maps become less reliable when a series of townlands yield to large areas of bog, mountain or water expanses. And in two of the baronies (that is, that part of Oneilland that bounds Armagh barony), not only is the size of the total area grossly underestimated but the whole of the outline and its naming pattern 'appears as if in a mirror-image with east and west reversed'.[48] Clearly the first county to be surveyed records the most problems. Differences in the quality of the surveyor's skills also emerge, with the best-surveyed baronies likely to be the work of the accomplished Raven. But whatever their deficiencies, the forfeited lands of Ulster had been transformed onto paper.

Despite these limitations, there is something wonderful, almost magical about the end map products. Each of the barony maps is produced in glorious Jacobean technicolour. Hill and mountain are shaded in brown, green and purple. Lakes are variously represented by using a stippled wave-like pattern, while coasts are also 'waterlined'. Like many other maps of the period, the rivers are rather swollen blue lines, green tree symbols march for woods, and bogs are shown by a reedy brown wash. Churches, castles, roundtowers and homes are rendered in profile or perspective drawings (see Fig. 3.3 and Fig. 3.4).

The most crucial elements in the mapping are the colours and symbols used to show the proposed allocation of the various units into their respective proportions. 'Each greater proportion is coloured yellow,' explains Andrews, 'with two small concentric circles drawn in red at or near its centre (these symbols being interpreted as raths or bawns by some modern writers unfamiliar with [Ridgeway's] "summary note"): medium proportions are in violet, with a circle divided by a bar: and small proportions in carnation with a circle enclosing a dot. Church lands are coloured green, abbey lands indicated by a small circle surmounted by a double cross'; a single cross 'refers to those townlands already granted to temporal proprietors before the survey was made, while lands assigned to forts, towns, Irish freeholders and Trinity College, Dublin, are distinguished by being left uncoloured'.[49] In addition to this dazzling array of colours and symbols, a single fateful red dot was placed on each townland, almost certainly as an aid in checking and counting up these basic chess pieces as they are allocated to each new estate or proportion.

And so for the first time in history, the fundamental building blocks of the whole territorial system of the Irish are laid bare in map form for almost a whole province. The actual colouring of the maps for presentation to 'his majesty for the division of Ulster' took place early in 1610.[50] By mid-March six volumes containing these striking maps of each of the plantation counties were ready for the king's inspection. The die was cast and the historical geography of Ulster and Ireland was to be profoundly and utterly changed. And whatever about other mapping deficiencies, the Bodley survey did provide a clear method for marking out and defining the new estates.

In April 1610, the confiscated lands were transferred by lot to the incoming proprietors. An integrated baronial map (probably finished in late March 1610) and since called the Hatfield map was most likely used as a guide to decide the future of the individual baronies. This map was almost certainly a central part of the final planning of the plantation, since in its overview it distinguished for each barony 'the three categories of the plantation scheme – English; Scots; servitors and natives'.[51] Thus three ethnic categories came to be incised onto the map and also into the social fabric and minds of the people. This Hatfield map helped to disperse most strategically and to segregate these ethnic groups across the Ulster countryside (see Fig. 3.5 for the overall patterns achieved).

By contrast, the Cotton map of the six plantation counties is most relevant and startling in showing for the first time the location of the new proportions, including the names of the planters to which these new estates were assigned. Bartlett's

3.5   Summary of the details of the Ulster plantation, 1609–13 (adapted from Map 5 by T.W. Moody and R.J. Hunter in *A New History of Ireland III* pp. 198–9)

wonderfully detailed provincial map of the ancestral lands of the old inhabitants of Ulster is still in the mind's eye as one inspects the Cotton Ulster map. It is most likely that the specific Bartlett maps of Ulster and parts of Ulster constituted an integral part of the original seventeenth-century State Paper Collection that also housed the plantation county volumes.[52] This cartographic conjunction throws into sharp relief how sudden, complete and radical – in a word, how brutal – was this transformation of the contours of Ulster's landowning and political worlds. On the Cotton map,[53] right across Ulster, one can now track the new owners – Sir Alexander Hamilton, Sir Hugh Wirrall and Lord Burghley in Co. Cavan; Sir Edward Blennerhassett, Thomas Flowerdew and Henry Henning in Fermanagh. The College of Dublin's estates turn up in most counties. For Co. Armagh, the estates of planters such as Henrie Acheson, James Craig and Richard Rolleston are defined and named, as are Robert Steward's, Sir Thomas Ridgeway's and Sir George Hamilton's in Tyrone. The county of Coleraine awaits the London companies; while all of Inishowen falls to Sir Arthur Chichester. Co. Donegal's new estate owners include John and James Cunningham, Sir Morrice Barkeley and James McCulloch.[54] Accounting and mapping now join forces to turn paper landscapes back into landed territories – but now transformed into individually owned new estate units. The landlord era has begun in Ulster.

These barony maps (Hatfield, Cotton, Bodley) allow us to excavate the knowledge of other worlds, a knowledge, one could argue, that came to be subjugated by the new philosophy about landownership, economy and markets that had

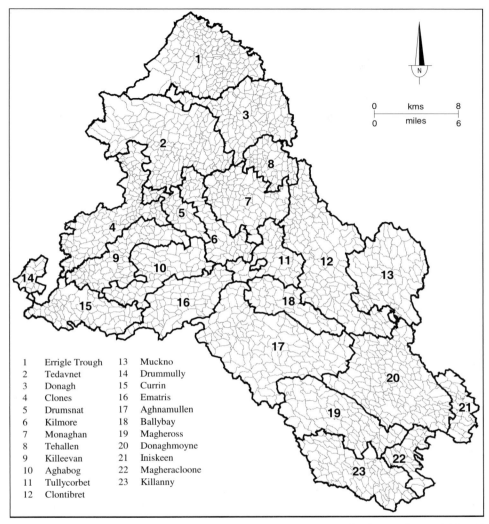

1	Errigle Trough	13	Muckno
2	Tedavnet	14	Drummully
3	Donagh	15	Currin
4	Clones	16	Ematris
5	Drumsnat	17	Aghnamullen
6	Kilmore	18	Ballybay
7	Monaghan	19	Magheross
8	Tehallen	20	Donaghmoyne
9	Killeevan	21	Iniskeen
10	Aghabog	22	Magheracloone
11	Tullycorbet	23	Killanny
12	Clontibret		

3.6a   Co. Monaghan's Irish territories (c.1591); its many townlands nestling within 23 civil/medieval parishes (Reproduced from the work of Patrick J. Duffy: see reference 55)

followed on from the plantations. These maps, taken in conjunction with other surveys carried out at the time, allow us to gain insight into how the Irish understood, organized and 'mapped' the landscape. One of the most striking aspects of these Bodley maps is the revelation of the cellular, nested nature of the ballyboes, polls and tates, which we now call townlands. For the first time, via these maps, the dramatic and impressive architecture of the Irish territorial system is revealed. Patrick Duffy's maps of Co. Monaghan's Gaelic territories (see Fig. 3.6a and Fig. 3.6b) also graphically demonstrate this achievement.[55] Significant, too, is the phonetic rendering of the placenames of these fundamental landholding, administrative units. The English-language rendering of these placenames is highly authentic and much more reliable than Petty's later efforts.[56] So the

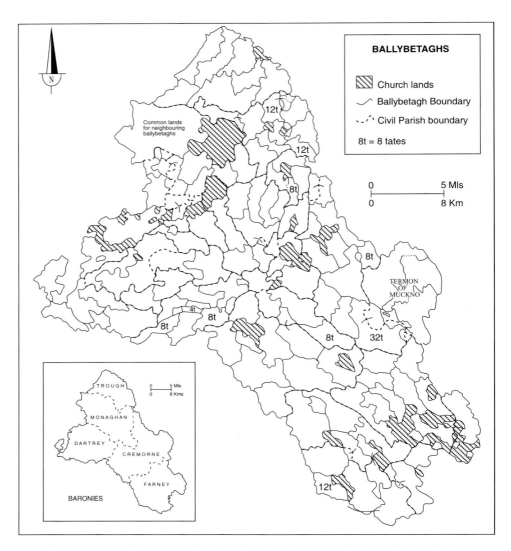

3.6b   Co. Monaghan's Irish territories (c.1591); its ballybetaghs and Church lands (plus baronies)
(Reproduced from the work of Patrick J. Duffy: see reference 55)

sounds of this story-laden, early seventeenth-century landscape are not lost.

All of this points to the surveyors' strategic use of key Irish informants and the
quality of the oral evidence gathered from them in the making of these maps. In
practically every description of the making of the Bodley survey, local voices and
expertise are to the fore. Davies tells us of 'the ancient natives, especially such as
had been rent gatherers and sergeants to the Irish lords' who acted as key guides
and informants for the surveyors.[57] Another commentator described how the
commissioners had 'caused the natives to tread out the confines of every territory
before them; and to set down the number, names, rents and owners of every ballibo
and parcel within every precinct'.[58] Elsewhere we are told 'that commissioners had

selected out of every barony, men, able to nominate, mere and bound every parish, ballibo and ballybetagh'[59] to help out – however reluctantly perhaps – with the survey. These 'jurymen' were the most able and educated in their communities. For example, Davies reports that the local jury in Limavady in 1609 comprised fifteen sworn men, thirteen of whom 'spoke good Latin and that readily . . . They conceaved their verdict or praesentment in a singular goode forme and methode.'[60] It may also be very significant that the majority of these 'gentlemen of good education and family' were members of the erenagh class (hereditary Church officials).

The Ulster Irish, then, had their own 'scholars' and 'surveyors' who knew the names, shapes, boundaries and values of a hierarchy of territories. They had a most intimate knowledge of their own dynamic landscapes and could translate this oral knowledge into a language that the English cartographers could turn into map form. Key players here were the heads of the ballybetaghs – the heads of subsepts – who acted as middlemen and rent collectors between the ordinary farmers/kinsmen of the ballyboes and the sublords (uirríthe) and lords of the territories.[61] As a result, today we can read from these barony maps the names of the ballyboes, tates and polls as faithfully remembered by the most expert criochairí (boundary surveyors) and maoir (bailiffs) of the Irish lords. For Clankelly in Fermanagh we read off the tate/townland names Kilturke, Clonmoilan, Cloncarne, Dromyeskie and Tategormegan. For Dungannon barony we encounter Kilmore, Galbolis, Gortnaboly, Dristernan and Dirrikill (see Fig. 3.7 and Fig. 3.8). And to these Irish-speakers (whose voices we can still hear from the maps), the placenames are not only markers of individual townlands, but are layered with meaning and stories. In one sense, each townland name subverts the plantation map by providing a doorway into other worlds of memory and myth. And the place of each townland or ballyboe is known within the larger units of the ballybetagh and the territories of the uirríthe, while for the hereditary elite classes of the Irish lordship, clearly such intimate territorial knowledge (or 'mapping') is known for the lordship as a whole.

This Gaelic territorial and social system was dominated by corporate kin-groups with greater or lesser economic, political and social power. Power was expressed mainly in the control of land, cattle and labour. The expansion of dominant clans at the expense of weaker kin-groups was achieved within a well-defined and well-established territorial lattice, where parish and ballybetagh boundaries reinforced one another.[62]

Beneath the ballybetagh, the basic building block was the ballyboe or townland, which itself was further divided into subunits. Most characteristically, the septland or corporate kin-estate comprised a ballybetagh of twelve to sixteen townlands, or fractions or multiples of these units. The ballybetagh or its equivalent was the primary territorial vehicle of the ruling kin-group and it was subdivided or added to in response to population or political pressures, including kinship group expansion or contraction. Hence, one finds fractions of the ballybetagh – a quarter or a half a ballybetagh – constituting a kin-based estate. Less frequently one finds multiples of ballybetaghs constituting very large kin-estates. For example, in Co. Tyrone Philip Robinson notes that the norm for a Gaelic estate – of which there were 30 examples – was a single ballybetagh of 16 townlands (38 per cent out of a total of 79 septland estates); 6 estates (7.6 per cent) contained more than 16 ballyboes, while 43 estates (54.4 per cent) contained various units of less than 16 ballyboes; of the latter, the majority were either 4, 8 or more often 12 ballyboes.[63] Oscillations in the social and political power of various kin-groups were, therefore, orchestrated and managed within a very stable yet flexible system of territorial units.

There is a significant gap between the Bodley survey and local topographic knowledge and use. This is suggested by how the mountains and upland blocks of land were 'mapped'. Since these kinds of lands appeared to be separate from the townland network proper, their 'subdenominations' and placenames were not included. However, this does not mean that the intimate micro-geographies and land-use potentials of these mountains were not well known to the local Irish. For Co. Tyrone, most lowland townlands had their associated upland pastures.[64] Further west, work on the 1585 Composition Book of Connacht, the detailed townland taxation survey, demonstrates the intimate relationship between lowland communities west of the Corrib and highly specific, clearly delineated and named upland pastures in the mountains of Connemara.[65] So hidden worlds and hidden landscapes sometimes escaped the imperial eye of the map.

Likewise, what appeared to some English commentators as anarchic, random and exceptionally high levels of mobility amongst Irish agriculturists was often in reality part of long-established local and regional rhythms, as cattle and people moved to and from the summer grazing pastures at the beginning and the end of the season. Such hidden geographies were also very much in play when the lords and sublords mobilized their armies. The townland and ballybetagh network constituted a well-orchestrated arena for both military mobilization and organization – both for supplying the requisite number of soldiers and in providing a recognized command structure.

As far as we know, the Irish did not use maps. 'Measuring/overseeing' with the eye (do reir sultomhuis) and walking the land may have been the critical skills for assessing the size of small areal units and their land-use potential.[66] Besides, the systematic, almost formulaic, use of easily identifiable and named landmarks – whether of fords, roads, ditches, rocks, trees, streams or wells – facilitated the careful and precise description of territorial boundaries. Precise knowledge of the location of borders, on a whole series of scales, was an essential skill in the culture. Named sacred or venerated trees, large stones and stone cairns deliberately set down as crucial markers of land boundaries were particularly favoured in topographic descriptions.[67] Of the many documents of this kind, the volumes of the Civil Survey provide the most complete, and most eloquent, not to say poetic, definitions of territorial boundaries at a whole series of levels from the farm unit to the 'county bounds' themselves. For example, 'by the oathes of good and careful men' of the barony of Clanwilliam in Co. Tipperary the following is a partial description of the boundaries of the parish of Rathleyney:

> And first beginning on the south west by an Antient ditch called Kleynacoran . . . by ye Ditch called Cleyskaghnagon . . . And from Loghagonnell by a gutter to the heighway called bohirgortnaganny bounded by Grantstown afforesd, and from that

heighway by an Antient heigh lane to the fford called Aghbohirnafeibuy bounded
by the lands of Kilfeikill afforesd and from the sd. foord along the sd. heigh lane to
a hill called Knockane Itarra in the west of the parish and from the sd. hill to the
ditch called Cleynacoran afforesd in the south west where wee first begun.[68]

The Civil Survey and comparable survey documents are full of such rich boundary descriptions, which still await detailed research.

Such knowledge is not confined to knowing the boundaries of a hierarchy of
named territories within the Irish townland/ballybetagh/parish system. It must
be related to the fusion of geography and genealogy that made up the Irish ethos
of landowning and landholding. For the local inhabitants, especially for the key
middlemen, each of the townlands was located within a genealogical 'chart',
which read off who the current owner or occupier was, and how such a family
group fitted into the overall genealogical and territorial structure. And not only
the current owner/occupier. Local knowledge amongst the Irish farmers,
sergeants and rent-collectors extended back in time to include the history of the
ownership of each ballyboe and how these changed with the waxing and waning
of the main kin-groups in the region. This land memory involved not only a
recognition of the history and landholding patterns amongst families but also
knowledge over the middle and long term of how the names of places are actually
changed to reflect these oscillations in kin-group power.

Work by Patrick Duffy on both the 1591 and 1606 inquisitions of Co. Monaghan
– which recorded the names of all the landholders in the county and the territorial dispositions of their lands – confirms these interpretations. Duffy notes that
changes in townland/tate names are more common than boundary changes. He
confirms that Thomas Raven's tate maps of Co. Monaghan show that in approximately fifty cases (16.2 per cent of his total) 'tates corresponding with modern
townland areas were differently named in 1634'. In addition, the various sources
that refer to tates by name between 1591 and 1641 occasionally append an 'alias'
form, 'reflecting the possible impact of changing ownership in earlier generations'.[69] Likewise, at the higher ballybetagh level, the shifting of land between
different branches of septs is suggested by such units having different names at
different times. At a higher level again, the *Dindshenchas* points out the elite
knowledge of the poets and brehons who tell of the changed meanings of some of
the great names across Ireland, whether of capitals like Tara, or of lakes and
harbours such as Loch Dachaech/Port Laírge. Nollaig Ó Muraíle's work also
confirms the mutability of some Irish placenames.[70]

Here we encounter a significant difference between the Germanic/Anglo-
Saxon use of placenames and the Irish/Gaelic tradition. The wider literature
suggests that once the Germanic placename forms become fixed in space and in
the minds and texts of the people, they remain constant in that form, enduring
and stable.[71] This is not necessarily the case with Irish townlands and their names.
In particular, the family names attached to placenames beginning with generic
prefixes such as Acar-, Bally-, Farran-, Lis-, Rath- and Tate- could be changed with
changes in ownership. Townland units functioned as the building blocks of the
large corporate kin-estates. In this game of competing kin-groups (that is, taking

into account the chance factors that followed on from family size, sudden deaths, gender structure, subsequent land divisions, as well as the enduring effects of clans expanding their landed domains) the chess pieces of the townlands may shift to another owner or may be combined in a different combination with higher order territories. In the process, nomenclature may come to reflect the changing political geography and at a variety of scales: for example, in the survey of the lands of Tyrone in 1609 'the names and quantities of divers "balliboes" and town-lands had been altered by the late earl, and so made uncertain'.[72] In short, the townland and ballybetagh names, especially the second non-generic suffix of the placename, can be transformed with the changing history and occupation of the local territories. Put another way, the dynamic and evolving character of landownership and occupation is often reflected in the name changes.

The local jurymen, bailiffs and especially the farmers could read off land-use potential from the townland names, as well as the very numerous smaller named land parcels within the townland: for example, the range of generic names in Co. Monaghan represent subtle environmental variations in the region's topography – such names include *cor* (pointed hill), *tulach* (hill), *cnoc* (hill, small mountain), *cabhán* (hollow), *lurga* (ridge), *ard* (height), *éadán* (brow), *mullach* (summit), *tón* (back), *gréach* (mountain flats). Other names too are measures of ecological variety and land potential, such as *cluain* (meadow), *eanach* (marsh), *srath* (flat place) and *achadh* (field).[73] Land in the Irish tradition was not measured in terms of a stan-dard, geographical unit like the acre, but of land-use potential, for example, its capacity to sustain so many cows and related cattle herd. Townland names subsumed (in either their prefix or suffix) generic elements, which signalled the nature of the terrain – whether bog, meadow, marsh, mountain, wood, arable, pastoral, stony or watery. Again, according as these landscape characteristics were transformed by human intervention, name changes would often follow in the Irish (as opposed to the Germanic) tradition of naming places.

As Sir Josias Bodley observed, the locals knew quite well the customary rents and renders of each townland unit, including the transactions and social and terri-torial hierarchies that went into making up such rent charges and food renders. Indeed, it is almost certain that the original townland units were specifically created for military, taxation and mustering purposes. Ireland had long been a highly militarized society and never more so than in the turbulent sixteenth and seventeenth centuries. The heavy dues levied to support the lordship's military capacity in the form of cavalry, gallowglass and kern were levied on the ballybe-taghs and the townlands. In addition, in O'Neill's mensal lands near Dungannon, key service and military families like the O'Hagans, O'Quinns and O'Devlins were obliged to supply essential victuals of oats, oatmeal, mutton and hogs to the lord's table.[74] Katharine Simms confirms a similar pattern of food renders to Maguire of Fermanagh.[75]

In short, both the economic and military potential, as well as the rents that were due out of very specific local and regional territories, could be read off from the names of townlands upwards to the ballybetaghs and the sublordships, each with their own special names and carrying capacity. The higher the status of the Irish landholder, the greater this 'map'/knowledge extends, until we reach the level of the great lordship.

At the apex of the great lordships in Ireland we encounter the greatest concentration of both material power and knowledge. This is so at O'Neill's settlement at Dungannon, O'Donnell's at Donegal, McMahon's at Monaghan, Maguire's at formidable Enniskillen, O'Reilly's town of Cavan, or O'Rourke's base at Dromahair. Outside Gaelic Ulster comparable foci existed to the south: from O'Connor's Sligo, through O'Farrell's Longford and Mac Murrogh's Borris, to O'Brien's Ennis and O'Sullivan Beare's stronghold at Dunboy. This lordship power was expressed in the style and strength of the lord's residence and in the size of the surrounding settlement; but also in the geographical expertise that the lord, his military officers and stewards had, and in particular, the poets, brehons and *seanchaithe* (custodians of local tradition) held. By definition, the *seanchaithe* and the brehons were 'map-makers' or geographers of a narrative kind. The brehons' function as legal adjudicators meant that their regional knowledge of the landholding/landowning system and its territorial hierarchies was both geographically very extensive and chronologically accurate. The brehons were immersed in the laws of the land – the *fénechas* – and had carried out a long apprenticeship in the study of Ireland's diverse and rich law texts to reach the position of, say, chief brehon. If they lived to a good age, some of them had vast experience of handling adjudications and making legal recommendations about many units of land across the relevant territory. The locally trained *seanchaithe* were responsible for recounting, remembering and recording the history and traditions of their territory and had a special obligation to sustain a memory of landownership patterns and changes. The expertise of the brehon and the *seanchaí* was often combined in local land dispute adjudications. The poets and bards too – the despised 'rhymers' of the Elizabethans – underwent a long literary apprenticeship, and were trained in the poetry and *dindshenchas* of the territory, the country and the families who ruled the land. And as elites who circulated freely all over the island, the poets and brehons had a specially powerful 'topographical' view and knowledge of the country as a whole.[76] Such elites epitomized in their offices and skills the deep-rooted territorial ideology of Gaelic/Irish society (see Fig. 3.9).

The fortunes of those two professional classes, however, diverged with the completion of the English conquest. The legal skills of the brehon were progressively acculturated to the prevailing canon and common law, which allowed many of the practitioners to make the transition to work under the imposed English legal system. The fortunes of many of the classic bardic poets were very different. Some such poet-priests and monks became leaders of a cultural and religious revival that ensured that the post-Reformation European norm *cuius regio, eius religio* emphatically did not apply in Ireland.[77]

Finally we come to the long line of chroniclers and annalists – the great memory-keepers of peoples and territories. Initially, the annalists were monks or friars; but by the later Middle Ages learned secular families, especially those trained in *seanchas* (history and place-lore) were also involved.[78] Territorial information was preserved in written genealogies, law texts and books of bardic and

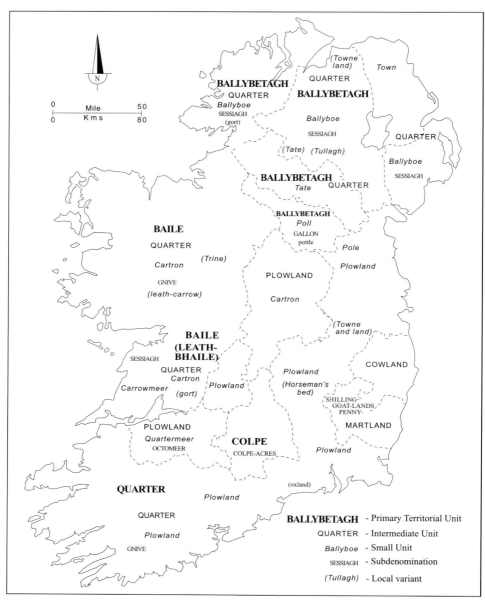

3.9   Territorial hierarchies in Gaelic and gaelicized Ireland up to the early/mid seventeenth century (adapted, in part, from Thomas McErlean's work: see reference 62)

historical poems. Likewise, land and territory-related matters were recorded in rentals and charters. The annals recorded a detailed chronology of the achievement of key dynasties, their territorial rights, their battles, defeats and victories; also their allies, including their important and strategic marriage and fosterage alliances. They recorded not only the history and geography of the key ecclesiastical and secular elites but also provided insights about the hereditary service clans, such as the brehons, historians, medical specialists, poets and smiths.

The most famous annals – *Annála Rioghachta Éireann: Annals of the Kingdom Ireland* – belong only in part to this long tradition of chronicle-keeping but they differ from the older annals in that they are a synthesis of previous annals and other historical sources. These Annals are part of the many texts produced in the first half of the seventeenth century – often by emigrant Irish writers – that contribute to the growing consciousness of the Irish as a unified Catholic (as well as ethnic) community. Like Céitinn's outstanding *Foras Feasa ar Éirinn* (1634), the Annals added to a literature that sought to integrate the Gaelic and Old English interests into a 'single ethnic' nation.[79] These Annals match the poignancy of Bartlett's vignettes with their own narrative descriptions of the fall of Gaelic Ulster and Ireland: for example, volume 5 of John O'Donovan's translation of the Annals averages seven pages a year between 1501 and 1588,[80] whereas in the final volume (from 1589 to 1616), which represents the epic story of O'Donnell's and O'Neill's battles with the English forces, each year requires a narrative of around twenty pages. Towards the end, the Annals stumble: there are no entries for 1610, the very year when the plantation of Ulster is finally mapped out, planned and executed; and there are no entries for 1612, 1613, 1614 or 1615, just when Ulster was receiving its first major influx of English and Scottish settlers under the plantation scheme. After a silence of four years, the Annals deliberately close with the death of O'Neill in Rome in 1616:

> Although he died far from Armagh, the burial place of his ancestors, it was a token that God was pleased with his life that the Lord permitted him no worse burial place, namely, Rome, the head [city] of the Christians. The person who had died was a powerful mighty lord, [endowed] with wisdom, subtlety and profundity of mind and intellect: a warlike, valorous, predatory, enterprising lord, in defending his religion and patrimony, against his enemies . . . a lord with the authority and praiseworthy characteristics of a prince, who had not suffered theft or robbery, abduction or rape, spite or animosity, to prevail during his reign; but had kept all under [the authority of] the law, as was meet for a prince.[81]

O'Donovan's translation of these Annals is one of the supreme feats of scholarship in nineteenth-century Ireland. And central to his achievement – to that recovery of a lost land – is O'Donovan's brilliance both as a topographer and a genealogist. He belongs to a long line of Irish scholars, *seanchaithe*, brehons, chroniclers and poets who were and had to be skilled topographers and genealogists – good 'map-makers' of a specific kind. The English shrewdly recognized these skills in the sixteenth and early seventeenth century and set out to turn these key literati to English ways and laws; or else – as the Spaniards had done to their equivalents amongst the Aztecs and Incas – to eliminate these most skilled spokespeople, to confiscate or burn their annals and manuscripts and to silence their voices, poems and songs.[82]

The Annals of the Four Masters fall silent in 1616. The Gaelic Irish territorial system (including its townland *names*) fossilized and froze around the same time, while the *written* state records continued to forge and flatten these territorial names into new English-language shapes. The central territorial unit of the corporate kin-estate – the ballybetagh – was the key casualty in this demise (see Fig. 3.9, p. 78, and Fig. 3.10).

Figures 3.9 and 3.10 seek to summarize the territorial strategies and ideology of a dynamic Gaelic and gaelicized society. Figure 3.9 illustrates both the general features of such a territorial system and its regional expressions. The primary territorial unit or 'estate' of the corporate kin-group is that of the ballybetagh or its equivalent. The 'quarter' represents an intermediate territorial unit, usually comprising either an entity of 4 townlands if the ballybetagh is constituted of 16 townlands/ballyboes, or a 3-townland entity if the ballybetagh or its equivalent is a 12-townland unit. Thirdly, there is the basic building block of the ballyboe/tate/ploughland, which eventually is standardized island-wide as the 'townland'. Beneath the townland unit is a whole variety of subdenominations (and subdenominational names) comprising various fractions of the townland units. Such fractions probably enclosed and referred to discrete areas of varying land use (arable, pasture, woodland, bogland, upland) within the townland.

Figure 3.9 also reveals island-wide variations in the relative integrity and dynamism of such a Gaelic or gaelicized territorial ideology and system by the early to mid-seventeenth century. In Ulster, this territorial system is still very much in operation – although more weakly expressed in the more normanized/anglicized communities of Down and Antrim. Likewise, Connacht and Clare (as well as the adjacent regions of north Tipperary) have sustained a dynamic territorial system, although the terminology varies with the *baile* or *leath-bhaile* (half-baile) as the primary territorial unit. Gaelic west Munster also appears to have retained a vibrant territorial system centred on the quarter. In contrast, a more feudalized Leinster reveals only fragments of a Gaelic or gaelicized territorial system, although the 'martland' and 'cowland' of parts of Wexford, Carlow and Wicklow still indicate residual vitalities at this subprovincial level.

Figure 3.10 represents a generalized 'view' or 'map' of the territorial organization of the *oireacht,* or lordship. The lordship is here represented as comprising five territories, the core region of the Gaelic lord and the surrounding four territories ruled on his behalf by the *uirríthe*, his kin-related subordinate lords. These are the lord's 'strongmen', his brothers or cousins who command their 'fiefdoms' on behalf of the lord, gathering in and transmitting money and food rents (including many cows) to the lord and co-ordinating military and hospitality functions for the lord. These *uirríthe* resided in a castle-cum-tower-house, which acted as the centre of the settlement structure in their regions and were supported in their organization of these territories by local clan-leaders in their specific ballybetaghs, who, in turn, held certain ceremonial, military and administrative duties at this level.

The lord's core territory – which covered an area of at least one-fifth of the lordship and the best land to boot – was focused on an impressive castle/tower-house, with its associated houses, cabins, bawns, out-houses and green. Such a settlement had quasi-urban functions and was often to become the site for a county town under English rule. This was the place where the surplus of the lordship was gathered in, consumed, celebrated and displayed. Rhymers, harpers and pipers

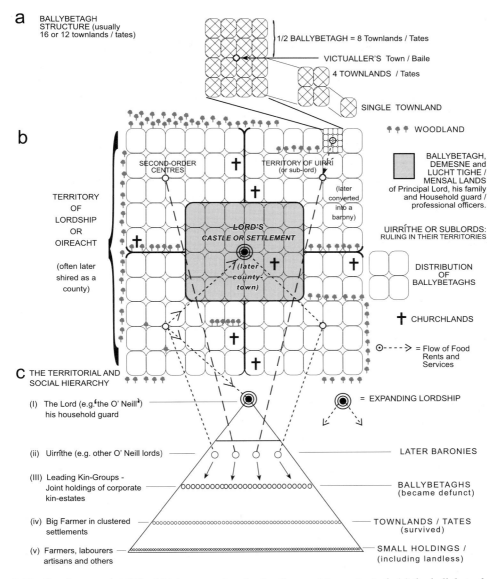

a BALLYBETAGH
   STRUCTURE (usually
   16 or 12 townlands / tates)

1/2 BALLYBETAGH = 8 Townlands / Tates

VICTUALLER'S Town / Baile

4 TOWNLANDS / Tates

SINGLE TOWNLAND

♦♦♦ WOODLAND

b

SECOND-ORDER CENTRES

TERRITORY OF UIRRÍ (or sub-lord)

(later converted into a barony)

LORD'S CASTLE OR SETTLEMENT

(later county town)

TERRITORY OF LORDSHIP OR OIREACHT

(often later shired as a county)

BALLYBETAGH, DEMESNE and LUCHT TIGHE / MENSAL LANDS of Principal Lord, his family and Household guard / professional officers.

UIRRÍTHE OR SUBLORDS: RULING IN THEIR TERRITORIES

DISTRIBUTION OF BALLYBETAGHS

✝ CHURCHLANDS

⊙ - - - > = Flow of Food Rents and Services

c THE TERRITORIAL AND SOCIAL HIERARCHY

(I) The Lord (e.g. the O'Neill) his household guard

◉ = EXPANDING LORDSHIP

(ii) Uirríthe (e.g. other O'Neill lords)

LATER BARONIES

(III) Leading Kin-Groups - Joint holdings of corporate kin-estates

BALLYBETAGHS (became defunct)

(iv) Big Farmer in clustered settlements

TOWNLANDS / TATES (survived)

(v) Farmers, labourers artisans and others

SMALL HOLDINGS / (including landless)

3.10 Sketch-maps (c.1600) of Irish ways of understanding and 'mapping' of: (a) the ballybetagh; (b) the lordship/*oireacht*; and (c) the territorial and social hierarchy, down to the 'tate', 'poll' 'towne and lands'

must have lived close by, as did key horsemen and kerns. The lord also had other castles-cum-garrisons throughout the lordship with specific functions such as controlling river crossings or sea-lanes and supervising the gathering of the lord's taxes from the fishermen.

Ballybetaghs adjacent to the central stronghold comprised the lord's own *uirrí* lands, the demesne lands which he farmed as was his right as lord and the *lucht tighe* (or mensal) lands for the provisioning of the lord's table (as well as some

Church lands). Such prestigious and wealthy ballybetaghs were held by the lord's key service clans. For example, in O'Neill's Dungannon heartland in the fertile Lough Neagh lowlands the corporate kin-estates of O'Neill's *lucht tighe*, members of his household guard, were to be found. These included the O'Donnellys, hereditary marshals of O'Neill's army; the O'Devlins, responsible for the maintenance of law and order; the legal family of O'Hagans, who held the ceremonial right to inaugurate The O'Neill, and the O'Quinns, chief stewards and administrators. As a general principle, the most prestigious kin-groups which were closest to the lord are found in the most favoured locations. Weaker and more distant or discarded kin-groups are marginalized to the edges of the territories, closest to the woodland or wetland borders. Hereditary Church lands – particularly important in Gaelic Ulster – could occupy either very good lands or strategic buffer locations between rival clan territories.

In this profoundly aristocratic, 'caste' conscious and highly stratified society, territorial organization and landownership were ruled by the iron laws of kin and status obligations and not by market forces. This essential interweaving of geographical closeness or distance with genealogical closeness and distance is central to the whole territorial and social structure of lordship. Its nuanced geographies were well understood by all its inhabitants. No diagram, however, can 'map' the geographical and temporal depth of the complex of delicate marital, fosterage and other alliances that determined the relative strength and political power of a lordship.

The ballybetagh constituted the fundamental landowning building block of this sophisticated, flexible, dynamic territorial system. One or more ballybetaghs constituted the corporate estate of a specific sept/clan. However, as we have seen, given the expanding clan-lordship system and other dynamics, the ownership of specific ballybetaghs or fractions thereof could shift. Hence, as Figure 3.10 shows, the ballybetagh had its recognized fractions of a 'half' or a 'quarter' which represented transactional territorial units in the Gaelic system. The customary ballybetagh comprised a total of sixteen townlands, most of which were characterized by a clustered settlement headed by a gentleman or big farmer. He administered this townland for the sept leader and organized the yeomen, husbandmen and numerous labourers within his townland domain. He also transferred the agreed rents in money and kind from the townland to the head of the ballybetagh and agreed on the number of soldiers to be billeted at this level. It is likely that the hard-working landless populations of these townlands constituted close to 50 per cent of the total population of a lordship. My guess is that the head of the ballybetagh, or more likely his sergeant, the gatherer of food rents and services from at least sixteen townlands, may have often acted as the local 'innkeeper and hospitaller,' one of the classic, enduring middlemen/brokers of Irish society.

This Irish system of territorial organization survived as long as an ideology centred on the needs of the kin-groups prevailed, and the system of lordships and sublordships functioned as overall controls on the society.[83] Even before the Ulster plantation, such a kin-centred culture was breaking down across Gaelic and gaelicized Ireland according as new legal agreements, expanding market forces and opportunistic new leaseholders and purchasers eroded the system. But the planning and implementation of the Ulster planter estates made the ballybetagh redundant. The ballyboe, by contrast – the basic building block – was retained but transformed to constitute a new leaseholding unit or farm of so many acres. In short, the townland unit was now constructed to serve new functions.

The statutory English acre takes over as the measure for allocating Ulster planter estates. Most estates were far larger than intended, and often came close to the kind of unmanageable units that had characterized the Munster plantation. But whatever the vagaries of estate size, the old Gaelic system of assessing land in terms of land-use potential now gradually gave way to the standard acre measure. The acre and the leaseholding townlands were invariably valued in monetary terms, so that they could now be shifted and sold like stocks and shares as they were released from the bonds and burdens of a kin-based system. And so, the socio-political entity of the ballybetagh was lost in this new world of rents and markets; and it disappears from the record forever.

In the early decades of the seventeenth century, therefore, the Irish brand of 'mapping' and territorial organization was being made redundant. It was primarily literate and verbal, not graphic and perspective-based. And it can be said to have sustained a scholarly geographical imagination, which – through the schematic listing of key landmarks – was able to demarcate and define the boundaries of the provinces and plot Ireland as whole by tracing the coastal landmarks of the provinces all the way around the island.[84] 'Tracing' is an ancient Irish pastime – the tracing of kinsmen and women and their land-histories. 'Tracing' the outlines of Ireland and its constituent parts via key landmarks was also part of this vital oral tradition.

The evidence of the experienced local juries in the Civil Survey returns highlights the centrality of memory in this oral culture. Even in areas long settled and feudalized by the Anglo-Normans, as in south Tipperary, the Irish names and boundaries of ancient property units – comprising one or more *colpes* (the equivalent of the ballybetagh) – are rendered in great detail. Whether following natural or man-made linear features such as stream, bog, wood, bank or lane or marked out by ditches, trees, stones and stone heaps, the local informants knew and recorded every intimate detail. Such clearly bounded units, whether in single or multiple-ownership, were often coterminous with the parish. Similarly, along the line of Gaelic or gaelicized territories stretching from Kilnamanagh to Ikerrin (see chapter 9), the boundaries of the corporate kin-estates of the O'Dwyers, the O'Fogartys of Inch and the O'Meaghers of Killea are faithfully delimited. In Killea, fourteen O'Meaghers hold joint-ownership of what comprised the whole parish territory. Memory and 'narrative mapping' are even more conspicuous in the most Gaelic parts of north Tipperary. Here, despite both the intrusion of the Anglo-Normans and the later expansion of the O'Kennedy clans, the jurymen are adamant in naming and defining the four ancient *tuatha* (smaller socio-political territories below the lordship) of Upper Ormond as Quiryn ó Glysane, Quirinitlea, Quirin ó Meara and Quirin McDaniell. It is most likely that all these territorial names and their boundaries were close on a thousand years old by the mid-seventeenth century.

In the Gaelic tradition, the description and transmission by oral memory of such ancient territorial entities and their patterns of ownership was as valid and as authentic as a legal parchment of similar age in England.

North and west of Tipperary, in the Gaelic and gaelicized lands of Thomond and Connacht, the names and boundaries of the *tuatha* and those of the *bailes* (corporate kin-estates) still survived into the mid-seventeenth century (see Fig. 3.9, p. 78). Nevertheless, their functions were being steadily eroded as the ideology and values of a kin-based, part food-rendering and deeply aristocratic society yielded to the cumulative impacts of deepening market forces, the ideology and practice of individual property ownership and the slow but steady expansion of English legal and administrative systems. 'Conquest by law' is a crucial strategy here. However, the ghosts of the *tuatha* survived in the shape of the parishes. The latter had begun life as the ecclesiastical arm of the still politically vital *tuatha* of the Middle Ages but they had now come to occupy a more dominant role in local societies. Similarly, the ecclesiastical deaneries survived the demise of the larger territories known as *triocha céad* (Gaelic military-cum-territorial divisions: later cantred/barony) and often overlapped in shape with the new barony with its very critical jurisdictional and administrative functions.[85]

The elimination of the *tuath*, *baile*, ballybetagh and colpe, as well as a host of smaller territorial entities, is the equivalent to creating new empty spaces or territories into which the colonists could pour a new ideology of writ-based social, economic and legal relationships based on the administrative units of the civil parish, barony and county. In short, a new uniform land law is writ large across the landscape. Administrative centralization, the spread of a market economy and the crucial geographical expansion via new court-houses and centres of an imposed law all helped erode the functions of the older territorial structures. However, nothing was more forceful in dealing a death blow to these old territorial and social structures than the formal plantation. That was a very different kind of mapping.

The 'outsider' view of the perspective map that links Ptolemy, Mercator, Bartlett, Raven and Petty created a very different Ireland. It was this 'outsider' perspective – backed up by innovative surveying instruments – that completed the mapping of plantation Ireland in the seventeenth century. This plantation mapping constituted a dramatic shift in the way places were represented, scaled and reproduced. A sequence of further plantations led to the 'seizure of native-owned estates and the introduction of British colonists'.[86] These began with Wexford (1610), Leitrim and Longford (1619), parts of Westmeath, the west half of King's County and parts of Queen's County, followed by O'Byrne's county in Wicklow in 1637–8 (see Fig. 3.11). In the earliest stages of the Wexford plantation it appears that the 'Ulster' model of estimating areas without a proper measured survey was attempted. But this was soon followed by a proper field survey, where the meres and bounds of the confiscated area were 'set forth and trodden with the chain':

> Henceforth the laying on of the chain was like a mystical rite, the agrarian equivalent of baptism or coming-of-age, which gave binding force (almost literally at the

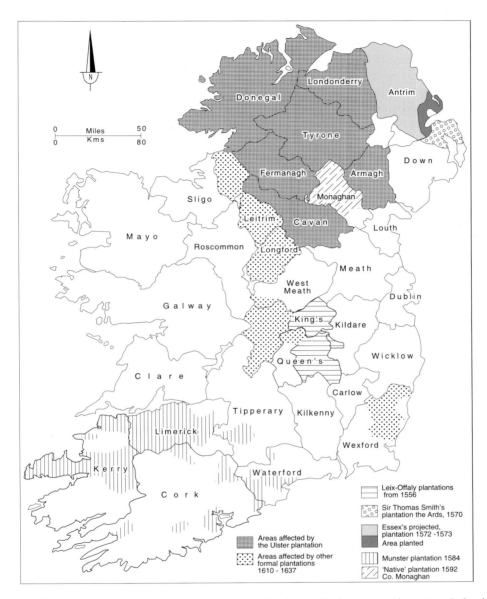

3.11   Plantation regions in sixteenth-century and also first half of seventeenth-century Ireland (adapted from Map 2 [p. 77] and Map 6 [p. 220] from *A New History of Ireland III*)

moment of survey, metaphorically forever) to the process of perambulation and which put the seal on one Irish townland after another as ready to be owned, occupied and civilized.[87]

The meres of Co. Longford were subsequently trodden with the chain, as were those of Leitrim, Queen's County and Westmeath. Measured geometric and numerical precision was the order of the day as each of the townland boundaries was traversed, its area mapped, its name noted and anglicized. Plantation Ireland was now being mapped down to the minutest detail.

The stubborn townland unit endured in plantation ledgers, on the maps, in the rent-rolls and on the ground in the lives and minds of the people. Each townland had a name, a history and a series of stories attached to it. The past was thus never fully eroded by conquest and plantations. The placenames and the landmarks of the townland and other aspects of the wider topography were still available for future interpretations and mobilizations – not just names like Aughrim, Benburb, Clontarf, Dromcree, Drogheda, Lurgan, Portadown and Tara, but also the names of each small townland locality. With about 62,000 townland names and numerous subdenominations, the Irish landscape is an infinitely and richly story-laden landscape. Simple names like Behagloss, Bawnmadrum, Boulabane, Camblin, Shankill, Kylemore and Kilcash still reverberate with meaning and memory. Seamus Heaney is helpful here:

> Our farm was called Mossbawn. *Moss*, a Scots word probably carried to Ulster by the Planters, and *bawn*, the name the English colonists gave to their fortified farmhouses. Mossbawn, the planter's house on the bog. Yet in spite of this Ordnance Survey spelling, we pronounced it Moss *bann*, and *bán* is the Gaelic word for white. So might not the thing mean the White moss, the moss of bog-cotton? In the syllables of my home I see a metaphor of the split culture of Ulster . . . Mossbawn was bordered by the townlands of Broagh and Anahorish, townlands that are forgotten Gaelic music in the throat, *bruach* and *anach fhíor uisce*, the riverbank and the place of clear water. The names lead past the literary mists of a Celtic twilight into that civilization whose demise was effected by soldiers and administrators like Spenser and Davies, whose lifeline was bitten through when the squared-off walls of the bawn and demesne dropped on the country like the jaws of a mantrap.[88]

In the final section of this chapter, the conceptualization and use of natural resources by the map-makers and the settlers they served is compared with how the Irish imagined, used and organized the same resources. This dialectic can be most fruitfully explored through an analysis of woodland geographies between *c*.1550 and *c*.1730.

Woodland: Fortress, Asset, Metaphor and Memory

> *Cad a dhéanfaimíd feasta gan adhmad?*
> *Tá deireadh na gcoillte ar lár*
> *níl trácht ar Chill Cais ná ar a teaghlach*
> *is ní bainfear a cling go bráth.*

> What shall we do for timber?
> The last of the woods is down
> There is no talk of Kilcash or the Butlers
> And the bell of the house is gone.[89]

This well-known Irish poem of the mid to late eighteenth century mourns the disappearance of the woodlands of south Tipperary and, by inference, Ireland as a whole. The poem laments the passing of a familiar wooded landscape of holly, hazel and ash – a landscape laden with memories of the hunt, of sport and relaxation generally, as well as memories of woodland as a crucial resource for all aspects of living and farming. It describes a naked landscape – bare patches of rock and stone. The great trees of the wood are also a metaphor for the old ruling family of the Butlers, and the poem laments the loss of leadership and patronage provided by such a distinguished family. Finally, the poem points to the loss of the culture associated with the woods, the bell tower of the great house and its chapel and people. The bell can be extended to mean 'voice' or 'voices' calling to pray, to work, to play. In short, the poem evokes the bare and silent landscape that once was crowded with people chatting and sporting, loving and fighting in a familiar, warm and wooded land.

From an English settler's perspective, the same landscape looked very different: a landscape cleared of woodland meant a landscape cleared for victory – where the stumps of trees represented a new field won for farming; where the conquered (perhaps ruined) tower-house meant a defensible space where a new house could be built. The new space represented a more secure and visible world that did not threaten attacks or burnings as did the formerly hidden and unknown world of the woods, home of the woodkerns and 'rebels'. The cleared landscape meant that the local Irish could be identified, monitored and checked; and could not remain elusive and footloose behind a frontier of woods. For the English officials and colonizers, Irish woodlands had come to mean threat and danger; and the term 'woodland Irish' was a synonym for 'wild Irish', who were to be broken, tamed and enframed.

Thus, the woodland and forest had come to mean one thing to the Irish and Old English defending their patrimony, and an altogether different thing to the colonizing New English and Scots seeking spaces for new houses, profits and livelihoods.

Kilcash is the anglicized form of Coill Cais – the wood of Cais. Woodland and shrubland names abound in Irish toponomy. There is a total of just under 2,000 townland names that begin with such forms as Crannach/Crannagh (tree abounding), Craebh/Creeve-Creevagh (branchy or bushy land), Garrán/Garrane (a shrubbery), Coill/Coillte, Kil/Kyle/Kilty (woods), Muine/Money (a brake or shrubbery), Ros/Ross (wood) or Scairt/Scart (a cluster of bushes).[90] In addition, there are well over 2,000 townland names whose first element refers to the most characteristic tree in the wood or place. Doire/Derry (oakwood) makes up a total of 1,300 townland names of this type; related renderings such as Dar/Darragh make up a further 300. There is at least a further 500 townland names whose first element comprises such features as Beith/Behy (birch), Cuilleann/Cullion (holly), Coll/Collon (hazel), Fuinnsean/Funshin (ash) and Sceach/Skagh (the whitethorn or haw tree). Then there are as many townland names again where the second element denotes woodland, shrubland or tree names: for example, Adare, Barnacullia, Ballymoney, Ballygarrane, Coolattin and Clonenagh, Lisfuncheon, Kildare, Edenderry and Moycullen. At the very minimum, woodland, shrub, tree or bush names are incorporated into around 15 per cent of all townland names. Patrick W. Joyce goes so far as to claim that 'if a wood were now to spring up in every place bearing a name of this kind, the country would become once more clothed with an almost uninterrupted succession of forests'.[91]

It is that vast memory bank of townland names that we must now excavate, so as to explore other dimensions of vanishing Irelands in the early modern era. We will argue that woodlands and trees were integral elements of Irish culture up to the mid-seventeenth century. Such woodlands constituted one of the essential fortresses for Irish culture in the face of aggressive English expansion.[92] For example, a late-1580s description of Irish counties notes of Fermanagh that there is neither good towns or buildings of importance 'for they rely upon the strength of their country and woods'.[93] While they lasted, the woods were integral to the Irish war tactics since most of their battles were strategic perforations of the enemy's lines of communication followed by a swift retreat to their wooden fortresses. Woodlands were subsequently transformed by the new settlers into assets, products and farms – only to become a memory and a metaphor for the Irish.

It is clear that woodlands and forests had been an integral part of Irish life for centuries, indeed millennia (see Fig. 3.12). In 1600, it is estimated that one-eighth (12.5 per cent) of Ireland comprised wooded or forested areas.[94] Historian Eileen McCracken based her estimate on a detailed analysis of the relevant contemporary maps, surveys and other documentation; but she did not use Bodley's maps for the plantations of Ulster as a source, which she may have been prompted to exclude on the grounds that they were not fully reliable. Indeed woods are completely, and mysteriously, absent from four baronies – part of Strabane, Clankee, Fews (which is a woodland name – *fiodh* and its plural form *feadha*) and part of Oneilland. However, the other barony maps do represent woodland. For example, in the barony of Clanawley in Co. Fermanagh only half a dozen (that is, around 10 per cent) of its non-Church-land townlands are represented as not containing woodland. In Knockninny in the same county again only around 10 per cent of the townlands are presented as not containing any trees or woodland. In nearby Clankelly barony, about one-third of the townlands appear without any tree or wood symbols, although it is significant that three extensive woodlands are shown extending along its northeastern and western borders. In contrast, in the more developed and densely settled barony of Dungannon about 40 per cent of its ballyboes appear not to be wooded.[95] As Philip Robinson notes in relation to the Bodley maps: 'the reliability of the wood pattern may be questioned: firstly as to the extent to which the tree symbols on the 1609 maps are the result of accurate assessment by the inquisitors; and secondly as to the uniformity of the assessment barony by barony'.[96] Yet given his intimate knowledge of seventeenth-century Co. Tyrone and its topography, Robinson judges that the woodland distribution shown on the Bodley maps is a reliable one, one which is confirmed by other available evidence from contemporary maps, surveys and descriptive accounts.

However schematic a guide, the Bodley maps provide us with an image of the distribution of woodland. More importantly, these maps show that the available woodland is an integral element of many townlands; and also, one assumes, of the larger territorial structures in which they are embedded. The ideology of Gaelic/Irish territorial organization emphasized community access to a wide

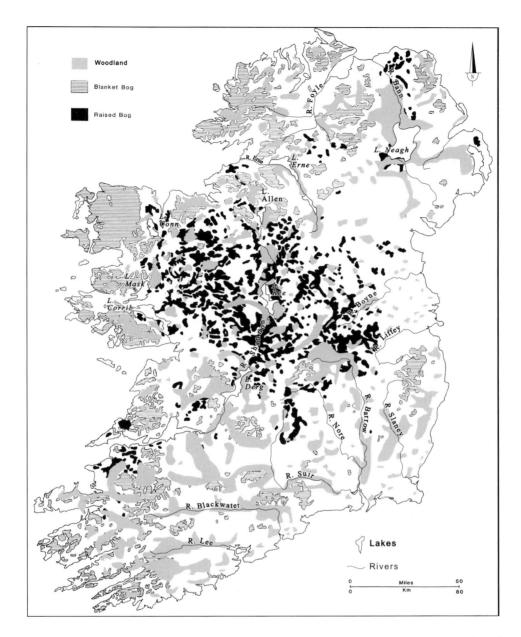

3.12   Distribution of woodland (and bogland) in Ireland *c.*1600 (woodland distribution adapted from the work of Eileen McCracken: see reference 7)

range of natural resources.[97] The ballybetagh/*tuath* structure had also sought to incorporate as wide a range of potential land categories from upland to lowland, arable and grassland, water sources and river meadows. Woods were clearly an integral part of the skilful territorial organization of the resource base in Ulster and in Ireland generally before 1600 (see Fig. 2.19, Pl.1m, and Fig. 2.20, Pl.1o).

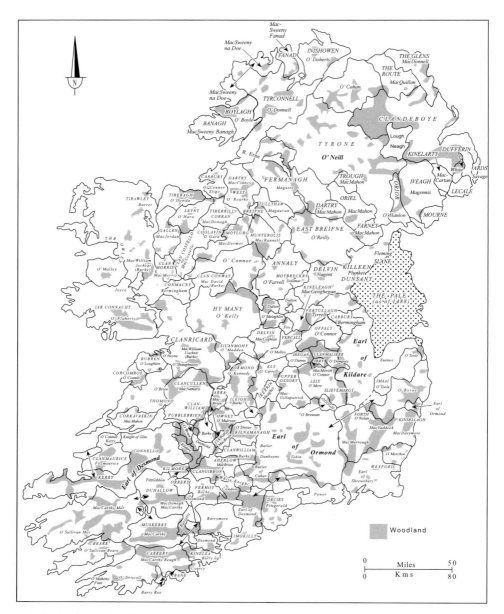

3.13   The relationships between the surviving woodland distribution (*c*.1600) and Irish lordships (1534) (Lordships as depicted by K.W. Nicholls in Map 1 [pp. 2–3] of *A New History of Ireland, III*)

It is striking how often the tree symbols on Bodley's maps march along town-land boundaries and particularly along stream and river borders. And while the maps are clearly inconsistent as to the detail presented of barony boundaries, it is notable how important woodlands are in defining such boundaries. Apart from the borders of Clankelly, woodland also features on the frontier both between Tullyhaw in Cavan and Co. Leitrim and between Tullyhunco in Cavan and north

Longford. Even as late and as incomplete a source as the Down Survey maps demonstrates the regularity with which baronial boundaries incorporated wood-land – whether in north Longford, along the Lagan valley between Down and Antrim, along the south Monaghan border between Farney and Co. Louth, between Barretts and Fermoy in Co. Cork and between Duhallow in the same county and the adjacent baronies of Kerry and west Limerick.[98]

When we examine McCracken's map of woodland for *c*.1600, we have to recog-nize a shift in the scale of representation: a map at this level of generalization must necessarily overlook the small woodland copses associated with many townlands in the plains, even within the Pale; and furthermore, the notion of large blocks of impenetrable woodlands – as suggested by the symbols on the map – has to be modified. The McCracken map, therefore, probably exaggerates the extent of such woodland areas. Even the most extensive woodlands – apart from their deepest undisturbed interiors where the goshawk survived – were part of a named network of pathways, townlands and larger territorial units. A similar change in levels of generalization can be seen between Bartlett's provincial map of Ulster (1602–3) as compared with his much more detailed map focused on east Tyrone and north Armagh (see Figs. 2.19 and 2.20).[99] The latter map shows about one hundred different strands of woodland – both large and small – in this specific region. His map of Ulster as a whole shows only about one-quarter of that number of woodland units for this same region. Bartlett's more detailed map of the east Tyrone/north Armagh region suggests that around 16–18 per cent of that land is still wooded territory.

An equally critical feature of what the map shows is the intimate relationship demonstrated between the woodland and other aspects of local culture. For example, we find that 'Neale McCormock of the O'Neales of Clandeboye' is 'chief of these woods' of Kilultagh. Likewise, 'Rowrie McBriane of the McGenises' is mapped as chief of the woods of Kilwarlin that border the Lagan river. It should therefore be stressed that Irish settlement and woodland were not mutually exclu-sive areal entities – rather they coexisted and complemented each other, even in areas with higher densities of population. The greater woods, impenetrable and impassable to the stranger, were familiar worlds to those born and bred to their 'uncharted' geography.

At the higher territorial level, one could argue that woodlands, especially along or around significant rivers and lakes, constituted the cores of lordships (see Fig. 3.13).[100] This is the case for McCarthy More (Lough Leane), McCarthy of Muskerry (along the River Lee), McCarthy Reagh of Carbery (River Bandon), McDonagh McCarthy of Duhallow (River Blackwater), Mac Murrogh Kavanagh (straddling the Slaney), Maguire (Lough Erne), the O'Donnells (Lough Swilly, east Donegal), O'Rourkes (Lough Allen in Leitrim), Roches of Fermoy (middle Blackwater) and the Clandeboy O'Neills (Lagan valley). It is scarcely a coincidence that woodlands are often associated with the core areas of essentially Gaelic lordships rather than those of the Old English.

Woodlands also acted as deliberate frontiers between lordships and sublord-ships, running along the border between two competing political entities. The later sixteenth-century county maps of Monaghan illustrate the importance of woodland boundaries between MacMahon's lordship and the territory of O'Neill. Woodland along the River Maine separated the Gaelic lands of McCarthy More of south Kerry from the more normanized Desmond palatinate in the north. Woodland territory along rivers could be frontiers as well as cores – as between the core of Ormond's lands north of the River Suir and the lands of the Powers and Fitzgeralds south of it; along the Shannon, as between the O'Kellys of Hymany and the Anglo-Norman lordships of Westmeath, and between the O'Farrells of Longford and the O'Connors of Roscommon. The great woods east and north of Lough Neagh also acted as buffer-lands between the Clandeboy O'Neills, O'Cahan of Derry and Tyrone's O'Neill. Likewise, local woods separated the lands of the Clanwilliam Burkes and O'Dwyers in Tipperary, as well as between the Clanwilliam/Limerick Burkes and the Mulryans along the Limerick/Tipperary border. In many of these instances, it is noticeable how often woodlands acted as buffer-territories between Gaelic and Anglo-Norman lordships.

McCracken's map portrays woodland distribution c.1600 just at the point when the assault on the woodlands by the New English and Scots landowners and settlers was to take on a marked intensity. Behind this map lies the extent of woodland clearance already achieved by the Tudors since the mid-sixteenth century. The destruction of Irish lordships and woodlands marched together.

The strikingly precise Laois-Offaly maps of c.1561–3 are each dominated by the green of the woodlands (see Fig. 3.14). As John Andrews and Rolf Loeber have warned us, the precise determinants of the extent of the midland woodlands shown requires both a realignment of the Tudor map with the more exact OS database and an examination of the related contemporary documentation on woodland acreages.[101] In addition, maps at this scale exaggerate the extent of woodland, especially on its borders. Nevertheless, a preliminary grid-square analysis conservatively suggests that close on one-quarter of the Midlands was wooded.

At the macro level of the Laois-Offaly map it is striking how often the woodland dominates the river valleys, for example that of the Barrow and its tributaries, also the Nore and the Boyne. The woodland frontier along the new 'Leis/Offalie countie' boundary is very broad and extends deep into the foothills of Slieve Bloom as well as in long linear fashion to the north of the Dunne territory of Yregan. The woodland abuts on islands of bogland and clings to and penetrates the upland regions of Slievemargy, the northern edge of the Castlecomer plateau, Cullenagh, as well as Slieve Bloom to the west. Nestling in between the woodlands and the streams are both the bogs and the well-settled *tuath*-like territories, coloured green and light brown respectively. Village and church settlement is also beautifully delineated, including the mainly timbered houses and wooden castles. This is a striking panoramic view of a Gaelic-Irish world just as it begins to be torn asunder by English conquest and colonization.

The assault on these Gaelic lordships was intensified and merciless from the early 1550s. When Lord Deputy Thomas Ratcliffe, later earl of Sussex, returned to

England in 1557, he left the then treasurer, Henry Sidney, in his place. The Annals record, for example, that the treasurer made a concerted assault on Fircall to take vengeance upon Molloy 'for his protection of the woodkernes and other insurgents'.[102] On this occasion the whole country from the Wood (Coill Mór) eastwards was ravaged and churches were burned. Sidney came back a second time in the same year of 1557 and 'burned the territory and cut down the woods and gave neither rest or peace to Molloy'.[103] Here Sidney and his captains waged a ferocious war against the Irish, who turned out against them – including the O'Connors, the O'Mores, the O'Carrolls, as well as the O'Molloys.

The Laois-Offaly maps were constructed a few years after these twin prolonged assaults by Sir Sidney on the midland Irish and their woods. The map in Figure 3.14 shows in striking detail the very detailed square outline of Fort Protector, with its single southwestern donjon, as well as Fort Governor to the north. It also shows in dramatic red the seats of some of the major planter settlers. Most particularly the map depicts, with a series of close-knit black lines, the crucial passes through the woods, as well as key crossing points. Twenty-five passes in all are shown driving west into MacGeoghegan country in Westmeath, most particularly driving westwards and northwestwards through the great woods along the Barrow and Slieve Bloom, as well as creating essential pathways westward through south Queen's County.

Both the map and known English strategic objectives demonstrate not only the drive to cut back the woods and fastnesses of the Irish, but also to establish visible and well-guarded lines of communication and trade. The objective was to facilitate the movement of armies, food supplies, goods and trade across a landscape that was being turned (via its new red-lined settler towns and settlement) into a regular market economy. In January 1567 both Philipstown (the early Fort Governor) and Maryborough (Fort Protector) were dignified as market towns and two years later became county boroughs that returned two members to parliament.[104] What was an old, rather self-sufficient, Gaelic woodland region would increasingly be ruled by sheriffs and courts and be made to bow to the dictates of rule from London via Dublin. Yet local resistance remained stiff and persistent.

The drive to clear the marchlands/woodlands gathered speed as the war against the Irish lordships intensified and reached a peak in the last two decades of the sixteenth century. In 1579, during the Desmond rising/rebellion, Sir Warham St Leger wrote to Lord Burghley proposing to employ 4,000 English soldiers (apart from those already in the field) to cut down and burn the woods of Aherlow, Drumfin, Glenmore and Glenflesk in Munster. This drive was obviously not successful, for six years later Sir John Perrott, the provincial president of Munster, was still proposing that the Munster woods be cut down, so as 'to deprive the rebels of their places of succour'.[105] However, the putting in place of the first Munster plantation greatly facilitated the first major commercial assault by the new planters on Irish woodlands. Led by people like Walter Raleigh (who imported 200 English timber workers to his Youghal/Blackwater estate), Henry Pine in Shillelagh and others, including Dutch entrepreneurs, the cutting and exporting of the timbers of these regions was massively accelerated.[106] A pattern of timber exports had been already established by Old English and Irish of the old port-towns of the southeast in the fifteenth and sixteenth centuries.[107] The two great zones of late sixteenth-century wood exploitation and export by the newly colonizing English were the Cork/Waterford and Wexford regions.

Large scale woodland clearance and devastation thus began in the 1590s. Commentators are agreed that, after the defeat of O'Neill and the Irish order *c*.1603 and the imposition of the 'peace', the assault on the woodlands of Ireland was greatly intensified.[108] After military conquest and the administrative reconstruction of the country, came legal, economic and ecological imperialism. A plantation colonial economy saw the great extent of Irish woodlands cleared at a speed and with a ruthlessness that was never witnessed in England itself, although the woodlands of England were gradually diminishing during the seventeenth century.[109] The improvement of forest and commons remained state policy in the second half of the seventeenth century and the coppicing of woodland remained a central conserving feature. Although England's woodlands had been reduced, they remained integral and significant elements of the eighteenth-century local landscape. As Oliver Rackham observes, 'at most only a tenth of the Irish woodland of 1655 was still there 180 years later, compared to at least three-quarters in England'.[110] As early as the first decades of the eighteenth century, Ireland experienced a wood famine, rather like some developing countries today. Its woodlands vanished forever – the landscape was denuded and radically reshaped.

By 1603, the new conquistadors were in secure possession of Ireland. This consolidation and solidification of English rule over all of Ireland for the first time opened up the country to new economic values and new forms of development. Apart from arguing for and legitimizing woodland clearance for military/strategic purposes, planters and settlers did not see the woodland as an integral element in a grass-subsistence, food-rendering economy. Rather, they saw the woodland as a vital economic resource, ready for rapid exploitation, a quick source of profit, as an engine of economic growth and – once cleared – as providing valuable farmland for commercial cattle, sheep and dairy farming.

Ireland's frontier-colonial status in the first half of the seventeenth century is made quite clear by the extent to which the new owners, merchants and settlers brushed aside a number of legislative measures geared to protect the woodlands and, in particular, the crown's strategic interest in these resources. For example, the London companies were attracted (partly at least) to investing in Derry 'on the strength of its woodland resources'.[111] The crown wished, however, to reserve to itself the ownership of the woods of Glenconkein, along the Bann, and Killetra, beside Lough Neagh. The London companies declared 'that only as lords of the soil could they ensure conservation of the timber', which, they agreed, they did not intend to sell.[112] The woods were then granted to the London companies on condition that they should only be used for building and other necessary purposes in Ireland. But from the beginning, staves were manufactured in these woods and exported illegally by agents of the London companies' Irish Society. In 1610, when the Londoners came to the region, the woods were both thick and extensive; but by the 1630s 'a man might see a mile through them'.[113]

It is clear that the woods of the London companies were cleared with the connivance of first the City's wood ward and later its overseer of the woods. However, the same blind eye operated at the highest levels: in 1611, Lord Deputy Chichester admitted his inability to control the stave trade of the port-towns, and so did not enforce an injunction going back to 1596 that forbade stave-exporting from Ireland to England; he opposed attempts to control the stave trade as late as 1625, arguing that the developers should be given the right to export staves to the rapidly expanding city of London.[114] His successor, Thomas Wentworth, first earl of Strafford, while earning increased revenue for the king by imposing an export licence on the staves, also managed to facilitate exemptions from the regulations not only for others but also for his own exports out of the great woods of Shillelagh.[115] Earlier still, an English Act of 1621 prohibited the felling of any timber within ten miles of either the sea or any navigable river in Ireland,[116] but like many statutory restrictions and injunctions, this Act was never anything but a dead letter. Legislation was totally ineffective, at least on the Irish colonial frontier, where local rules applied. The government's earmarking of trees for state purposes – as in Shillelagh and elsewhere – never materialized. This is nowhere better illustrated than in the outcomes of the navy's interest in Irish oak woodlands and the rather different interest of local colonial magnates. It is, nevertheless, both ironic and logical that Ireland's 'wooden fastnesses' – the great defensive shields of Irish/Gaelic culture – were to help enhance England's navy, its 'wooden walls', which was soon to give that country such maritime supremacy in the world.

Two specific surveys of Irish woods were undertaken on behalf of the navy. In 1609–10, Philip Cottingham, a shipwright, was authorized to inspect the woods of the south of Ireland. He managed to mark 16,000 trees in the woods of Co. Cork and Co. Wexford to be reserved for naval use. For example, part of the woods along the 'Kinsale' (Bandon) river were supposed to be reserved for the crown and were earmarked for the navy by Cottingham.[117] But private interests and companies prevailed. The British East India Company established a settlement at Dundanion, below Inishannon, in 1612, and brought in 300 English to work at its shipbuilding and iron-smelting works, using the woods of the surrounding countryside.

The naval interest in the Bandon region ran into opposition from others involved in the timber trade, none more formidable than Richard Boyle. Although Boyle did nod in the direction of state needs by supplying some timber for the navy from his woods in west Cork and on the Blackwater, his massive, private timber-dealing interests – which saw him record transactions involving about 4 million staves alone between 1618 and 1628 – resulted in much encroachment of woods earmarked for the state's navy.[118] Just as Boyle was actively exploiting the woodlands of the Bandon estuary, the crown also attempted to retain wood for the navy around the Lee estuary.[119] However, the greater part of these woods went to feed Boyle's numerous ironworks, or was turned by him into pipestaves.[120] Likewise, it was proposed that the woods along the Blackwater below Mallow should be reserved for the crown, since the river was navigable from there to the sea. But once again most of these woods fell under Boyle's control, as did woods earmarked for the crown along the Bride and Blackwater rivers. Boyle was one of the greater timber exploiters – not only for staves, iron-smelting and tanning but also for glass-making. He epitomized the new, ruthless, innovative colonial buccaneer.[121]

The second survey on the Irish woodlands was made for naval purposes by another shipwright, Philip Bronsdon, in 1670–1. His reports are interesting 'both as regards the value of the location of Irish woods and the difficulties involved in extracting the timber'.[122] In contrast to Cottingham's reports of 1609–10 (when there were vast resources of timber in accessible maritime and riverine locations), by the early 1670s nearly all the good quality timber woods that still survived were inaccessible and in difficult locations. Only the woods along Kenmare Bay were extant to provide a ready-made naval source, since here the timber needed only to be transported a mile or so to the harbour.[123] Elsewhere, along the Bann, in the Glencar and Glenfin woods in Co. Kerry and particularly along the Shannon river, the cost of transporting the timber overland for export to England was prohibitive. Such woods could only be exploited *in situ,* and that is what happened: these woods were destroyed by the charcoal/iron industry.

By the 1670s, the insatiable iron forges, bark-strippers and stave-makers had gone a long way towards destroying the Irish woodlands. And the woods surrounding Kenmare Bay (which Bronsdon had reserved for naval use) went instead into the great ironworks established in 1670 by Sir William Petty. Even for this great statist, private gain transcended the state's needs and desires.

For Petty, the final conquest or, as he preferred to call it, the final and complete 'reform' of Ireland, would have to be economic.[124] Already, a quasi-Industrial Revolution was taking place over the first half of the seventeenth century. The flavour of the period is nowhere better expressed than by Eileen McCracken:

> In the east–west valleys of Cork and Kerry lay miles and miles of forests that were to enrich the Boyles, the Pettys, the Whites and for a short period, Sir Walter Raleigh: forests which in the first part of the 17th century were to cask nearly all of the wine that France and (to a lesser extent) Spain would produce, which would float as the hulls of many of the East India Company's ships and which until the mid-18th century would fuel the insatiable furnaces of the ironworks that lined the river valleys and which would provide the bark for the tanners of Killarney.[125]

The key industries that exploited the woodlands were casking, shipbuilding, iron-works and tanning. South Munster was only one of the great regions of cask-making, albeit the most strongly linked with the continental trade. The second major region of stave-making centred on Shillelagh in the Slaney valley. In 1606, Chichester had observed that these woods were of sufficient size to furnish the crown with timber for shipping and other uses for the next twenty years.[126] Instead, they were to make wealthy many of the great iron and timber merchants of the town of Enniscorthy – mostly involved in the export of staves to England. In the north, the stave-making export trade was centred on Derry, Coleraine and, to a lesser extent, Belfast, where it was strongly linked with Scotland.

Although not in itself a major industry, it appears that Irish shipbuilding underwent a significant revival at the beginning of the seventeenth century. Small, privately owned shipyards using local woods, coexisted at Belfast, Carrickfergus, Coleraine, Cork, Derry, Groomsport, Glencarn, New Ross, Sligo, Wexford, Youghal and Whitehouse. Indeed, the navy itself established temporary shipyards at Kinsale and Haulbowline Island in Cork harbour. But shipbuilding paled by comparison with the ironworks in its impact on Irish woods. The destructive use of Irish woods – with no attention to coppicing and sustainability – meant that Irish charcoal was very cheap and this cheapness even offset the cost of importing raw ore.[127] By the mid-seventeenth century, Dutch naturalist Gerald Boate records that 'it was almost incredible how much timber an ironworks used'.[128] Almost three-quarters of the seventeenth-century iron forges in Ireland were established before 1641 and almost two-thirds of all ironworks originated in that century as a whole. McCracken's maps identify the great regions of the early iron industry – south Munster, south Leinster and east Ulster – while the later exploitation, especially in the eighteenth century, is concentrated in more remote pockets along the Shannon, in north Connacht and northwest Ulster.

Another consumer of woodland was the farming industry. One of the three key exports of Ireland in 1600 was hides, described as 'the produce of an uncommercialised livestock production'.[129] Tanning was a very old Irish industrial activity, but its character, distribution and intensity changed significantly during the seventeenth century. Because of the damage the tanners could wreak in a wood, legislation both in the early Irish laws and by the New English from the sixteenth century onwards sought to limit both the locations and the numbers of tanneries. In 1628, the barking of trees for tanning was actually forbidden; and again in 1634, when it was stated that the barking of living trees 'by lewd and mean persons' was more prevalent than it had ever been.[130]

There was a massive expansion in the tanning industry after the Cattle Acts of the late 1660s, which prohibited the export of live cattle from Ireland. In consequence, the number of tanned hides increased from 106,300 in 1665 to 217,000 in 1667. In his *Political Anatomy of Ireland* (1672), Petty notes there were as many as 20,000 shoe-makers (and brogue-makers, including their wives), and 10,000 tanners and curriers 'and their wives' in Ireland.[131] These figures provide a rough guide to the scale of the industry, and hint at the havoc that the brogue-makers wreaked in the bark-stripping of the woods. The trees when stripped would often be left to rot, or be burned to clear the ground for farming.[132]

Tanning and cattle-rearing were both ancient activities. The economic and cultural capital of the earlier Irish lord – with his traditions of feasting and hospitality – consisted mainly of livestock, food products, food rents and hides. But in the early seventeenth century we witness a dramatic shift towards commercial cattle production for export.[133] With the conquest and lull in hostilities, the cattle trade was able to flourish despite the efforts of some woodkernes, who continued to steal and destroy cattle into the 1620s. As a result, the first four decades of the seventeenth century saw livestock exports expand considerably. By the late 1630s, cattle exports probably exceeded 30,000 per annum. With the revival of the trade after the Confederate Wars (1641–9) and Cromwellian conquest (1649–58), as many as 50,000 cattle and 100,000 sheep were shipped from Ireland to England in the early to mid-1660s.

The huge expansion of the cattle and sheep trade meant that the conditions for a more commercially oriented agriculture had developed. With a greater emphasis on better breeding, field husbandry, marketing and modes of trans-shipment, it became quite an agri-business. This expansion of the cattle trade increased the pressures to 'waste' the shrubby, wooded pasturelands. The newly emerging 'rancher'-style economy was further enhanced by new owners at mid-century, uncertain of their titles to land and seeking quick returns via the further commercialization of the cattle and sheep trades. This was another major factor in woodland erosion.

The commercialization of pastoral production also meant a very significant intensification of the number and locations of fairs and markets. The increase in the number of licences granted to hold fairs and markets throughout the country by the Dublin government at the beginning of the seventeenth century was partly an attempt to formalize an existing situation, and partly an acceleration in the pattern and distribution of fairs and markets.[134]

The great focal points of these trading activities were the new towns and villages – freshly built and spreading dramatically across a refurbished Irish landscape. Centuries of urban growth on the European mainland had been telescoped into a few decades in Ireland. Irish towns prospered in the first half of the seventeenth century: of the 89 charters of towns still existing in 1834, 55 of them (70 per cent) were granted between 1603 and 1641, as few as 10 per cent before 1603, and 20 per cent were granted after 1660 (see Fig. 3.15 on p. 99 and Figs. 12.3a, b and c on Pl.2o). L. M. Cullen and T. Jones Hughes have documented in depth the rich legacy of planned towns and villages created across so much of Ireland, while Patrick O'Flanagan has detailed the propulsive role of so many of these landlord-inspired settlements in the fostering of trade via market and fair foundations.[135]

The boom nature of the Irish economy in the first four decades of the seventeenth century cannot be doubted. Many of the new towns and villages, built to accommodate new settlers in the various plantation regions, involved houses built in the half-timbered style. Such house types were being introduced at the beginning of the sixteenth century, but they became much more fashionable with the influx of English immigrants at the end of that century and beginning of the next.[136] Such half-timbered houses had already been part of the old urban scene in places like Kilkenny, Drogheda and Dublin, where the earlier wattle-and-clay houses were replaced in the Elizabethan era by half-timbered types. But it was in the new towns of Ulster and other plantation regions that the greatest drive to use local woods for house frames was most noticeable – in the building of the city of Derry and the town of Coleraine, as well as in smaller towns and villages such as Strabane and Bellaghy. Particularly striking are Raven's maps of the new architecture of the villages of the London companies.[137] New mansion houses also came on stream, incorporating much of the famous native oakwood – for example, Chichester's mansion in Carrickfergus, Sir Henry O'Neale's at

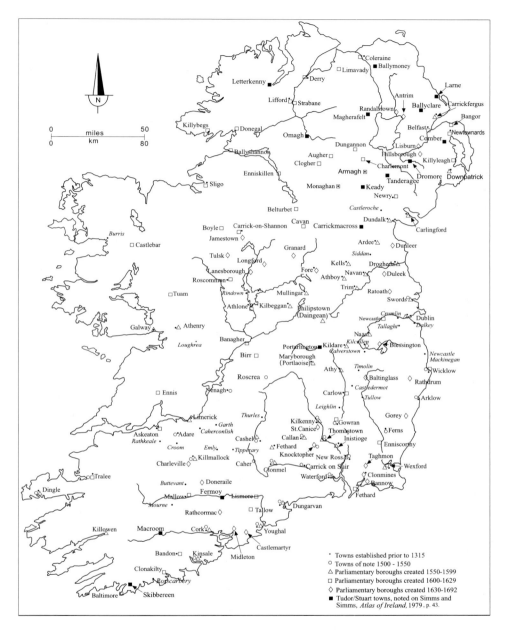

3.15 Geographical expansion of urban foundations from the medieval period to end of the seventeenth century

Killylough, and that of the Warings of Waringstown. Then, after the great fire of London in 1666, oak was shipped in vast quantities from Ireland to help rebuild the city. By the time of the Commonwealth (1649–59), we see the first signs that timber was not so universally or readily available for house-building, since settlers were now only permitted to cut trees for house construction under license.

By the 1720s timber had to be imported; by the 1730s, people lost their cattle during the winter months for want of wood to make sheds in which to shelter them.[138] Their world had changed beyond all recognition.

All of this points to a further nexus between conquest and woodland. The first half of the seventeenth century was clearly the greatest era for plantations proper – from Ulster through Longford, Wexford, King's County and Queen's County, and Leitrim, not to speak of plans for the plantation of Connacht and parts of Clare and north Tipperary (see Fig. 3.11, p. 85). All of these plantations were accompanied by surveys, which detailed, amongst other things, the forest resources of the plantation regions. And there were still powerful woodland zones – both profitable and unprofitable – in these counties: for example, the plantation surveys show that in Co. Longford the woods (of all kinds) comprised around 16.5 per cent of the total area; the territory of the (later) combined baronies of Ballybritt and Clonlisk in King's County had an area of woodland as high as 18.6 per cent of the total acreage.[139] Even as late as 1654, the 'barony descriptions of the Civil Survey for Co. Leitrim mention "great stores of underwoods and shrubby woods" and of oaks and other timber trees in every barony except [coastal] Rosclogher'.[140] Leitrim seems to be one of the last of the most heavily wooded counties in Ireland. Wexford was another, where despite the already heavy exploitation of timber resources, the country of the Duffry and the borderlands of Carlow and Wicklow were still heavily wooded. So was south Wicklow as a whole, with extensive woods stretching from Shillelagh eastwards through Rathdrum to the coast at Arklow.[141]

These plantations involved both sponsored and independent settler migrations. The scale of immigration into Ireland in the seventeenth century was enormous: the average rate, peaking at 8,000 per year in the 1650s, 'probably made it the largest stream of migration in the entire north Atlantic world'.[142] Immigration to Ireland in this period probably equalled the entire flow from Britain to America, even exceeding it in the decades before the 1640s, when America was still unknown and problematic. As many as 100,000 British settlers migrated to Ireland between the years 1603 and 1641; this scale of immigration resumed in the 1650s, the late 1670s and again in the 1690s.[143] In 1600, immigrants of English or Scots descent probably constituted no more than 5 per cent of the total population of Ireland. By 1641, this had risen to 18–20 per cent; and by 1700, it was in the region of 27–30 per cent. Ireland was therefore the country with by far the greatest level of immigration in the whole of seventeenth-century Europe.

This immigrant population was the main driving force in woodland colonization, industrial development and urban creation. The immigrants were by no means confined to the plantation zones – unsponsored migration was at least as important as that sponsored by planter landlords. From Raleigh's time in the Youghal region, timber workers were most often English, working to piece rates as fellers, lathe-turners, sawyers, wainsmen, timber squarers and overseers. On the rivers, men worked at rafting the timber and working the cots. Back upstream, other men carted the timber to the rivers using oxen or horses. Iron-making required the iron-masters who supervised the colonies of mainly English, but also including some

Dutch and Walloon workers. Included here were the skilled furnacemen and hammermen and the more poorly paid fellers and charcoal burners. It is also likely 'that women were employed in such tasks as carrying buckets of charcoal from the tip to the furnace'.[144] Beyond these worlds were the brogue-makers, brewers, carters, coopers, cot-makers, cattle dealers, coach- and carriage-makers, dairymen and women, glass-workers, house-builders and frame-makers, farm leaseholders, stave-makers, sawyers, shipwrights, tenant farmers, trappers, wainscot-makers and wood rangers. Orchestrating all this feverish economic activity were the landowners, merchants, government officials, naval suppliers and exporters.

The final nexus between conquest and woodland clearance was the creation of new farmland. In the 200-year span between 1530 and 1730, Ireland's worked agricultural land was enlarged by up to one-fifth.[145] The settlement and infra-structural history of these former extensive woodland/shrubland regions is still to be written.

In this chapter, I have used the dialectic between (i) mapping as a colonial instrument for conquering and more particularly for planting and settling Ireland; and (ii) the centrality of memory and the oral/aural tradition in govern-ing the complex, embedded relationships between Irish populations and their landscapes and territories as a way of enlarging our understanding of the chang-ing historical geography of late sixteenth- /early seventeenth-century Ireland. As part of this theme, I have used the story of the uses and destruction of the wood-lands as a metaphor for both the uprooting and displacement of so many of the Irish ruling elites and their ways of living and the construction of a new colonial society and economy.

The period from c.1570 to c.1640 ushered in one of the most revolutionary phases in the whole of Ireland's cultural history. The shiring of so many new counties and the creation of further layers of administration and rule at the barony and manorial court levels progressively undermined the older territorial and legal systems of rule. However, there is little doubt but that the introduction of full-blooded plantations – involving elaborate planning, detailed mapping, the introduction of new landed elites and settlers, the creation of many new planta-tion towns and villages and the intensification of a market economy – was central to this transformation. Figure 3.11 (p. 85) highlights the geographical extent of these plantations beginning with Laois-Offaly, then the highly significant province-wide plantations in Munster and Ulster and culminating in what might be called the routinizations of plantations across much of southeast Leinster and the northern Midlands during the first four decades of the seventeenth century. Almost equally important were informal 'plantations', settler infiltration and the widespread exploitation of a wide range of economic opportunities in farming, commerce and industry. And by 1637, Strafford had briskly paved the way via legal stratagems and a comprehensive mapping programme for the proposed plantation of most of Connacht and north Tipperary (see Fig. 4.1, p. 108).

As we have seen, the scale and geographical extent of immigration into Ireland in this period was phenomenal. With it went the whole series of infrastructural, social, economic and cultural changes detailed above. The country is literally opened up via woodland clearance, road- and bridge-building, and new village and town foundations to the greater commercialization and monetization of all aspects of life. This is particularly true of the Gaelic and gaelicized regions – less so in the long urbanized and more market-oriented economies and societies of the mixed Old English/Irish regions in the northeast, east and south, as well as the old heartland of Connacht. Yet everywhere, or almost everywhere, the pressure on both the old Irish and the Old English is to change, adapt and assimilate – to learn English, to dress in the English manner, to accommodate to the norms and demands of the English common law, to attend the Anglican parish church and support the burgeoning market economy with their labour, rents and services.

In 1600, Ireland was, at least in part, a woodland culture. By the 1720s/1730s that cultural base was fundamentally shattered and Ireland was then undergoing a wood famine. Jonathan Swift captures the degradation of local Irish populations in his classic description of them as 'Hewers of Wood, and Drawers of Water'.[146] This era represented the nadir point for both Gaelic/Irish culture generally and for its woods; and is fittingly the beginning of an era known as that of the Protestant Ascendancy. One of the great ironies is that the descendants of the planters who destroyed and exploited the woods came to be the great custodians of newly planted trees – 'For the house of the planter/Is known by the trees'.[147] And on what was now a relatively bare if heavily regimented and reconstructed stage, the Gaelic/Irish culture was beginning to slowly reconstitute itself, albeit in rather different forms.[148] Behind these reformations and stories lies the deepest chasm in the historical geography of early modern Ireland – the 1641 rising/rebellion, the ensuing Confederate Wars and the Cromwellian conquest and settlement. It is necessary now to trace the geography of these cataclysms – to explore the cultural tectonic forces that made for a shaking earth and left us with that great mid-seventeenth century rift in Irish culture and society.

4

The Transformation of Ireland 1641–1654
Wars of the 'Body Politic'

*Ag so an coga do chríochnaigh Éire
's do chuir na mílte ag iarra déarca.*

[This was the war that finished Ireland
and scattered the thousands begging.]

Seán Ó Conaill[1]

Not these my people, of a vainer faith
and a more violent lineage. My dead
lie in the steepled hillock of Kilmore
in a fat country rich with bloom and fruit
. . . so many fences stretch between our minds.

John Hewitt[2]

In the bulky files of the Irish Folklore Commission[3] only one name from Irish history occurs more often than Oliver Cromwell – that of Daniel O'Connell. O'Connell, who spent much of his long life working in and for Ireland, is seen as the great hero and exponent of both democratic political life and Catholic nationalism in Ireland. In contrast, the republican Cromwell – who spent less than a year on Irish soil and who is undoubtedly one of the great architects of English nationalism – is seen in much Irish folklore as the great demon/destroyer/conqueror. It could be argued that Cromwell's regime achieved in a decade (1649–59) what previous administrations had sought to achieve for more than a century. What the Tudors and Stuarts aspired towards and partially achieved in Ireland between the 1530s and the 1630s, Cromwell's military and civil administration came close to full implementation during his brief republican/Commonwealth Interregnum. This involved the hammering of Ireland into a new shape and the forging of new territorial and social structures, which even on the grand European scale, could be compared only with achievements such as those of Napoleon.

The Cromwellian 'revolution' in Ireland was deep, intense and multifaceted; and Ireland is still – in part at least – the inheritor of what happened in the 1640s and 1650s. We need to look at the consequences of the rising/rebellion that began in late October 1641 and ended with the surrender of the last western outpost on Inisbofin in 1653, because two major cataclysms radically transformed Ireland's cultural and historical geography in that decade.

For many Protestant settlers much of the pain and trauma of the Confederate War years were concentrated into the early and mid-1640s. The early months of the rising/rebellion brought them face to face with terrifying experiences: husbands and wives were to see members of their family or those of their neighbours' murdered or brutally treated; farms were plundered, castles and mansions attacked and besieged while a number of their towns and villages went up in flames. Numerous Protestant refugees, panicked by fearful rumours and threats, fled to safe places either within Ireland or across the Irish Sea. Not all reached places of security. And some could not face the terrors of the war and displacement and 'died of the frenzy'.[4]

Likewise, some Catholic villages and communities suffered either severe military depredations or populist Protestant 'revenge' atrocities (or both) in the years before the Cromwellian conquest. But the war that finished 'Catholic' Ireland and sent thousands of displaced persons either begging or overseas is the Cromwellian war, which culminated in the Acts of Settlement and the banishing of the Catholic elites and their retainers to Connacht. We get rare glimpses of the traumas associated with these huge displacements. We can tell the story of Molly Hore, who, with her husband and family, received instructions to leave their sturdy north Co. Dublin castle and farm and move west to Connacht, a land they did not know – a remote and threatening land. Molly Hore could not face the prospect of being so uprooted and having to move to the west. She committed suicide.[5] Hers is just one of the many stories of personal, family and communal tragedies that pile up and replicate across the island.

The geographical evidence to document the distribution, scale and intensity of these two cataclysms differs considerably. As Toby Barnard summarizes:

> whatever violence was offered to the Protestant newcomers in 1641 could hardly have surpassed the brutality, casual and calculated, meted out to the Irish in the preceding century and in the last stages of the Confederate Wars. However, the 1641 massacres were distinguished from these other episodes by the thorough and effective methods by which they were publicized.[6]

The maltreatment of Protestant individuals and communities is vividly documented and preserved in the many county-by-county volumes of the depositions, recording Protestant losses and experiences over the first half of the 1640s. Selective abstracts from these depositions formed the basis of key propagandist tracts and texts in the early and mid-1640s. The related Cromwellian court examinations – which revisit this evidence in the early 1650s to establish the guilt of the 'rebel' leaders and the perpetrators of the violence – provide further extensive documentary accounts. There are no remotely equivalent and geographically comprehensive records of the sufferings of the Catholic Irish communities either during the 1640s or early 1650s. As with all wars, to the victor belongs not only the spoils but also the power and prerogative to dominate, establish and preserve the record, and to tell the story. It is therefore a challenge to excavate the silent spaces and voices of this crucial period, so as to dismantle 'the architecture of silence' that surrounds these awful events. This chapter will attempt to clarify the story by showing how these depositions and examinations are profoundly relevant, not only to understanding the experiences and attitudes of the Protestant settlers, but also the behaviour and attitudes of many of the Catholic Irish during and after the rising/rebellion.

I begin with a provisional overview of the rising/rebellion. This is followed by a detailed examination of the problematic nature and use of the 1641 Depositions and the later Cromwellian examinations as forms of evidence. Using these depositions and examinations, both the geographical nature of the wars fought over identities and territorial control of the body politic are then explored in some depth. A final section summarizes the devastating effects of the Cromwellian conquest and associated famines in Ireland.

The 1641 Rising/Rebellion – An Overview

The recent work of historians – particularly that of Nicholas Canny and Michael Perceval-Maxwell – provides us with a clear picture of the contexts, origins and geographical expansion of the 1641 rising/rebellion.[7] From the beginning, I am embroiled – like the combatants of the seventeenth century – in questions of language, terminology, perspectives, and values. Much of the literature on this period refers to the 1641 'rebellion'; other commentators discuss the 'rising'. But like Doire/Derry/Londonderry, we need to 'splice' the description and talk about the 1641 rising/rebellion. From most Irish points of view the event is an uprising; from the British point of view it is a rebellion. I will continue to refer to the event as the 1641 rising/rebellion.

In this initial exploration, I hope to summarize the contexts, the origins and geographical expansion of the rising/rebellion. Attention must be paid to the class composition of those involved, the decentralized nature of the war and its territorial structures, the operation of state terror, as well as the ferocious treatment meted out by some of the Irish to the settlers, especially the English settlers, at the outset of the war, and the subsequent reactions and reprisals following on from such horrific encounters.

What has been known as Ireland's mid-seventeenth-century civil war is part of a wider European theatre of politics and warfare: not only are the Irish wars linked to continental currents and conflicts but they are implicated in a series of wars that embraced the three kingdoms of England, Scotland and Ireland. These conflicts are a double-island affair: with reverberations, rumours, peoples and armies moving back and forth between Scotland, Ireland and England. England is tearing itself apart at the same time and Scotland too is deeply riven. This is the greatest revolutionary period in English history – it ended in January 1649 with the beheading of the English king, Charles I. And these dramatic events herald a constitutional and administrative revolution.

At the end of its extraordinary struggles, England becomes a republic with Cromwell as lord protector of the Commonwealth from 1649 to early 1658.[8] Scotland mobilizes to express and defend its independent beliefs from England and the Anglican episcopacy and has its own 'Bishops' wars. The earliest of these

Scottish wars was concerned with gaining religious freedom, which is practically achieved by the end of the 1630s. Scotland thus broke free from the Church of England and established the supremacy of the Presbyterian Church. The example of the Scottish struggle for religious freedom was to have a significant impact on the Irish Catholic population, especially its elites.

One of the great questions about the 1641 rising/rebellion, which broke out in that year on 22 October 1641, relates to the identity of those who participated in the planning stages and to the timescale involved in the actual preparation for war. Perceval-Maxwell would argue that three groups were involved in the planning: the northern Irish, the Palesmen and the continental Irish.[9] To begin with, there was a northern 'plan', a northern 'plot'. And once again we are ensnared by language. Which words to use: was it a 'plan' or a 'plot'? First, the northern plot/plan appears to be the key to the initiation of war: a core group of leaders – Lord Conor Maguire of Fermanagh, Sir Phelim O'Neill of Armagh and, in one perjorative description, 'that grand hell-hound' Rory O'More,[10] who had estates in Armagh as well as Kildare – were important players. Second, there was a segment of the Old English Catholic gentry of the Pale, who were involved from the beginning.[11] And third, there was a continental plan or plot. Central figures here are Eoghan Rua O'Neill and Luke Wadding. O'Neill was an officer in the Spanish army in the Netherlands and was involved in correspondence with his O'Neill cousins in south Ulster and with key clerical figures in Flanders and Rome. He will return to Ireland to lead the northern Irish forces in the summer of 1642.

These three strands eventually interconnect. The northern and the continental strands are intertwined from the beginning, and they involve – albeit reluctantly at the start – some of the Palesmen. This is the first time that the Old English of the Pale and the old Irish combine. Forty years earlier, the Old English of the Pale were actively involved in putting down the Ulster rising/rebellion led by Hugh O'Neill, when the Old English were still part of the establishment, still seeing themselves as part of the administrative, political and military elite who ruled the country. Now for the first time (and indeed forever) they break ranks and join the rising/rebellion. We are talking here about planning amongst the leaders, about the gentry, about the still powerful landed group who led the rising/rebellion in most regions, and who knew that they were risking all in this extraordinary endeavour.

Many of the clergy too belonged to families of the Catholic gentry; and the Catholic landowners were patrons and protectors of the clergy. It is doubtful if the rising/rebellion would have spread on the geographical and social scales it did if the Catholic clergy had not been so deeply involved. Clearly, the highly mobile and educated clergy were key players in establishing effective connections between Catholic Europe and Ireland. Priests, friars, bishops all played a part. Some parish priests were very active; a few tried to stand aside. As in any major crisis, some people agreed to act, some hesitated, some refused. Most particularly, the hardy mendicant orders, led by the Franciscans (and the Dominicans), appear to be everywhere. A letter dating from that time to Luke Wadding declared: 'there is not an army or a regiment, not a province or a county, not an angle of land, not a camp or a meeting, not a single expedition or a battle, that the friars were not in midst of it . . . Such zeal for the promotion of the Catholic cause do I find in my subject friars that they need reins rather than the spur.'[12] The local clergy and friars were on the ground in the cities and towns, in parishes, in each of the surviving or recovered monasteries and abbeys. The mobility, poverty and ubiquity of the friars also facilitated 'spying' on enemy fortifications and lines of support. They provided a critical diffusion network and translation mechanism for the ideas and objectives of the rising, as well as pressurizing loyal Irish lords (and their soldiers) to join the rebellion. Likewise, leading Churchmen attended vital international, national and provincial meetings, while acting as critical lynchpins between continental and insular Catholicism.

Such clerical involvement in war was not unusual. It was the norm at a time when Reformation and Counter-Reformation armies battled across much of Europe, battles that were not just political but also religious. The seventeenth century in Europe is an era when religious belief and adherence is taken seriously. There is fanaticism on all sides. In Ireland the Catholic clergy was no exception. In Scotland, the Presbyterian clergy helped lead the revolt against the Anglican bishops in the Covenanting movement; in the years before 1641, Scotland had its own kind of religious war.[13] Ireland, therefore, already had seen a neighbouring clergy of a different denomination and ethos heavily involved in battles for religious freedom. Some of these Presbyterian ministers were to play important roles during the 1640s in the reconstruction and expansion of Presbyterian communities across the north of Ireland. Clergy on all sides were crucial in the Irish battle. On the Anglican side one need only note the key ideological roles played by such Church of Ireland pastors as Robert Maxwell and Henry Jones, first dean of Clogher and later bishop of Kilmore, who drove the agenda of the 1641 Depositions with great ideological fervour and energy.

From the Catholic Irish point of view, the first fear related to property loss. Ireland had already seen a whole series of regional and county plantations (see Fig. 3.11, p. 85). From the mid-1630s, Strafford had been planning the plantation of Connacht and of north Tipperary and, in preparation, this vast western region had already been mapped in great detail (see Fig. 4.1).[14] Strafford was threatening property rights, and one wonders what the existing landowners in the west thought of the detailed work of the map-makers, led by the now well-established Thomas Raven. In one sense, all Irish property was being threatened by an array of doubtful legal stratagems pursued by grasping New English interests. As Pádraig Lenihan comments, 'Such institutional land confiscation in peace time (1603–1641) . . . would simply not have been considered in England or even Scotland.' Ireland was different: successive governors from 1603 onwards pursued 'what was, in effect, a radical course of colonization . . . reshaping Irish society to create in religion, language and society, a replica of England'.[15]

Second, there were widespread fears about a further loss of religious freedom. Catholics were already severely discriminated against in the state. In this period of high anxiety, the Scottish army, which won the battle for Presbyterianism in Scotland, and the parliament in London, where the Puritans were continuing to

4.1   *A Mappe of the Province of Connaght* and north Tipperary, and excluding Co. Leitrim (almost certainly the index map of counties, baronies and parishes from Strafford's survey 1637) By permission of the Board of Trinity College Dublin (MS 1209/70)

increase their power, were both seen to further threaten the limited toleration of Catholicism. News and rumours flowed swiftly in both directions across the Irish Sea in the mid-seventeenth century. Parliamentary speeches and resolutions were quickly relayed to Ireland and deepened feelings of anxiety about the freedom to exercise Catholic worship. The struggle to gain basic religious guarantees from Charles I was regularly dogged by indecision, obstacles and frustrations.[16]

A third major anxiety related to the continued erosion of the administrative powers and privileges of the old elites. Historically, the Irish, and more particularly the Old English, had access to pivotal positions both in local and central government. By the late 1630s much of this power had already been lost. Practically all of the officials in Dublin and most administrators in the counties were of New English extraction. From the point of view of a New English official, the objectives of the domain of government and administration had to be kept secret to be effective, and if the Irish, and more especially the Old English, were still involved in the government of Ireland, they would discover England's secret interests and strategies for the island.

There were other concerns. The New English officials who had gained control of the Irish government apparatus in Dublin used the outbreak of the Irish rising/rebellion to forge links with the extreme group of English parliamentarians. These Dublin officials had two key objectives: to ensure the continuation of the plantations, and, in the process, to continue the consolidation of Protestantism and Protestant rule in Ireland. In England, there was now a standoff between the crown and parliament. England was breaking apart, with one party for the king and one driven by the radical Puritan parliamentarians who are eventually headed by Oliver Cromwell. These radicals, spurred on by extremists like John Pym, 'identified their parliamentary cause with a grandiose Irish plantation that made Strafford's ambitions in Connacht look moderate in the extreme'.[17]

The stakes were very high in these wars in both Ireland and England. As the 1641 rising/rebellion grew and changed in its first months, objectives were shifting.[18] Among the Irish Catholic elite there was growing pressure to regain their equal rights, not only political and religious but also civic – including the right, for example, to be allowed to purchase land in planted regions, which they had been prohibited from doing in Ulster after the plantation. They were seeking liberty of religion and religious expression; and eventually they sought the repeal of all anti-Catholic legislation. What they wanted was a charter for full citizenship for the 'mere' (or pure, unmixed) Irish. One of their powerful motivations was a strong objection to appointment of English 'strangers' (often perceived by the Irish as of lower class origin) as officers in county and government positions, originally the preserve of the old elites. There was a deep sense of deprivation at no longer having access to secure positions in the judiciary and other government offices.

Smouldering beneath everything, right through the period of apparent peace (1610–40), was the persistent threat to land titles – threatened by the operation of government commissions, by Wentworth, and threatened by every New English officer ready to use every 'quirk and quiddity' of the law to find flaws in old land titles.[19] So, the Irish were burdened with memories of recent plantations, the prospect of more proposed plantations and an ongoing insidious legal imperialism. Local and regional grievances of varying intensity – depending on the recency, the effects or the threat of plantation and immigration, the varying leadership impact of Catholic gentry and clergy and uneven levels of economic and social dislocation, which were all sources of resentment – were the mobilizing factors, the powerful undercurrents that lent force to the combustion that made the 1641 rising/rebellion and the later Confederate Wars.[20]

The epicentre of the rising/rebellion was in south Ulster. The early conquests by Sir Phelim O'Neill and his allies can be seen as reversing Mountjoy's key advances against Hugh O'Neill in the early 1600s. The first strongholds to be captured were Dungannon castle, Fort Charlemont, Fort Mountjoy, Cookstown, the Drapers' castle at Moneymore, Dungiven, Tandragee and, somewhat later, the towns of Armagh and Newry (see Fig. 4.2).[21] By the end of November 1641, the co-ordinated Ulster Irish forces had moved swiftly and in a number of different directions to command much of south Ulster and had penetrated into south Down and north Antrim between December of that year and February 1642. However, Strabane and Newtownstewart – vital stages on the way to Derry – had by then been regained by the Laggan settler regiment led by Sir William Stewart. Sir William Cole had earlier held Enniskillen. Most significantly, the core area of Ulster Scots settlement, first in north Down and south Antrim, and then over the

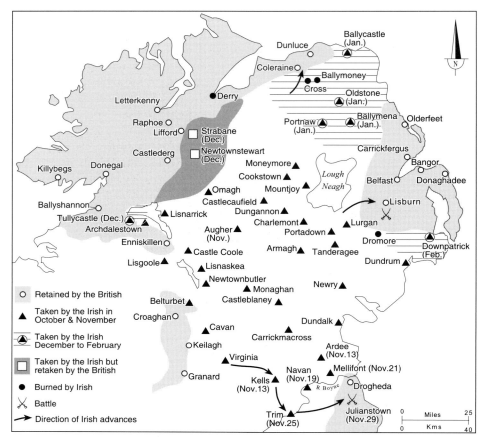

4.2 Early geographical expansion of the rising/rebellion 1641–2 (adapted from Map 3 [p. 215] Perceval-Maxwell; see reference 7).

whole of east and south Donegal, along the Foyle and Finn valleys and north Co. Londonderry, had either never yielded or rallied strongly to push back the persistent early Irish assaults.

Part of the early strategy of the leaders of the rising/rebellion was to attack the areas of English settlements and fortifications and deliberately to avoid disturbing the Scottish quarters. Indeed, Phelim O'Neill's clever use of what turned out to be a forged commission, purported to have been issued and signed by the king, explicitly excluded attacks on Scottish settlements. By early 1642, this ruse and strategy had rebounded. The core areas of settler resistance in the north were those regions held by the Scots. These were to be supported strongly by the crossing over of General Robert Monro's Scottish Covenanter army in the spring of 1642 with the aim of protecting (and indeed – as it turned out – augmenting) the interests of the Scottish settlement.[22]

Meanwhile, and partly because of the force of settler resistance in the north, the focus of the rising/rebellion had already swung southeastwards by mid-November. Figure 4.3 provides a picture of the geographic expansion of the rising/rebellion

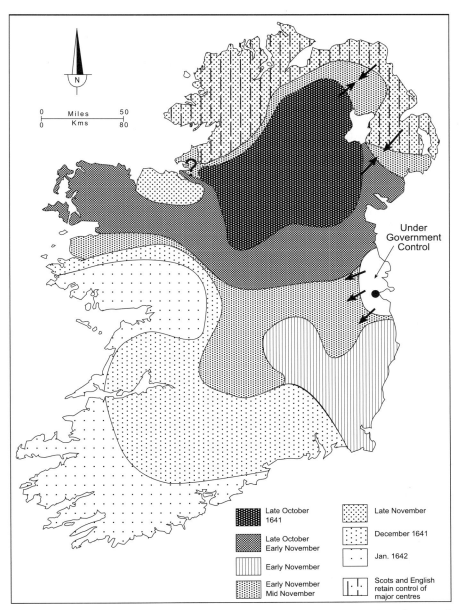

4.3   The geographical expansion of the rising/rebellion island-wide, 1641–2 (adapted in part from Map 4 [p. 253] by Perceval-Maxwell; see reference 7)

island-wide. As this map shows, by mid-November Westmeath and Meath have been drawn into the conflict. As 'rebels' from south Ulster pushed south, the 'United Lords' of the Pale were reluctantly drawn into the war. By the end of November, Laois, Carlow, Wicklow and Wexford were very much involved. The insurrection in Kildare, Offaly and Kilkenny really gathered momentum by late November after the victory of the Irish at Julianstown and following on from the example of their northern Palesmen. Most of the Munster counties, led by Tipperary, 'rise in rebellion' by December. In the northwest, both Leitrim and Longford should be seen as integral if extended components of the earlier 'Ulster' phase of the rising/rebellion in October. Roscommon was also rapidly engulfed, while Sligo and Mayo exploded in conflict by January 1642 as bitter memories of English abuse and tyranny under the Binghams surfaced. The earl of Clanricard endeavoured to keep Co. Galway peaceful, and slowed down but did not halt the spread of the rising/rebellion further south in Connacht.

Figure 4.3 maps out the timing and spread of the so-called 'popular' uprising, as evidenced, in particular, by attacks on, and robberies (and sometimes the murders) of Protestant settlers. However, counties like Wicklow, Wexford, Carlow and Tipperary experienced very early and deliberate expressions of 'rebellion'.[23] Likewise, knowledge of the Ulster rising/rebellion itself spread very rapidly throughout the island. The rising/rebellion spread so quickly because there was significant prior planning and, for example, Leinster groups were involved in the planning/plotting stage. It was, therefore, the spread of a well-coordinated and quite sophisticated movement. The military organization and co-ordination of the rising/rebellion was driven by gentry leaders, while at the rank-and-file level there was often a vicious popular uprising, which the gentry found difficult to channel and contain.[24]

Immediately after the capture of the first key strongholds in middle and south Ulster by Phelim O'Neill and other Irish gentry leaders, a popular rising/rebellion occurred, which involved the pillaging and expulsion of the settlers. This began with 'the mobbing and despoiling of all the English thereabouts [in the barony of Dungannon], beating and abusing all that offered to resist'.[25] As deponent James Stewart reports: 'about the 23rd of October the Irish within the county Cavan rose up in arms and robbed and spoiled all the British that dwelt in the county'.[26] Nicholas Canny describes the nature of these attackers: 'The typical offensive involved an armed group of Irish descending upon a Protestant settler family and demanding, at knife point, that they forsake their home and farm and surrender their moveable goods. Killings usually occurred only where Protestants resisted.'[27]

It is likely that the escalation of violence into a number of grievous atrocities followed on from a series of 'rebel' defeats at Augher in Tyrone, Lisnegarvey in Armagh and, later on, at Ardee in Co. Louth. After the reverse at Augher, where the Scots and English combined to defeat the insurgents, the Irish 'showed no restraint against either the Scots or English'.[28] More particularly, the first victory over the insurgents at Lisnegarvey – where the victorious settlers are said to have killed 700 of their Irish assailants – is seen as a crucial turning point in the local wars. The bloody-mindedness of the settlers in taking revenge after the battle was reciprocated by the slaughtering of many defenceless Protestants at Portadown and elsewhere. As historian Marianne Elliott explains: 'the Catholic leaders, however, very quickly lost control in what fast became a total breakdown of order in Ulster. . . . However moderate the aims of the initial Rising, that breakdown of order generated vigilantism. Popular indiscipline gave rise to localized vendettas.'[29] Likewise, some Irish murders of undefended Protestant tenants represented reprisal killings following on the indiscriminate brutality of the government forces rampaging through Kildare and mid-Leinster. Indeed, it is most likely that the spread and deepening of the rising/rebellion among the Catholic gentry in parts of Leinster and Munster actually followed on from the ground-up popular rising and in part was motivated by a need to control and channel the popular conflagration.

The creation of the Confederation of Kilkenny was also in part a response to the need to establish centralized direction and command of a rising/rebellion that looked likely to get out of the control of the gentry and the clergy.[30] The founding of the Confederation in June of 1642 followed on from a meeting of the leading clergy and prominent gentry leaders, who agreed on an oath of association that would unite the Confederate Catholics of Ireland into a single body. In effect, a national government was established with well-defined political and military structures. Functioning as a sovereign administration, this Confederation had as its prime function the waging of war 'for the defence and advancement of Catholic interests in Ireland'.[31] As Perceval-Maxwell notes, what followed was the clash of 'two ideological juggernauts, English nationalist expansionism and Catholic religious supra-nationalism'.[32] The Confederation lasted from 1642 until 1649 and is fundamentally important as the single example, before 1922, of Irish self-government.[33]

This distinction, however, between a gentry-led rising/rebellion and a popular, bottom-up rising may be too sharply drawn. The extent to which local and often disaffected lesser gentry were involved in the popular rising needs further clarification. More significant perhaps is the vital middle level (both structurally and geographically) provided by the clergy and friars. A recurring feature in Ireland's historical and cultural geography is that Church structures and personnel often provided a vital geographical infrastructure as well as an equally vital mobilizing force in the spread of ideas and in providing motivation and local leadership. Many local clergy and friars emerge as counter-cultural figures. Thus the clergy and key members of the lesser gentry, as well as strong tenant farmers, provided the crucial strands from which the rising/rebellion was knit into a single force.

The controversial 1641 Depositions provide us with a remarkable body of evidence which allows us to listen in to the voices, experiences and traumas on each side of the political/religious divide.

The 1641 Depositions: The Construction of Memories

The 1641 Depositions comprise thirty-one county volumes with an additional two volumes of related material included to complete the collection. These thirty-three manuscript volumes of evidence are confused, confusing and controversial. Constituting the results and findings of five distinct and different processes of evidence collection over the period 1641–54, they are confused in so far as these diverse materials have been regrouped, rearranged and amalgamated into single county volumes.

As historian Aidan Clarke has documented, the five categories of evidence include: first, and most importantly, the sworn statements of Protestant deponents as to the 'robberies and spoils' committed against the settlers themselves, as well as the 'murders and massacres' inflicted upon them.[34] Many of these specific depositions were made in the first two years of the rising/rebellion but depositions were still taken up to the end of 1647. These depositions, drawn up by the appointed government commissioners headed by the tireless and highly partisan 'chief investigator' Henry Jones, served two key purposes. As Clarke notes, 'its formal function was to register claims and to issue certificates of loss to the Protestant deponents. Its informal function was to act as an information gathering system.'[35]

The second component of the depositions comprises a set of copies of the originals made in the late 1640s by Thomas Waring, clerk of the Commission. The third category of evidence consists of the Munster component of the depositions, specifically headed by Philip Bysse, newly appointed archdeacon of Cloyne, under the authority of a special commission and collected between March 1642 and August 1643. (Bysse – like some earlier map-makers and collectors of evidence – was murdered early in the summer of 1643.) These special arrangements for Munster were made to offset the previous absence of such depositions from the southwestern province.

The fourth component of the collection 'consists of sworn statements made by individuals; captured Irish and Old English as well as refugee Protestants, by coercion as well as by choice' before some state officer. These documents deal almost exclusively with supplying 'information about the activities of the rebels, about their governmental and financial arrangements and the condition and disposition of their armies'.[36]

The fifth, and clearly the second most important, component of these documents consists of Cromwellian examinations taken in the context of high court proceedings, which were established to hear and determine all murders and massacres of any Protestant or other person. These formal Cromwellian courts were held in a variety of county locations – for example, Cashel (Co. Tipperary), Carrickfergus (Co. Antrim), Granard (Co. Longford) – throughout the country from the middle of 1652 until 1654. To add to the confusion, it seems that there were also some earlier 'examinations' held in the mid-1640s.

It may be concluded, as Clarke observes, 'that the archive consists of five separate groups of papers, brought together as a working collection to service [Cromwellian] judicial proceedings during and after 1651 and subsequently shuffled, in or before 1741 (when presented to Trinity College, Dublin), to conform to a single county arrangement'.[37] The shuffling, internal scrambling and amalgamation of the five distinct sources of evidence covering the period from 1641 to 1654, therefore, makes for some difficulties of analysis. The total effect is 'kaleidoscopic and baffling' – and the apparent repetitions, numerous conflicts of evidence and the sheer mass of detail makes it very difficult to get an overall view.[38] Material from the different counties is highly uneven – both in content and in the times when the evidence was taken. Some of them contain many later

Cromwellian examinations; 'some have hardly any; some have many "informa-
tions" while others may have none'. In sum, no two volumes 'have a similar
make-up and they have defeated both sampling and generalization'.[39]

The greatest difficulty with the depositions is the passionate controversies they
have generated over the centuries and especially the controversial use made of
selected abstracts in the highly charged 1640s and early 1650s. Here we enter that
difficult arena of not only the construction and perpetuation of selective memories
but also the kinds of reactions and prejudices which such selectivity inspires, not
just in the mid-seventeenth century and after, but down to our own time. It may
be that the original intention behind the taking of the depositions was a genuine
attempt to record the real grievances of the discomfited Protestant families. But
over time, they became documents of conquest.

In 1741, wishing to mark 'the centenary of the bloody massacre', Bishop John
Stearne of the diocese of Clogher presented this extraordinary collection of documents to Trinity College, Dublin. Stearne had inherited these papers from Henry
Jones, his mid-seventeenth-century predecessor in both the bishop's see and the
vice-chancellorship of the university.[40] Thus the tumultuous events of 1641 and
afterwards were being formally remembered in 1741 as these crucial documents of
memory were deposited, catalogued and preserved in Trinity College Library.
However, the depositions were already well known, since extracts concerning
their most horrific and dramatic happenings had been widely promulgated for
propaganda purposes. In that way, they were heavily implicated in, as well as
being a partial record of, the traumatic events of the 1640s and early 1650s. They
serve both as a memory of trauma and as an instrument of conquest, confiscation
and plantation.

Efforts to understand what happened, and when and where it happened in
1641 (and after), has generated much passionate disagreement. The depositions
naturally form the central site for this contestation over behaviour, morality and
world views. On one side, the depositions were seen as 'pretexts for indicting
and outlawing the Catholic landholders throughout Ireland, dredging up and
encouraging the wildest stories of horror and maltreatment in a crude propaganda exercise to give not merely "the rebels" but the Irish nation and the
Catholic religion a bad name'.[41] On the other side, the depositions were seen as
compilations of the events of the time, 'to preserve the memory of the dead and
to note the names of their murderers'.[42] As Clarke argues, both these views
converge in stating that the purpose of the deposition commissioners was 'to
take evidence upon oath to keep up the memory of the outrages of the Irish to
posterity',[43] to provide both a formal narrative for the perpetuation of the
memory of the violence done to Protestants, as well as a careful listing of the
names of the rebel assailants.

From the beginning there is a recognition that the battle was not only about
land, power and religion but also about memory. After Bysse was killed in
Munster, the preservation of the vital tranch of depositions he had collected was
carefully and diligently attended to in turn by such key establishment figures as
Lord Inchiquin, the secretary to Sir William St Leger, Sir Philip Perceval, and

(possibly) Lord Digby. 'The deponent (Richard Gething) remembereth very great care to have been taken and much caution given to preservation of that trunk.'[44] Whatever the original intention behind the setting up of the deposition proceedings, the immediate use made of such evidence determined more precisely what their functions were to be. Henry Jones was the first to use the evidence of early depositions selectively in a report, which 'was openly designed to elicit relief funds from England and may well have been intended, as it was certainly used, to promote investment in the reconquest of Ireland under the Adventurers Act of February 1642'.[45] The standardization of the narrative of the '1641 massacres' had begun.

Already in 1641–2, the evidence of the depositions was critical to identifying Irish landowners implicated in the rising/rebellion. Even as early as December 1641, scarcely one month after the rising/rebellion had begun, the Dublin lord justices remarked that land confiscation would follow quickly on the suppression of the insurrection.[46] Another powerful New English figure, Edward Loftus, publicly wagered that 'Irish Catholics would be stripped of their lands and religion before the year 1641 was out'.[47] This New English group never imagined that these processes would take another thirteen years. But they were watching and waiting to seize opportunities for their expansionist English/Protestant/nationalist agendas. Questions may be raised, therefore, about the ulterior motives behind the taking of the depositions.

The propaganda wars began a week after the beginning of the rising/rebellion as the first of many pamphlets, entitled *The Last Newes from Ireland Being a Relation to the Bloody Proceedings of the Rebellious Papists There*, appeared on the streets of London early in November 1641.[48] By the following month, parliamentary propaganda had turned the widespread killings of settlers into a massacre myth, which would eventually legitimize the bloodiest of reconquests ever seen in Ireland. Less than a year later, Robert Maxwell, a Church of Ireland clergyman from Armagh and one of the most important deponents whose evidence runs to many pages, reported that 154,000 Protestants had been murdered in the Ulster precincts alone, where 'waves of innocent bloud crouds up in heaps'.[49] A year later this 154,000 figure was very widely disseminated when a House of Commons declaration on the rebellion and the numbers massacred was read in all the Protestant churches. By 1644, the growing legend of the total number of Protestants massacred had reached a quarter of a million; and in John Temple's *The Irish Rebellion* (1646) the numbers returned as massacred rises to 300,000.[50] Toby Barnard explores in depth the reverberations of this book's messages, 'with its blend of circumstantial detail, its professed objectivity, its parade of method and evidence – and because it accorded so well with the preconceptions about Ireland and the Irish encouraged by more ephemeral accounts since 1641 and, no doubt, by word of mouth from the refugees – it exerted a strong and hateful influence'.[51] Moreover, Temple's book stirred up 'earlier sedimentary deposits of prejudice left by previous wars in Ireland'.[52] Temple's was the most influential text on the rebellion and went into numerous fresh editions not only in the seventeenth but also in the eighteenth and nineteenth centuries, especially wherever it

appeared that 'the Protestant control of Irish government and society was threatened by Catholic demands for a recovery of some of their lost power'.[53] John
Milton – whose stern views of the Irish were deeply influenced by Spenser's *View*
– then enlarged the figure to 600,000 Protestants massacred – he multiplied
Maxwell's figure by four, since he assumed that the latter's figure only related to
the province of Ulster.[54]

Tracts describing the barbarity of Irish insurgents streamed from English printing presses from late October 1641, communicating lurid and sensational tales of
atrocities. Between 1 October 1641 and 30 June 1642 over 250 news tracts (or close
on 25 per cent of Thomason's collection) dealt with Ireland. By the latter half of
1642, only 6 per cent of such tracts deal with Ireland, less than 4 per cent in 1643
and 1644, and by 1645 Irish news had been reduced to a mere 10 tracts (2 per cent
of the total). The avalanche of news tracts about Ireland in these crucial months
leading to the outbreak of the English Civil War ensured that the English nation
was kept more than fully informed about the Irish rebellion, with escalating alle-
gations of 'barbarous cruelties' committed by Irish Catholics against English
Protestants. The same Irish Catholics are regularly described as 'barbarous rebels',
'cut-throats' and 'blood-thirsty Papists' in such atrocity stories which historian
Keith Lindley agrees were 'generally wildly exaggerated accounts of actual events
if not sometimes complete fabrications'.[55] True or not, these stories were widely
believed throughout England and Wales according as rumours and fears of an
intended Irish invasion of England flourished. Even parts of the West Riding of
Yorkshire went into a panic and 'the peoples [*sic*.] hearts failed them with fear'[56]
when a mistaken report of an Irish rebel advance was reported. Ardent Protestants saw these events in Ireland and those threatened for England as part of a
wider continental Catholic conspiracy to eliminate Protestantism. The Irish
massacres were interpreted therefore as part of a wider European pattern of
Counter-Reformation assaults and threats.

By the mid-eighteenth century more sober estimates of the Irish massacres and
the number of innocent Protestants murdered had emerged. A figure of 40,000 had
by then assumed some orthodoxy, although the Anglican clergyman Warner – one
of the few to have carefully examined all the evidence *in situ* – had strongly
argued for one-tenth of that figure, that is, around 4,000 murdered.[57] Canny's
view that 'Attempts to measure the intensity of popular [Catholic] animosity
against Protestant and Protestantism in Ireland by calculating the numbers who
were killed in the entire conflagration are now seen as futile' seems a wise counsel
today.[58] But in the 1640s and 1650s selective abstractions from the depositions
entered deeply into shaping the military, political and cultural geography of the
new English and Irish worlds emerging under Cromwellian rule.

It is important that we see the ideological reasons that lay behind the collection of evidence and much more particularly the strategic use made of the 1641
Depositions to create a grand moral-historical view of English rights and Irish
guilt. It is also important to emphasize that the evidence of the depositions had
been collected over a twelve-year period, in very different contexts and conditions and often under different rules and procedures, which led to a lot of mixing

of memories and statements.[59] It is recognized that many of the deponents were reporting at a time of great pain and trauma, not to say hysteria. Nevertheless, I think one can negotiate ways through such evidence to get at some of the more authentic descriptions of and responses to what happened, as experienced from the British/Protestant side of the frontier.

The depositions proper involve the presentation of the evidence of the Protestant settlers, of their losses and how they suffered in the early months and years of the war. There are, in effect, no such Catholic depositions to tell their side of the story. However, the Cromwellian examinations for Co. Antrim reveal glimpses of some of the early retaliations and of murders carried out against the local Irish Catholic population. But, overall, the depositions and the later examinations reveal little of the traumas suffered by the Irish Catholic population, which was often severely repressed and terrorized both during and immediately after the ending of the wars of the 1640s. We get some angles on people's experiences of the war; but the lens is still narrowly focused.

Some picture of the fate of the Catholic population may be gleaned from sources outlined below. We know a little of 'the excessive and indiscriminate brutality of Charles Coote's expedition to Wicklow' (and south Co. Dublin),[60] characterized by hangings and village burnings. Likewise, St Leger carried out a similar early and brutal campaign in mid-Munster, which brought a number of formerly loyal old Irish and Old English lords into the rising/rebellion.[61] We know of the massacres of the Irish in Co. Antrim at Islandmagee and Carrickfergus, where the Scots 'gave out that they had a warrant from the King to murder all the Irish'.[62] We know that in Templepatrick in south Antrim an Irish couple sought refuge 'from the fury and violence of such who had soon before slain many of the Irish inhabitants in these parts'.[63] Retaliatory massacres of Ulster Irish at Templepatrick and Islandmagee were not isolated incidents:[64] some 500 people, mostly women and children, were reportedly killed in a revenge attack in the Mourne Mountains in Co. Down, and another 295 in Fermanagh. In the Mourne incident Sir James Montgomery could not contain his men, for they 'had seen their houses burned, their wives and children murdered so they were like robbed bears and tigers and could not be satisfied with all the revenge they took', and instead of open battle, as Montgomery wished, they attacked the Irish from the rear, 'being full of revenge . . . most partys killing many and giving no quarter'.[65] Elliott is of the view that this period decimated many Ulster Catholic families and that an 'analysis of those of the Fews in Armagh shows a numerical decline of between a third and four-fifths'.[66]

As the war developed and settler consolidation of power in northeast and northwest Ulster deepened, we know that the by-now minority Irish often lived in fear of reprisals and that killings of Irish tenants occurred. Sir Audley Mervyn's detailed account of the putting down or containment of the rising/rebellion in counties Donegal, Londonderry, Tyrone and Fermanagh confirms that between late October 1641 and the end of 1642 – through surprise rallies, putting insurgent garrisons to the sword when captured, defending key sites such as Ballyshannon and Coleraine, in foraging and raiding for cattle, in raiding skirmishes, battles and reprisals – as many as 4,500 to 5,000 of the 'rebel enemies' were killed, slaughtered, executed.[67] For some Irish it may well have been safer to enlist in Monro's Scottish army after it was reported that at the Route in north Antrim 'the Scotch army killed all the Irish as they came along'.[68] At the height of the early fury, the truth is more likely to have been that 'without difference or distinction the Irish killed all the English and Scots that they could lay their hands on and the English and the Scots did the like to the Irish'.[69] James Turner, one of Monro's captains in 1642, was to lament that in the war 'the cruelty of one enemy cannot excuse the inhumanity of another'.[70]

We know about these atrocities; but we have no area-based depositions to tell us of the consequences of the lord justices' edict of June 1642 implying complete and merciless reconquest: 'We have hitherto – where we come against the rebels, their adherents, relievors and abettors – proceeded with fire and sword, the soldiers not sparing the women and sometimes not the children.'[71] Likewise, we have no depositions to tell us of the human consequences of the unrelenting raiding by the Laggan army and the Scots against the Irish of mid-Ulster during 1642–3, where nothing was left in Kinard (Caledon, Co. Tyrone) 'but some angry dogs and embers'.[72] Nor of the effects of the intensification of these raids in mid-Ulster in the winter of 1644–5, which resulted in a large scale exodus of possibly 30,000–50,000 Ulster Irish refugees, who fled southwards not only to north Connacht and north Leinster but even reached as far south as the Iveragh peninsula in Co. Kerry.[73] We catch these and other fleeting glimpses of the outnumbered local Irish often 'living in fear'. Much of the rest is silence.

Nevertheless, the depositions proper do help us to get inside Ireland in the early 1640s, to feel and share the people's fears, the hysteria, the traumas, the tragedies, the heroism, the failures and the betrayals that characterized that whole conflagration. This is a war where the late medieval, Reformation, Counter-Reformation and newly modernizing forces meet and clash in complicated ways. It is an astonishing focal point in Ireland's historical geography.

By contrast with the historians' accounts – which suggest that one can separate fact from fiction in these times[74] – I would argue that the cultural geographer and anthropologist might take a different path. When reading the depositions one is struck, not so much by the rational sets of behaviour as by the recurring use of myths, symbols, folkloric images and motifs, the use of prophecy, and a whole range of cultural strategies and instruments that do not fit the usual interpretations. Masks, flags, emblems, banners, forms of disguise, motifs, code words, and other cultural techniques flourish. It is a colourful, gruesome and extraordinary period, steeped in strong beliefs coupled with uncertainties and fears, where paranoia and the paranormal often become the norm.

A powder-keg of beliefs, emotions, attitudes and concepts emerges from a reading of the depositions: there are numerous beliefs and rumours, for example, about the key aristocratic and military leaders: that Charles I 'the King [of England] was in the north of Ireland and that the King would march against the Protestants';[75] that Sir Phelim O'Neill had a picture of a crown on his body which signified that he was to be made king of Ireland; that he was prayed for at mass in Armagh as king of Ireland; likewise, the myth was circulated that Phelim O'Neill was that 'little light' that would arise in Ulster as prophesized by St Patrick and he 'should drive away all the mist and darkness out of the Kingdom'.[76] Religious prophecy was fused with political propaganda. There is a merging of mid-seventeenth-century military strategies with ancient myths and folklore. In Armagh there is a rumour that 'a great man was coming out of Spain and that they daily expected the coming approach of Owen McArt [O'Neill] of the ancient Irish race . . . to be head and rule this Kingdom'.[77] Dreams, hopes and fantasies flared. Later on, deep in the Midlands there were rumours flying that Eoghan Rua O'Neill's 'army in the north consisted of one million men'.[78] There are other rumours and reports of reinforcements – some as large as 40,000 men – arriving by sea from Spain or France or Flanders. In the Midlands, an Irish captain named O'Molloy states that 'we may thank the ould *Calliogh* for this',[79] that is, thank her for a local victory and the spoils that went with it. As Gearóid Ó Crualaoich has documented, such ancestral loyalties strongly persisted with regard to the Irish otherworld realm, including 'loyalties to the name and legends and the authority of the Goddess – and more specifically to the *Cailleach/Hag* persona – in its benign and nurturative as in its destructive and threatening forms'.[80]

There are references too in the depositions to the use of omens and symbols of retribution. Strange visions and apparitions were 'commonly seen on the waters of Belturbet . . . and some of them a year after the English were drowned there'.[81] The local Irish of Fermanagh are reported as believing that after the drownings at Belturbet both 'the fish and the English had gone away together'[82] and left Lough Erne. Elsewhere it is reported that their own gardens had fallen barren 'since they fell into rebellion'.[83] There is a wider view that these omens of abnormality and infertility were signs that God was visiting retribution on the Irish for their sins of pillaging and murder. One can hear echoes of the ancient belief that the land cannot prosper and be fertile because of 'bad' leadership and foul deeds. There is equally a Protestant-settler view that God is punishing them as well.

As against these fears, there is clearly a powerful resurgence of regional feelings and loyalties: the Catholic Fitzgeralds are to become earls of Kildare again, the O'Reillys are to be kings of Cavan; the whole county of Leitrim is given to O'Rourke by the king; the O'Connor Don should be made king of Connacht; the Maguires and MacMahons should once again be made kings of Fermanagh and Oriel (Monaghan).[84] Only once in all of the depositions, at Limerick, is it intimated 'that it was the Irish intention to have a free state of themselves as they had in Holland and not be tied unto any King or Prince whatever'.[85] In contrast, Nicholas Michaell reports from Co. Cavan that the rebels said 'they had an Irish King among them and they regarded not King Charles the King of England'.[86] But it is likely that the view among the majority of the Irish explained involvement in the rising/rebellion as being due to 'the justice of our cause, which is for the maintenance of his Majesty's Prerogatives, our liberties and religion, which is so much trodden under foot, that most of this kingdom are resolved to sacrifice their lives in defence thereof'.[87] The Confederate Catholics of Ireland 1642–9 confirm the above sentiments as represented in their motto, *Pro Deo, pro Rege, pro patria unanimis* (For God, King and Country together).[88]

God is drawn into battle on both sides of the frontier: some Protestants in Armagh 'could not have endured but God Almighty gave them still extraordinary strength and patience';[89] 'All honour to God Almighty who fought our battles' is how Sir Audley Mervyn describes Protestant successes;[90] in Queen's County the refugee Protestants managed to get safely to Maryborough 'with God's help'. And in the same county 'the women of the Popish Irish around Maryboro fasted and asked penance during the war for the good future of the Catholic cause' – in some instances 'solemn fasting for three days in the week [was] constantly observed'.[91] In King's County the insurgents are reported as saying, 'this is God's justice/ Escore o ye shin' (Is cóir ó Dhia sin).[92] A planter victory could not be achieved 'but God so assisted us'.[93] Masses were constantly being said in the gentry houses for the success of the Catholic cause. An inspirational commander of cavalry troops in the Leinster army, Garrett 'Crón' Fitzgerald wore three Agnus Dei (Lamb of God) tablets encased in silver across his upper body and 'had such confidence in the divine virtue of those holy things that he would not trouble himself to wear any armour: "these", he said, [were] "surer than any [armour] how steely, soever, which was true for true believers"'.[94] Before the battle at Julianstown, the Irish troops – 'dear sons of St. Patrick' – were exhorted by their clergy to 'strike hard the enemies of the holy faith'.[95] Catholic soldiers scored the sign of the cross on their bullets to be effective; and when going into battle they were motivated by the speeches of priests, by having holy water sprinkled on them, and by prayers and invocations later 'found quilted in the doublets of the dead'.[96] Millenarian predictions, often going back to Colmcille's prophecies, were a regular feature. The papal nuncio, Rinnucini, was to observe: 'I find these people much given to belief in these foolish predictions.'[97] The use of prophecy, then, is seen as 'not just a propagandist device but the ramifications of a deeply ingrained fatalism'.[98] Either way, religious symbols entered deeply into the war.

On the Protestant side of the frontier there are terrifying happenings, experiences and fears. There is terror at the stories of 'massacres'. We learn about the terror of hearsay in Co. Roscommon, where stories of atrocities in faraway counties Londonderry and Antrim relate how houses and towns were burned there and 'great numbers of murdered British Protestants [were] thrown upon heaps and stripped naked both men women and children and saw the very dogs feed upon some of their carcasses as they lay there unburied most barbarously wounded, massacred and some of them hewed to pieces'.[99] John Wheelwright reported from Co. Cavan 'and further saith that he had heard it credibly reported by divers people in Dublin that there died of the robbed and stripped people in Dublin aforesaid (after they came thither out of the country) the number of seven thousand odd, betwixt the tenth of December 1641 after the rebellion began and the feast day of Easter then following'.[100] As anthropologist Michael Taussig has observed: 'in a climate of terror, it is not the events themselves that are the progenitors of war. It is the telling of the violence, its narration that in turn produces more terror. What matters for fear is how it passes from mouth to mouth.'[101] Reported speech and stories of terrible deeds and rumours of further terror to be enacted circulated among the Protestant communities.

By looking at the distribution of reported 'murders/killings' in the depositions where no actual location for such an event is given, and by examining the uneven distribution of the ratio of murders reported to the number of deponents making such reports, one might assume that it would be possible to come closer to an understanding of the regions and counties where rumours and exaggerations abounded.[102] Such a cumulative analysis suggests that the Ulster/Leinster/Connacht borderland – specifically the counties of Cavan, Fermanagh, Leitrim and Longford – is one such region. County reports from Meath, Queen's County, Wicklow, Waterford and Kerry also suggest a higher level of hearsay and exaggeration in the returns. On the other hand, one could argue that the reasons why there is greater imprecision in the reporting for certain regions may relate to where the settler communities were so dislocated and disturbed that it did not facilitate the emergence of a fully reliable picture of the violence and displacement inflicted on them.

In the final analysis, however, the critical issue is not the actual reliability of the stories told but what the Protestant settlers believed to be true. Our central concern is to discern the level of terror, hysteria and paranoia that characterized the Protestant communities, and to understand how such communities came to construct and fabricate stories of their common experiences, trials and fears; in short, to gauge how these communities, gave shape and meaning to the levels of violence and displacement that they experienced. Their later reporting of events and conversations represents retrospective, sedimented interpretations and rationalizations of events and discussions that happened months or even years before.

In an age when a print culture is taking off, the terror is passed on not only from mouth to mouth, but from page to page, with the pamphleteering, the parliamentary edicts and the books published about these events. There are multiple narrative levels where stories are told, retold, elaborated, transformed, synthesized (and often manipulated) both to serve the larger political agendas and to cement the ideology of the group. The retrospective forging and fabricating of the stories often constructed the accidental and chaotic into things planned and rationally carried out. In that way, the solidification of the stories told gradually fabricate and forge a certainty of explanation, which, fuelled by prejudice and memory, perceives the plotting of death and destruction from the other side. We can be sure that the same processes were at work on the Irish Catholic side, particularly at the local level, even if the evidence is less forthcoming.

It could be argued that an analogous process is taking place in my construction of the narrative. One is always involved in a dialogue with the historical documents and later interpretations – sifting, selecting, judging, balancing, attempting to present a multilayered, diverse and moving picture of places, lives and events, which in the end escape and defy final description and exploration. But hopefully this enlarges our understanding. There is always the danger that the very manner by which we tell the story imposes too much order and clarity on it, and too little awareness of how complex and chaotic the human realities were on the ground.

The wider European literature on death and destruction in the Thirty Years War may be helpful, where it is suggested that the strongest possible language of death and destruction is that used by the local claimants and reporters, 'because this seemed to be the only language adequate to deal with the magnitude of events'.[103] The historian John Theibault has emphasized that 'these claims of destruction were embedded in social processes and interactions which lend these claims/descriptions plausibility and compelled the central authorities to accept that they could be plausible'.[104] One could argue that a like process of interaction, persuasion and prompting took place between the deponents across Ireland, the mainly Dublin-centred commissioners, the English parliament, and public opinion generally. Later pamphleteering and writings about these events made the suffering real not only for those who wrote about it, but also for those who read about it. For example, as late as 1652, the four parliamentary commissioners sent to arrange the terms of the Cromwellian settlement explained how Henry Jones – reintroducing his highly selective abstract of the 'barbarous . . . cruel, murders and massacres' of 1641 – had succeeded in overcoming their temptation to leniency: 'so deeply were [we] all affected . . . that we are much afraid our behaviour toward this people may never sufficiently avenge the same: and fearing lest others, who at a greater distance, might be moved to the lenity we have found no small temptation in ourselves', they sent a lengthy extract from Jones's depositions to deter parliament from making concessions.[105] A collective memory of the awful events of the war was constructed, which accepted as real the experiences of the common people.

As argued above, the rhetoric of death, destruction and displacement in Ireland as returned in, and abstracted from, the depositions is not simply a symptom or description of the war – it becomes itself a major part of the war. It enters into the refinement of English and Irish Protestant ideology, the shaping of policies and the further working out of the war down to Cromwell's revengeful conquest of Ireland and into the terms of the subsequent land settlement.

In interpreting these situations, the work of anthropologists, who have assessed the origins, forms, and behaviours surrounding ethnic hatreds and their expression in horrific bodily violence, is especially helpful. Anthropologists are particularly insightful in describing and interpreting how the contemporary narratives, stories, memories of events – especially those dealing with extreme violence – are constructed and function. The repetitive, almost formulaic, rendering of many of the stories in the depositions, with the use of similar motifs and images, initially inclines one to question their validity, their reliability. But in so doing we forget how often these stories had been shared between surviving families, neighbours and friends before reaching the written form of the deposition. The events had been debated and distilled – biblical allusions to betrayals, persecutions of a chosen people and wanderings in the desert are integrated into stories that sometimes take on the character of a morality play. So also in those accounts, a collective history of a particular kind was being created, 'not only a description or evaluation of the past but a subversive recasting and reinterpretation of that history in fundamental moral terms'.[106] As Liisa Malkki describes it, neither history nor myth but a combination – what she calls a mythico-history – is what is generated in such situations of extreme ethnic violence.[107] Told and retold, and often reproduced in the

depositions, such similar, recurring, formulaic, historic accounts are thus characterized 'by repetition, thematic unity and the sense of a collective voice, a collective
consciousness'.[108] Such a narrative continually emphasizes boundaries: 'them' and
'us', 'Irish Papist' and 'English Protestant', 'good' and 'evil'. A parallel and opposing set of recurring narratives obviously emerged on the other side of the frontier.
So both the 'Irish' and the 'English' came to be ruled by their contesting categorical
imperatives about violently opposed notions of right and wrong.

In this wider anthropological literature, comparisons have been made of
accounts of other victims of extreme violence in a whole variety of geographical
and historical situations. Malkki confirms that narrative accounts of atrocities seem
to converge on formulaic key themes and assume clear thematic forms. She
concludes that both the perpetuation and the memory of the violence may be
formalized – that is, both are culturally determined and routinized forms.[109] Both
the ritualization of the violence itself and the related formulaic ways of telling and
retelling the story of the violence are a feature of widely divergent ethnic atrocities.

In reading the depositions, therefore, we must recognize that we are dealing
with ideologically specific and often powerful narratives that give us one view of
the state of affairs – however valid and genuine it may appear to one side of the
divide. Our evidence and our information about what was happening in localities
between 1641 and 1652 is heavily dependent on the depositions and later examinations.[110] Our perceptions are strongly shaped, therefore, by the actual
geographical distribution of the New English settlers (see Fig. 4.4). We are hearing
voices only from where the New English and some Scots have settled. We are not
hearing very much about peoples and territories outside of their spheres of influence. We are hearing less from a number of Ulster counties and regions where the
rebellion/rising was either never really allowed to take off or rapidly put down,
whereas the number of deponents is probably overrepresented in south Munster,
especially for Co. Cork.[111] The result is that there are large narrative and
geographic gaps and biases in the stories that have survived. The prime witnesses
and storytellers are the New English settlers – gentry, parsons, tenant farmers,
merchants, soldiers, widows, artisans. But if we listen very closely, we can
recognize that a lot of 'Irish' intentions, behaviours and attitudes are being
recounted and reported upon. I put 'Irish' in quotes because the New English
storytellers/deponents have imposed this ethnic classification. The ethnic category
of 'Irish Papist' is in the first instance an English 'colonial' creation. No longer is
the simple term 'Irish' only used to refer to the ancient occupants of the island. The
ethnic-cum-religious classification 'Irish Papist' is intended to marginalize and
belittle the Irish by seeing them as 'idolatrous, barbarous' people. It also eliminates
any distinction between the old Irish and the Old English. Likewise, in telling the
story, we may be reinforcing the ethnic categorization 'Irish', which may for this
period be a little too flattening and monolithic. Did some of these reported 'Irish'
people see themselves as 'Irish'? Or more as people of O'Neill's or O'Reilly's clan,
or people of, say, Connacht or Munster or Leinster? On the other hand, the record
also suggests that a consciousness of being Irish – of being an 'Éireannach' – was
deepening everywhere.[112] We hear the Irish voices, but through a filter of British

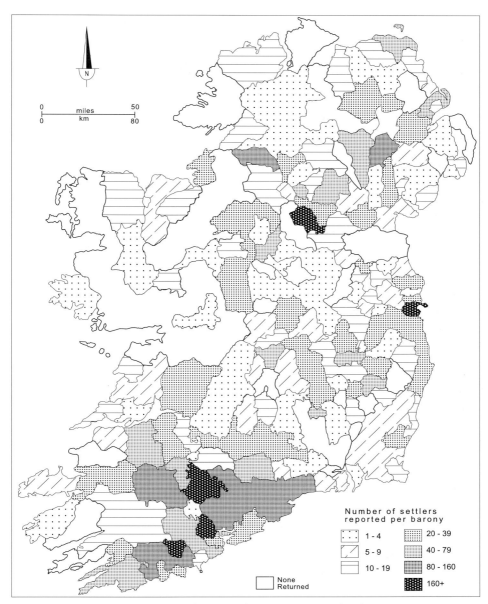

4.4   Geographical distribution of settlers by barony, as reported in the 1641 Depositions

settler views, through a form of translation and telling which is often a second- or third-hand retelling.

These materials are absolutely unique to seventeenth-century Ireland. They are unique because one can listen in to the conversations of many ordinary people as they struggle with conflict, fear and trauma: we can hear the words they used, we can get the rich local ethnographic detail; we can map intimate details of life and death. We can feel the pain and the traumas, we can come close to penetrating to the core of people's own experiences. Despite their later misuse and politicization, many of the depositions represent unique, deeply human as well as geographically localized perspectives.

As mentioned earlier, records of such Irish voices are particularly rare for the period. Even the records of the deliberations of the Supreme Council of the Catholic Confederation at Kilkenny – what we might call the deliberations of an 'Irish Catholic Parliament' – have been lost,[113] and these represented the views of a ruling and highly educated elite. It is even more difficult to get a feeling for what was happening amongst the ordinary Irish on the ground. There are some tracts and pamphlets but very few compared to those generated by English propagandists.

Our question, then, is this: how do we find ways of listening to and catching other voices? How do we arrive at the hidden, the concealed truth of mid-seventeenth-century Ireland's chaos, such as Daniel Corkery attempted in *The Hidden Ireland*[114] to construct his version of a vital and creative eighteenth-century Ireland that similarly never appeared in official records?[115]

Wars Over Identity

The rationale for the wars of identity that exploded after 1641 has deep roots. In chapters 2 and 3, we saw something of the English conquest of Ireland and consequential policies of 'normalization' and assimilation that had been gathering greater force since Elizabethan times, but most particularly from the early decades of seventeenth century onwards. The radical and widespread transformation of Irish society and, in particular, the pressures arising from a market economy involved enormous personal and family adjustments, displacements, disorientations, as well as some opportunities. The foundation of a wide variety of towns and villages across many regions in Ireland from the mid-sixteenth century onwards is symbolic of the dramatic social, cultural and economic changes. The English administrators and settlers sought to turn Irish space into another England. The coexistence of either a planned linear or triangular settlement in a central fertile location, with the enduring, surrounding topography of gnarled townlands and rapidly diminishing and residual woodland on the edges, is a recurring motif across the island (see Fig. 4.5), and symbolizes the juxtaposition of very different ways of living.

There was much sifting and shifting of local populations; and the size and dynamism of new settler precincts must have added to local tensions. The generation of new wealth under an expanding market economy left many of the old elites and middle classes at a disadvantage. For many of the older gentry, the sharpness and strangeness of the transition was too severe; and many were left mortgaging their properties to new landlords or leaseholders, selling off valuable assets like woodland and seeking to match their lifestyles to that of newly emerging landed elites, and often incurring heavy debts. Likewise, at the parish and townland levels, the rapid commercialization and monetization of the farming economy also involved problems of heavy rents, heavy labour dues and, indeed, indebtedness at this scale also. Part of the animosity expressed by the locals against settlers and very specifically against Church of Ireland pastors related to their role as moneylenders.[116] Their command of local tithe income was a further aggravation.

At the macro scale, the power vacuum following Wentworth's execution (after May 1641) saw a deterioration and fragmentation of political power within Ireland and exacerbated England's constitutional crisis. A number of political forces sought to manipulate 'national' identities both within Ireland and in Britain: a radical old Irish Catholic group, a loyal if deeply Catholic Old English axis, the Ormondists (who were of a number of religious persuasions), royalists, pragmatists, those leaning towards the Puritan faction in parliament, and in the north of Ireland an embryonic Presbyterian regional culture whose aspirations were inspired by the Scottish Covenanters (as they were feared by Irish Anglican forces). On the wider European level, there were continuing doubts in England about its main continental Catholic rivals, as well as fears and doubts about the viability and safety of the Irish borders on its western flank. And at a wider level again, a globalizing Atlantic economy was gathering momentum, reverberating into markets, towns, farm economies, technologies and industries in Ireland. In addition, the increasingly self-confident and more radical members of the Irish diaspora on the Continent were advocating notions of a separate Irish Catholic identity in the homeland. Following the formal and informal plantations, there were greatly increased population/immigration pressures in Ireland, which ulti-mately manifested themselves in violent collisions between a privatized concept of landownership, on the one hand, and a family/clan-based concept of landownership, on the other. The acceleration and conjuncture of all these forces, therefore, exacerbated the propensity for violence in Ireland. And, with the initia-tion of the rising/rebellion proper, the subsequent disruption and eventual collapse of the economy added further uncertainty to an already 'abnormal' and disturbed world.

Anthropological literature strongly suggests that the specific conditions where group violence between previous social associates occurs are associated with particular forms of uncertainty regarding identity.[117] The Ireland of the late 1630s and early 1640s, and especially its Catholic population, was subjected to multiple uncertainties over identity: over access to systems of territorial administration, over religious and political freedom, and over property. Wider geographical forces were centrally involved in adding to uncertainties. In mid-seventeenth-century Europe, the greater speed and intensity with which both material and ideological 'goods' circulated across national boundaries created a new order of uncertainty in social life. The scale of the Irish scattering to Europe from 1580 onwards is one manifestation of the transformed social and cultural geography of western Europe (see Fig. 3.1, p. 57). The increase in the power of the state and the size of its armies is another.[118] We have already seen the complex and varied levels of interactions, including stories and memories, that ebbed, flowed and throbbed between Ireland/Scotland/England. Adding fuel to this ideological uncertainty were the tumultuous polarities of the Thirty Years War and the rapidity with which knowledge – religious and political – of events in France, Spain and the Low Countries percolated back to Ireland and Britain.

Tudor England had insisted on purity of religion and language – to be a loyal, obedient subject required one to be Protestant and English-speaking. The new English nation-state sought to extend such hegemonic control over Ireland's culture and political life. This policy intensified under James I (1603–25), who regarded the Irish Catholics as, at best, half-subjects.[119] In an era of growing absolutism, conformity to the monarch's religious affiliation reigned supreme. English nation-building required 'normalization', conformity and loyalty. Consequently, if somewhat episodically, the Irish Catholic population was subjected to intense physical, legal, economic and moral pressures to conform to the Anglican model and attend Church of Ireland services. The challenges and threats to Irish Catholic identities were immense.

From the 1580s, and certainly by the 1620s, Counter-Reformation Catholicism had begun to establish deep roots in the Irish towns and countryside. The role of the European seminaries, continentally trained priests, the ideology of the Counter-Reformation and knowledge of what norms prevailed for Catholic worship and practice in the Catholic countries of the Continent sharpened the edge of the Catholic experience of the abnormal in Ireland – where the Church was outlawed, mass was offered in homes and not in elaborate churches and where the paraphernalia of the old liturgy had been dismantled in the now Anglican-controlled parish churches.[120] Add to this the growing politicization – at home and abroad – of Catholic spokesmen (poets, clergy and friars) about the reality and integrity of the Irish Catholic nation, which fostered in the people a mentality that stressed resistance to the subjugation and displacement that was entailed by the English conquest.

The above scenarios are essential to any understanding of the explosion of animosities that Catholic groups directed against their Protestant counterparts in the early phases of the 1641 rising/rebellion. One of the most emphatic and regular motifs that emerges from a reading of the depositions is the centrality of mass-going to the Catholic population. The Tridentine reforms had clearly bitten deeply by 1641.[121] But there was a further factor in the intensity of this Sunday mass observance, for mass-going had become a central symbol of political identity for Irish Catholics. It was a badge of defiance, a statement of resistance; and the sites of mass celebration – whether in gentry or merchant houses, barns, makeshift chapels, or in the open air – had become central places for creating community and 'national' cohesion. These were now not only central places for the diffusion of Tridentine ideas of behaviour and observance, but also for the dissemination and absorption of ideas enhancing people's awareness of and identification with the Catholic nation. The long-term deepening of opposition between the 'Irish' and the 'English' was characterized by mutually conflicting and competing constructions of their ethno-religious categories.

With the explosion of violence that followed on from the rising/rebellion, the depositions from practically every county report on the enormous repression and intimidation that prevailed in local communities to force Protestants to attend mass, to conform to the Catholic norm and thus deny their own Protestant/English heritage. The intensity and ubiquity of this form of intimidation is striking. It could be argued that the Catholics were reciprocating in kind the pressures placed on them in earlier decades to conform to the Protestant norm. After October 1641, the battle about what was 'normal', the battle about what was central and integral to the identity of the country, was engaged in such a way that it left enduring bitterness afterwards on both sides.

'They [the Protestant families] are turned to mass' is a frequent refrain in the depositions for many counties. In Mountrath in Queen's County the Perrys and Goslings and Richard Grace, burgomaster, are 'fallen away to mass', while in the county of Kildare, the earl of Kildare, Lady Anne Colley and her sons are described as 'gone to mass'.[122] Defections by Protestant vicars are reported: a James Kevan, vicar of Castlecomer, 'hath revolted to masse and hath joyned himself with the Popish faction'; in Limerick, Sir Robert Tirrell left his castle and linked up with the insurgents; while Teige O'Grady, chancellor of Emly, had likewise 'gone to masse'.[123] Sir Thomas Esmond of Wexford 'was at the Protestant Church very often and seemed to be a protector but from the present rebellion is fallen from that religion and turned Papist and the deponent was told by some of the said Sir Thomas's own tenants who said they were at mass with him'.[124] It is reported of 140 despoiled Protestants at New Ross that 'they [the rebels] imprisoned them, putting ropes around their necks to hang them if they would not turne to mass'.[125] Others were accused by deponents of being 'backsliders from the Protestant religion' and are 'now abiding among the rebels and going to mass'.[126] In Co. Leitrim O'Rourke offered to give John Cooke 'his goods back if he would go to mass'.[127] Similar offers were made to Protestants in Co. Clare. Even Sir Henry Bingham of Castlebar, 'being hurriedly turned to masse, [is] gone away to live among the Irish Papists within Thomond'.[128] And the pressure to conform also extended to some old Irish, as in Queen's County, 'who formerly went to church [and are] now gone [back] to masse'.[129]

There are equally striking examples of deep Protestant belief – where individuals demonstrated great faith and would not yield to intimidation, would not conform, 'would not goe to masse'. They insisted on defending a different religious norm and on defending their own identity. Joan Brydges, widow of Nicholas Brydges in the county of Kildare, declared that 'she went not to masse but they [the rebels] said if I should marry a Papist and let my son be a captain I might do well and enjoy much'. Her recorded response is that 'She had but a life to lose, let her soule be safe and doe as they please.'[130] In Galway, Joseph Hampton was told 'the King and all England will go to Masse and so must you if you go to England yourself . . . Whereon I replied I humblie thank your lordship for the love [he was speaking to the Catholic archbishop] but my Lord, I have eight children and before any child shall say their father renounced the faith and religion he brought up therein, I will die a thousand deaths.'[131] To fall away, to revolt, or 'to turn to the mass' was seen by some deponents as a betrayal of both their religion and their whole being.

With the exception of the Cavan/Monaghan/Fermanagh borderlands, it does not appear that 'turning to mass' was a significant feature in Ulster. In contrast, in both the Midlands and south Leinster, and particularly in the core area of Munster, stretching from Limerick, north Cork, southwest Tipperary into west Waterford, that is, in the regions of the oldest plantations, the pressures on Protestants to conform were very intense. As far back as the 1590s, the Munster towns had led the revolt against attending Protestant services, reverting to the public display of attending Sunday mass.

Parallel to the pressures on the Protestant community 'to turn to mass' was the treatment meted out to Protestant church buildings and, in particular, to the Bible, then seen as the supreme symbol of the Protestant faith. The Irish Catholic population had seen or remembered their fathers and mothers recalling the impact of the English Reformation laws and edicts on the parish churches – the stripping of the altars, the breaking of the altar rails, the burning of images, shrines and relics, and the destruction of abbeys and friaries. Likewise, they had seen what they regularly described in the depositions as the new 'heretic' religion established, which in its turn abhorred 'graven images' and made central the reading and knowing of the Book. The martyr figure of Mrs Nicholson of Queen's County stated she 'would rather lose her life before her bible should be burned'.[132] Yet even though the Tridentine Catholic priest was to include among his religious belongings his copy of the Bible, such niceties counted for little at the height of the mass violence in late 1641 and early 1642. In practically every county, there are references in the depositions to the tearing up of bibles. They were torn 'in pieces with the most horrible indignation' by rebels outside the market-house at Mountmellick, while elsewhere in Queen's County the pages of the Bible were 'thrown on the highway' and left whirling in the wind.[133] In Co. Armagh a deponent was told by an eyewitness that after stripping some Protestants, 'they [the rebels] laid the said Bible on the privy parts of some of them in contempt of same'.[134] In Co. Cavan 'all the Protestant books, such as Bibles and the rest that were not of the Romish stamp . . . were burned in great heaps at the High Cross of Belturbet'.[135] Here is a striking opposition between the centrality of the images and rituals surrounding the ancient and durable high cross and a religion that was perceived by Catholics as stripped down to the single Book – the Bible. The insult to the Bible is complete in Kilkenny, where it is reported by a deponent that the bibles were torn up in the shops and used 'as waste paper to wrap in sope, starche, candles and other wares'.[136] Tearing up the bibles meant tearing up and attacking the source of the Protestants' beliefs, their power, their certainties.

Attacks on Protestant churches, ministers and the desecration of church property (including the burning of altars and pews) occurred in all four provinces but particularly in mid and south Ulster, midland and south Leinster and parts of Munster. Churches were attacked from Ballintoy in Co. Antrim, through Armagh, south to Fethard-on-Sea in Wexford and a number of churches in west Waterford including Dungarvan. At Fethard-on-Sea, 'they [the rebels] cutt the pulpit cloth and the Minister's books in pieces and strewed them about the churchyard and caused the pyper to play whilst they danced and trampled them under their feet and called the Minister dogg and stript him of his clothes'.[137] A disproportionate number of Protestant ministers were murdered, many suffered significant material losses, evicted, as they were, from their residences, and some were badly treated. Robert Nicholl and his family at Skreen in Co. Meath were robbed and all of them 'stripped to their very skirts and smocks'.[138] And in Co. Kilkenny one minister, a stranger, when faced with 'the implacable fury against all the Protestants', died 'distracted in all his wits'.[139] Indeed, it is noticeable from the depositions how often the local Protestant clergyman is the first target for assault and expulsion – whether in Antrim, Meath or Wexford. The animosity towards the Protestant minister was intense: Mr Fitzgerald of Baldongan in Co. Dublin is reported as saying 'that he did hope shortly to see every Minister's neck as long as his arm'.[140] The petitions to the House of Lords by the Ministers of the Gospel in Ireland suggest that close on half of their members ended up in distress in the early 1640s.[141]

The depth of the ethno-religious divide is nowhere better revealed than in the treatment of parish graveyards. Here we encounter deep feelings about ancestral burial grounds, as well as deep division over beliefs and rituals. In a number of locations scattered throughout the island – from Fermanagh in the north, through Kildare town and county, King's County, and on into counties Limerick and Wexford, priests and friars either were involved in digging up the bones of the 'heretic' Protestant dead and removing them from the sacred precincts, or they instructed their parishioners to do so. It was a source of great distress for Protestant families to see the bones of their fathers, mothers, or uncles and aunts so disrespectfully treated, sometimes burned, sometimes thrown to the dogs or dumped on the roadside or in rivers and hedges.[142] For example, in Bailieborough a deponent reports that the murdered Protestants were buried in the open fields, since 'they were not Christians and were not worthy to be buried in any church or churchyard'.[143] Likewise, in the difficult frontier county of Fermanagh, the desecration of Protestant graves was accompanied by statements that 'heretics must not be buried in hallowed ground'.[144] The Catholic clergy were insistent that where this had happened, their bones had to be removed before the sacred ground could be reconsecrated. In this age of Puritanism, extremism and fanaticism, we enter the territory of 'cultural purification' – one group is 'pure' and is involved in rituals of sanctification and purification, while the 'other' is seen as polluting the sacred ground.

The depth of the ethnic divide does not stop at objects and places of religious adherence. It is all-embracing and includes not only religious distinctions but equally ethnic/national categories as well. In the 1641 popular rising/rebellion, ethnic insults fly fast and thick: the 'English heretics' were 'God's enemies' and such 'Protestants served the Devil'.[145] This polarization in propaganda and ethnic stereotyping is total. Deponents report that the term 'English doggs' is regularly used by the Irish.[146] Phrases such as 'it was no more pity to kill the English than to kill dogs'[147] provides a mirror-image to English attitudes when they held the upper hand. As the fury of the rising/rebellion grows, the depositions detail a progressive denial of the humanity of the settler people – a process which was no stranger to the Irish themselves. The abusive term 'othnick' or 'ethnick' is applied

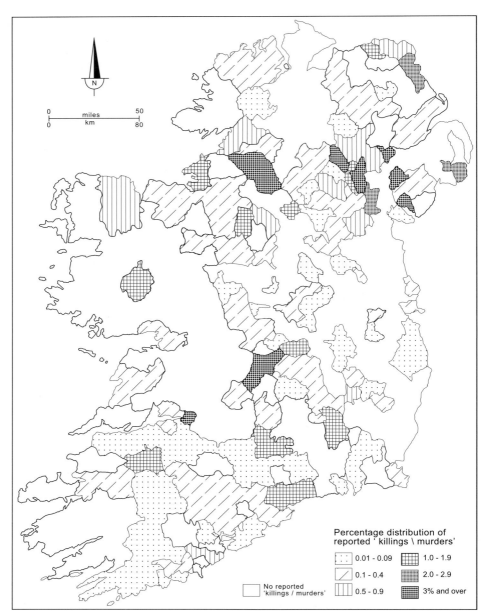

4.6   Generalized summary of the relative percentage distribution of 'killings/murders' per barony, as reported in the 1641 Depositions

by the Irish to the settlers.[148] In Kilkenny the insult is reciprocated when it is said that 'the Irish kept their promises as badly as "Ethnicks" or Turks would'.[149]

There is, therefore, a hugely hostile reaction to the incursions of the English newcomers. The local Irish see themselves as the ancient occupants of the land and the English 'as a race of foreigners'. On a sharp frontier in Queen's County it is stated that 'the English should never come in amongst them [the Irish] and they would make use of them for so longe as it lasted and would keep the upper hand for as long as they could'. Another major motif is that 'English blood should fructify Irish land'.[150] Figure 4.6 provides a generalized summary of the relative distribution of 'murders/killings' reported by deponents over the island after 1641.[151]

Counties Armagh and Fermanagh experienced the greatest number of murders – the twin cores of a crescent of violence stretching from north Antrim on through Cavan/Monaghan, which included parts of south Leitrim and north Sligo. Elsewhere, atrocities and murders were far more dispersed and far fewer in number, with the exception of particular concentrations in key contested frontier locations such as at Birr, Belturbet, Boyle, Castlecomer and Cullen (Co. Tipperary); where convoys were attacked, as at Shrule on the borders of Mayo/Galway, and at isolated but large English concentrations at the Silver Mines and Cashel in Co. Tipperary. However, there were many localities where no murders occurred. Close on 85 per cent of the Irish baronies record settler presence, yet four out of every ten of these baronies do not report any murders. In Connacht and Leinster, six out of ten baronies do not record any such atrocities. The opposite is the case for Munster and Ulster, where almost two-thirds of the respective baronies record murders. The overall distribution of murders is, therefore, far more concentrated. One can identify a number of key frontier regions where the cumulative impacts of the popular rising/rebellion were most severely felt – in a south Ulster region that also embraced the edges of Co. Meath, northwest Longford and extending westwards into central Roscommon and south Leitrim; a midlands zone stretching from much of Kildare into west Offaly and extending southwards to mid-Laois and Fassadinin in Co. Kilkenny; the west Waterford/southwest Tipperary settler region, the Limerick-Shannon region, and a final bitter frontier in southwest Cork and south Kerry.

The spiral of 'ethnic' violence unleashed by the Irish after October 1641 – as confirmed by Figure 4.6 – left a number of localities in Ireland where the landscape was littered with often mutilated dead bodies: Protestant settlers were murdered in their homes, in the fields, on streets, on bridges, in prisons, as well as members of convoys who tried to get to safe places, whether from Leighlinbridge to Ross and Waterford, or from Belturbet via Virginia (Co. Cavan) to Dublin. Men, women and children were hanged, stabbed, drowned, starved or otherwise so illused by strippings and expulsions as to result in death. Some died of exposure to the winter cold.

As we have seen, one striking feature of the deponents' descriptions of these brutal murders and atrocities is their similarity, their rather repetitive format. Whatever the source of the stories told, there are enduring motifs: Elizabeth Martin's report of horrific violence in Cullen, Co. Tipperary, includes that of a pregnant mother whose body was ripped open 'till the child fell to the ground'.[152] This obsession with the hanging or stabbing of the woman with child is a central motif; and symbolizes (amongst other things) the drive by the Irish to eliminate a future for the settler population. The greatest number of such murders occurs across south Ulster and the adjacent Connacht/Leinster borderlands. This was an area where a rapidly expanding settler frontier of young and fertile families was pushing into new territories and where the intrusion of 'the stranger' was likely to be most fiercely and emphatically resisted. Other recurrent motifs include the persistent stabbing and pricking of bodies with pikes and knives, the mangling and quartering of the bodies, including the cutting off and mocking of the genitals of some male victims. Martha Piggott reported the death of her husband Captain John Piggott:

> Butchered and murdered this examt's husband and her said son before her face, herself and said two grandchildren standing naked in the room as spectators of that inhuman massacre and the rebels not contented with sundry mortal wounds in his body given by them but also (modesty would blush to relate it) this examt's husband lying dead and breathless upon the ground some of these cruel execution-ers slitted and scarred his private parts in many pieces.[153]

A symbol of settler potency and fertility is dealt with grotesquely and ritualistically.

Another powerful image is the stripping of settlers' clothes, their being expelled from their homes and farms and exposed to the rigours of winter snow and frost. Although some of the early strippings related more to the robbery of clothes and monies concealed on the victims, the dominant image is of a further degrading and humiliation of the victims in a ritualized way, especially when such strippings took place as refugees fled in convoy to try to reach safe havens.[154] Stripping is reported for most counties. It is a most noticeable feature in a zone stretching from north Antrim along the Bann into north Armagh and Fermanagh. In Connacht, stripping is strongly represented only in Co. Leitrim. It is a far less frequent occurrence in Leinster, except in the Laois/Offaly/north Kilkenny region. In contrast, it is wide-spread in Munster, particularly in the Munster plantation regions but also including parts of south and west Clare. In King's County there is a report of '22 widows who were stripped starke naked. . . . And then they covering themselves in a house with straw, the rebels then and there lighted strawe with fire and threw amongst them of purpose to burn them where they had been burned or smothered but that some of the rebels (more pittiful than the rest) commanded those cruel rebels to forswear'; this group of women lay naked in the woods from Tuesday to Saturday 'as in frost and snow the snow long lay upon some of their skins unmelted and some of their children died in their arms'.[155] In Castlecomer the stripping of the Protestant women settlers saw the local landlord, William Wandes-forde, give to 'many of the stripped people fustian to make their skirts and smocks to cover their nakedness'.[156] The ultimate objective of stripping was the humilia-tion and dehumanization of the English population.

Figure 4.7 provides a summary of the island-wide distribution of a range of atrocities and events documented in the depositions and, in some additional cases, in the Cromwellian examinations. Reported losses of property, stock and personal belongings, 'murders/killings', 'rebel' talk, the desecration of church property, instances of settlers 'turned to masse', stripping and other cruelties, as well as inci-dents of burning and pillaging are mapped. There are three outstanding regions of devastation and settler disruption and displacement. First, the core of the Munster province – with foci around the cities of Cork, Limerick and Waterford – reveals a

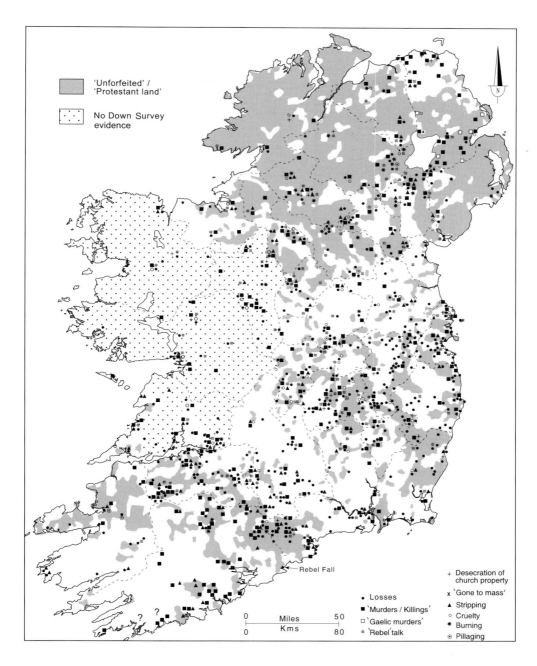

4.7   Distribution of a range of atrocities and events, as reported in the 1641 Depositions. Over much of the island, this map clearly shows a not unexpected high correlation between areas of 'Protestant land' and settlement and vulnerability to attack – noticeably on the margins of such settler regions and most particularly where Irish and settler populations were juxtapositioned geographically and less evenly balanced. On the other-hand, over much of north-west Ulster, South Antrim and East Down, the evidence strongly suggests a far greater impunity to attacks and/or a much earlier mobilisation of effective defence networks.

major region of disturbances stretching from south and mid-Clare through most of Limerick county, north and mid-Cork, and also including south Tipperary and much of Waterford. The evidence suggests that north Clare and north Tipperary, as well as a more extensive zone in southwest Munster, was less disturbed, or more correctly, was characterized by a very small settler population to begin with.

A second, large and strikingly compact zone of settler dislocation comprises much of mid-Leinster, stretching from Dublin westwards through Co. Kildare to Offaly and Laois and also including the northern edges of Kilkenny, Carlow, Wexford and all of Co. Wicklow. It is likely that the extent of pre-1641 settler penetration into the non-plantation zones of Leinster has been underestimated in the literature. On the other hand, the evidence suggests that much of south and mid-Wexford, Kilkenny, Louth, Meath and Westmeath were far less affected by either settler colonization or disturbances.

The third zone of major dislocation lies in Ulster. It is linked to the Leinster borderlands in a vector joining Navan to Kells, which reveals the line of the insurgents' advances in late 1641. The distribution of losses, expulsions and murders in Ulster is concentrated in a number of core locations – from north Antrim and northeast Londonderry along the Bann, including both the Antrim and Tyrone countrysides flanking Lough Neagh and linking the English settlement of the Lagan valley on into Armagh, mid-Monaghan and Cavan, with strong extensions into the Connacht/Leinster borderlands as into mid-Sligo, south Leitrim and north Longford. In Connacht there are settler outliers and disturbances in pockets in central Roscommon and Mayo. There is also a small epicentre of disturbances, which includes the Galway city region and extends northwards. However, the greater part of Connacht – without any significant settler presence – remains clear of depositions. On the other hand, for significant areas in Down, mid-Antrim and the greater northwest Ulster region, including much of counties Donegal, Londonderry and Tyrone, the evidence available suggests early settler organization and resistance and less devastation (See Fig. 4.7).

The ambition to expel or 'root out' the English from the kingdom is often articulated in biblical terms as an attempt to 'drive them all into the sea'. Others go further, promising that, having reconquered Ireland, 'they would [afterwards] go to England to assist the King' and 'cut off all the Puritans'.[157] Such threatening statements were frequently quoted by Irish Protestant refugees when they reached England and added further to the heightened terrors and fears in that kingdom of an invasion by the 'blood-thirsty Irish'.[158] On the Irish side, the dream is that 'Ireland would not be conquered these thousand years',[159] so that Colmcille's prophecy would be fulfilled that Ireland would drive back the conquerors. In all these reports, the motifs of expulsion and ethnic 'purification' run deep: 'they would root out all the English and Scots whom they called heretics out of Ireland and not leave one of them here'.[160]

The victims who reflected on what they heard, experienced and witnessed knew that something other than religion was at stake here, and that 'whatsoever the Irish should pretend, it was the determination of the said Irish to take away root and branch of the English nation'.[161] In short, the English and the Scots were deemed to be alien; and the slogan 'Ireland for the Irish, England for English and Scotland for the Scots' should prevail. Such 'rebel talk' – 'we must never be subject to the English nation again'[162] – is recorded in the depositions for every county; but is most conspicuous in three core areas of the rising/rebellion– from mid-Ulster to the Connacht/Leinster/south Ulster borderlands, from Dublin through to the southern midlands of Leinster, and from Co. Limerick through north Cork and south Tipperary to Waterford city.

Core issues of ethnicity bedevil the 1641 rising/rebellion – issues surrounding purity of descent, language, religion, and naming. The rising/rebellion is about redefining boundaries at a whole variety of geographical scales. It reflects the uncertainties and fears amongst the Irish (still only an embryonic nation) about their identity. It may also reflect concerns about the level of acculturation already taking place with the English and Scottish settlers. Buried anxieties about the problems of mixing – mixing of languages, mixing of settlements and farmlands, intermarriage, pressures to conform (at least outwardly) to English-imposed legal, military and religious norms, the mixing of styles of dress and address and the anglicization of personal, family and placenames – all now surfaced. Indeed, one of the most striking single phrases from the many depositions is the rebel claim 'that Virginia will become Aughanure again'.[163] The Irish drive is for clarity, for a separate cultural world with its own ancient integrities intact – in violent opposition to 'the other', 'the enemy', 'the English people and language and religion'. In short, the recognition and fear of further assimilation to English cultural norms acted as a catalyst for defining and emphasizing key ideological differences.

The cumulative picture is of an Irish population, driven by the uncertainties and injustices of recent months, years and decades, seeking to clarify its world and to distinguish clearly its identity and existence from that of the English planter/settler community. In a sense, the Irish are seeking a form of purification, a kind of counter to the potential Puritan purging of Ireland that threatened them. Irish Catholics justified the rising/rebellion in the first instance as an act of self-defence against English/Puritan intentions for their homeland:

> We the said Catholics and loyal subjects to his Majesty, do probably find by some acts, to pass by them the said Parliament, touching our religion, . . . Also by threat to send over the Scottish army, with the sword and the Bible in hand against us that this whole and studied plot was, and is, not only to extinguish religion (by which we altogether live happy) but likewise to supplant us and raze the name of Catholic and Irish out of the whole kingdom.[164]

The English historian Conrad Russell has observed that this quotation 'could not easily be improved upon' as an accurate perception of Puritan intentions.[165] Hugh O'Reilly of Cavan is reported as saying that 'the English thought to cutt the throats of the Irish for their religion but the Irish would prevent them and cutt their throats first for their religion'.[166] The suspicion and fear of clandestine planning of terror by one group (Puritan/Protestant/English) against the other (Irish Catholic) acted as a catalyst for counter-violence against such anticipated attacks.

In sum, the justification for the rising/rebellion came down to: 'we either drive our enemies out of this land or be driven out ourselves'.[167]

To claim that the Irish were motivated to purge the land of the existing and incoming settlers may appear to be an extreme interpretation. Yet there is much evidence to support it. A central motif running through the reports in many depositions and examinations of Irish intentions stresses that even young boys – as in Queen's County – were seen to be 'very bould in their robbing, telling John Grissell and the rest of the English be gone out of this country and if they would not be gone within a short time, they should be hanged'.[168] What seems to be intended at the height of the fury of the early popular rising/rebellion is an act of purification and clarification – Ireland to be a Catholic state for the Irish people, 'na hÉireannaigh'. The Catholics 'would have their Church, land and kingdom to themselves'; for many Irish insurgents the drive is to reverse the plantations, to reoccupy ancestral lands,[169] castles and parish churches, to recover positions of privilege in local and central administration, so as not to leave even the lowly position of petty constable in English hands.[170] Their resentment of Protestant colonization and dominance of the local economy means that not only are further immigrant incursions to be resisted but existing immigrant settlement is to be uprooted and dispersed. As Friar Madden explained to the local minister in Portumna: the commotion was 'grounded upon a national quarrel and inveterate malice which the Irish had to the English'; the Irish would 'stand for themselves if the King did not help', and 'they wanted all their churches in their own hands'.[171]

Seen in this light and in the context of the dreams and hopes of the oppressed Irish, their brutal treatment of many Protestants takes on a certain macabre logic. The drive by the Irish to regain control of their land, identity and rituals, and so radically reduce the uncertainties prevailing for them in the Ireland of the late 1630s, lies at the heart of the execution and expulsion of the settlers. This drive to expel 'the alien' faltered, especially in the strong Scottish quarters of the northwest, where the rapid mobilizing of the Laggan's forces consolidated settler control of Donegal and east Londonderry and west Tyrone and established fortified bridgeheads to push back the rebel forces in mid and south Ulster; and in the northeast, where, after a series of bruising and brutal engagements, the line of the insurgents' advance faltered at Lisnegarvey/Lurgan. This north Down and south Antrim settler region is consolidated and further strengthened by the coming of the Scottish Covenanter army under General Monro in the spring of 1642 (see Figure 4.2, p. 110). Henceforth, and often with the severest techniques and slaughter – for example, the recapture of Newry from the insurgents was followed by the putting down of some of the local inhabitants by fire and sword – the Scottish forces were to help not only recapture but clear spaces for further Presbyterian Scottish colonization.

The drive to clear out the 'stranger' faltered wherever a sufficient number of settlers – under strong local leadership – managed to consolidate and defend a series of safe towns, castles and fortified houses scattered through the 'rebel-dominated' countryside, whether in Athlone, Arklow, Birr, Carlow, Coleraine, Cullen, Duncannon, Drumrusk, Dundalk, Edenderry, Iniskeane, Manorhamilton,

Maryborough, Newmarket, Newry, Newtownhamilton, Tralee, Trim or Youghal. Most significantly, the Irish drive to oust the 'alien' intruder faltered in both the Dublin Pale region, where the government forces reassumed military control, and in the Cork 'enclave', where Inchiquin O'Brien (Murrogh of the Burnings) and the lord president of Munster, the aggressive St Leger, consolidated Protestant defences in a triangular area around Cork, Kinsale and Bandon. Dublin and Cork would provide vital bastions and springboards for the Cromwellian reconquest (see Fig. 4.8).

There was very little middle ground. According to the depositions, the Irish Catholic treatment of those 'of its own' that remained 'church-' rather than mass-goers was unequivocal: like Thomas McGranald of Leitrim/Sligo, they were hanged without mercy. James Goldsmith, a former priest, now a Church of Ireland pastor in Mayo, was well aware that the Irish reserved the deepest hatred and contempt for people like him. Equally, any of the backsliding Protestants who later sought re-entry into the Protestant fold got short shrift. Irish insurgents strongly encouraged Irish Catholics to desert from the government forces; but in battle Irish commanders offered no quarter to renegades, turncoats or 'any Irish Catholic in enemy ranks'.[172]

Nevertheless, throughout the depositions there are numerous examples of Catholic clergy and lay people who are remembered for being generous to Protestant settlers in peril. In Antrim, James Steele escaped, the saving of his life ascribed to a priest named O'Donnell.[173] John Wisdom, the parish clerk in Armagh, eventually escaped to Dublin in an open boat, put in at Skerries and was kindly treated by John Malone, a Jesuit priest described as a 'friar'.[174] And in parts of the Pale, particularly in Co. Meath, it is reported that they were 'loath to take arms against the Protestants, their neighbours and friends'.[175] In Cavan, George Butteven reports that some of the more merciful Irish gave them some small pieces of cloth to hide their nakedness. In the same county Richard McSymonds, 'his late neighbour, an Irishman and one who had been a soldier in the Kingdom for the late Queen Elizabeth, perceiving the deponents' weakness – did, out of meere pity – take in his wife and child to his own house'.[176] In Co. Londonderry, when the shocking details of a murder carried out by Owen O'Gillane became known, it was reported in the depositions as 'so offensive that the priests in masses did three times curse the said Gillane for the fact'.[177] In King's County, as elsewhere, there are references to the Irish who extended genuine courtesies to the English on several occasions.

But these exceptions only prove the rule. While confirming that individual Irish could behave generously, they equally highlighted how the categorical ordering of 'good' and 'evil' behaviour, as between English and Irish, was deeply rooted in fundamentally opposed world views. Some deponents were given to attributing every evil that befell them to the power of the priests and bishops, right up to papal influence. There are a number of references implicating the clergy and friars in instigating the people to rise against the 'heretic English'.[178] As we have seen, long-standing English attitudes to the Irish, especially the Gaelic Irish, were essentially hostile.

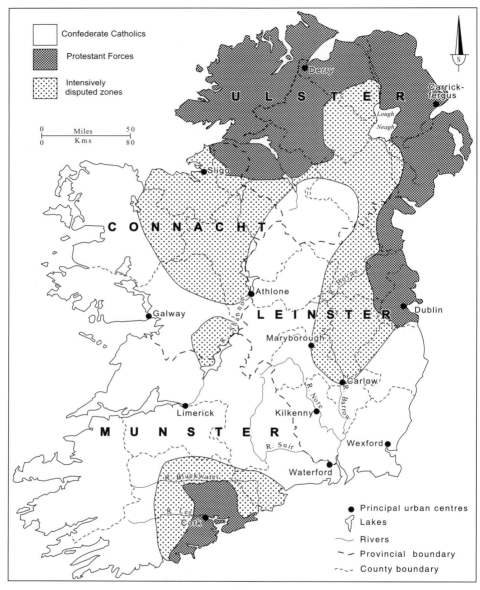

4.8   The battle for territory between Catholic and Protestant forces, 1642–9 (based on the work of Lenihan and Ó Siochrú: see reference 15 and 226)

The mutual enmities between the Irish and English were both renewed, fabricated and reinforced by the many levels of the '1641' historical discourse – from the ordinary witness making depositions to the highest officials with their own clear agendas. Henry Jones and John Temple are key propagandists here. As Barnard has argued and documented, their writings and actions exerted a profound and long-term effect on the collective memory of Protestants. Equally, memories of Protestant deliverance and victories, and of Irish evil-doing and defeats, were absorbed into the liturgical calendar of the Church of Ireland, 'which, accompanied by military flourish and celebratory bonfires, brought great content to the Protestants and shamed the Catholics'.[179]

Wars Over Territorial Control

In the 1641 rising/rebellion, the battle for territorial control was exercised firstly at the level of the individual person – as shown by the strippings and 'murders/killings' recounted in the previous subsection. Parallel to this ran a battle for control of key local economic units such as farms, shops and artisan workshops and forges. The whole Irish landscape was a battlefield – from parishes, castles and mansions, estates, through villages, towns and garrisons, sprawling outwards to larger territorial units such as the barony, the county and the province to embrace ultimately the entire island. And beyond that again the war was carried on at a British–Irish scale. Using the depositions, this section will explore the wars for territorial control in this ascending order of geographical levels.

The motivating force for some of the local participation in the war was the drive to reoccupy townland farms sequestered by Protestant farmers, so 'that never a one but a Papist should possess a foot of land again in Ireland'. As in every war, opportunists were at hand seizing the main chance. But most were involved in regaining ancient tenancies, ancestral lands and residences: for example, in Co. Kildare, where William Collis reports losses to the McKegans, who 'were ancient owners of Balliagh and were furridly put off it by the planta-tion';[180] likewise, Rory Maguire in Fermanagh is reported as saying: 'They would have their lands again.'[181]

The stripping and robbing of the farms of cattle, sheep and horses, while sometimes simply a rustling or looting exercise, was often geared to supporting the food needs of the Catholic army. For example, in the siege of Drogheda wheat crops confiscated from Protestant farms were turned into bread to support the besieging army.[182] At the very least, however, these raids were intended to under-mine the economic power of the settlers. Elsewhere, the victualling of Irish armies with Protestant corn was also a feature. The returns made to the commissioners by the Protestant farmers reveal a diligent, thrifty and enterprising population used to keeping accounts and farm records. The scale and diversity of the material losses returned point up how powerful, wealthy and dynamic many Protestant settlers had become by the late 1630s. The reasons proffered by the local insur-gents to their victims/deponents for the robberies varied: the O'Farrells of Longford showed a high level of originality in claiming that they were seizing goods and cattle in lieu of rents due to the O'Farrells since the beginning of the Longford plantation (1617); in Armagh they claimed that 'the land of Ireland was theirs and therefore they would have the English goods'.[183] Clearly a sense of the growing economic and social inequalities between the favoured settler population and the marginalized Irish generated much resentment and jealousy. In some instances, especially at the popular level, the raids and robberies reflected a drive to turn the new political and social order upside down.

A recurrent feature that emerges from the various depositions is that the women are seen to be 'as fierce as the men'.[184] Nicholas Canny, Margaret MacCurtain and Mary O'Dowd have written at length on this theme.[185] Women assume leadership positions in a number of incidents: they are warriors, hucksters, lookouts, administer juries, are passionate about liberty, are equally eloquent in insulting and mocking the settlers; and sometimes they celebrate the inversion of the social order by wearing the fine garments and assuming the airs and graces of the erstwhile 'lady of the manor'.[186]

Since the primary function of the depositions was to record the losses incurred by Protestants, it is not surprising that the greatest number of items documented relate to their material losses, including items of clothing. The geography of losses provides, in part, a surrogate measure of the distribution of settler properties and wealth over much of south Ulster, Leinster, Munster and Connacht. The great number of losses recorded for Co. Cork alone ensures that Munster reveals by far the greatest concentration of settler farms, goods and other properties. Apart from Cork, the main settler losses in this province stretch from the coastal and Shannon estuary regions of Clare through much of Co. Limerick, southwest Tipperary and much of Waterford, especially its western component.[187]

The strength of settler properties and wealth in Leinster, especially mid-Leinster, is a very noticeable feature of the depositions, with the lists of farm losses headed by Co. Kildare. The details for Leinster reveal a significant divergence between the distribution of material losses and the distribution of atrocities committed. In particular, counties Louth, Meath, Kildare, Wexford and much of inland Wicklow reveal significant settler losses without any accompanying acts of violence. East Leinster, therefore, may represent a region where Catholic seigniorial and clerical power exerted selective control over the popular rising/rebellion. South and mid-Ulster records a good scattering of losses. Much fewer losses are recorded for Connacht, apart from Co. Roscommon and pockets elsewhere in Sligo, mid-Mayo and the Galway city hinterland.

Significant losses are incurred by major landowners and leaseholding tenants in many locations. Likewise, bishops, deans, archdeacons, and ministers of the Anglican Church appear very frequently in the lists. Government officials, sheriffs, borough-masters and schoolmasters also appear, as do merchants, millers, master brewers, tanners, clothiers, weavers, yeomen, sheep- cattle- and grain-farmers, overseers, felt-makers, apprentices, wheelwrights, coach and harness-makers, slaters, innkeepers, park-keepers, butchers, ironworkers, stewards, goldsmiths, silk weavers, skinners, fishmongers and parchment-makers. The depositions point to the fullness and diversity of a maturing English settler community, albeit a community under stress and in much disarray.

The apparently wanton destruction of Protestant properties – the burning of farmhouses and mansions, the razing of enclosures, the digging up of gardens, the killing of English breeds of cattle and sheep – while appearing to contradict the argument that the locals were seeking to regain their economic power, may point to a deeper symbolic motive, namely to wipe out the cultural capital of the colonizer, as epitomized in such key landscape symbols as the Big House, the new

Anglican churches, slated dwelling houses, the early enclosures, tree and garden plantations, orchards and hedges. These symbols later came to signify the expansion of the British Empire everywhere.[188] These, complete with the tennis courts, bowling greens and fishponds, were seen as key signifiers of the masterful, civilizing English way of life. Dutch writer Gerald Boate comments on the deeper meaning of this erasure of English landscape symbols in Ireland:

> Before this 'bloody rebellion' the whole land, in all parts where the English did dwell, or had anything to doe, was filled with goodly beasts, both Cowes and Sheep, as any in England, Holland or other the best countries of Europe: the greater part whereof hath been destroyed by these barbarous, the natural inhabitants of Ireland, who not content with to have murthered or expelled their English neighbours . . . endeavoured quite to extinguish the memory of them, and all their civility and good things by them introduced into that Wild Nation.[189]

The destructive forces unleashed against the colonizer can be interpreted as an attempt by the Irish to exorcise the face of the settler – at the parish level, to exorcise the symbols of the 'heretic' Church; at the level of the landscape as a whole, to eradicate from their memory the icons of an intrusive culture that had reshaped and alienated ancestral lands, dwelling places and even their very names.

The battle for territory was fiercely fought at the level of the parish. One of the most striking and most persistent features of the depositions – whatever the county volume consulted – is the extent to which the parish is recognized as a place of residence, a place of social organization, a place of communal identity and, in particular, a place or field of intimate information flows. Deponents of the early 1640s, as well as examinations and witnesses of the early 1650s, regularly identify a person as coming from a certain parish; they refer to the behaviour of parishioners; and strikingly, too, they indicate local settler knowledge of the precise Gaelic names of their Irish neighbours and attackers.[190] Their parish church was a focal point of identity for the Protestant community: some were newly erected in the plantation regions by new landlords, so as to cater for the incoming settler populations; many were the ancient pre-Reformation churches. The latter, if used and refurbished, were regular targets of attack by the insurgents. Some of these churches indeed (for example, at Armagh and Clones) came to function as the last bastions of defence for the beleaguered local Protestant community; and some of the worst atrocities of the early, most brutal, period of the war were carried out either in or adjacent to such churches.[191]

The motivating drive of the local Catholic clergy and religious was to regain the territorial and settlement infrastructures of the pre-Reformation Church, and especially the revenue (including the tithes) accruing to parish jurisdictions. Hence, there is a number of references to bishops, vicar-generals and priests reoccupying older cathedrals and churches, and to the apparent reoccupation of monasteries and abbeys closed after the Henrician Reformation and the subsequent dissolution of these institutions. The recovery of the parish tithes was very important to the war effort of the Catholic Confederation in Kilkenny:[192] parish priests were obliged to provide two-thirds of tithe income to the Kilkenny 'administration', and some were rather reluctant to do so. Over broad swathes of territory in Munster, Leinster (outside the Pale) and much of Connacht, the ancient parish reverted to local Catholic control. In Ulster the footholds were weaker and weakened further according as Church of Ireland and more especially the dynamic Presbyterian communities came to dominate local regions.

There was also a battle for control of the civil parish administration. With the rising/rebellion, the functions of the parish constable were invariably held by Catholic representatives in the insurgent-controlled centres and regions. These played an essential part in tax collection at the parish level. In addition, they played vital roles in mobilizing local populations and in channelling information, instructions and personnel from one parish to the next. In all of their activities, crossroads and bridge-point meeting-places also played important roles in rebel organization and communication, as did the country inn and public houses. In addition, some parish churches acted as sites for the swearing of oaths of association to the Catholic Confederation: 'ye mass doors of ye parish of Rosslare were shut and ye said oath administered to all sortes of people before their departure from Mass'.[193]

The centrepieces of English (and Scottish) settler colonists and estates were the plantation villages and towns, the castles and mansion houses. As the rising/rebellion spread southward from Ulster a number of reports in the depositions describe the burning of these towns and villages as a blazing landscape lights up the night skies. In the barony of Dungannon, a deponent saw 'many towns burning in the night' and a Daniel McGowne 'being at Ballymoney' saw 'all the country on fire'.[194] The planter mansion house and village of Vintner-stown, Co. Londonderry, was burnt. Armagh was partially burnt; the castle at Portadown pillaged; Lurgan, Clones and Dromore were burnt. Further south, Carlow was not captured but the assault on the town included an attempt to burn it. In Co. Cork, Mitchelstown mansion house and town was eventually demolished, as were a large number of other castles and Big Houses. Insurgents took over the town of Mountmellick, confiscating all Protestant weapons and household goods. The town of Roscommon was captured and burnt, and that of Elphin besieged. When the town of Galway was captured, 'the English rebels' were disarmed; and the depositions claim the Galway Catholic merchants were assisted 'by the rude and barbarous multitude of rebels of Ere [Iar] Connacht', who were employed 'to rob, murder and strip the English'.[195] Enniscorthy castle was handed over to Sir Morgan Kavanagh, while Conor O'Brien captured Dromoland castle because he knew 'where the key was hid'.[196]

The Catholic Confederation managed to capture every inland town of consequence in Ireland with the exception of Trim.[197] But the Protestant settlers defiantly held on in the crucial coastal footholds and springboards of Derry, Coleraine and Carrickfergus in the north; Drogheda and Dublin in the east; Bandon, Cork, Kinsale and Youghal in the south. Although punctuated by a number of key battles, the wars of 1642–9 consisted for the most part of bitterly fought sieges of the often isolated Protestant castles, fortifications and mansion houses scattered through Confederate-dominated territories. In the bitter borderlands of north

Connacht, William Crofton's Templehouse held out in north Sligo; Castlecoote like-wise survived in Co. Roscommon, supported by Athlone castle to the south. When the O'Farrells besieged Castle Forbes in Co. Longford, Dame Jean Forbes was the valiant defender, and she reports in the depositions 'that the number of 220 poore robbed and distressed British flying to her for savour and saffetie of their lives, she harboured and received within the same castle'.[198] The siege lasted from 2 November 1641 to 2 August 1642, 'at which time she and they stooping to a most miserable and woeful want of victuals were informed to desert and leave the castle and had quarter to come to Trim and from thence came to Dublin'.[199] Further south in King's County, the King's Fort at Banagher and Geashill castle were under siege, as was Knocknamease castle, where the defenders were 'very glad to eat the flesh of horses, dogs and cats'.[200] At the long siege of the frontier town and castle of Birr, surrounded by four insurgent camps of the O'Molloys, the Coghlans, the O'Carrolls and the Ormonds, '900 some men, women and children endured . . . paying 20/- for a suckling colt and 2/- for the blood and entrails of a horse'.[201] There were ten Protestant garrisons in Co. Limerick in the winter of 1642–3 and British-defended castles were then at least as densely distributed across Cork and Kildare as Queen's County and King's County.[202] If Protestant settlers had not developed a siege mentality before 1640, the battles and sieges of the next decade ensured that they now did.

Urban settlements were, clearly, crucial battlegrounds for control of territory, property and the local body politic. The market-house and sessions-house were key public sites and meeting-places to make proclamations, to promulgate war propaganda, to humiliate local Protestant settlers, to burn bibles and other Protes-tant objects – in short, to command spaces, including the gaols, which had previously been seen as the ruling preserve of the settler-incomer. Market days were particularly important for promulgating information and instructions about the war effort. Catholic organization in these towns was a major feature in this revolutionary period, with each urban parish characterized by a range of functionaries to serve both the Catholic religion and the cause of the 'Catholique army' by collecting tithes, property and excise taxes. If regained by government forces, the towns in turn became showpieces of state power and terror. The public hangings of 'rebels' and priests – such as Father Higgins at Naas and insurgent leaders in Youghal – were mainly urban spectacles. And in the northeast and northwest the expansion of the Presbyterian Church saw new kirk foundations. Indeed, in July 1644 a Presbyterian church was erected and a congregation estab-lished in Belfast.[203] New anchor points were being established at key sites – symbols of settler recovery and their new-found sense of security.

It was the clergy, and especially the more mobile friars, and the local lords who provided the crucial links to the next territorial level – the baronies and deaneries. In many parts of Gaelic and gaelicized Ireland, the English-inspired barony displaced the smaller lordships and the deaneries of the Catholic Church. And, like the parish, it is striking how important a place the barony occupied in the life and knowledge of the local ruling elites in the mid-seventeenth century. We are fortunate that the depositions (especially the examinations for both Co. Wexford

and Co. Meath) reveal the details and the centrality of the barony in terms of military mobilization, food supply and local government. In Co. Meath and north Co.
Dublin we see how Lord Gormanston, Nicholas Preston, acts as the leader/pivot
of a military organization which mobilizes many of the adjacent baronies. Details
about the organization of companies in the barony of Duleek, the half-barony of
Kells and Slane, as well as Dunboyne, are provided, while the captains in other
baronies are also named. Nicholas Dowdall reports on how the collectors from the
barony of Duleek organized the provision of 'cows and corne' for the besiegers of
Drogheda.[204] In Co. Meath, each lord was assigned a barony to organize. The lord
of Slane was responsible for nominating captains within his barony. Lord
Gormanston established four captains in Duleek barony, while the earl of Fingall
organized a further four captains in the barony of Skreen. A warrant was issued
from Lord Gormanston via the sheriff of Meath to the collectors of food and taxes
in each of the baronies. While the infantry was raised at the barony level, the
cavalry of 120 horsemen was raised at the level of the county, each barony designated to raise so many horses from their local gentry stables.

The evidence of the depositions is that, from Co. Wexford, through Co. Kildare
to counties Down and Antrim the barony was a significant unit of military organization and local government: a public meeting of the barony of Ballaghkeen in Co.
Wexford was held to raise men for the defence of the county and for tax collection;
in the barony of Toome in Co. Antrim a meeting of the Irish took place to organize
the local forces. Other incidental information from the depositions points up the
importance of the barony even in the western counties of Leitrim, Roscommon and
Sligo and, to a lesser extent, Mayo. In Co. Roscommon meetings were held to agree
the army captains of each barony and in Co. Sligo the first actions to mobilize were
at the barony level. The baronies were also crucial units for tax collection. Each
barony supported two commissioners of the Catholic army. But here, as elsewhere,
there were problems with the return of monies by officials and collectors.

Hilltop gatherings in the baronies are also notable focal points: for army
mobilization; for public meetings to generate continued support for the
rising/rebellion; and as sites for electing representatives to county and provincial
councils. The hill of Tara was such a focal point; as was the hill of Croftie near
Drogheda. In Co. Louth the hill of Tullagh was a meeting-place, as was that of
Garristown in north Co. Dublin. Baronial meetings were also held on hilltops in
Co. Wexford. Interestingly, the organization of the Scottish militia to resist the
advance of the rebels was convened at the ancient meeting-place of Tullyhoge in
Co. Tyrone.

The houses of the gentry were crucial meeting-places in the organization of the
local wars. It is claimed that the clergy were always in attendance – as they were
at the key hilltop public meetings – to provide not only political but also ritual
leadership. But equally, the Big Houses of the planter gentry were significant in
organizing defences against the insurgents and in inspiring the many local settlers
to join the government forces to defend Drogheda and other key state bastions.[205]

The county was a central unit of both identity and organization during the war;
and it was one of the sharpest battlegrounds for local government control

between the competing 'state' entities – the Dublin New English administration and the Kilkenny Confederation. The figure of the sheriff – the shire-reeve – is of course pivotal to the military, judicial and administrative functions of the county. The retention or capture of this position by the rebel forces was crucial to county mobilization and control of county taxation. In some cases, as in counties Cavan, Longford and Sligo, the existing sheriffs – an O'Farrell, an O'Reilly and a Crean – simply switched allegiances and proceeded to support the rising/rebellion and later the Kilkenny administration. In some cases, as in Fermanagh, Monaghan, Louth, and Armagh, the sheriff's functions were assumed by the leaders of the insurgents – such as the MacMahons, O'Neills and Maguires – as were the governorships of other key towns. In Co. Meath the sheriff was part of the rising/rebellion amongst the gentlemen of the Pale, seeking to implement the directives of the ruling council under Nicholas Preston's command.

Co. Wexford presents the most detailed and clearest picture of the exercise of county functions under a Confederate government.[206] The elected representatives, as well as their functions and activities, on the County Council are detailed, demonstrating that county councils existed long before 1898. A strong democratic tradition of representation had much deeper roots in these older counties. From parish constables to county representatives, a clear and viable system of local government was put in place – which, like parallel structures in counties Kildare, Wicklow, Carlow, and King's County, also functioned to implement the directives of the Leinster Provincial Council based in Kilkenny. One of the most innovative features here is the imposition and collection of a poll-tax in the Leinster counties in 1644. The Co. Wicklow depositions actually detail the poll-tax contributions to be paid by the representatives of the different social grades in the county, and Co. Carlow records the raising of 'Pole-money' following orders from the council in Kilkenny.[207] Counties like Wexford also issued warrants for the raising of horses and provisions and for mobilizing and organizing the county militias. Likewise, the local judiciary were reconstituted under the 'rebel' county administration. The latter process was seen as a central, restorative process. It is clear from the depositions that the Irish deeply resented their subjugation via English-dominated courts and juries, sites for the 'theft of power' using judicial proceedings.[208]

Counties were crucial units in tax collection. Cash receipts of the Confederate government between 1642 and 1644 points up some dramatic and crucial features of regional variations in county administration and their capacities.[209] Allowing for some defects in the Confederate returns, it is the Munster and south Leinster counties that dominate in the formal returns. This was the Confederate heartland. Tipperary is the leading contributor, followed by Limerick and Kilkenny, then Wexford, Clare and Kerry. Cork is weaker, since the core of the county (running from Cork city northwards to Mallow, southwest to Kinsale and east to Youghal) is under Protestant control. And Waterford is weaker, given the settler resistance in the western part of that county.

We have a more detailed picture of the burden of taxation in the Leinster counties for the later year of 1647. Since the Confederate territory did not then include Dublin and Louth, much of Meath, Kildare and Queen's County, Kilkenny (22.5

per cent) was the leading Confederate Leinster contributor to the tax burden, followed by Wexford (18 per cent) and Westmeath (15 per cent). King's County, Wicklow and Longford ostensibly occupy middle positions; but returns for counties Longford and Westmeath are skewed downwards to allow for the quartering and impact of O'Neill's army in the north Leinster region. Carlow, Queen's County, Meath and Kildare had the weakest Confederate tax bases in Leinster.[210]

In Connacht, only Roscommon was a contributor to Confederation revenues; and in Ulster, Cavan and Monaghan were the only two counties still under Confederate control and able to make any contributions. Elsewhere in Connacht, Confederate local government failed to put down roots; and the situation in Co. Galway was affected by the earl of Clanricard's control and influence in southeast Galway. Interestingly, the Confederate administration did not expect to collect in cash from west of the Shannon – rather, the contributions were expected in kind, especially in beef.

We are dealing here with two different kinds of Ireland in revolt; and with a regional fracture that, apart from personal animosities and the ethnic divide, further undermined the Confederate government. The least urbanized northern and western counties were not yet heavily involved in a cash economy – the mobilization of large cash resources to support and feed a large (and sometimes unnecessarily inflated) army, such as that of Eoghan Rua O'Neill's, was not possible. Likewise, the ratio of cavalry to infantry seems somewhat weaker for the northern army. By contrast, the long-urbanized and shired counties of Leinster and Munster (where they are not under New English control) were far better placed to organize, mobilize and provide in cash for the needs of very large armies, which by then were the norm in seventeenth-century European wars.[211]

Not surprisingly then, there is a strong regional distinction between those counties (in Leinster and Munster particularly) which played a central role in the organization of the war and in providing a strong and steady territorial base for tax revenue, and the most recently shired counties of the west and south Ulster, where urbanization was weaker and mobilization of war resources had to take a different path. This situation constituted one of the main problems for O'Neill's northern army – he had to move constantly southwards into east Connacht and north Leinster to feed his army, thus aggravating the whole war effort.[212]

Nor is it surprising to find that the depositions and examinations reveal that the Gaelic sept organization (involving different modes of territorial organization and the mobilization of mainly food resources in kind) figures prominently in these northern, western and midland regions. If one maps the sept/clan names that regularly turn up in the depositions, they stretch from the interwoven kinship networks of the Kavanaghs, O'Byrnes and O'Tooles of south Leinster, the Brennans of Idough and on to the west Midlands, where the septs of the Dempseys, Molloys, O'Carrolls, O'Dunnes and O'Mores still retained great vitality; northwards from the O'Hanleys along the Shannon, the O'Farrells of Co. Longford, O'Connors of Sligo and the Burkes of Mayo, to the O'Reillys, 'kings of Cavan', the O'Rourkes, 'lords of Leitrim' and the O'Neills, 'kings of Ulster'. In all these regions, the residual clan structures were still mobilized to effect the rising/rebellion.

These Gaelic (and gaelicized) worlds underpinned the war effort by rather different methods than the Ireland of the hybrid Old English worlds to the south. The differences between Preston and O'Neill were not only differences of personality and war strategies; they were not only about clericalist versus secularist perspectives, they had their own deep cultural geographies – they were rooted in different mentalities, modes of territorial organization and modes of consumption. In 1652, an Anthony Preston testified before Sir Robert Meredith, chancellor of the Exchequer, that one of the ordinances made by Supreme Council at Kilkenny related to 'the taking away of all distinction and comparison between the old Irish and the old English'.[213] But ordinances could not change such deep cultural differences. The Cromwellian conquest and its aftermath was to be the most effective hammer for forging a single Irish Catholic nation.

This is not to argue that the armies mobilized in the south and east of the country did not often have a strong kinship structure (as well as a tenant base). The large army rapidly mobilized by Lord Mountgarrett – Ormond's grand-uncle – from Tipperary and Kilkenny could be described as a private Butler army. The mobilizing of the Brown and Rossiter regiments in south Wexford was achieved by medium-sized landowners from a sizeable array of middling tenants.[214] Similarly, the Barrys and Roches mobilized their own tenants and kinsmen in north Cork, as did the MacCarthys in west Cork under key leaders such as Viscount Muskerry.[215]

Gentry leadership in defence of Protestant interests is very noticeable. Apart from the key leadership role of Sir William Stewart at Newtownstewart, it is clear that William Cole also provided a key anchor point at Enniskillen; we read about victories of Lord Conway's troops at Lisnegarvey and Lurgan; Lord Mountgomerie won back territory in Oneilland barony in north Armagh; local tenants are incorporated as ensigns in Captain Aldworth's forces at Newmarket in Co. Cork; and we read about the relief of the castle of Rathbarry in the south of the county, then under the command of Arthur Freke, 'a Dorsettshire gentleman, being then in great distress'.[216] The son of the earl of Cork, Roger Boyle, Lord Baron of Broghill, fought a powerful campaign in Munster from July 1642 onwards.

When, however, we read about the earl of Ormond's government-cum-royalist army in Westmeath with its 7,000 foot, 1,500 horse and 200 waggons, we know we have shifted to a different geographical and human scale that not only involves the provinces and island of Ireland as a whole but now operates at a trans-insular level, embracing the civil war in England as well as in Ireland.[217] The ultimate battlegrounds were three: the provinces, the island of Ireland, and beyond the seas, the battle for control of three 'Kingdoms' of England, Ireland and Scotland.

The Confederate government and army replicated in part the English colonial model and also built on much older antecedents to establish four provincial councils – for Ulster, Leinster, Munster and Connacht. It is likely that if Drogheda – the capital and 'local town' of the Catholic gentry of the Pale – had been recaptured from the government forces early in 1642 that it might have functioned as the capital of Confederate Ireland. It was not recaptured and it was Kilkenny – the wealthiest inland town, deep in the heartland of the wealthy core communities of south Leinster and Munster – that became the capital of the Catholic Confederate administration. There was an impressive level of democracy at the gentry level, as each county and borough elected members to their respective provincial councils and elected their provincial delegates to Kilkenny. At Kilkenny, the Supreme Council, or Executive, was established with Lord Mountgarrett as president. From Kilkenny, statutes and ordinances were issued for the government of the country. The key military structures were based on the provinces: Leinster's army was headed by Thomas Preston; Munster by Viscount Taafe, Connacht by John Burke and Ulster by O'Neill.[218] The provincial councils were also involved in strategic taxation moves to support their armies – including, as we have seen, a poll-tax in Leinster – and a highly innovative strategy of taxation on other goods.

The story of the wars of the time at national and international levels has been told by many historians, most notably Patrick Corish, Pádraig Lenihan and James Wheeler.[219] Over the period 1642–9, Ireland's 'shaking sod' was host to a bewildering range of distinct armies. To the northeast Monro's Scottish Covenanter army commanded a large part of that countryside, concentrating on achieving the goals of the Scottish parliament in defending the Ulster Scots and keeping close to Scotland. To the northwest the resilient Laggan army consolidated and deepened its power, sometimes expanding the frontier southwards against the Irish forces. O'Neill's large Ulster army – with or without Confederate agreement – could not survive in south Ulster alone and impinged heavily on the limited Irish resources (and goodwill) of Connacht and north Leinster. The Confederate goal of seeking to establish not only four provincial armies but also a single mobile national army was never realized, although the very modern Leinster army under Preston – given its strategic middle location on the island – sought to fill the gap on a number of occasions.[220] Ultimately the Confederation controlled quite a large standing army – close on 20,000 soldiers at its peak in 1645–7 – an impressive achievement given its relatively poor financial base. But deep regionalist affiliations and political (as well as class) factionalisms severely weakened any concerted Irish war effort.

As the war dragged on, the different provincial armies – particularly O'Neill's – often seem as intent on consolidating their own territorial power bases as effecting larger island-wide goals. In 1642, a strong government counter-attack against the Ulster and north Leinster forces did not receive sufficient support from the well-stocked armies further south.[221] Just as the Munster army achieved the necessary growth to parallel the strength of Ulster and Leinster armies in mid-1646, it disintegrated into factionalism between the clericalist and more secularist wings. Lord Inchiquin held the Cork Protestant enclave, firstly for the king, then the parliament, then the king again; but ultimately this Cork core region was to stand with the parliamentary forces. Meantime – and probably most crucial of all – the Protestant earl of Ormond doggedly retained the core government army base in and around Dublin. He continued to complicate Confederate strategy by constantly delaying negotiations with Charles I, and in the end showed his hitherto well-concealed moderate parliamentary leanings by handing over Dublin to the English parliamentary forces,[222] led by Michael Jones in 1647. (Jones was a brother of the ubiquitous Henry who had 'ferreted out and catalogued the gruesome details of the massacres'.[223]) Ormond's gift was not only to Jones but also to

Oliver Cromwell. Thus by mid-1647 'the Confederates faced an army almost three times larger than they had faced the previous winter'.[224] And the scale of the English parliament's intended reconquest of Ireland was signalled by the financing of its armies at the rate of £30,000 per month – an allotment that dwarfed annual Confederate expenditure of £70,000 at peak army strength in 1646.[225]

Figure 4.8 (see p. 140) shows how little the Confederate campaigns achieved – and how little territory was actually gained, despite all the hardships – between 1642 and 1647. It is Lenihan's judgement that the key strategic mistake of the Confederation was to concentrate too much resources, attention and time to winning back Ulster and parts of Connacht instead of securing the core regions of Dublin and Cork, thus preventing the parliamentary forces from gaining easy access to these two key strategic foci in the east and south.[226]

As in previous Irish wars, the English navy – in this case, that of the parliamentary party – controlled the Irish waters, not only the Irish Sea and Celtic Sea but also along the west coast, as in the Shannon estuary. Wexford was the naval headquarters for the embryonic Irish Catholic state and the key focus for the importation of arms and ammunition from Antwerp and elsewhere on the Continent. Other ports under Confederate control (for example, Dungarvan and Galway) also maintained their own direct links with continental suppliers from Dunkirk and elsewhere. Of the townsmen of Galway it was reported that they 'did furnish the Rebbels of the four provinces of the Kingdom with powder when there was none to be had for them anywhere'.[227] Clearly the Irish Sea constituted a critical battle zone against the ever-increasing power of the English parliamentary fleet. It was also a crucial propaganda zone: news and people travelled quickly by boat and ship between Dublin and Co. Down to the north, and between Dublin and Wexford to the south, as well as east–west across the Irish Sea. Some deponent witnesses were also struck by the rapidity with which Irish news filtered back and forth from Flanders; for example, one deponent gives evidence as to how soon Eoghan Rua O'Neill knew that Dublin Castle had not been captured in the earliest phase of the rising/rebellion,[228] being therefore earlier and better informed than some of the distraught English Protestant settlers in south Ulster who not only feared that Dublin had fallen but also – believing Sir Phelim O'Neill's propaganda – that the king had betrayed them to the Irish (and maybe to the Scots as well). The critical links in the Irish/Flanders chain of information flow were the clergy.

We come now to the final level in the territorial organization of the war, that is, the supranational world of the Counter-Reformation, which still often spoke in Latin and which, through the elaborate network of Irish seminaries and emigrant urban centres, turned Ireland's war into a European war. The dioceses overlapped and reinforced the secular county structures that supported the war; and the archdioceses more or less coincided with the secular provincial councils: those of Armagh, Tuam, Cashel and Dublin. The depositions tell that Dr Malachy O'Queally, archbishop of Tuam, went on circuit throughout his province – like the old provincial kings – to urge opposition to the English and the reclamation of the rights and lands of the pre-Reformation Church.[229] Bishop Heber McMahon of

Clogher actually succeeded Eoghan Rua O'Neill as head of the northern army after the death of O'Neill. The depositions also provide insights about friars linking up between provinces – moving from Connacht to check out the war situation in Westmeath and Leinster and vice versa. And the international scale of events emerges in people like Fr Richard Barrett, a Jesuit and Spanish preacher, described as an agent of the Irish in Iberia.[230] These supranational linkages are especially epitomized in the central role played by key bishops on the Supreme Council of the Confederation and the constant communication maintained with Irish colleges on the Continent, particularly with Rome, where Luke Wadding occupied a key facilitating role and from which the fateful decision to send Rinuccini as papal nuncio to Ireland was made.

Intercontinental links were not confined to one side. English and Scottish forces in Ireland also had close bonds with the Protestant armies of the Low Countries, the German Palatinate and Scandinavia.[231] Likewise, English Puritans and Calvinists perceived the 1641 Irish rising/rebellion as another instance of a host of persecutions that confronted European Protestantism in the early seventeenth century. Thus, the Irish insurrection, for example, 'gave rise to charitable collections in the United Provinces [of the Netherlands] for suffering Irish brethren in Christ'.[232] A series of English sermons and tracts portrayed the Irish rising/rebellion as part 'of a much grander Counter-Reformation design against the Godly'.[233] This view prevailed, not only among sympathetic Calvinist communities in England and Scotland, but also among their counterparts in the Netherlands, Switzerland and Germany. As much as £30,000 was collected by the Dutch Calvinists alone to assist 'the Protestant cause' in Ireland; and of twelve ships loaded with grain and victuals, all but one reached Ireland safely. But these goods did not always reach the suffering Irish Protestants, 'but ended up in soldiers' stomachs, being used to feed the parliamentarian forces in Ulster'.[234]

However, the narration of these stories in the depositions, where the territorial components of the rising/rebellion are broken down into their respective parts, obscures how interwoven and interconnected all these levels of operation were. One might argue that the Book of Kells, with its interlacings, is a useful metaphor to emphasize both the rooted depth and the reinforcing, intertwined nature of the Irish kinship linkages which fused the local popular rising, the gentry rising and that of the Catholic clergy into a single, cumulative force that stretched and looped from the local townlands and parishes on to Louvain and Rome. But the Book of Kells also has its fractured lines and introverted beasts that loop back to bite their own tails – a useful metaphor for the factionalism and lack of unity in the overall Irish military and political organization. Nevertheless, in comparative European terms, the achievement of Confederate Catholic Ireland was impressive. It had most of the attributes of seventeenth-century statehood: it controlled two-thirds of the island and exercised the governmental functions of raising taxes, waging war and concluding treaties. Its functioning as a sovereign government was quite developed and complex, with regular general assemblies (parliaments in all but name) at the apex of a network of provincial, county baronial and parish councils, and it lasted seven years.[235]

The English state apparatus in Ireland, that is, the capacity to maintain a regular and (usually) routine administrative and military machinery, stood in good stead to the Protestant capacity to resist after the early onslaught of the rising/rebellion – as did the fortifications, garrisons and urban strongholds that had been newly created across the Irish landscape in the previous 60 to 100 years. But kinship linkages for the settlers were also crucial to give them heart and hope – the fictive kinship of belonging to a still ruling English Protestant nation and also the deep bonds of kinship based on blood enabled many to survive and transcend the traumas of the wars. The settlers also had their deep divisions; but by the end of the Confederate Wars they had in Cromwell one single commander who would hammer both Britain and Ireland into a new shape. Prior to Cromwell, war-torn Ireland was a highly fractured reality because power was so dispersed. Cromwell's regime would put an end to all that.

The Cromwellian Conquest, Famine and Plague

Cromwell's conquest of Ireland (1649–50) was relatively swift, ruthless and often brutal. In a country where no less than four armies had been locked in stalemate situations for close on a decade, Cromwell's nine-month campaign saw the conquest and forging of the three provinces of Leinster, Munster and Ulster into a single jurisdiction. Only Limerick, Waterford and Connacht were left for Henry Ireton, Cromwell's son-in-law, to subdue after the latter's departure in May 1650 to begin his triumphant campaign against Scotland. The Cromwellian conquest of Ireland was an integral part of the imperial expansion of the English state. Cromwell, the Independents, and the New Model Army came to Ireland with an attitude inherited from the English Puritans – that Irish Catholics must pay a price for the 1641 'massacres' – and so they came imbued with the enduring Spenserian view that a scorched-earth policy was required.[236] Their ideology was one of conquest, confiscation and colonization.

Cromwell's victory in the Second Civil War in England allowed the parliamentarians to focus their attention and resources on the conquest of Ireland. The parliamentary navy was modernized and streamlined and quickly saw off the attempt of the royalist navy under Prince Rupert to control vital approach routes into Ireland, cut off royalist and Catholic support from the Continent, and protected the large English convoys sailing to Ireland.[237] In putting down the coalition of Irish royalist forces under Ormond's leadership, the parliament expended £3.8 million between 1649 and 1653.[238] Cromwell led a well-drilled, well-fed and experienced New Model Army of 12,000 men, with a 900-horse artillery train to haul cannon, powder, munitions and ordnance repair equipment. Over 100 ships and a war chest of £100,000 backed up this well-planned strategy.[239] The Cromwellian conquest of Ireland was, therefore, a triumph of logistics in which the new Commonwealth maintained a steady flow of supplies, money and manpower to Cromwell's army in Ireland.

Unlike the cautious Ormond, who lacked the military vision to recapture Dublin from Michael Jones in the months between March and July 1649,

Cromwell was a brilliant military leader who moved his army swiftly and simultaneously on a number of fronts, who mobilized a well-organized combination of land and sea support systems to great effect and who paid close attention to the morale of his soldiers whether on the move or in garrison.[240] Arriving in Dublin in August 1649, he moved rapidly northwards towards Drogheda. This city was stormed by Cromwell's troops on 11 September. The brutal execution of more than 2,000 soldiers after the capture of Drogheda clearly signalled Cromwell's intent to conquer Ireland by terror, if needs be. The fall of Wexford in October 1649 was a major coup for Cromwell and represented a massive loss of key Confederate naval resources, including warships and tons of supplies.[241] The notion that the October slaughter of the defenders and townspeople at Wexford was a consequence of his soldiers running amok does not tally with Cromwell's reputation as the commander of a highly disciplined army. He did nothing to prevent the slaughter. The message was being sent out loud and clear to all of royalist/Catholic Ireland, especially to its cities and towns, what lay in store for them when the New Model Army arrived at their gates. After Drogheda, Trim and Dundalk yielded to Cromwell without a fight; and after Wexford, New Ross soon surrendered, opening up south Leinster and Munster to Cromwell's advance by land.

Once Drogheda, Trim and Dundalk had fallen, Cromwell dispatched Colonel Robert Venables northwards to establish a landbridge to Sir Charles Coote's Derry and to clear Ulster of forces loyal to the royalist cause. Lisnegarvey, Antrim and Belfast were taken without a siege, as 'most Protestants in eastern Ulster evidently decided to surrender to the parliamentary army and accept its terms rather than to continue the struggle on behalf of the King who was allied to a Catholic coalition'.[242] Coote soon took Coleraine, massacring most of the garrison, and later Carrickfergus. The swift Cromwellian conquest of Ulster was achieved between August 1649 and early 1650 – in a situation where O'Neill's large army played little part. O'Neill himself died suddenly in November 1649.

In south Munster, after Cromwell had won the allegiance of Lord Broghill, the garrisons of Cork and Youghal soon defected to the parliamentary cause; Bandon and Kinsale also capitulated.[243] All the major ports of both Munster and Leinster, with the exception of Waterford and Limerick, were now under Cromwellian control; and the major links between the Catholic/royalist forces and the Continent had been severed. Cromwell's initial strategy of controlling maritime Ulster, Leinster and Munster, was almost complete and the spatial circuits of the Irish armies were being severely reduced.

After a short stay in winter quarters, Cromwell moved swiftly in late January from Mallow to Fethard in Co. Tipperary, which surrendered on good terms. In a series of pincer movements he closed in on Clonmel, and the capital of Confederate Ireland, Kilkenny. Meanwhile, Colonel John Hewson, appointed by Cromwell as governor and commander of Dublin, moved south across the Barrow and, joining Cromwell and Ireton, first took Gowran, and after a series of assaults, the old Ormond Butler town of Kilkenny fell to Cromwell.[244] Despite Hugh O'Neill's valiant defence of Clonmel, the Tipperary capital was captured but not without large English losses. With the heartland of Confederate Ireland now under his control, Cromwell instructed Ireton to take command in Ireland. The locals at Youghal still point out the site where Cromwell's ship waited for him to sail to Bristol on 27 May 1650. He then travelled by land to reach London by 1 June 1650 to prepare for his conquest of Scotland.

By then, the Catholic military prospects 'were next to hopeless; but the uncompromising Puritanism of the men who ruled the English Commonwealth prevented the war from ending in the Summer of 1650'.[245] Cromwell had provided the lead on this matter, for it was his view that the Irish 'unprovoked put the English to the most unheard of and most barbarous massacre (without respect of sex and age)'. It was the Irish, he declared, who 'had caused the current war because they had ungratefully risen against the English who had brought the blessings of civilization and religious light to Ireland'.[246] Cromwell had made his deep hostility to Catholicism crystal clear: 'I meddle not with any man's conscience. But if by liberty of conscience you mean liberty to exercise the mass . . . that will not be allowed of.'[247] Clearly, both Cromwell's strong religious beliefs and his understanding of the 1641 rising/rebellion shaped his thoughts and actions towards Catholics in Ireland. Under his rule, priests were executed simply because they were priests: 1649 (19) and 1651 (22) saw the high points of martyrdom for Catholic priests killed or executed.[248] The institutional and building fabric of the Counter-Reformation Catholic Church was ripped apart and dismembered under Cromwell's reign. Nevertheless, it is Wheeler's view that it was the New English commanders, such as Sir Charles Coote and Roger Boyle, 'who conducted the most brutal operations against the Catholic forces. They, far more than Cromwell, made the conquest an ethnic war.'[249]

Ireton captured Waterford and Duncannon in mid-August 1650; Limerick yielded after a five-month siege in October 1651; and Galway surrendered in May 1652. But, according as the Irish armies fragmented, local guerrilla resistance intensified. The Cromwellian conquest had now entered its bloodiest and dirtiest final phase. A slow war of attrition ensued as the grinding down of Irish opposition by the Cromwellian military machine spread death and destruction throughout the island. After Cromwell's departure from Ireland, the English resorted to a policy to 'smoke and starve out' the still 'rebel-infected' areas of the country. For example, Leinster appears to be conquered by 1650–1, yet 'Cromwellians admitted they only controlled about half of the province'.[250] Unlike the earlier phase of the war (1641–8), English punitive expeditions and raids now devastated those parts of Ireland that had been spared the ravages of the war before 1649. A civil administration of four commissioners was established in October 1650 who divided the country into six precincts (later stabilized at twelve). In each precinct a military governor oversaw both counter-insurgency and revenue-raising measures.[251]

The barony was a critical geographical unit in this programme of Cromwellian monitoring and repression. As early as February 1650, 'the impossibility of identifying kindred willing to admit to the misdemeanours of their relatives explained the need for the proclamation . . . whereby the pound of flesh was to be taken from "all inhabitants of the said barony that suffers rebels to go without hue and cry"'.[252]

The effects of such legislation on the ground is vividly outlined by the Irish poet Éamonn Mac Donnchadha an Dúna:

Tories *ghuirid d'fhuirinn an tsléibhe,*
's an fear astig gan choir gan chéim air
caithfidh a íoc gach ní dá ndéineann
an tory amuith má bhíonn a ghaol ris.
muna bhfuil gaol dá thaobh re féachain
nó an costas do shoichfeadh an t-éileamh,
is dá mbiaid gan fios cia rinn an t-éireach,
Caithfidh an tír an díol so 'dhéanamh'.

Tories close to the team of the mountain
And the man inside with no rights or status
Or authority over them, must pay for
Everything they do. If he is related to
The tory outside, or if no other of his
Kindred can be found, or if no
One knows who should pay the levy,
Then the whole country must pay.[253]

The language of power is exercised here with the use of the pejorative term 'tory' (Irish, *tóraidhe*), meaning, raider/outlaw/bandit. A series of Cromwellian proclamations sought to penalize the relatives of these 'tories', the inhabitants of the respective baronies where crimes were perpetrated – ultimately, the whole 'papist' community. The poem also suggests that the prosecution of tories represented a surrogate policy by the parliamentarian forces and administration to persecute and if possible to liquidate the Irish.[254] The intensity of the levels of prosecution are powerfully evoked in this verse, which relies heavily on the imported English words:

Transport transplant mo mheabhair ar Bhearla
Shoot him, *kill* him, strip him, *tear* him.
A *tory*, hack him, hang him, *rebel*,
A *rogue*, a *thief*, a *priest*, a *papist*.[255]

The impact of Cromwellian counter-insurgency tactics in Irish populations and landscapes have been well documented by historians.[256] The Cromwellian takeover of hundreds of garrisons previously held by the Confederates and royalists throughout the towns and countryside did not end the war. Thousands of armed Confederate soldiers, who had been scattered by the defeat of their armies, took to the bogs, woods, loughs and hills, from whence they attacked 'English supply columns, tax collectors and small military units', as well as settler farms.[257] By April 1651, the commissioners for Ireland decided to launch a still more ruthless campaign against the tory threat.

Many but not all of the so-called tory bands were remnants of the Confederate forces led by senior officers from aristocratic lineages such as the O'Neills, the

Kavanaghs, the O'Dwyers, the Ryans and the Fitzpatricks.[258] What is involved in this 'tory' terminology is the criminalization of this guerrilla form of resistance by official government edicts and actions. This type of pejorative terminology became a feature of the Interregnum Commonwealth period.[259] To deny these resistance groups all information and supplies 'from sympathisers living close to English garrisons', the commissioners ordered

> that all and every person and persons whose parents, husbands, sons or brothers are in actual rebellion . . . or live in any woods, bogs or other places . . . do within fifteen days remove themselves, their children and families out of the said garrisons and places adjacent within two miles distance of every respective garrison.[260]

Garrison commanders were ordered to destroy any houses that might be used to shelter 'tories' or their kin within two miles of the garrisons and towns. The English objective was to drive any Irish still in arms into the remote parts of the country, where they would do least harm to both the English settlements and to the increasing number of war-weary Irish who were ready to accept Cromwellian military occupation and security in protected zones and get on with their lives as farmers and workers.

Subsequently, these policies were intensified as the commissioners decided to demarcate the 'rebel'-controlled areas (as distinct from the 'protected' zones) and to declare these areas 'free-fire zones' in which English forces could destroy any person or habitation without cause, other than the fact that a person or building was in a designated area. Thus, all or part of the counties of Carlow, Cork, Kilkenny, King's County, Queen's County, Tipperary, Waterford, Wexford and Wicklow were declared to be excluded from English rule and protection.[261] As historian John Morrill notes: 'summary execution and transportation for living in a place where attacks on Commonwealth soldiers took place is further evidence that war changed its visage as it left England and Wales'.[262]

So the country was divided into 'protected' areas for populations who wished to live peaceably under the protection of the English army, and 'outlawed' areas 'beyond the line' or 'free-fire zones', where places and persons were excepted and excluded from the protection of the parliament of England. In these latter areas, punitive expeditions were led to destroy crops, cornmills, fortifications and settlements and so marginalize the resource bases of the guerrilla forces still further. For an entire year (1652) the English waged these brutal campaigns against women and children, as well as against the armed men. But they failed to end the 'tory' threat.[263] The spatial circuits of the Irish forces – their room for manoeuvre, subsistence and support – were, however, being slowly eroded.

Likewise, the growing administrative efficiency of the Cromwellian government in Ireland is demonstrated by a ruthless policy of surveillance. In order to identify and prevent the insurgents infiltrating across the line from outlawed to protected areas, seeking supplies, information and further recruits, the Cromwellians carried out a series of impressively comprehensive local censuses in protected areas – as in south Co. Dublin for 1650–2.[264] These censuses document in astonishing detail the composition, physique, age and sex of each of the adult inhabitants of every townland and village. Constant vigilance was exerted so that the Cromwellians could keep track of movements within clearly defined zones. The construction and elaboration of this highly efficient surveillance system slowly ground down resistance, confining the outstanding pockets of opposition to ever-smaller circuits. By the late 1650s 'tory-hunting' had become a kind of sport for the victors, akin to fox-hunting.

Thus, from 1649 onwards (intensifying during the early 1650s) these grindingly slow, counter-insurgency tactics operated throughout those parts of Ireland where the parliament did not exercise full control and full military occupation. This scorched-earth policy produced famine conditions. Up until 1649 much of the war had been focused on the disputed areas between the Confederates and the opposing royalist/government/parliamentarian and Covenanting forces in limited regions of Leinster, Munster and Ulster (see Figure 4.8, p. 140). In these regions, the comings and goings of large armies either seeking food supplies or destroying them for strategic purposes created near famine conditions – nowhere more poignantly than in mid-Ulster, which set up a major outmigration of refugees to other provinces. The intensification of the war after 1647 also led to devastations and near famine conditions in a number of other areas. By 1648, 'famine now threatened to consume the entire country' with 'so great a dearth of corn that Ireland had not seene in or memorie, and so cruel a famine which hath already killed thousands of the poorer sort'.[265] After Cromwell's coming, extensive regions in Leinster and Munster and Connacht – long under Confederate control – now faced the full rigours of war. Massive and lengthy sieges around Waterford, Clonmel and Limerick led to a rapid reduction in food supplies as well as many casualties. Ireton, travelling a 150-mile circuitous route from Waterford to the siege of Limerick, observed in that summer of 1650 that he passed through districts extending 30 miles 'with hardly a house or any living creature to be seen, only ruins and desolation in a plain and pleasant land'.[266]

The deadliest killer, however, was the bubonic plague – a continental European phenomenon originating in Spain. The plague reached Galway in the summer of 1649, a tragic reminder of the intimate and regular connections between that still-important western port and the Iberian world. An estimate for early 1650 indicates that some 20,000 had died from the disease in Galway city and county alone. Petty indicates that when at its highest, in the summer months, Dublin city had plague deaths of around 1,300 per week. There was no general abatement of the plague between 1649 and 1652 and in some regions not until 1653.[267]

The bubonic plague is a warm-weather disease, spread by the movement of rat-borne fleas and is deadliest in a situation where the population is already malnourished.[268] The prolonged, widespread and intense nature of the Irish wars – especially after the arrival of Cromwell – ensured that many Irish populations were left vulnerable to the spread of such diseases. Forcing or herding people into protected zones, armies involved in rapid movements exercising burnt-earth policies, other Catholic refugees on the move from the towns where they had been excluded – all added to the swift spread of the disease. Famine conditions likewise disrupted expected patterns of behaviour, leading to forced migration, much overcrowding and other conditions facilitating the spread of epidemic disease.[269] Since the plague is most voracious in urban or village situations, the nucleated centres were hit hardest.

The nucleated village world of the south, the Midlands and the east of the country (see chapter 6) also provided areas of population concentration where the disease could flourish. And it was in these highly populated zones of Munster, Leinster and east Connacht (which constituted the core of the regions 'beyond the line') that the plague was most virulent. The earlier pacification of Ulster, which was less urbanized and had a more scattered settlement structure, helped that province escape the worst ravages of the disease. But elsewhere the disease was rampant and it clearly leaped over the boundaries of cities, towns and large villages to spread into the surrounding countryside. In Scotland, by contrast, the bubonic plague was confined to the towns (where it made for a 15–20 per cent mortality rate) but did not spread into the countryside, so that its overall effect was a reduction of only around 2 per cent of the total population.[270] In Ireland its impact in areas of rural Connacht, rural Co. Dublin and south Co. Wexford and elsewhere confirms that it also wreaked havoc in the open countryside. 'Cromwell's pestilence' spread far and wide.[271] It lasted three to four seasons at the very least (1649–53); it was associated with war-induced population movements and famine; and, since there was no epidemic in the preceeding half century in Ireland, it exerted an exceptionally heavy toll.[272]

Attempts have been made to come up with a picture of levels of the mortality due to disease and famine. Lenihan takes a sample of five areas: a rural area within a protected zone (south Co. Dublin); a rural area from 'beyond the line' (north Wexford); a city that was not besieged (Dublin), and one that was (Limerick); as well as the evidence of age structures from Transplantation Certificates for Co. Waterford.[273] Between 1649 and 1653 he estimates that south Co. Dublin suffered a 15–20 per cent decline. In the outlawed region of north Wexford the mortality rate may have been as high as 80 per cent, but minimally 50 per cent; in a besieged city such as Limerick, at least one-fifth (20 per cent) of the population had died of the disease/famine (Cork, Galway and Waterford probably suffered similar rates of decline). Dublin's population, though the focal point of new British immigration in the 1650s, probably declined by 12–15 per cent. Overall, Lenihan suggests a minimum population decline due to plague and famine of 15–20 per cent over the period 1649–53.[274] Since the child and teenage mortality is calculated at the unlikely level of zero in Lenihan's estimates from age structure evidence, it could be argued that the more likely overall mortality figure due to plague and famine lies in the 20–25 per cent range.

To take account of total wartime population decline from October 1641 to 1654, we have to include: (i) the numbers of Protestants killed in the early months of the rising/rebellion; (ii) the larger numbers who died of famine and exposure as refugees in the countryside, in garrisons, in the besieged towns and in cities such as Dublin; (iii) outmigration of many Protestant refugees to Scotland, England and Wales, although reflux movements back into Ireland from the mid-1640s may offset part of this figure; (iv) the many reprisal killings against Catholics in the areas where the Protestant militias regained early military control; and (v) the ongoing killings that followed the brutalities on all sides. Ulster suffered exceptional losses of life in the earlier years of the 1640s.

Military operations are estimated to have directly caused over 100,000 casualties, while thousands of soldiers also died of hunger and disease in the garrisons or camps.[275] The final English solution that allowed for the demobilization of the remnants of the Confederates armies (1652–4) was to facilitate the transportation of 35,000–40,000 Irish soldiers to serve in Catholic armies on the Continent. Earlier, during the 1640s, about a further 20,000 Irish soldiers were shipped overseas to serve either in British, Spanish or French armies. As many as 15,000–25,000 other Irish men, women and children were likely transported in the infamous sweeps carried out by Cromwellian agents and merchants to find cheap labour for the plantations in the West Indies and Virginia. Even the Cromwellian army (the best fed and best financially supported army engaged in the war) saw 37 per cent of its soldiers die, some in battle, but more from the plague between March 1649 and July 1652.[276]

Most commentators are agreed that the period 1641–54, especially the final Cromwellian phase from 1649 to 1654, created what can only be described as a demographic disaster in Ireland.[277] We will probably never learn the full scale or the geographic distribution of that population disaster. Central European researchers can map in detail the geography of the Thirty Years War and note the variations across Germany and the Holy Roman Empire where there was more than a 66 per cent population decline (for example. in parts of Mecklenburg, Pomerania, Saxony and the Rhineland). Likewise, there were extensive regions of population decrease of the order of 33–66 per cent dispersed across this huge territory.[278] We are not yet even close to making such a map of mortalities for Ireland between 1641 and 1654, although the prediction made by Clanricard early in the war that Ireland would become another Germany in terms of death and destruction seems to have been well founded.[279]

William Petty – the most original demographer/statistician in seventeenth-entury Europe – made his own estimates of population losses in Ireland soon after the Cromwellian conquest. According to his estimate, Ireland lost 616,000 out of a total (1641) population of 1,466,000. In his assessment: 167,000 Catholic Irish died by the sword and by famine during the war; a minimum of 275,000 (and perhaps as many as 400,000) died from the effects of the plague of 1649–53; and 112,000 Protestants died between 1641 and 1652 (with perhaps as many as 37,000 dying in the very early phases of the war). In short, Petty estimates a 42 per cent decline in Ireland's total population between 1641 and 1652.[280]

Given more recent research, I now take the view that the population of Ireland in 1641 was possibly as great as 2 million (certainly not less than 1.8 million). In this scenario, Petty's population-loss estimate of 616,000 would constitute a reduction of 31–34 per cent. Wheeler is of the view that we should take Petty's estimates very seriously and not only of Catholic losses but also his figures for Protestant deaths. He agrees that it is most likely that no more than 4,000–5,000 Protestants were murdered in the early months of the rising/rebellion; but he also agrees with the English historian Samuel Gardiner's view that many more Protestant refugees 'were slain and allowed to die of starvation in the first two or three years of the war'.[281] Louis Cullen agrees with the notion of a demographic disaster during the later plague years. He places the associated total population loss at between a third and a fifth and more likely the latter figure.[282]

If the overall level of mortality after 1649 is of the order of 20–25 per cent, and given the effects of the earlier murders, sieges, battles, skirmishes, reprisals, famines, outmigrations and transhipments between 1641 and 1654, the likely scale of the overall decline comes closer to one-third of the population. If we further associate a minimum total population figure for Ireland in 1641 of 1.8 million, this suggests a population loss close to 600,000. With these guesstimates we are coming close to the adjusted Petty estimates. And if we assume that a 33 per cent loss is evenly distributed between Catholic and Protestant, and taking Petty's Protestant/Catholic ratio in 1641 of 2:11, this gives a total Protestant population of around 327,240 in 1641 and a projected Protestant population loss, of 109,080.[283] The proportionate Catholic loss was of the order of 490,920, that is, one-third of 1,472,760. If, however, Ireland's overall population in 1641 was as high as 2.0–2.1 million, then absolute population losses were likely to have been greater. The reduced population of Ireland in 1652 is thought to be no more than 1.3 million.

This was 'the war that finished Ireland', that is, Catholic Ireland. More than 10,000 Catholic landowners forfeited their estates – whether large or small – under the new draconian Commonwealth legislation. Only a fraction of this group, along with family members, retainers, servants and some tenants, trekked west via Athlone and Loughrea to register for land entitlements in Connacht. A total of 45,000 people may have been involved in these epic journeys (see Fig. 4.9) in the winter of 1653/1654 with many stragglers arriving in 1655.[284]

However, in the vast social upheaval it is quite clear that a significant majority of these old landowners and their kin (well over two-thirds) did not transplant; or if they did so, they decided to return to their old localities as head-tenants/Catholic middlemen in the now fully triumphant landlord system with its regimented, compact estate structure. Others of the old landowners were dead, some had gone mad; some emigrated or had been hanged, banished or transported. Judging by the statistics compiled by W. H. Hardinge for the now missing Transplantation Certificates, it was the Munster counties (minus Cork) headed by Tipperary that saw the highest numbers of transplanting old elites. Outside of counties Kilkenny, Wexford and Westmeath, the Leinster counties suggest a greater disinclination to move to Connacht and this was most particularly the case for the counties in Dublin's metropolitan shadow.[285] We have few details of the geographic movements of the Ulster transplanters; but Corish suggests that they 'settled in the inhospitable lands of Leitrim though this had been assigned to the [Cromwellian] army'.[286]

As noted above, 35,000–40,000 officers and soldiers from the dismantled Irish armies (and some wives and children) set sail for the Continent to serve abroad. Perhaps 15,000–25,000 others – some of those owners who would not transplant, those who had filled the town gaols to overflowing in the counter-insurgency phase, women, children, the unemployed, and the now growing number of beggars and vagrants – were dispatched to the American and West Indian colonies. Bishops and priests were killed, imprisoned, exiled, or else moved furtively in disguise, heroically serving local communities. As many as 100 Catholic clergy either died in prison or were executed under Cromwellian rule and a further minimum of 1,000 were sent into exile.[287] Overall, the closely knit, interwoven Catholic landowning, military and ecclesiastical elite-worlds had been shattered and scattered across the Old and New Worlds.

On the ground, many of the ordinary tenant farmers, craftspeople and labourers had been retained to work to support the new superstructures of the Cromwellian state. They had been spared uprooting and expulsion to Connacht, according as the views of the planter and pamphleteer Vincent Gookin and the old Protestant elite won out over the radical and punitive drive by the Cromwellian officer class (as articulated by Colonel Richard Lawrence), which was bent on creating an

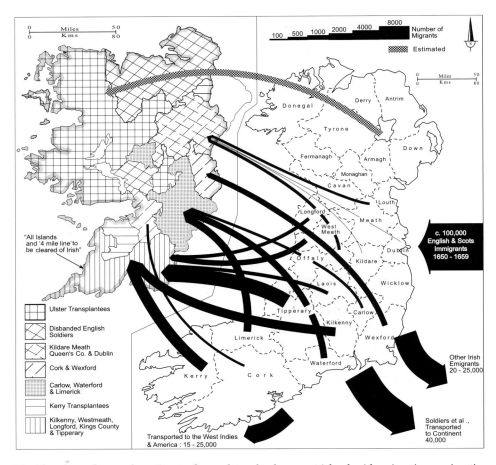

4.9   The planned transplantation to Connacht and subsequent island-wide migration, emigration and immigration 1650–60 (sources: see references 15, 266 and 267)

absolute *tabula rasa* – a totally English world of tenants and landowners east of the Shannon, with the 'treacherous' Irish penned in the far west between the sea and the Shannon.[288] Instead, the Irish tenants, artisans and labouring classes remained, for the most part, undisturbed. They were glad to see the end of the wars – glad to know that soldiers of whatever hue would not be descending on their villages and townlands, robbing, burning, killing and looting. As the economy recovered, in Corish's droll phrase, 'there was little else for it to do',[289] some of these tenants and craftspeople gained more lucrative niches in this opportunistic society.

Recovery took place in a shattered landscape because, in the later phase of the war (1650 to 1653), the Cromwellian armies had deliberately laid waste the land as a military tactic. By the end of the war, grain cultivation had almost ceased and livestock had to be imported into a country famous for its cattle herds. Former agricultural landscapes were reduced to 'heath, furze and furry pasture, occasioned by the great waste'.[290] In war zones such as northeast Kildare and north Wexford, the Civil Survey documents the ruination and destruction of the great majority (80–85 per cent) of castles and mills, in contrast to the more peaceful southern ends of both these counties.[291] Figure 4.10 shows the equivalent contrasts between war-torn north and mid-Tipperary and the more peaceful southern parts of the county. In northeast Kildare the value of buildings in 1654 had been reduced to as little as 3.5 per cent of their 1641 values.[292] Petty's assessment of the devaluation of the total building stock in the country between 1641 and 1654 at one-fifth may, therefore, be a substantial underestimate.[293] Likewise, in war-torn towns, like New Ross, Kilmallock and Kilkenny, 43 per cent, 26 per cent and 14 per cent of their respective tenements were in ruins.[294]

As in all wars, those of 1641 to 1653 show significant variations in their impact on regional economies and landscapes. North Ulster recovered reasonably rapidly from the very destructive early phases of the war – certainly it was in this period that Belfast was to outstrip its rival Carrickfergus as the great port of the northeast. Derry city also benefited from a war economy. Dublin city and region began to recover by 1647, while in the southeast, the Confederate ports of Waterford and Wexford and their hinterlands – including the capital, Kilkenny – also prospered for much of the war period. In South Munster, the victualling roles of Cork and Kinsale helped sustain their economies. Of all the cities, Galway was to be most shattered by the Cromwellian conquest, although the disruption of the economic life of most of the southern cities – excluding Dublin – was immense following on from the expulsion of its Catholic inhabitants and especially its merchants – from the city of Cork in 1644, from Drogheda and Wexford in 1649, and from Kilkenny, Clonmel, Waterford, Limerick and Galway in the early and mid-1650s.[295]

Under the Commonwealth, the state kept a careful watch on all religious activity. As Corish notes, 'specifically "popery" and "prelacy" were excluded because they were "idolatry" and were therefore forbidden by scripture'.[296] Neither the adherents of the Church of Ireland nor Presbyterian forms of worship and administration could accept the basic tenets of the ruling Independents with their commitment to the congregational principle. Nevertheless, they learned 'to reach a practical accommodation with the Commonwealth' government and its officials

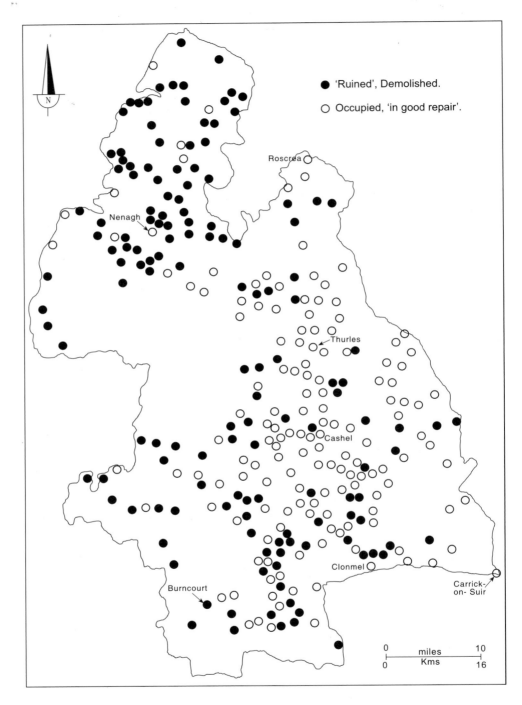

4.10 The state of castles-cum-towerhouses in Co. Tipperary in 1654 (based on details abstracted from Civil Survey volumes for Co. Tipperary)

and ministers.[297] Through skilful mediations and compromises, the government appointed close on 400 state-salaried ministers from all Protestant denominations – including Baptists – between 1651 and 1659. Later, the parish system was allowed to be restructured and gradually the restoration of the tithe was put in place.[298]

On the political level, the administration of Henry Cromwell (Oliver Cromwell's son) saw a consolidation of the economic and political power of the old Protestant elite as the foundation for the Protestant Ascendancy was firmly put in place.[299] Finally, the Catholic majority – and especially its elites – was now totally excluded from the political process, not to be included again until 1829, with Daniel O'Connell and Catholic emancipation. Catholics had seen their electoral rights and privileges of office and representation gradually whittled away from the time of Henry VIII onwards. These processes had rapidly accelerated over the first half of the seventeenth century. Now they reached their full expression of exclusion. So, from the point of view of the Catholic political elites, this is the beginning of a long night.

The abiding memories of these awful decades have haunted Anglo-Irish (and indeed Catholic–Protestant) relations ever since.[300] The great shock to the Protestant communities came in the early months and years of the war. They were to remember and indeed commemorate the 1641 'massacres', their expulsions, illtreatments and tribulations as refugees in isolated garrisons and towns, where they often came near to starvation, and so had instilled in their psyche an enduring fear of sudden rebellion and the need to be always vigilant in Ireland. For the Catholic communities, the early expectations and hopes of liberation were shattered in the later phases of the war. They remembered the vicious reprisals. They remembered Cromwell at Drogheda and Wexford and the military brutalities that characterized 'the savage war of peace' after 1650. They remembered too – at home and abroad – the subsequent uprootings and dislocations. It was a brutal war that brutalized many of its participants. There was enormous pain on both sides; but each group nursed and perpetuated only the memories of its own pain. Few were capable of empathizing with the other's experience.

Meanwhile, in 1653–4 unfinished business had to be attended to. More than half of the island, some 11 million acres, had to be planted anew, mainly with New English owners and settlers. An early attempt at assessing and mapping the distribution of land available for forfeiting and planting – the Gross Survey – had been a failure.[301] The jury-based Civil Survey for twenty-seven counties (excluding the already Strafford-surveyed counties of Connacht and Clare) provided a comprehensive narrative record of the hereditary estates – the crown, ecclesiastical or unforfeited estates – while also comprehending all corporate and lay estates and possessions.[302] But a fully colonial Ireland, in the grips of a military occupation and dictatorship and now to be subject to an all-embracing plantation, required comprehensive island-wide mapping at a scale detailed enough to allow for the transfer of townlands and estates from the old to the new elites. Into this large information gap stepped the precocious, original and enterprising William Petty. To achieve the goals of the Cromwellian plantation, the military conquest was to be matched by a full cartographic conquest.

5

William Petty and the Construction
of Cromwellian Ireland

The young men chanted beside the public way:

Is there any sorrow like ours
who have forfeited our possessions
and all respect.

And the virgins of the Parrish of Killmainham
hung down their heads.

Thomas Kinsella[1]

How that full cartographic conquest was achieved has been described in William Petty's own words:

> Whereas surveyors of land are commonly persons of gentile and liberall education, and theire practice esteemed a mistery and intricate matter, farr exceedinge the most parte of mechanical trades, and withale, the makeinge of theire instruments is a matter of much art and nicety, if performed with that truth and beauty as is usuall and requisite. The said Petty, consideringe the vastnesse of the work, thought of dividinge both the art of makeinge instruments, as alsoe that of usinge them, into many partes, vizt., one man made onely measuringe chaines vizt., a wire maker, another magneticall needles, with theire pins, vitz., a watchmaker, another turned the boxes out of wood, and the heads of the stands on which the instrument playes, vizt., a turnor; another, the stands or leggs, a pipe maker; another all the brasse worke, vizt., a founder: another workman, of a more versatile head and hand, touches the needles, adjusts the sights and cards, and adaptates every peece to each other.
>
> In the meane tyme scales, protractors, and compasse cards, being matters of accurate division, are prepared by the ablest artists of London.
>
> During the same tyme, alsoe, portable tables, boxes, rulers and all other necessaryes, as alsoe small Ffrench tents, were provided to enable the measurers to doe any buissnesse without house or harbour, it being expected that into such wasted countries they must at some tymes come.[2]

By such minute instruments did Petty make visible what was previously unseen and unknown – that is, the distribution and layout of properties across the whole island. And such was the method and order that Petty brought to bear on this vast work of mapping almost the entire island of Ireland after the Cromwellian regime gained full military and administrative control of the country by 1653. Indeed,

Petty was not only the mastermind behind the first full field-survey and *mapping* of any European country, he was also the mastermind that cut through the jungle of difficulties that faced the Cromwellian administration in *allocating* the appropriated lands to the restless New English adventurers and the highly combative and much more numerous Cromwellian officers and soldiers.

The complex negotiations about, and the specific modes for, allocating and distributing the lands to the conquerors was in the end mainly Petty's achievement. Having penetrated to the core of the Cromwellian administration in Dublin and been given access to the growing state archives of a powerful centralizing bureaucracy, he used this opportunity both to construct the so-called '1659 Census' and to write his *Political Anatomy of Ireland*. Petty was, therefore, centrally involved in constructing our knowledge and images of seventeenth-century Ireland, in cartographic, narrative and statistical forms, as well as literally carving out the boundaries and spaces of landownership that were to endure for well over 200 years. These achievements made his reputation in Ireland. Elsewhere, Petty was to achieve fame as a pioneer in the study of demography, economies and the state. He was a founding member of London's Royal Society (see Fig. 5.1).

The Cromwellian Settlement: Surveying Context

The Cromwellian settlement was the culmination of a century of English plantation policy and practice in Ireland. The Adventurers Act of 1642 – which offered 2.5 million statute acres of profitable Irish land as a return for private investments of £1 million in the conquest of Ireland – was the precursor to the Commonwealth Acts of 1652 and 1653, which came to define the parameters of the Cromwellian settlement. The 1642 Act clearly anticipated the confiscation of insurgent Irish lands in all four provinces and also anticipated widespread 'rebel guilt' well before the 1641 rising/rebellion had actually moved across the whole island.[3] As it turned out, the MPs and merchant adventurers of London and other English cities advanced (only) one-third of £1 million. Yet, by 1652, they anticipated a return of about 1 million Irish (plantation) acres on this investment. Later Acts of the 1640s encouraged army officers to either invest or allow part of their payment to be made in land. However, it was only in the early 1650s, as the Irish resistance was worn down, that the Cromwellian government arrived at the conclusion that the only way the administration could pay off its massive debts of £2.5 million to £3 million was with confiscated Irish land. The English Commonwealth decided that Irish land should pay for both the costs of revolution at home and repression in Ireland.[4] The massive cost of reconquest after 1649 had generated the economic pressure for a total confiscation of Irish lands. Apart from the adventurers, major pay arrears to the army grew day by day, as well as debts to other public creditors. As Karl Bottigheimer and Patrick Corish have emphasized, the central motive for the massive confiscation of Irish lands was, therefore, economic and fiscal – while Henry Jones in his *Remonstrance* provided a kind of moral imperative for a severe rather than a lenient treatment of the Irish.[5]

The Act of Settlement of 12 August 1652 in its preamble notes that it was not the intention of the parliament to extirpate 'the entire nation' but that pardon as to life and estate would be granted to 'the inferior sort'.[6] The treatment of those of rank and quality – particularly the landowners – would be very different. Five groups – because of their inferred insurgent status – were condemned to death and their lands confiscated. Under the first clause alone approximately half the adult male population was judged liable to the death penalty. This draconian legislation was directed almost exclusively against Catholics; and it was so framed that no person of any property could hope to escape.[7] The 'total reducement' and settlement of that nation was now to be speedily affected.

Behind the framing of the Act, however, a number of assumptions had to be teased out and key decisions arrived at. The Cromwellian commissioners in Ireland had proposed that the land debts of the adventurers could be settled in a compact plantation in any one of four groups of counties – in the south and west (including Clare and Galway); the southeast; the northwest (including Leitrim and Sligo); or the east of Ireland. In addition, they envisaged the establishment of a 'new Pale' defined by the Boyne river to the north and the Barrow to the east. These proposals indicated that, as late as April 1652, the ultimate solution of transplanting the Irish to Connacht had not yet been finalized.[8] Either way, the adventurers were not very enthusiastic about the proposal; neither were they very anxious to settle in Ireland until they had received more guarantees and privileges and were confident that the final resistance of the Irish forces had vanished. They also baulked at later proposals in the summer of 1652, which required them to settle and plant their lands within three years or lose their rights to such land.

By December 1652, the final shape of the planned Cromwellian settlement began to emerge. Partly to offset the security fears of the adventurers, the commissioners recommended that the army and those private investors should jointly occupy a total of ten counties, each county to be divided in half between the two groups. These counties stretched north–east to south–west across the middle of the country, from Antrim, Armagh and Down in Ulster through Meath, Westmeath, King's County and Queen's County in Leinster, and including Tipperary, Waterford and Limerick in Munster. The county of Louth was held in reserve as a security to guarantee the adventurers' share. Note that none of the Connacht counties now figure in this solution. By this time the fateful idea of transplantation to Connacht was on the horizon. The counties of Cork, Dublin, Kildare and Carlow were to be reserved for government use – including the payment of its public debtors. The Boyne/Barrow boundary was to see the passes along these two rivers further secured. Exclusive of Connacht (initially) and (eventually) large swathes of well-planted Ulster, the confiscated lands of the remainder of the country were also to be made available to satisfy and settle the army (see Fig. 5.2).

The phenomenal transformation of the economic, cultural and political geography of Ireland was thus planned: (i) a new Pale; (ii) a middle zone to be settled with yeomen soldiers, officers and adventurers; (iii) an already well-secured north of Ireland; (iv) an isolated and segregated Irish quarter west of the

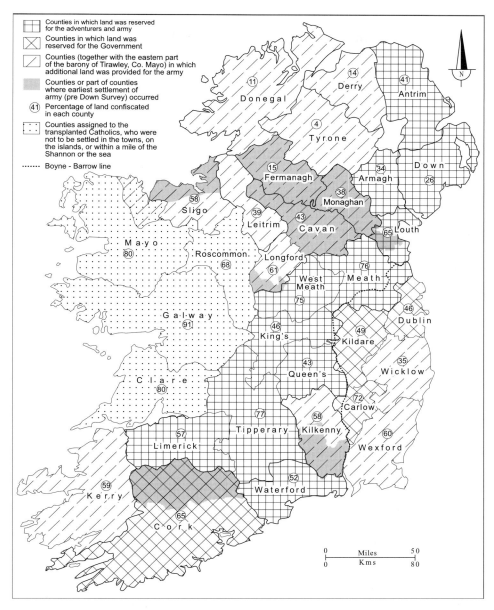

Legend:
- Counties in which land was reserved for the adventurers and army
- Counties in which land was reserved for the Government
- Counties (together with the eastern part of the barony of Tirawley, Co. Mayo) in which additional land was provided for the army
- Counties or part of counties where earliest settlement of army (pre Down Survey) occurred
- (41) Percentage of land confiscated in each county
- Counties assigned to the transplanted Catholics, who were not to be settled in the towns, on the islands, or within a mile of the Shannon or the sea
- ······ Boyne - Barrow line

County labels and percentages shown on map:
Donegal (11); Derry; Antrim (41); Tyrone (4); Fermanagh (15); Armagh (34); Down (26); Monaghan (38); Sligo (58); Leitrim (39); Cavan (43); Louth (65); Mayo (80); Roscommon (68); Longford (61); West Meath (75); Meath (76); Dublin (46); Galway (91); King's (46); Kildare (49); Queen's (43); Wicklow (35); Clare (80); Carlow (72); Tipperary (77); Kilkenny (58); Wexford (60); Limerick (57); Waterford (52); Kerry (59); Cork (65)

```
0        Miles        50
|————————————————————|
0        Kms          80
```

5.2 'Regional planning' and the Cromwellian land confiscations (1652–3) (adapted, in part, from Map 9, p. 358 by Patrick J Corish in *A New History of Ireland, III*)

Shannon to be established, with the reinforcement of defences along the line from the headwaters of the Shannon to the Sligo coast; and (v) a four-mile exclusion zone for the Irish was to be created around the whole Connacht coast and along the extent of the west banks of the Shannon. The Irish were not to be allowed to live in the towns, or the garrisons, or to trade. Debates still raged about whom of the Irish should be transplanted. Crucial revisions were made in July of 1653 for the transplantation of *all* the Irish to Connacht before 1 May 1654 – including those Irish who were technically innocent at least of showing disfavour to Cromwellian rule – to ensure the better security of the Commonwealth and to clear the spaces for the incoming planters.[9]

The whole island of Ireland lay at the mercy of the Commonwealth. The lands of royalist Protestants were also to be included. However, an ordinance of September 1654 allowed such Protestant 'delinquents' to compound – pay a fine – for their estates, which, for the most part, they never managed or were required to pay. Likewise, an early plan to transplant the Ulster Scots southwards into Tipperary, Kilkenny and Waterford never got beyond the blueprint stage. Cromwell was clear in his mind that the crucial political division was between the Irish Catholics and the rest. In effect, 'forfeited' or 'confiscated land' came to mean, as it appears so consistently on the Down Survey maps, Irish Catholic land. The Down Survey maps outline, but do not map 'Protestant land'. The land itself had become imbued and imprinted with religious-cum-ethnic-cum-political values (See Fig. 4.7).

It was Petty's achievement, via the Down Survey, to map Ireland more accurately and comprehensively than had ever been done previously. But to gain this eminence, Petty had to displace Benjamin Worsley, the surveyor-general. The instructions attached to the Commonwealth Act of 1653 required 'the exact and perfect survey and admeasurement of all and every the honors, baronies, castles, manors, lands, tenements, and hereditaments, forfeited by force or virtue of all or any of the said Acts'.[10] But the instructions further allowed that – since it was intended to satisfy the adventurers, soldiers and officers and have 'Ireland planted with as much expedition as maybe' – in a shorter time a gross survey might be undertaken, to be followed by a more exact admeasurement.[11] It was Worsley's fate to be in charge of this Gross Survey.

Petty's lengthy *History of the Survey of Ireland Commonly Called the Down Survey*, as well as his early powerful summary of the survey, survives; whereas Worsley's version of the story is not available to posterity. In truth, Worsley (as illustrated by his detailed surveying instructions to Petty and his Down surveyors) was no mean surveyor. It should be recognized that when Worsley set out to supervise the Gross Survey the government had no real knowledge either of the total acreage of each county and barony, and, more critically, had little if any knowledge of either how much forfeited land was available to settle its debts or where precisely such lands lay. It was a potentially chaotic situation, especially since all vested interests were pressing for a speedy settlement. Worsley was, therefore, working under enormous pressure to bring in rapid survey results. He did the late 1653 Commonwealth administration some essential service by quickly providing it, via the Gross Survey figures, with estimates of the confiscated land (but including the unprofitable with the profitable) not only for the ten key counties to be shared between the soldiers and adventurers but also for the remainder of the island. The provision of these estimates allowed for the critical and early determination by lottery of which baronies in each of the ten counties would fall to the soldiers and which to the adventurers. It is clear that the actual division of these counties was based on Gross Survey figures of the amount of confiscated land available in the respective baronies. A first stage in the redesigning of the Irish land chessboard had begun.

Worsley's Gross Survey proceeded not only by estimation: stage two included careful, mapped admeasurement. Hardinge notes the survival in précis of the original warrants of payments made to specified surveyors, which prove that significant blocks of land – coming to a total of 571,000 Irish acres – in the counties of Cavan, Cork, Fermanagh, Kilkenny, Longford and Sligo – were admeasured and mapped. These were certified as correct by Worsley, 'which is conclusive evidence that the field books, maps and their reference sheets, came into the custody of the Surveyor General'.[12]

These surveys – and possibly those of Co. Monaghan and Co. Louth – were completed by the summer of 1654. It is almost certain that they were specifically carried out to facilitate the disbanding of close on 5,000 soldiers, agreed on towards the end of 1653 and implemented early in 1654. This disbanding was accompanied by fears on the part of all concerned – the government, the army and the adventurers – that there would be insufficient land to meet all debts. These fears were exacerbated by the initial estimates provided by the Gross Survey, which (as it turned out) severely underestimated the amount of confiscated land that would become available for settlement. As a result, the first disbandment and settlement of soldiers was accompanied by a downward revision of rates attached to the value of lands of different counties and provinces. However, it is also clear that this early allocation and distribution of lands to a segment of the army was attempted too far in advance of adequate planning, and it led, in Hardinge's words, 'to great discontent being expressed by the soldiers at the inaccuracies of many kinds that vitally affected their interests'.[13] Discontent arose in part from administrative deficiencies, in part from doubtful levels of devolution in decision-making about property allocation, but it also arose from very problematic decisions made by the surveyors as between profitable and unprofitable land.

The government now moved to improve its knowledge base by instigating what is now called the Civil Survey, distinguished from the Gross Survey, since the latter was under military control whereas the former was managed by the civil/legal authorities. These were empowered to convene courts of survey, involving knowledgeable local juries at the barony scale, to describe in narrative form all manors, lands, and tenements forfeited to the Commonwealth since 23 October 1641. Church and crown lands, as well as baronial lands claimed by any English or Protestant proprietors, were also to be included. The urgent priority attached to the distribution of lands to the soldiers (and the consequent reduction in the government's monthly pay bill) meant that the appointment of the first Civil Survey commissioners in June 1654 related to the ten strategic counties reserved equally for soldiers and adventurers. Subsequently (late July 1654), a further seven counties, specifically allocated for the satisfaction of the soldiers – Kilkenny, Wexford, Donegal, Kerry, Londonderry, Longford and Tyrone – were issued with commissions. The 'government' counties of Dublin, Cork, Carlow and Kildare, as well as Louth and Wicklow – that is, the new Pale – received later commissions, and the last recorded Civil Surveys (of June and September 1656) were carried out in Leitrim and Monaghan.[14]

The Civil Survey was a bureaucratic exercise in describing and defining many other things apart from property lines. It ignored the subtle cultural distinctions and perceptions of the older populations – they were all characterized, and henceforth would be categorized, as 'Irish Papists'. A system of ethnic categorization and stratification is therefore embedded in these documents of conquest. Such categorizations provided the contextual framework that shaped and bounded future social relationships between these groups. The Civil Survey also sought to reduce the complexity of localized areal measures to a single formula – the plantation acre – while also seeking to bring order to the wide range of territorial entities that the surveyors met as they travelled across arable and pastoral land, bogland and mountains. Hence, the future importance of that most crucial of property units, the townland.

Early results from the Civil Survey pointed out that more confiscated land was available for allocation than had been estimated in December 1653. Consequently, the army demanded a better land return on its arrears and reverted to the rates prescribed in the 1642 Act. The adventurers had been given control of the disposition of barony lands among themselves. They continued to use the estimates from the Gross Survey (in conjunction with their own private surveys), 'a dim light to guide them in their plantation of a darkly labyrinthine Ireland'.[15] Chaos was likely to prevail.

Into this maelstrom of conflicting interests, advices and estimates came William Petty. It is likely that Petty's coming to Ireland as physician-general to the Cromwellian army and as personal physician to the lord deputy was not prompted as much by his medical interests as by his drive and desire as 'colonist-physician' to acquire and apply his method to the quasi-laboratory situation which he perceived to be the Irish condition. His interest lay more in the health of the body politic. Petty saw it as both an honour to carry out the Down Survey as 'a service for a victorious army, the first that ever totally subdued Ireland', as well as a duty, so that 'the same noble army might not be abused by an absurd and insignificant way of surveying then carrying on by Mr. Worsley'.[16] With supreme self-confidence, Petty assaulted the position of the surveyor-general by arguing with and convincing the powers-that-be that the Worsley-led mapped admeasurement involved excessive payments to the surveyors, provided no mode for examining or verifying, nor offered any security for the correctness of the work. Most particularly, Petty criticized the Worsley strategy of only measuring the 'scopes of forfeited lands . . . under one surround'.[17] In contrast, Petty proposed that the whole landscape should be measured, both according to its civil boundaries – that is, baronies, parishes and townlands – and also by its natural boundaries of rivers, mountains, ridges, rocks, loughs and bogs 'as answeringe not onely the very ends of satisfyinge the Adventurers and soldiers then in view, but all such future ends whatsoever as are usually expected from any survey'.[18]

Worsley's main objection 'against the performance of so vast a work in 12/13 months' was that he considered that such an island-wide survey would be 'the business of as many years'. Petty set out to convince 'many worthy persons that what they had been told [would] be some seven years' work, might (to their great accommodation) be dispatched in one'.[19] He was well aware of the great importance Cromwell and the Commonwealth placed on the satisfaction and disbanding of the army, so that the soldiers should with as much 'expedition as possible be put in possession of their lands'.[20] Worsley's instructions to his surveyors – while meeting the terms of the 1653 Act's instructions – only dealt with mapping the boundaries of the forfeited lands and contributed nothing in Petty's view to 'the memory of the ancient bounds of baronies, parishes, etc. nor to order and to regulate the intended [Cromwellian] plantations'.[21] Petty's emphasis in his mapping strategy was on the permanent record of physical and territorial boundaries rather than the existing estates' boundaries, which were now going to be radically transformed by this plantation. Likewise, Worsley's method did not provide for the subdivision and mapping of the shape of the properties as allocated to their new owners. In contrast, Petty would contract to first survey the forfeited lands, and parallel to this, subdivide and map the new properties and instruct his 'instruments' (that is, his surveyors and their assistants) on the ground to mark on the landscape the new property boundaries he had already marked on the Down Survey maps. In effect, each soldier's particular proportion and quantity of land could be confirmed and set out without another survey. Petty's vision, therefore, far outstripped Worsley's solid but pedestrian way of doing things.

After much coming and going – including obstructions by the plodding Worsley and the older breed of surveyors now being surplanted by Petty's farsighted division of his labour force, which included employing hardy Cromwellian soldiers as measurers – the Army Committee were pleased to acknowledge how Petty had ingeniously cut through the 'perplexities and difficulties wherein that affair [of survey and land distribution] was involved before the Doctor appeared in it'.[22] In the army review, Petty brought logic, clarity and economy to the process. He would carry out the mapping of Ireland in less time, at less cost and more comprehensively.

On 11 December 1654 strict articles of agreement were drawn up between the army and Petty. These were brought to the Council Chamber, where

> very many of the chief officers of the army . . . being present, and after a solemne seeking of God, performed by Colonell Thomlinson, for a blessing upon the conclusion of soe great a business were, with some little alterations about the money and some discourse about the army leavying their pay, finally assented to the articles of agreement between Benjamin Worsley, Surveyor General on behalf of the Commonwealth and Doctor William Petty on the other part.[23]

Thus – with solemn ritual and blessings – the most thorough mapping survey of Ireland was initiated to complete the conquest. The army officers had come to realize that a sure survey would be the foundation on which all their future property rights would rest. Having agreed these articles with Petty, possession of the survey was given to the army and with it possession of the lands.

The agreement reached was 'that the lands to be sett out for the payment of the armyes arreares and other publicke debts be surveyed downe as is proposed by

Dr. Petty'.[24] Petty was to be paid £7 3s 4d. per 1,000 acres of forfeited profitable lands mapped (the army contributing 40 per cent of these costs; the state the remainder). Church and crown land, as well as all unprofitable lands, were to be surveyed at £3 per 1,000 acres. Petty was thus to reduce Ireland's forfeited lands to a scale of 40 perches to the inch. He was also contracted to produce a set of barony maps. In the end, he surveyed twenty-nine counties in whole or in part, only omitting the counties so well surveyed under Strafford (Galway, Roscommon and most of Mayo).

Thus, the Down Survey came to be Ireland's Domesday Book. The final pages of each of the barony maps were to include indexes of 'Names of Irish Papists, Townes Names, Gleabes, Bishopps, Deanes and Chapter Lands, Crowne Lands, and Woods' and 'Observations as Castles, Weares, Mills, Ffords, Passes, Bridges, Abbies, Churches, Mines' and ruins.[25] To Dr Petty, the old land and its people was like a dead body – ready for a kind of anatomical carving up by the instruments of survey, for cutting up into new pieces, for replanting and nurturing, so that its former reputed flourishing condition could be restored.

Mapping the Island and Its Properties

The Strafford survey of the late 1630s had already mapped all of the province of Connacht in a highly effective and meticulous manner, based solidly on the quarters (townlands), parishes and baronies (see Fig. 4.1, p. 108). It had involved two powerful surveyor-leaders – Thomas Raven in Connacht proper with his thirty surveyors, while the very able William Gilbert worked with twenty-two surveyors in Clare, north Tipperary and parts of Co. Limerick.[26] It seems to me that Petty was made aware of this survey at an early stage – it was already being sought out for the Loughrea commissioners for the transplantation of the Irish to Connacht. It provided, both in scope and surveying methods, a useful preliminary model for the enterprising doctor – and with the assistance of one of his key surveyors, Patrick Raggett, Petty was to build on its achievements for his Down Survey work in north Tipperary. Petty had the foresight to envisage a completion of the mapping of Ireland by surveying not only the forfeited lands of the other three provinces but *all* other lands, so as to provide the government with an up-to-date picture of the country's baronies and their boundaries. He saw that beyond the requirements of the Cromwellian plantation he could advance the state's knowledge and management of the whole island, its provinces and counties, as well as its baronies and parishes.

Petty convinced the army and the government of his mapping strategy by stressing that he would guarantee reliable and workable results. He devised better field books, a more robust compass needle and a more simple method for the estimation of acres in the field. But his greatest originality was in the organizational arena – he marshalled close on a 'thousand hands' like a good conductor, dividing the whole art of surveying into its component parts: fieldwork; protracting; casting; reducing; the finishing and ornamentation of the maps; the writing of the accompanying tables and columns; and, crucially, the subsequent examination to ensure *'the truth of the fieldbooks* [my emphasis]'.[27] Great care was taken to double-check the surveying procedures; surveyors were sworn in by oath to properly perform their duties; and certificates as to the quality of the work undertaken by the surveyors were provided by Petty's key lieutenants and examiners: Thomas Taylor, Edmund Lucas, George Baldwin, John Vise, William Morgan, William Trevis, Rice Lloyd and William Brundenel.[28]

So under a military government with absolute powers, Petty initiated a military-style, modern survey, first dispatching his team of surveyors and assistants (including fifty foot soldiers) into the adjacent counties of Dublin, Kildare and east Meath. Worsley was instructed by the Council of State to issue warrants to get meersmen (or 'bounders') to point out the boundaries, to establish which garrisons 'did everywhere lye most conveniently for their defence', as well as providing guards for securing the respective persons to be employed in this endeavour.[29] In parallel, the commissioners of the County Civil Surveys were to provide Petty and his team of surveyors with abstracts or lists of forfeited lands to be surveyed in their respective counties and baronies. The agents or representatives of the army were required to attend these commissions so as to expedite the work in the particular counties where their lots had fallen. Crucially, Petty was given access to all other government records and surveys that might be of assistance in his work.[30] Monitoring all of these activities was a committee of army officers who were established to supervise the final regimented subdivision of lands among the soldiers. In short, the whole apparatus of the military government was at Petty's command to ensure the rapid completion of a comprehensive and accurate survey (see Fig. 5.3 and Fig. 5.4).

Nevertheless, it took all of Petty's enormous energy, organizational ability and will power to bring this vast undertaking to a successful conclusion. Apart from the intrigue and incessant infighting at the centre of power in Dublin, Petty encountered numerous setbacks and difficulties in the field. Beginning with the survey of Co. Dublin, Petty discovered that the mapping of this very particular late medieval landscape involved laborious and time-consuming surveys of very small, scattered plots of land – much smaller than the '40 acres or over' areal units he had contracted to survey. Petty was also to find that the work of the commissioners of the Civil Survey did not always keep pace with his surveyors' needs for vital information as to which were the forfeited lands: missing or faulty abstracts meant retracking for second surveys and resurveys, so that Petty felt like 'a master of a shipp who had contracted to export one hundred tun of goods' but 'is bound to make a hundred voiages to performe the said contract'.[31] His surveyors also encountered difficulties in determining boundaries and acquiring the necessary local expertise in certain counties and baronies that were most wasted and depopulated 'in the recent wars', problems accentuated by 'the rapidity of the transplantation' and the removal of soldier/guards for service in England and Scotland. Adding to his headaches, some surveyors pawned their instruments and/or went absent without leave or were attacked by local tories.

The definition of 'profitable' *vis-à-vis* 'unprofitable' lands constituted another challenging and persistent problem for Petty. Given the perceived gap between

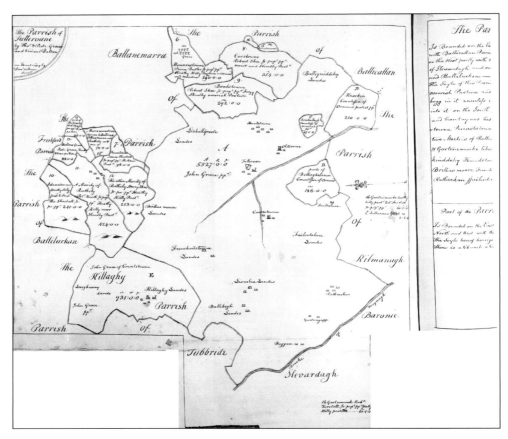

5.3   Example of Down Survey mapping at parish scale of Tullaroan, Co Kilkenny (1655)

the amount of forfeited land available for plantation and the amount of debt to be cleared, it was vital to the Commonwealth, the army and the adventurers that as much forfeited land of a profitable quality be found to satisfy all the demands. The 'unprofitable lands' of wood, bog and mountain were not to be included in the debt/acreage equation but thrown in for good measure. Hence the second article of the agreement between the Commonwealth and Petty: that 'the said Doctor shall exactly survey and distinguish . . . between all lands as is profitable and all lands which is unprofitable, the end that the said profitable land may be exactly knowne'; and in the surveying of all unprofitable lands, Petty was also required to promise faithfully 'to describe the nature and bounds of same, especially where the same boundeth upon the profitable land, and to sett down good grounds for returning and adjudgeing the same for unprofitable'.[32]

Given the foundational status of the Down Survey in land allocation, these map definitions of 'profitable' and 'unprofitable' constituted legal statements of great importance.[33] Hence the challenge facing Petty and his surveyors in the field of moving from instruments of quantitative measurement (such as the compass and chain) to qualitative assessment of land values. For the surveyors on the ground

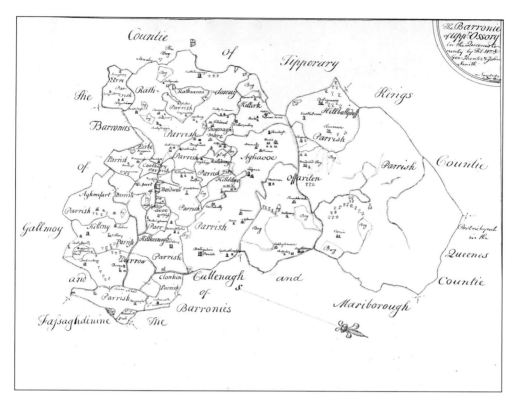

5.4   Example of Down Survey mapping at barony level of Upper Ossory, Queen's County (1657)

the definitions of land quality were achieved by a combination of 'the best of our judgements and the best information we could get [locally]'.[34] Such judgements were invariably subject to controversy and dispute. When officers and soldiers found themselves allocated properties where the designated 'profitable' lands looked decidedly 'unprofitable' to them, the complaints against Petty began. The fact that Petty was paid more than twice the rate for surveying the profitable lands led to the charge that he inflated such figures. These disputes not only erupted in relation to specific property allocations but also reverberated upwards to the level of the provincial allocations to the different regiments. Sir Hierome Sankey, Petty's inveterate enemy in the army ranks, along with Colonels Richard Lawrence and Robert Barrow, challenged Petty's assessment of land values in Munster – 'that the said Doctor imploying drunken surveyors, unprofitable land had been put uppon the army as profitable'.[35] In particular, they sought to have some of the south Kerry baronies excluded altogether from the official allocations and the Munster army component to be compensated by the addition of the good lands of Crannagh and Galmoy from Leinster's Kilkenny. The army agents for the Leinster and Ulster provinces objected to such a move and countered with their own proposals. The Council of State ruled that the *status quo ante* should prevail and Petty's map definitions of land quality stood. In the end, very few if any legal cases were brought against Petty on the score of land quality definitions. The great majority of the army officers trusted him and his survey. Yet the classification of the Kerry lands still seems strangely at odds with the rest of Munster.

The greatest difficulty facing Petty arose because the work of the Down Survey outsped the capacity of the army to agree on its modes of subdivision and on what rate-per-acre they would accept in satisfaction of their pay arrears.

Rumours abounded about the amount of land available for confiscation. The initial Gross Survey returns seriously underestimated the amount of land available. Early returns from the Civil Survey indicate that a greater amount of land was available for confiscation. By July 1655 the Down Survey returns for most counties had come in, 'whereby it evidently appeares that the lands doe hold out above a *third part more* than did the estimate in the civill survey [my emphasis]'.[36] All the time government remained uncertain if it could satisfy all its debts – not only those incurred in Ireland's civil war but also England's. With the news of more land coming available, the army officers insisted on being paid according to the rates of the 1653 Act, that is, they sought full satisfaction. Throughout all of this seesawing and infighting, the adventurers clung to the returns of the Gross Survey. They had the advantage that their needs had been prioritized and that since only 1,500 persons were involved, land allocation could be made per individual rather than per troop and regiment. In contrast, on the army side, over 30,000 soldiers still had to be satisfied in the division of the lands.

Petty's primary brief was to map the baronies allotted to the soldiers in the ten counties – from Antrim to Waterford – designated to be shared with the adventurers. But the government had also allocated to the officers and soldiers the outstanding forfeited lands of counties Kerry, Donegal, Wexford, Kildare, Kilkenny, Londonderry, Longford, Tyrone and Wicklow. Likewise, the remaining undisposed forfeited lands in Carlow, Dublin and Cork were to go to the army. After completing the mapping of the baronies allocated to the soldiers in the ten counties, Petty also surveyed counties Wexford, Kerry and Donegal in 1655, as well as much of Longford, Kilkenny and Kildare. Dublin had already been surveyed. Londonderry, Tyrone, south Cork, Carlow and Wicklow were completed early in 1656 (see Fig. 5.5).

The most complaining elements of the army, as Petty saw it, were allocated lands from mid to late 1655 and the remainder received their lands in 1656. Despite the lack of synchronization between the actual Down Surveys and the subdivision of lands to the officers and soldiers, Petty notes that 'there came to the Doctor, orders upon orders, exceeding thicke to make ready the surveyes: both bookes and platts, of the lands to be sett out to the forces now to be disbanded and which were to be kept in whole or halfe pay untill the same were done'. Yet by 'the speciale and extraordinary mercy of God, the said surveyes, and surveyors to subdivide [and demarcate the new properties] were in such readiness upon the several respective spots [allotments], that not a penny of unnecessary pay was continued by any occasion of unreadiness herein'.[37] Petty also sought to meet his obligation to each officer and soldier allocated holdings of 1,000 acres or over – to provide them with a map of his new property.

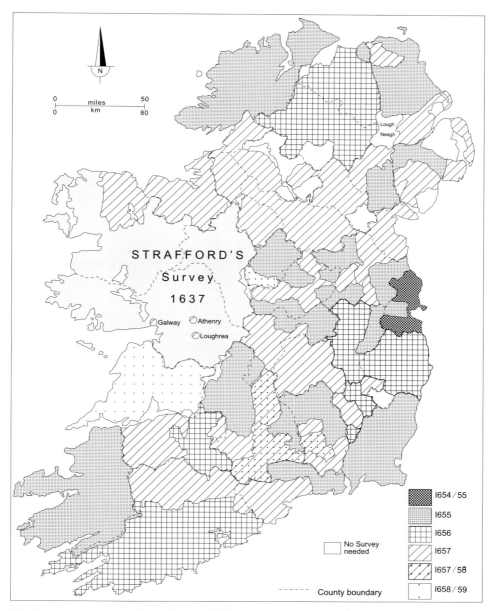

5.5   The progress of the Down Survey, 1654–9 (source: see work of W.H. Hardinge, especially Appendix E, pp 45–99, reference 12)

The quality and comprehensiveness of the proprietorial and mapping data that Petty provided to the Cromwellian administrators is demonstrated in Fig. 5.6. Adapted from Hardinge's table of 'Irish Plantation Acres, Profitable and Unprofitable, Admeasured as Forfeited in each Barony',[38] this map shows in much detail the extent and depth of the Cromwellian confiscations as revealed by Petty's surveys. The first striking feature is the number of baronies from

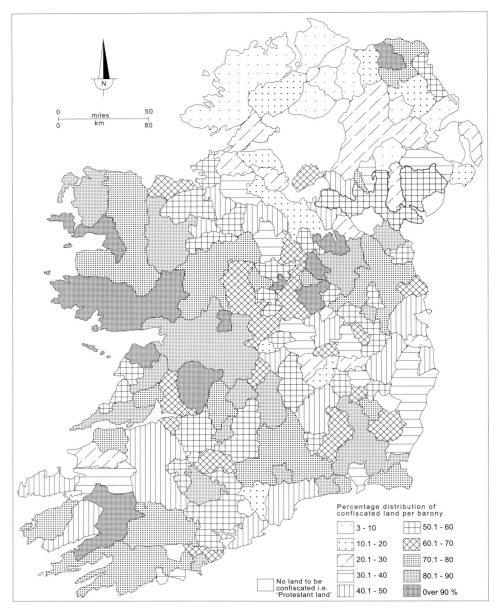

5.6   Details of the distribution of confiscated land per barony in Ireland of the mid-1650s (source: calculated from Hardinge's Appendix E, pp 100–104, reference 12)

Kinalmeaky in Cork through Shillelagh in Co. Wicklow and Farney in Co. Monaghan on to much of Co. Tyrone, where no confiscations were required, since all the land was already 'planted'. Secondly, the cumulative and still geographically expansive impact of the Ulster plantation is revealed as the frontier of planter settlement and landownership extends well into northeast Connacht and into pockets in north Leinster; only southeast Ulster retains a buffer role, with over 50 per cent of the land now awaiting confiscation. The impact of the Munster plantation shows strongly in the west and south of the province, while it is clear that both formal and informal plantations in midland and southwest Leinster have made a deep impression on patterns of landownership. There are three great regions of confiscation: the Pale territory of north Leinster; much of Connacht and Clare; and a great belt of formerly strong Catholic landownership levels from Tipperary to south Wexford. Two other outliers of confiscations emerge in southwest Munster and north Antrim. This map clearly and succinctly summarizes the impact of the Tudor and Stuart plantations – formal and infor- mal – while highlighting more than half of the remainder of the island, which is to come under Cromwell's hammer.

The senior officers of the army were the ones to dictate the pace and pattern of the Cromwellian land distribution and settlement of the military. Many of the ordinary soldiers did not wish to stay on as small landowners and even in the first disbandment of late 1653/early 1654 there was a lively market in their debentures (that is, certificates of debt to soldiers to be paid in land). By 1655–6, this market in soldiers' debentures had depreciated and they could now be purchased at one- quarter of the original rate. The officers – as well as the existing Protestant landowners and speculators, especially those in the Ulster counties – were the great beneficiaries of these transactions. Yet the Council of the Agents for the army still pressed the government for more land, arguing that there was insufficient land allocated to meet their full demands. So in a piecemeal fashion, with army agents for their respective provinces still squabbling about the distribution of surpluses and the transfers of baronies from one province to another, the govern- ment claimed more lands to satisfy the land hunger. All the lands in Connacht exempted from the Irish, those around the garrisons and the towns, near the sea and the Shannon in the so-called 'four-mile' (later 'one-mile') line were now designated for army settlement. Eventually all of counties of Sligo and Leitrim (consequently surveyed by Petty as late as 1657), as well as the barony of Tirawley in Co. Mayo, were added to the army's plantations. The squeeze was now on the west bank of the Shannon; and the transplanted Irish received even more cramped and reduced allocations (see Fig. 5.5 and Fig. 5.6).

In Petty's discourse on the history of the Down Survey (and his involvement in the related Cromwellian land settlement) the trauma of this transplantation does not figure. There are scattered references to waste and depopulated countrysides, the lack of meersmen, the odd attack of tories on his surveyors, but the rest is a deafening silence. However, outside the walls of Dublin Castle (Petty's Down Survey headquarters) and beyond Petty's discourse, the traumatized Irish elites, merchants and some of the tenant population were facing either forced internal migration or emigration and sometimes execution. Under the Commonwealth, the whole of the island had become a huge chessboard on which the 'game' of plantation and transplantation was played. Draconian legislation had to be im- plemented – 11 million acres had to be cleared of its original owners and occupants and space made for the new conquering elites. Plans might have to be adjusted, further commissions and commissioners appointed, some of the Loughrea commissioners in charge of the transplantation to Connacht might have to be sacked for oppressive and/or irregular measures, including the acceptance of influential bribes from the wealthiest of the Irish elites seeking a better deal in that province, requirements that the wives and retinue of transplanting landowners be permitted to stay behind to harvest the spring and summer crops of 1654, all might be allowed. But whatever the variations, revisions and indecisions, the relentless reconstruction of the island's property proceeded apace.

Very few of the thousands of active insurgents who were condemned to death by the first article of the Act of Settlement 1652 were actually executed but many, perhaps 40,000, were shipped overseas. Likewise, many of the landowners who would not transplant were thrown into prison. Some were made an example of and executed by hanging but most were subsequently released on condition that they did transplant. All the while the grip of the military tightened around the residual but persistent resistance of the Irish tories. Quick fortunes were made by a number of speculative planters and government officials who leased the extensive lands and urban properties that still awaited formal plantation between the early and late 1650s, while in the Protestant quarters of Ulster, part of the Pale and south Munster, long controlled by local and/or government militias, consolidation of Protestant landownership and tenant occupation proceeded without necessarily always first receiving formal clearance from the Dublin administration.

Some Catholic tenants, likewise, consolidated their own local power bases in this uncertain post-war situation. As we have seen, the original edict that all the Irish Catholic population should be cleared west of the Shannon was gradually relented upon; but the climate of fear and threat was such that many Irish sought the nearest waterside to escape to other worlds. The overseas scattering of the Irish – later known as the Wild Geese – had now begun its long journey in earnest. English assessments of the need for labour and a clear realization that Irish labour would be far cheaper than the equivalent labour supplied by English immigrants (obviously needed to fill the places of the Irish if transplanted) meant that as the 1650s progressed, more realistic adjustments were made as to who would be obliged to transplant and who might be permitted to remain. Numerous requests to be allowed to retain Irish tenants, artisans and labourers flooded into the Dublin administration from the representatives of the 'reserved' counties, as well as from Wexford, and indeed from most counties.[39] The game plan had to be adjusted, and this, combined with the massive sale of soldiers' debentures, ensured that the dream of a more comprehensive and deeper settlement of English Protestant soldier yeomanry faded.

It is, therefore, important to note that the transplantation to Connacht met with massive, if mainly passive, resistance. Petty's maps fail us here. Connacht contained about 5,000 freeholders in 1641. Admittedly, perhaps a third of these holdings were of less than 100 plantation acres. Of the remaining bigger landowners, it appears that about one-third were officially recognized as transplanters. Munster is likely to have had around 4,000 landowners with over 100 plantation acres in 1641; yet only one in eight ends up in Connacht. Leinster probably contained about 2,700 bigger landowners in 1641; only one out of five appears in the Connacht list of transplanters. Allowing for both the attrition of the wars and outmigrations (forced or otherwise), the above figures strongly suggest the extent to which former landowners – big and small – remained in their localities and survived as major leaseholders or tenant farmers. The Sweetman family of Wexford is a classic example of a former major landowning family, members of which prospered as major leaseholders. The Tobin family of southeast Tipperary is another. Examples abound. Despite the Cromwellian storms, and despite the drastic changes at the ownership level, a great many old Irish families held their ground, survived, and adapted to the new landlord regime.

Nevertheless, the clearances continued, nowhere more deeply and traumatically than in the towns – the wealthy Atlantic city of Galway was stripped of its enterprising merchant traders and was not to recover fully from this Cromwellian purge until the later twentieth century. The Irish of Kilkenny were expelled, as were those of Clonmel – for example, in 1640 the population of the walled town of Clonmel was overwhelmingly Catholic; by 1660, 75 per cent of its population was English and Protestant.[40] A series of forced migrations is thus initiated. Figure 4.9 (see p. 162) summarizes not only the planned transplantations to Connacht but also the major patterns of transportation and emigration of Irish Catholics out of the island. Over the 1650s, this exodus is clearly offset by very significant immigrations from both Scotland and England.

The 'Great Transplanting of the Irish' to Connacht – orchestrated by the commissioners at Loughrea and Athlone – appears initially as a very disorganized, not to say, chaotic enterprise. The commissioners had at their disposal Strafford's excellent 1637 survey of the province, and, it appears, the commissioners authorized some of their own private surveys as well. In addition, they received the Transplantation Certificates from the 'refugee' Irish landowners, as returned to the regional Revenue Commissioners. More particularly, the so-called Black Books (including the 1641 Depositions and critical reports from the deliberations of the Confederation of Kilkenny) were made available to enable the commissioners to make their judgements about degrees of guilt and punishment.[41] What the record does not show is the number of 'insider deals' done between the government officials and the most influential transplanters as the land market and land allocation came under the swirling pressures of bribes, land exchanges and political intrigue of all kinds.

A few generalizations can be made, however, on the basis of Robert Simington's great work on the records of the transplantation.[42] The planned reallocation of transplanting landowners from particular counties in Leinster and Munster to specified baronies within Connacht was not achieved. The process was recognized, at a later stage, as impractical even by the government. The best managed county in this respect was Co. Clare, where one-third of the transplanters from the other provinces were settled in their designated baronies. Co. Roscommon saw about one-fourth of the landowners transplanted from outside the county settle in their specified locales. Galway saw only one-fifth so placed. As for Co. Mayo, the situation was almost totally chaotic and unregulated. Less than 5 per cent of the transplantees from the other provinces actually settled in their allocated baronies. The further away from the centres of control at Athlone and Loughrea – and the later the process of allocation – the greater the free-for-all.

It is often not recognized that local Irish landowners *within* Connacht were also obliged to transplant within their own county and province. As much as 91 per cent of the lands of Co. Galway and 80 per cent of those of Clare and Mayo were forfeited. Just under 70 per cent of Roscommon's lands and 60 per cent of Sligo's lands were likewise confiscated – whereas in Co. Leitrim the figure at 39 per cent is much less. As much as 40 per cent of the total number of transplantees in Co. Clare involved local elite families – this figure climbs to 45 per cent in Roscommon and in Co. Galway over half of the new land allocations involved local families being forced to move. Connacht was the scene of enormous disturbances, dislocations and great pain. The congestion of the districts and counties of the west had begun.

A detailed analysis of the transplantation records confirms that across a large swathe of territory – from south Roscommon (Athlone barony) through much of north and central Galway, including Moycullen barony to the west, as well as the three northwestern baronies of Co. Clare – there is almost a complete match between the amount of lands forfeited and lands allocated to transplanters under the Cromwellian administration. Indeed, in the Co. Galway baronies of Kilconnell, Killian and Tiaquin – as well as the Burren in Co. Clare – it appears that there was more land allocated to the transplanters than was officially forfeited in these baronies. It may be no coincidence that this pile-up occurred in regions in and around Athlone and Loughrea – the administrative centres for the Cromwellian implementation of the transplantation (see Fig. 5.7a)

In south Mayo, mid-Roscommon, south Galway and mid and east Clare, around 90 per cent of the lands available under the forfeiture rules were allocated to new Catholic transplantees. In contrast, in north and west Mayo, Ballynahinch barony in west Galway and all of the south Clare baronies only around 70 per cent of the forfeited land is accounted for in this way. There is a noticeable slippage in the quality of the transplantation allocations in those regions most remote from the Athlone-Loughrea centres. We are left with a picture of overallocations in this core of the province and many anomalies on the northern and southern flanks. Not surprisingly, it emerges that Co. Galway received almost half (42 per cent) of all the transplantees, Co. Clare (22 per cent) and Roscommon (15 per cent). Co. Mayo only received 12 per cent of the total. It is also clear that in the most important middle zone, a far higher proportion (around 66 per cent) of the transplantees are local and have been moved within their own county, whereas over much of Mayo, south Clare and north Roscommon (see Fig. 5.7b) these proportions are far less (between 20 and 45 per cent).

Officially, just under one-fifth (908,708 statute acres) of Connacht was not forfeited. This included 61.1 per cent and 42.2 per cent respectively of the already planted or partially planted counties of Leitrim and Sligo. Whereas only 8.4 per cent of Co. Galway remained unforfeited, as much as 24.3 per cent of Mayo, 25.6 per cent of Clare and 32.2 per cent of Roscommon remained unforfeited, confirming either the existing strength of New English and/or Protestant interest in these latter three counties or lands designated for army settlement. These figures include the one-mile line allocations along the Shannon and the western seaboard. However, the baronial analysis (discussed above, see Figure 5.7a), which demonstrates a significant underallocation of forfeited lands to transplanting Catholics, confirms that close on 30 per cent of Connacht was either allocated to the army or acquired/retained by existing New English/Protestant interests. Major beneficiaries here included Justice James Donnellan, Sir Charles Coote, Lord Ranelagh (Arthur Jones), Sir Robert King and Lord Henry Cromwell. This geographical expansion of the Protestant interest was particularly true of north Mayo, most of the Shannonside baronies and, with the exception of northwest Clare, all of the coastal baronies. The Cromwellian administration of the plantation of Connacht was far more effective than the literature has suggested. The transplanted Catholic landed community was clearly penned in and contained in a very effective geopolitical strategy.

In terms of the transplanting counties, Tipperary leads the way with 19 per cent

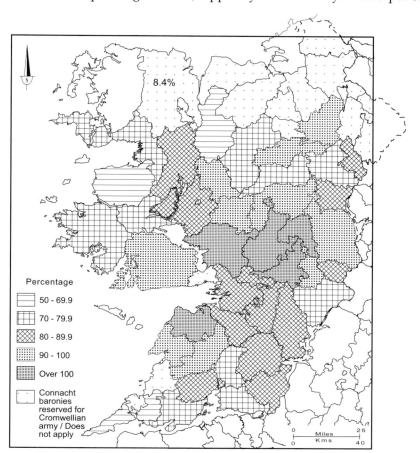

5.7(a)   Proportion of forfeited land in Connacht and Clare actually allocated to Catholic transplantees (source: calculated from materials provided in R.C. Simington, reference 42)

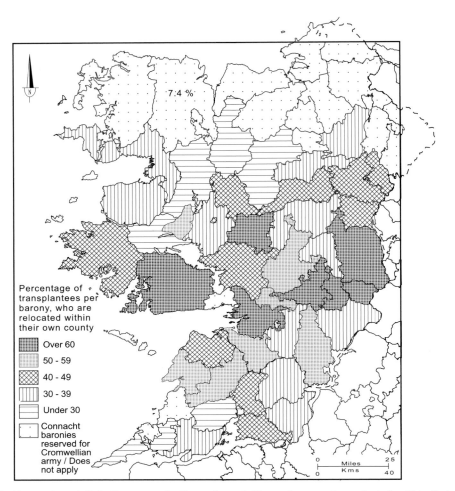

Percentage of
transplantees per
barony, who are
relocated within
their own county

Over 60

50 - 59

40 - 49

30 - 39

Under 30

Connacht
baronies
reserved for
Cromwellian
army / Does
not apply

7:4 %

Miles

Kms

0   25

0   40

5.7(b)   Proportion of Catholic owners in Connacht and Clare who were transplanted within their own county (source: as in 5.7 (a))

of the total number of transplantees. There is also a close correspondence in the numbers detailed for Tipperary in Hardinge's Transplantation Certificates and those recorded as receiving land in Connacht.[43] Limerick county comes second with over 9 per cent of the transplantees – but the numbers transplanting here represent more than a 30 per cent reduction on the numbers recorded in Hardinge's Transplantation Certificates. Historian Chris O'Mahony's intimate analysis of the Limerick evidence suggests that only about half of those due for transplantation actually crossed the Shannon.[44] Likewise, Co. Kilkenny, with 7 per cent of the transplantees, shows a 50 per cent reduction on the number expected to move as per Hardinge's certificates. Co. Kerry is the most extreme example of the latter trend – only 1.1 per cent of the country's transplantees came from this county, which represents a fraction (one-fifth) of the Hardinge total due for transplantation from that county.

Co. Meath ranks fifth with 7.5 per cent of the total of transplantees. But here, as with the other counties of the Pale (Kildare, 2.3 per cent; Dublin, 2.9 per cent and Wicklow, 0.7 per cent), Hardinge's figures are seen to be incomplete. It is clear that many of the Catholic landowners in this region – if they could not avoid transplantations in the first instance – registered within their own precinct (Dublin). Co. Cork, with 6 per cent of the transplantees, also clearly fits this latter pattern of registration – only one-quarter of its transplantee families are returned in Hardinge's table. In the other big transplanting counties – Wexford (7 per cent), Westmeath (6 per cent), Waterford (5 per cent) and King's County (4 per cent) – there is a much closer correspondence between the Hardinge figures and the records of the transplantations to Connacht. The remaining five Leinster counties – Carlow, Longford, Louth, Queen's County and Wicklow – together only account for 5.3 per cent of transplantations, reflecting, for the most part, longer histories of either formal or informal plantations. And the nine Ulster counties together only produced 2.6 per cent of the transplantees – by 1653 there were very few Irish landowners left to transplant in the northern counties. Galway ranks third of all counties, with 9 per cent of transplantees, Roscommon had 2.1 per cent, Sligo 1.8 per cent, Clare 1.7 per cent, while Mayo contributed only 1.3 per cent of total countrywide transplantees who were obliged to move outside their own county boundary.

Figure 5.8 summarizes the overall origins of the transplantees to Connacht. Regional discrepancies in the enforcement of Commonwealth regulations – and the importance of local patronage such as that of the earl of Ormond – influenced this geographical patterning. Nevertheless, it is clear that it is the most revolutionary counties in the heartland of Confederate Ireland – stretching from Galway to Wexford, with Tipperary as the central axis – were being punished most severely for the rising/rebellion. It is also striking how this core zone corresponds with the region containing the highest densities of tower-houses and later comes to be recognized as the heartland of hurling. This is the region where a hybrid 'middle-nation' – born of the integration of Gaelic and Old English Catholic families – was already emerging by 1641. This region of resistance and political leadership was now to be dismantled and disempowered via massive land transfers. However, as with much else of the Cromwellian settlement planning, this strategy was only partially successful. Co. Tipperary and its adjacent counties remained only half-conquered (see chapters 8 and 9). But I anticipate.

Still the battles raged about the division of the spoils both between and within the adventurers and the army. In this rarefied world of claims, counter-claims and divisions, Petty was regularly accused of both advantaging his own army friends (as well as himself) and of all forms of skullduggery in his exercise of the surveying and the critical release of lands for settlement. Yet, when the army brought a rigorous system of refereeing to bear on the Down Survey, setting up a Committee of Examination to test its reliability, Petty brought fifty surveyors into the Council Chamber to answer questions and provide demonstrations, according as their field books, plots and protractions were scrutinized. Worsley even sought his own additional examination (completed 18 August 1656), which in the end consisted of minor quibbles, all of which Petty casually dispatched in face-to-face meetings at the Council table. Much of the Commonwealth's so-called 'forfeited lands' had been mapped and dissected into the smallest parcels, like chess pieces to be re-allocated across the Irish gameboard. The stakes were high and after the survey came the critical distribution of the land. The survey was now utilized for the purpose for which it had been set up – to pay for the Commonwealth's massive debts in allotments of Irish land.

Petty had delivered on the promise to survey over two-thirds of the country with extraordinary rapidity and with a level of accuracy unsurpassed at that time. His reward, apart from money payments and the formation of a new landed dynasty (that of Lord Landsdowne/later earls of Shelbourne), was the achievement of immortality as Ireland's greatest map-maker.

Distributing the Confiscated Lands

So began the systematic divvying up of the country. Thomas Larcom, writing in the mid-nineteenth century, could find no analogy, not 'even in the planting of a modern colony'.[45] Petty was now not only head physician to the army, and secretary to Henry Cromwell, but also one of the clerks of the Council of State and director of the Down Survey. Despite the challenges made to the integrity and quality of his Down Survey by some army officers, the army as a whole was sufficiently confident of both his ability and probity that it selected Petty as one of the three commissioners to be put in charge of the subdividing and allotment of lands to the army (May 1656).

The task facing Petty and his colleagues was formidable. The completion of the earlier part of the Down Survey actually followed on from the first (1653–4) disbanding of part of the army, which appears to have been accomplished in a highly irregular and confusing manner. Petty, writing a few short years after these events, described these earliest attempts at planting the soldiers as obscure. Writing 350 years later, we can only concur. All we can say is that the army's choice of Petty was a sensible, even essential, move. Petty's abilities as a conceptualizer, his capacity to take a bird's-eye view of Ireland as a whole and his organizational powers all came into play once again as he reflected, deliberated and decided on the complex issues of land distribution. As Larcom rightly notes:

> in truth it is difficult to imagine a world more full of perplexity and uncertainty than to locate 32,000 officers, soldiers and followers with Adventurers, settlers and creditors of every kind and class, having different and uncertain claims on lands of different and uncertain value, in detailed parcels sprinkled over two-thirds of the surface of Ireland.[46]

The earliest settlement of the officers and soldiers had been made in a hurried fashion. No account of what was then done 'did ever appear as a light into what was further to bee done'; some soldiers had been satisfied as to their full allowance or rate, yet all this process left, in Petty's description, 'many scraps of baronies . . . which were imperfectly settled down [planted]'.[47] Throughout all of this time the Court of Claims – dealing with the Catholic Irish claims – had been meeting and making adjustments. Committees for agreeing debentures and a whole battery of other commissions were all acting, interacting or not interacting. Likewise, the army officers had failed to resolve even their own internal differences. Such was 'the ragged condition the affaire was in . . . and . . . with other uncertainties of debt and creditt, as allsoe [many] clashing interests' that Petty inherited.[48]

Even before his appointment as commissioner, Petty voluntarily took pains and time to think through the issues. He wanted to see this 'great and memorable worke well transacted'.[49] And despite the presence of two fellow commissioners (Gookin and Miles Symner), it is clear that the management of the calculations, along with the invention of the method and means to put the general directions of the Commissioners of Distribution into practice, lay wholly with Petty.[50] A second key meeting of the army officers with Petty took place early in July 1656, when Petty's solutions to quotas, distributions and the use of reserved lands gave that large assembly of officers 'such satisfaction that it hath proved the ground of whatsoever hath since been done' and 'composed the clashings then in being'.[51] Or so Petty claims. Larcom details the masterly generalizing view that Petty took and propounded of the whole question of land distribution, not only in relation to what land had been allocated in 1653 and 1655, but what remained to be done from 1656 onwards:

> he first restored the whole army, by calculation [of all debts/arrears] to the state it was in 1654 when they cast their lots: then [he] ascertained what lands were disposable, in pursuance of all Acts of Parliament and ensuring orders of Council, separating those [lands], which for any cause it was necessary to reserve, from the remainder which were disposable, obtaining the immediate authority of the Council on doubtful points, and the concurrence of the army by adjustments amongst themselves where such would afford satisfaction and facility.[52]

Both the state's and Petty's need for method and order was realized in the vast collection of Cromwellian ledgerbooks, which forty clerks, working under Petty's tireless direction, now put together. In short, thirteen categories of books were compiled to complete and document this major phase of land distribution. Petty hoped that these books would 'contain a compleat and regular account of this great affaire'; but further noted that 'the explanations of which papers and the aforementioned operations would require a treatise of itselfe'.[53] We do not, unfortunately, have such an explanatory treatise. Besides the original books of the Down Survey, which Petty noted

> have been several times turned over, there hath been made by us certain neat bookes as large and voluminous as the said bookes of surveyes, containing the number of reference, proprietors names, lands names, number of acres profitable, each in a distinct and proper colume; together with the columes for decrees of the Court of Claimes; private grants, orders of suspensions, doubts of the Civil Surveys, former disposures, with the respective rates of each land act to whom disposed; and lastly, a colume of such lands as wee judge absolutely cleare and fitt to be sett forth.[54]

In effect, Petty thus created the template for the Books of Survey and Distribution.

Further books also dealt with a list of all the debentures, the books of distribution for the allocations made in 1653 and 1655, books on court rulings about land, suspensions, private grants, Civil Survey 'doubtful' lands, possible Commonwealth lands not yet measured, and books of other private surveys besides the Down Survey. Most importantly, Petty (and his fellow commissioners) had made distinct books of all the 'neat/clear' lands by themselves, 'fitted into lists of contiguities, and standing in the same order wherein they must be sett forth [to the army]'.[55] Paralleling these neat books were large books of all the army debentures admitted for satisfaction, reduced into specific lists and likewise arranged in the same order wherein they must be satisfied. The debentures of each officer and soldier could thus be matched to the geographically contiguous land lists.

Agents for each regiment were issued with a list or file of contiguous lands, detailing the contents of each townland or part townland allotted to that regiment as well as lists of debentures belonging to or affixed to each troop and company within such a lot. The lands of each regiment's lots were then distributed according to the rules and judgements laid down by Petty and his two other commissioners and/or as agreed with the army agents. Rules for the distribution and subdivision of lands amongst the army were laid down, modified, revised. A key stipulation was that a whole regiment allocated its respective lot (in specified provinces, counties and baronies) was required to set down continuously and contiguously and not to scatter over the county. Each regiment was required to settle and plant where the lands of the previous assigned regiment ceased. The several regiments, troops and companies were to draw further lots as to where individual proportions should fall. Disbanding troops were therefore advised 'to plant together and not dispersedly' where possible, so that the officers and soldiers of each troop would try to settle in a way that made for 'the better security and maintenance of the public peace and their respective interests'.[56] We may imagine a troop (or what was left of a troop) setting out from the local garrison with their officers to ride to their respective plots and begin the process of building a new life in a mainly hostile countryside.[57] What had begun as a military conquest, had become a military-style property system and settlement.

In early January 1657, the commissioners were still trying to tidy up the loose ends of this stage of the Cromwellian land distribution. Apart from questions of outstanding priorities and dealing with 'concealed land', they stressed there was still not enough land to satisfy existing claimants, not to speak of future ones. So the commissioners sought direction from Council with regard to the distribution of surplus lands, as in Co. Kildare, and an anticipated surplus from the adventurers' land in Co. Louth.

Parallel to Petty's work as commissioner of distribution and having completed the first stage of the Down Survey relating to the army lands, Petty and Worsley were now jointly authorized by the Council to carry the work of the Down Survey to a further stage. It was felt necessary that the forfeited lands in the baronies of the ten counties which had fallen by lot to the adventurers, as well as other forfeited lands in the counties of Louth and Leitrim, should now be surveyed. Equally important, the forfeited lands set to the first disbanded soldiers in 1653 and 'such other lands escheated to his Highness [Oliver Cromwell] and the Commonwealth as yet not admeasured should be forthwith admeasured by an exact survey'.[58] The Council of State in Dublin was therefore stressing the need not only to survey the adventurers' lands properly but also the lands allocated so 'irregularly' to the disbanded soldiers in 1653–4. Such survey work began over the second half of 1656 and was completed in 1657 (see Fig. 5.5, p. 179).

In January 1657 Petty, in conjunction with fellow commissioners Gookin, Symner and Ralph King, was appointed to enquire into the state of the adventurers' lots. Indeed, these commissioners of distribution now insisted that no more land claims were to be entertained until they would 'wholly perfect the several accounts wee have to make and until the Adventurers and disbanded of 1653, their lands bee returned by the surveyors'.[59] Clearly a tidying-up process was in operation here, as Petty sought, with the aid of the Distribution Board, to be fair in the distribution of lands to all legitimate claimants. The specific '1653' lands included baronies in the counties of Cork, Kilkenny, Longford, Louth, Cavan, Monaghan, Fermanagh, Sligo, and even Mayo. This final mapping drive was also to include the residue of forfeited crown and ecclesiastical lands in twenty-three counties that still remained unsurveyed, as well as the plotting of forfeited lands within the Liberties of Galway and Athlone. The net was closing in, even on lands west of the Shannon.

As the survey of the baronies that were allotted to the adventurers was completed, the army proposed to the Council of State in Dublin that Petty be sent to London to finalize the settlement of the adventurers. Up to then the adventurers had insisted that the findings of the Gross Survey – which had provided barony totals of confiscated land by early 1654 – and their own privately sponsored surveys were adequate for the division of lands in their allotted baronies. It is clear that this process had run into many difficulties: some adventurers complained of deficiencies in their allocations; others – though not complaining – clearly had received well above their legitimate allocation. All of this time the army – fiercely competitive with the adventurers in the allocation of Irish land – were rightly convinced that the original ten half counties allotted contained a sufficient security for the whole debt of the adventurers. Consequently, they sought to have any surplus lands in these counties (particularly those of the forfeited lands in Co. Louth) released and allocated to the constituency of the army.

Between 1653 and 1658 the Committee of Adventurers at Grocers Hall in London controlled their own land distributions. The mode of distribution was that this committee should fill each half county 'like a sack' to its agreed allocation, then move on to the next county.[60] Figure 5.9 illustrates the highly geometric mode of distribution adopted for Co. Tipperary, as in the other counties. Petty's job was to assure the adventurers of the goodwill of the Dublin government and that 'such [adventurers] who made advantages of the present confusion may be discovered and that such as have only their just rights may be confirmed therein, and that such Adventurers as want it may be speedily relieved'.[61] He was also to confirm that 'if any be due', the army was to receive the surplus of lands.

Petty arrived in London in May 1658, preceded by libellous charges and

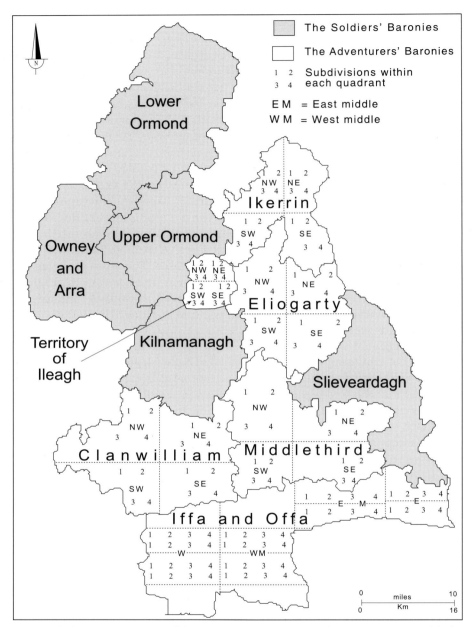

5.9   Example from Co. Tipperary of the geometric mode adopted for the distribution of forfeited lands to the adventurers (adapted from map [p. 386] in J.P. Prendergast, reference 41)

malicious rumours both about his person and his performance as a surveyor and distributor of Irish lands. Yet, after a number of debates in Grocers Hall, Petty succeeded in getting the Committee of Adventurers to agree that their allotment of lands should be subject to revision and that Petty's survey of their lands – 'which was equal in quality to that on which the allotments to the army had been made' – should be adopted for the allocation of land to the adventurers as well. All the while, Petty had to overcome the original adventurers' views that their own survey was authentic; that they had the right to purchase 'whatsoever they had taken more than their due'; that they should be confirmed in the places where they had settled, 'notwithstanding irregularities in doing same' and were not bound to account or show to the state what lands each of them were possessed of. That, in effect, they could disregard and 'overthrow the state's survey', since the Committee of Claims at Grocers Hall was the only true, legal administrators of the allocation.[62]

The twenty principles of the agreement between Petty (acting for the state) and the adventurers was published on 21 August 1658. It emphasized the powers vested in the lord deputy and Council of Ireland 'to assigne unto each Adventurer what lands by name shall be applied to his particular satisfaction', 'that the [Down] Survey is more favourable to the Adventurers than their owne . . . And lastly the said survey, although it were very faulty, because it is authenticke, universall, uniforme and regular, is the most safe rule that the Adventurers can goe by.'[63] Since the power of the lord deputy and Council was the only legal power to make land distributions, and their survey the only authentic survey, it followed that only what was done according to their rules and methods would provide a legal foundation to the adventurers' properties in Ireland. In no other document relating to the conquest of Ireland is the fundamental role of the mapped survey as the foundation stone of plantation so clearly stated. The Down Survey map is authentic, universal, uniform and regular – its 'writ' shall run. Two centuries later, Larcom was to write that Petty's Down Survey 'stands to this day, with the accompanying books of distribution as the legal record of the title on which half the land of Ireland is held'.[64]

On 31 August 1658 the adventurers at Grocers Hall agreed to the principles of distribution as formalized by Petty. And the trust the adventurers now placed in Petty was such that they asked the Council in Dublin that 'the said Doctor be appointed to transact the above mentioned affaire, born in the belief of your Lordships and your petitioners [of him] being a person of whose ability and integrity your petitioners have received good satisfaction'.[65] Just as the army had complimented Petty and his strategies by awarding monies towards the first stage of the Down Survey, now the adventurers agreed that there should be a levy of three half-pence

> upon every Irish acre, profitable and unprofitable, for which the respective Adventurers should have their ultimate particular allotment certified, together with mapps attested by the Surveyor-General, and orders of the Council for possession, to be paid by the respective Adventurers unto Dr. William Petty, all the time when such particular allotments, orders and mapps, should be altered and issued, and not before.[66]

The adventurers rightly saw that Petty, given his enormous command of both the details of the survey and the modes of land distribution, was the person to give their business in Ireland rapid dispatch. Hence their eventual choice of Petty as the sole member of a Commission for the Distribution of Land to the Adventurers, for 'we cannot but, upon our experience of his work and accomplishments, repose in him under your Lordship the sole trust of the said Adventurers' settlement'.[67]

However, a minority of the adventurers, opposed to these proceedings and principles, hired counsellors-at-law to state the case against 'the Petty agreement'. Matters were not finally resolved until early in 1659. As it happened, time was running out for the full implementation of the Cromwellian settlement – Oliver Cromwell died in September 1658. Bottigheimer is of the view that Petty went to London in May 1658 to convince the adventurers that a resurvey of their own lands was in their own interest as well as that of the state. He takes the view that Petty was shortly *thereafter* employed in the work of such a survey that 'it was allegedly completed by the end of 1658';[68] in fact, the state survey of the adventurers' land had been authorized as far back as the summer of 1656 and by far the greater part of the adventurers' baronies had been fully surveyed by the end of 1657.

Petty had gone to London with a very clear view of land arrangements in these baronies, which he had been examining since January 1657. In dealing with the adventurers in Grocers Hall, he was able to demonstrate his method of using neat books for the particular purpose of 'setting out the land' to the prospective owners. As Hardinge has emphasized, Petty kept for his own and the state's use his original, massively detailed 8 x 10 feet or 6 x 6 feet square baronial surveys.[69] The fact that many of the official barony surveys of the adventurers' land were not formally received in the Surveyor-General's Office until 1659 does not mean that Petty was not in a position more than a year earlier to start refereeing and negotiating solutions to impasses created by the previous overzealous dependence of the adventurers on the results of both the highly uneven Gross Survey and their own private surveys.

What still remains to be determined is how effective and complete Petty's intervention was in the distribution of the adventurers' lands; and the extent to which the 'injurious irregularities' that had accompanied the adventurers' own distribution had been corrected by the end of 1659. Bottigheimer's view that Petty did not intend to stand the existing allotment on its head 'only to squeeze it into a more compact form' is almost certainly true – 'to doe the same by any unnecessary removalls, but rather to continue att small matters', for 'it is not the desire of the Lord Deputy and Council . . . to alter the distributions formerly made by the Adventurers where there appears noe manifest injury'.[70] Bottigheimer is probably correct also in arguing that 'the Settlement conceived in the act for adventurers of 1642 never reached a conclusion'.[71] But whether it had grown so great and complex that 'like some gorged beast proved unable to digest what it swallowed' remains a moot point.[72] The army was determined that if a surplus of land was being held by the adventurers, that such matters be rectified. When Petty was sent to London by the Dublin Council, it was, among other things, to acquaint the adventurers that Dublin was determined to establish a fair distribution of lands; and to establish what surpluses might still be available to achieve their ends. The groundwork had already been done during 1657; certainly the mapped surveys (and possibly the neat books) were available for Petty to both rectify injustices both in the distribution as between different adventurers, and the distribution of the surplus lands. He was in a good position to tweak and bend the property jigsaw to these ends. It is therefore likely that much more was achieved in the frantic years of 1658 and 1659 than Bottingheimer allows for.

As we have seen, the adventurers were allocated lands in three counties in Ulster – Antrim, Down and Armagh; four counties in Leinster – Meath, King's County and Queen's County and Westmeath; and three counties in Munster – Limerick, Tipperary and Waterford. Five out of ten of the adventurers' land allocations went to the Leinster counties; four out of ten went to the Munster counties, with just under one out of ten to the Ulster counties.[73] However, it is both noticeable and interesting that the Ulster allocations were very compact – with only a small number of adventurers involved and with Sir John Clotworthy, William Hawkins and Maurice and George Thompson the big gainers. By way of contrast, Co. Tipperary saw land allocations to as many as 225 adventurers, while Queen's County and Co. Meath each were allocated 167 adventurer settlers and Co. Westmeath 151. What is not so clear is how many of these adventurers actually settled in their respective baronies.

The names of *tituladoes* (that is, landowners, merchants and professionals) as listed per barony in the Petty-inspired '1659 Census' allow some tentative generalizations to be made about the scale and geographical depth of the adventurer settlement. Fortunately for the barony of Rathconrath in Co. Westmeath many of the *tituladoe* names are accompanied by the entry 'Adventurer'.[74] Thus, we have a more precise picture of the number who had settled in that barony by *c.*1660. Of the total number of adventurers who were allotted land in that barony, just under 30 per cent are returned as settled residents. However, this figure may not be a representative one for the adventurer settlement in Ireland as a whole for two reasons: first, because it constitutes a rather rare instance where the subscribers from a single corporation (Dartmouth) were not scattered over a wide number of baronies, as was the norm in the lottery, but were rather allotted lands within a single barony; second, the figure of 28–30 per cent actually resident in the barony may be somewhat enhanced by Westmeath's location within the more 'protected' Dublin orbit.

A preliminary analysis of a comparison of the surnames and Christian names from the full list of adventurers who drew land in Ireland (a total of 1,043) with named *tituladoes* in the 1659 Census suggests the number of settler adventurers resident in their allotted barony was somewhat less for the ten counties than for Rathconrath.[75] Since some of the very small adventurer grantees would not necessarily make it onto the *tituladoe* list, we cannot assume that the evidence from the 1659 Census is fully comprehensive. In addition, it is clear that this listing of *tituladoes* for the different baronies in the different counties is not always either fully consistent or reliable. Recognizing these limitations, it would appear that close on 60 per cent of the adventurer grantees had not settled in their allocated baronies by 1660. Only about one-fifth had actually settled. The striking feature is the number of adventurer settlers who were absentees from their lands but living in Ireland – mainly in Dublin city and its hinterland but also in the other major county towns and port-cities. Clearly some of the adventurer settlers in 1660 still preferred to live (and sometimes trade) in the protected quarters of the walled cities and towns and manage their lands from a distance. A clear majority of them, however, had not crossed the Irish Sea but had either leased or sold on their allotments.

Only about half the adventurer grantees are confirmed in the ownership of their lands by the Acts of Settlement of Charles II in 1662.[76] The intended plantation of over a thousand New English landowners into ten allocated counties had been diluted substantially. Just as a majority of the ordinary soldiers had sold out their interests to either the officer or existing landowning classes, so many of the adventurer investors sold out and did not settle. Once again, the original aims of the Cromwellian settlement had been compromised.[77]

Such, in outline, was Petty's central involvement in what was the most epic and monumental transformation of Irish life, property and landscape that the island has ever known. He had surveyed to a high degree of accuracy (down to town-land, parish and estate levels) all but three counties of the island. The whole Cromwellian settlement of Ireland depended for its success on precise and rapid knowledge of the amount and location of land subject to confiscation. It took Petty to provide that knowledge.

This detailed mapping of Ireland was a pivotal aspect of the wider process by which power was lost by the old elites and created and sustained for the new planters. The Down Survey maps throw into sharp relief the places of implantation; and they demarcate the territories of the new Cromwellian estates – key instruments for the territorial control of land and people over the next two centuries. Less well recognized but equally important, Petty's was the organizing and calculating brain that cut through the increasingly confused undergrowth of claims, counter-claims and disputes that threatened to engulf the massive task of transforming the ownership of well over half the island. His clarity of thinking, his practical and mapping knowledge of the whole country, his dedication to serve the state's interests, his accounting skills and love of numbers, his organizational genius and passion for order were so impressive as to convince sceptical and suspicious army officers, as well as shrewd and frustrated London MPs and adventurer merchants, that he could be trusted and that he knew what he was doing. If Cromwell achieved the military conquest of Ireland, Petty was the one who masterminded the completion of the Cromwellian plantation and settlement. Without him, the settlement would have been achieved more slowly, been characterized by a far greater degree of confusion and irregularity, and accompanied by far more legislation, delays and chaos. And the Restoration might then have ensured a very different state of affairs.

Petty had come to Ireland to advance his knowledge of human affairs and especially to apply that knowledge to assist the British state in the government, management and reorganization of a newly conquered land. No other European intellectual of this era had the practical experience of wrestling with the complex and dangerous business of a land confiscation, which, one could argue, was matched in scale and ruthlessness only by twentieth-century Soviet Russia's land appropriations. Out of the furnace of that encounter, Petty had gained many new insights, forged many new ideas and concepts and had not only mapped but also left his stamp on the island's landscapes. By 1659–60 he was ready to create radical new images and narratives of that conquered land that was also becoming his home. But first he needed 'numbers'. He needed to devise a way to count the people and make a 'census'.

One of Petty's major motives in this was to determine the relative proportions of Irish Catholics and English (and Scots) Protestants on the island. Through a highly imaginative use of the 1660 poll-tax, Petty constructed his census.[78] What the census confirmed was that, not only had a substantial number of the old Catholic gentry families survived in Munster and Leinster, but that quite a number had slipped back home from 'exile' in Connacht as well. And while the census confirmed the overwhelming control now exercised by the planters in the major port-cities and county towns, it also revealed the resilience of old Catholic merchant families and populations in many of the small and medium-sized towns outside of Ulster. Most telling, for Petty, was the still enduring demographic power of the Irish Catholic population, despite both outmigration and its now highly marginalized position in the society and the economy. The demographic balance between Protestant and Catholic was to remain an enduring concern for Petty. It returned to haunt him in his last years, as he contemplated the succession of James II to the throne and the consequent threat to newly established landed dynasties like his own.

6

Society, Settlement and Immigration in Mid–Seventeenth–Century Ireland:
The Evidence of the '1659 Census'

> In every village is a castle, and a church, but bothe in ruyne. The baser cottages are
> built of underwood, called wattle and covered some with thatch and some with
> green sedge, of a round forme and without chimneys, and to my imaginacōn resem-
> ble so many hives of bees about a country farme.
>
> Luke Gernon[1]

'Not perhaps since the days of early Celtic colonisation had a movement of this
kind, emanating from abroad, left such a lasting impression on Irish life.' This is
how Jones Hughes describes the impact of the climax phase of landlordism in
Ireland.[2] The roots of this movement belong to the late sixteenth and seventeenth
centuries. Then Ireland's status as a fully fledged colony of Britain was confirmed
and Ireland's global position shifted from the outer edge of the European periphery to a strategic location on the great Atlantic routes to the New World. The social
and settlement geographies of seventeenth-century Ireland mirror these radical
changes, reflecting an uneven amalgam of late medieval, 'modernizing' and 'New
World' landscapes and mentalities.

Once its limitations are recognized and other sources of evidence (such as the
hearth-money records) are used in conjunction with it, the 1659 Census[3] provides
an enormous stimulus to our understanding of these complex cultural worlds of
late medieval/early modern Ireland. Recognized now as a 1660 poll-tax, the
Census allows for an analysis of the interconnections between population densities, economy and ethnicity; it facilitates an exploration of the interrelationships
between settlement and social hierarchies and also allows for a detailed assessment of the varying impact of New English and Scottish settlers on the whole
fabric of Irish society. For the purpose of this chapter, many of the problems[4] associated with the poll-tax[5] can be circumvented by avoiding absolute totals and
concentrating attention on a series of interbaronial comparisons.

Population, Economy and Ethnicity

I begin by looking at the interconnections between population densities,
economies and ethnic distributions. Figure 6.1 revises the pattern of population
densities as suggested in the poll-tax returns by incorporating the deficiencies

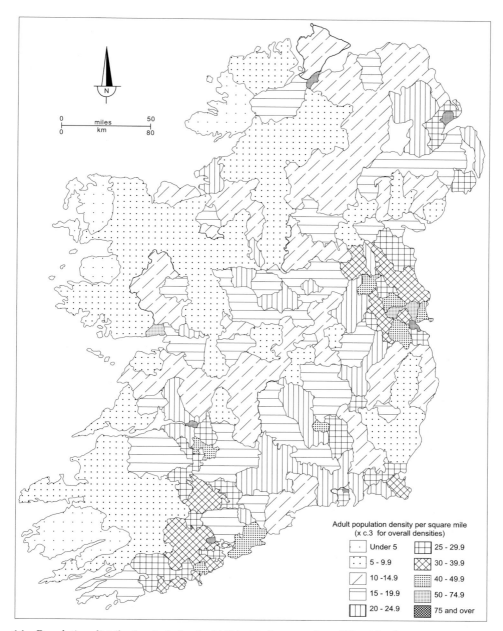

6.1   Population distribution in Ireland *c*.1660 (with the exception of Fig. 6.5, all maps in chapter 6 are based on materials from the '1659 Census')

noted above and elsewhere.[6] The most striking alteration is in the northeast, where the greater depth and extent of old Irish and planter populations is empha- sized. A higher density of settlement is also confirmed for east Donegal and the Sligo hinterland.[7] There are no striking alterations in population patterns over the rest of the island, apart from the inclusion of the estimated populations of the four missing 'census' towns of Carrick, Cashel, Clonmel and Fethard,[8] which more strongly emphasizes the hearthland of south Tipperary.[9]

I have adopted a number of strategies to fill in the gaps on the map for those counties with no 1660 poll-tax returns. Tyrone and Wicklow have hearth-money returns for the 1660s, which allow for a reasonable interpolation of 1660 densities at the barony level.[10] Counties Cavan, Galway and Mayo – with no solid population figures until the nineteenth century – present far greater difficulties. In this context, estimated county populations – based on computer projections from the 1672 hearth-tax receipts[11] – have been redistributed amongst the relevant baronies in proportion to the percentage number of denominations returned for each barony in the Books of Survey and Distribution. While allowing for the greater antiquity of the townland network, a comparison of the 1660 barony returns, with their respective townland densities for the adjacent counties of Clare and Roscommon, suggests that such an exercise is reasonably predictive (± 0–5 per cent) of 1660 population distributions.[12] Use of denominational proportions from the Books of Survey and Distribution would appear to understate the population densities of the more accessible modernizing baronies, while overstating those for the less urbanized, more remote territories. In short, the townland densities antedate the shifts in population consequent upon rapid economic developments in the late sixteenth- and especially the first half of seventeenth-century Ireland. The estimates are, therefore, further modified to take account of the urban populations of specific baronies. The patterns suggested for the missing baronies in counties Cork and Meath are more robust and are based on evidence from the Civil Survey, Books of Survey and Distribution and other taxation details from the 1660s.[13]

The mid-seventeenth-century population patterns are dominated by a number of maritime regions, each interwoven with its own distinctive array of outside connections (see Fig. 6.1). The Pale region – with a salient westwards into Westmeath – stands out as the zone of highest population density. Dominated by the needs of the expanding capital of Dublin (and those of England beyond), this mixed-farming/tillage region of north Leinster was full of market towns, mills, castles, stone houses, weirs, roads and bridges – in short, a well-furnished economic region.[14] Co. Meath's status in this region is well documented, its market towns and diversified agricultural economy of commercial grain, sheep and cow/cattle production focused on the port-city of Drogheda. Indeed, rural population densities are often twice as high as they were either before or after the Great Famine.

Between the Midland bogs and the hills and woods of the Wexford/Wicklow borderlands, the upper Liffey and Barrow valleys form a bridgehead into a second region of population concentration along the riverine lowlands of the southeast. Here, under the long-standing patronage of the Butler lordship and pivoting around the port-city of Waterford, substantial rural communities and solid inland towns had crystallized along the navigable waterways of the Nore, Suir and Barrow. Kilkenny is the anchor county here, its tillage economy specializing in rotations of winter and spring grain.[15] On the western side, south Tipperary had

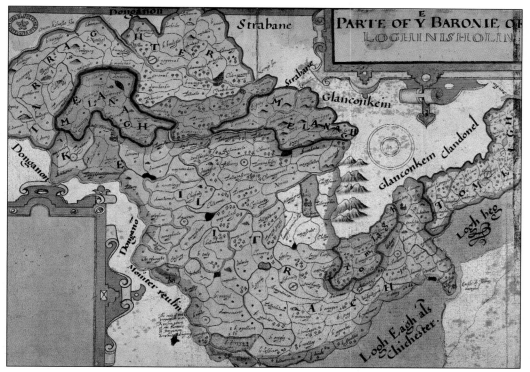

Plate 2a, fig. 3.3 Example of Bodley survey for barony of Loughinsholin, 1610 (Co. Londonderry). By permission of Public Record Office, London (MPF 47).

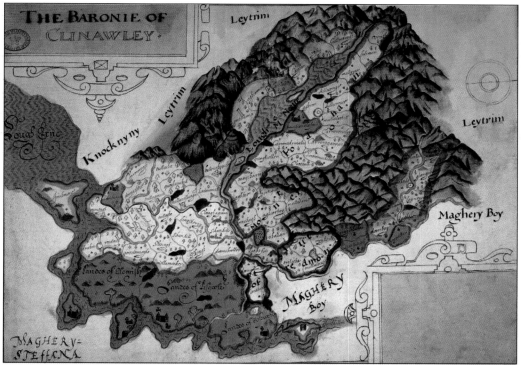

Plate 2b, fig. 3.4 Example of the Bodley survey for barony of Clanawley, 1610 (Co. Fermanagh). By permission of the Public Record Office, London (MPF 4).

Plate 2c, fig. 3.7 Tates/townlands of the barony of Clankelly, 1610 (Co. Fermanagh). By permission of the Public Record Office, London (MPF 45).

Plate 2d, fig. 3.8 Ballyboes/townlands of the (part) barony of Dungannon, 1610 (Co. Tyrone). By permission of the Public Record Office, London, (MPF 45).

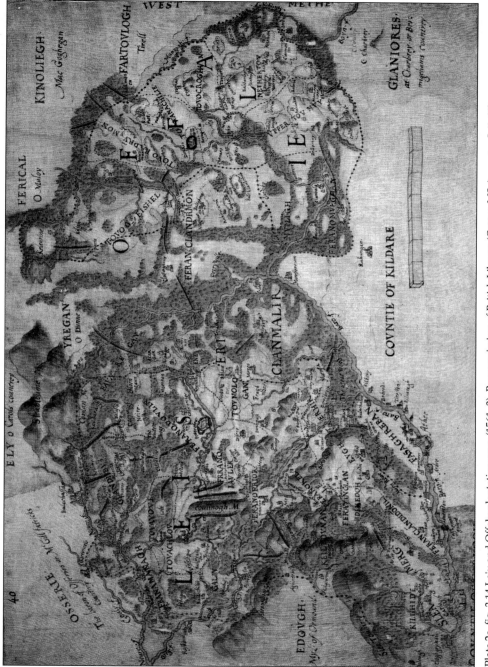

Plate 2e, fig. 3.14 Leix and Offaly plantation map (1561–3). By permission of British Library (Cotton MS Augustus I. ii. 40).

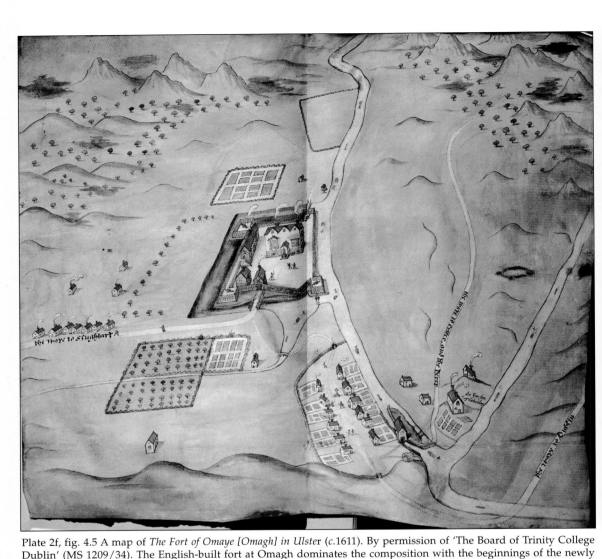

Plate 2f, fig. 4.5 A map of *The Fort of Omaye [Omagh] in Ulste*r (c.1611). By permission of 'The Board of Trinity College Dublin' (MS 1209/34). The English-built fort at Omagh dominates the composition with the beginnings of the newly incorporated and enclosed town/main street of Omagh shown to the south of the Elizabethan fort. This fort in turn had supplanted the Irish power-centre of the *Sliocht Airt Uí Néill*. The broken remnant of the stone tower-house of the O'Neill *uirrí* is shown near the island bridging point close to the mill and the inn, the key junction-point of rivers and roads that had long made Omagh an important central place. Here is the key meeting place of the fish-abounding rivers of the Camowen, and the Drumragh to the south, tributaries feeding into the River Strule which (beyond the map) joins the River Foyle to the north. Omagh is shown as the centre of an old road system that drives eastwards to Dublin via Dungannon and Armagh, northwards to 'Liffer and Derry' and westwards via Slught-art on to Castlederg. However, the most striking feature is the regularity and order of the built/designed-world at the centre – the strong fort with its bastions and cannons, the substantial Governor's house, the geometric tree-plantations and recreation ground, and the emphasis on well-bulit 'chimneyed' English houses with their neat gardens and enclosures – all symbols of the English-mode of possessing, commanding and occupying new territory. Armed soldiers and busy settlers populate the centre. In sharp contrast is the emptiness of the surrounding unnamed townlands (of Lisnamallard, Gortmore, Killybrack, Dergmoney and others beyond) which may be said to signify the 'emptying' of the power of the Art O'Neills and their lineage. On the edges are irregular strands of woodland bordering the foothills of the mountainous territories of Mid- and West Tyrone, suggesting another world both different to and remote from the emphasis on the new order and rule at the centre.

Plate 2g, fig. 5.1 Portrait of the younger William Petty by Isaac Fuller. By permission of the National Portrait Gallery, London.

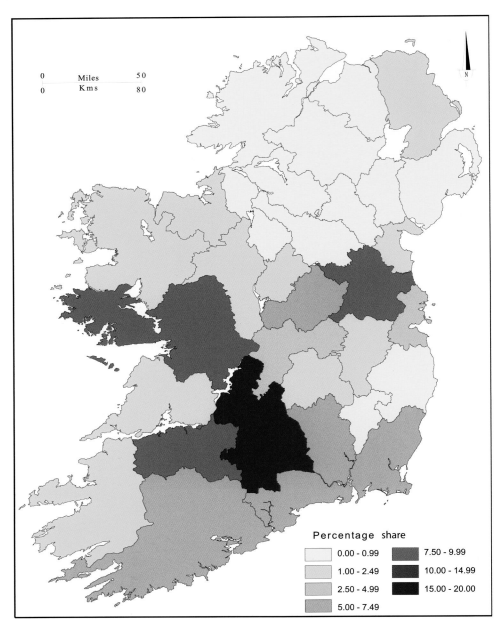

Percentage share

0.00 - 0.99	7.50 - 9.99
1.00 - 2.49	10.00 - 14.99
2.50 - 4.99	15.00 - 20.00
5.00 - 7.49	

Plate 2h, fig. 5.8 Geographical origins of the Catholic Irish transplanters obliged either to move to Connacht or to another county within that province (source: as in 5.7(a)).

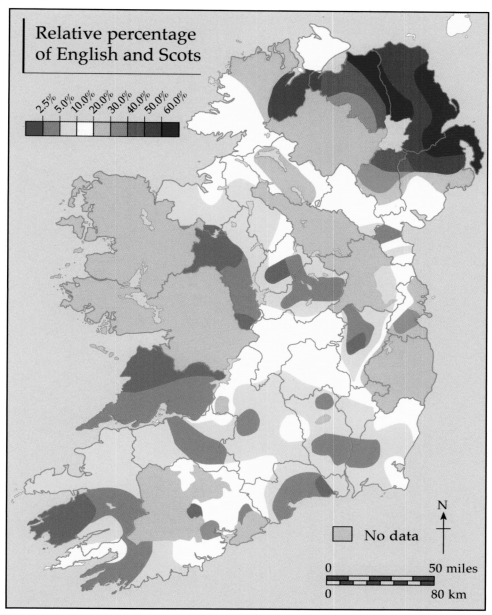

Plate 2i, fig. 6.6 Relative distribution of 'English/Scots' in 1660 (reproduced from *Atlas of the Irish Rural Landscape*, figure 44, p 25).

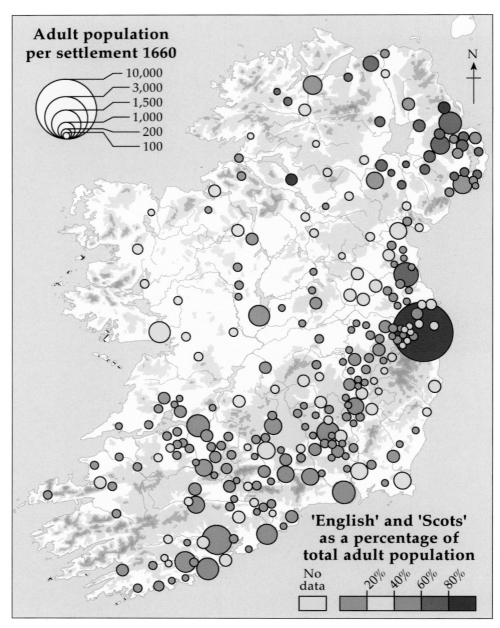

Adult population per settlement 1660

— 10,000
— 3,000
— 1,500
— 1,000
— 200
— 100

N

'English' and 'Scots' as a percentage of total adult population

No data

20% 40% 60% 80%

Plate 2j, fig. 6.7 Distribution, size and ethnic composition of cities and towns, *c.*1660 (reproduced from *Atlas of the Irish Rural Landscape*, figure 12, p. 185).

Plate 2k, fig. 8.8 Portrait of James Butler, First Duke of Ormonde by Peter Lely.

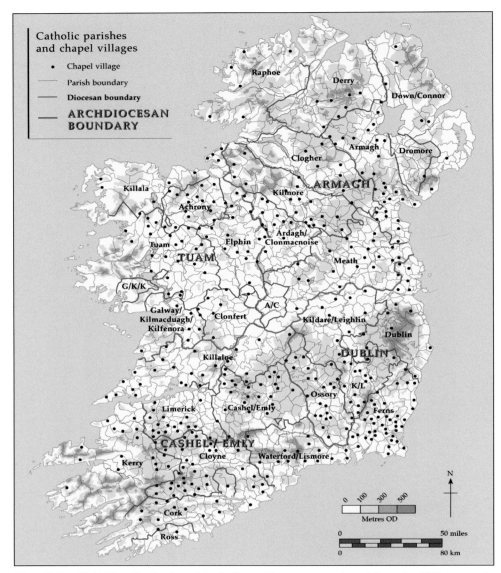

Catholic parishes
and chapel villages
- • Chapel village
- —— Parish boundary
- —— Diocesan boundary
- —— **ARCHDIOCESAN
BOUNDARY**

Raphoe

Derry

Down/Connor

Armagh

Clogher

Dromore

Killala

Kilmore

ARMAGH

Achrony

Ardagh/
Clonmacnoise

Tuam

Elphin

Meath

TUAM

G/K/K

A/C

Galway/
Kilmacduagh/
Kilfenora

Clonfert

Kildare/Leighlin

Dublin

DUBLIN

Killaloe

Ossory

K/L

Limerick

Cashel/Emly

Ferns

CASHEL / EMLY

Kerry

Cloyne

Waterford/Lismore

N

Cork

0 100 300 500
Metres OD

Ross

0   50 miles
0   80 km

Plate 2l, fig. 10.11 The distribution of Catholic parishes as reconstituted from the 1650s onwards
(reproduced from the original in the *Atlas of the Irish Rural Landscape*, Figure 30, p. 194).

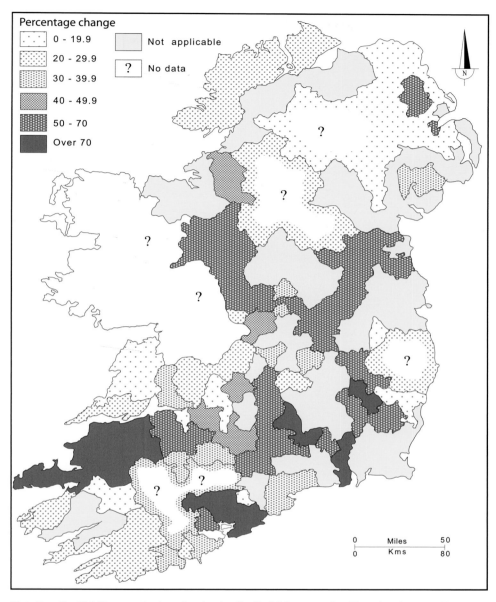

Plate 2m, fig. 11.2 Patterns in the adoption by Gaelic Irish gentry families of mainsteam European first/Christian names (*c.* 1660).

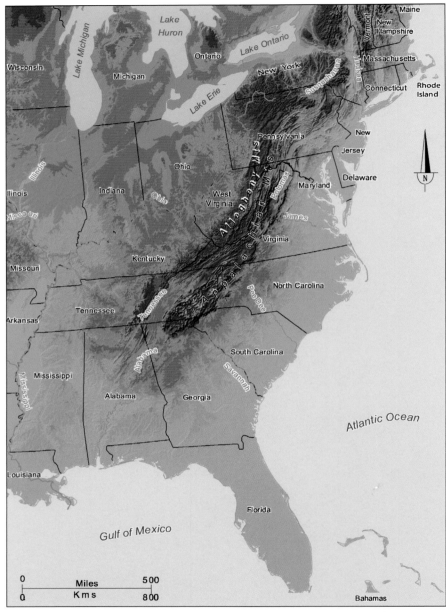

Plate 2n, fig. 12.1 Eastern North America: main physiographic features (courtesy of U.S. Geological Survey and U.S. Census).

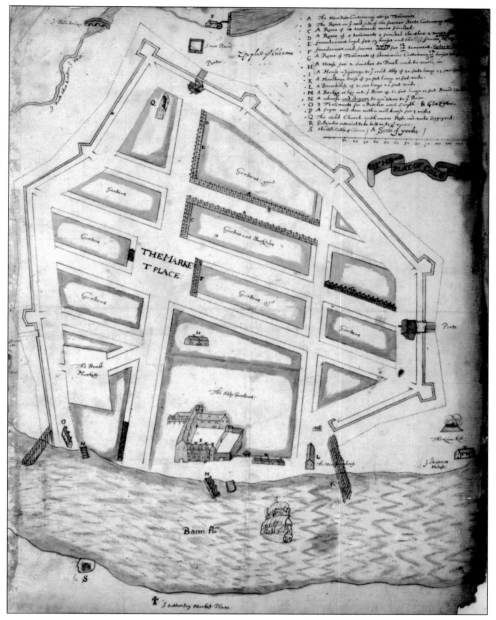

Plate 2o, fig. 12.3 (a) 'The Plat of Coleraine' *c.* 1611. Reproduced with the permission of 'The Board of Trinity College Dublin' (MS 1209/24).

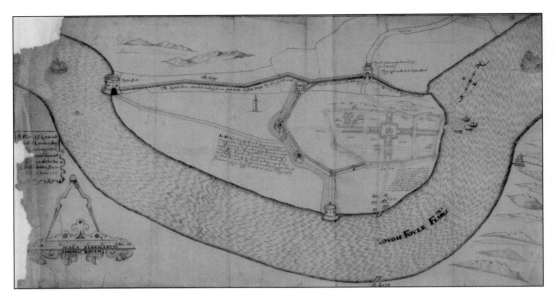

Plate 2o, fig. 12.3 (b) River Foyle and City of Londonderry, 1625, by Thomas Raven. Reproduced with the permission of 'The Board of Trinity College Dublin' (MS 1209.24*).

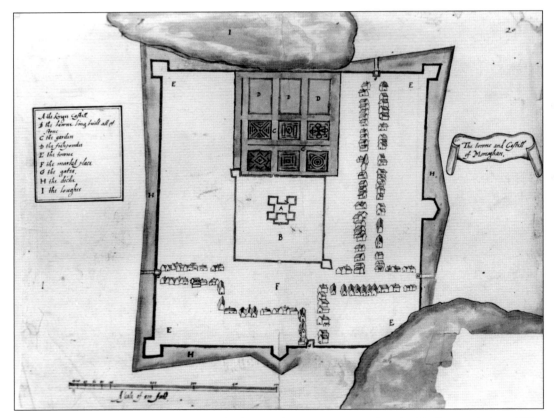

Plate 2o, fig. 12.3 (c) The Towne and Castell of Monoghan, *c.* 1611. Reproduced with the permission of 'The Board of Trinity College Dublin'.

Plate 2p. fig. 12.8a View of Stradbally House and Gardens (Anonymous). (Private Collection): Photographic Survey, Courtauld Institute of Art. This painting provides a bird's eye, almost cartographic, view of the landscape of the Big House – in this case Stradbally Hall, Co. Laois – and the adjacent landlord village of Stradbally. It provides a fine example of the classical geometric style of Big House landscape design of the early decades of the eighteenth century. The avenue and bridge to the front and the long sweeping vista to the rear were laid out in 1714 while the elaborate waterscapes are even earlier. The axial design of the long avenues emphasise the centrality and power of the Big House and its landlord – in this case Mr Cosby who is seen arriving by coach and six horses at the bottom right of the painting. At a respectable distance from, yet intimately aligned with the Big House is the redesigned linear village of Stradbally with its market house and square, estate-workers and shopkeepers. On the horizon is shown the ancient but now defunct O'More stronghold of Dunamase. Indeed Stradbally stands in the heartland of the historic territory of the O'Mores of Laois. An O'More founded a Franciscan friary here in 1447. Captain Francis Cosby – seneschal of Queen's County – made a large house out of this friary after being granted these O'More lands in the Laois-Offaly plantation. The 1740s painting, therefore, depicts the 'modernising' triumphant landscape of landlordism superimposed on this old Gaelic territory despite the stiff and persistent resistance by generations of the O'Mores to the earlier and resilient plantation settlement.

Plate 2p, fig. 12.8b State Ball at Dublin Castle in 1731 by William van der Hagen (Private Collection). In the spacious and elegant surroundings of the most prestigious site of Irish administration, with its ornate ceilings, classic pillars, obelisks, paintings and glittering chandeliers, the Lord Lieutenant and his distinctively attired Lady surrounded by members of the Privy Council and Kings Bench initiate the ritual of the ball. The fashion and style of the European court is a dominant motif. In the foreground, flanked by the protective shield of ceremonial guards, the bewigged male members of the establishment in all their English and French silk finery move freely about, conversing and discussing business while a great tiered array of females sit with arms folded, looking on at the proceedings. This space of representation thus epitomises the realisation of the apex of achievement by members of the new Protestant Ascendancy in Ireland. This highly structured, elitist and gendered social space was mirrored in microcosm all over the island by the Big House and its world of elegance and exclusion. It was in the same year of 1731 that the Irish House of Lords – aware of concerns about the growing development of Catholic Church structures – established a survey of 'the State of Popery' all over the island.

also a sheep and cattle economy, while the use of the territorial term 'martlands' in Carlow/north Wexford signals the prevalence of cattle in this commercializing mixed-farming region. The remainder of Wexford was also a tillage land special- izing in summer corn, while the southern halves of Laois and Kildare were also active in mixed-farming/arable enterprises.

The power of the Munster province is further revealed by the port-dominated regions of Cork and Limerick. The sea-enriched baronies on each side of Cork harbour underpinned the agricultural surpluses – especially of grain – that found their way to the growing city of Cork and the still vibrant ports of Kinsale and Youghal. Figure 6.1 also identifies the labour-intensive granary lands of 'Roche's country' in mid-Cork. The wider Cork hinterland – now geared to dairying and cattle production for the growing Atlantic economy – is linked by Kilmallock to the Limerick port region. This core area has positively affected the fortunes and populations of south and east Clare – indeed, Clare as a whole benefited from its sandwich location between the late medieval 'city-states' of Galway and Limerick. Gernon's description of Limerick villages with their haggards stacked with corn captures the density of life in these lime-rich Munster lowlands.[16]

The city of Galway, looking out to the Atlantic and the Iberian world, shows up as more isolated, a weaker (and weakening) axis of population concentration in the west. On the other hand, the solidity of the settlement of mid and south Galway should not be overlooked. The map underestimates the quality of the land stretch- ing northwards from Ballinrobe, through to the Moy valley and curving eastwards to embrace the relatively well-developed coastal hinterland of Sligo. The early seventeenth-century spread of both new and refurbished market foundations high- lights the penetration of commercial forces into this western region.[17]

The most striking changes from the late medieval pattern of population concen- trations emerge in the northeast. An embryonic core of planter settlement and economic power is already consolidating in a triangular region between north Down, Armagh city and Coleraine. Arable, mixed-farming and pastoral zones had emerged in this area, where a new urban network had cemented economic and cultural links with Scotland and northern England. A secondary core is emerging around the city of Derry and east Donegal, with salients of further development indicated along the Bann valley, fanning southwestwards through the Monaghan corridor into the hearthlands of counties Cavan and Fermanagh.

Between the most densely populated maritime regions and the areas of sparsest and least stratified populations, a number of transitional areas can be identified. Co. Wexford exhibits an enduring trinity of regional qualities. There is the frag- mented, crowded tillage lands of Bargy and Forth, described in harvest-time as looking like 'a well-cultivated garden'.[18] There is the mixed-farming middle zone with its moated sites and placenames pointing to its marchland hybrid character. North Wexford, in turn, forms part of a pastoral wooded region incorporating much of Wicklow and the adjacent borderlands of Carlow and Kildare – once resilient Gaelic territories, now deeply disturbed by the wars, famine and ongoing successful planter colonization. The less disturbed grazing hearthland of na Déise (Decies barony) in west Waterford emerges clearly. Equally emphatic is the woodland/bogland core of the Gaelic and gaelicized Midlands. To the west its borderlands extend into north Tipperary and the southern flanks of Co. West-meath. The pastoral areas of north Clare, north Galway and much of Roscommon and Leitrim appear as areas of similar status. Finally, a wide crescent of territory with moderate to low population densities – in lands which yielded 'very little grane without much store of manure and labour'[19] – curves from south Down across the broken drumlin country of south Ulster and swings northwards again to embrace part of Derry and all of Inishowen.

The far west region emerges as distinctively in the mid-seventeenth century as it does in the mid-nineteenth century, but for different reasons. Its areas (with the greatest densities on T.W. Freeman's pre-Famine population maps) are often the least densely settled parts of mid-seventeenth-century Ireland.[20] Much of Kerry (with a core in the Iveragh peninsula) and Mayo, west Clare and west Galway were then the least populated parts of the moist Atlantic peripheries of northwest Europe. The Sligo/Galway/Roscommon and Longford/Leitrim/Cavan border-lands, and west Donegal and its inland extension into the Sperrins of Tyrone also belong to this world. Jones Hughes has noted that most of these areas 'only experi-enced close and permanent settlement by farming people at a very late date and these late colonisers were probably evicted from adjoining more desirable regions'.[21] As the seventeenth-century evidence confirms, the great centres of stable enduring rural cultures in Ireland were not in these far western lands.

In summary, violent contrasts and subtle gradations characterize the picture of population densities and levels of economic development in mid-seventeenth-century Ireland. The inclusion of county boundaries in Figure 6.1 highlights the internal contrasts even within single counties. In Co. Cork, for example, population densities were probably eight times as great in coastal Imokilly as inland Duhal-low. North Co. Dublin had ten times the rural densities of west Donegal. Other sources reveal the extent to which practically all the townlands of counties Limer-ick and Kilkenny were already intensively settled and cultivated, whereas around two-fifths of the townlands in counties Clare and Roscommon were still not permanently settled.[22] Such lands were to provide opportunities for later coloniza-tion and settlement but they then formed part of a world where the permanently settled lowland communities exercised seasonal rights over extensive upland and wetland territories.[23]

Territorial polarizations and gradations in the distribution of Irish family names has much to tell us about deep-seated regionalisms in Irish life.[24] The poll-tax listing of the most important Irish family names for each barony allows for the mapping of the relative distribution of Gaelic and Old English names. It also permits the exploration of relationships between population densities, social structures and cultural backgrounds. Apart from the northeast, Fig. 6.2 confirms the correspondence between the zones of highest population density and the areas of enduring Anglo-Norman and mixed Norman-Gaelic settlement.[25] The Old English Pale area emerges again but in this case apparently more Boyne-valley-based. As with the big farms of the nineteenth century,[26] the strength of the population with Gaelic names over much of Louth, south Meath, Dublin and

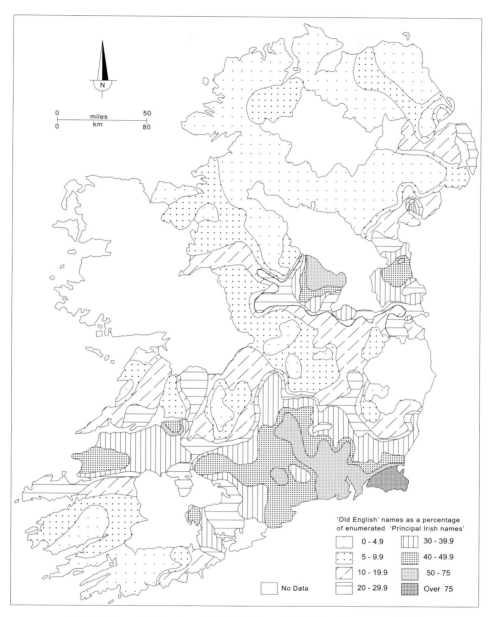

6.2   Relative distribution of Old English and Gaelic family names *c.*1660

particularly Kildare is striking. The mid-seventeenth-century evidence also establishes the spread of medieval settlement and culture in southeast Ireland. Outside of the northwest and the southwest of the province, Figure 6.2 emphasizes the strength of Norman naming patterns over Munster. But what the map does not reveal is the infinitely subtle gradations in the rendering of the same Anglo-Norman names as they work their way inland and westwards into such gaelicized lands as north Kerry, not to speak of the naming and cultural permutations that characterize Connacht.

The strength of the Gaelic tradition so close to Cork city is a feature of Figure 6.2. The Gaelic hearthland of the southwest is as clear and as extensive in 1660 as it was in 1260. The introverted Gaelic hearthland of Laois-Offaly and its border-lands stands out, as does the weak Norman imprint in the wetter lands of northeast Connacht, in north Longford and all of Ulster, outside of east Down and Antrim. The map confirms the hybrid areas in Irish culture where the most coveted lands were fought over by Norman and Gael and where the deepest levels of assimilation between the two traditions emerged.[27] East and north Cork, north Kerry, most of Limerick, much of mid-Tipperary and Laois belong to this 'middle nation', as do all the lands bordering the north Leinster core of Anglo-Norman settlement. Figure 6.2 also suggests the regional diversity, demographic power and resilience of these Old English worlds in the first half of seventeenth-century Ireland. Flexible in lifestyle and language, the Old English were still skilful enough to hold onto and indeed expand their control of key properties and posi-tions until the traumas of the Confederate War and the Cromwellian settlement stripped them of the material bases for their distinctive culture and ideology.[28]

Population and family naming patterns derived from this poll-tax evidence strikingly mirror Kenneth Nicholls's map of Irish lordships in 1534.[29] While the political superstructures had changed between 1534 and 1660, the poll-tax reveals the surviving substrata. The ancient marchland from Cooley to Athlone and beyond, the solidity of the Gaelic societies of the Midlands, southeast Lein-ster and southwest Munster and the relatively autonomous society of the O'Brien lordship in Clare all recur. The absence of details for counties Galway and Mayo in 1660 is a great loss – these too, if available, would likely reveal the enduring character of the gaelicized Norman heritage of south and middle Galway and the lowland hearthland of Mayo. But what the lordship and poll-tax patterns most clearly suggest for late medieval Ireland is the fusion of a number of relatively powerful port-centred economic regions with the administrative/political super-structures of the great lordships. Beyond these core territories were the rural-based, less stratified and generally (though not invariably) smaller political lordships.[30]

Settlement, Society and Status

By 1660 the poll-tax reveals that an English legal and administrative network had been thrown across the whole island. The power bases of all the lordships have been dismantled, as the now universal superstructure of counties dominate the scene. While the barony and the parish were the next two levels below the county, the smallest administrative, fiscal and landholding unit of all was the townland. One of the great attractions of the 1660 poll-tax is the emergence, for the first time in Irish history, of a picture of the population structure at the townland level all over the island. English power to rule, tax and count had by now penetrated to this fundamental level. This 1659 Census document also provides us with a legacy of the placenames as they were rendered in the mid-seventeenth century.[31] The poll-tax figures thus allow us to probe more deeply into the patterns of settlement and social stratification at this the most intimate of scales, while also indicating the relevance of parochial, baronial and county structures in a study of the settlement and social hierarchy.

Combined with an analysis of materials from counties Kilkenny, Limerick and Meath, a detailed survey of all the available mid-seventeenth-century evidence for Co. Tipperary[32] suggests a threefold classification of 1660 townland population returns. The small minority of very extensive and essentially rural townlands in Co. Tipperary that return adult populations in excess of 40 are exceptional. Clearly, large townland size does not necessarily mean bigger townland populations.[33] However, it will be demonstrated that in 1660 at least three-quarters of Co. Tipperary's townlands with an adult population of 40 or over (that is, a total population of 120 and over) did contain nucleated settlements in the mid-seventeenth century (see chapter 9). Such settlements housed more complex social structures – comprising servant, artisan, farming and service populations, as well as lay and/or ecclesiastical elites. It is more difficult to make as clear a statement about the settlement characteristics of townlands with adult populations of 20–49 (total 60–119) but at least half of these townlands in Co. Tipperary then hosted nucleated or agglomerated settlements. With some exceptions, townlands with less than 20 and particularly less than 10 adults were clearly not as diversified in social and institutional structures – irrespective of whether their settlement form was clustered or scattered.

Correlation of settlement details from the Down Survey parish maps for the barony of Crannagh in Co. Kilkenny with the 1660 poll-tax returns confirms the above patterns.[34] All of the barony's mapped townlands with adult populations over 40 were characterized by more complex nucleated settlements, usually comprising both a church and a castle; the great majority of mapped townlands with an adult population of 20–49 had at least one nucleating element at the centre of the settlement and that was usually a castle/tower-house. In contrast, only one of the six townlands containing clustered settlements and an adult population of 10 or less exhibited any such institutional foci. Recent aerial photographic work has confirmed the deserted status of many of these seventeenth-century settlement foci in counties Tipperary and Kilkenny, while Jack Burtchaell has clearly demonstrated the exceptional combination of forces that allowed for an almost identical range of nucleated and clustered settlements to perpetuate themselves in the southern baronies of Co. Kilkenny.[35]

It is also worth noting that three-quarters of the nucleated settlements identified by Patrick O'Connor in his work on the Civil Survey for Co. Limerick, and whose populations can be confirmed in 1660, reveal adult populations in excess of 40.[36] Indeed, it is no coincidence that 80 per cent of all townlands with like populations in the barony of Clanwilliam contain tower-houses and/or churches, a pattern that can be confirmed for the baronies of Coshlea, Coonagh, Kenry, and Small County.[37] The combined evidence from Co. Meath's Civil Survey and Down Survey and additional information from the Edward Roberts 1659 estate maps all confirm a settlement and social hierarchy for the baronies of Duleek, Skreen and Ratoath that is clearly replicated in the 1660 poll-tax returns.[38]

The following analysis is, therefore, based on the twin assumptions: (i) that the bigger the townland population returns, the greater the possibility of a more stratified population; and (ii) the greater the likelihood that at least some of that population lived in a more nucleated as opposed to a more scattered form of settlement. It should also be pointed out that wherever the poll-tax returns only one population figure for two or more named townlands, it is assumed for the purposes of this analysis that more than one settlement is involved. Using these assumptions, my strategy here is to provide general clues to island-wide variations in social and settlement hierarchies. Detailed local studies would be required to examine all the local intricacies of society and settlement of the period.

Figure 6.3 indicates the relative distribution of townlands returning 40 adults or more, that is, a total townland population of over 120 in 1660. Co. Tipperary, for example, exhibits three distinct patterns of townland population size. In the southeastern baronies of the county, well over 20 per cent of the total number of townlands had populations in excess of 120. Here, in the best and historically the most secure land in the county, with a good communications network by road and river to Waterford port, a dense network of substantial market towns and a compact 'manorialized' property structure dominated in 1641 by individual landowners of Anglo-Norman descent.[39] These lorded over a zone of commercialized mixed-farming specializing in wheat, barley and sheep production. The bigger townland populations in this region were, therefore, strongly related to an arable-intensive economy, where labourers, artisans and other service classes underpinned a complex settlement and social hierarchy. The more pastoral upland barony of Slieveardagh on the borders of Co. Kilkenny was still emphatically village-dominated, whether these 'villages' were farm clusters, mill-hamlets, castle-hamlets or church-hamlets, fully blown manorial centres or small market/fair towns.[40] This Tipperary region supported vibrant parish centres, although absentee landlordism and the earlier spread of sheep farming had already left a number of 'lost/deserted villages' in their wake.

Southeast Tipperary was on the western edge of a wider belt of high farming and a developed settlement and social hierarchy that had matured in a time of feudalized centralization – where a manorial village economy, substantial farmers, markets, mills, fairs and towns were long-standing features of the society. The central hearthland of Kilkenny county was part of this world, as were the rich tillage lands of the Barrow and the village-studded lands of east Co. Kildare and south Co. Dublin. This was the nuclear area of large settlements, often still set amongst open fields long nurtured by the industrious hand of the laborious husbandman. A core area in south and mid Co. Louth was equally an essentially medieval landscape of villages and associated farm clusters. The Boyne valley might also be interpreted as another great spine of settlement nucleation.[41] This, therefore, was not only a society of gentry, farmers and merchants but – as other census evidence indicates – also of labourers, ploughmen, husbandmen, cowmen, horseboys, smiths and weavers and even its smaller towns had their maltsters,

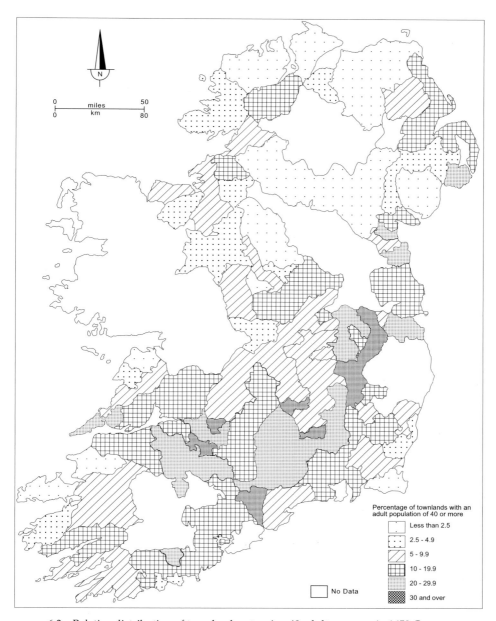

6.3   Relative distribution of townlands returning 40 adults or more in 1659 Census

millers, tanners, butchers and innkeepers.[42] The nuclear area of Leinster is further revealed by a consideration of the distribution of townlands with over 20 adults (60 people or more): in south Kildare and north Carlow, over 60 per cent of all townlands contain such levels of population concentration and there is a broad belt of territory stretching from west Dublin beyond north Kildare and stretching into the southern parts of Laois and most of Kilkenny where well over 50 per cent of townlands are in this category – as they are in most of Co. Louth. This Leinster core region is therefore outstanding in settlement terms in 1660.

On the southwestern flanks of Co. Tipperary, west Waterford also has a strong pattern of villages and towns – an older nucleated pattern here is strongly augmented by New English planters and immigrant craftsmen in the ironworking settlements and the refurbished towns. North Cork and much of east Limerick were also studded with a hierarchy of towns and villages. O'Connor has given a conservative estimate of 65 nucleated villages for Co. Limerick.[43] Given its great density of tower-houses and their often adjacent house clusters, one is not too surprised to find that east and mid-Limerick emerges with one of the most elaborate settlement hierarchies in the whole country, full of what the Civil Survey describes as 'Irish Townes'. Plantation processes clearly intensified this settlement hierarchy. Outliers of these high density settlement patterns included the diverse regions of peninsular Moyarta in Clare, coastal Imokilly and inland Kinalmeaky in Co. Cork.

At the other end of Tipperary, in the lakeland/midland baronies of Owney and Arra and the two Ormonds, a weak nucleated settlement pattern is evident in this region long dominated by Gaelic lords. This mosaic of lowland, bogland, woodland and hills was on the margins of a commercialized economy in the seventeenth, as in the nineteenth century. Remoteness, the lack of an urban hierarchy, the fragmentation of landownership patterns in a more Gaelic world, the dominance of a pastoral economy in what is often 'small oats and cow country', and the scattering of a wide range of institutional foci (churches, castles and mills) in different townlands within single parishes – all had combined to produce a more dispersed, less stratified and less populous settlement pattern. Under 10 per cent of these denominations held populations in excess of 120. The dispersal of population here often involved the scattering of communities within and between townlands in small clusters of two, three or four houses.

The Gaelic or gaelicized lands of na Déise, west Cork, south and mid-Kerry also reflect similar processes. Northwards from the Ormond lowlands in Tipperary, a wide belt of equivalent settlement and population structures dominate the wet Midlands on each side of the Shannon with an even more emphatic levelling off in townland populations in Garrycastle (Offaly), north Roscommon, south Sligo and south Donegal. Apart from coastal and southern Galway and a relatively narrow strip through central and coastal Mayo, it is likely that similar patterns prevail over the rest of Connacht – as they clearly did in northwest Clare. On the other hand, many of these same baronies emerge with over 30 per cent of townlands with adult populations in excess of 20. For example, the status of Rathvilly and Forth in Carlow and Scarawalsh and Bantry in Wexford – significantly located on the borders of the rich south Leinster spine of nucleation – is seen to be strongly enhanced at this level, as are the other parts of Munster named above. Likewise, the southern halves of Longford and Roscommon emerge as areas with quite a number of lower order settlements, as do the baronies of Beara in Cork, Tireragh in Sligo and Tirhugh in Donegal. The boost in the settlement structures of these coastal baronies reflects the importance of the sea for fishing, coastal trading and the enhancing of the productivity of the coastal lands in general. The recent upsurge in ironworks and forges produced an additional widespread boost to local settlement structures.

Co. Tipperary has a third important region of moderate population densities, where from 10 to 19 per cent of townland populations exceed 120 and where over 40 per cent exceed 60. This middle band of settlement is in a zone of mixed ecology containing much good land but also some hill, wood and bogland. It is also a zone of old and newly emerging towns where mixed-farming, a mixed settlement structure and a mixed ethnic heritage are evident. Much of Co. Meath appears to belong to this hybrid zone as well. Here a very mixed farming economy sustained over 90 manorial villages, 45 castle-hamlets or 'fortified clusters', over 50 non-fortified farm clusters, as well as a substantial number of solid independent farmsteads.[44]

Figure 6.3 suggests that parts of north Kerry and west Limerick, the southern half of Co. Clare, some baronies in south and north Kilkenny, much of Laois and indeed all the baronies bordering the dominant core of settlement along the Barrow and the Liffey are characterized by similar mixtures of settlement. The Down Survey parish maps for the barony of Crannagh in Co. Kilkenny reveal the complex array of nucleated settlement items that characterize this plateau-interfluve country west of Kilkenny city. The axis of a moderately well-developed settlement hierarchy also extends westwards through Co. Westmeath and north-ward to the Cooley peninsula. Further north a combination of medieval and planter settlement boosts the settlement structures of parts of east Antrim and east Donegal. The old settled baronies of Ards and Lecale are also on the edges of this wider settlement region, whose rhythms and lifestyles seem to belong more to a southeastern than a northwestern culture world. All the evidence from the late sixteenth and early seventeenth centuries suggests a greater integration of these hybrid zones with the revitalized (if short-lived) centres of Old English power.

The seventeenth-century settlement evidence suggests that a dialectic exists between the cultures of the northern and southern halves of Ireland.[45] Stretching north of one of the oldest and most persistent territorial divides in Ireland, the poll-tax evidence identifies this final settlement region, which stretches north of a line from the Cooley peninsula to the Cavan/Meath borders, through mid-Longford and mid-Roscommon to reach the sea around Clew Bay. Exclusive of the few coastal foci discussed already, this region was profoundly characterized in 1660 by a scattering of settlements and societies. The few glimpses we get of the local rural societies from the early hearth-money records[46] also suggest a much less stratified population – it was a society of farmers, labourers, herds, shepherds, carpenters and rabbit-catchers. The historical absence of a nucleated settlement tradition is made starker in this zone of rapid and recent urbanization. This essentially Gaelic, pastoral, and subsistence world sustained the most integrated territorial hierar-chies in Ireland until the turn of the seventeenth century – stretching seamlessly from the greater and lesser lordship through the ballybetagh to the ballyboe or its equivalent at the base. These kin-centred structures were broken only by the plan-tations of Ulster.[47] Then, such corporate sept estates – with partible inheritance and the regular redistribution of townlands as central features – were stripped down and recombined into the indivisible, commercially oriented, manorial estates of the new landowners. A private property system was now married to old territorial frameworks.

The surviving Civil Survey and Down Survey for Ulster baronies regularly stress that 'a few creaghts [cabins] are scattered about ye said parish' and in some instances they note that a parish contains no buildings but 'removable creaghts' for 'the Irish inhabitants always lived in creaghts which they remove from place to place to enrich the small plots of arable for tillage' (Orior, Armagh).[48] The barony description for Orior is also instructive: 'The soil is good for breeding cattle and corn and steeds but not for sheep and there is but a small part thereof that yields any kinds of grane and not without good store of industry and labour because the land is very strong, the unforfeited part is in the plain and is much better land.' In the drumlin country of the parish of Creggan in the Fews, the description notes that 'the Curroghs' (meadowlands) encircle 'the small hills wherein natives live'. Patrick Duffy's interpretation of Raven's maps for south Monaghan captures most of the essential features of the settlement pattern in this broader region:

> the poor clustered hamlets reflect the Gaelic mode of settlement in the shadows of the residual pattern of rath settlements . . . The peripheral mills presumably reflect the comparatively marginal impact of a grain economy . . . The intrusive landscape element was represented principally by the embryonic form of Carrickmacross town . . . the links between the little town and the surrounding countryside were presumably slight, represented mainly by a few country houses belonging to English undertakers.[49]

The relatively sparsely distributed residences (some few of stone) of the local lords had been important foci for larger settlements here. Yet in this region, which had never experienced a deep integration into a feudalized European economy (as much of the south and east had), it is striking how sacred places – parish or diocesan centres, monasteries, nunneries or abbeys – acted as the gathering points for peoples and settlements in this northern region where Church land was more extensive and less subject to secular control than elsewhere.

On a broader front, Figure 6.3 cannot reveal the rather different forces making for nucleation further south. In the Pale area and in north and mid-Leinster generally, the roots of a richer village culture may have been older, deeper and more strongly based on a tillage economy. The patterns of nucleation in the tower-house-studded lands of southwest Leinster, all of Munster and south Galway may have been more complex, in some cases more recent, and almost certainly had more to do with the growth of a commercialized mixed stock-rearing/arable economy in the later medieval period.

Likewise, Figure 6.3 cannot highlight the expanding zones of big independent farmsteads in the hinterlands of the port-cities and towns. The barony of Gaultier in east Waterford was a land of scattered, slated and chimneyed farm-houses;[50] and other Civil Survey evidence points to the existence of large independent farms in the Clonmel, Cashel and Kilkenny hinterlands. Similarly, a belt of individualistic farming in Co. Dublin radiated into the eastern half of Co. Meath. East Ulster too – and certainly the Bangor and Holywood areas – was full of substantial individual farms worked by planter tenants.[51] This latter pattern was likely based on pre-plantation settlement and landholding arrangements. Thus, the oldest and newest forces were pointing to a radical restructuring of society and settlement.

In short, the poll-tax evidence on population suggests: first, areas where ancient settlement and social structures were on the retreat; second, it pinpoints a number of regions with a mixed and resilient character; and third, it indicates other regions where new processes were emerging that were eventually to dominate the modern settlement framework. Crucial figures in the remodelling process were the planter landowners and merchants who likely saw Ireland as part of a dynamic frontier for both individual economic gain and wider colonial expansion.

Planters, Property and Power

Ownership and control of property was the central anchor of economic and political power in seventeenth-century Ireland. Property units were, therefore, critical territorial frameworks for shaping the location and character of human activities. The poll-tax allows us to identify and locate both the most prestigious people in the island – the so-called *tituladoes* – and to explore the relationship between these resident elites and the development of patterns of colonization and settlement hierarchies. The *tituladoe* entries are almost certainly a listing of the people who were able or were obliged to pay the highest taxes. Apart from the cities and towns, where merchants, army officers, members of the professions and borough officeholders are conspicious, the listing for the baronies is generally dominated by the leading landowners (and in some cases leading leaseholders) who are returned for the townland of their residence. A preliminary comparison of this list with the hearth-money, subsidy or other lists for counties Clare, Tipperary, Waterford and Armagh [52] confirms the relative reliability of these entries. On the other hand, for example, the lists for the baronies of north Longford, Louth and Monaghan still appear somewhat defective. Detailed local studies are necessary to tease out the full implications of these *tituladoe* entries.

As a crude measure of the distribution of the wealthiest and most powerful people – and hence the most stratified and privileged societies and landscapes in the country – the proportion of *tituladoes* per adult population in each barony was assessed (see Fig. 6.4). Two great belts of 'gentrified' territories emerge; on the one hand, the lands west of the Shannon (comprising most of Roscommon, most emphatically all of Co. Clare and also including, one assumes, much of Mayo and Galway); and, the rich lands of north and mid-Leinster on the other. In Clare and Connacht, the juxtaposition of many long-settled Gaelic and Norman families, other Old English and Gaelic merchant investors (from the cities of Limerick and Galway) and an increasing number of pre- and post-Cromwellian New English landholders and lessees was to endow this western region with a distinctive and densely concentrated ruling class.

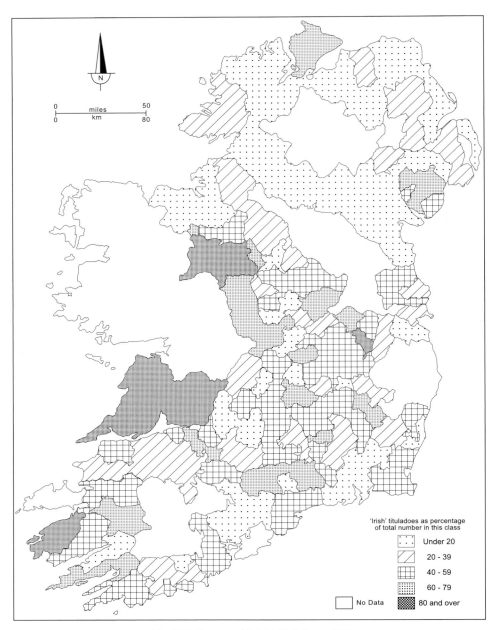

6.4   Distribution of 'Irish' *tituladoes c.*1660

The second region of 'gentry' concentration connects south Roscommon with Co. Westmeath, widens out into a belt of powerful people in the Pale region as a whole and stretches south along the Barrow corridor deep into Carlow. This region (together with east Galway) may well be the area where the greatest continuities in landownership patterns helped sustain older settlements and social hierarchies for much longer than we have imagined. Certainly this was the region with the most elaborate village and urban structures in the mid-seventeenth century.

Much of the rest of south Leinster, as well as east and south Munster, is also characterized by a moderate concentration of resident gentry, whereas the more Gaelic regions of na Déise, south Kerry and west Limerick reveal a less gentrified social stratum. Likewise, apart from east Down, and a mixture of old and new landlords in east Donegal and parts of Fermanagh, this recurring culture world stretching north of a line from Co. Sligo across to Co. Louth appears least top heavy in terms of a gentry and substantial rural middle class in this extensive zone of weaker settlement hierarchies. However, since this region was also likely to be the zone of greatest tax evasion, this interpretation will require further refinement.

We are on safer ground when analysing the ethnic background of the *tituladoes*. The most telling statement emerging from the poll-taxes is the strength of the new planter elite in the northern half of the island. Apart from Inishowen and the baronies of south Down, the country that lies north of a line from mid-Roscommon to mid-Louth was emphatically a region of Scottish and English elites. Indeed, the critical question over much of this region is the actual relative dominance of enterprising Scottish as opposed to English landowners and the implications of this ethnic dualism for specific patterns of immigration and settlement by these two planter groups.[53] The depth, extent and rapidity in the transformation of the power structures of this region leaps from Figure 6.4, emphasizing the cultural cleavages that followed on from this abrupt ascendancy by a new ruling class. The older society had lost its patrons and leaders – and Petty's county maps for this northern region in *Hiberniae Delineatio* (1685) starkly revealed the residual and scrappy character of the surviving Irish lands (see Fig. 6.5a and Fig. 6.5b). The poll-tax references to the officer rank of so many of the elite emphasizes the militarized nature of this conquered world. So do the early seventeenth-century town maps, which mirror intimately the subjugation of lands and peoples where the Norman had never penetrated.[54]

Figure 6.4 reveals the sharpness of the cultural and political frontier between this settler region and the rest of Connacht. Only the barony of Boyle acts as a buffer between the planted areas of Sligo-Leitrim and the outstanding density of old elites stretching south from Roscommon to Clare. Yet, even in Clare there is a small planter class along the Shannon estuary baronies – developers of both new towns and new economies. The most striking feature of the rest of Munster and Leinster is the mosaic-like distribution of different ethnic elites. There are localized power structures, social hierarchies and related landscape expressions in these provinces which makes generalization difficult. One can identify, however, an axis of New English control from south Co. Dublin through Wicklow into north Wexford (the core of the officially designated 'New Pale'), which extends westwards in a narrow salient into the Laois midlands. A second axis of New English control emerges in the immediate hinterland of Waterford city. East Cork (excluding Imokilly), Kinalmeaky and Carbery, not surprisingly in view of the Munster plantation, reveal a strong planter elite. But the overall pattern for both Co. Cork and the wider Limerick hinterland is a fragmented one. Michael

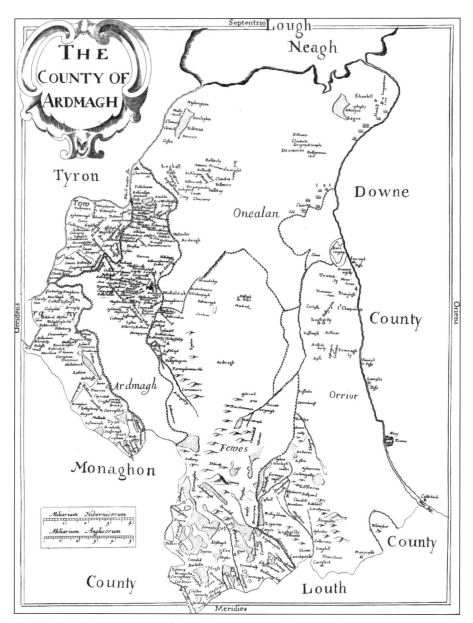

6.5a   William Petty's county map of Armagh, as constructed from the Down Survey (from his *Hiberniae Delineatio*, 1685)

MacCarthy-Morrogh's emphasis on the intermixed, fretted and piecemeal character of the English settlement in Munster is supported by this map.[55] The remainder of Munster and Leinster emerges as a battleground of interests – areas where often the planters' more narrow political ascendancy is matched by both the residual class power and greater population size of the older society. Members of the latter society still held on to powerful hinge positions in urban

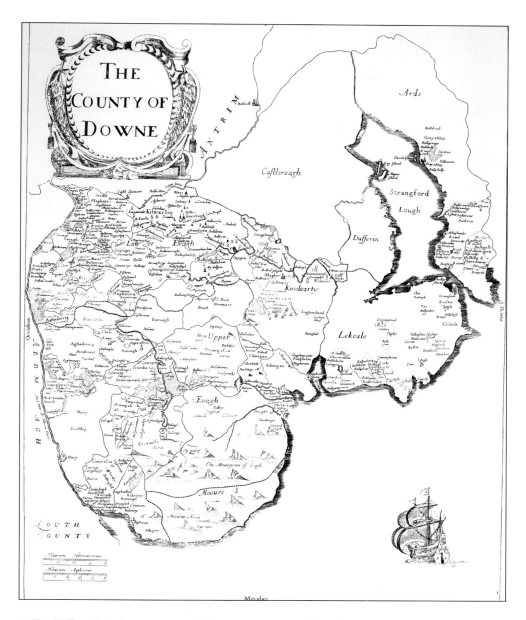

6.5b   William Petty's county map of Down, as constructed from the Down Survey (from his *Hiberniae Delineatio*, 1685)

and rural social hierarchies and ensured that the relative success of the new landlord-inspired economy would both depend on and be mediated by them. Over the southern half of the island, therefore, surviving territorial and social structures were often orchestrated to deflect the full brunt of colonial rule. The dominance of old or new elites also had a bearing on the extent to which settler immigration was a significant feature in their respective regions and towns.[56]

The 1660 poll-tax documents this process of settler immigration. As we have seen, it was William Petty who asked the vital question about the relative size of English/Scots versus Irish populations in each town, street, parish and barony. It is, therefore, certain that this ethnic categorization was carried out subsequent to the collection of the tax at parish level. Almost certainly Petty's clerks in Dublin were given instructions to abstract on a surname basis the members of the two broad ethnic groups – or at the very least, to abstract the surnames deemed to be Irish. This strategy formed the basis for that extremely valuable listing of the most important Irish family names at the end of each barony entry.

There has been much speculation as to what the terms 'English/Scots' and 'Irish' mean in the poll-tax abstracts. In many respects this categorization is a strong indication of religious allegiances but it is doubtful if this is the central goal of the classification. In some areas, but by no means all (given the existence of Gaelic-speaking Scottish settlers, the expansion of English, and the extent of bilingualism elsewhere), this classification may have a linguistic basis. But the distinctions made by Petty and the poll-tax abstracts are most likely of a sociopolitical nature. The classification appears to be primarily concerned with distinguishing the new settler populations from the older inhabitants, whether the latter were of Irish or Old English descent. In essence, this is a classification similar to that used in the Civil Survey, which distinguishes the 'Irish Papists', who were to lose their lands, from the new landowning elite of 'English (and Scotts) Protestants'. There is little doubt that the Old English are here categorized as 'Irish'; and increasingly, their own self-image was to reflect this externally imposed categorization. Significantly, the only place where it is deemed necessary to clarify that 'Irish' also includes 'Old English' is in the distinctive culture area of Bargy in Co. Wexford. Ó Murchú's research on Co. Clare and work on Co. Tipperary and elsewhere[57] confirms the relative reliability of the ethnic categorizations for most of the island.

The area where this ethnic categorization is most problematic is in Co. Antrim, east Co. Down and possibly the barony of Coleraine in Co. Londonderry, where there appears to be much confusion about Scottish and Irish names. The contrast between the returns for the raw frontier county of Fermanagh and the older, more intermixed populations of east Down and Antrim could not be sharper. The Co. Fermanagh returns are better for both Irish and settler names, it should also be noted – here there is no confusion about the identity of the Planter and the Gael. The abstracts not only provide a list of the principal Irish names for groups of parishes but also return the principal Scottish and English names as well. And typical of a frontier situation, only a limited number of recurring planter names – Armstrong, Johnston, Nixon, Eliot and Graham – are itemized. On the other hand, the barony of Antrim identifies 'Principal Irish names & Scotch [and] Their Numb'.[58] At the very minimum, half the names so identified in this barony are of Scottish origin. Similarly, for the barony of Glenarm, the list of the principal Irish names includes 'som[e] Scotch'. Again, at least four out of every ten names are of Scottish provenance. The list for Massereene barony only refers to 'Irish names'; yet a MacLysaght-based analysis of these names confirms that, at the very least, one-fifth are clearly Scottish names.[59] Likewise, one-third of the 'Irish names' in the barony of Toome, and one-half in Belfast and Dunluce/Cary/Kilconway appear to be Scottish-derived. Whatever the linguistic situation on the ground, it is unlikely, therefore, that the proportions of Irish versus English/Scots in these baronies are correct from an ethnic point of view. Figure 6.6, therefore, incorporates a minimal adjustment of the returns to give a more realistic distribution of the ethnic groups in this region.

In a wider European context, the scale and diversity of seventeenth-century immigration into Ireland is staggering. Spanish migrants to continental Latin America may not have equalled the number of migrants that Ireland received in the century after the 1590s. This migration involved three neighbouring peoples from the larger island, converging westwards on land and opportunities in a smaller insular world. Apart from some later attrition in the southwest and the Midlands, the evidence suggests that this pattern of immigration had already been so solidly established by 1660 as to survive intact into the late twentieth century. Raymond Gillespie and Philip Robinson have skilfully explored the origins and maturation of this settlement for Ulster as a whole.[60] In particular, Robinson has highlighted that the deep-rooted nature of this settlement grew out of the planters' familiarity with, and adaption of, pre-existing territorial, economic and other institutions. This may have been particularly true of the successful colonization of so much of the northeast by independent Scottish migrants.

Figure 6.6 summarizes at the barony scale the level of immigrant penetration and consolidation in Antrim, most of Down, north Armagh, much of the county of Londonderry, east Donegal and a core around the lakes of Fermanagh. It highlights the cutting edge of a southwestward moving frontier as it spilled over into the less densely populated edges of Connacht and the northwest Midlands generally. This advancing front was running up against an old Gaelic world and in the process deflected some of the older populations further south into Omeath in the Cooley peninsula to the east, and on to the Galway/Clare borderlands and the islands to the west. New frontier nucleations had emerged such as the Scots planter town of St Johnstown in Co. Longford and in pockets elsewhere, as in Carrigallan and Manorhamilton in Co. Leitrim. This map assumes that the missing populations are divided proportionately between Planter and Gael but there is a strong possibility that the strength of the tightly knit Scots Presbyterian communities is still underestimated.

The poll-tax assists us in identifying the core areas of polarization in the newly planted territories (while also pointing to the possibilities for colonizing previously unsettled, if extensively grazed, townland units). The poll-tax evidence allows one to identify the townlands occupied by English/Scots populations only. Consequently, a kind of segregation/dislocation index can be calculated that further refines our view of the hearthland of the colony. This core of planter settlement pivots around three interlocked areas – east Co. Londonderry, coastal and mid-Antrim (information is missing at this level for south Antrim), and north and central Armagh, where 18 to 28 per cent of all townlands enumerated for these regions appear to be the sole preserve of the settlers. A domain or intermediate area with 8 to 12 per cent of townlands segregated can be identified for the remainder of northeast Ulster, with secondary cores of equal strength emerging in east Donegal and Fermanagh. The fringe of this extension of Scottish and English cultures into the north, that is, where less than 6 per cent of the townlands are segregated, can be identified for Inishowen, west Donegal, south Armagh and parts of mid-Down. Overall, Co. Down is quite striking in its admixture of populations and the densely populated lands of Ards and Lecale register no segregated townlands. Its rich variegated societies and landscapes appear to have had more assimilative powers than much of the rest of Ulster. Further south along the Connacht/Leinster border-lands, settler expansion was less compact and more individualistic in nature and for the most part represented the infilling of settlement within already populated townlands – outliers in what must have been a hostile world.

The second most powerful core of planter settlement pivoted around the Pale region and Dublin city – a cockpit of diverging interests, where Irish, Old English and a variety of settler elements congregated around the richest prizes. Apart from a strategic northern coastal salient, planter settlement had only limited success in the rich hearthlands of north Leinster. But to the south and west a new wide band of a significant minority population was well established, reaching right across Laois, Offaly and the edges of north Tipperary to reach the Shannon at Limerick, and on the other flank, curving southwards to colonize the west Wicklow/north Wexford borderlands. This too was an enduring settlement, which laid down a whole range of new nucleations on the edges of north Munster at Cloghjordan, Borrisokane and Birr and on the edges of the Midlands generally through Castlecomer in Kilkenny to Dunlavin in Co. Wicklow and Gorey in Wexford.[61]

Third, there was a southwestern core of settlement, pivoting round Cork city and the Munster plantation precincts. However, the barony-based map obscures the expansion of settlers southwestwards – as they followed the rich fishing grounds along the coasts of west Cork and south Kerry. The integration of this south Munster region into a wider economic context is symbolized by the inland frontier town of Bandon – an outlier of the English West Country woollen indus-try and a pivot for future colonization westwards.[62] Unlike the other two settler regions, however, this Munster plantation – with the exception of the wider west Cork area – was initiated in an already long-settled, well-developed region. In addition, much of this gentry- rather than soldier-led colonization was begun in an earlier period when religious/political affiliations were not as deep or as divi-sive as they were to become in mid-seventeenth-century Ireland. It would appear that the shock of 1641 and longer term processes of assimilation were to absorb much of the fringes of this southern settler area into the old body politic – and nowhere more emphatically than in that most assimilative of counties, Limerick. But much of this lay in the future. Southwest Munster, given its mixed heritage, was to underpin the most innovative and wealthiest overseas English settlement anywhere in the seventeenth century.[63]

The most enduring colonial contributions and populations were, however, in the towns – and towns were, as always, the central instruments of imperial expansion and control. The poll-tax allows us to make a more than tentative identification of the distribution and size of these urban settlements, while also providing a picture of the ethnic composition of the urban populations. Dublin's primacy is one obvious feature of Fig. 6.7 – a position of dominance that had been, for the most part, achieved by a possible fivefold increase in population between *c.*1600 and 1660. Its primacy is also suggested by its list of *tituladoes* (624), which is as large as the elites of all the other Irish cities and towns put together. Then, as today, it was the dominant governmental, legal, military, financial, industrial, commerical and educational centre – full of lords, judges, attorneys, merchants, army officers, distillers, clothiers, clerks and innkeepers.

Cork had achieved second place in the urban hierarchy by 1660, outstripping Galway and Limerick, which had ranked second and third in the early 1600s. Cork too, with the expulsion of its old merchant families outside its walls, had a large new elite population (144) especially active in its dominant role as the import centre of south Munster. Waterford, Limerick (and Galway? for which we have no 1660 poll-tax) were of almost equal rank and population and all retained a significant minority of the old merchant families. Drogheda, Carrickfergus, Youghal, Kinsale and the growing city of Derry were also important port centres with a substantial number of wealthy taxpayers. Kilkenny was the most significant inland city with its own complex economic structures, supporting as it did a wide range of shops, services and small industries (see chapter 8). Figure 6.7, therefore, reveals three types of regions with different urban structures and lifestyles: areas with an elaborate urban hierarchy in the east, the south and increasingly in the northeast; areas with a still developing urban hierarchy running through the Midlands and on the borders of the feudalized world generally; and the remoter areas, where urban settlement hierarchies and ways of living were still only in their infancy.

The most telling aspect of Fig. 6.7 is not only the primacy of Dublin and the larger port-cities but also the conquest of Dublin and indeed the conquest of all the large port-cities and county towns by immigrant peoples and elites. The Cromwellian settlement was not only to make for massive property transfers in the countryside. More significantly, Cromwellian policy and independent economic processes saw the radical acceleration of planter command of urban properties, agricultural surpluses, external trade and a whole range of political and administrative offices based in the cities and towns. Underpinning this urban ascendancy were the officers, the soldiers and the elaborate garrison fortifications that had been grafted on to the walls of these old cities and towns. Although the poll-tax is markedly deficient in its enumeration of all garrisons, it is still impressive how often the enumerated military rulers turn up in the cities and bigger towns. Even more striking still, running through this strategic middle belt of the country – from Carrickfergus, Magherafelt and Charlemont, through Boyle, Roscommon and the great garrison pivot at Athlone, and on to Thurles, Mallow, Cork, Kinsale and Bantry – the soldiers' barracks is a prominent and sometimes an overwhelming element in the urban setting. In Roscommon, for example, the civilian population, for the most part local, is close to being outnumbered by the English soldiers of the garrison.

Such control made for a radical restructuring of the social geography of cities and towns. The medieval city of Kilkenny provides a dramatic example of this process. In the core of the city, in the High Street and elsewhere, over 72 per cent of the population was of planter stock. In the ring of urban settlement around the core, 40 per cent of the population were settlers, while in the outlying Liberties of the city 24 per cent were 'outsiders'. Similarly the core of Cork city had been lost, yet Shandon was still 72 per cent Irish. A core/domain/periphery structure characterized even the largest cities. Expanding Irishtowns characterized the urban scene everywhere. The deep divisions of the post-Cromwellian society were most sharply chiselled into the narrow confines of the urban fabric.

A second major feature of Fig. 6.7 is the almost exclusive dominance of the planter population in these often newly planned urban centres in Ulster. Apart from the newly created towns, which must have been literally outstanding features of this hitherto rural world, the surviving secular centres and more especially the diocesan towns, such as Clogher, Dromore, Kilmore and Raphoe, were now solidly in the hands of the planter. Only within some older towns of east Down (Downpatrick, Strangford and Ardglass) and in the more outlying cities of Armagh and Derry was a substantial Gaelic population represented. There are equally vivid contrasts between the wealth of the strong, comfortable, planter towns at the core – not only Larne and Belfast but also Antrim, Ballymena and Lisburn – with their bigger houses and developing market, fairs and communications networks – and the rudimentary and isolated frontier towns like Enniskillen, where over 80 per cent of the population was of planter stock. Here and likewise in fortified Monaghan (see Fig. 12.3c, Pl. 2o), Carrickmacross, Ballyshannon and Lifford, the poll-taxes and the early town maps highlight the sharpness of the clash between the planter townsmen and the remnants of the rural order. Beyond this region, the towns with a 20 to 40 per cent planter population highlight the great buffer zone stretching from south Down across to Sligo and Roscommon. Figure 6.7 also illustrates the strength of planter settlement in the episcopal capitals, and new planter towns elsewhere in the country. Everywhere, too, the poll-tax notes the powerful role of the resident landlord in patronizing these centres of administration and trade.

Finally, Fig. 6.7 reveals a more hidden urban Ireland, where the often walled, sometimes small but always socially and morphologically complex borough towns of the south and east still retain an overwhelming proportion of older town dwellers. East Limerick is typical of this resilient urban world of Munster – Cork county's urban ethnic mix reflects a more exposed settlement history. In Leinster – and particularly along the western edges of Wexford, in Kilkenny, Kildare, Meath and Westmeath – an older corporate tradition of urban living also survived. And so another lesson emerges from the poll-tax pages – these old and battered towns had weathered the storms of the medieval period and were in place to benefit from the upswing in the economy from the sixteenth century onwards. Clearly, it was these elaborate and enduring urban societies that helped sustain the population densities and more complex rural settlement hierarchies outlined above. Figure 6.7, therefore, provides a dramatic illustration of the coexistence on the island of very different urban cultures.

The 1660 poll-tax evidence, then, stresses how much of the foundations of modern Ireland had been laid down and firmly put in place by the mid-seventeenth century. It was a ragged framework, where old worlds, transitional worlds and, literally, new worlds coexisted within and between areas as small as two or three adjacent streets or parishes.[64] Sharp polarities are evident in many places and at many levels, not least where the Scottish borderers along the Fermanagh frontier faced 'the men of Connacht'. On the other hand, the mosaic-like qualities of so many patterns point to the tensions and creativities that sprang from new encounters. And so a whole series of retreating, stable, embryonic and transitional culture regions are identified – regions of devastation and despair, regions of sustained continuities and hope, regions of powerful intrusions and enterprise, and regions with hybrid, ambivalent qualities.

After 1660, the forces of massive economic and demographic growth, the deepening of external political control and the profound island-wide impact of what Jones Hughes has termed landlordism[65] were to transform, if again unevenly, these seventeenth-century patterns and lifestyles. The poll-tax evidence is, therefore, of immense significance to the study of seventeenth-century Irish life and its later transformations. Once its limitations are recognized and other sources of evidence are used in conjunction with it, the poll-tax is enormously fruitful in unravelling the stratas and stresses, territorial and societal, that made up later medieval/early modern Ireland. It also helps us to reclaim and enlarge our vision of seventeenth-century Ireland and, through that, our vision of ourselves and where we have come from.

II

REGIONAL CASE-STUDIES

7

Dublin County
Changing Social Geographies in the
Sixteenth and Seventeenth Centuries

> The eastern triangle is the geographical nucleus from which men have seen their best chance of commanding the whole country. And yet the same district is also one of the most vulnerable parts of Ireland, the longest break in its defence of mountain ring, with the estuaries of the Liffey and the Boyne to beckon the invader onwards.
>
> J. H. Andrews[1]

Strategic borderlands often nurture key central places and regions. Dublin city and county are good examples of this process. It was only with the creation of the Hiberno-Norse overlordship in the tenth century that these ancient buffer lands (between the Laigin to the south and the southern O'Neill to the north) were merged into a single, powerful region centred on the city of Dublin. Anglo-Norman rule – both secular and ecclesiastical – strongly consolidated the role of this pivotal region. Even at the height of the late medieval Gaelic resurgence, Dublin county remained solidly within the Pale, except for its southern flanks on the edge of the Dublin and Wicklow mountains, where a great reservoir of Gaelic culture maintained what was officially described as 'a land of war' in sharp contrast to the sheltered conditions in 'the land of peace' in the Pale.

New English rule in the early modern period was to change all that. Using Dublin as a fulcrum, the New English set out to conquer, colonize and rule the whole island. This process was accelerated from the 1530s when the machinery of government located in Dublin was elaborate and so designed that in theory at least it could comprehend the whole island.[2] Thus, for much of the sixteenth century, this core region's governmental potential was translated into a powerful reality, according as the English state, using Dublin as the strategic hub, first established a military conquest and then proceeded to either revive or initiate the administrative machinery necessary to achieve the conquest and control of the whole island. Beginning in the mid-sixteenth century, Dublin city and county – as the cockpit of the struggle for the control of government – became crucial spring-boards for the extension of English colonization into the enlarged Pale of the Midlands, the Wicklows and beyond. The first half of the seventeenth century saw the consolidation of military and administrative control over all the island.

These monumental changes reverberated with varying intensity throughout the country and elicited a wide variety of responses within Dublin city and in the smaller towns, villages and townlands of Co. Dublin. This chapter analyses the fragmentary documentary evidence available to re-create the changing social and cultural life of Co. Dublin in the later sixteenth and seventeenth centuries, and particularly in the traumatic years between 1630 and 1670.[3] The key documents for this study of Co. Dublin are the 1654 Civil Survey and the Down Survey maps of 1655–6. The 1660 poll-tax returns for this county are augmented by the comprehensive demographic details available from a highly specialized Cromwellian survey of the population of south Co. Dublin in 1650–2. The early seventeenth-century visitation reports of the Anglican archbishop of Dublin also provide many useful insights.

I begin the story by providing an overview of the long-standing environmental, economic and cultural conditions that shaped the character of Co. Dublin. Then the changing social geographies of the county over the sixteenth and seventeenth centuries are examined at three levels. First, I shall explore the changing geography of the great estates and the elite landowning class. The beginning of Co. Dublin's modern story stretches back to the dissolution of the monasteries in the mid-sixteenth century. The secularization of former Church land between 1540 and 1640 is therefore a major theme, as is the contrasting social worlds, of the old and new elites. Second, the battle for control of the county's parishes, churches and villages in the increasingly bitter post-Reformation era is examined. Third, the social life of individuals, families and tenant households is explored with particular reference to the unique insights into the occupational, naming and kinship structures that the very special census of south Co. Dublin in 1650–2 provides. For all three levels – that of the estate, the parish and townland – the impact of New English colonization and control on long-standing social, cultural and settlement patterns will be kept in focus.

Culture, Economy and Environment

Despite its relatively small size, the county of Dublin contained a fascinating variety of physical conditions, economic possibilities and cultural topographies in the sixteenth and seventeenth centuries. The story of its people in this period involves a dialectic between the lifestyles of land and sea, the nature of social interactions between the people of the mountains and lowlands, the city and county, and the arable and pastoral cultural areas. An enduring engagement between Gaelic, Anglo-Norman and New English social structures and value systems is a central theme, as is the recurring northern-versus-southern elements in the county's (and city's) culture.

Co. Dublin is located in the southern half of the only extensive coastal lowland in Ireland. Elsewhere, an upland perimeter predominates but here along the east coast the drift-covered limestone lowlands face eternally eastwards across the Irish Sea towards England and Wales. Since the Viking era, the city of Dublin has been the main filter of external impulses to the rest of the region, although the local hinge function of smaller maritime settlements such as Dalkey, Bullock, Dún Laoghaire, Ringsend, Clontarf, Howth, Portraine, Rush, Malahide, Holmpatrick and Skerries should not be underestimated. The Vikings emphasized the county's peninsulas and islands for coastal traffic by rebaptizing the many landmarks stretching from Dalkey through Howth and Ireland's Eye to the Columban island of Lambay and the Patrician port and parish of Holmpatrick. The impact of the coastal maritime culture is suggested by the fact that 2 per cent of Dublin's adult population was involved in some kind of maritime occupation at the end of the seventeenth century.[4]

A 'northside'/'southside' dialectic was well developed in the mid-seventeenth century in Dublin city and county. The southern 'half' of the city was much more densely peopled and developed; the northern 'half' was represented by the single parish of St Michans, which in 1660 constituted only 13.4 per cent of the city's population.[5] The modern reclaimed harbour area was still an extensive coastal delta, where the Tolka and Dodder rivers, as well as the Liffey, debouched into the sea. An outlying gravel ridge provided for one of Dublin's expanding outports at Ringsend – the placename (combining an Irish word, in this case 'rinn', with its English meaning 'end') points to the hybrid character of this focal region. Across from Ringsend is the magnificent bay of Dublin, whose draped creation pivots from the ancient rocks of Howth in the north to those around Dalkey to the south. Further southwards lay the graceful curve of Killiney Bay and a lowland corridor stretching into the new county of Wicklow. This lowland, hemmed in by the imposing bulk of the Leinster granite, is never more than five miles in width. Extensive coastal lands in the north of the county are subdued and open, characterized by low, till-covered limestones and fringed by post-glacial spits and sand dunes (see Fig. 7.1). The Tolka, Ward and Delvin rivers, as well as a series of other minor but locally important millstreams, make their way seawards at Ballybough, Baldoyle, Malahide, north of Donabate and below Gormanston. In areas of few streams, as in the barony of Coolock between Clontarf and Swords, seventeenth-century farmers ground their corn in a variety of horse-, wind- or tide-powered mills. Major rivers, and particularly the Liffey, housed tucking (woollen) mills and some brewhouses on their banks.[6]

Inland, north Co. Dublin is characterized by gently rolling landscapes, merging into the central lowlands and the Boyne valley beyond. Here one is struck by the role of the early Christian Church as a fixing point for so many later settlements. Finglas to the south and the large monasteries of Swords and Lusk further north dominated these good arable lands, acting as the springboards for the spread of Christianity and parish formation in their hinterlands.[7] In the far north and west of the county, more resistant old red sandstone and ordovician shales and slates provide the backbone for a series of striking hills that run from Garristown and south of Naul on to Baldungan and the more rugged coastlands near Balbriggan. From these hills, the Cooley peninsula and the plains of north Leinster command one's view – beckoning the invader, as Andrews says, to turn northwards and inland, a feature emphasized by the density of townlands containing the early medieval term 'town' in this area.

Two further significant physical features should be noted. The first is the 'vale of Dublin', where the Liffey and Tolka rivers cut into rich drift lowlands. Here a

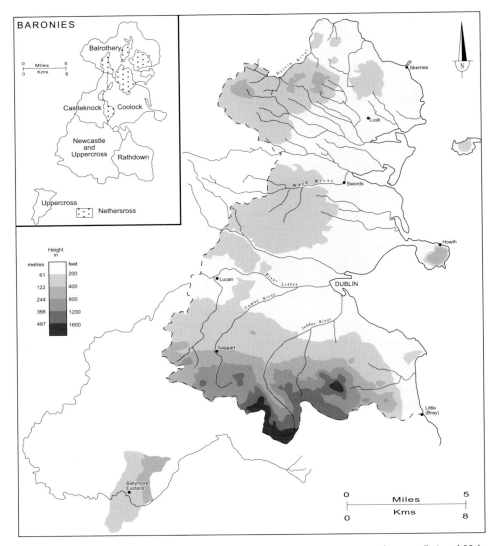

7.1   Location and topography of mid-seventeenth-century Co. Dublin (see references 5, 6 and 22 for main sources used in making these maps of Co. Dublin)

series of historical foci at Kilmainham, Crumlin, Ballyfermot, Clondalkin, Grangegorman, Chapelizod, Palmerstown, Lucan, Castleknock and Glasnevin highlights the role of the early Christian and medieval Church as the generator of key settlements in this region. The second major feature is the granite mountains of the south in which the Liffey itself rises, curving westwards by Ballymore-Eustace (still part of Co. Dublin in the mid-seventeenth century), before beginning its long circuitous route to the sea. Here too the Griffeen, Camac, Dodder and Owendubh rivers have their source and here the upper level of drift had helped generations of farmers to push settlement up the valleys of Glenasmole and Glencullen.

Throughout their history, the Dublin mountains have provided a scenic, pastoral and unruly backdrop to the regulated world of the vale of Dublin. Along the 'marchlands' between the 'land of peace' and the 'land of war' in the hills, a line of strategic villages is found – from (Little) Bray and Donnybrook through Rathfarnham, westwards to Tallaght, Saggart and Rathcoole and on to Newcastle and Ballymore-Eustace. These villages marked the southern edge of the Pale in the sixteenth century. But culturally and economically they played an integrative role as bridgeheads between the cultures of the mountains and the plains, between a land of cows, turf, and timber, on the one hand, and a land of corn, on the other – between a world dominated by Irish names and a more hybrid feudal world in the lowlands beneath.[8]

Beyond the Tolka river to north Co. Dublin, townland names show a preponderance of early medieval English-based placename endings, as in Porterstown, Scribblestown, Robswalls and Coldblow. This culture zone is part of a core region of Scandinavian and Anglo-Norman colonization, which pushed in along the Boyne and its tributaries pivoting around Drogheda – one of the leading corn ports of the medieval period. The distinctive character of this northern half of the county had already been emphasized by its specific regional name – Fingal – reflecting the impact of Viking rule and settlement in the region for over 250 years. In the mid-seventeenth century its distinctiveness was still commented upon in terms of its specific speechways and 'archaic' lifestyles.[9] Often referred to as the breadbasket of Dublin, Fingal's strategic importance to the New English-dominated city did not go unnoticed by Eoghan Rua O'Neill, who in 1647 ravaged the country between Castleknock and Drogheda, then containing 'the goodliest haggards of corn that ever were seen in those parts'.[10] In the high medieval period, episcopal manors like Finglas made much more profit from milling than their southern equivalents like Clondalkin. The movement of cattle was restricted on the northern manors – here arable lands were highly prized and cattle were kept in their place.[11]

Unfortunately, a distinction between arable and pastoral lands is not made in the Civil Survey for the barony of Nethercross and no such returns exist for the baronies of Newcastle and Uppercross.[12] While allowing for these difficulties, close on 70 per cent of Co. Dublin was then classified as 'arable' – land capable of producing good tillage crops. This proportion of arable land ranged from 80 per cent in the barony of Castleknock to 62 per cent in Rathdown barony in the south. Balrothery, Nethercross and Coolock oscillated around the mean of 70 per cent, while it is likely that the other southern baronies of Newcastle and Uppercross would have exhibited returns more similar in character to those of Rathdown.

Pastoral parishes were aligned along the northern and southern edges of the county, centred on Tully, Kiltiernan, Kilgobbin and Whitechurch in the south, and included Holywood, Balscaddan and particularly Balrothery parish in the northern barony of the same name (see Fig. 7.6, p. 251). The coarser coastal parishes of Donabate, Portmarnock and Howth also had an excess of pastoral over arable lands. The arable lands are in the hearthland of the county, stretching from Lusk and Garristown in the north, southwards through Swords and Finglas, and westwards along the Tolka and Liffey valleys, including the outlying parishes of Old Connacht and Rathmichael to the extreme south.

The distribution of cornmills, as evidenced by the Civil Survey returns, provides other clues to the nature of local economies. In the county as a whole, there were 50 cornmills, suggesting a minimum adult population per mill of about 240. (By the late 1640s, however, many of these mills were in ruins.) The wider Pale area contained two milling regions – one along the Boyne valley and its tributaries (south Meath and much of lowland Co. Louth) – the other along the Liffey valley and including the coastal hinterland of Dublin city between Coolock and Rathdown. These two arable regions were connected by the main road from Dublin to Trim along the Ward river. In contrast, western and northern parts of Co. Meath and pockets in north Co. Dublin and southeast Co. Meath were less committed to grain production and milling, as was much of the hill country around the borderlands of modern Co. Wicklow. The significance of sheep and wool is suggested by tucking mills along the Delvin and especially along the Liffey valley – as well as along minor streams as at Killiney, close to the wool of the Wicklow mountains.

Regional variations in the founding of fairs also demonstrate local contrasts in economic activities. The core world of old fairs is south of the Liffey – from St Kevin's outside the gates on the south of the city through ancient Donnybrook to the early fair sites at Palmerstown, Newcastle, Fieldstown and Rathfarnham. Here a higher proportion of castle sites had accompanying bawns – valuable enclosures for cows, cattle and sheep. To the north, only the widely spaced fairs of Swords and Garristown are likely to be of older vintage, although St Margaret's benefited from a fair foundation as early as 1612. In the second half of the seventeenth century, expansion of a commercial pastoral economy in Dublin's hinterland is indicated by increases in the number of annual fairs at old centres, by the emergence of new fair sites between Swords and Dublin city at Clontarf, Clonturk, and Luttrellstown, and by the spread of fairs throughout much of the north county from Kilsallaghan, Ballyboghill to Lusk and Balrothery. Expansion of a more commercialized pastoral economy on to the edges of the Dublin mountains is reflected in new or revitalized fair sites at Saggart, Carrickmines and Laughnanstown. Bringing up the rear with fair foundations in 1718, 1755 and 1766 respectively are Finglas, Rush, and Skerries/ Balbriggan.[13]

There was obviously an intensification of a mixed-farming economy as the seventeenth century progressed, and a growing bias towards cattle, sheep and cow production. The overall impression of mid-seventeenth-century Dublin is of a gradation from a more pastoral south through to a more dominant arable core, with minor pastoral niches on the northern and maritime edges. Mixed farming was probably the dominant mode, with corn production, dairying and sheep production occupying significant components of overall agricultural output. The relatively weak evidence from summaries of Transplantation Certificates – with returns for only ten Dublin proprietors – supports this interpretation.[14] Despite the devastation of war, famine and disease, Co. Dublin and the wider Pale region were characterized in 1660 by the highest population densities in the island.

Retrospective use of the 1660 poll-tax returns can help us to refine our ideas about the economic landscapes of mid-seventeenth-century Co. Dublin.[15] While a complex range of factors affect variations in population densities (some of which, such as size of estates, the distribution of villages, gentry elite, and artisanal and industrial activities, will be examined later), labour supply was a critical factor at this time. Intensively cultivated arable zones required greater labour inputs than equivalent areas geared to extensive pastoral activities. From an assessment of the ratio of a single adult per number of Irish plantation acres in each parish (see Fig. 7.2), it is clear that there are three regions of very high population density: (i) in north Co. Dublin in the parishes of Portraine, Swords and Malahide; (ii) in the Dublin city hinterland from Howth, Kilbarrack, Raheny, Glasnevin, Clonturk, Grangegorman and the rural parts of St Kevin's and the Liberties of Dublin; and (iii) along the southern coastlands in Killiney, Tully and part of Rathmichael. These core areas of highly populated parishes are surrounded by a second tier of slightly less highly populated parishes – including Garristown, Clonmethan, Holmpatrick, Lusk east and west, and Holywood – as well as parishes in the north of the county and an outer ring of parishes in the Dublin metropolitan region which includes Ballyfermot, Kilmainham, Donnybrook and Monkstown. In the extreme south of the county, only the parish of Old Connacht fits into this category (see Fig. 7.6, p. 251).

The least densely populated parishes (presumably those most directly involved in pastoral activities) included Balrothery, Ballyboghill, Portmarnock and Killastee to the north. There was no such parish in the wider city hinterland. In contrast, a belt of less densely populated parishes swept from Clonsilla in the west to Rathcoole and Calliaghstown in the southwest and Kilgobbin in the southeast. This region included most of the baronies of Newcastle and Uppercross. Here Newcastle and Clondalkin, it would appear, had the relatively highest density populations – where corn crops were still important – while at the other extreme, literally 'beyond the Pale', were Kiltiernan, Saggart and the upland halves of the parishes of Tallaght and Rathcoole. Even as early as the 1330s, the ratio of pasture to tillage in these parishes was about six to one.[16]

On the whole, the evidence suggests a dialectic between the city hinterland and coastal parishes, on the one hand, and inland parishes, on the other. The former parishes were richer and more densely populated: they constituted the core region of arable production that stretched from Holmpatrick in the north to Killiney in the south. The less densely populated, peripheral and pastoral parishes curve from Balrothery in the extreme north through Ballyboghill and along the west and southwest of the county. Alternatively, one could postulate a basic north–south dialectic, with a mixed farming economy to the south of the Liffey and Tolka and the intensive tillage lands of the northern half of the county. The distribution of old fair sites and cornmills supports this distinction between the cow-centred mixed farming culture of the south and a land of haggards, barns and 'chaffehouses' (thatched cabins) to the north.[17]

Dublin's overall attractiveness to migrants and its wide-ranging assimilative role is demonstrated by the fact that it is part of one of three major cultural regions

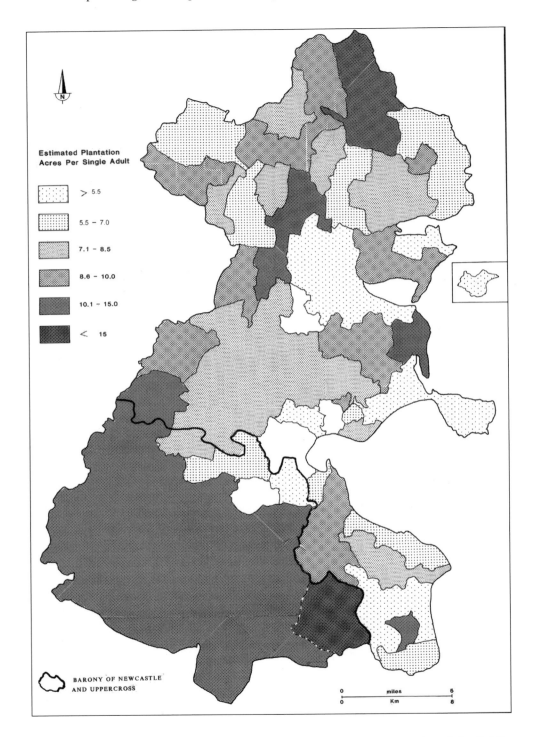

7.2   Distribution of the ratio of plantation acres per single adult in the parishes of Co. Dublin in 1660

in mid-seventeenth-century Ireland characterized by greatest diversity of Irish surnames per head of adult population. Unlike, for example, the introverted Gaelic Midlands, where over one-quarter of the total Irish population bore one of the surnames of the prominent families enumerated in the 1660 poll-tax, Dublin surnames suggest a more complex social structure. Excluding New English names, only 15 per cent of the total number of Irish surnames are composed of the most prominent family names listed in baronial summaries and this percentage falls as low as 7 per cent in Castleknock barony.[18] Dublin accordingly belongs to one of the three culture regions where there is much surname (and cultural) diversity – namely the Leinster coastlands, centred on Dublin and extending through Wicklow into Wexford, where there is also a great variety of immigrant names; the northeast of Ireland, centred on Co. Down, is another such region; and the southwest, especially Co. Cork, is a third such region. No other area in Ireland, not even the northeast, had such a range of outsider names, both New English and Welsh in origin, as Dublin.[19]

Another indicator of the reach of Dublin's migration and information fields is the distribution of lands held by its monasteries at the time of their dissolution. Whether mapping these lands or the distribution of villages and tenements held by the monks or the relative valuation of these properties and lands, it is obvious that the county itself constituted the core for all these criteria – the domain is the counties of Kildare, Meath and Louth (as well as the former south Co. Dublin lands later incorporated into Co. Wicklow). The sphere of outlying cultural connections has a southern and southeastern bias, with Wexford, Waterford and Tipperary represented, but there are few connections with the remoter Midland counties of Leinster. Cork and Limerick are very much on the edge, while the cultural worlds of Connacht and Ulster appear very remote in the sixteenth century.[20] Dublin's seventeenth-century island-wide hegemony is not yet in sight but the crucial transformations of the mid-sixteenth century laid the foundations for such control, not least in terms of the progressive transformation in the composition and ethos of its ruling official and merchant elites, a process already begun in the mid-sixteenth century and completed between 1630 and 1670.[21]

Prelates, Property and Power

Co. Dublin is exceptional within the Pale region and within Ireland in the extent to which its landowning and settlement structures have been for so long controlled by ecclesiastical interests. Just under 47 per cent (104,000 statute acres) of Dublin's total of 222,710 acres were owned by the Church until 1540–1. Over half of this Church land (51 per cent) was actually owned by the archbishop of Dublin. In essence this prelate held close to one-quarter (24 per cent) of the real estate of Co. Dublin up to the Reformation of Henry VIII, although much of this land was in the hands of freeholders paying a chief rent to the archbishop.[22] A further 8 per cent of all the county's land was held by the Cistercian abbey of St Mary's, 6 per cent of all Church land by the cathedrals of Christ Church (mainly) and St Patrick's, and the remainder by nine religious houses of men, three houses of women and two small leper hospitals. Three-quarters of this ecclesiastical land had already been granted to the Church in pre-Norman times. We are therefore dealing in this county with a landowning structure of enormous continuity. The conservation of powerful territorial structures over such long periods of time must also have decisive implications for the nature of society and settlement locally. Equally important, the exceptional amount of Church land in Co. Dublin provided an ideal opportunity to post-Reformation English monarchs to utilize these confiscated lands to consolidate and expand their control of the most pivotal core-region on the island.

The other half of the county's land was dominated by long-established medieval families of the Pale led by the St Lawrence family of Howth, second in rank only to the archbishop within the county. Then followed Talbot of Malahide and Garristown and the numerous expanding branches of Barnewalls from their anchor points at Castleknock and Drimnagh, the Plunketts of Dunsoghly and Portmarnock, and the Fitzwilliam family – historic wardens of the marches – in the south county. In this last region, descendants of other marcher families, Harold, Archbold and Walsh, who had established a *modus vivendi* with the 'Irish of the Mountains', occupied key properties. The Walshes of Carrickmines are described in the early seventeenth century as 'of large and ancient stock, men of note in this metropolitan county, with land rich and plentous in corn and cattle'.[23] Intermixed amongst these were recent landowning families such as the Suffolk family of Wolverston.

There was a number of smaller gentry families scattered throughout the county, some with their origins in the merchant and legal world, like Seagrave of Finglas, Ussher of Donnybrook, Fagan of Feltrim and Bathe of Drumcondra, while there were particular constellations of smaller gentry in Newcastle and Balrothery baronies.

There were four royal manors at Newcastle, Saggart, Esker and Crumlin, mainly administered by middlemen, except for Crumlin with its own system of 'tenant rule'. Each of these parish-manors had functioning court machineries, as evidenced by Edmund Curtis's edition of the court book of Esker and Crumlin for the early seventeenth century.[24] Dublin's merchants and aldermen had always been landholders and leaseholders, especially of monastic and episcopal land. They, with many legal families, were conspicuous Big House dwellers along the main roads and especially in the beautiful vale of the Liffey, as well as along the Tolka. Finglas, in particular, was a favourite resting place for some of these bigwigs. But the most outstanding territorial institutions were properties under control of the archbishop, the cathedrals and the major monasteries.

Three features characterize the changing geography of landownership in Co. Dublin over the period 1541 to 1641: (i) the growing secularization of property ownership generally; (ii) the insertion of New English settler families (the majority being descendants of key Dublin Castle administrators) into the landowning mosaic; and (iii) the consolidation of the property bases of the leading gentry families of the Pale. These three factors increased the wealth of these secular lords, a wealth reflected in greater emphasis on education and social responsibility and a marked improvement in lifestyles, quality of housing, furniture, dress and diet.[25]

These changes were predicated on the massive curtailment of the former landed wealth of the archbishop of Dublin, the complete dissolution of Dublin's monasteries, and the redistribution of their extensive lands. Christ Church and St Patrick's retained landed power under the new dispensation and in 1641 a further 1,400 plantation acres of glebe and parsonage land were retained by the newly established Church in the old parishes. Crown revenues were substantially improved by these changes and a lucrative trade in the leasing of land was manipulated by the crown and its New English officers to consolidate the centralizing state's power in the Pale region and eventually throughout Ireland.[26] The Cromwellian conquest and settlement are not the pivotal points in the evolution of the modern property, social and settlement frameworks of Co. Dublin. In this metropolitan region, key processes of reconstruction had been initiated more than a century earlier with the dissolution of the monasteries and the whittling down of Church power under the reigns of Henry VIII and Elizabeth.

The Civil Survey estimate of the acreage of the county as a whole seems to be defective by the order of around 30 per cent.[27] Although some of this underestimation was obviously concentrated in the extensive mountain lands in the south, there is also a severe underestimation of some of the cultivated and better arable lands. The estimated size of the estates of leading landowners must be mentally transformed by the order of around 25 per cent to get a more reliable picture of their actual extent. For example, the leading landowner was Sir Adam Loftus, with an estimated 8,290 plantation acres (13,264 statute acres) – a more reliable estimate would be in the 16,500 statute acre range (see Fig. 7.3). The archbishop of Dublin was returned in the Civil Survey as holding 5,000 plantation acres; the St Lawrence family of Lord Howth 3,913 plantation acres; Nicholas Barnewall of Turvey 3,240 plantation acres; and Sir William Parsons 2,675 plantation acres. A common denominator between the four leading landowners is that they were all major holders or gainers of ecclesiastical land.

The story of the Loftus family is examined in greater detail below. This extensive estate had been built up by the first Adam Loftus, a Yorkshireman who, in the latter part of Elizabeth's reign, ended up as archbishop of Dublin and lord chancellor, the supreme legal officer in the state. His heirs were beneficiaries of the confiscation of the attainted third Viscount Baltinglass/Eustace lands at Rathfarnham (and they built a new mansion house there in in 1583); they also benefited from later encroachment upon extensive episcopal land in Tallaght, Creevagh and Whitechurch parishes. The ancient family of St Lawrence had expanded from an already solid base in Howth parish to acquire monastic lands in Baldoyle, Raheny and elsewhere. The influential Barnewall family of Turvey built up a vast estate, not only from the acquisition of monastic land such as that of the nunnery of Gracedieu but also by acquiring and leasing large segments of extensive old episcopal manors in the parishes of Swords and Lusk.[28] Sir William Parsons was typical of the new adventurers coming to Ireland, untiring in his pursuit of office, land and income and quickly becoming a man of influence and wealth in the county;[29] he too was a beneficiary of a cunning legal assault on former episcopal lands in the south of the county.

In the following discussion, I will look first at Protestant-held land and then examine the changing geography of the Catholic landowners.

It is difficult to be precise about the actual extent of the archbishop of Dublin's lands in 1640. For example, Dean Jones of Elphin is credited with over 342 acres but as the subtext in the Civil Survey notes, the dean was a leaseholder of land belonging to the archbishop.[30] It is probable that quite an amount of land actually owned by the archbishop was let out in extremely long leases and there are a number of examples of such leasing arrangements noted in the Civil Survey, especially for the barony of Nethercross. Luke Netterville (himself a landowner and an important figure in the 1641 rising/rebellion) is identified as a major lease-holder of episcopal lands.[31] But it is also probable that some such episcopal land is returned under the name of the leading long leaseholders without any reference to the archbishop's interests. The figure of 5,000 acres for the archbishop's estate is therefore a minimum estimate. Whatever the figure, the land of the archbishop of Dublin had undergone a massive reduction from the original figure of 53,200 acres in 1540–1. The Anglican Restoration after the Commonwealth Interregnum elevated the fortunes of the archbishop – he gained an estimated 2,207 acres in the 1660s.[32] More correctly, perhaps, the archbishop reasserted legal ownership over some former episcopal lands, especially in the parishes of Swords, Lusk and Finglas, which had slipped from the prelate's immediate grasp in the turbulent 1640s. Some of the archbishop's lands had been used to augment the landed resources of the newly founded Trinity College. A further 1,516 acres of Church land was restored by c.1670, while the dean of Christ Church directly held an estimated 1,115 acres at the time of the Civil Survey.

The Loftus family estate headed the list of New English Protestant landlords in Co. Dublin in 1640. The Loftus of Rathfarnham and Barnewall of Turvey families are examples of opposite poles of attraction in the socio-political geography of the Pale region c.1640. Their marriage, kinship and professional alliances illustrate the contrasting social geographies of, on the one hand, a New English settler family and, on the other, a long-established Old English family of the Pale. Figure 7.3 highlights the distribution of New English and Protestant land in Co. Dublin in 1640 and indicates the extent of the Adam Loftus estate in the south of the county. Adam Loftus I was an influential figure in policy-making and implementation. He was a zealous reforming figure in the Anglican Church, anxious to establish a like-minded university in Dublin and, above all, an ardent promoter of the policy of extending English culture over the whole island. The marriage alliances of his sons, grandsons, daughters and granddaughters illustrate how successful he was in inculcating these colonial values. A grandson to the archbishop, and son of the soldier-colonist Sir Dudley Loftus, who concentrated the family estate around a new mansion house at reconstructed Rathfarnham, the Adam Loftus of the 1640 Civil Survey was himself a landowner and a government officer (vice-treasurer), was Puritan in outlook and yet a friend of Thomas Wentworth. His estate, and particularly his castle at Rathfarnham, was a bulwark for settlers in 1641, offering

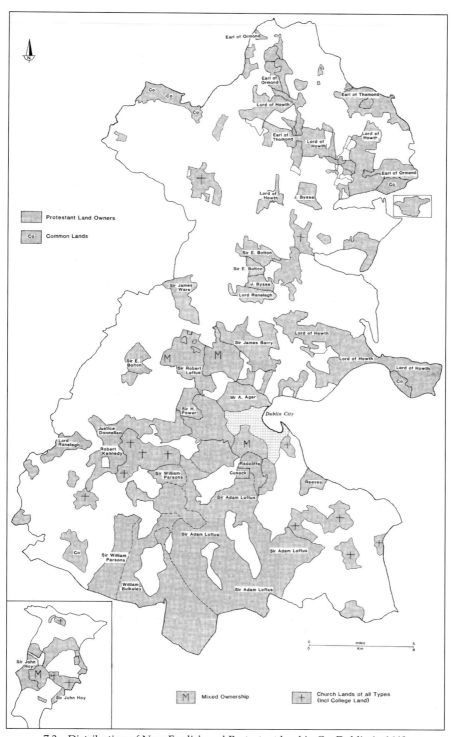

7.3   Distribution of New English and Protestant land in Co. Dublin in 1640

strong resistance to the Irish forces of south Co. Dublin. He was also a planter of new settler families like the Butterfields; before and after the Restoration, he continued to plant his townlands with English settlers, like Dixon, Gibson, Hudson and Greene.[33]

The marriage networks of his uncles and aunts, as well as those of his immediate family, reflect an almost exclusive identification with the now burgeoning New English frontier colony, extending linkages all over the island, apart, that is, from the still relatively autonomous Gaelic territories. These networks stretched north to the new planter family of Bagenal in Newry, Co. Down, and south to the strategically placed Colclough family of Tintern Abbey, as well as a specific Loftus family expansion into the lands of the Hook peninsula. This network expanded westwards in a complex mesh of alliances across the Dublin region and deep into the Queen's County/King's County planter class of Colley (twice), (Moore), Duke, Digby, Hartpole, Wakeley, Cosby, De Renzi, and Warren. Eventually this Loftus social world linked up with descendants of the Munster plantation (Berkeley of Askeaton) in the deep south and later still with descendants of aggressive Ulster Scots planters (Philips of Newtown Limavady and Hamilton of Killeshandra) in the north.[34] The connections of a landed magnate like Adam Loftus extended over much of colonial Ireland, showing a remarkable degree of intermarriage with related settler families as they established their landed and social power locally, contributed to the solidification of a distinctive and exclusive colonial culture and presented a shield of resistance to cultural impulses from the old elite, whether Gaelic or Old English.

Sir William Parsons, a lord justice, was the second leading landowner in this new alliance. One of Adam Loftus's daughters married a son of Sir William's and another married his cousin's son, Sir Lawrence Parsons of the town of Birr (for a while known as Parsonstown), who had acquired an extensive estate in the former Ely O'Carroll territory. Smaller New English landowners included Sir Edward Bolton, chancellor of the Exchequer, with an estate of 1,144 acres between Swords and Lusk, Sir John Hoey, with 1,124 acres, mainly in the Ballymore-Eustace region, John Agar on the old Church lands of Grangegorman, with 930 acres, the recorder John Bysse, with 678 acres at a number of locations, and another ally of the Loftus family and also an archiepiscopal family, that of Bulkeley of Old Bawn, who held 584 acres in Co. Dublin alone. Sir James Ware, government official, friend of Ormond, historian and keeper of manuscripts and genealogies, represents a bridging figure in this scenario, with his 364 acres mainly in the parish of Ward.[35]

The total amount of Protestant land in Co. Dublin in 1640 was an estimated c. 44,000 plantation acres, or around 33 per cent of the total acreage of the county (see Fig. 7.3, p. 237). One-quarter (c.11,000 acres) of this Protestant land belonged to the 'conforming', mainly Old English group. Heading this transitional social group was the earl of Ormond – his bailiwick was anchored further south in the counties of Tipperary and Kilkenny, another social world of close kinship and marriage alliances. The Civil Survey records he held around 800 acres in Dublin, centred on the manor and old parish of Rush. The O'Briens, earls of Thomond, held one of the most stable property blocks in the county – the parish of

Holmpatrick. The parish territory had been constructed into an ecclesiastical property in pre-Norman times, continued as the estate of the local priory until the dissolution, when it was granted to another influential Kilkenny legal family, the Cowleys, and was emphatically intact in the 1640 Civil Survey, as in the Restoration under the administration of the earl of Thomond and his tenants.[36]

The St Lawrence family of Howth and Lord Howth held the largest estate of Old English Protestant families. Here the impact of port geography may have had its own cultural effects. Howth had become one of the main places of embarkation and arrival of New English officers and administrators.[37] The St Lawrences acted as their hosts in their comings and goings to and from Dublin: progressively their sons were educated in England and the main branch assimilated to Protestant culture. Another significant landowner with an Old English name, Sir James Barry, established an estate at Santry with 1,160 acres, partly on Church lands originally granted to the Plunketts of Dunsoghly. Smaller Protestant landowners in this middle group included Sir James Donnellan and Robert Kennedy, an Exchequer official, both in Castleknock parish, Sir William Ussher, Robert Dillon of Cappock, George Aylmer of Aderry and Henry Power on the edge of Kilmainham. The families in this group occupied a middle ground between the cultural geography of a family like that of Adam Loftus and that of the Barnewalls of Turvey, the leading Catholic landowners of Co. Dublin.

The marriage, kinship and professional relationships of the Barnewall family at Turvey may be used to illustrate another social geography, which rarely, if ever, touched that of the Loftus milieu, and which highlights the interweaving of Old English Catholic landed gentry and their legal kinsmen – the traditional administrative elite of Dublin city and the wider Pale region. This network was centred on the city and county of Dublin but included most of counties Kildare, Louth and Meath, with outliers in Co. Westmeath and elsewhere. Nicholas Barnewall, later created first Viscount Kingsland, was the holder of the most extensive block of Catholic property in north Co. Dublin (see Fig. 7.4) – so extensive that there are references in the Civil Survey to the 'outlands' of his property stretching from the east coast near Portraine to the western county boundary at Palmerstown and Fieldtown.[38] Nicholas Barnewall was the son of Patrick Barnewall, a leading advocate against the recusancy laws of 1613 and a great grandson of another Patrick Barnewall, the staunch defender of Old English elite interests in the era of the dissolution of the monasteries. Nicholas Barnewall's father was married to a daughter of Sir Nicholas Bagenal's of Newry; his Uncle John was married to a daughter of Alderman Henry Cusack's of Dublin, a woman who was in turn the widow of Christopher St Lawrence, seventh baron of Howth (she later married John Finglas of Westpalstown). Nicholas Barnewall's aunts had married into the Finglas family of Westpalstown (twice); the St Lawrences of Howth; rather exceptionally into the recent settler if Catholic family of the Mastersons at Ferns; the Plunketts and Fitzgeralds of Meath, including the family of Lord Dunsany; the Draycotts of counties Louth and Meath (the Barnewalls had long-established landed connections with Co. Louth); the Delahides of Co. Meath; the Dillons, first earls of Roscommon; and the legal landed family of the Bealings.[39]

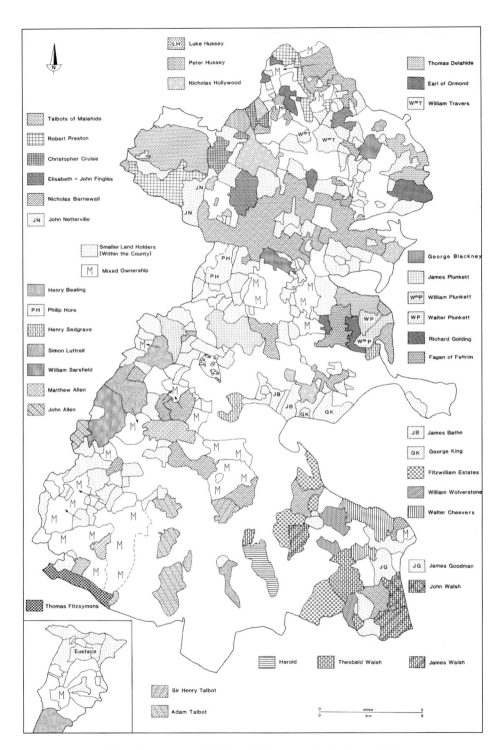

7.4   Distribution of Old English lands in Co. Dublin in 1640

These marriage alliances reflected the influence of class and geographical proximity within the Pale. In north Co. Dublin, Turvey, Westpalstown, Howth and
Gormanston (just across the border in Meath) were the main hubs of this elite
world, whose influence radiated out into Louth, Meath and Kildare. The caste-like
quality of the network is revealed by the scale of intermarriage between landed
and legal families. As Donald Jackson notes, 'the various branches of the
Barnewalls had themselves held numerous administrative offices',[40] and with this
galaxy of legal connections it is not surprising that the family was to produce some
of the greatest legal practitioners of sixteenth- and seventeenth-century Dublin.
Their in-laws belonged to the same milieu, the Draycotts, master of the rolls,
Fitzgeralds and Dillons, barons of the Exchequer, justices like the Delahides, and
the Bealings with a solicitor-general in their ancestry. Other Pale families like the
Talbots, Plunketts and Eustaces also act as justices, including chief justice on the
King's/Queen's Bench. Such control of legal and administrative processes
ensured that the Old English were well capable of defending and advancing their
interests up to the 1640s.[41]

The sustained power of the Old English Catholic landowners in Co. Dublin is
evidenced by the fact that they held 91 per cent of all Catholic land in the county
– and Catholics generally still had over 60 per cent of the county's land in 1640.
The Barnewalls of Turvey were therefore at the centre of a relatively tight network
of Catholic nobility, lawyers and officeholders of the Pale – very different from the
Protestant Loftus colonial network that stretched more loosely across the frontiers
of settlement over the island. Family reactions to the 1641 rising/rebellion were
radically different. Nicholas Barnewall's sisters had married two of the main 1641
leaders of the Irish, Rory O'More and Luke Netterville; other sisters had married
into the Aylmer family of Lyons, to Christopher Fleming, baron of Slane and to
his brother James. Nicholas's own high status is reflected in his marriage to the
daughter of the twelfth earl of Kildare, a widow of Rory O'Donnell, earl of
Tyrconnell.[42] The interlocking connections between the Barnewall, Preston and St
Lawrence families were reinforced when the sixth Viscount Gormanston married
Nicholas Barnewall's eldest daughter. Barnewall, then, was close to the top of the
Pale social hierarchy, characterized by a dense network of relationships, built on
land, offices, marital alliances, prestige, political influence, shared leisure
pursuits, wealth and material possessions. It was a milieu generally sympathetic
to Counter-Reformation culture, a supplier of personnel to religious orders such
as the Jesuits, yet still loyal to the crown.[43] Striving to be spiritually loyal to the
pope, while simultaneously remaining loyal to the secular power of the king, the
Barnewalls, like many of the Old English, were impaled on a cross of contradictions between 1641 and 1660: whilst two of his brothers-in-law were active in the
rising/rebellion, Nicholas himself went to England to support the king, as did
some other leading Palesmen like Talbot of Templeogue, St Lawrence of Howth,
and, as we have seen, the powerful earl of Ormond.

In 1640 as in 1660, the Barnewalls of Turvey headed a phalanx of Old English
Catholic families with estates of at least 2,500 to 5,000 statute acres. These landholders had profited from the redistribution of Church land, further emphasizing

the centrality of former monastic and episcopal lands in the county. (see Fig. 7.4, p. 240).

Luttrell of Luttrellstown was one such family. Well-connected and with much legal expertise, the Luttrells had expanded to include the monastic lands of Coolmine and Tallaght, bringing their total to an estimated 2,030 acres. The Luttrells had a sixteenth-century chief justice in the family; they conformed to the Established Church in the later sixteenth century but were increasingly Catholic in ethos in the first half of the seventeenth century.[44] They were connected by marriage to the Barnewalls, St Lawrences, Goldings, Cheevers and Plunketts of Dunsoghly, as well as Dublin merchant families such as the Seagraves. Although transplanted in 1655, the Luttrells returned after 1660 and intermarried with such new families as the Newcomens, symbolizing their integration into the new political order, which saw their estates augmented by a further 614 acres after the Restoration (see Fig. 7.4).

Christopher Fagan of Feltrim, a member of a Dublin mercantile and mayoral family, had successfully augmented his estate to an impressive total of 2,254 acres by 1640, picking up pieces of Church land all over the county, especially in the parishes of Lusk and Swords. The agile Fitzwilliams of south Dublin were not only beneficiaries of post-Reformation land reallocation (as at Kiltiernan) but benefited from archiepiscopal patronage in the late medieval period in the acquisition of four manorial estates at Merrion, Baggotrath, Booterstown and Dundrum. They were also leaseholders of Church lands, including those of Christ Church at Simons Court. Their cultural position on the south side of the walled city was similar to that of St Lawrence at Howth; proximity to the city meant that they were heavily involved in leasing lands to New English officers such as St Leger and Sir John King in the Baggotrath area, as well as providing the only strategic grazing lands for the horses of the large Dublin garrison.[45] They broke with their kinsmen, the Prestons, in 1641 and gradually acculturated to the new order, becoming the great landowners of south Co. Dublin and the enlightened developers of Merrion Square and Fitzwilliam Square.

The old family of Finglas of Westpalstown expanded their estate to 1,577 acres between 1540 and 1640; the Hollywoods of Artane also gained the old Church lands of Clonmethan, ending up with an estimated 1,392 acres. James Bathe's estate in Drumcondra was essentially a product of ecclesiastical grants – reflecting the power of this cultivated mercantile/legal/military family. Philip Hore's estate at Kilsallaghan of 1,500 acres and that of the original legal family of the Bealings with 1,382 acres had solid cores but also benefited from smaller Church property acquisitions in the Swords region in particular. The estates of the Talbots seem least augmented by Church lands, their total of around 1,654 acres solidly based in the old lands of Malahide and later those at Garristown. Transplanted to Connacht, they resumed ownership of Malahide after the Restoration. Patrick Sarsfield's estate at Lucan was less affected by Church grants; originally a Meath family with Dublin mercantile connections, the Sarsfields had acquired their Lucan estate of over 1,500 acres following the attainder of a branch of the Kildare Fitzgeralds in the sixteenth century.[46] The long curve of the Sarsfield family fortunes followed from a high point of involvement with the crown when Lord Fitzwilliam and Patrick Sarsfield surveyed the bounds for the creation of the new county of Wicklow in 1605; the estate and house were under Cromwellian occupation in the 1650s; only a fraction of the estate was recovered in 1660 and in 1693 a famous son was to die on a continental European battlefield.

Eighteen Old English Catholic landowners held a further 16 per cent of the county, with estates estimated at between 1,000 and 2,500 statute acres. Included here were two Plunkett families, James Plunkett of Dunsoghly (1,220 acres) and Walter Plunkett of Portmarnock (626 acres), as well as Robert Preston of Balmadun (1,060 acres), Luke Netterville of Corballies (1,084 acres) and Christopher Cruise of Naul (670 acres), all solid, middle gentry landholders in the north of the county. There are three Barnewalls in this group, James of Terenure, with 900 acres, Mathew of Bremore, with 747 acres, and Peter of Drimnagh, with 654 acres. Other south county families included John Walsh of Old Connacht, with 923 acres, Garrett Archbold of Stillorgan, with 870 acres, Thomas Fitzsimons of Calliaghstown, with 720 acres, and Henry Talbot of Templeogue, with 670 acres (see Fig. 7.4).

This group also includes a collection of recent immigrants now deemed to be 'Irish Papists', who had acculturated away from rather than towards the new establishment order. Walter Cheevers held Monkstown (850 acres), Lawrence Nottingham held Ballyowen (832 acres), and George Blackney held Rickenhore (718 acres). This group also included James Allen, with 730 acres, and Mathew Allen, with 823 acres; the Allens (Alens) were descendants of New English Churchmen and administrators in the mid-sixteenth century and heirs to Church land at Palmerstown and St Wolstans.[47] The Wolverstons of Stillorgan, with 532 acres, were a Suffolk family which also belonged to this acculturating group.[48] Henry Seagrave of Cabra, with 923 acres, is the last of this group who managed to hold on to positions and lands and yet remain devoted Catholics. For several generations before 1640, the Seagraves were prominent in the episcopal and judicial world of the city, as well as its commercial and mayoral life. In receipt of Church lands in Finglas, Walter Seagrave changed his residence from Finglas Wood to a house nearly five times its value at Little Cabra. As Myles Ronan notes:

> this was a house of Jacobean design and decoration, valued at £1,400: It was built of stone and roofed with tiles, was very extensive, and had a brewery, dairy and coach-house. It was furnished lavishly with every refinement of the period. On the walls were oil paintings of the Last Supper and the Last Judgement . . . The Seagraves appeared to have adhered to the Catholic faith, yet they were allied by marriage with prominent Protestant families and were praised for their good and kindly dealings with Englishmen. This great house of Jacobean refinement was a meeting place for priests, Jesuits and Friars. [49]

There were another 32 Old English Catholic landlords with estates estimated between 500 and 1,000 statute acres within the county. Lord Trimleston and Lord Gormanston were landowners outside the county. Many were cadet branches of Old English families discussed above; others were local small gentry families, like

Locke of Colmanstown, Russell of Brownstown, Conran of Wyanstown, Harold of Harolds Grange, Meaghe of Kilmactalway and Bermingham of Lusk. These landowners, as well as 36 others with estates estimated between 200 and 499 statute acres who included such families as Golding of Raheny, Caddle of Naul, Delahide of Loughshinny and Taylor of Swords, were crucial lynchpins in the local social and settlement hierarchy and bridges between townland communities and the biggest gentry houses.

Such then was the overall pattern amongst the old elite of the 1640s. In terms of family names, the Barnewalls emerge as the leading group in the county, with 8 representatives in the landowning class, followed by the Eustaces (mainly in the Ballymore-Eustace region) who had 7. The Plunketts had 5 families in the Dublin landed class; the Walshes, the Dillons and the Russells had 4. There were 9 families with at least three separate estates – Fagan, Delahide, Ussher, Talbot, Fitzwilliam, Allen, Conran, Kennedy and Nugent. There were 14 other Old English families which appear at least twice as landowners – Goodman, Cusack, White, Dongan, Mill, Wolverston, Aylmer, Bealing, Netterville, Purcell, Hussey, Begg, Bermingham and Preston. And there were close on 50 other gentry families which were represented at least once in the Dublin landed world of 1640 – families like Jacob, Carbery, Travers, Fitzrury, Warren and Browne, which provided solid foundations for an elaborate social hierarchy.

However, the Dublin landownership scene was not at all a self-sufficient one. Co. Dublin was obviously part of a wider culture region of the Pale, which actually constituted one single property, information and marriage field for the Old English. In Duleek barony alone in Co. Meath there were at least 34 landowners who had either landed interests in Dublin or else were based in Co. Dublin with landed interests in Co. Meath.[50] It was a similar situation in the barony of Ratoath, with overlapping property interactions amongst the Plunketts, Fagans, St Lawrences, Barnewalls, Delahides, Cruises, Talbots and Seagraves, as well as Protestant interests in the shape of Sir William Parsons, Sir William Ussher and Sir James Barry. The Catholic gentry of Dunboyne, Deece and Moyfenrath had equally significant interactions with the Dublin landed world, a pattern weakening but by no means absent in the baronies of Navan, Kells and Fore, and in Magheragallon and Slane as well. There were also links with the baronies of North and South Salt and Naas in Co. Kildare.[51] The lands of Clane and Connell were transitional in this property matrix. On the other hand, south Kildare, as represented by the baronies of Kilkea and Moone, clearly belonged to a different culture and land market.

Figure 7.5 summarizes the complicated landownership patterns in 1640 by, first, identifying all the estates of Protestant landowners, whether located on or outside of old Church land. Second, it also shows the parts of Old English landed estates which benefited from the dissolution of the monasteries and acquisition of episcopal lands.[52] Third, it maps the cores of Old English estates outside of these Church lands that had been the dominant element of the Dublin property and settlement scene since pre-Norman times. The New English were by no means wholly dependent on Church land and had expanded well outside of it. South Co.

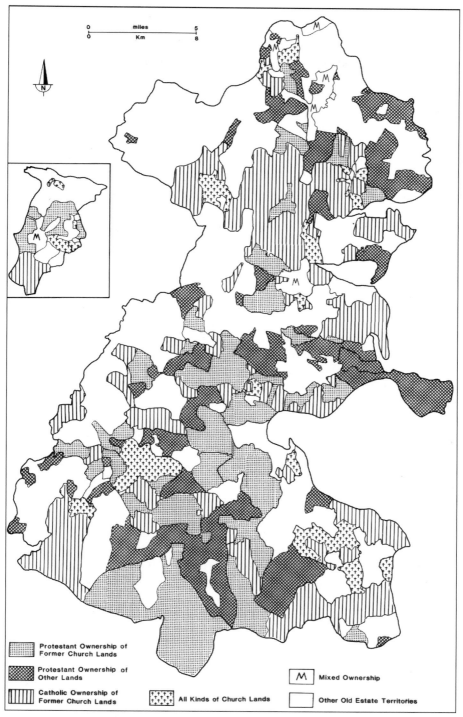

7.5 Distribution of both Protestant and Catholic estates in Co. Dublin in 1640 and their relationship to former Church lands

Dublin, coinciding with the expansion of the Pale frontier, was controlled by Loftus and Parsons and their allies, while a galaxy of other New English interests competed for the highly valued smaller estates around the city walls, especially in the southern parish of St Kevins and the manor of St Sepulchre. In mid-county the St Lawrences dominate to the east, with Sir James Barry of Santry and a cluster of Old and New English families competing in the Castleknock region. In the far north, it is the earls of Thomond and Ormond who fill the picture, with the Bolton estate in the centre and only a small scatter of New English interests in the rest of the north and west of the county.

Figure 7.5 illustrates how Church land was used to bolster the fortunes of the Old English elite. Walter Cheevers occupies the old Cistercian lands of Monkstown, while the Fitzwilliams, Walshes and Barnewalls obtained former Church lands in or near the Dublin mountains. The Church lands of Rathcoole are held by a clique of Old English landowners, some speculative in character but the majority local and probably representing former leaseholders on this archiepiscopal manor. Further north, descendants of the Allens hold Palmerstown and St Wolstans. The Fagans and the Plunketts are the beneficiaries in central Co. Dublin, while across the northern half of the county the Barnewalls of Turvey stand out as major gainers, followed by the Nettervilles, and a cluster of smaller gentry families such as Bermingham, Conran, Dowdall, Cruise, Caddle and Hussey.

The cores of long-established Old English estates are also identified in Fig. 7.5, which highlights Church lands that stayed intact. Deansgrange and adjacent townlands remain as part of the estate of Christ Church cathedral, while the episcopal manor of Clondalkin, and to a lesser extent that of Finglas, still reflect in their property structures the survival of the older episcopal order. On the other hand, the episcopal lands of the now mosaic-like parishes of Swords and Lusk have been reduced, while the manors of Dalkey and St Sepulchre have been broken up. In the south county, the estate cores of the Fitzwilliams at Merrion and Baggotrath and the Walshes of Old Connacht and Shanganagh can be identified, as can the residual power of the Harolds, ancient wardens of the marches, holding on near the mountains at Harolds [Marley] Grange but cut off from the lowlands that ran towards Harolds Cross. The cores of the Barnewall estates at Terenure, Drimnagh and Castleknock emerge around the parish of Mulhuddart, as do those of Bealing, Plunkett, Fitzrury and Nottingham. Plunkett at Dunsoghly and Hore at Kilsallaghan dominate a cluster of smaller properties north and east of Mulhuddart, while on the eastern coastal lands Talbot of Malahide reigns supreme. In the far north the Talbot's control in Garristown is significant. Robert Preston is the central figure in the old parish centre of Balmadun. The northern half of the barony of Balrothery is controlled by smaller gentry, Cruise and Hussey at Naul, and other branches of Barnewall in Balrothery parish, as well as Travers, Blackney, Walsh of Kinnure and others. Whereas the large and middle gentry generally managed to survive the traumas of the Cromwellian settlement, a majority of the lesser gentry fell by the wayside. At least 70 of such Catholic landowners in Dublin were not restored to their lands. A similar pattern prevailed in Co. Kilkenny and elsewhere.[53]

Conspicuous losers in the new order were Blackney of Rickenhore, who lost 664 acres of his lands mainly to Sir George Rawdon, who had gains of 479 acres in the county by *c*.1670; the Conran brothers lost out to the archbishop of Dublin, as did Mathew Begg, the Russells, Gawdons and Husseys, while William Travers's lands passed on to Lord Fingal and Lord Fitzharding, the latter holding 1,373 acres in the county by *c*.1670. The estate of the Finglases of Westpalstown broke up, part going to the in-laws, the Barnewalls, the rest scattering locally. Sir Audley Mervyn took over the Robertstown Talbot landed interests to amass 1,106 acres, while Major Alexander Staples (with a total of 285 acres in 1670) also cut into a signifi-cant part of old Talbot lands in Garristown. Robert Preston of Balmadun and Richard Golding of Kinsealy lost out to Lord Kingston who amassed an estimated 1,107 acres by *c*.1670. Lord Fitzharding gained Walter Plunkett's lands at Port-marnock, while other smaller gentry losses occurred on the lands of Richard Pentony and Patrick Cusack of Blackhall farm near Balbriggan. The ubiquitous duke of York, acquiring a total of 6,441 acres in the county after the Restoration, gobbled up the lands of Luke Netterville, Cruise of Naul and Delahide of Loughshinny. The core of the Hore estate went to Sir George Lane (with 730 acres, *c*.1670), although Hore stayed in the game by acquiring 679 acres elsewhere. Much of the Bathe estate in Drumcondra and the King estate at Clontarf were swept aside by the march of New English interests out from the city. To the west the Sarsfields lost 1,250 acres of their Lucan estate. In contrast, the astute duke of Ormond trebled his lands in north Co. Dublin to 2,200 acres, while, island-wide, his power grew as the lord lieutenant of Ireland for Charles II.

In the south county, the older marcher families were stripped of their landed power. John Kennedy of Rochestown lost out to Patrick Mapas (already holding land in 1640 at Castleknock), while the Goodman estate was reconstructed by Sir William Domville. The Walshes of Carrickmines lost out to the earl of Meath (gaining 632 acres by 1670) and Roger Jones (holding 584 acres in 1670). The last Harold of 'the Grange of the March' gave way to Sir Maurice Eustace, now long adapted to the new social order, who gained 703 acres. These changes further consolidated the power of New English interests along the southern flank of the county. In place of the many marcher families which had for centuries held the line against the 'Irish of the Mountains' was a fresh frontier of New English gentry who would make the half barony of Rathdown a glittering landscape of Anglo-Irish culture for centuries to come.

There were other changes across the county but especially in the northern half of the barony of Balrothery and the south and southeastern part of the county. Although around 44 per cent of New English lands already held in 1640 had been consolidated and expanded, it is surprising that not one of the New English landowners of 1640 were major gainers after the Restoration. A second feature is that a crucial 37 per cent of the lands of the county had permanently changed hands by *c*.1670, that is, after the turmoil of the Cromwellian settlement and the Restoration, as evidenced by the Books of Survey and Distribution. The cultural processes making for change by the 1660s were the augmenting of the estate of the archbishop of Dublin, and the recovery of other Church lands, as well as the consolidation of estates of leading landowners, like the Barnewalls, and the expansion of the property of powerful players, like the duke of Ormond. As noted, new players in this landed chess game were also Lord Fitzharding, Sir William Domville, Lord Kingston, Sir Audley Mervyn, Sir George Rawdon, Alexander Staples, Roger Jones and George Lane. Dublin's hearth-money records of 1664 point equally to the consolidation of New English leaseholders and landowners in the region.[54] Dublin county retained its attractiveness for all groups as the struggle for the most lucrative prizes intensified in the later seventeenth century. Overall, the Protestant interest in all its forms had increased its share of Dublin real estate from around 44 per cent to around 60 per cent of the total by 1670.

One of the most striking features of Co. Dublin is that close on 40 per cent of rural properties had stayed in the hands of or had been acquired by the old Irish and Old English Catholic landed gentry. Of the over 140 gainers of new lands by the 1660s, only half gained additions of less than 100 acres. Of those gaining additions of 250–500 acres, half had Old English family names and had been intimately involved in the Dublin land market for centuries. Likewise, of the group gaining 100–250 acres, 20 out of 38 were experienced players on the Dublin landed stage. Co. Dublin, and especially its northern half, as well as significant parts of counties Kildare and Meath, maintained a complicated property structure until the late seventeenth century. The 1660 poll-tax provides evidence of the survival of Old English gentry in the Pale region. There are two other clusters of Old English gentry survival – one from south Wexford through counties Kilkenny and Tipperary and on from Waterford into east Cork; the other is a small focus along the southern shores of the Shannon estuary, which extends northwards into east Connacht. But the major zone of Old English gentry survival is in the wider Pale region.

In Ireland as a whole the Restoration left the Protestant landowners in a very dominant position. By 1669, Catholics had only been restored to about one-third of the lands they held in 1641. In 1688, Catholics only held 22 per cent of the land and close on half of this share was located in the lands of Connacht and Clare – granted to the transplanted Catholics under the Cromwellian settlement. That the Catholic gentry of Co. Dublin still managed to regain two-thirds of their properties in the Restoration period and held on to about two-fifths (38 per cent) of the county's land speaks to the highly distinctive character of this metropolitan region.

That distinctiveness arises from a number of factors. Long before 1641 the Gaelic Irish had not been significant players in the Dublin land-market – rather the tightly knit Old English Catholic elite of the Pale controlled the territory from their privileged positions as landed gentry or as government officials or merchants. Indeed, they had been major beneficiaries of crown patronage via the former exclusive Church lands. After the 1641 rising/rebellion, the pro-government forces established rapid military supremacy in the Dublin region. The freedom or inclination for rebellion on the part of some of the Old English Catholic elite was therefore severely curtailed. They could thus happily prove their 'innocence' after the Restoration. More particularly, in the early Restoration period, the long-standing landed, mercantile and legal power and astuteness of this regional elite meant that these major Old English landowners were in the best position to engage in the politics of defending their own interests. Proximity to Dublin city and the centre of government decision-making also greatly helped. Proximity to Dublin city also meant that during the Cromwellian Interregnum, leading Cromwellian officials-cum-regicides came to be significant landowners in the region. Such lands often reverted to the original Catholic owners immediately on the Restoration. In addition, it appears that 'the estates of at least eleven Catholic proprietors' actually evaded segregation even during the Cromwellian era.[55] All these factors distinguished Dublin city (and the Pale region generally) and made for striking continuities on many estates, and thus helped to sustain ancient parishes, villages and modes of living in the eighteenth century.

The Books of Survey and Distribution show that many of the old elite families emerged more strongly after the Restoration. The Barnewalls had consolidated their landed power by a further 966 acres, while Henry Talbot of Templeogue gained 304 acres. The traumas of the Commonwealth were not in the end to disturb the landed position of the major Pale families. However, their political power was fast on the wane. When the widow of the executed Luke Netterville remarried, she did so to Sir Richard Bolton, lord chancellor, a near neighbour occupying old Church land at Brazil. He obviously belonged to the new administrative and legal order. This conjunction exemplifies the complex pathways taken by members of the Old English Pale families in the years between 1540 and 1660. These Palesmen had been defenders of English culture and interests and had marched and supplied soldiers, horses and carts against the O'Neills of Ulster and other Gaelic families in the latter half of the sixteenth century, yet ended up on the sidelines or in rebellion in 1641–60. The descendants of these families were scattered, some holding and indeed improving their ground, some doing so but more weakly and some marginalized in the new Restoration order. The story of a Patrick Scurlog of Rathcreedan near Rathcoole is instructive of the fate of smaller landowners. In 1599 he was having his son schooled at Trinity College to be educated in 'the English religion' and to acquire 'English apparell'.[56] By the 1640s the family was in 'rebellion'; by the 1660s the Books of Survey and Distribution records their swift demise.

Parishes, Communities and Settlement Hierarchies

Despite the traumatic effects of the Reformation and other state interventions, the parishes of Co. Dublin remained important institutions shaping society and settlement through the later sixteenth and seventeenth centuries, and parishes were still the basic units for tithe assessment and collection, as they were for the making of the Civil Survey and Down Survey. The 1660 poll-tax and the hearth-money returns were made at the parish level. Parishes often continued as crucial landowning and leaseholding units. Their religious functions bifurcated in the aftermath of the Reformation but parochial interests, established over the centuries, still exerted influence over social institutions and settlement hierarchies in their localities. In leisure activities such as hurling, the parish was a forum for relaxation. As in Co. Kilkenny, the parish functioned as a legal administrative unit and often had its own manorial court – a feature that survived best in the northern half of the county and in episcopal manorial parishes.[57] A number of parishes retained residual functions in relation to control of access to common lands, whether these were the petty commons at the heart of the parishes or the massive belts of mountain pasture to the south. Well over one-third of parishes fronted directly on to the rich resources of the sea or the River Liffey and even some inland parishes, such as the deanery of Taney (Dundrum), retained rights to fishing tithes into the early modern period.[58]

The first striking point about Dublin county's parishes is the pre-eminence of pre-Norman parish names, possibly pointing to early parish formation. Whereas in the city – long the fulcrum of Anglo-Norman rule – parishes called after continental saints outnumbered their Irish equivalents by over four to one, the picture is radically reversed in the county (see Fig. 7.6). Co. Dublin, in fact, exhibits a higher proportion of parish names with roots in the era of Celtic Christianity than does Norman Co. Kilkenny. At least 70 per cent of all parish names had their roots in the early Christian era, from Balscaddan (Baile na Scadán – the town of the herrings) in the north to Shankill (Sean Cill) and Tully (Tulach na n-easpog) in the south. Balmadun (Baile Mac Dun), Kilbarrack (Cill Berech), Donnybrook (Domhnac Broc), Donabate (Domhnac Mite), Malahide (Mullach Ide), Rathcoole (Rath Cumhaill), and Taney (Tigh Naithi) are all parish names. Only around 14 per cent of parish names are medieval in origin or later translations of older Irish names. The sole clustering of this group of medieval parish names is in the north-west of the county from Holywood through Fieldstown and Palmerstown to Garristown, an area which, taking into account the high density of names ending in 'town', seems to be a zone of primary Scandinavian and Norman colonization. Here new lands were laid out geometrically – to judge from the shape of the townlands – in a wetter, forested region. The smaller area from Castleknock to the Ward bears certain settlement similarities with this northwestern region. Finally, about 15 per cent of parish names are hybrid in character, part-Irish part-Viking/part-Norman, as in Balrothery, Holmpatrick, Baldoyle, Balgriffin, Castleknock and, more doubtfully, Rathmichael.

The above evidence confirms the geographical influence of the early Christian Church in this part of Ireland. It could be argued that all of Co. Dublin is essentially a coastal world, characterized internally by a series of smaller peninsular regions from Bremore (Lambrecher, Church of the Bees) in the north through Portrane (Port Rachrann – Reachra was the ancient name for Lambay Island) and Portmarnock (Port Mo Ernoc or Ernan) to the rich early Christian settlements at Killiney (Cillinion), Shankill and Bray (Bre Chualainn) to the south. Inwards from the smaller peninsulas were the famous ecclesiastical centres of Lusk (Losc), Swords (Sord), Finglas (Fionnglas), Dublin (Dubh Linn), Clondalkin (Cluain Dolcan), Saggart (Teach Sagart) and Tallaght (Tamhlaght). Rather like the monastic borderland strongholds from Clonmacnoise to Roscrea, the persistence in the Dublin area of a north–south political buffer zone may have augmented the region's role as a focus of early Christian monasteries. Competition between the

Parishes of Dublin

Balscaddan

Balrothery

Naul

P.of Balmadun

Holmpatrick

Garristown

Hollywood / P.of Balmadun / P.of Hollywood

Baldongan

Ballymadun

Westpalstown

P.of Lusk

P. of Lusk

P.of Lusk

Tipperkevin

Palmerstown / Clonmethan

Ballyboghill

Ballymore Eustace

Portraine

Ballybought

Donabate

Kilsallaghan / Killossery

Killeek

Swords

Malahide

P.of Finglas

Ward

Mullhuddart

P.of Finglas

St. Margarets

Cloghran

P.of Swords

Portmarnock

Santry

Santry

Balgriffin

Baldoyle

Clonsilla

Castleknock

P.of Finglas

Glasnevin

Cloghran

P.of Finglas

Raheny

Howth

Lucan

Clonturk

Clontarf

P.of Aderry

Palmerston / Chapelizod

Kilmainham

Parishes of City of Dublin

Esker

Ballyfermot

Drimnagh

St. Kevins

Kilmactalway

Crumlin

Donnybrook

Clondalkin

Newcastle

Rathfarnham

Rathcoole

Taney

Monkstown

Kill

Saggart

Tallaght

Killiney

Calliaghstown

Whitechurch

Tully

Cruagh

Rathmichael

Kiltiernan

Connaught

| 0 | miles | 50 |
| 0 | kms | 80 |

7.6   Distribution of medieval and civil parishes in Co. Dublin in 1640

Patrician north and the cults of St Brigid and St Kevin from the Leinster south may have added to the vitality of religious foundations in the region.

This legacy was to be complemented, reinforced and transformed by the Normans and their officer corps of bishops and clergymen. For the most part, they were inheritors rather than creators of ecclesiastical structures. For example, Westpalstown parish is named after Roger Westpayle, who occupied the land of the O'Caseys of Fingal, but the church of the new parish was pre-Norman in foundation.[59] The Normans' two major contributions were to crystallize further the territorial nature of parochial life and to dominate the reformed monasteries of Dublin city. This latter achievement resulted in transfer of surpluses from rich rural parishes to monastic houses in the city.

However, the greatest geographical contribution that the Normans made was linking the ecclesiastical territory of the parish with the economic unit of production – the manor. This process was accompanied by rededicating the church to St Mary, frequently the Blessed Virgin Mary, or other mainland continental saints such as Nicholas, Margaret, or Catherine, one of the favourite saints of the Normans of Fingal.[60] Geographically, this dual strategy reinforced the functions of head settlements of the parishes, where parish church and manorial castle acted as twin pillars of society and settlement for centuries. One can identify sixty manors located at either parish centres or chapel-of-ease sites, a figure complemented by the number of mills in the mid-seventeenth century.[61] These manorial sites, built mainly on early Christian foundations, sought out maritime and riverine locations.

The majority of the parishes of Co. Dublin were thus distinctive landowning entities, a feature that reinforced the role of the parish as a focus of territorial life (see Fig. 7.6). As late as 1640, one half of parishes were exclusively owned by either a single landowner or a centralized episcopal/royal manorial administration, with the local seneschal, steward or bailiff still in place. For example, Clondalkin's complex property structures were parish-based, as were those of Crumlin, Finglas, Rathcoole, Saggart, Kilmainham and Ballymore. Exceptions to this general arrangement include the parish of Taney in Rathdown barony, where expanding Fitzwilliam power broke up the old ecclesiastical unit. The enormous parish of Tallaght was a cockpit of competing interests between New English owners like Loftus and Parsons and Old English families such as Talbot and Luttrell. The royal manor of Newcastle was fragmented in its ownership structure but the parish core reveals a complex property arrangement with its origins in earlier manorial administration.[62] The episcopal lands of the unwieldy parishes of Swords and Lusk had become a landownership patchwork, repeated on the archiepiscopal manors of Donabate and Clonmethan. Balscaddan and Balrothery were parishes of small property owners and the landownership structure of Castleknock had long been fragmented between separate townlands. However, the area of greatest complexity was on the northern edges of Dublin city, with property and parish boundaries in a state of flux, as at Coolock, Glasnevin, Clonturk, Killester and Raheny.

Other parishes reveal close relationships between parish territory and a single administration or ownership pattern. Thus, the Talbots dominated the parishes of Malahide and Garristown and the earl of Thomond lorded over the old priory lands of Holmpatrick, and Walter Cheevers over those of Monkstown. Walsh dominated in Old Connacht, George King in Clontarf, Allen in Palmerstown, Sarsfield at Lucan, St Lawrence in Howth, Baldoyle and Kilbarrack, Plunkett in Portmarnock, Sir James Barry in Santry, and Eustace in Tipperkevin and Ballymore-Eustace.

In the light of these interlocking ecclesiastical, proprietorial and economic functions, it is not surprising to find – as in Norman Kilkenny and south Tipperary – that the townland boasting the parish name is the leading centre of population and settlement throughout Co. Dublin in 1660. The nucleating and demographic power of the *caput* of the parish is far greater in Co. Dublin than in either south Tipperary or Kilkenny. Eighty per cent of Dublin's rural parishes are dominated by the townland bearing the parish name.[63] From Balscaddan, Balrothery and Garristown in the north, through Ward, Malahide, Cloghran-Swords, Baldoyle, Santry, Raheny, Balgriffin and Coolock through to Saggart, Tallaght, Ballymore-Eustace and Kilgobbin in the south, the parish settlement structure pivots around the nucleated parish centre (see Fig. 7.6).

It is easier to identify the exceptions that defy this rule of the power of the parish centre than to list all the dominant parish centres themselves. Kilmactalway, which never appears to have been a manorial centre, with an adult population of 17 in 1660, has given way to the feudal centre of Milltown with 24 adults in 1660 but with a much larger population in 1650. The parish centre of Esker (21 adults) yields to Ballyowen (30), dominated by the landlord family of Limerick Nottingham. Kill-of-the-Grange yields to Walsh-dominated Loughlinstown (72). The Cheevers-dominated village of Monkstown is a large parish centre (64 adults), yet is smaller than the garrison-port of Bullock (110). The Walsh-dominated castle-hamlet at Shanganagh (74) has ousted the declining centre of Shankill (44), while the now dilapidated parish centre of Clonmethan (12) yields to the manorial church centre of Fieldstown (47). Holywood (6) has lost out to the other old manorial church centre of Grallagh (26), highlighting, like Fieldstown, the importance of chapel sites as focal points of settlement. Clonsilla (27), one of the newest parish centres, is outstripped by the feudal power of the Luttrells of Luttrellstown (31) and by the monastic settlement of Coolmine (40) (see Fig. 7.7).

The unique census-like materials for parts of south Co. Dublin for 1650–2 provide tantalizing glimpses of the social structure of these parish settlements.[64] This sample of 47 townlands comprised around 15 per cent of Dublin's county population. Two types of parish settlements can be identified here: first, the largest settlements such as Tallaght, Newcastle and Lucan, and second, the more average sized parish settlement centre such as Palmerstown, Esker, Kilmactalway and Ballyfermot. Both types are characterized by a gentry presence, a significant small farmer labourer/cottier group, a substantial number of smiths, carpenters, tailors and brogue-makers and the usual array of male and female servants. However, bigger places like Tallaght or Lucan with an adult population in excess

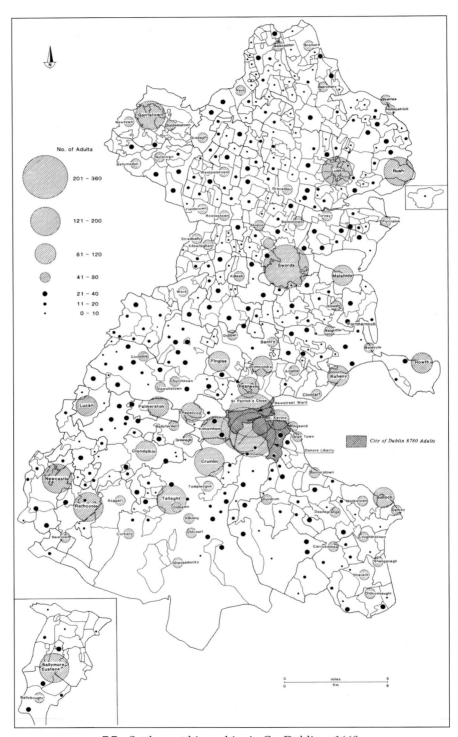

7.7   Settlement hierarchies in Co. Dublin, *c.*1660

of 100 (that is, a total population of 300 plus) had more specialized services and functions – the miller, the maltster and/or the brewer are likely residents, special-ized artisans like the mason and the slater appear, as do the butcher and/or the innkeeper and a more specialized domestic and outdoor servant class. Widows and spinster women are far more likely to be independent heads of households in the larger settlements. This was also true of the Tipperary evidence.[65] Finally, larger centres attracted poorer men and especially beggar women, living on the edges in the smallest cottages.

The Down Survey adds to our image of the village of Lucan by noting that 'here there is a very faire house, a chappell, some thatch houses and Cabbins and a good Stone bridge crossing the river Liffey', while at Rathcoole' stands two old castles and very good habitable houses and Cabbins with the ruins of a chap-pell'.[66] John Dunton, an acerbic observer, describes seventeenth-century Rathcoole as 'a country village with two indifferent inns and six miles from Dublin'. He comments on the general practice of planting

> an ash and some other tree which will grow big in the middle of the village. In some towns, these trees are old and very great and hither all the people resort with a piper on Sundays or Holydays in the afternoon where the young folks dance till the cows come home (which by the way they will do without anyone to drive them).

Dunton notes that while the dance goes on the 'elder people sit close spectators telling stories of their own like feats in days of yore and now and then divert themselves with a quill of sneezing or a whiff of tobacco'.[67] The capacity of the seventeenth-century parish village such as Rathcoole to attract a 'congregation' for a wide range of leisure activities was no less than its twenty-first-century equivalent, the chapel village. Dunton notes the role of the parish in sport and especially in hurling:

> at this sport one parish sometimes or barony challenges another: they pick out ten, twelve or twenty players a side and the prize is generally a barrel or two of ale which is brought into the field and drunk off by the victors on the spot, though the vanquished are not without a share of it too . . . this is commonly upon some very large plain, the barer of grass the better, and the goals are 200 or 300 yards one from the other; and whichever party drives the ball beyond the other's goal wins the day . . . At some of these meetings two thousand have been present together. They do not often play football, only a small territory called Fingal near Dublin the people use it much and trip and shoulder very handsomely.[68]

Dunton provides a less than complimentary picture of the parish centre and town of Malahide:

> it contains about thirty ordinary huts in all and not one without several little chil-dren who sprawl about the fireplace . . . One Jones's house was the Inn and that but a poor ordinary place . . . One Father Gowan or Smith as he called himself, à la mode de Angleterre, happened to be in the Inn at our arrival, where hearing he was a priest of the parish, I engaged his company with us at dinner for I had never seen any of their clergy before.

He has much more to say about baptisms, wakes and funerals, as well as religious practice on Sunday, where 'more appearance of devotion among the laity at celebration of their Mass is not everywhere to be found'.[69]

The resilience of the parish and parish centres is a feature of both post-Reformation and post-Cromwellian Ireland. However, the fate of the medieval churches is another story. Ronan's work on the Anglican archbishops' visitations of 1615 and 1630 contains insights into the state of the churches and religious activities in the first part of the seventeenth century.[70] The massive decline in number and quality of parish churches is the first feature of these reports. In the city of Dublin and the deanery of Taney 71 per cent and 78 per cent of all parish churches, which were in good repair in 1531, were still in good condition in 1615. On the other hand, the northern deanery of Swords shows a decline of 34 per cent in the number of good quality parish churches over the same period, while the deaneries of Ballymore-Eustace (57 per cent), Bray (including part of south Co. Dublin, 54 per cent) and Leixlip (including part of west Co. Dublin, 54 per cent) show massive declines in the number of parish churches still in working order. On the fringes of the diocese in Kildare and parts of Wicklow, decline in the status of parish churches is devastating; 82 per cent of the parish churches in the deanery of Castledermot were already in decay by 1615.

The survey of 1630 by Archbishop William Bulkeley pinpoints a further decline in the number and quality of parish churches and in the quality of the Reformation clergy and their mission. In 1630, after close on a century of Anglican control, in all of Co. Dublin there were only 13 out of 68 parish churches still in full repair. These were Donnybrook, Cloghran-Swords, Donabate, Killossery, Holmpatrick, Balscadden, Newcastle, Lucan, Rathcoole, Tallaght, Crumlin, Finglas and Monkstown. The parish churches at Howth, Clonmethan, Lusk, Ballyboghill, Clondalkin, Kilmactalway, Aderry, Tully, Deansgrange and Kill were still in operation but in need of repair. Yet between 1615 and 1630, the staggering number of 79 diocesan churches had become ruined. This included the ancient parish church at Swords, which 'by the neglect of the gents of the parish, who were recusants, is lately fallen flat to the ground, and noo parte standing onely some part of the bare walls'.[71] The parish churches which disappeared after 1615 now joined the far greater number of parish churches or chapels-of-ease that had ceased to function before 1615. In the diocese as a whole, only 35 per cent of the parish churches in use in 1615 were still in good repair by 1630. Churches of the suppressed monasteries suffered most in this process of decline.

The many infrastructural problems of the post-Reformation Anglican Church in the Dublin region were exacerbated by clergymen holding down a plurality of parishes, by massive absenteeism from parochial and pastoral duties and by the initial problems of a generally poorly educated clergy.[72] There were additional problems arising from the stubborn refusal of the majority population to support the new state Church and its appropriated infrastructure. Bulkeley's visitation in 1630 regularly notes the failure of the 'recusant' or Catholic tithe farmers to support financially either the local vicar or to help maintain the fabric of the parish church. Indeed, the opposite was often the case, as reflected in the withholding of tithes. For example, in Portraine, it is noted that 'John Finglas, gent' detains 'tenn acres of land belonging to the church'.[73] In Kilsallaghan Philip Hore is named as 'keeping away the gleabeland from the vicar',[74] while in Howth, 'Lord Houth, the heires of Bealing and Bealingston and others' are accused of detaining from the vicar '20 acres of land, 12 houses and 55 shillings cheefe rent due to him and heretofore received by his predecessors'.[75]

In the diocese of Dublin in 1630, over 40 per cent of tithes were the property of Catholic tithe farmers.[76] The evidence from the Civil Survey would suggest that for Co. Dublin alone in 1641 at least one-third of tithe income remained amongst older Catholic families, some of the most important titheholders being landowners like Lord Barnewall, Simon Preston, Christopher Fagan and Walter Cheevers. New landowners like Sir John Bysse, Viscount Moore and Adam Loftus were also holders of tithe incomes.[77] Whatever the denominational breakdown of tithe ownership, there was much withholding of tithe incomes from local vicars. In the city of Dublin in 1630, 84 per cent of tithe incomes went directly towards support of the local Anglican clergy as stipends for vicars and curates. The city was the active core of the Anglican Church in the diocese. The deanery of Swords ranks second, yet with only 38 per cent of its tithe income going to support local Anglican clergy. Newcastle and Leixlip deaneries are weakly supportive to the extent of only transforming 29 per cent and 28 per cent of total tithe incomes into vicars' stipends. The deanery of Taney follows with only 22 per cent of total tithe income used in this way. Thus Swords, Leixlip and Taney deaneries were transitional areas in the Anglican cultural region of Dublin diocese. Clearly, outside of the immediate Dublin city hinterland and a few outlying parishes such as Finglas and Rathcoole, material support for the new Reformation Church and its officers was quite weak. The resilient power bases of old gentry families and the survival of a significant proportion of Catholic tithe farmers were inhibiting factors.[78]

However resilient the old gentry families, yeoman farmers and local communities were, Catholic worship and clerical support had to withstand the dissolution of the monasteries, the alienation of parochial territories and buildings and the loss of substantial incomes deriving from glebelands and tithes. Archbishop Thomas Fleming describes the situation in 1632:

> At the present time we enjoy some slight toleration whilst exercising our religion in private houses; but to the great detriment of the Catholic faith all the public chapels and houses of the religious orders have been confiscated by the Government . . . There is no district in this diocese which cannot conveniently have a priest. The religious orders strenuously cooperate with them in administering to the spiritual wants of the faithful – living as obscurely as possible according to the rule, and maintaining the regular discipline as far as the circumstances of the present times allow.[79]

Bulkeley's visitation illustrates a number of other features in relation to the role and status of the Catholic Church at this transitional time. First, the visitation adverts to the significant role of local Catholic gentry houses in hosting migrant friars and priests and in providing the main focal points for masses. It is true that a large mass house 'of nine couples [rafters] longe covered with strawe'[80] had already been built at Garristown under the patronage of the Talbots; there was likewise 'a common Mass howse, frequented publicly since the proclamaçon in the towne of St. Margarets',[81] as well as a third mass house in Monkstown (under the patronage of Walter Cheevers).[82] However, the overall pattern is Sunday mass attendance in the Big Houses: in Swords, at Taylor's house, 'where unto there is great concourse of people on Sundayes and holydaies';[83] in Kilsallaghan at Philip Hore's house; in Howth at the house of Richard St Lawrence of Corstown; in Westpalstown the parishioners 'resort to the howse of the Lady Dowger [sic.] of Howth';[84] in Holywood and Naul in the houses of Caddle and Cruise; in Lusk in the house of the farmer Dermot of Raheny; in Rush on the lands held by George Delahide; in Baldongan at Nicholas Fitzwilliam's house, 'unto whom all the inhabitants round about doe resort to hear Mass';[85] in Baldoyle at Thomas Fitz-simons, the tithe farmer's house; in Portmarnock at Walter Plunkett's house; in Malahide at Talbot's house (he was also the farmer of the tithes); and in Balrothery in the gentry houses of Mathew Barnewall at Bremore and Elizabeth Finglas at Stephenstown. Mass in Balscadden was celebrated in the dwelling house of George Taafe of Grange; in Clondalkin in the house of Browne of Nealstown, 'who is a greate abettor and maintainer of fryers and preists';[86] and in Esker in the house of Limerick Nottingham of Ballyowen. In Tallaght parish, mass was frequently celebrated in 'the towns of Ballyneskorney, Balliman, Kilnarden and Jobstowne, some tymes in one mans house, some tymes in another, in those townes',[87] while in the Templeogue area the Talbots of Belgard and Templeogue, Reillys of Tymon and Archbolds of Knocklyon were all patrons of priests and friars and hosts for Sunday mass. In St Margarets and Finglas, the Plunketts, Barnewalls and Seagraves were patrons of the Church. The gentry supported other aspects of religious devotion in the middle of the seventeenth century. For example, Patrick Fagan of Feltrim decorated an octagonal building of 'graceful style' built over a holy well near Balgriffin devoted to the Blessed Virgin Mary and 'had its inner walls covered with frescoes'.[88]

Without exception, therefore, the old gentry and some yeoman farmers provided the basic infrastructure for the reconstruction of the Catholic Church and for the maintenance of patterns of worship and devotion. The surviving names of the priests are instructive – Cahill, Doyle, Barnewall, Drake, Shergall, Begg, Duffy, 'Mr. Clarke' ('as they call him'), Connell, Harris, Gargan, Fitzgerald, Reilly, Comyn, Murrochoe and Byrne.[89] The landed elite and patrons of the Church were essen-tially descendants of medieval settlers, yet half the priests – like those of Co. Kilkenny – bore names of old Gaelic families from the region. One meets the same diversity in schoolmasters who were patronized by local gentry.

There are, however, gaps in the records of activities of religious personnel for this period. In some parishes, as in Lord Barnewall's bailiwick at Donabate, it would appear that the vicar had been forbidden by the local lord to reveal either his stipend or the names of local friars and mass priests. The names of Catholic patrons and pastors are less forthcoming in the stronger Protestant parishes – as at Lord Thomond's domain at Holmpatrick, where no details are provided. In the belt of plantation settlement and settler consolidation in the New Pale of south Co. Dublin, the state of the Catholic Church is less clear.

Overall, between 1613 and 1630 there was a contraction in the influence of the Anglican Church over Co. Dublin, with sometimes locally high losses in congregations, as at Swords. Finglas parish and church is the staunchest focal point of the new faith, with 150 regular communicants. To the south, a second belt of Anglican Church attendance stretches from Donnybrook (60 communicants) and Deansgrange (24) through Taney (20) to twin peaks at Rathfarnham (60) and Tallaght (60–80) and on to Saggart (30), Rathcoole (30), Newcastle (30) and Kilmactalway (12), to peter out in Lucan, with 5 communicants. Apart from Howth (30) and Holmpatrick (20), the Anglican congregations of north Co. Dublin were few and far between.[90] The distribution of 'English', as defined in the 1660 poll-tax, reveals a similarly constricted distribution (see Fig. 7.8).

The long-term social and settlement implications of these Church structures are less clear. The majority of settlement centres that acted as old focal points of parishes were still reasonably vibrant in the 1660s. In the difficult year of 1698 – when 85 per cent of Irish priests, belonging to regular orders, were 'shipped to foreign parts' – there were still 27 'Romish clergy' working in Co. Dublin, which meant about one priest for every two and a half medieval/civil parishes.[91] This was a less favourable ratio than in the smaller populations of counties Louth, Kildare and Wicklow, yet a total of sixteen large Catholic parish units were now in place in the county. We get a small glimpse of longer term implications of these changes from John Rocque's superb county map of 1763.[92] It is not a fully comprehensive source, as it missed the Protestant church in Finglas, as well as missing out some Catholic chapels, for example, at Garristown. The overall balance, however, between church sites mapped is sufficiently reliable to allow conclusions to be drawn about the religious situation in the period that marks the ultimate achievement of the Protestant gentry in Ireland. One can identify 26 Anglican parish churches in the county as a whole – a situation marking some improvement on the numbers of adherents and status of the Church in the 1630s. There are at least 21 Catholic chapels shown on the map, as, for example, at the hamlets or villages of Balmadun, the Grange of Ballyboghill, Old Connacht, Booterstown, Saggart, Clondalkin, Crumlin, Holmpatrick, Leixlip, Luttrellstown, Blanchardstown, Cloghran, Baldoyle, Howth and Malahide. The first of the lonely chapels in the countryside is shown between Damestown and Napstown in north Co. Dublin.

A number of points emerge from this preview of the mid-eighteenth century. First, Rocque's map is incapable of portraying the reality of a hidden Catholic Church of stations, patterns and other devotional practices.[93] Second, the Established Church has improved its position and built a number of new parish churches at Clontarf, Castleknock, Dundrum and Swords. And finally, Rocque's map shows the growing dialectic between adjacent villages and communities, one 'colonial' and the other 'indigenous' in character, one centred on the Anglican church, the other on the Catholic chapel.

Striking examples of this dual pattern are Tallaght *vis-à-vis* Saggart, Rathcoole and Clondalkin, and the juxtaposition of 'colonial' Castleknock and 'Catholic'

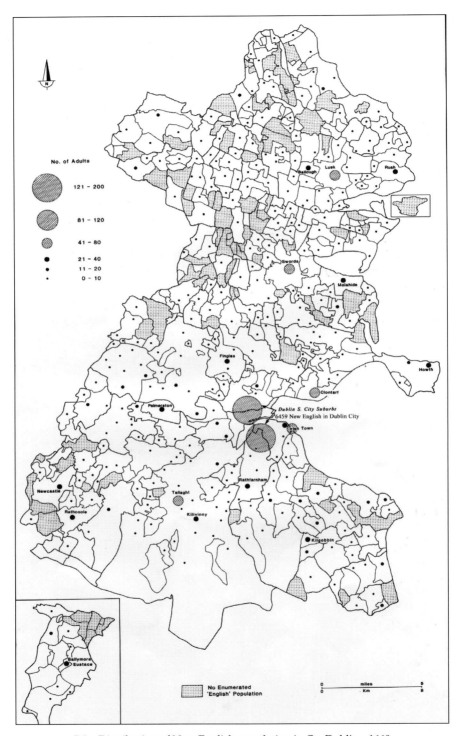

7.8   Distribution of New English population in Co. Dublin c.1660

Blanchardstown. There are six villages or towns – Clondalkin, Clonsilla, Swords, Lusk, Balrothery and Skerries – where the two churches and the two traditions are located together. Otherwise, settlement and social distinctions between the two major cultural traditions in Co. Dublin had widened since the mid-seventeenth century. The most important geographical point is that for both denominations, old villages provide ready locales for their churches and congregations. This was not only true of the Anglican Church but also of the new Catholic Church, which built its chapels in the old villages, especially in those that had been least affected by the seventeenth-century settlement and which remained, like the chapel at Malahide, under powerful Catholic patrons like the Talbots.

Townland Placenames, Occupational and Household Structures

At the foundations of this culture and society, increasingly influenced by the needs of a burgeoning capital city and ruled locally by a diverse group of land-lords, leaseholders and parish clergy, were the individuals, families and households of the townlands. The townland denominations are referred to as 'places' in Petty's 1660 poll-tax abstracts and constitute the most fundamental territorial building blocks. Townland names evoke a heritage of settlement and cultural development from the early medieval period – the related 'bally' and 'town' names are mainly medieval in origin and dominate the distribution of townland names in the county. The more gaelicized 'bally' zone is conspicuous along the southern edges of the county, as well as in pockets in the Liffey valley, on the borders of Castleknock and Coolock baronies and along the northern coast-lands. A striking 'town' zone stretches in a narrow belt across south Co. Dublin to expand into a compact block in the Castleknock/Clonsilla area, and northwards to the Meath border and beyond.

The most interesting feature of the late medieval placename legacy is the strength of other descriptive townland names in English. Extending out from Dublin city are intriguing belts of names. Along the southeast coast are Forty Acres, Smotscourt, Priestshouse, Galloping Green and Deansgrange; southwards along the old road networks to the county border at Newcastle is a vector that includes Bluebell, Yellow Meadows, Newlands and Brownsbarn. There is an axis of these placenames along the Liffey and Tolka valleys, from Castleknock through Blackditch and Yellow Walls to Coldblow and St Catherines Park. The northern half of the county has a series of pathways along which distinctive English placenames have travelled – along the coast from Grange, Broomfield and Robswalls and north to Newhaggard and Blackhall to Strifeland and Castle-land; along the main routeway through Swords from Forrest Great and Little through the many English names for open-field areas around Swords on to Lissenhall and Colecot to Holywood and Grange in the north. To the northwest, Cardiff's Castle, Cold Winters and Bishopswood point the way to Co. Meath. Extreme versions of this trend are revealed in placenames like Passifyoucan, Efferknockstown, Willies Rush, Bog of the Ring and The Ffullams, hinting at the depth of an English-speaking cultural world in this region. On the other hand, toponyms proper are relatively rare in this deeply humanized land.

The 1660 poll-tax abstracts identify 500 settled 'places' or townlands. Just over 60 per cent contain an adult population of under 20 (that is, a total population of under 60), 25 per cent contained adult populations of 20–39 (that is, a total population of under 120), and 15 per cent were inhabited by 40 adults or over (that is, a total population of greater than 120 persons). Within this framework, one can distinguish three regional types of settlement hierarchies. To the south, the baronies of Newcastle and Uppercross (22 per cent) and Rathdown (22 per cent) – the most exposed areas of the Old Pale – exhibit the highest proportion of townlands with adult populations of over 40. It is this buffer region that was most studded with castle foci up to the 1640s. At the other end of the spectrum, the more peaceful north of the county – the baronies of Balrothery and Nethercross – has well above the average number of townlands with adult populations under 20. In Nethercross barony, 73 per cent of all townlands had such small populations, while the proportion was 67 per cent for Balrothery. Indeed, in these northern baronies, townlands with an adult population of less than 10 comprise 42 per cent of the total in Nethercross and 35 per cent in Balrothery. A critical factor here is the large size of the episcopal manors of Lusk and Swords, ruling extensive areas of small farm hamlets. The middle belt of baronies from Coolock (29 per cent) to Castleknock (39 per cent), closer to the city's influence, has an above average concentration of townlands with medium-sized adult populations (20–39). It is no coincidence that this region is characterized by many independent smaller property holders (see Fig. 7.4, p. 240 and Fig. 7.7, p. 254).

Parish centres, often in combination with gentry rule, were major generators of settlements with an average adult population of 60. Despite the traumas of Cromwellian settlement, the independent factor of gentry residence – whether Old English or New English – also boosted townland population size. Townlands with 40 adults or more were in a minority (15 per cent) in the county, yet the average size of townlands with a gentry residence was 43 adults. In Newcastle and Uppercross, for example, 46 per cent of gentry townlands had an adult population of 40 or over, 28 per cent contained 20–39 adults and 28 per cent returned smaller adult populations.

The 1650–2 Census of parts of Newcastle and Uppercross provides detailed insights into the nature of these townland communities, often dominated by lesser members of the gentry.[94] It is difficult to distinguish between gentry and big farmer households; these two classes graded into one another, revealing similar household structures. For example, the new settler John Nicholson in Tallaght is described as a farmer but his household composition suggests a 'gentrified' structure. Some families described as gentry have household structures no more complex than the bigger farmers. Allowing for this ambiguity, there are at least 31 gentry families enumerated in the Census. The composition of this gentry group reveals new names not apparent from analysis of landownership alone. Occupation of land by major leaseholders as opposed to owners is a crucial variable at this time.

One finding that confirms this leasehold factor is the emergence of the Byrne family at this gentry level, a factor obscured in an analysis of landownership alone. Indeed, the virtual absence of landowning families of Gaelic origin is a striking feature of Co. Dublin, very different indeed to, say, the landowning world of north Tipperary. Byrne emerges as the second most common gentry family name with three representatives, one less than the tenacious Archbold family. Archbolds are more conspicuous at the lesser gentry level than at the strictly landowning level. A family with more than one gentry representative is Barnewall, which was equally entrenched at the top levels of landownership. There are 15 other gentry names ranging from Brereton through Sarsfield to Ussher and Walsh but a number of Gaelic/Viking names, hidden at the top level, also emerge – Doyle, McDaniel and Kennedy. There are also at least 4 settler gentry in this group – Dixon of Butterfield, Bulkeley of Old Bawn, Nicholson of Killininny and Loftus of Belgard. Twenty-four out of the 31 gentry families are associated with townland adult populations of over 40, 3 with the 20–39 group and 4 with less than 20 adults.

The Barnewall household – dominating the village of Shankill with a total adult population of 128 – is typical of the bigger gentry situation. This household includes 21 persons, headed by Mary Barnewall, widow of Robert Barnewall and a sister of another Barnewall, seventh baron of Trimleston. She has 2 sons and 3 daughters. Amongst her household staff are a bailiff, labourer, footboy, gardener and driver, ploughholder, horseboy, cowherd and swineherd. There are also 5 female servants, undifferentiated as to function. The Tirlagh Birne house, which dominates the townland of Milltown, Uppercross barony, with a total adult population of 72, reveals other variations on this gentry theme. Tirlagh himself is a bearded hundred-year-old, his wife is eighty and his married son has two sons. His household workforce includes a ploughholder, 2 taskers (foremen?), a weaver, driver, fosterer, 2 cowboys, a smith, bullockboy and gamekeeper, as well as an array of other male and female servants, including wives of the leading workmen – the ploughholder and the tasker. The settler family of Bulkeley of Old Bawn (a settlement with a total adult population of 130) is also a complex three genera-tional household with other kin such as sisters and cousins represented and a clearly differentiated series of female servant roles identified.[95]

In a minority of examples, a gentry household may stand alone in a townland. Robert Cusack, member of a leading mercantile family in Dublin, lived in the castle/mansion house of Rathgar with his wife, son and daughter, as well as two men servants, a maid, another female servant 'to the said Robert', and two poor women of unidentifiable status (almost invariably the poor are associated with either a small town or a gentry townland).[96] The total adult population of Rathgar is 10, all inhabitants of a single gentry house. Likewise, the adult population of the townland of Blundelstown was represented by the single gentry household of Nicholas Hart.[97]

This unique Cromwellian census, therefore, permits generalizations about the nature of townland social structures in the different population ranges. In town-lands of under 20 adults, there were at least three types of social structure. First, there are townlands with tenant cottiers in some kind of partnership group, with their wives and male and female servants. Second, and more characteristic of the baronies of Balrothery and Nethercross, are townlands with a single farmer (occupying a better house, *vide* the Civil Survey), with his labourers/smallhold-ers (living in 'chaffe-houses') and their associated male and female servant groups. Third, these smaller townland populations may be headed by a lesser gentry family, sometimes with one or two labourer/cottier households but invariably involving a more diverse group of female and male servants, as well as possibly poorer women.

In the middle group of townlands with adult populations of 20–39, there are three main types of social structures. Many townlands are headed by one big farmer, with a great number of assisting labourers/cottiers and a complex array of servants. A few artisans such as a smith and/or a carman may also be represented. The second type of social structure at this level is the gentry-based household with assisting labourers/smallholders, and specialized servant functions, such as watchman and gamekeeper as well as artisans. A third and more unusual type comprises a miller/carpenter, with some labourers and a greater number of artisans.

The structure of townlands with over 40 adults has already been partially discussed in relation to parish centres. Non-parish-centred townlands of this type tend to be gentry-dominated. Such a townland hosts a large number of cottiers and especially labourers, the servant composition is complex and more artisans are represented. Key management people, such as the bailiff, steward or 'hayward' of the townland, are also found. However, other kinds of social structures are repre-sented at this top level. Crumlin, while having gentry representation, is permeated by a solid small farming/artisan class. Deansrath, an old ecclesiastical tenant unit, has many labourer/small farmers and a few artisans. Dalkey, while containing gentry households, is dominated by its 'husbandman' group.[98]

The Census is also helpful in teasing out the overall occupational structure of Co. Dublin in the mid-seventeenth century. The sample is an inland one (only one fisherman from Shankill is represented), so there is a bias away from maritime occupations which would be evident along the coast. There are problems with identifying the occupational structures of some townlands, notably industrial Kilmainham, Rathfarnham with its estate village, as well as Ballyfermot and Bally-owen. This sample appears to be overly biased in favour of larger settlements; it may overrepresent gentry, servants and artisans, while underrepresenting labour-ers and cottiers. However, there is little doubt that it provides unique insights into the occupational structure of Co. Dublin in this period. The hearth-money records of 1664 now and again reveal similar structures. Carmen, cowboys, tailors, glovers, tenants, smiths, weavers, shepherds, soldiers, herds, ploughmen, sieve-makers, slaters and dairymen still peep through these impersonal records.[99]

Whatever the boundary between lesser gentry and big farmer – the term 'farmer' in 1650–2 is then confined to a distinct 'yeoman' type – these two groups are the dominant strata in the sample, with a total number of *c.*76 households and a slight bias in favour of the big farmer. Beneath this group came the husband-man/cottier group with *c.*111 households – this would be described as the middling small farmer group in today's terminology. The labourer group –

involved in manual work on bigger farms and gentry holdings, while also working their small crofts and gardens – make up the bottom layer of this agricultural landed working class with c.192 households.

Perhaps the most striking feature of the mid-seventeenth-century social structure is the overwhelming importance of the servant class, both male and female. There were c.202 man servants and c.295 maid servants listed in the sample – the vast majority single, and this, as David Dickson has argued, made for a significant proportion of celibate men and women in this early modern society.[100] There was a further c.168 specialized domestic and farmworkers, which included ploughholders (30), cowherds (36), drivers/drovers (24), swineherds (13), gardeners (9), ploughmen (9), shepherds (6), nurses (5), watchmen (4), horseboys (4), bullockboys (4), bailiffs (3), footboys (3), as well as stewards (2), brewers (2), taskers (2), cooks (2) and 1 hayward and 1 gamekeeper. Two fosterers and two foster mothers should also be included here, reminding us, as MacLysaght has shown, of the continuing role of fosterage.[101]

There were c.142 artisan households led by carmen with 25 representatives, followed by smiths (21), carpenters (17), tailors (16), brogue-makers (16) and weavers (15). These groups were essential and eternal figures in the rural landscape. In an area without bogs, 8 furze-cutters made their living, as did 2 basket-makers and 2 sieve-makers. There were 6 shoe-makers (not yet so critical an artisan group as brogue-makers), 2 glovers, 2 knitters, a comb-maker, cooper, hooper, mason, rope-maker and tanner. And there were still a few descendants of a hunter-gatherer culture – 1 fowler, 1 fisherman and 1 coney [rabbit] catcher.

In contrast, members of a shopkeeper service class were few and far between in these more self-sufficient local communities. Only 18 members of the group were enumerated: 6 butchers, 4 millers, 3 grain merchants, 2 maltsters, only 1 innkeeper (where were the others?), 1 linen draper, and 1 snuff merchant. Bringing up the rear of household heads were 28 widows, 14 spinsters of independent means, as well as 9 poor women and 2 beggarmen, one named Patrick Farrell and one whose name Phelim MacArt suggests a long march southwards. In sum, 6 per cent were gentry or big farmers, 9 per cent husbandmen and cottiers, 16 per cent labourers, a staggering 54 per cent servants of various kinds, 11 per cent artisans, with the remaining 4 per cent made up of shopkeepers, widows, spinsters and the very poor.

A surname analysis of the various strata illuminates other aspects of the social structure. Some of the poor women were local or regional in origin, such as, for example, Gormley Keohoe, who resided at Newcastle; some may have come from further afield, such as Kath Kearney at Belgard and Mary Heelan at Gallanstown. Margaret Clandonnell, a poor woman with a dwelling in Tallaght, suggests an Ulster background. The small shopkeeper service group is obviously not a local class – only one of the more common names in the region are represented at this level. For example, Thomas Morrin is a glover, Nicholas Harford a miller, yet Cahire McDonnell is a 'sneezing merchant'. No family name occurs more than once in this group. In contrast, carmen are rooted in their localities and communities – Toole, Doyle, Byrne and Purcell all occur more than once.

The overall social structure of the region clearly emerged in family names of female and male servants and work people. Amongst female servants, there were 32 Byrnes, 14 Doyles, 8 Walshes, 6 Kellys, 6 Murphys, 6 Tooles, 6 Allens, 5 Kavanaghs and 5 Keoghs. A majority of women derived from the general region, with a northward drift from the Wicklow mountains also indicated. The proportion of female servants whose names occur more than once outnumber single instances of family names by a ratio of 1 to 0.69. On the other hand, since as many as 125 separate surnames emerge in this servant class and since 41 per cent of these surnames occur only once, the long-range migration of some members of this group is suggested.

Amongst male servants, Byrne (34) heads the list, followed by Doyle (9), Murphy (8), Lawlor (6), Cullen (6) and Kavanagh (5). Again much of this group is locally born. Sixty-one per cent of male servant names occur more than once, outnumbering single instances of family names by a ratio of 1 to 0.64. Overall, there is little difference between male and female servant naming patterns, although there is a slight tendency for female servants to be more diverse in naming patterns and geographical origins. It is clear, given the overall age/sex pyramid of the population, that there has been substantial inmigration into south Co. Dublin of the younger adult age groups, especially those between the ages of 19 and 35.

A stratification of servants' occupations and an examination of surnames of those who worked for gentry or big farmer households reveal further nuances in this middle rank servant group. Byrnes jointly hold the lead with Doyles, each with 6 representatives, followed by Nolans (3) and Tooles (3). Six other local names are represented twice. On the other hand, 94 servants appear in the group, each with a different surname. Based on this surname evidence, it would appear that only one-quarter of the higher ranking servant group came from nearby parishes – many others had migrated from much further afield. Some were Welsh and English emigrants who had been brought with their masters and mistresses into a new land.

The artisan group is much more local than this higher ranking servant group. Nine Byrnes head the artisan class, followed by 4 Doyles, 4 Murphys and 4 Nolans, with 12 other family names occurring at least twice. On the other hand, since 56 per cent of all artisan names occur only once, a fairly extensive and diverse migration field is also suggested. Among the crofter/labourers, the Doyles (9) master the Byrnes (6) for the first time but the other key names, Murphy (6), Toole (3), Carroll (3), Nolan (3), Farrell (3) and Gormley (3), are recurring regional names. Not surprisingly, the labourer/crofter group is much more rooted than the mobile artisan class, with 55 per cent of its surnames recurring more than once in the sample, as opposed to 44 per cent of artisan names. The husbandman/cottier tenant class is somewhat similar, although the Byrnes (16) reassert their supremacy over the Doyles (8), with Tooles (5) and Kellys (5) also conspicuous. Recurring names account for 52 per cent of all surnames in this class, which is very similar to the labourer group.

Excluding the small shopkeeper group and the higher ranking servant class, there is a remarkable consistency in the naming structures of male and female servants, artisans, labourers and small farmers. Overall, Byrne outnumbers Doyle by two to one and they in turn repulse the challenge of Murphy and Toole by a further two to one, with Kelly, Walsh and Keogh also strongly represented amongst the top names.

The real break in the class and family structures comes with the farmers. Amongst the farming class the ubiquitous Byrne is no more conspicuous than Walsh, Shippy and Lawless and the run of farming names suggests either a spread downwards from landed families or the emergence of a new settler farmer class. When we reach the gentry level in the sample, the dominant group here is medieval in origin and closely connected with the set of landowners and merchants already discussed. Co. Dublin was a highly stratified rural society in the late medieval and early modern period. Only the Byrnes and a few other families managed to maintain a bridge between the deeply divided worlds of the gentry/big farmer, on the one hand, and the cottager/labourer servant, on the other.

Further clues to the structure of local rural communities in mid-seventeenth-century Co. Dublin are provided by the Census details relating to household and kinship structures. Children under twelve had been excluded from this survey, so it is impossible to determine the overall distribution of households where husband and wife did or did not have children under this age. Close on 12 per cent of the total sample of c.592 households were nuclear families, that is, with children over twelve years of age) and close on half of this group had at least one servant in the home. A further 42 per cent comprised either a husband and wife (24 per cent), a husband and wife with one servant (10 per cent), or a husband and wife with more than one servant (8 per cent). The majority of these households were likely to have had children either at the time of the survey or at an earlier stage in the life cycle. Over 7 per cent of the sample may be said to exhibit a gentry-type household, involving a wide diversity of servants and retainers. Nearly 16 per cent of the households could be described as actually or potentially incomplete, characterized by a single parent with servants (4 per cent) or a single unmarried heir with mother and/or sisters and/or servants (5 per cent). Siblings as heads of households with parents and/or servants comprise a further 5 per cent, while the remainder comprise single men or single widows or spinsters.

The household structures of mid-seventeenth-century Dublin (and Ireland) were more diverse than their modern equivalents, with only 31 per cent having a simple nuclear family. Households involving two generations and/or servants and other siblings comprised a further 6 per cent; around 4 per cent of the total number of households comprised two sets of husbands and wives; and 4 per cent involved a number of widows living together or with others. Finally, about 11 per cent contained more complicated combinations of servants/kinsfolk/lodgers living under the same roof. Overall, this was a rural society characterized by complex webs of relationships within households, townlands and wider parish communities.

Evidence of extended kinship structures and the degree of 'openness' in townland communities can also be extracted from surname analysis. The greater the repetition of the same family names within the same townland, the more likely that closer kinship links existed. Put another way, the greater the diversity of surnames within a settlement, the greater the possibility of a more open, less introverted social structure. However, it is clear that townlands of different population size have different possibilities of exhibiting recurring family names. It is therefore necessary to divide townland units into the three categories already identified – those with less than 20 adults, those with 20–39 adults and those with 40–79 adults – as well as the additional category of those with over 80 adults, and analyse the level of recurring family names in each of these groups.

The smaller the townland population, the less likely the possibility of repetitive family names and this is confirmed by townlands with an adult population of less than 20. In four such cases, there is no repetition of the family name at all, while in one case the proportion of family names recurring out of the total number of surnames in the townland is 31 per cent. The average is 11 per cent. In the adult population group 20–39, the range is from 0–44 per cent, and the mean is 23 per cent. Climbing the social and settlement hierarchy to the 40–79 group, the range is from 14 per cent to 66 per cent, with the average proportion of recurring family names constituting 46 per cent of the total number of names. The overall pattern is therefore a doubling of the incidence of recurring family names from low to highly populated townlands. In the largest settlements of over 80 adults, the range is from 29 per cent to 66 per cent, with the average proportion of recurring family names amounting to 47 per cent. In the two highest population settlement groups, there is no significant difference in the indicators of extended kin networks.

However, the critical element in this analysis is the divergence in kinship structures within settlements of the same size. Here a striking geographical pattern emerges (see Fig. 7.9a). Apart from Byrne-dominated Irishtown, where half the family names occur more than once, all other settlements along the Liffey valley and the routeway westwards display weaker kinship structures than would be predicted from their settlement size. Thus, from Kilmainham through Ballyfermot, Palmerstown, Rowlagh, Deansrath, Ballyowen, Backstown, Lucan and Westpalstown there is a lower than expected incidence of recurring family names. This is a belt of country in Co. Dublin characterized by more open, less kinship-dominated social structures. The impact of traffic and communications along major routeways and gentry household structures may have been particularly influential in shaping this pattern.

A second belt of weaker kinship structures stretches from Rathgar through Rathfarnham on through Ballimount, Newlands, Jobstown and Grange to Old Bawn. These settlements show lower frequencies of recurring family names than would be expected from settlements of their size. A Big House culture, a major routeway to the southwest and a minority of new settler families in this belt may have dissolved more rooted kinship structures.

In contrast, two regions in south Co. Dublin reveal stable kinship and social structures, suggested by recurring family names. Between the Liffey and the Newlands belt in a zone beginning at 'clannish' Crumlin and stretching through Curtlagh, Nealstown, Kilshogue, Milltown, Gallanstown and on to Loughtown

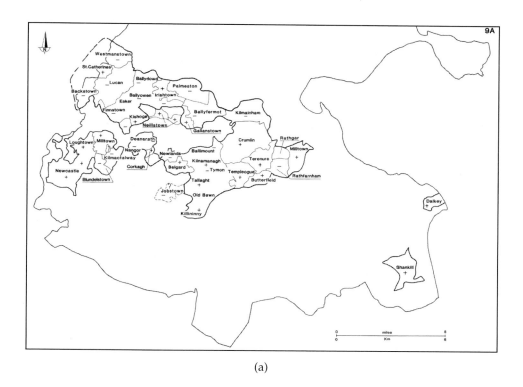

(a)

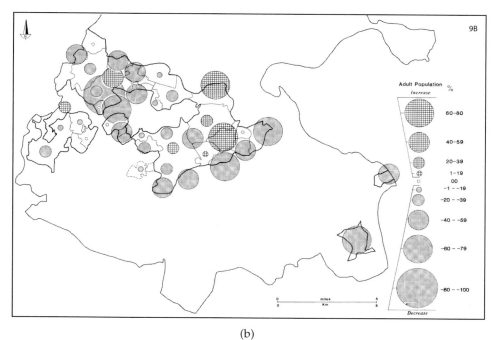

(b)

7.9   (a) Kinship structures in south Co. Dublin 1650–2
       (b) Population change in south Co. Dublin between 1650–2 and 1660

and Newcastle, a belt of more powerful localized family structures is revealed. To the south, Newcastle connects up with lands at the foot of the Dublin mountains running from Killininny through Tallaght, Belgard, Kilnamanagh on to Butterfield and across to Dalkey and Shankill, where another series of communities emerges with high levels of recurring family names. Byrne dominates in much of the baronies of Rathdown and Uppercross; Doyle achieves a local prominence in a middle belt from Rathfarnham to near Tallaght, while the western half of the barony of Newcastle is dominated by a different suite of family names, suggesting an old cultural distinction between the southeastern and southwestern edges of the county.

Finally, these Newcastle barony materials provide illuminating details on the overall structure of the population. The total number of households and individuals give an average household of 4.08 persons (exclusive of children then under twelve who were not enumerated). This figure indicates a large household size, although it should be remembered that there is a bias in the sample towards more populated townlands with substantial gentry and farmer households. Gentry households were complex and included a minimum of 7 adults. There were at least four instances of gentry households of over 20 adults.

A second feature, which Dickson has emphasized, is the size of the resident servant class, male and female, in non-gentry households. This was a critical demographic feature, since around 24 per cent of the total number of adult females were unmarried servants residing in wealthier households. Dickson has also identified crucial differences in the average age at first marriage of women and men – women marrying at the relatively early age of twenty-three, while their husbands were likely to be at least five years older. Irish rural society was therefore potentially more patriarchal than its English equivalent.[102] On the other hand, it is significant that women, especially those in the artisan and labourer/cottier classes, tended to retain their own family names after marriage.

Odd glimpses of the traumas of the 1640s and early 1650s are also suggested by the sex ratio of different townlands. Whereas the overall ratio of female to male is even, with a slight preponderance of women, there are divergences from this norm. In the village of Dalkey, 61 per cent of the adult population is female, and in the townland of Ballydowd, this proportion is 66 per cent. Rathfarnham's adult female population constitutes 57 per cent of the total, in Terenure, 65 per cent, and Tallaght, 57 per cent. Although large settlements like Tallaght and Rathfarnham had a tendency to attract more widows and spinsters, the hidden traumas of the 1640s and early 1650s had probably left their mark on these populations. The details, therefore, of local dislocations, famine/plague deaths and migrations in the war years still remain a mystery for Co. Dublin and for Ireland – hidden behind these brief numerical summaries.

In the 1660s, the Restoration did not make for dramatic changes in the social and cultural topographies of Co. Dublin. True, the Talbots were back in Malahide, the

Wolverstons in Stillorgan, Barnewalls at Bremore, Cheevers in Monkstown, Garret Archbold at Jobstown and George Foster at Ballydowd. The hearth-money records of 1664 suggest that about 20 of the old gentry regained access to their ancestral townlands, displacing sideways recent Cromwellian settlers.[103] The hearth monies also show that at least 40 other members of the old gentry class held their ground from the Cromwellian period – certainly all of this group were already living in their old residences by 1659–60. In addition, nearly 50 members of the New English gentry, solidly entrenched in 1660, were confirmed in their respective residences by the mid-1660s. However, the most striking feature of the 1664 returns is the emergence of at least 90 other English gentry, merchants and major leasehold families in the county, reflecting the expansion of the new ruling elite in the second half of the seventeenth century, whose houses radiated out along the major routeways.

Finglas had become one of the most fashionable centres for gentry settlement outside of the city, with 10 major hearth-money taxpayers in 1664. Clontarf entered a new phase, marking the initiation of a significant movement of gentry into this part of Coolock barony – from Drumcondra through Clontarf and on to Raheny. Kilmainham exhibits rapid population growth in the later 1650s and 1660s and the hearth-money records with their mills and forges highlight its industrial functions. Chapelizod had developed into an industrial suburb with a burgeoning linen industry (see Fig. 7.8, p. 260).

On the other hand, the impact of famine, disease, dislocation and uprooting of old populations consequent on the events of the early 1650s left their mark on other settlements. It is useful to compare the status of settlements covered so completely in the 1650–2 Census with the situation by 1660.[104] A number of striking patterns are revealed (see Fig. 7.9b). From the 1650–2 sample of 47 townlands, an overall reduction of 25–30 per cent of the adult population is suggested by 1660. Allowing for some economic recovery in the late 1650s, this is a staggering reduction. The sex ratio of some of these settlements in 1650–2 already reflected population disturbances in the 1640s. However, not all townlands reveal reductions: Crumlin's population increased by 33 per cent between 1650–2 and 1660, and Kilmainham's by a massive 64 per cent. Nearby Terenure saw an increase of 38 per cent, and other places that recorded increases included Ballyowen, Backstown, Templeogue and Kilnamanagh. The overall distribution of gains and losses shows a juxtaposition of settlements with large gains or high losses; local displacement and highly localized migration patterns may therefore be a feature of the turbulent 1650s.

Sixty per cent of the townland sample reveal decreases in population. For example, Butterfield seems to have lost 78 per cent of its population, Old Bawn 49 per cent and Killininny 41 per cent, and in these three cases some of the reduction may relate to outmigration of new immigrant families. Elsewhere, a clear correlation exists between the loss/displacement of old gentry patrons and their retainers and the emergence of newer less sympathetic landlords. Dalkey village declined by 48 per cent (from 84 to 44 adults) and this must reflect the disappearance of the old gentry family of Miles Byrne. In Shankill there is a reduction from 128 to 40 adults (69 per cent). Here displacement of the Barnewall family must have had a decisive impact. The new landlord figure, Evan Vaughan, clearly ruled over a different kind of place to that of the Barnewalls. Lucan, now without the Sarsfields, also suffered a 28 per cent decline. Thus, in at least half of the cases of townland depopulation, disappearance of old gentry households and patrons is a factor.

But there were other factors. The likely reduction in the population of Tallaght (a decline of 26 per cent) and Newcastle (a decline of 21 per cent) may relate as much to the part these places played in the rising/rebellion as to local gentry displacement. Certainly Newcastle's decline from a strategic town on the west of the city of Dublin to its 'shabby village' status in the eighteenth century owes much to the traumas of the 1640s and 1650s, although the decline in its original garrison function was also a factor, since the old Pale boundary was dissolved with New English expansion in the later sixteenth century.[105]

Elsewhere, major settlement and population shifts were from the interior to the coastlands. The parishes of Ward, Mulhuddart and Kilsallaghan suffered irreparable war damage in the mid-seventeenth century and never recovered anything like their old population densities, even in the immediate pre-Famine period. This area suffered much destruction of castles and churches and the associated trauma is poignantly revealed in the suicide of Molly Hore of Kilsallaghan on hearing of the intended transplantation of her family to distant lands beyond the Shannon.[106]

Overall, the evidence from Co. Dublin emphasizes the exceptional conserving role of long-established and powerful ecclesiastical interests that sustained enduring territorial entities like the parish, the related parish-village structure and the associated worshipping local community. After 1541, the secularization of the exceptional amount of Church land in Dublin led to the consolidation of an increasingly powerful New English settler class, which grew out of the now centralizing and anglicizing Dublin Castle administration. Ironically, these confiscations also led to the further consolidation of the landed, if not the political, power of the great Old English families of the Pale, which, for the most part, became the patrons of a vital Counter-Reformation Church in the wider region.

Indeed, one of the most striking conclusions to emerge from this survey is the level of resistance shown to the Anglican Church and its officers by the Catholic community at a whole series of levels in the social hierarchy – from the great landed patrons at the top, through the lesser gentry and big farmers who sheltered the priests and friars, made their bigger homes available for the saying of Sunday mass and who – by withholding either incomes and other Church revenues – deliberately and systematically undermined the new 'heretic' Church.

The inability of this New English administration and its local representatives to win over or seek to win over the allegiance of the Old English elites of Dublin county and the Pale therefore constitutes the most significant assimilative failure of this era. If the New English had attempted and succeeded to assimilate rather than alienate the majority of these key Catholic merchant families of Dublin city and the great landed and legal families of the wider Pale region, the history and human geography of Ireland could and would have been very different. However, it may well be that the gap between the mentalities and culture of this early modernizing and highly mobile New English class and the deeply rooted and more conservative Old English Catholic world was already too great to be bridged. Perhaps more to the point, as the New English tightened their grip on the military and economic administrative control of the country, the vested interests and ambitions of these two key political groupings inevitably led to divergence and collision. In the end, their increasingly harsh religious struggle was partly a reflection and partly a cause of the anxieties and bitterness that accompanied the decline of one kind of civilization (that of the late feudal Old English) and the rise of a new, modernizing, commercial/early capitalist culture, led by the New English officials and colonizers.

Whether old landed patrons survived or lost out in this new order is also poignantly revealed in the varying fortunes of Dublin county's villages and hamlets, as shown by an analysis of key documentary sources from the beginning and the end of the decade of the 1650s. Likewise, it is clear that war-induced famine and plague made for highly uneven demographic patterns locally. The complexities of family and household structures and, in particular, the predominance of a servant class in the composition of the common people, nevertheless, points to enduring social hierarchies and work practices. Likewise, deep and significant class differences within the rural communities are revealed as between the gentry/big farmer class, on the one hand and the small farmer/cottier/labouring classes, on the other. By way of contrast, one can also track the vectors of modernization along the main routeways out of Dublin city, while the communities off these highways still reveal more localized and tighter kinship structures.

Growth flowed outwards along the roads from the 'second city of the empire' with the blossoming of old and new settlements along the northern and southern coastlands. Much of this was yet to happen when that brilliant cartographer John Rocque mapped the county in the mid-eighteenth century.[107] Rocque reveals the durability of Co. Dublin's rural settlement structures, while also pointing out new 'ribbon' developments of settlements along main roads. It was the Georgian building boom of the later eighteenth and early nineteenth centuries that finally transformed this archaic rural world. There was a massive expansion of demesne building in the county after the 1750s. At least fifty old settlement sites of north Co. Dublin were privatized by such demesnes. These Big Houses and high-walled enclosures obliterated forever many old worlds with roots deep in the medieval period – those same worlds whose contours have been explored and mapped in these pages.

8

County Kilkenny
Territorial, Social and Settlement Hierarchies

One can still feel this Norman influence. It hangs almost palpably in the air of some parts of the country, distinctive and unmistakable, chiefly in the east and south-east. In such counties as Kilkenny, where this influence lasted long and was least disturbed, even by the disastrous upheaval of the Reformation, the very nature of the people is patently different to that of the contiguous county of Tipperary. Even the people of south Tipperary, which was more effectively colonised than north Tipperary, appear, to me at any rate, clearly affected by that prolonged foreign reign. . . .

In the rich country around [Kilkenny], the farmhouses have an air rather of Wessex than of Ireland, solid cutstone barns, finely arched, with all the marks of a tradition of good husbandry such as old trees, straight ditches, orchards and kitchen gardens. There is over the land the fragrance of long memory of stable conditions, so different to the harsh south and west where the generations have lived for centuries from hand to mouth and have only in our time cut free from the gnawing fears of poverty and famine. For the story of many parts of Ireland, there are no records; here there are many; rent-rolls and charters that take us back to the Middle Ages.

Sean O'Faolain[1]

Sean O'Faolain's portrait of Kilkenny as the Wessex of Ireland is a powerful image of this Leinster county. Another literary figure, Frank O'Connor, describes Kilkenny as the loveliest of Irish counties 'still a 13th-century country which you can imagine as the setting for the *Canterbury Tales'*.[2] Most people's perceptions of the county is of the rich core area that stretches out in all directions from the ancient city of Kilkenny. We have to remember, however, that there are many different facets and aspects to this compact county, which for the most part is coterminous with the diocese of Ossory. There are striking, sometimes unexpected, variations in altitude, in quality of land, in aspect, landscape furnishings, social structures and cultural heritage across the county. While constituting a hearthland region in the southeast of Ireland, the county of Kilkenny extends into and shares in the history and landscapes of the more open Midlands and the Pale region of the province of Leinster. It is bounded, traversed and enhanced by the two sister rivers of the Nore and the Barrow, which converge on the town of New Ross, and which, in combination with the River Suir, sweep beyond Waterford city into the great harbour of the same name. The two vital urban centres, New

Ross and Waterford, have influenced the economic and social life of south Kilkenny for close on a millennium.

On its eastern borders the hard Caledonian line of the Lower Palaeozoic rocks, represented by the striking Blackstairs, has bent the alignment of the northern half of the county. In place of the typical east–west alignment of the Armorican, characteristic of south Kilkenny, the trend swings round to north–east and south–west, as in the topography of the coal country of Castlecomer and the extension of the Slieveardagh hills into the county. This hearthland county of the southeast is also a border zone in both physical and cultural terms, marking the boundary between the Armorican and Caledonian worlds and that of the Ossorians and the Munstermen (which now finds expression in the often bitter rivalry between the two hurling counties of Kilkenny and Tipperary).

As compared to the adjacent counties of Tipperary and Wexford, Co. Kilkenny has a more muted and subtle landscape. Its mountains, the so-called Walsh mountains in the middle south of the county, never rise higher than 294 metres (970 feet). Elsewhere, its gently rolling landscapes are broken by the often steep hill country of both Brandon and the countryside west of Graiguenamanagh, by the more gentle extension of the Slieveardagh hills into the baronies of Crannagh and Galmoy to the northwest and by the extensive Carboniferous plateau country of Castlecomer to the northeast. Given the apparent ubiquity of rolling landscapes, the dominant feature of Co. Kilkenny still remains its central limestone plain drained by the Nore river and its tributaries, which stretch from Ballyragget in the north to Ballyhale in the south and eastwards from Callan to the more modern Goresbridge on the Barrow. A second important lowland zone lies within the bend of the River Suir to the south of the Walsh mountains but this area narrows considerably in the countryside between the city of Waterford and the town of New Ross, from Slieverue to Glenmore and beyond.

Kilkenny's central location and its weak topographical boundaries have facilitated access from all sides: for example, along the Barrow valley, where it opens out into the plains of Gowran, the gap to the north between Ballyragget and Durrow, the corridor to Upper Ossory via Galmoy; the powerful King's river axis cutting through the middle of the county and opening into Tipperary and the valley of Slievenamon; the narrow gap from Ballyhale through Mullinavat to Waterford city, not to speak of Kilkenny's main corridors along the Suir, Nore and Barrow valleys. Away from these more accessible places are peoples of the often bleak, wet, cold hills of the Castlecomer region, the warmer lands of the dry upland county around Tullaroan and Clomantagh, the difficult terrain that stretches across the southern portion of the county from west of Rosbercon to almost the gates of Kildalton demesne at Piltown and the often late settled country of the hills of Brandon, Coppenagh and Freagh. It is, therefore, important to recognize that Kilkenny has been and is a varied land.

The primary objective of this chapter is to explore (and seek to reconstruct) the nature of economy, society and settlement across this varied county in the pre-Cromwellian era; my secondary objective is to sketch in the differential impact of the Cromwellian conquest and assess the territorial, social and settlement consequences flowing from this radical transformation in the status of the city and county of Kilkenny and the consequent displacement of so many of its old elites. In all of this, Kilkenny's place in the wider regional and island-wide context of the seventeenth century is kept in focus.

In the absence of the Civil Survey for the greater part of the county (but not the city) of Kilkenny, the key sources for this endeavour are the Down Survey maps of 1656–8, the poll-tax abstracts of 1660 (the 1659 Census),[3] the Books of Survey and Distribution,[4] as well as seventeenth-century inquisitions[5] and the Ormond Deeds.[6] Equally essential to these efforts is the reconstruction of historic landscapes and societies via fieldwork and the very rich oral heritage of a county that has been so well served by its historians, notably William Carrigan[7] and Owen O'Kelly.[8]

Environment and Economy

The greater part of Kilkenny is good agricultural land. Its hearthland is the champion lands stretching from Freshford through Ballinamara, Odagh and Mayne in the north, on through Dunmore and around the immediate Kilkenny city hinterland to broaden out into the most extensive and richest belt of land stretching right across the county from Callan in the west to the Barrow valley. The names of the core medieval parishes here (see Fig. 8.2, p. 282) – Burnchurch, Clara, Danesfort, Dunbell, Earlstown, Ennisnag, Gowran, Kells, Tullaroan – echo to the richness and variety of the lands, landscape furnishings and developed social structures of this culture hearth. There are pockets of equally superb farming land to the north at Lisdowney and Ballyragget and to the south from Dunnamaggan across to Knocktopher and especially in the rich belt of land that stretches from Owning in the west through Fiddown and on into the 'village' world of Pollrone and Portnascully to cross the Blackwater river into the strong parishes of Dunkitt and Gaulskill.

Flanking these core areas are the more extensive regions of medium quality soils, which already sustained a more commercialized agricultural economy in the mid-seventeenth century. Much of the baronies of Galmoy and Crannagh fit into this middle category, as do the western and southwestern parishes of Fassadinin, the southern half of Gowran and large areas of Ida. Parishes typical of this category of medium quality land include Fertagh and Clomantagh to the northwest, much of Castlecomer, Rathcoole, Kilderry and Shankill to the northeast, Powerstown, Kilfane, Inistioge, the Rower, Ballygurrim, Kilmakevoge and Kilcolumb to the east and southeast, while the borderland with Tipperary stretching from Mallardstown to Owning also fits into this regional category. In contrast, the wetlands of the parishes of the Castlecomer region, including Dysart, Muckalee and Mothell, the hill country around Graiguenamanagh and Clonamery and the rugged lands of the Walsh mountains from Listerlin in the east to Aghaviller in the west provide a much tougher and less flexible environment for agriculture, with their stickier soils and often poorer drainage (see Fig. 8.1).

In the broadest terms, therefore, Kilkenny can be characterized as containing three major physiographic regions – a rich, flexible, lowland core, flanked to the

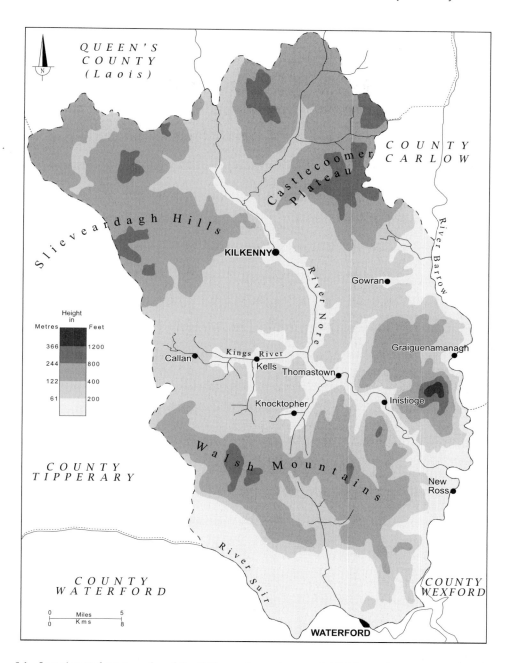

8.1   Location and topography of Co. Kilkenny (see references 3,4,5,6 for main sources used in the making of these maps for Co. Kilkenny)

north by an intermixture of ridge and lowland country with a less well-developed river system, and to the south by tough upland country surrounded by good lowland stretches, drained and enhanced by powerful river systems. Water power derived from the upper Nore and its tributaries the Nuenna and the Dinin to the north, the numerous small tributaries of the Barrow in the Gowran region, the extensive tributary system of the Nore in its middle and lower regions, including the King's river, and in the south from the Blackwater and other very minor tributaries of the Suir and Barrow drove the wheels of the many grain and tucking mills that were the cogs around which the economy of seventeenth-century Kilkenny revolved.

Details of the local economies of Kilkenny are rare for the mid-seventeenth century. The residual evidence from the Down Survey maps and other sources confirms the dominant milling functions of the country that stretches south from Kilkenny city eastwards to Callan and on to Thomastown and Inistioge in the southeast.[9] This was also the zone of the greatest concentration of smaller towns. Kilkenny city, with a population of over 4,000,[10] was the 'imperial' capital of the northern one-third of the county; Waterford and to a lesser extent New Ross and Carrick-on-Suir dominated the southern and southeastern one-third of the county; while in the middle a rich countryside supported a cluster of closely packed smaller towns. Callan was the largest of these, with a population of over 1,000,[11] then followed by Thomastown, Gowran, Kells and Knocktopher. Inistioge and Graiguenamanagh in turn benefited from, and acted as springboards for, internal and external trade along the tidal reaches of the Nore and Barrow. Waterford city and port provided Co. Kilkenny with its gateway to the outside world.

An inquisition at Inistioge provides glimpses of the nature of the local economy in the early seventeenth century. After the confiscation of the monastic lands, the new lord here was Viscount Butler of Tullowphelim, who owned the former priory of Inistioge and its lands, in addition to quite a number of houses, orchards and gardens intermixed amongst the lands of the burgesses and people of the town. A clear distinction between the demesne lands of the landlord and the burgess lands is made but it is also clear that in a wood of 120 plantation acres (called Kilclondowne) 'the burgesses of Inesteok have common pasture, subboscage, the cutting of copse and boughs of trees', while in certain mountain-lands called Knockerowry and other lands 'the community of the town of Inisteok have common pasturage, wherever they are not enclosed or new meadows'.[12] Inistioge had in 1607 at least two watermills, 'one of which is called the upper mill at which the burgesses and townspeople of Inisteoke must grind their corn, and must also supply workmen to repair "the weares" and ponds called the "myllponds" of their own mill, and workmen and vehicles to draw mill-stones and materials for the repairing of the mill', with the landlord Viscount Butler supplying food to the workmen while involved in these activities.

The salmon fisheries of the River Nore were clearly an important and highly valued local resource. We also catch glimpses of some of the more important slated dwelling houses in the settlement, including the principal house of the manor of Inistioge, the 'kill-' or butcher-houses, the bakeries, the hardware shops and other artisan functions, as well as the many thatched houses of the ordinary farmers and artisans and including a significant number of widows who lived in the town. It is clear that the orchards and especially the gardens of the individual townspeople were a very important part of the local economy. Likewise, the burgesses and townsmen of Inistioge were required to serve two days ploughing on the lands of Viscount Butler, 'one day at the sowing of the wheat, and another day at the sowing of oats'. Every burgess was further required to provide one draught horse for the carrying of three loads of wood to the house of the viscount, 'only on the Feast of the Nativity of our Lord each year',[13] and the burgesses and community supplied workmen annually to assist in the making of the lord's hay – a pattern repeated on many other properties in the county. The burgesses of the town were required to pay to Viscount Butler a stipulated rent for every tenement in Inistioge, as well as serving at a court baron every three weeks, and a court leet, with a view of frank pledge, once a year. The landlord received the fines and pledges of the tenants of the manor of Inistioge. And like other medieval towns of Kilkenny, Inistioge still kept its walls and gates – to mark the boundary between two kinds of territories and social worlds – not yet fully exposed to the solvent forces of a highly developed commercial economy that would integrate town and countryside in an ever more powerful and all-embracing way.[14]

The Civil Survey details for the city of Kilkenny highlight a vibrant local urban economy in the 1640s, as well as the critical role of the city in the northern half of the county.[15] The cathedral church for the diocese of Ossory and the castle head-quarters of the Butler lordship acted as the twin pivots of the main business streets, with their associated substantial houses, gardens, orchards, well-cared-for stables and cowhouses. The sessions-house and the county gaol epitomized the key role of the city as an administrative and legal centre. The city was then domi-nated by the three merchant/professional families of the Archers, the Rothes and the Shees. There was a close relationship between city and countryside, with the latter providing agricultural surpluses and the former a wide range of goods and services, as emphasized by the wide distribution of breweries, bakeries, butchers and tanneries (the last on the fringe of the Hightown) in the city, as well as the numerous merchant-tailors, weavers, glovers, leather- and shoe-makers, stone-masons and carpenters. But the most important pointer to town–country relationships is the dense distribution of the highly valued cornmills owned by the leading merchant families, which dominate each side of the River Nore below Kilkenny city. The regional role of the city is symbolized by the many retail shops, inns and lodging houses and its coal and wine houses point to the importance of long distance trade. Located almost equidistant from Dublin and Cork, Kilkenny city was a major centre of interprovincial business between Munster and Leinster. Details of meetings of the members of the Confederation of Kilkenny in the 1640s reveal both the rich furnishings and level of civilization amongst the merchant and professional families of the town before the Cromwellian conquest,[16] as well as Kilkenny's powerful hinge-position at the national and international levels.

Overall, it would appear that a mixed economy prevailed throughout the region, with cows and cattle occupying an important part in Kilkenny's farming life – clearly its upland areas were more geared to pastoral pursuits, as the distrib-ution of castle bawns confirms. Likewise, the Ormond Deeds now and again provide glimpses of the important role of cows, sheep, pigs and even goats in local economies. There were strict rules at parish (and townland) level regarding the grazing of common grasslands, and the impounding of stock in lieu of rent or the king's taxes is a recurring feature in the sheriff's accounts for the county in 1637.[17] The slow expansion of a commercial pastoral economy and the improvements in the landscape generally are suggested by the imparking and enclosure of a few townlands in the vicinity of some of the landowners' tower-houses or mansions. Orchards were also significant landscape features in the core of the county. But it is also clear that an open-field tillage economy and the production of grain crops, especially of wheat, barley and oats, was the dominant feature over most of lowland Kilkenny. In Hardinge's summary of the Transplantation Certificates, Kilkenny dominates the south and east of the island in the production of winter and spring grain crops: as high as 41 per cent of all winter grains and 33 per cent of all spring grains returned by all of the transplanting elites for the country emanated from Co. Kilkenny.[18] Ploughmen, plough horses and harvesters were, therefore, key figures in the yearly cycle of most Kilkenny townlands. Grain crops were central to the diet of the poor, while providing a regular cause of conflicts between local farmers with regard to the hedges that seasonally bounded their tillage strips. Contrasts with some of the best lands in Co. Tipperary were very sharp in this regard. Again the Transplantation Certificates reveal that one-third of all sheep returned by the island's old elite came from pastoral Tipperary, suggesting a level of sheep production in Tipperary about twelve times that of Kilkenny.

The overall evidence from the Transplantation Certificates suggests that Kilkenny county as a whole occupies a second rank position in terms of cow production in the mid-seventeenth century, well behind Cork but second only to Meath and Laois of the Leinster counties. It was one of the leading grain producers, ranking fourth amongst a cluster of five leading counties, which was headed by Wexford, Meath, Louth and Laois. In terms of sheep production, it clearly lagged far behind the leading counties, including Tipperary, but sheep production was still important, as is evidenced by the significance of tucking mills in Kilkenny's seventeenth-century landscape.

Parishes, Property and Power in 1640

Property and parish units provide crucial territorial structures for shaping the location and character of most human activities. The adjacent counties of Tipperary and Wexford reveal a threefold gradation of landownership, with Gaelic lands in varying partnership combinations in the north and northwest, a hybrid Gaelic/Old English landownership pattern in the middle and the individually owned Old English properties of the south and southeast. In sharp contrast, Kilkenny is emphatically an Old English property world in 1640 and was so long before the seventeenth century. The early grants of knight's fees for the county, as documented by Eric St John Brooks, highlight the solid and deeply localized feudal units that had been established in the north and middle region of the county by c.1200. Most of the land grants came to correspond to the structure of the medieval parishes.[19] The regions of the baronies of Knocktopher, Ida, Iverk and Gowran in the east and southeast, on the other hand, were initially granted to their feudal lords as large 'baronial' entities. Here again, however, in areas like Dungarvan one can document the filling in of the parish and manorial structures by the 1280s. Clearly, the high medieval period saw the fleshing out of a stable landowning and parochial framework throughout the whole county.

Up to the 1640s, therefore, the most enduring and most stable of all property and administrative frameworks was the territorial structure of the medieval parishes. Figure 8.2 illustrates the distribution of the nineteenth-century civil parishes – the lineal descendants (in the great majority of cases) of the medieval parish network. But it is clear that the territorial roots of this durable parish network is older still. John O'Donovan's mid-nineteenth-century Ordnance Survey letters are full of the stories of the early saints, monks and bishops that impressed themselves so deeply on the topographies and the minds of the people of pre-Norman Kilkenny.[20] Looking at the placename geography of the parishes, a striking feature is the number and density of medieval parish names that retain their Gaelic forms, whether beginning, as the majority do, in Kill (Cill) or Dysart (Diseart), while many others incorporate old saints' names, as in Tibberaghny (St Fachtna), Rathkieran (St Kieran), Tiscoffin (St Scuitin), Tullaroan (St Ruadhan of Lorrha, also reflecting the Midlands linkages) and the much more obvious parish names of Columbkill, Kilcolumb and Kilbride. A second ancient category of parish names derives from more 'secular' territorial units, such as Dungarvan, (Bally)Gowran, Dunkitt and Odagh. A third, much smaller group of parishes – Glashare, Clonamery, the Rower and Aghaviller – are essentially topographic names.

On the other hand, it is clear that the deepest impact of the Norman culture – as judged from the capacity of the Anglo-Normans to either anglicize or create new parish names – was, as one would expect, in the core area, from Kilkenny city, south through Castleinch, Grange, Burnchurch, Earlstown and Mallardstown, reaching close to the foothills of the Walsh mountains, where significantly the hybrid parish name of Ballytobin is found. This zone extends eastwards through Jerpoint and Ballylinch to Thomastown and Graiguenamanagh and bends northwards again to embrace Powerstown, Blackrath, St Martins and St Johns. There is a secondary zone of weaker impress to the north, stretching from Castlecomer through Grangemaccomb to Freshford and Borrismore. To the south the gap from Jerpoint to Waterford city is weakly connected by Gaulskill, while near Carrick-on-Suir the parishes of Whitechurch and the more upland Owning infer the cultural gradations and subtleties along the Tipperary/Kilkenny borderlands. Overall, there is clearly a strong regional stratification of parish names, with much of the hills and fringes of the county retaining the names of ancient territorial divisions and, more particularly, early Celtic Christian denominations.

Continuity of placenames, however, should not be assumed to mean continuity in culture from pre-Norman times. Just as the first names of many of the old Gaelic families of Kilkenny increasingly show the influence of medieval Christian naming patterns, so too with the dedications of many parish churches, chapels-of-ease and their associated sites of veneration and pilgrimage, such as holy wells. The O'Donovan letters and Carrigan's four-volume history (1905) indicate that about twice the number of churches were dedicated to continental European

8.2   Distribution of the civil parishes and baronies in Co. Kilkenny, 1640

saints, compared with the remaining churches that clung stubbornly to devotion to the older Celtic saints. Thus the deeper cultural transformation of so much of the county is emphasized by the transformation in church dedications and devotions in parishes like Killamery, where the holy well is dedicated to St Nicholas, the holy well of the parish of Ballinamara indicates devotion to the Holy Trinity,

Kilmocar to Our Lady, Rathbeagh has St Catherine's well, Ballycallan has a pattern to St Michael, and Dunnamaggan's devotion is to St Leonard. As many as 8 holy wells are dedicated to Our Lady, 4 to St John 2 to St Martin, and a Cambro-Norman connection is commemorated by at least 2 wells devoted to the Welsh St David. The resilient Celtic saints are led by Kieran (5), followed by Brigid (2), her dedications, in turn, indicating Ossory's interconnections with Kildare and Leighlin and east Leinster generally. An overemphasis on the meaning of the parish names, however, obscures the political and cultural advances of the Anglo-Norman/Old English into the foothills and the hills of Kilkenny, as evidenced not only in church dedications and holy wells but also in the spread of roadside shrines and crosses and in the continuing strength and capacity of parish communities to retain figurines or statues of their local saint into the nineteenth century, a feature very different to the Gaelic west, where few such representations are encountered in a culture equally devoted to the cult of the saint.

The centrality of ecclesiastical structures to late medieval/early modern Kilkenny is also highlighted by the role of the bishop of Ossory as a landowner and as a powerful figure in Kilkenny city (especially in the ancient independent borough of Irishtown), while surrounding townlands like Chancellorstown still bear witness to the might of the officers of the diocese. Likewise, the manor of Freshford and its mansion, Uppercourt, were essential parts of the episcopal order until forfeited and handed over to a leading Kilkenny family, the Shees. Elsewhere, the abbeys and monasteries of Graiguenamanagh, Jerpoint, Inistioge and Kells, and even smaller places like Fertagh, exerted a powerful cultural influence in their localities. They were also major landowners until their estates were confiscated in the mid-sixteenth century – to augment the landed power of Ormond and his henchmen. The post-Reformation era ushered in a long period of uncertainty and ambiguity.

By 1640, over 30 of the 147 medieval parishes identified in Fig. 8.2 – usually the smaller ones – appear to have been absorbed and integrated into larger parochial entities. The creation of bigger and often more unwieldy parishes had already begun. Likewise, the tithes of many parishes moved further out of the ecclesiastical sphere and into the hands of lay patrons. As early as 1619 the tithes of as many as 47 parishes or part-parishes were under the direct leasing control of the earl of Ormond,[21] one other indication of the cumulative expansion and consolidation of Butler power over the previous three centuries.

Much of Tipperary and Kilkenny effectively formed a single Butler lordship administered as a single powerful unit of political and economic integration from c.1350 onwards.[22] The Butlers had also become the dominant landowners in the towns of Roscrea, Nenagh, Thurles, Caher, Gowran, Knocktopher, Inistioge and Callan, thereby controlling the core areas of the economy. Following on from an aggressively expansionist strategy, the Ormond Butler lands of Kilkenny practically commanded all the frontier territories of the county – lapping up to the county boundary in all cases except where the wide expanses of the lower Suir and Nore/Barrow river systems already performed a defensive barrier function (see Fig. 8.3). In addition, the earl of Ormond in part commanded the rich middle

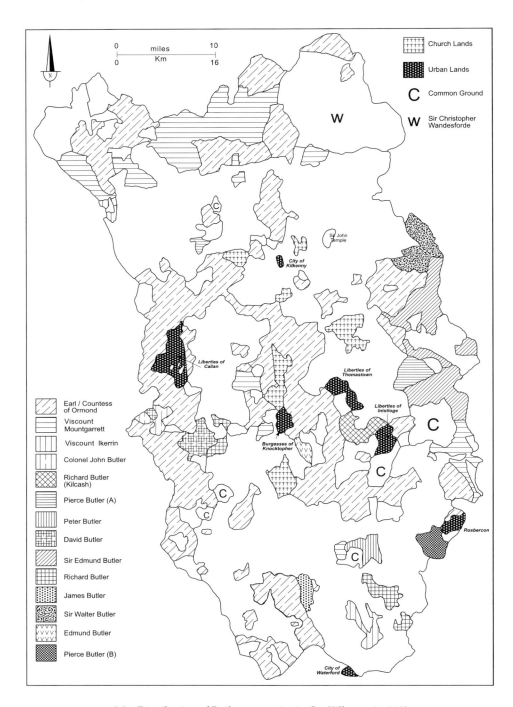

8.3   Distribution of Butler properties in Co. Kilkenny in 1640

core of the county from Dunmore in the north to the former monastic lands of Jerpoint, while also holding the strategic lands along each side of the navigable stretches of the Nore. Adding a further shield to the towns and better lands were the remaining key Butler families. Lord Mountgarrett – later an important Confederate leader – dominated the lowlands along the strategic territories fronting the former Gaelic zone to the north. To the east, the frontier lands and former abbey lands along the Barrow river were held by Sir Edmund Butler (7,559 plantation acres) and the Butlers of Paulstown (2,785 plantation acres).[23] Likewise, other key Ormond allies – the Graces to the northwest with 9,690 plantation acres and the Purcells (4,955 plantation acres) and the Cantwells (3,116 plantation acres) to the northeast – reinforce in depth this northern frontier. And underneath the Butler overlordship, the head-tenants on the individual manors (usually on leases of twenty-one years) were for the most part lesser Butlers, members of other leading Old English landed families, such as the Comerfords, or leading members from the professional and merchant classes of Kilkenny city. These key elite families were invariably involved as officers in local government and as legal and administrative officials for the earl of Ormond in either Co. Tipperary or Co. Kilkenny. Indeed, some such families as the Comerfords, Archers and Cowleys worked as lawyers in the Dublin crown courts.[24]

The remainder of the rich central lowlands of Co. Kilkenny was dominated by Norman families such as the Shortalls with 3,745 plantation acres, the St Legers, whose leading member George held 1,935 plantation acres, and the Blanchfields, whose Sir Edmund held 2,332 plantation acres – each family commanding a long-established territorial domain. Also, leading (but often absentee) merchant families of the city of Kilkenny and allies and kinsmen of Ormond – the Shees (Robert had 4,884 plantation acres), the Rothes (Sir Robert held 2,385 plantation acres) and the Archers (Henry held up to 6,737 plantation acres) – further dominated the lowland scene. In addition, the bishop of Ossory held over 5,000 plantation acres scattered throughout this lowland core (see Fig. 8.4). To the south, the complex hierarchical territories of the highly gaelicized Walsh family (the 'Lords of the Mountain') extend right across the county from Tibberaghny in the west to near Rosbercon in the east. Here Robert Walsh alone held over 10,000 plantation acres. Other key centres in this tough upland region were manned by members of the extended kin-group of the Walshes. This kinship strategy was also characteristic of all the major families in Tipperary, Kilkenny and elsewhere, revealing the interweaving of 'Gaelic' and 'feudal' strategies of land management and social control, particularly where the management of cattle was more central to the economy. The remainder of the south is dominated by long-established landed families: the Forstalls (Robert held 1,152 plantation acres) dominate in the parishes of Ballygurrim and Kilmakevoge; the Fitzgeralds (with 1,534 plantation acres) are lords of Brownsford and Gurteen; William Gaule held 1,631 plantation acres around Dunkitt and Gaulskill; Edmund Daton, near modern Piltown, controlled 2,179 plantation acres; while families like the Denns (Thomas with 2,708 plantation acres) and the Freneys (Thomas with 2,082 plantation acres) are also strongly represented. Some descendants of Waterford merchant families, such as the Strangs (Peter held 3,035 plantation acres), and the Grants (David held 709 plantation acres), are well-established in the lands fringing the lower courses of the navigable rivers.

Co. Kilkenny was therefore dominated up to the 1640s by a long-established territorial, political and social hierarchy, headed by the earl of Ormond, who directly ruled over 50,000 plantation acres from the castle at Kilkenny and indirectly exerted great landed and territorial power throughout the whole county. The next level in the hierarchy was represented by the highly influential figure of Lord Mountgarrett with close on 20,000 plantation acres. Then came a third layer of eight major owners, John Grace, Robert Walsh, Sir Edmund Butler, Henry Archer, John Bryan, the bishop of Ossory, Philip Purcell and Robert Shee, each with estates of 5,000 to 10,000 plantation acres. Beneath this group was a further eleven landowners, headed by Thomas Shortall, with 3,745 acres, and completed by George St Leger, with 1,935 plantation acres, who controlled estates in the 2,000–4,000 plantation acre range. Underneath this group were a further sixteen landowners with estates from 1,000 to 2,000 plantation acres. This group included 3 Fitzgeralds, 2 Butlers, 2 Walshes, 1 Strang, 1 Grant, 1 Purcell, 1 Dobbin, 1 Sweetman, 1 Comerford, 1 Shortall, 1 Walton and 1 Dalton. Then came the smaller landowners, 22 with estates from 500 to 900 plantation acres, from William Drilling with 900 plantation acres to Thomas Grant with 507 plantation acres; a further 29 held estates from 330 to 490 plantation acres, beginning with James St Leger holding 486 plantation acres down to Joseph Walsh holding 335 plantation acres. A further 41 smaller landowners held estates/farms from 100 to 280 plantation acres and at the bottom of the landed hierarchy, with less than 100 plantation acres, were men as diverse as Lord Ikerrin with 93 plantation acres (his vast patrimony was across the border in Co. Tipperary) down to a John Cantwell with 24 plantation acres.

It should also be stressed that this landed hierarchy was criss-crossed by many marriage and kinship alliances, connected in a spiralling series of networks that centred on the family of the earl of Ormond. The total list of landowners included at least 13 families each of the Walshes and the Butlers, 11 Shortalls, 8 St Legers, 7 Fitzgeralds, 6 each of the Archdeacons (Codys) and Graces, 5 each of the families of Forstalls and Dobbins, and 4 each of the Comerfords, Denns, Grants, Rothes and Shees. At least three Blanchfield families are represented, likewise the Purcells and Strangs, while at least two landowning families each came from the Cantwells, Sweetmans, Gauls, Freneys, Kealys, Aylwards, Howlings, Bryans and Cowleys. Fifteen other family names are represented at least once amongst the landowning elite.

The county as a whole, therefore, was a land of closely linked groups of long-resident proprietors, deeply rooted for the most part in their respective territories, with wide-ranging marriage and kinship linkages with the adjacent families both within and outside the county. Each family ruled a local 'fiefdom', their estates, manors and townlands often managed by members of the extended kin-group. An analysis of the diversity or lack of diversity of Irish family names per barony in Ireland, as itemized in the 1660 poll-tax, reveals a very compact,

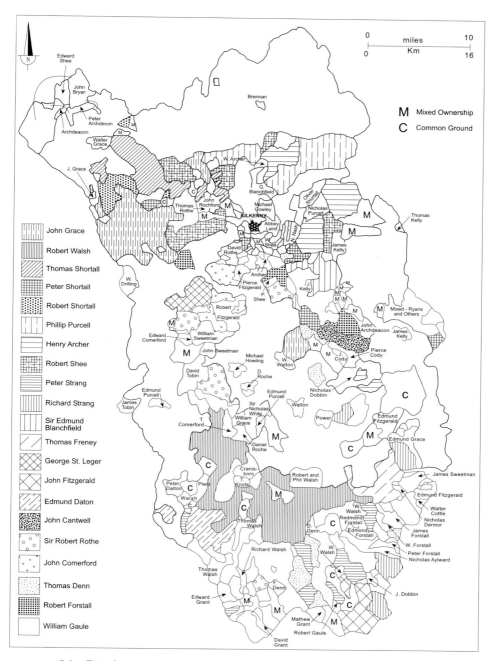

8.4   Distribution of other Old English-owned lands in Co. Kilkenny in 1640

tight-knit clustering of recurring names for much of Kilkenny. The county was second only to the introverted Gaelic Midlands in the limited range of Irish family names represented. It was the close-knit world of landed and legal-cum-administrative families and their associated property units that produced in turn, one could argue, the critical framework for the hierarchy of towns, villages, hamlets and farms that characterized this deeply humanized part of Ireland (see Fig. 8.3 and Fig. 8.4).

The Gaelic lands of Kilkenny, in contrast, had almost disappeared by 1640 – in the previous sixty years the vast patrimony of the O'Brennans of Fassadinin had been whittled down to a pathetic 60 acres by the insidious penetration of the earl of Ormond and his Old English cohorts and finally obliterated by the creation of the great modern estate of the Wandesfordes centred on the old manorial keep of Castlecomer, soon to become a classic landlord/middleman town.[25] Only the Ryans from their hearthland in Idrone in Carlow kept a resilient, if residual, foothold in the Leighlin parishes of east Co. Kilkenny. But here again Ormond power via newly established garrisons pushed the Kilkenny county boundary eastwards to reduce both the threat from the Barrow borderlands and the jurisdiction of both Co. Carlow and that of the Kavanaghs. In the extreme northeast the Bryan family (a branch of the Idrone O'Byrnes of Carlow but now clearly assimilated to the Old English order) manned the gap on the edge of the former woodlands and boglands of the Gaelic fastnesses to the north. Yet the property map does not reveal the conditions of life for the majority of the population. Beneath the Butlers, Shortalls, St Legers and other Old English landowners, the surviving hearth-money records of the 1660s bring up the families of Cahills, Hennessys, Phelans, Keeffes, Meaghers, Murphys, Brennans, Brophys and Delaneys, interwoven in complex tenurial and kinship webs throughout the townlands, villages and towns.[26] Despite the severe reduction in the power of Gaelic lineages, such as that of the O'Brennans, O'Ryans and Kavanaghs, the Gaelic substratum remained very deep here and we must now turn to the occupation of the land and its settlement structure to catch a glimpse of the total population at mid-century.

Settlement and Social Hierarchies

Seventeenth-century documents are only incidentally concerned with describing aspects of settlement and social structure. Reconstruction of these patterns for Co. Kilkenny therefore involves the careful combing (in the absence of, for the most part, the Civil Survey) of what the Down Survey maps have to offer, combined with a retrospective use of what the 1660 poll-tax and, to some extent, the early hearth-money records reveal. Again settlement details from all these sources are uneven and sometimes fragmentary.[27] For example, with the poll-tax returns, the population size of some parish/manorial centres like Fertagh may be inflated, as it may include the populations of satellite hamlets and outlying farms in a single total. On the other hand, separate returns for two or three townlands where the settlement focus converges at the meeting-place of these two or three townlands, as at Knocktopher, tends to depress the relative status of such centres in the settlement hierarchy. Making allowances for these deficiencies, a relatively clear picture of the settlement hierarchy can be constructed for Co. Kilkenny from the poll-tax returns (see Fig. 8.5). The superimposition of the Kilkenny Down Survey maps on

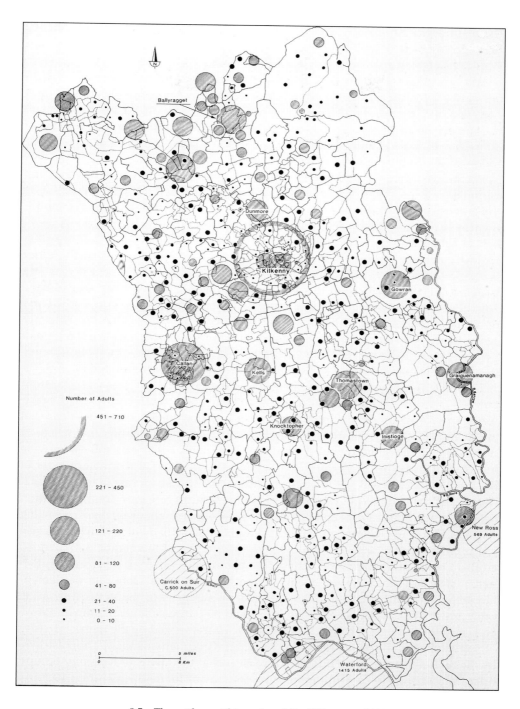

8.5 The settlement hierarchy of Co. Kilkenny, *c*.1660

the mid-nineteenth-century six-inch OS maps of the county is also helpful here –
highlighting how often old settlement centres have been buried under landlord
demesnes created mainly in the eighteenth century. The juxtaposition of seven-
teenth- and nineteenth-century maps further reveals the well-defined contrast
between the *evolved* versus the *planned* landscapes and between societies that have
been less disturbed and those that have been clearly reorganized and regimented.
A comparison of these maps shows regions of great continuity and regions of
deep transformation, mirroring in place the sharp polarities in Irish society that
followed on from the Cromwellian conquest.

Locating Kilkenny's settlement and social structure in its wider regional and
national contexts, one may note first that Kilkenny occupied a central position in
the wider region of the east and southeast, where a more hidden urban Ireland is
revealed in the mid-seventeenth century. The Kilkenny towns belonged to a wider
belt of urban culture, where these often walled, small but socially and morphologically complex borough towns still retained a preponderance of the older
Catholic stock of townspeople.[28] Kilkenny's towns, like many of the old and
battered towns elsewhere in this wider region, would therefore appear to have
weathered the storms of the late medieval period and were still sufficiently
dynamic to benefit from the upswing in the economy from the mid-fifteenth
century onwards. As elsewhere in this eastern and southeastern cultural region of
Leinster, these Kilkenny urban societies helped to sustain the population densities and more complex rural settlement hierarchies in their hinterlands.

Second, when placing Kilkenny in its wider regional context, it is also clear from
poll-tax and other evidence that much of Kilkenny, like south and east Tipperary,
was part of a wider belt of high farming and a developed settlement and social
hierarchy 'which had matured in a time of feudalised centralisation – and where "a
manorial" village economy, substantial farms, markets, mills, fairs and towns were
longstanding features'.[29] Within Co. Kilkenny 48.5 per cent of the total number of
the townlands returned in the poll-tax contained 19 adults or less (a total population of less than 60), 36 per cent were in the 20–39 adult category (total population
60–119), while 21.5 per cent contained over 40 adults (total population of over 120).
The baronies of Ida, Crannagh, and Knocktopher had settlement hierarchies closest
to the county norm, with a slight underrepresentation of townlands with over 40
adults. On the other hand, the richest core baronies of Gowran, Kells, and Shillelogher reveal a much more evenly balanced and more elaborate settlement
hierarchy, with about one-third of all townlands in each of the three population
categories noted above. These then appear to be baronies with the most mature
and complex settlement hierarchies and those characterized by the highest density
of solid substantial towns, including Gowran, Graiguenamanagh, Thomastown,
Inistioge, Kells and Callan. It is therefore clear that the towns of Kilkenny occupy
fulcrum positions in sustaining the rural settlement hierarchies in their vicinity:
they are both the gathering points and the stimulus towards the more intensive
production of grain and cattle surpluses in their hinterlands.

To the north of the county, the baronies of Fassadinin and Galmoy are each relatively exceptional in population/settlement terms – frontier Galmoy is dominated

by settlements at the upper end of the spectrum (38.1 per cent of its townlands contained over 40 adults), while Fassadinin's middle level settlements (20–39 adults) are well above the county average. Among the northwestern frontier parishes, it is also striking how often a castle was attached to the parish church, as at Rathbeagh, Threecastles, Clashacrow and Thornbrack. None of this is very surprising given the buffer role these northern baronies played in protecting the rich Ormond-dominated lowlands to the south. David Edwards has amply demonstrated how after the Mac Giollapadraigs (Fitzpatricks) had withdrawn the entire territory of Upper Ossory from Co. Kilkenny's and Ormond jurisdiction, the earls of Ormond proceeded to sever the county's ancient links with this strong Gaelic dynastic region and established a new and stiff frontier all across the north Kilkenny border from Urlingford to Castlecomer.[30] After 1515, these northern lands became a heavily defended military zone, castles were either newly built or further strengthened and the earls of Ormond required the local lords to provide military service in return for land grants. Partially gaelicized, the Old English families of the Archdeacons (Codys), Shortalls, Graces and Purcells constituted tightly interwoven 'clannish' family groups across this northern frontier land, combining strong 'traditions of lordship, kinship and resistance to outside interference'.[31]

Most significantly, the two peaceful baronies dominated by large cities, that is, the Liberties of Kilkenny and the barony of Iverk to the south, controlled respectively by the cities of Kilkenny and Waterford, have a much weaker settlement hierarchy, with almost 70 per cent of all denominations in both baronies containing less than 19 adults. Likewise, in the more peaceful, more feudalized and developed parts of Co. Kilkenny, as around the town of Kells and in the Liberties of Kilkenny, it is clear that many large fields and gardens are not permanently settled but are worked from a distance, belonging, it would appear, to a wider territorial framework of manorial, demesne or burgess lands.

Overall, however, Kilkenny reveals a very high level of occupation of land units, as compared with some western counties, where less than half of the enumerated townlands were permanently settled in the mid-seventeenth century. In this context Kilkenny is clearly even more closely settled and occupied than neighbouring Tipperary. In baronies such as Iverk, Knocktopher, Kells and Shillelogher there is well over 90 per cent occupation of all enumerated land denominations – only the barony of Slieveardagh matches this intensity of settlement in Co. Tipperary. In Callan and Galmoy up to 85 per cent of all land units are settled, with most of the remaining baronies showing an occupation rate of around 70 per cent. The overall impression is of a well-settled, well-worked countryside characterized by a close network of landscape furnishings and boundary markers.

However, this summary of baronial patterns only provides a general picture of society and of social and settlement structures. They say little about the detailed arrangement of settlement and the construction of society at the townland level. In seeking to advance the story of Kilkenny's settlement and social structure at this townland scale, it may be useful to revert to the analogous situation in mid-seventeenth-century Tipperary, which is well documented: three kinds of village nuclei have been identified there – the parish-church-centred village; the castle village or hamlet, that is, centred on the tower-house; and the manorial-type village, where church and castle (and sometimes mill) are located close together.[32] In addition, parts of Co. Tipperary were characterized by non-nucleated, that is, loosely knit, agglomerated, farm settlements, which are sometimes referred to as farm clusters. Other parts were characterized by a greater dispersal of settlement and society. The Tipperary evidence also suggested that most of the nucleated villages, whether of parish, tower-house or manorial type, contained a more stratified and, in particular, a more significant artisan component than did the more lowly clustered farm settlements.

The analogy with Tipperary permits us to make tentative generalizations as to the nature and form of the mid-seventeenth-century settlement hierarchy. The evidence for Kilkenny is far richer on the cartographic side but weaker in terms of social details. Unlike Tipperary, where only one barony (Slieveardagh) is adequately covered by the Down Survey parish maps, there is an outstanding series of barony maps for the whole county of Kilkenny, in addition to parish maps for four baronies as well as for the Liberties of Callan and Kilkenny. In particular, the barony maps for Crannagh and Ida (two of the most representative baronies in the county) are particularly instructive. Surviving traces of Down Survey maps from the Quit Rent Office, now in the National Archives, also provide additional sources of information for other baronies.

The evidence for Co. Kilkenny points overwhelmingly towards the dominance of a nucleated/clustered settlement pattern in the mid-seventeenth century: for example, out of a total of 70 settlement units on the barony map of Ida, 61 or 85 per cent are of village or hamlet type – some are centred on a castle and/or church, others are simply clustered settlements without any visible nucleus.[33] This is still village country today and allowing for the growth of new clustered settlements in its hilly regions in the late eighteenth and early nineteenth centuries, perhaps 50 per cent of the seventeenth-century villages still survive. On the other hand, the northern barony of Crannagh – now mostly bereft of farming villages – was emphatically a world of villages and hamlets in the 1650s.[34] Correlation of settlement details from the excellent Down Survey maps for this barony with its 1660 poll-tax returns confirms the relevance of the latter to settlement analysis (see Fig. 8.5, p. 289, and Fig. 8.6). All the barony's mapped townlands with adult populations of over 40 were characterized by complex nucleated settlements, usually comprising both a church and a castle; the great majority of townlands with an adult population of 20–39 had at least one nucleating force at the centre of the settlement and this was usually either a castle/tower-house or large stone house. The limited Civil Survey evidence confirms that the stone slate house at Damnagh was the centre of a rural hamlet of 30 cabins, Ballycallan castle had 24 cabins attached, while 15 cabins were located beside the 2 'chimney houses' at Corrohy.[35] In contrast, only one of the six settlements containing clustered settlements and an adult population of 10 or less exhibited any such institutional foci. Recent aerial photographic work has confirmed the deserted status of many of these seventeenth-century settlement centres in Crannagh. Although the surviving barony

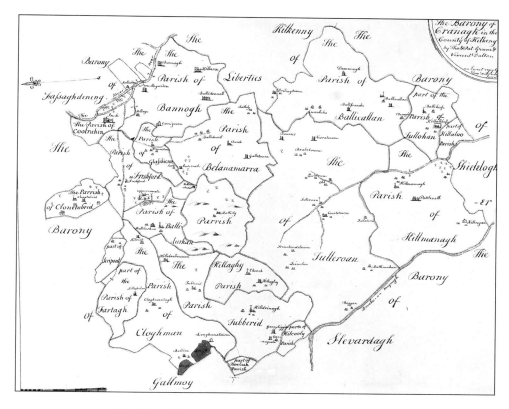

8.6   Down Survey map of the barony of Crannagh (1655)

map for Iverk is clearly quite uneven and incomplete, examination of its Quit Rent parish maps, in conjunction with the barony map, confirms the ubiquity of its village structures, a unsurprising finding given that the region still retains 36 farm villages into the early twenty-first century. The scattered settlement structure of Fassadinin today contrasts with William Nolan's detailed interpretation of its settlement structure in the mid-seventeenth century. He notes that the cabin was the most numerous settlement item then found in Fassadinin *c.*1654 (other settlement items included castles, bawns, churches, cornmills, tucking mills, houses with chimneys, stone houses and thatched houses). But the collections of cabins were almost always recorded in conjunction with 'more substantial edifices such as castles, churches, thatched or stone houses or bawns – they were not found in isolation'.[36] As Nolan notes, the cabins were the dwelling places of the dependent 'tenantry' (and their labourers). The extent to which such settlement concentrations involved a continuation of a 'demesne style' of farming requires further study.

The folk evidence is almost overwhelmingly couched in terms of a village culture not just in south Kilkenny but also in the north. Owen O'Kelly in his very useful book *Place-names of Co. Kilkenny* identified the sites of at least forty deserted villages.[37] In the villages of south Kilkenny today – as at Ballytarsney near Mooncoin – the locals regularly refer to the village as 'the street', while in the north of the county the old village between Cloneen Bridge and Courtstown in Tullaroan parish is still known as 'Carroll's Street'. The widespread view that the Irish have no word for 'village' should now be dispensed with: the term 'sráid' (or 'sráid bhaile') has long functioned as the term for 'village' – including the farm village – and the modern use of the term 'street' is not only known in counties like Kilkenny but also as far afield as Clare, Mayo and Monaghan. O'Kelly notes numerous instances, as in Killeen (parish of Kilmanagh), where 'there is an old graveyard called "Seanchill" and also a field called "sean-sráid", "the old street"'; according to O'Kelly, 'the latter name denotes an old deserted village everywhere throughout the county'.[38] Likewise, in Kildrinagh there is 'a place called "sean-achadh", "the old field" also called "the old street" where stood the old town of Kildrinagh'. Similarly, there is a number of references to '"páirc na sráide", "the street field", evidence again of an old hamlet'. Another indication of the deserted village is the field-name 'sean-bhaile', as in Corstown in the parish of Bally-callan.[39] The terms 'faiche' (green), 'garrai/garraithe' (gardens) and references to forge fields (especially if adjacent to castle and/or church sites) may also provide additional evidence of other deserted villages and hamlets. Lythe's early map of the southern half of Ireland (1569) confirms this village distribution for both Co. Kilkenny and much of lowland Leinster.[40]

While the folk evidence provides confirmation of the desertion of certain hamlet or village sites, it is by no means a comprehensive source or memory bank. For example, the Down Survey parish map of Tullaroan indicates the existence of at least ten hamlets or villages in the mid-seventeenth century, while only two are revealed by the assiduous research carried out by Carrigan and O'Kelly of the local folk traditions. Indirectly, therefore, the uneven oral traditions point to a much higher level of desertion in the county, especially in its northern and central parts. Aerial photography is also confirming this pattern. Likewise, even a cursory inspection of the Ormond Deeds confirms the service functions (including the presence of butchers, tailors, weavers, clerks and others) in a number of places in Kilkenny, such as Listrolin, which are now deserted.[41] Like the Elizabethan fiants for Tipperary, these documents confirm the diversity of occupations at the local parish level. The frequent juxtaposition of a large central townland in the parish with its nucleated settlement and outlying townlands on the edge of the parish, seemingly characterized by the settlement of a big farmer and his labourers, suggests a more complex settlement story.

The 1660 poll-tax is the first reliable, if indirect, indication of the settlement hierarchy after the Down Survey maps of 1654.[42] Although carried out at the end of one of the bloodiest episodes in Irish history when Kilkenny city (and its county), as the *caput* of the Catholic Confederation, was one of the cockpit regions in the conflict and in spite of the turmoil of the Cromwellian settlement itself, it is still striking how many of its most populated denominations coincide with the residence of a *tituladoe*. I have sought to examine the relationship between gentry residence and population size in all of Kilkenny's townlands. This analysis illustrates one other factor in the relatively weak settlement hierarchy of Iverk, for in an area that is dominated by the estates of the duke of Ormond and the

Cromwellian Colonel John Ponsonby, only 36 per cent of the relatively few higher order settlements are patronized by a gentry family. These southern lowlands did not support a significant community of gentry families. Fassadinin's settlement hierarchy, even more emphatically dominated by two great landlords, the duke of Ormond but more particularly the Wandesfordes, is likewise less well patronized by local resident gentry. In no other barony does the ratio of gentry to higher order townlands (over 40 adults) go beneath 50 per cent and in Galmoy, Ida, Knocktopher, the Liberties of Kilkenny and Shillelogher close to over two-thirds of all the larger settlements are associated with gentry residence. A third notice-able feature is the gentry patronage of middle order townlands (20–39 adults), especially in the wealthiest core baronies of Kells, Shillelogher, Crannagh and the Liberties of Kilkenny – Ida and Iverk occupy a middle position on this spectrum, with Fassadinin (understandably) and Gowran less well patronized by gentry at the middle levels. (After the Restoration, gentry levels in Gowran are again restored to an expected level with the return of a number of key Butler and other Old English families.) Ida, Kells, Shillelogher and Crannagh also display a rela-tively strong gentry presence and patronage even at the lower levels of the settlement hierarchy (less than 19 adults). In the absence of comprehensive Civil Survey details as to the location of owners of castles in Kilkenny in 1654, the above correlations would also seem to reinforce the Tipperary Civil Survey evidence as to the strong relationship between landlord patronage, tower-houses and higher population concentrations in such townlands.

These landownership patterns were often closely tied into the parochial network. This parish framework is the oldest in the county and a powerful lattice for shaping local identities. The parish unit not only organized life at the religious level and functioned as a territorial unit for the collection and payment of tithes, it also func-tioned as a more 'secular' administrative unit: the peoples of the different townlands in the parish were obliged to maintain things like the parish penfold, to keep watch on the common grasslands (if these existed at the parish as opposed to the joint townland level), to assist in the maintenance of 'the King's highways' if they passed through the parish, and to respect the offices of the parish constable or his petty constables.[43] Up to 1640, therefore, the parish functioned as a relatively powerful ecclesiastical, economic and administrative unit, although its ecclesiasti-cal function had been often bifurcated by the Reformation and its aftermath.

It is therefore not surprising that the parish unit often supported a strong central settlement. To relate parish and village geographies in this county, an analysis of the distribution of parishes whose centres either have greater or equal population size to all other townlands in such parishes was carried out. In both counties Tipperary and Kilkenny there is a clear, recurring correlation between parish vital-ity and settlement strength with the better lands. With some notable exceptions, it is striking how the highly valued grain-producing and mixed-farming regions of the core areas of Kilkenny sustain a more vigorous parish life and associated parish centres. Equally instructive are exceptions on the better land, where the strong nucleating role of the local landed families reduce the power of the parish centre. The dominance of the landlord residences as key focal points – as with the

Fitzgeralds of Gurteen (parish of Rathpatrick), the Bryans of Bawnmore (parish of Erke) and the Blanchfields of Blanchfield's Park (parish of Kilmacahill) – reduces the status of their respective parish centres. Likewise, it is clear that in the hill-plateau country of Crannagh and Fassadinin and the area of the Walsh mountains to the south, the greater scattering of settlement in such pastoral regions often left the parish centre in a relatively weaker position. In addition, the weaknesses of parish centres along the edges of the Liberties of Kilkenny and the middle Nore valley highlight the already lost centres and villages of the late medieval period in places like St Martins, Blackrath and elsewhere. Such parishes suffered both from absentee church administrators and absentee landlords.

While recognizing the twin pillars of settlement structures that parish adminis-tration and landlord patronage provided, it is noticeable by the early and mid-seventeenth century that the balance had often swung in favour of the defen-sive military arm of the settlement, a not too surprising development given the turbulence of sixteenth- and early seventeenth-century Ireland. One pivot of the nucleated settlement structure – the parish church – was under stress both before and particularly after the Reformation. Yet the extraordinary power of the twin anchors of castle and church – with the military/political arm increasingly becom-ing more important – still provided the main *raison d'être* of the community structures in Co. Kilkenny as late as the mid-1660s. The longer term consequences flowing from the belated, if effective, implementation of the Reformation, partic-ularly the effects of the Cromwellian conquest and settlement and the subsequent greater commercialization and pastoralization of the economy (with its associated processes of privatization and enclosure), were to rupture this twin alliance with a thoroughness that allows one to speak of the 'lost worlds' and 'lost villages' of Kilkenny. But, as in life, things were not as simple as that: there were also commu-nities and regions of greater continuities and adaptabilities as, for example, in south Kilkenny. To try to understand this complex pattern, I now turn to the impact of the Cromwellian conquest and settlement.

Settlement Implications of the Cromwellian Conquest

Prior to 1641, Kilkenny formed one of the richest, most developed parts of Ireland. This county was inhabited by a close-knit group of landed proprietors who were resident on their own lands and who managed their own territories and peoples. With some notable exceptions, these proprietors were Catholics of Anglo-Norman descent. By the end of the seventeenth century this class had been largely supplanted by New English Protestant landlords, many of whom were Cromwellian officers and soldiers, whose arrears of pay had been satisfied by grants of land, and a substantial number of which were to become absentee landowners. A great transformation had taken place, particularly in the patronage of local communities and their settlements. Here I look at some of the processes and patterns that underpinned this transforma-tion in terms of landownership, settlement and social mores in the county.

To begin with, however, it should be noted that this transformation has deeper roots than in the Cromwellian period. Edwards has documented the penetration and expansion of centralized state power into the Ormond lordships in both the Elizabethan and Jacobean eras.[44] So despite the power of the Ormond Butlers and a deserved reputation as the greatest collaborators in Ireland with the English crown, the Ormond lordship nevertheless was deeply affected by the royal assault on all regional lordships and power-holders across the island. From the time of Elizabeth, 'crown officials in Dublin became less tolerant of the privileged position of the Ormond territories and began working tirelessly to undermine the earldom'.[45] More particularly, in the 1610s and 1620s, when the government's anti-Catholic programme was at its height, the lordship was overthrown under the less sympathetic rule of James I. Far more than in the Elizabethan period, the central government was determined to protestantize as well as anglicize local and regional power structures.[46] Edwards has also argued that as James Butler, the twelfth and most famous of the earls of Ormond, rose to power in the central administration, befriended Thomas Wentworth and made a number of damaging concessions regarding both lands and official positions in Co. Kilkenny, which added further to the centralization of state power, his authority in the lordship and county deteriorated rapidly.[47] He was seen as not seeking to ensure – in the time-honoured fashion – the consent of the other key power-holders in the lordship, whether gentry or merchant, to change, but rather like the government, he was seen as riding roughshod over customary powers and rights. He was thus regarded as a partner in the system of misrule by the central government – as part of the English governmental machinery, which did not rule via assemblies but rather by dictat. So the great majority of Co. Kilkenny's power-holders rose in rebellion in 1642 and not only against the unjust Dublin administration but also against the earl of Ormond, who was described as not only a traitor to his blood but also as an enemy of the political traditions of the Ormond lands.[48] What followed was the establishment of the Catholic Confederacy at Kilkenny, the Confederate Wars and Cromwell's capture of Kilkenny city in March 1650.

From that conquest came the comprehensive source-materials that only a centralizing imperial state could have collected at this time. These documents have helped us to unearth the hidden worlds of pre-Cromwellian Kilkenny. These same documents must also be seen for what they were, namely, instruments of conquest and administration of 'new' territories and peoples. The Down Survey maps are in the first instance concerned with the identification and demarcation of existing property units. On that basis, the chessboard was redesigned partly in order to pay off the soldiers and adventurers who had ensured the Cromwellian conquest. Likewise, the great ledgers of the Books of Survey and Distribution are an accounting exercise for many other things apart from property units. Cromwellian planters regarded themselves, as Barnard observes, 'as the chosen instruments of providence and looked upon their conquest as theirs by Divine Right . . . The Irish offended their political (Republican) and religious (Puritanical) prejudices. The Irish were Papist and Jacobites and so inferior and alien.'[49] A system of ethnic signification and stratification is therefore embedded in these documents of conquest and such categorizations provided the ideological framework that shaped and bounded future social relationships between these two groups

The poll-tax and hearth-money records must also be seen for what they set out to achieve, the first to act as paymaster to the Irish garrison and the second, reaching into almost every home in the country, to support the superstructure of the Restoration state, which now came to impinge even more deeply on Kilkenny county and which until the early seventeenth century had been shielded by the earls of Ormond in their almost autonomous control of the 'lordship'. The New English were a varied group: some were early seventeenth-century English government officials, many were soldiers and officers of the Cromwellian army, some were essentially adventurers and speculators in land and money, and others were simple ordinary people probing for a better home. All these newcomers must have seen the landscape and resources of Kilkenny afresh; they saw themselves as belonging to a growing commercial nation and came with notions of exploitation and gaining wealth – most were still relatively insecure and getting rich quickly was an important priority. They settled in areas of which they had little previous knowledge. They had no sense of their chosen region's past histories; they were concerned with creating their own futures and the existing lands, peoples and placenames they encountered were simply the instruments towards that achievement.

The striking changes in the composition of juries at the county and barony level is one illustration of the new legal order. The anglicization and protestantizing of local government was now complete. This new political/legal order is nowhere better epitomized than in the county town of Kilkenny, which now, more than ever, became the fulcrum of the state's rule in the county, further supplanting the once almost exclusive powers of the earl of Ormond. The dramatic transformation in the population structure of the city of Kilkenny also clearly reflects these changes. The most significant inland city in the country, this regional capital had long been dominated by powerful Old English and other merchant families, had its own complex economic structures, supporting a wide range of shops, services and industrial activities, including as many as eighteen mills. New English control was to make for a radical restructuring of the social geography of the city. In the core of the city, in the High Street and elsewhere, over 72 per cent of the population was of planter stock as early as 1660. In the surrounding ring of urban settlement, 40 per cent of the population were settlers, while in the outlying Liberties of the city 24 per cent were newcomers to a county where the New English comprised *only* 7.8 per cent of the total adult population. Initial infiltration into such county towns was in the administrative, legal, military, political and ecclesiastical spheres, but by the 1660s it was the merchants who dominated – men like Wareing, Warren, Wheeler and Haydocke – the new leaders of the economic order whose merchant wealth was to help many of them acquire extensive estates in the surrounding regions. Kilkenny, like most county towns, was thus radically restructured.

As we have seen, the forces of transformation were not all compressed into the Cromwellian period. The expansion of Old English power and influence under the expressed direction of the earls of Ormond over the previous century had paved the way for later intrusion. It was the post-Reformation takeover of the parochial glebelands that first initiated a small scattering of new immigrants into the region. Likewise, overspill from the earlier plantations of Laois and Offaly was to affect the northern edges of the county – a process that underpinned the greatest rural concentration of Protestant populations in these border parishes in the eighteenth century. Similarly, the 1641 depositions indicate the deliberate introduction of a minority of New English tenants, miners and leaseholders by both old modernizing and new landowners. The establishment of state-supported garrisons at places like Lodge Park and Knocktopher also brought in new people, as did rapid growth in the urban functions of the frontier town of Castlecomer. Clearly, Kilkenny city's central position in the new episcopal order provided additional impetus for immigration and expansion from these old metropolitan foci – a process reflected in new leasing patterns on the episcopal lands of the bishop of Ossory.

Figure 8.7 outlines the broad pattern of landownership c.1670. The now restored duke of Ormond had actually increased his extensive holdings from 55,000 to 58,000 plantation acres in Kilkenny. This fact, in conjunction with the restoration of Lord Mountgarrett, the survival of the extensive Grace estate in Crannagh and the continuation of the extensive Wandesforde estate in Fassadinin, meant that a sizeable proportion of Kilkenny's real estate did not figure in the Cromwellian settlement. Grantees benefited especially from the dismantling of the lands of many of the lesser Butlers, of the great Walsh estate in the south and practically all the other medium and small sized estates held by the great phalanx of middle order Old English gentry. There is, therefore, a close correlation between the areas of Cromwellian settlement and Fig. 8.4 (see p. 284), which depicts the non-Butler lands of Co. Kilkenny in 1641. Thus, a solid group of Cromwellian estates at the 500–3,000 plantation acre level did emerge amongst the Baker, Blunden, Bradshaw, Bushe, Loftus, Warden and Warren families. Families like the Cramers of Ballyfoyle, a number of lesser branches of the Cuffe, Deane and Jones families, the Horseys at Kilcrony (now Greenville), Mathews at Bonnet-stown, Johnstons at Clara, Villers at Dunnamaggan, the Woods at Baile na Lochan (later Woodsgift), the Webbs at Baile na Rince (later Webbsborough) and the Wheelers of Lyrath were also to dig their heels in. The creation of a Protestant Ascendancy in Kilkenny, then, given the relative weakness of an earlier New English presence, was overwhelmingly a function of the settlement of Cromwellian families. On the other hand, of the seven to eight estates over 5,000 plantation acres it would appear that only the Cuffe and Ponsonby families were to become perma-nently associated with the county – the former at Inch (Dysart) and the latter at Kildalton and the landlord village of Piltown.

A more detailed examination of the distribution of the new Kilkenny *titula-does*/gentry in the 1660 poll-tax provides further clues to the critical priorities of the ruling group in the mid-seventeenth century. First, control of the county and episcopal capital is a central feature of this design. As illustrated elsewhere at the national scale, the Cromwellian conquest was, above all, a conquest of Dublin, all port-cities and county towns such as Kilkenny by immigrant elites and peoples.

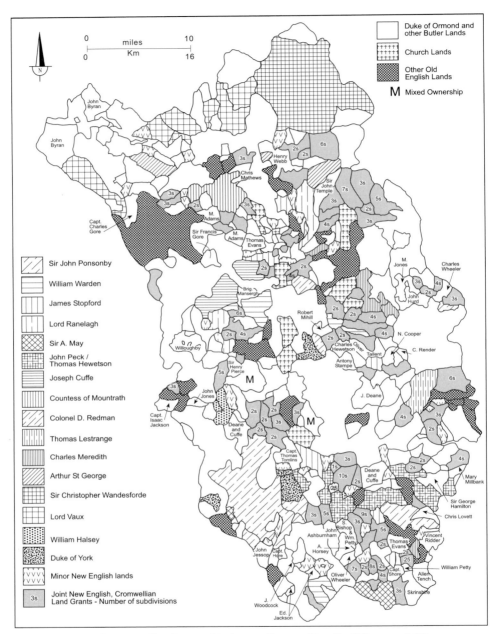

8.7   Patterns of landownership in post-Cromwellian Co. Kilkenny *c*.1670

Island-wide, the Cromwellian settlement had not only made for massive property transfers in the countryside; more significantly, Cromwellian policy and independent economic processes saw the radical acceleration of planter command of urban properties, agricultural surpluses, the export trade and a whole range of administrative and commercial positions in the cities and county towns.

The second major feature of the Cromwellian elite distribution in Kilkenny is the control of key communication lines in the country. Unlike the older lordship, which had to administer and defend its own boundaries, the New English elite could depend on the central state for this now broader function – in any case, much of this land was still held by the Ormond Butlers. The New English elite came to concentrate its control not only in Kilkenny city but also its hinterland in all directions: moving north through Ballyragget to the Midlands, northeast by Freshford and on to mid-Tipperary; northeastwards via Castlecomer and east-wards along the rich core area to Gowran and the Barrow, southwestwards along the corridor from Callan and Clonmel, while also controlling the navigable stretches of the Nore within the county and the lower stretches of both the Suir and the Barrow. Clear access from the city south to Waterford port is also main-tained, as is a central east–west axis along the northern foothills of the Walsh mountains. Thus, the Cromwellians not only achieved landed control and control of the centres of trade but also the essential road and river networks that opened out from Kilkenny to Dublin and Waterford and the Atlantic markets beyond. Here we see the further articulation of all modes of communication to better serve the market economy. The early decades of the seventeenth century had already seen a renewal and expansion in the markets and fairs in the lowland core region centred on Kilkenny city and secondly around Waterford city. The second half of the seventeenth century was to see the incorporation of the rest of the county, especially the hill country from Freshford (1675) in the north to Kilmoganny (1706) in the south, into an expanded market and fair network, according as the drive towards commercialization of the agricultural economy gathered momentum.

By the mid-1660s the triple alliance between the new ruling military/political order, the landed-commercial system and the Established Church had stabilized and consolidated its geographical bases. Burtchaell's work on the distribution of the New English in the southeastern counties in 1660 highlights the central role of the towns, the fanning out of the settlers along the major routeways and the resid-ual impact of the outlying garrison centres, still there to wipe out the pockets of resistance that survived in the woodlands and the hills.[50] The greatest regional concentration of settlers was in the triangular core region that linked the hinter-lands of Kilkenny city with those of Callan and Graiguenamanagh. This triangular core funnelled southeastwards to New Ross via the Nore valley. Two other secondary areas of settlement were in the extreme north of the county and in the southern parishes of Iverk and Knocktopher.

The corollary of the geography of this revolutionary transformation in the distri-bution and composition of elites was a geography of dislocation and trauma for the majority of the old landowners and urban middle classes. These were required to make themselves, their families and their retinues of stock and other material wealth known to the Revenue Commissioners before trekking to their new alloca-tions in Connacht. The Kilkenny group was led by such people as Walter Archer of Gowran, Nicholas Aylward of Aylwardstown, Thomas Butler of Kildellig, John Cantwell of Cantwellscourt, Philip Purcell of Ballyfoyle and Pierce Walsh of

Ballyhubbock.[51] Essentially, all major and minor landowners were included in the transplantation, with the exception of the earl of Ormond, and his closest kinsmen and allies. Analysis of the summary forms of the Transplantation Certificates highlights the zones of greatest potential dislocation and clearly mirrors the zones of greatest Cromwellian landed dominance, as shown in Fig. 8.7. The main areas of dislocation included the parish of Erke in Galmoy, the lands from Tubrid through Freshford and northeastwards to Castlecomer, extended southwards into the parishes below the Castlecomer plateau and on into the plains of Gowran, southwestwards through Inch and Tullaherin, and on to Tullamain and Killamery and turned eastward from the southern parish of Fiddown into Knocktopher and Dunkitt. There was also some disruption in the River Barrow parishes of Ida, along each side of the Nore valley and curving around the hills of Graiguenamanagh to rejoin the zone of change in the middle Barrow valley.

The transplantation summaries do not tell the whole story: less than one-third of this group actually moved to Connacht. Many of the remaining two-thirds hung on locally, hoping for restoration via the restored duke of Ormonde (Fig. 8.8). Thus, in 1660 the old gentry in Kilkenny controlled the parishes of Clonamery, the Rower and Dungarvan in Gowran barony and much of the middle lands of Ida, including the parishes of Ballygurrim, Kilbride, Kilmackevoge and Kilcolumb. Elsewhere, in lands controlled by the Butlers, old elites dominated such parishes as Killaloe, Coolaghmore, Dunnamaggan and Kells, while also still competing with the new Cromwellians along the Kilkenny city/Waterford port axis. Likewise, a great belt of old gentry survived in much of Crannagh barony, apart from the strategic northern axis through Freshford, while some also survived on the borders of Galmoy and Fassadinin in north Kilkenny.

The 1664 Ormond list of dispossessed landowners in the county identifies close to a hundred members of the former elite families who were still hoping that, through the good offices of the duke of Ormond, they would be restored to at least some of their lands.[52] Only a few families, particularly those at the top of the social hierarchy who through their substantial wealth, social position and political influence at the highest levels, were able to renegotiate a place in the sun. The great majority of landlords were not restored: with them went the patronage of not only the poets and the harpers but also many of the old settlement foci and their populations. The Reformation and its aftermath weakened some of the old villages but it was the uprooting of the old landowner patrons in conjunction with the economic forces unleashed by a new elite under a new economic order (mercantilism) that finally shattered many of them.

In this context, it is relevant to note that the surviving village world in south Kilkenny is a world with few, if any, demesnes – clearly it was north and middle Kilkenny where landlordism struck its deepest roots, as evidenced by the reconstituted towns and villages of this region, as well as the dense distribution of landlord demesnes. Thus practically every demesne in Galmoy barony was built on former focal points and a similar pattern prevails elsewhere. Already in the 1660s a new order of settlement was emerging, as at Balleen (Lodge Park), Coolcashen (Fayle) and Bawnmore, while the surviving estate maps of Co. Kilkenny point to a climax phase of demesne creation between the 1730s and the 1760s. A preliminary analysis suggests that close on a hundred of Kilkenny's demesne lands are built on the sites of former village settlements. In place of the old village communities, parklands and high walls were built, enclosing forever the lost worlds of the seventeenth century. The newly constructed, more stratified and more ethnic-based social structure was therefore to have a very clear geographical expression. Social and cultural distance was matched by a growing spatial separation of the classes – of the elites from the commoners, and of the farmers from the labourers.

The reverberations of such change were to echo into the nineteenth century. Kells was to shrink to a small village, Newtown Jerpoint was to disappear completely, as were a whole host of parish centres throughout specific regions of the county, especially in the rich core in the middle and northern parts of the county. On the other hand, places like Ballyhale, Ballyragget and Inistioge were relocated or reconstructed, while new landlord villages were to emerge at John-stown and Goresbridge. I have detailed in chapter 9 the depopulation of the Tipperary lowlands and the massive expansion of settlement along the roads and in bogland and upland regions between the 1650s and the 1850s.[53] It is clear that these processes were already in motion in the two counties between the 1650s and the 1670s – probably at a much swifter pace in the more pastoral county of Tipper-ary; more slowly but with similar long-term results in parts of Co. Kilkenny. The local and regional displacement of populations was often linked to the disappear-ance of the old landlord patrons.

I have identified the contrasting regions in seventeenth-century Ireland where old elities or new elites were pre-eminent.[54] The sharpest contrasts appear between plantation Ulster and the regions 'reserved' to the Irish in Connacht. But much of east and south Leinster and east Munster emerges as a battleground of conflicting interests. Here, members of the older society still held on to powerful hinge or middlemen positions in the urban and rural social hierarchies and ensured that the relative success of the new landlord-inspired economy would both be based on and be in part mediated/negotiated by them. These generaliza-tions may apply particularly to those parts of Tipperary and Kilkenny where the duke of Ormond and, more particularly, the other Butler families and those of their allies survived as landlords for lengthy periods after the mid-seventeenth century. The again highly influential duke of Ormonde retained a massive 130,000 plantation acres in Tipperary up to the early eighteenth century and likewise held close to 60,000 plantation acres in Kilkenny.[55] The survival or restoration of the Grace, Mountgarrett, Galmoy, Blanchfield and other smaller estate units often sustained local communities in their respective areas.[56]

It follows that the comparison of the 1660 poll-tax with those of the hearth-money records four years later would reveal intriguing regional variations in the dialectic between the Cromwellian and the older forces at work in local commu-nities and regions.

In the barony of Fassadinin there was a further solidification of the Cromwellian settlement between 1660 and 1664, witnessed especially by the survival of the existing Cromwellians and the emergence of new Cromwellian families at the upper (two hearths plus) level. Nolan confirms this pattern for the end of the seventeenth century, when the barony was solidly in Cromwellian hands; even the second duke of Ormonde was selling off his interests here by the 1690s.[57] Similarly, in Galmoy along the edges of the solidly planted midland belt of Laois-Offaly, a further solidification of the New English Cromwellian settlement was in motion between 1660 and 1664. In contrast, the Grace-dominated barony of Crannagh was to remain remarkably stable and resilient, with the old gentry families keeping a firm hold on their territories. The Liberties of Kilkenny also witnessed the further solidification and extension of an already well-established Cromwellian presence and likewise the rich barony of Shillelogher. It is clear that the old core of the county had already been transferred to a completely new group. Knocktopher is a transitional barony where both landed traditions are consolidating in different parts of the barony. Apart from the intensely colonized part of the Kilkenny city hinterland, it is evident that the restoration of some of the major Butler families (including Lord Galmoy) and their allies in Gowran saw a shift in favour of the old gentry families in the eastern half of this region and the consequent relocation elsewhere of some of the new Cromwellian grantees. Ida and Iverk remain for the most part unchanged between 1660 and 1664; Ida showing a striking balance between the power of the two elites, whereas Iverk, given the dominance of the duke of Ormonde and Ponsonby, saw little change as its crescent of small Cromwellian grantees along the Suir held their ground.

There are further complications in landownership and landholding patterns, with significant implications for societal and settlement structures. The first is absenteeism. Only about 20 of the *c.*200 Cromwellian grantees in Kilkenny were to become so permanently associated with the county through residence and political representation as to form its Protestant Ascendancy.[58] Much work needs to be done to tease out early and continuing levels of absenteeism amongst the new owners of land but it is clear that it was of a very significant order in counties like Kilkenny and Tipperary. The lands of absentees Lord Ranelagh, the countess of Mountrath, Lord Vaux, the duke of York, Sir William Petty, Sir John Temple, and indeed many others, were clearly managed from a great distance (see Fig. 8.7, p. 300). However, we need to qualify the meaning of 'absenteeism' here. The fragmentation of properties as a result of much land speculation at an island-wide scale was a consequence of the Cromwellian conquest. For the first time this specific conquest opened up the whole island to country-wide land acquisition and speculation. The second factor that compounds the landownership patterns is illustrated in Fig. 8.7, namely the subdivision of old compact properties amongst numerous grantees. This was to further complicate what was already a highly complicated property framework.

These two factors, absenteeism and the break-up of compact property frameworks, were also to have significant implications for levels of settlement continuity and reconstruction, for the development or non-development of demesnes or landlord villages, for the encouragement or non-encouragement of the influx of 'improving Protestant head-tenants', and for the survival or non-survival of old ways of managing territories and societies. Clearly, family, tenant and settlement continuities in south Kilkenny were related to higher levels of landlord absenteeism, as well as to other factors. Likewise, the degree to which the survival of both old landlord patronage and parish structures in the richer lands of Kilkenny actually inhibited the spread of enclosures, the greater commercialization of the agricultural economy and the decline of the old village structures needs to be assessed in more detail.

In any event, the most crucial continuities were not at the elite levels. The evidence here suggests that Kilkenny (like Tipperary) was only half conquered. The hearth-money records for both counties point up the continuing strength of the middle and lower levels of the old society and also pinpoint how sharp were the contrasting patterns of settlement in the mid and late 1660s. The limited Kilkenny hearth-money evidence for 1664 suggests a similar pattern to Co. Tipperary, which surfaces even more emphatically at the time of the Williamite Wars in 1688–91. Then under the short-lived reign of James II, the Irish in Kilkenny only managed to define sixty Cromwellians as 'rebels' and a number of these were the widows of landlords 'who were absent from the kingdom'. In contrast, on the defeat of the Jacobites, nearly 300 of Kilkenny's old elites, with some farmers, clerks, and blacksmiths, were outlawed.[59] This list of 'outlaws' shows the strength of the Brennans of Fassadinin – gone as landowners, yes, but clearly a dominant force as middle gentry and local power-holders in Castlecomer and adjacent parishes. Likewise, the Shortalls are still deeply embedded in the life and power structures of north Crannagh, even if none of them is to survive officially as landowners. The list of those outlawed also highlights the power of the old families in baronies like Gowran; indeed, the list is in part a pointer to the last drive by the old 'feudal' group to regain the high ground. Judging by the list and distribution of names, the southern half of the county appears to have been less involved and less turbulent this time, a factor that may have further shielded this part of the country from later confiscation and infiltration. It is also clear how the core leadership of the Jacobite movement lay with the merchants, surgeons and other gentry families of the city of Kilkenny. Close to 20 per cent of all the Jacobite 'rebels' resided in the city. The failure of the insurgents meant that the Williamite conquest and confiscations would complete the Cromwellian conquest with a ruthlessness and a finality that would not be challenged at the political level for at least 100 years. However, underneath the landownership levels, stubborn tenant farmers, shopkeepers and artisans were constructing their own strategies of adaptation and resistance.

This chapter has set out to investigate and reconstruct the transformation of the territorial, social and settlement structures of Co. Kilkenny over the seventeenth century. In many respects it is a story of a relatively sharp transition from an already transformed 'feudalized' order to a more 'modern capitalist' order. At the territorial level, the old lordship of the Ormond Butlers is effectively dismantled and the English state – through the enhanced role of the county sheriff, the English court system, the Established Church and the planting of a new elite – comes to dominate.

At the parish level, the appropriation by the new colonial Church of the old parochial territorial structures, buildings and incomes necessitated a slow but, in the end, radical reconstruction on the part of the modernizing Catholic Church of its own parochial and settlement arrangements.

At the property level, the close-knit networks of the Old English landowners is, for the greater part, dismantled, as a new and much smaller Cromwellian elite (now backed by the military power of the state) takes over and seeks to reconstruct this conquered world in their own image and for their own purposes. The older, more feudalized social structure, underpinned by a powerful Gaelic substratum and interlaced by clan kinship strategies in land management and social control, is also partially disrupted and fragmented.

And at the settlement level, the medieval nucleated settlement patterns, pivoting around the castles of the lords or the parish churches or both, are now subject to erosion, as many of the lords are displaced and as the Church of the majority is forced to seek new centres of worship.

Overall, there is now a growing spatial segregation of ethnic, class and status groups, according as the development of the demesnes, the expansion of the number of compact, independent farms and the emergence of the roadside cottages split apart class and status groups that formerly had often lived close together in the one village or hamlet. Cutting across and augmenting all these processes is the deep-seated transformation of the economy as the countryside and the reconstituted towns are increasingly integrated into a world geared to production for outside markets.

These different processes, however, work in a very uneven way across the varied physical and cultural topography of mid-seventeenth-century Co. Kilkenny. The south and southeastern part of the county within the tidal reaches of the Suir, Nore and Barrow reveals a combination of very special conditions which allow the older social and settlement structures to interface with and to assimilate the new forces without that much trauma or displacement. The survival of both the duke of Ormond and some other Old English families as landowners in this region, the significance of local gentry families as middlemen, the high level of 'non-improving' absentee landlords, including merchants from Waterford city, the availability of off-farm employment in the nearby towns and city, the tradition of sending sons and daughters into ecclesiastical occupations, as well as outmigration to Newfoundland and elsewhere, all combined – with an associated conservation of language, customs and religious institutions – to allow these societies and villages to reproduce themselves without too much disruption.[60] The middle third of the county is a transition zone in this context, its social and settlement structures clearly more radically reconstructed; yet its towns (with the exception of the county capital) remain firmly in local control and many old farm villages, townland and kinship networks survive here also. The northern baronies of the county were most transformed, reflecting the impact of the Wandesforde estate and coal-mining (particularly in the Castlecomer region) and the overspill of strong settler influences in the northwest from the Laois-Offaly plantation region. The middle and northern zones reveal by far the greatest erosion of old farm clusters and especially of nucleated villages.

Again, these generalizations have to be qualified. There are complications due to the topographies and social structures of seventeenth-century Kilkenny. For example, if one looks at the continuity in the occupation of old parish sites by the Catholic Church, other gradations emerge: the main corridors of the county seem most subject to change and dislocation, whereas the hill country and the fringes of the county generally (as along the Tipperary/Kilkenny border) reveal much greater continuity at this parish/community level.

There is a stubborn resilience in the character of Kilkenny: it is a land where Gael, Norman and New English have clashed and perhaps fused and cross-fertilized in quite an extraordinary way. Unlike most pre-Reformation Irish cathedrals, St Canice's in Kilkenny still provides a sense of continuity and inclusiveness, which embraces the Butler tombs and the Banim brothers, and which, like the city of Kilkenny itself, transcends the deep fissures of the post-Reformation period. Equally deep levels of assimilation are characteristic of the Kilkenny countryside, the smaller towns and amongst its peoples. The Statutes of Kilkenny had forbidden the descendants of the Anglo-Norman/Old English from mixing or marrying with the Irish or even playing hurling. Yet some of the best hurling stylists in Kilkenny still bear names like Barry, Comerford, Power, Forstall and Walsh, others bear names like Carey, Phelan, Larkin, Murphy and Fennelly. These hurlers dance through history, mocking all official and exclusive definitions of who they are and where they come from.

9

County Tipperary
Property, Patronage and Population

> East Munster is of unusual interest to the student of changing spatial relationships
> as an example of an area of convergence where some major strands in Ireland's
> history have met. County Tipperary forms the heart of this area.
>
> T. Jones Hughes[1]

In reconstructing the human geography of mid-seventeenth-century Ireland, I
recognize that the ownership and control of land was the central fulcrum of
economic and political power. Property units also provided crucial territorial
structures for shaping the location and character of most human activities. The
central objective of this chapter is to explore the interrelationships between property units and the settlement and occupational structures of Co. Tipperary,
particularly over the period 1640–70. I begin the story by identifying some of the
essential factors shaping living conditions within the county in this turbulent era.
In the conclusion I shall assess briefly the settlement consequences flowing from
the Cromwellian conquest and the emergence of the new landowning elite.

Geographers greatly appreciate spatially comprehensive source-materials,
which provide a comparative perspective for all parts of their study area. The
richest sources for studying and reconstructing mid-seventeenth-century Tipperary derive from the Cromwellian settlement and the growth of a central state
bureaucracy. The Civil Survey for Co. Tipperary, edited and with a comprehensive introduction by Robert Simington, is a rich, deeply layered and ambiguous
document, which reveals the ancient tenures, land measures and territorial divisions of each parish and barony in the county (see Fig. 9.1).[2] It allows one to
reconstruct the proprietorial geography and tithe contributions of each parish in
1640, and provides much evidence on land-use potential and land valuations, as
well as elementary settlement details for 1654. An increasingly more comprehensive picture as to the distribution, density and composition of the population
in the county emerges from the poll-tax (1660) and hearth-money tax (1665–7)
records,[3] though, like the Civil Survey, these records are not without their limitations and ambiguities.

In all of this, we need to remember Jones Hughes's opening generalization and
observations about Tipperary's crucial location on the island: its experiences are
not those of Dublin, Meath and the Pale region to the east nor, say, that of Galway

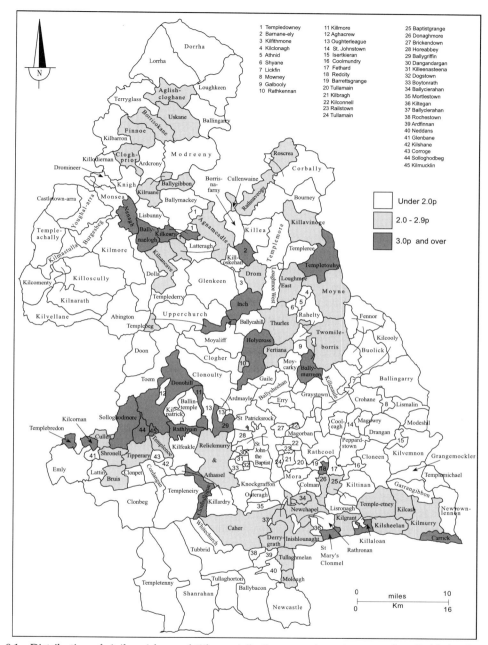

1 Templedowney	11 Killmore
2 Barnane-ely	12 Aghacrew
3 Kilfithmone	13 Oughterleague
4 Kilclonagh	14 St. Johnstown
5 Athnid	15 Isertkieran
6 Shyane	16 Coolmundry
7 Lickfin	17 Fethard
8 Mowney	18 Redcity
9 Galbooly	19 Barrettsgrange
10 Rathkennan	20 Tullamain
	21 Kilbragh
	22 Kilconnell
	23 Railstown
	24 Tullamain

25 Baptistgrange
26 Donaghmore
27 Brickendown
28 Horeabbey
29 Ballygriffin
30 Dangandargan
31 Killeenasteena
32 Dogstown
33 Boytonrath
34 Ballyclerahan
35 Mortlestown
36 Kiltegan
37 Ballyclerahan
38 Rochestown
39 Ardfinnan
40 Neddans
41 Glenbane
42 Kilshane
43 Corroge
44 Solloghodbeg
45 Kilmucklin

Under 2.0p

2.0 - 2.9p

3.0p and over

9.1   Distribution of civil parishes and tithe contributions per plantation acre of profitable land in Co. Tipperary *c.*1640, (see references 2 and 3 with regard to sources used for all maps in this chapter and see back to Fig. 5.9 for distribution of Co. Tipperary baronies))

or Mayo to the west. It was (and is) a significant region in the middle of the country, where the tensions and battles between Irish and intrusive forces have been both sustained and creative. It is a key hearthland region.

Environmental, Demographic and Economic Contexts

In 1666–7, four core areas in Co. Tipperary are distinguished by high population densities (see Fig. 9.1). A primary core area exists along the lower Suir valley, pivoting around the towns of Clonmel and Carrick-on-Suir and extending westwards to reach Ardfinnan. A second more extensive zone embraces northern and western Clanwilliam and extends into the southern edges of Kilnamanagh from upper Donohill to Ballintemple/Dundrum. A third core area dominates much of central Eliogarty, with twin population peaks around Thurles and Fithmone. A fourth high density zone appears in the lowlands of Upper Ormond, centred on Nenagh town and also embracing the north-facing parishes of the Arra region and the rich lakeland district of Killodiernan and Kilbarron in Lower Ormond.

In sharp contrast are the relatively lightly populated areas, which include much of the difficult hill country and wet shrubby lowland areas of Owney and Arra and the southern hills of Upper Ormond. This lightly populated area also extends from Barnane and Borrisofarney through Kilnamanagh to incorporate the southwestern upland regions around the Galtee and Knockmealdown mountains. Relatively low population densities are also recorded for the woodland/bogland parts of the Lower Ormond parishes and equivalent zones along the northeastern border of the county, stretching from Corbally, Killavinoge and Templetuohy, through to the 'Great Bog of Ely' and reaching almost to the gates of Cashel. In this eastern half of Middlethird, and over much of Slieveardagh and Comsy, the general relationship between environmental possibilities – as reflected, for example, in the 1654 land values – and density of population is much more complex than in other upland/wet lowland regions.

Land-use potential in Co. Tipperary is carefully documented in the Civil Survey. Land described as 'arable' does not necessarily mean that such land was under tillage at the time of the survey but does indicate the flexible champion lands as, for example, at Kilruane and Donohill, which are described as 'suitable for arable or pasture'. The distribution of such champion land sharpens further our appreciation of the overriding strength of the lower Suir region, which includes the civil parishes of Carrick-on-Suir, Kilmurry, Kilsheelan, Killaloan, Powerstown, Lisronagh, Rathronan, Ballyclerihan, Newchapel, Abbeyinislounaght, Tullaghmelan, Neddans, Ardfinnan and much of Caher. It also highlights the great flexibility of the lands of western Middlethird and much of Clanwilliam. The distribution of arable lands in Eliogarty is more complex and this complexity also characterizes the remainder of the county.

To clarify the picture, it is useful by way of contrast to identify the profitable lands deemed suitable for pasture in the Civil Survey. Three regions stand out: first, the extreme southwest of the county, stretching south of Newcastle through Ballybacon, Shanrahan and Templetenny and including parts of Clonbeg and Templeneiry in the Glen of Aherlow; second, the great hill region of Kilnamanagh and its borderlands; and third, the cold Slieveardagh hills, with a core in the parish of Ballingarry. In all these regions, more than half the profitable land is deemed suitable for grazing purposes only. There are secondary grazing cores in the Slievenamon and Barnane areas.

There are also extensive transitional belts in Tipperary where 25–50 per cent of the enumerated profitable land is regarded by the Civil Survey jurors as most suitable for pasture. The remainder of Slieveardagh and much of the northeastern edges of Middlethird – particularly the parishes of Ballysheehan and Magorban – fit into this category and help to explain the sharp contrasts in population densities in this variegated barony. Likewise, contrasts with Eliogarty reveal extensive grazing lands in Thurles, Loughmoe, Callabegs and Rahelty, while also emphasizing the sharpness of the frontier between the arable lands of (Twomile) Borris and the grazing lands of the Slieveardagh plateau. Equally sharp is the frontier between tillage and pastoral lands in Owney and Arra, while on Lower Ormond's better lands, the propensity for tillage would appear to be as evident in 1654 as it is today.

Information in the Civil Survey on the distribution of tithe contributions in 1640 can help us to further refine our generalizations as to the forces affecting the distribution and density of population. The tithe contributions can be measured in pence per profitable plantation, or Irish, acre – the range is from over three pence per acre to under a half-pence per acre. The main burden of tithe payments fell on tillage producers, particularly those engaged in grain cultivation. The parishes of much of Ikerrin and Middlethird, which had average-valued tithe contributions per plantation acre (1.5 pence to 1.9 pence), would seem to indicate the mixed-farming/moderately populated regions. In contrast, the well-above average tithe values (2.5 pence to 3.5 pence) for all of the middle and lower Suir valley, north Clanwilliam, the eastern as well as the Suir valley region of Eliogarty and the whole Upper Ormond core linked to the old Church lands of Cloghprior, Aglish and Uskeane suggest the central importance of these areas in grain production. The grazier zones are confirmed by the limited tithe payments (under 1 pence per acre) for the lower valued lands of Slieveardagh, the western part of Iffa and Offa and south Clanwilliam, most of Kilnamanagh and Arra and Owney, while also including the fringes of the arable core of Upper Ormond, as well as the bogland/woodland zones of Lower Ormond. Most noticeable, however, are the lower tithe returns for the highly valued parishes of northern Middlethird (including Ballysheehan and Ardmayle) and the parishes of Drangan, Kilvemnon, Ballymackey, Templemore, Modreeny, Kilbarron and Aghnameadle, which indicate the possible accentuation of commercial pastoral production prior to the 1640s. The transition from arable to commercialized pastoral production is further highlighted in the founding of fairs (and markets) in these areas by the more enterprising landowners.[4] The most striking evidence of the importance of sheep in the economy is revealed in the Transplantation Certificates, where the average number of sheep returned per transplanting landowner in Tipperary is 14. This is four times that of the next highest county – Waterford – and twelve times that of the average per capita returns for all the counties of Munster and Leinster.[5] Over one-third of all the sheep returned by the former landowning elites of both Munster and Leinster were, therefore, coming from Tipperary.

The best evidence for long-term economic swings comes from the Civil Survey details relating to cornmills, tucking mills and other economic indicators. The contrast between areas where cornmills were still active as opposed to areas where cornmills were in ruins by 1654 is instructive. The location of the working mills is a veritable distribution map of the Tipperary river systems and their major tributaries. The Suir and its tributaries (the Arra, the Multeen, the Clodiagh, the Drish, the Clashawley and the Anner) dominate the pattern. In the southeast, the King's river and its tributaries are locally important, while the Nenagh river system also sees much activity in grinding the corn of the rich lands of Ormond. The areas where grain has retreated are even more instructive, indicated by ruined mills along the Kilmastulla and other smaller rivers draining to the Shannon and also along the northern and southern edges of the surviving arable core of Upper Ormond. The bridgehead country between Nenagh and the Suir valley likewise underwent a retreat in grain production, as did a whole series of parishes located on each side of the core milling zone that stretched along the Suir valley. Judging by their ruined mills, east Clanwilliam, much of Middlethird and the western and northwestern parts of Iffa and Offa had also yielded much ground to the spread of sheep and cattle.

Complementing this distribution were those tower-houses and stone houses with 'bawns' (walled enclosures for cattle) that dominate the strong pastoral zones, sweeping southwards in a curve from Bawnmadrum (Bourney) through Templetuohy, Moyne, Moycarkey, Graystown and Magorban and then fanning east and westwards to pick up a number of parishes along the Iffa and Offa, Middlethird borders. The 'bawn zone' also incorporates western Iffa and Offa and each side of the Arra river core of Clanwilliam. It then curves northwards again emerging conspicuously along the edges of the Upper Ormond arable core and with other key sites in Lower Ormond at Ballingarry and Terryglass. The tucking mills occupy key hinge points in the county – outside Fethard (one lately built by a Cromwellian), in Carrick, Clonmel, Abbeyinishlounaght (also built by a Cromwellian), around Caher at Lisseva, Kedragh and Cloghbridy, at Ballygriffin, Holycross and near Dromineer. Likewise, the centrepieces of a commercialized mixed-farming economy emerge where active cornmill, bawn and tucking mill distributions overlap. This overlap can be seen in Modreeny, Roscrea, Borrisoleigh, Thurles and Holycross, and even more emphatically from Ballygriffin, Cashel, Caher and Fethard, through to the primary axis of development that centres on the county town of Clonmel.

The cumulative evidence thus points to a highly variegated Tipperary. Clearly, long-established patterns of intensive economic activities – particularly in grain cultivation – were dominant in the favoured agricultural regions, and these, in turn, exhibited the highest population densities. Equally, there were well-grounded pastoral rhythms in the remoter upland and wetland regions, which made for the lowest population densities. The longer term trends certainly favoured cattle and sheep production, although it is evident that the local and regional demand for grain in the more urbanized zones of the southeast was quite substantial. The expanding urban frontiers in Co. Tipperary were in the west and north at Clogheen, Tipperary town, Roscrea and Nenagh and most of the new fair foundations were also in these regions, marking the growing penetration of the formerly sheltered Gaelic hearthlands by expanding commercial influences. In contrast, in the Old English core of the south and east of the county were the older, more durable urban worlds of Thurles, Fethard, Cashel, Clonmel and Carrick-on-Suir. These old towns exhibited much more complex morphologies and social structures than those found in the still rudimentary fair towns of the north and west. They also nurtured more elaborate rural settlement hierarchies in their hinterlands.

More recent short-term changes are also indicated in some of the unexplained population variations, which may relate to the military and famine depredations of the previous decades. A related major impetus for change was an economic one, as agricultural trends swung ever more sharply towards cattle and sheep production after the Restoration. While not placing undue weight on the demographic evidence between the 1659–60 and 1666–7 taxation returns, there does appear to be a general trend emerging which saw some of the richest core areas lose population relative to the more marginal regions. These marginal areas seem to gain population disproportionately even over this brief phase. Given the chaos that characterized the period from 1641 to 1660, these economic and demographic fluctuations are to be expected. A short-term shift from intensive to extensive forms of agriculture may therefore help to explain lower population densities in highly valued lands that returned well above average tithe contributions in 1640. One such example is Rahelty-Shyane, a parish that reveals a relatively high number of 'waste' or unoccupied houses in 1666–7 and which is described in 1654 as 'overmuch spent by ploweing'.[6] It is tempting therefore to suggest that the economic processes that were to dominate the next 150 years – the rationalization of landholding patterns and relative depopulation of the better lands, with associated significant increases in settlements and populations in the marginal areas – were already well in motion by the later 1650s and 1660s. To unravel other dimensions of these patterns and processes, we must now turn to look at the landowning elites who supervised both these populations and economic activities and who, in turn, were to be engulfed by the forces that revolutionized the landowning patterns of mid-seventeenth-century Ireland.

The Property Matrix

Figure 9.2 illustrates the distribution of the major property units of Co. Tipperary in 1640. The contrasts between the landownership patterns and practices of the Old English zone of south and east Tipperary and the more Gaelic north and west have been emphasized elsewhere.[7] While there was some mixed ownership of undivided properties in borderland locations in Ikerrin and Eliogarty and while Old English ownership patterns still remained intermixed in some parishes within the hinterland of Clonmel, individual ownership of property was a general feature in the Old English zones by 1640. In contrast, the dominant pattern in west and northwest Tipperary is a hierarchy of holdings shared by a varying number of kinsmen in complex partnership arrangements. As Aidan Clarke has noted, the Irish land system at this time was a hybrid one, with 'both traditional native and

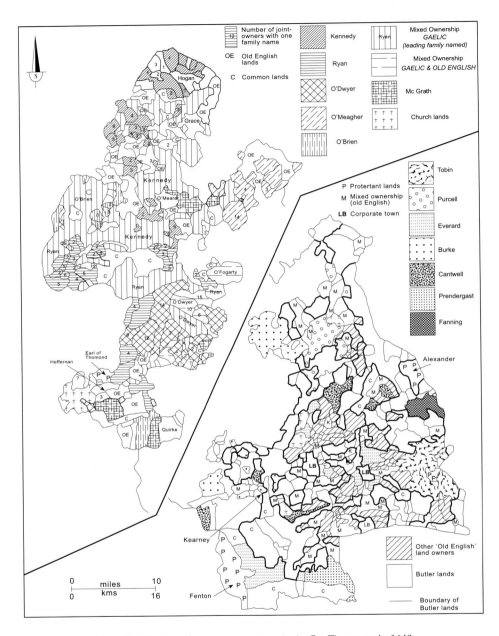

9.2   Distribution of major property units in Co. Tipperary in 1640

authentic feudal arrangements surviving in many places in varying stages of modification'.[8] The two extremes of land being held in common without partition in the 'Irish' manner, on the one hand, and land held according to the most elaborate stipulations of feudal overlordship, on the other, were to be found within Tipperary. A host of examples of the former arrangements can be cited from north and west Tipperary, while archaic feudal arrangements still survived, for example, in the Ballybacon-Newcastle region in the south of the county. The central objective of this subsection is to establish the size and respective distribution of these property units, as a prelude to understanding their impact on the human and, in particular, the settlement geography of the county.

The leading landowning sept in Co. Tipperary in 1640 was the Butlers. Over seventy Butler families owned land in the county, ranging from the earl and countess of Ormond (who between them directly controlled an estimated 85,000 statute acres), through to the second order Butler houses of Dunboyne, Ikerrin, Kilcash and Caher and down to the forty or so smaller Butler landowners controlling units of c.200–400 statute acres. The major components of the Butler lands are illustrated in Fig. 9.3. No map, however, can do justice to the complex mesh of management, kinship and marriage alliances that characterized these properties and families – relationships which the Cromwellian settlement certainly fragmented but by no means destroyed.

The political and economic power allied with the territorial extent of these Butler properties was initially a product of the overarching policy control exerted by the earl of Ormond from his two administrative centres – primarily from Kilkenny castle but also from his mansion house at Carrick. A second component was the intense rivalry that persisted between the major Butler houses, with representatives of each family expanding their properties right up to the final victory of the Cromwellian forces. As C.A. Empey has illustrated, the hammering out of the Butler lordship, with its power base in the productive riverine lowlands of the Suir, Nore and Barrow and pivoting around the great port-city of Waterford and its rich hinterland of solid inland towns, was one of the major achievements of the late Middle Ages in Ireland.[9] While the shift of the Butler power centre from Nenagh to Kilkenny in 1391 had highlighted the retreat of effective Butler control from its old hearthlands in north Tipperary, the 1640 distribution highlights, in turn, the subsequent consolidation of power in south and east Tipperary, and the ruthless reassertion of both Butler and crown control over the remainder of the county.

One function of this Butler territorial strategy was the control and protection of the towns and the maintenance of peaceful conditions for commercial agricultural production in their hinterlands. It is no coincidence, therefore, that, in addition to Carrick, the earls of Ormond controlled the key inland town of Thurles and the frontier manorial towns of Roscrea and Nenagh to the north, while also maintaining a keen interest in the county palatinate town of Clonmel. A second aspect of this territorial strategy was expansion into the buffer zones to the north and west and the solidification of boundaries on the edges of the old Gaelic hearthlands. The earls of Ormond had striven to solidify the northern and western frontiers with the Ely O'Carroll territories at Loughkeen, Modreeny and Roscrea and also with the other Gaelic lordships along the southeast facing slopes of the Barnane-Keeper Hill ranges. Careful land grants, strategic castle-building, as at Farneybridge and Ballysheeda, and the acquisition of extensive Church lands, as at Holycross and Athassel, were all part of this wide territorial strategy.

The management of these vast estates also had its own intricate internal geography. Of the seventy-five members of the Butler 'middle management team', which can be identified by looking at the major hearth-tax payers on the earl's manors and other properties in 1667, a little less than one-third were from junior Butler families, more than one-third were recruited from other Anglo-Norman families, one-fifth were from Irish families and the remainder were New English incomers.[10] Within this framework, it is striking how often Ormond utilized close kinsmen to man key frontier positions, as at Lorrha, Templemore and Donohill, while he bestowed responsibility for developing his towns to even closer kinspeople such as Mathew (Thurles). On the other hand, his more peaceful and commercialized estates of the east and southeast were more often administered by local Anglo-Norman families and sometimes included representatives of business and legal families from Kilkenny city itself. Ormond also played a key role in ensuring that some of his main Kilkenny allies were either restored to their old lands (as were the Cantwells at Dromineer), or were granted extensive Church lands (as were the Graces at Tyone and Cloghprior).

A second layer in the geography of the Ormond administrative system was represented by other major Butler houses. The Butlers of Kilcash were closest both kinship-wise and policy-wise to the earl of Ormond and controlled an estimated 8,000 statute acres under the southern slopes of Slievenamon, overlooking the richest vein of land in all of Tipperary. While centred on the parishes of Kilcash, Temple-etney and Newtownlennon, this family had also significant landed outliers in Knockgraffon, on the eastern edge of the Tobin lands in Comsy, in ancient Donaskeigh in Clanwilliam and most strategically in Lower Ormond at Modreeny and Ardcrony. Other close branches of the Ormond Butlers occupied smaller estates in Lower Ormond and more particularly in Eliogarty, where the Butlers of Nodstown (3,600 statute acres) and Moyaliff (300 statute acres) were located strategically at the apex of persistent pressures emanating from the foothills to the northwest, west and southwest. These two units then represented an old and crucial frontier between the Gaelic and Old English areas.

The second great cadet branch of the Butlers was that of the house of Dunboyne. By 1640, the core of these recently divided lands was centred on the wealthy manorial parishes of Drangan and Kiltinan, but also included other cores in Fithmone and Rathcool and included segments of the lands of Magowry, Crompsland, St John Baptists Grange, Tullamain, Railstown and Knockgraffon, totalling an estimated 12,200 statute acres. Old-established Dunboyne branches were represented at Ardmayle (3,800 statute acres), Cabbragh (1,600 statute acres) and Brittas (800 statute acres) in Thurles parish, while the more recently created Kilconnell estate (8,000 statute acres) emphasizes the massive scale of the original Middlethird core of the main Dunboyne lands. Likewise, the Ballinakill (3,200 statute acres), Killoskehan (2,500 statute acres), Clare (3,600 statute acres), Derryluskan (1,500 statute acres) and Widdingstown (1,500 statute acres) units point to the consolidation of the associated Dunboyne Butler estates in Middlethird barony in the later Middle Ages. This pattern also indicates an equally vigorous expansion into the northern borderlands, which complemented and reinforced the crescent of lands

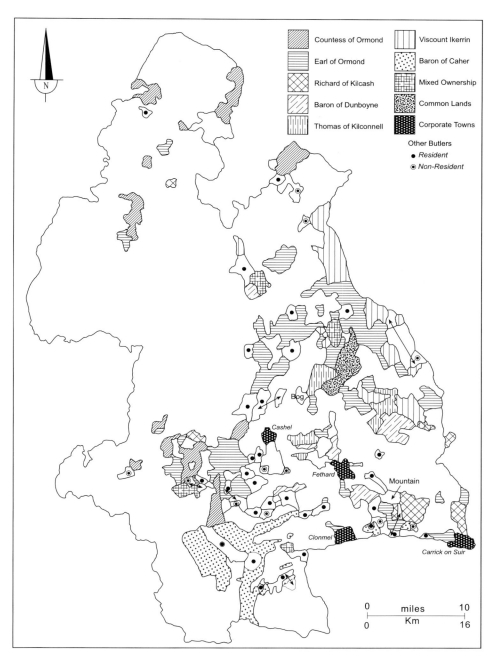

9.3   Distribution of Butler lands in Co. Tipperary in 1640

dominated by the earl of Ormond and, in the process, added further in-depth protection to the lucrative agricultural lands of the east and southeast.[11]

The lands of Viscount Ikerrin also reveal an interesting geographical arrangement. Centred on the parish of Lismalin, which overlooks the King's river,

Viscount Ikerrin's lands (*c*.26,700 statute acres) were mainly located in the baronies of Slieveardagh, Eliogarty and Ikerrin, and concentrated particularly on the eastern bogland/woodland flank, which in more turbulent times had come under pressure from the Gaelic lands of Clandonagh in Laois and indeed from further afield. This area was studded with substantial tower-houses and well-defended parish churches, as, for example, at the earl of Ormond's manor Buolick; Viscount Ikerrin had a secondary core here at Clonamicklon (Fennor); both face the woods and bogs of Ely, which stretched on into Cashel.

By far the most compact of the major Butler estates was that of the barons of Caher. This estate straddled a very interesting transitional zone that bounded the oldest core areas of Norman settlement along the Suir at Knockgraffon and Ardfinnan and reached westwards to front the former lands of the Whiteknight Fitzgibbons, traditional allies of the Desmond Fitzgeralds. The Caher estate had been gradually expanded to incorporate the more western manors of Rehill and Castlegrace and by 1640 comprised *c*.17,000 statute acres. Other branches of the Caher house were represented at Knocklofty (2,700 statute acres), Knockananamy (500 statute acres), Cloghbridy, Clonbrogan, Gormanstown, Mullaghneony, Bally-hustea and Rouskagh, while important outliers along the lower Suir were represented at Poulakerry (1,140 statute acres) and Ballynoran. In this most gaeli-cized of the Butler houses, the head-tenants or middlemen are invariably of old Irish extraction in the more pastoral western end, where the Slatterys, Lonergans, McGraths, O'Donnells, Connells and Hanrahans are particularly conspicuous – but in the old arable cores, it is the local Anglo-Norman families of English, Keating, White, Prendergast and Tobin which administer the townlands for the Caher Butlers.

The situation is different on Viscount Ikerrin's estates, where it is not too surprising to find that two-thirds of his head-tenants were of Old English descent, although the main old Irish families are the descendants of the gallowglass McSweeneys and the ecclesiastical/milling family of the Hogans. The Dunboyne estate, focused mainly on Middlethird, also reveals a fine equilibrium between the Irish (Shanahan, Kearney, Meagher and Ryan) and the Old English (Lawrence, St John, Britton, Tyrrell and Comerford). It should also be remembered that each of these major Butler houses had its second-level hierarchy of dependent houses, and this layer of Butler houses was concentrated mainly in the middle and lower Suir valley regions of Boytonrath, Dogstown, Outrath, Buffanagh, Lisnatubbrid, Ardfinnan, Temple-etney and Castlecoyne.

The territorial arrangement of the other Old English lands (see Fig. 9.2, p. 314) reveals two outstanding features. Apart from the Fethard-based Everard property (8,000 statute acres), the Moycarkey Cantwells (3,000 statute acres) and the St Johns of St Johnstown (3,800 statute acres), which were all in the rich hearthlands of Eliogarty and Middlethird, the other major Old English estates were located for the most part in the outlying pastoral regions. The Everard estate in southwest Tipperary, originally centred on Ballyboy (Tullaghorton), illustrates the new trends in estate development in early seventeenth-century Ireland. Its newly built mansion house at Ballysheehan (later known as Burncourt) reflected the wealth, confidence and extensive connections of this branch of the Fethard family. Along the Suir proper, the long-established Prendergast family had considerably extended their power base, establishing overlordship over land in three to four parishes around the manorial core at Newcastle (5,000 statute acres). Equally striking about the Everard and Prendergast properties is the managerial structure, with the major townland in each subunit on the estate dominated by other members of the main family. North of this latter zone, the Tobins lorded over the (old) territory of Comsy, with a main administrative core at Killaghy (Kilvemnon), which acted as the centre of the compact 10,500 statute acre property of James Tobin. Here also a tight-knit system of kinship networks was utilized to manage this complicated ecological zone, which takes in part of the Anner valley, the northern slopes of the Slievenamon and adjacent hills. Further north, two Fannings, William at Farrenrory (3,100 statute acres) and Michael at Ballingarry (2,500 statute acres), dominate this largely pastoral parish. In the northern march-lands of Eliogarty, the Purcells, barons of Loughmoe – where they had built a new mansion house – and their numerous relations had expanded their property bases, most notably along the western edges, through a process of purchase from Irish families in the parishes of Ballycahill, Templebeg and Moyaliff.

Further west and northwest, MacWalter Bourke of Borrisoleigh commanded a more hilly 9,500 statute acres, with only its immediate core area around Borris counted as good grainland – the rest was 'small oats' and cow country, where again a whole array of lesser Bourkes protected the frontiers to the north and south of this old distinctive territory of Ileigh. This hybrid zone reveals another case of a hierarchy of lands managed by family members. Here the balance was still struck in favour of primogeniture and estate concentration and the processes of subdivision were kept well in check. This contrasted with the more gaelicized Stapleton family in nearby Drom, where a 4,000 statute acre property had splin-tered under different pressures. Apart from a relatively compact zone of smaller properties south of Tipperary town, the remainder of their lands had been broken up. By 1640, only islands of propertied Bourkes survived in east Clanwilliam, reflecting the deep penetration of this area by Ormond and his cohorts following the Munster plantation. Beneath the veneer of the new overlordship, the Bourkes of Clanwilliam survived in great strength as middlemen and in 1667 they were second only to the Butlers in their occupation of more substantial houses taxed for two or more hearths in Co. Tipperary. Many smaller but highly lucrative Old English properties flourished behind the combined shield of both the Butler lands and these larger marchland properties in mainly pastoral regions. These were concentrated particularly in the east and middle parts of Iffa and Offa and dominated the historic core area of Middlethird and adjacent parts of Slie-veardagh, as well as the edges of the large Thurles manor to the north. Families with significant properties included: the Keatings at Nicholastown (2,000 statute acres) and Loughloghery (700 statute acres), the Crokes of Moylessan (1,600 statute acres), the Comyns of Tullamain (1,800 statute acres) and the Cantwells of Poynstown (1,280 statute acres).[12] These typified the highly dispersed local power structures of these parts of Co. Tipperary, whose owners were, as I shall later argue, powerful patrons of a close-knit system of nucleated settlements in their parishes.

Clanwilliam's complexity is emphasized by the presence here of extensive Church land around the old episcopal centre of Emly, where most head-tenants bore Irish names such as O'Grady and McGrath; by the solidity of the Heffernan clan in the rich lands of Lattin and Shronell; by the survival in the Glen of Aherlow of the O'Briens, the Quirkes and the O'Connors; by the strength of the Hogan family in the Anglo-Norman core of the barony and by the expansive power of the Ryan family – and especially its clerical branches – which dominate Solloghodmore, part of Tipperary town and Cordangan. Adding further complexity to a barony that saw the full blast of both deliberate plantation and commercial infiltration are the properties acquired by the descendants of the infamous archbishop of Cashel, Miler McGrath.

The McGrath lands in Clanwilliam (4,320 statute acres) and in Upper Ormond again highlight the new forces and alliances that were at work in Ireland generally, although more muted in Tipperary because of the dominance of the Butlers of Ormond. The McGrath influence, for example, may also have helped the medical/ecclesiastical family of O'Mearas of Toomevara to expand their Lissinskey estate, which is a striking feature of the Upper Ormond landscape in 1640, since it represents a compact, individually owned 'Gaelic' estate of over 9,000 statute acres. While Upper Ormond did not experience the same set of cross-currents as the more politically exposed Clanwilliam, the emergence and expansion of the McGrath, O'Meara, Butler and Grace properties, comprising 14.5 per cent, 10.8 per cent, 9.7 per cent and 6.7 per cent respectively of the barony's surveyed acres, indicate the power of the new consolidating forces in this rich zone.

Figure 9.2 does not however reveal that 11.6 per cent and 7.6 per cent of all properties in the barony were either recently purchased or mortgaged, with the main attrition taking place on the lands of the Kennedys, whose vast patrimony was gradually being eroded by the 1640s.[13] None the less, a previously powerful 'expanding clan' structure had still left the Kennedys holding 37.5 per cent of the surveyed area, with leading houses at Ballintotta, Killownine, Ballynaclogh and Traverstown. The old Norman family of de Mariscoes (Morris) hold 4.6 per cent of the barony centred at Latteragh and significant properties in Knockagh (Drom) and Castleleiny (Templeree). The remaining major landholders include the dynamic Ryans driving outwards in all directions from their Owney core and in this case intruded successfully in the Dolla/Templederry/Kilaneave area to command 7.7 per cent of the barony. The old erenagh family of the Gleesons control 5.2 per cent (mainly in Kilmore), while other smaller units are controlled by families like the MacBirragas (2.6 per cent). A final indicator of the new dynamic forces at work in this barony was the redevelopment of the Silver Mines by New English entrepreneurs, utilizing a highly skilled imported workforce. This workforce suffered substantial attrition in the 1641 rising/rebellion, highlighting the insecurities and uncertainties that underlaid the shifting property pattern.

Ormond Butler and allied expansion had been significant in Ikerrin and the size of Ballinakill bawn and castle points to the new forces at work here also. The crown, in the person of Strafford, surveyed this area for plantation purposes in the late 1630s, following the successful colonial incursions further north in the land of the Ely O'Carrolls, traditional overlords of the O'Meaghers in Ikerrin. The great O'Meagher stronghold was centred on Clonakenny (Bourney), where John held a compact individually owned estate of c.3,500 statute acres. Other powerful O'Meagher bastions survived in Killea, Corbally and Bawnmadrum (Bourney). Yet underneath the top layer revealed on the map, the leading head-tenants often bear Anglo-Norman names. Even in Killea – a classic case of fourteen O'Meaghers sharing in the ownership of the whole parish – the wealthiest family may have been the Bourkes of Killawardy. However, the reverse is true in the Old English-controlled lands in east Eliogarty, where the O'Meaghers were important hearth-tax payers. Witness also the strength of the O'Heyden family in Moyne (benefiting from rich episcopal relations), while likewise, the O'Fogartys had built up an extensive patrimony at Inch. The northern half of Middlethird, although clearly dominated by Old English properties, has also an extremely strong Gaelic stratum, including another important ecclesiastical family, the Kearneys. The Kearneys not only survive as landowners but are even more conspicuous as head-tenants and middlemen. The Carrans of Mobarnan were another major family here, while the two other successful families, the Sheas and the Neales, had long adapted themselves to the rhythms and necessities of a feudal order.

Kilnamanagh and Kilnelongurty also reveal the dynamic forces at work – particularly along the southern and eastern boundaries, which had been strongly colonized by the Normans in the early medieval period, partially lost in the Gaelic revival, and which again were coming under pressure from both the adjacent Old English and incoming New English entrepreneurs. In 1640, 11.6 per cent of these lands had been recently purchased. Amongst the O'Dwyers, the two leading families are clearly those of Philip at Dundrum (Ballintemple) and Anthony at Clonyharp (Clogher), who both occupy large single property units as demesne lands and who, like all major Gaelic chiefs, are still receiving substantial surpluses in the form of chief rents from the other O'Dwyer properties in the hills. In these latter areas, the most traditional co-ownership patterns in all of Tipperary are apparent. The scale of mortgaging in the barony – 19.3 per cent of all lands – also points to the dominance of traditional Irish practices in the exchange of properties. The core of this zone, therefore, represents one of the most integrated and most vibrant Gaelic territories to survive in mid-seventeenth-century Tipperary.

The barony of Owney and Arra reveals somewhat similar patterns and trends. However, proximity to Limerick city, the strategic importance of the Shannon waterways, the commercial importance of its woodlands and the absence of the Ormond tenurial shield may have all combined to make for an earlier infiltration by some New English elements. There is a noticeable expansion of commercial interests in the O'Brien territory of Duharra, particularly on the lowland edges, which is clearly aimed at the Hogan and lesser O'Brien freeholders. In the uplands, however, and along the Shannon-side core of their territory, the dominant O'Brien clan at Ballina and Castletown is very active in purchasing the lands of lesser O'Brien and other freeholders in the region. In the Ryan territories of Owney, landowning patterns are much more stable, with major Ryan strongholds at Tullagh and Cragg.

Finally, in the far north of the county, Lower Ormond barony, which was to undergo the greatest transformations after the Cromwellian settlement, reveals by far the most stable landownership pattern of all the Gaelic areas in 1640. Here, almost 90 per cent of all land transactions involved the transfer of ancestral lands to kinsmen. These figures, however, obscure the longer term processes of land acquisition by both the Kennedys and the great brehon family of the McEgans mainly through amassing Church lands at Lorrha and elsewhere. It also obscures the earlier reassertion of Butler power through both strategic acquisitions (the earl and countess of Ormond held 10 per cent of the barony in 1640) and the placement of allies such as the Graces (5.3 per cent), Cantwells (2.8 per cent) and lesser Butler families (5.3 per cent). Their often elaborate mansions contrasted with the older tower-houses of the Kennedys at Lackeen, Ballyhagh, Ballyfinboy, Carrigeen and Castletown. The Kennedys – in varying ownership permutations – controlled 41 per cent of the barony. The ecclesiastical family of the Hogans, with an old core at Ardcrony, had proved themselves equally versatile in the acquisition of Church lands, owning 10.2 per cent of the barony. The McEgans controlled a very respectable 11.2 per cent of the barony and in these changing times their legal astuteness saw them shift towards individual ownership of properties. One of their leading members – Constance McEgan of Killnalahagh – controlled an admittedly fragmented property of over 3,600 statute acres, while John at Cloghuston and Cormuck at Ballyknavine each owned c.900 statute acres. Yet the old hearthland of the family – Ballymacegan – was still shared amongst the leading members.[14]

Such then were the complex property structures of Co. Tipperary in 1640. It exhibited an extraordinary mosaic of arrangements; for the most part, it still demonstrated many elements associated with the parcellated sovereignty of the feudal order, as well as strongly residual Gaelic features. None the less, the palatinate lordship of the earl of Ormond and the lesser lordships within particular territories had seen a growing centralization of power at a series of levels. New English intrusions were also becoming more characteristic and were particularly prominent at the critical leaseholding level. However, the new order of things signalled the growing significance of merchant families in acquiring lands. These were represented throughout all the county but were particularly conspicuous in Iffa and Offa and Middlethird, the most urbanized regions. Slieveardagh emerges as the most stable property zone.

These ownership details are essential to the understanding of the settlement structure of the county. But property maps do not reveal the conditions of life for the majority of the population. Neither do they reveal that after the Ryans, Burkes, Butlers, Hogans, O'Dwyers and Kennedys, families bearing such names as Walsh/Brenagh, Donoghoe, Kelly, Connors and Murphy are more conspicuous in the hearth-money records than all of the other landowning families. There were many human geographies in mid-seventeenth-century Tipperary.

We must now turn to the occupation of the land and its settlement arrangements to catch a glimpse of the total population and to ascertain the extent to which these property structures shaped where and how the people lived.

Settlement and Work Patterns

The Civil Survey enumerates more than 1,760 land denominations for Co. Tipperary in 1654. The settlement 'denominations/townlands' enumerated for 1659–60 and 1666–7 drop to around 1,200 and 1,270 respectively. These figures are instructive. First, a distinction must be drawn between these settled units of landholding and those unsettled or unpopulated 'townlands or denominations' that were worked from a distance for tillage or for grazing purposes, as an 'outfarm' or as part of a larger 'open-field' system of territorial organization.

The barony of Owney and Arra appears to have the largest proportion of land units (50 per cent) permanently unpopulated. The Civil Survey indicates the utilization of the poorer upland units in this barony by owners/landholders living in adjacent or more lowland settlements; in contrast, the more densely settled baronies of Clanwilliam and Slieveardagh reveal the least discrepancies, with settled denominations comprising respectively 84 per cent and 92 per cent of the total number of denominations enumerated in 1654. The baronies of Upper Ormond (72 per cent), Lower Ormond (77 per cent) and Kilnamanagh (75 per cent) occupy a transitional position reflecting the availability of extensively used upland, woodland and bogland zones.

For Iffa and Offa (69 per cent), Middlethird (67 per cent) and Ikerrin (66 per cent), the proportion of townlands settled or unsettled may indicate a more complex array of factors. In the densely settled and thoroughly colonized barony of Middlethird, it is likely that these proportions highlight the integration of often relatively small land units – sometimes comprising single large fields – within a more large scale 'manorial' system of land management and land-use and this is also a factor in the long-settled normanized zones of Iffa and Offa, Eliogarty and Ikerrin.

A second lesson emerging from these figures is the recognition that Co. Tipperary had for many centuries been a well-settled land, characterized in the mid-seventeenth century by at least 1,200 clearly defined settlement communities. Nothing reveals this better than the preliminary parochial descriptions in the Civil Survey, which concentrate on the delimitation of the boundaries of the parishes. The range of landscape elements – highways, lanes, butts, marks, bushes, crops, firm banks, dry or wet ditches, quickset hedges – described by the old inhabitants, has passed down to us the intimate topographies of each parochial unit.

The combined evidence of the Civil Survey, 1660 poll-tax and the hearth-money records also reveals certain anomalies. The hearth-money records appear to be the most reliable and comprehensive in relation to the specific distribution of settled denominations, but here again one must scrutinize the evidence very carefully. For example, the hearth-money records return a relatively large household population (25 hearths – an estimated total population of c.140) for Ardfinnan – a not unexpected figure in the light of this ecclesiastical settlement's lengthy history and varied functions. In this instance, however, the Civil Survey provides more detailed evidence of the actual distribution of settlement in this unit, demonstrating that three or four of Ardfinnan's subdenominations were also settled. In short, the gradation of settlement in Ardfinnan (as in other units such as manorial Derrygrath), while still emphasizing the primary pivotal role of the ecclesiastical or manorial centre, is a more muted one than suggested in the hearth-tax returns. Problems may also arise that work in the opposite direction, as at Pallis and Graigue in Dorrha or at St Johnstown and Milltown/Cooleagh, where joint-settlement agglomerations may have been obscured by separate population returns. Similarly, problems arise where there is a convergence of a number of townlands on parish centres, such as at Ardcrony, Knigh and Borris(okane). Other evidence might suggest a concentration of settlement around these townland foci, whereas there is no suggestion of larger agglomerations forthcoming from the population figures, which are returned separately for each townland. The main burden of the evidence, therefore, falls on the hearth-money records and to a lesser extent on the 1660 poll-tax returns, both of which provide a less than crude picture of settlement distribution (see Fig. 9.4).

Additional inferences – especially in relation to the actual layout of settlements – can also be made from a perusal of the composite Down Survey/Ordnance Survey maps.[15] One obvious inference is that so much of the seventeenth-century settlement evidence is now totally enveloped by landlords' demesnes. Everywhere in Tipperary – and nowhere more emphatically than in Lower Ormond – the picture is blurred by the extensive embellished landscapes, whose creation often meant the clearing away of the older medieval settlement accretions and their replacement by the new geometric landscapes of the late seventeenth century and, particularly, the eighteenth century. These maps, therefore, reveal the striking juxtaposition of old evolved and newly planned settlements over much of Co. Tipperary, mirroring in the landscape the deep divisions of the post-Cromwellian society.

In 1667 such changes were only in their infancy. Then 36 per cent of all settled denominations (henceforth called townlands) were returned as containing 5 or fewer households, 30 per cent are returned as containing 6–9 households, and 34 per cent with 10 or more households. Townlands with the smallest number of hearths, that is, 5 or under, were disproportionately represented in the baronies of Upper Ormond (47.8 per cent) and Owney and Arra (45.2 per cent), with the barony of Middlethird (29.3 per cent) representing the other end of the spectrum. Intra-barony variation was even greater. The hilly, more wooded, and more pastoral country of the Knockmealdowns and the Galtees, the Glen of Aherlow, the predominantly Gaelic areas of Clanwilliam, the hills of Kilnamanagh, Owney and Arra and much of Upper Ormond formed one continuous line of smaller settlements along the western half of Tipperary. The eastern half of the county was much more varied. Slieveardagh was generally a zone of larger settlement units but sharp local variations existed, as, for example, between Kilvemnon and the neighbouring parishes of Lismalin, Cloneen and Modeshill. One can identify

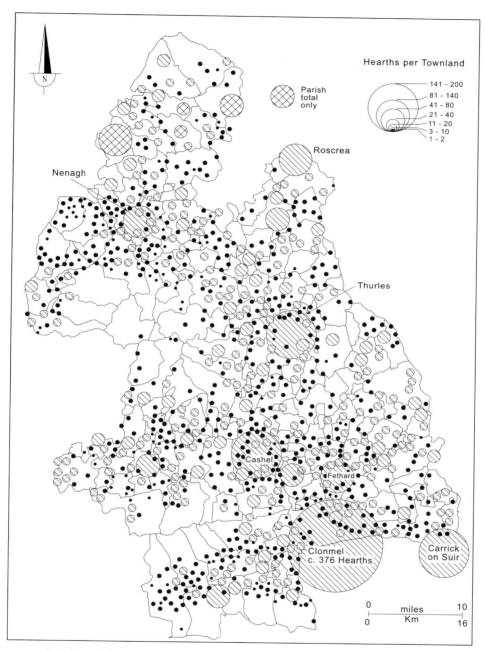

9.4   Population distribution and settlement hierarchies in Co. Tipperary, 1665–7

a second zone of a relatively high proportion of smaller settlement entities stretching from the transformed parish of Kiltinan in the south, through Peppardstown,
Graystown and Killenaule and linking up with the grazing/bogland parishes
along the eastern flanks of Eliogarty and Ikerrin (Templemore and Killavinoge

excluded). This belt reaches across Barnane to Toomevara/Aghnameadle. Lower Ormond reveals a highly uneven pattern reflecting its transitional character. With the exception of the parishes of western Clanwilliam and Slieveardagh, it is the highly commercialized/mixed-farming/Old English/private property zone of the Suir valley and its tributaries that reveals the largest settlement units and reaffirms that relatively sharp frontier with the eastern borderlands of the Kilnamanagh hills. This zone extends northwards through Holycross, Thurles, Inch, Drom and Templemore and reaches, via Borrisoleigh and Latteragh, into the rich lowlands of Upper Ormond, which, despite the resurgence of the Gaelic lordship, is likely to have retained a far more durable Anglo-Norman landscape impact.

That quite a number of such smaller townland communities lived in more compact/clustered settlements is strongly supported from a wide range of sources. The Down Survey maps for Slieveardagh clearly show that overlooking the Lingaun river in the parish of Newtownlennon, the three townlands of Clash-nasmutt (5 hearths in 1667), Attyjames (6 hearths) and Curraheen (9 hearths) were each characterized by a clustered settlement pattern. Similarly, further north at Currasilla (8 – Grangemockler), Rathbeg (12 – Fennor) and Grange (10 – Kilcooly), agglomerated settlement patterns are evident. Further north in Lower Ormond, the townland of Kilconyhinemore (5 – Ballingarry) is also characterized as a cluster of 4 (stone?) houses. Smaller settlement units also sometimes involved parish centres as at Ballinure (6) and Magorban (8), which are again shown on the Down Survey maps as small nucleations. 'Castle clusters' are shown for Ballykirine (6 – Croaghane), Noan (11 – Graystown) and Killusty (11 – Kiltinan).[16]

In the description of the parish of Clonoulty, there is a reference to a boundary 'mearing with the cabbins of Cleynaboule'.[17] There are also a number of references, such as the description of the small castle-centred Butler holding of Castlecoyne (9 – Mortlestown), which notes that 'upon the said lands stands the castle and some enclosures about the *Village* of Castlecoyne aforesaid beset with quicksets. . . . The said *lands* are at present waste without any improvement' (my emphasis).[18] This points more strongly to a nucleated rather than a scattered settlement pattern. Likewise, in Tullaghmelan parish 'the lands of each village [is] divided in parcels amongst the rest of the lands of said villages'.[19] While again recognizing the variety of uses of the term 'village' – and quite clearly this term is often used in the Civil Survey simply to mean townland unit – there is much circumstantial evidence to suggest in these specific cases that the jurors are making a distinction between the *lands* of specified denominations and the actual settlements ('townes'/'villages') that acted as focal points and gave their names to land denominations as well.

The above evidence, therefore, suggests a variety of agglomerated settlement forms from widely different environments located in seven of the nine baronies within the county. Even in Owney and Arra, where dispersal was the norm, infrequent descriptions in the Civil Survey highlight a greater concentration of settlement distributions within townland units characterized by co-ownership and joint management of undivided arable lands.[20] Some of the smallest agglomerations may therefore have comprised such kin clusters; some, as in Castlecoyne,

Ballykirine and Ballinree, involved the settlement arrangements associated with the management of a single townland by a resident farmer-owner and his part-ners/labourers; others involved, as at Curraheen, head-tenants, like Comerford with his two hearths, managing a townland in similar fashion; the majority, however, were probably associated with partnership farmers of 'husbandmen' status, working lands mainly for subsistence purposes.

Dispersed farm settlement was generally associated with the more substantial thatched and stone houses than with 'cabbins'. There is clear evidence in the hearth-money records for the existence of only a single farmhouse in quite a number of townlands and particularly those townlands in the grazier/sheep-farming parishes. There were many independent farm units in the lower Suir valley, as in Killaloan, Kilgrant, Mortlestown and Kilsheelan, also in Donaghmore, Kiltegan, St John Baptists Grange, Moratownkirke and parts of St Johnstown and Rathcool parishes in Middlethird, in the parish of Corroge in Clanwilliam, Templeree in Ikerrin, Aghnameadle in Upper Ormond and in a wide variety of examples from Owney and Arra.

The notion of the dispersal of populations and settlements, however, needs also to be examined at other levels. It is striking how close the association is between the fragmentation of ownership patterns and the scattering of population at the townland level, whatever the form of settlement within such townlands. The greater the fragmentation of ownership, the greater the scattering of population: that seems to be the general rule. For example, this was the situation for the nine O'Dwyer co-owners in the parish of Kilpatrick or other O'Dwyers at Toem and Donohill or the Ryans of Templebeg and Doon. Indeed, it should be emphasized that of the 1,300 or so landowners in Co. Tipperary in 1654, well over 60 per cent were concentrated in the four most Irish baronies of Upper and Lower Ormond, Kilnamanagh and Owney and Arra. In the last barony alone, there were over 250 such landowners. Such a splintered, flexible ownership pattern (as compared with, say, forty landowners in Slieveardagh) made for a wide dispersal of settlement over a large number of clearly distinguished townland units, unlike the rather different processes at work on large, consolidated, privately owned units (that is, estates), which acted both to reduce the number of separate settle-ment units and concentrate a much greater variety of resources, both human and material, at specific centres of control. Consequently, one rarely finds either such a scattering or such a number of settlement units in the parishes of southeast Tipper-ary – the upland parish of Whitechurch, the dairying parish of Templetenny and the bigger farms of the lower Suir excepted. Likewise, no such scattering of settle-ment occurs in the stable settlement hierarchies of Slieveardagh, while in castle-studded Middlethird only the strongest areas of Gaelic survival – as in the parish of Magorban – and the big sheep farms elsewhere break the pattern of a clear hierarchy of settlement concentrations. The variegated nature of Clanwilliam is highlighted by the discontinuous distribution of scattered or weakly hierarchi-cal settlement structures, as in the Ryan-dominated parish of Cordangan and in the woodland/upland parishes of the Glen of Aherlow, as opposed to the nucle-ated structures of the richest parishes in the barony.

Similarly, it is important to note the parallel dispersal of institutional foci (for example, church, castle, mill) in the most Irish areas. Again and again, as in the parishes of Lorrha, Borrisokane. Terryglass, Loughkeen, Kilbarron, Cloghprior, Kilmore, Ballymackey, Youghalarra, Burgess, Inchyofogarty and Moyaliff, and wherever the pastoral hill communities are found, there is a constant dialectic between the declining or stable parish centre and other centres or control exercised by landowners and millers. For example, Lorrha has still retained its old and now dilapidated monastic centre, but equally important in the mid-seventeenth century is the Butler fulcrum at Ballyquirk, the legal focal point at Ballymacegan, one of the Kennedy strongholds at Lackeen, and the lakeside strongholds of Portland and Annagh, then under Cromwellian control. Kilmore also has a lively series of settlement foci, which includes not only the parish centre but other castle and/or church centres, as at Ballycahill and Erenagh, the Silver Mines, leading Kennedy and O'Brien landlord foci at Dunalley and Tullaghedy respectively, and even the focal point of Dolla parish, which was actually located within the parish boundary at Kilboy. Whatever the settlement arrangement within such townlands, the striking feature – as compared with southeast Tipperary – is the dispersal of centres with diverse origins and functions between a large number of townlands.

Nucleated settlements can be confirmed far more confidently as the population size of townlands increase above the 10-hearth threshold to cluster around 14–20 enumerated households (see Fig. 9.4 p. 325). The Down Survey evidence for Slieveardagh – admittedly for one of the most stable landowning and least disturbed baronies – illustrates a strong pattern of settlement nucleation as at Killenaule (14), Fennor (14), Graystown (26), Clonamicklon (27), Mellison (15), Garrangibbon (14), Killaghy (21), Modeshill (24), Buolick (38), Kilcooly (38), Pointstown (14), Farrenrory (19), Croaghane (18), Coolquill (18), Rossnaharly (14), Lismalin (55) and Castlejohn (21). The surveyors are obviously rendering these large nucleated settlements in a symbolic way – generally showing five to six houses circled around the major nuclei of castle and/or church. At 'Kilcooly Towne', and to a lesser extent at Viscount Ikerrin's head settlement at Lismalin, a more regular 'street' pattern is suggested – not unexpectedly, given that these two settlements were the largest nucleations in the whole barony. Outside of Slieveardagh, other surveyors were less interested in providing any details regarding settlement arrangements. Nevertheless, it is significant to see the manorial parish centre of Moycarkey (20) in the adjacent barony of Eliogarty shown clearly as a major nucleation. Elsewhere, and almost in grudging fashion, the Down Survey confirms the nucleated status of both the towns of Thurles and Nenagh and the old parochial centres at Cloghprior, Ballynaclogh, Modreeny, Castletown-arra, Bonocum, Terryglass and Dromineer. It also confirms a nucleation of a street-like fashion at Kennedy's 'Lackeene Towne' in Lorrha and less emphatically at O'Meara's of Lissinskey (Ballymackey).[21]

The Civil Survey too eventually yields a few of its secrets as to the specific arrangement of settlements at this level in the population hierarchy. The description of the parish centre of 'Kilshane Towne' (22 hearths in 1667, including a forge) points to a small nucleation: 'the said glebeland is situated near to the village of

Kilshane upon the road from Kilshane to Tipperary. . . . The said glebeland had upon it two gardens, one thatcht house and a few cabins.'[22] In the parish of Holy-cross, there is a clear reference (supported indirectly by the limited Down Survey evidence) to the 'street-of Rathkienane (23)' with its castle and church.[23] Likewise, in the parish of Inchyofogarty there is a reference to the 'Streets of Upp Dovea (22) in this parish'; there is no clear evidence of a nucleus or focal point to this Upper Dovea settlement.[24] The Civil Survey may also provide a significant pointer to one aspect of the internal morphology of some castle settlements, with references like 'a quickset hedge that leads from the greene at Clonyharp (27)'.[25] There is also a reference to the 'greene' of the castle-cum-parish centre at Moyneard (9) and the 'greene of Ardfinnan', with 'its castle and the walls of a castle, ye walls of a stone house, and a bawn and a mill-greist and some cabbins and a weir on the river Shewir'.[26] Indeed, over 80 per cent of all the castle entries in the Civil Survey refer in similar fashion to their associated houses and cabins; but the specific spatial arrangement of these houses needs to be confirmed from other sources.

Supporting evidence is also available from other documentary sources, in folk tradition and increasingly from aerial photographic work. For example, the settlement arrangements associated with the much-battered old burgage town of Ardmayle (39) are put in doubt by the large number of subdenominations associated with this manorial parish centre; a contemporary description of reprisals in this area in 1641, however, points to a still surviving nucleated settlement, since a Captain Paisley (with some of his troops), 'marching to Armaile killed there, seven or eight poor men and women whom he found standing abroad in the streets near their doors inoffensively'.[27] In the parish of Templenoe and Donegore, the old placename of Grenane is returned with 15 hearths in 1667. Today, this area is characterized by a highly embellished landscape where a later landlord had obviously pushed out the old road network to expand his demesne. John O'Donovan's OS letters, however, note that a subdenomination 'called Cloghavadeen is said to have been a little village and the name is retained in that of a field in the townland of Grenane, near the site of the old castle'.[28] Finally, it is probable that the villages of the parish centres of Tullamain (19) and Boytonrath (21) and likewise those of Barretstown (15) and Ballyduagh (19) – all revealed as former nucleated settlements from aerial photographic evidence[29] – were deserted after, rather than before, the transformations of the mid-seventeenth century.[30]

The forces making for nucleation at this level (around 14–20 hearths) are therefore becoming clearer in the light of this evidence. The two most critical elements making for nucleated settlements were the presence of a landowner with his tower-house/castle (or less often, a substantial stone house) and a parish centre with its church, graveyard and glebeland. Where the landlord's control and that of the parish centre were combined (and indeed when augmented further by milling and other functions), the forces for settlement concentration were very great indeed. Under one-third of all settlements with 10 or more hearths, where a clear nucleus/or nuclei can be established (an estimated 280 sites), exhibited such an arrangement; a further 15 per cent indicated the autonomous nucleating power of either the parish centre or other ecclesiastical foundations. Equally striking, however, is the fact that almost one-half of these settlements pivoted around the autonomous centralizing power of the landowner, his castle/tower-house, reinforced in some instances by a mill or mills. The remainder of the nucleated settlements owed their existence to milling, bridging, marketing, mining, or other such single functions.

The evidence adduced here indicates that the power of the later medieval tower-house/castle as an autonomous force for concentrating settlement at specific nodes may require a closer examination. It is likely that such 'castle-villages' housed a much more stratified population, and, in particular, a more significant artisan component, than the clustered settlements described above. The late sixteenth-century Elizabethan fiants indicate that Castlegrace, Newcastle and Knocklofty included not only yeomen farmers, husbandmen and labourers but also horsemen, houndsmen, clerks, carpenters, butchers, tailors, weavers, harpers, blacksmiths, and in some cases – as at Newcastle and Knocklofty – even goldsmiths.[31] While there is no available evidence that would allow us to evaluate the range of artisan occupations represented in the other settlements at this level, the hearth-money records may provide a substitute measure for their relative distribution.

The returns on forges (that is, extra fireplaces taxed) does appear somewhat uneven. For example, only 4 forges are returned for the whole barony of Kilnamanagh (and a forge is not returned for Clonoulty, though there is evidence of one existing in this townland in 1641). There are strong suggestions, however, that enumerated forges often do provide another index of nucleation. Forges were scattered throughout the countryside or located in clustered settlements with smaller populations, as at Clashnasmutt near Slievenamon, yet 86 per cent of all forges enumerated in 1667 are associated with townlands characterized by 10 or more hearths and, indeed, 60 per cent are associated with townlands with 25 or more hearths. The forge and the smith may therefore often provide a clue as to the whereabouts of other artisans.

As one moves up the population hierarchy, the presence of ovens (and bakehouses) is also more conspicuous, reflecting a greater proportion of labourers and other agriculturally non-productive sectors dependent on the purchase of bread in the nearby village. Another more unusual index of possible village status is the far greater proportion of women householders who are returned in the hearth-money records for specific settlements. They likely survived by carrying out a range of service functions, including the age-old one of the huckster/small-town trader, in such settlements.

The intimate relationship between landlord patronage and settlement size reflected the accumulation of rent surpluses at the centre of such estates, and the need for professional and military support in the management of large property units. It also indicates the greater need for a wider range of services and, in the turbulent decades of the late sixteenth and mid-seventeenth centuries, the desire for greater protection and security on the part of the weaker segments of the population. Kenneth Nicholls's suggestions as to temporary agglomerations around strongholds in these turbulent times is relevant here, although it may be more useful to see this period as one characterized by 'refugees' fleeing the open countryside and settling, as their equivalents did in later famine times, on the edges of existing settlements.[32]

Even allowing for the religious and settlement schizophrenia that was to emerge in Ireland following on from the Reformation,[33] the Catholic parish centre, with its glebeland and graveyard and its often dilapidated church, did not yield immediately to the new forces swirling about it. Historically, parish centres were powerful settlement foci and community anchors. Indeed, long after their demise as active parish centres for the great majority of the population, these places were to retain (and many *still* retain) their most powerful centralizing function as burial places and the centrepieces, therefore, of the most elaborate ritual in the Irish countryside – the funeral. In the mid-seventeenth century, therefore, the parish centre could still sustain, if more weakly, both separate organizational structures and some centralizing influences. When combined with the more dominant secular functions of the major estate centre and still powerful landowning patrons, the parish centres were likely to be quite substantial settlements.

An examination of 'parish and village' geographies in Tipperary in the mid-seventeenth century suggests that a total of 93 (55 per cent) of the parish centres were still powerful nucleating forces; in 77 cases (45 per cent) they were no longer the dominant element. In two-thirds of the former parishes, the townland bearing the parish name still returned an above average (that is, 10 hearths or more) population. In assessing their autonomous role *vis-à-vis* the castles/tower-houses, it would appear that while about one-third of the parish centres were weak nucleating forces, quite a significant minority (around 45 in number) provided the *raison d'être* for nucleation in settlements with an average household population of around 14.[34]

The status of such parish centres is further enhanced when combined with the legally defined manors with their additional court and administrative functions, or in what may be termed 'manorial-style' villages. Excluding the manorial parish centres that are clearly of urban status, the average size of the remainder of the manorial-type village centres was around 20 hearths or a total population of around 110. It is also relevant to note that 40 per cent of all the forges enumerated are concentrated among the manorial-type villages. At this level, one is also more likely to find additional functions, such as those ancillary to milling, and furthermore, an increase in the proportion of resident women householders.[35]

Figure 9.5 examines the distribution of parishes whose centres were either more important than or equally as important as other townlands in such parishes. What is striking about this distribution is the recurring polarities between better and poorer land, and more particularly, between tillage and pastoral land. With some notable exceptions, it is instructive to note how the higher valued grain-producing mixed-farming, single property zones extending from the lower Suir to the core parishes of lowland Upper Ormond sustained a much more vigorous parish life and associated parish centres. Equally striking is the relative weakness of the parish centres in the pastoral zones of the Glen of Aherlow, the uplands of Kilnamanagh, Upper Ormond and Owney and Arra (with the exception in the last case

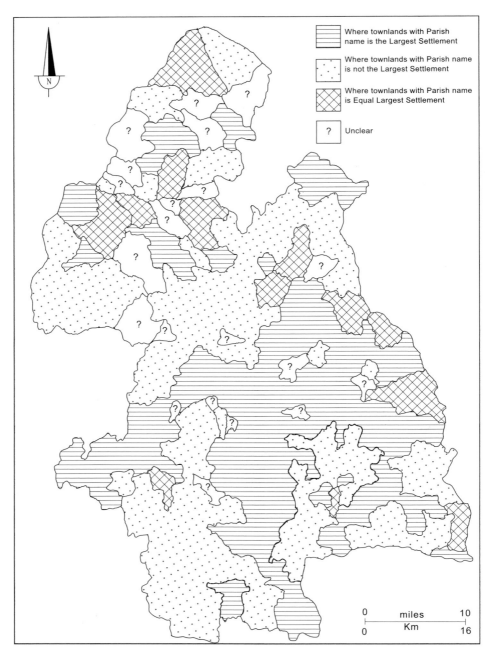

9.5   Distribution of the pattern of relationships between parish centres and settlement size, 1665–7

of the parishes of Castletown, Youghal and Burgess and the half parish of Kilmas-tulla). This belt of weakness also extends across to the eastern boundaries of Ikerrin and Eliogarty. The picture for Lower Ormond is less than clear. Overall, it is a curious mosaic, with the parish of Cloghprior, Uskane and Ballingarry most supportive of large parish centres. However, here again, as in the parishes of Borrisokane and Finnoe, the population returns may actually obscure the size of the parish foci. Most of the exceptions on the better lands of Iffa and Offa, as at Derrygrath and Ballybacon, point to the stronger nucleating power of local landed families like the Keatings of Nicholastown and the Butlers of Gormanstown. On the other hand, the weaknesses of parish centres along the borders of Iffa and Offa and Middlethird highlight the already 'lost centres' of the late medieval period at Donaghmore and elsewhere – that is, parishes that had not only suffered from absentee church administrators but also absentee landlords. The map also shows the transitional status of parishes that lie between the well-nourished manorial or manorial-style villages in the core areas and the essentially scattered settlement structure of the more pastoral regions.

The independent nucleating role of the tower-house is particularly obvious at the middle level of this rural settlement hierarchy, more powerful than that of the church centres *per se* but obviously somewhat weaker than the manorial or manorial-style parish centre. The average size of this castle-village (exclusive, that is, of around 50 castle foci with less than 10 hearths) is around 17 hearths or a total population of around 100.[36] This group of settlement units again accounts for 40 per cent of all the forge entries, but given their greater numbers, this leaves about two-thirds of these units with no evidence as to artisan composition. Again, while the evidence is rather incomplete, there are at least 25 parishes where other churches are associated with these non-parish-centred castle settlements. Quite clearly the two Hackett families of Kilballyherbery and Ballytarsney are benefi-ciaries/patrons of churches separate from that of the parish centre at Ballysheehan, as were the O'Meaghers at Clonakenny (Bourney), the O'Mearas at Lissinskey (Ballymackey), the Butlers at Ballycahill (Kilmore), the O'Dwyers at Rathkienane (Holycross), the O'Briens at Pallis (Youghalarra), the Fennells at Ballygriffin (Religmurry), the Crokes at Mellison (Buolick), the Everards at Kilnockane (Rathcool) and Rathmacarthy (Tullamain), the Brittons at Killusty (Kiltinan), the Tobins at Kilnagranagh (Cloneen), the Butlers at Ballynoran (Kilmurry) and the Kearneys at Ballyduagh (Railstown). It is likely that this list could be augmented and there is more than a hint that the greater scattering of churches is a feature of the more pastoral Irish regions.

While recognizing the twin pillars of settlement support that parish adminis-tration and landlord patronage provided, it is also noticeable how the balance seems to have swung in favour of the secular arm of the settlement – a not too surprising development, given the turbulence of post-Reformation Tipperary. Indeed this trend may have predated such changes. The Down Survey evidence for Slieveardagh, for example, seems to point to the greater attractive/protective force of the landlord's tower-house than that of the parish church *per se*. At Croaghane, it is clear that the focal point of the nucleation is around the castle, similarly at Graystown and Garrangibbon, and even more emphatically at Viscount Ikerrin's headquarters at Lismalin. At Buolick there is also a strong suggestion that the new (reconstituted?) settlement pivots more around the tower-house than the earlier parish church (of the formerly more extensive burgage town). Further north, the admittedly more fragmentary Down Survey evidence suggests a similar gravitation at Terryglass, Dromineer and Castletown-arra. The host of examples where the tower-house and its accretions dominate the parish, as in the uneven dialectic between Ballinakill and Rathnaveoge, Dundrum and Ballintemple, and Killaghy and Kilvemnon, suggests further movement down this road of secular/military dominance.

The opposite end of this sacred–secular dynamic also points to the strength of the relationship between landowner patronage and settlement size. It is seen in its most striking form where landowners are actively extending their proprietorial control, encompassing and enveloping adjacent parishes and, in the process, weakening the settlement hierarchy. Prendergast expansion from Newcastle into adjoining parishes seems to have weakened these settlement structures, as some, though by no means all, of such townlands are now managed from a distance. More particularly, the expansion of property zones in Middlethird by St John, Everard and some Fethard merchant families seem to have further weakened settlement structures and parish identities in what was, in any case, a weak zone of parochial management.

Ownership of extensive belts of land by absentee merchants from Clonmel, Waterford and Kilkenny generally resulted in a weaker settlement infrastructure. It is not surprising, therefore, to find that the parishes of Mullaghabby and Tullaghmelan are enumerated for the mid-seventeenth century as part of (Prendergast's) Newcastle parish and that there is much confusion about the size and status of a whole string of smaller parishes in the hinterlands of Cashel and Fethard. In all, it would appear that around 30 parishes had already lost a strong sense of identity by 1667.

One anchor of the nucleated settlement structure – that of the parish church – was under stress both before and, more particularly, after the Reformation but the extraordinary power of the twin pillars of castle and church – with the military arm becoming more and more important – still provided the main *raison d'être* of the settlement structure of the county even as late as 1667. The longer term consequences flowing from the Cromwellian settlement were finally to rupture that twin alliance with a ruthlessness and a thoroughness that now allows one to speak of the 'lost worlds' of seventeenth-century Tipperary.

Settlement Implications of Cromwellian Conquest

In 1640 the cultural geography of Tipperary was a highly varied one. The distribution of surnames (see Fig. 9.6) highlights the polarities between Irish and Anglo-Norman areas and the many intervening transitional zones. Analysis of first names further indicates that the tide of acculturation and assimilation was running in favour of the 'middle nation' or 'Old English' in this their final expansive phase before the traumas and dislocations of 1641–54.[37]

Unlike the earlier Norman conquest, the ruthless Cromwellian conquerors or their New English/Scottish predecessors proselytized every corner of the county and the island and as zealous revolutionaries, attempted to superimpose new

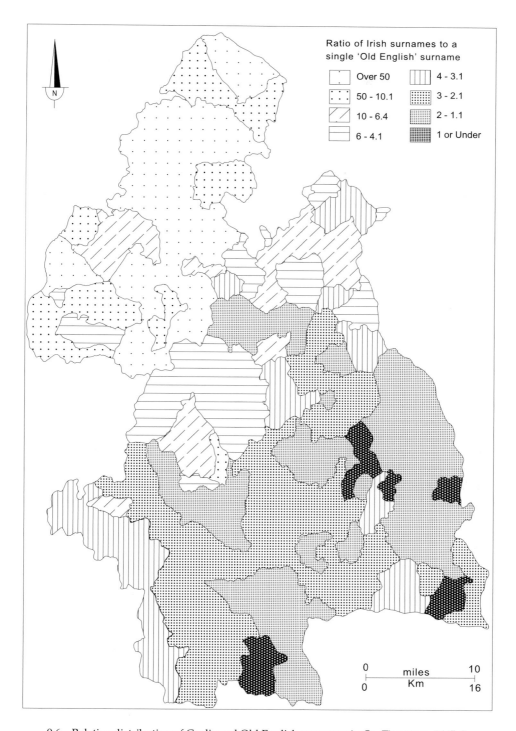

9.6   Relative distribution of Gaelic and Old English surnames in Co. Tipperary, 1665–7

models of religious, linguistic, legal and economic behaviour. What this chapter analyses are the hidden worlds of pre-Cromwellian Tipperary, using comprehensive source-materials that only a centralizing state – working with impressive bureaucratic efficiency in a new colonial setting – could have produced at this time in European history. These same documents, which help us to reveal the local diversities in the economy, in naming procedures and in settlement structures, must also be seen for what they were originally designed to achieve. The Civil Survey and Down Survey were in the first instance concerned with the identification and demarcation of existing property units before redesigning these chessboard pieces to pay off the soldiers and adventurers who had won the Cromwellian conquest. The first mark of conquest is generally boundary definition.

Conquest, therefore, not only involved a classification and appropriation of property units and their associated rent surpluses, it also meant a reclassification and renaming of places and peoples.[38] The lyrical quality of the parish topographies mainly derives from the many placenames embedded and perpetuated in these accounts. Yet here, as on the Down Survey maps, such placenames are rendered in standardizing English. The same process was at work on the family surnames as the newly centralizing state bureaucracy reshaped the worlds it encountered to better fit its image of what a 'proper' language, economy and society should sound, work and behave like.

The hearth-money records must therefore be seen for what they set out to achieve – a taxation system reaching into almost every home of Tipperary and extracting additional surpluses to support the superstructure of the state apparatus that now came to impinge so deeply on the county. Its instruments were the New English, acting out of self-interest, but also seeing themselves as representatives of the centralizing imperial state. They were profoundly imbued with notions of superiority, improvement and civility, a part of that wider movement of colonizing Europeans who were then plundering much of the world for its riches.

We need further research on the social backgrounds, motivations and general ethos of the varied groups and individuals that are collectively labelled Cromwellian. Suffice it to note here that they must have viewed the Tipperary landscapes afresh; they came with notions of exploitation and of gaining wealth; they belonged to a growing, expansive nation; and they were to leave a deep impression on the landscapes and societies into which they intruded.

The new political/legal order is nowhere better epitomized than in Clonmel, which now, more than ever, becomes the fulcrum of the imperial state's rule in Co. Tipperary. Not surprisingly, Clonmel had by 1667 the highest proportion of enumerated New English (49 per cent) of any Tipperary town and this figure had been significantly augmented since 1660, when W.P. Burke estimated the immigrant population at about one-fifth of the total.[39] The initial infiltration into the town was in the administrative, legal, military/political and ecclesiastical spheres, but by the 1660s it is the merchants who dominated – men like Richard Hamerton, Richard Moore and John Perry – the new leaders of the economic order whose mercantile wealth allowed them rapidly to acquire extensive estates in the

Clonmel region. Seventy-eight per cent of the wealthiest inhabitants of Clonmel in 1667 (that is, occupying two or more hearths) were of New English stock; they literally occupied the houses of the old merchant families but brought into these homes radically different assumptions and world views. They then attempted to remake Clonmel and its hinterland in their own image.

These forces of transformation were not all compressed into the Cromwellian period. The expansion of Old English power and influence under the express direction of the earl of Ormond over the previous century had paved the way for later intrustions. As the Civil Survey for Co. Tipperary highlights in its list of Protestant lands in 1640,[40] it is the post-Reformation takeover of the parochial glebelands that first introduced a wide scattering of new immigrants into the county. The strength of the Established Church in Lower Ormond and the adjacent parishes of Owney and Arra, Upper Ormond and Ikerrin pointed to a substantial infiltration over the first half of the seventeenth century of new settlers moving into this region, particularly along the edges of the planted baronies of Ballybritt and Clonlisk in the then Queen's County. Similarly, the 1641 Depositions indicate the deliberate introduction of New English tenants by both old and new landowners.[41] The modernizing families of the Everards in southwest Tipperary, the Ikerrin Butlers at Lismalin, as well as a number of New English – Fenton in Templetenny, Percival in Clonoulty, the earl of Cork in Arra, Warters in Cullen, Waller at Grenane, Esmond in Garrangibbon, St Leger at Cashel and Baker in Solloghodbeg – had all been responsible for introducing new tenants and initiating new settlements. The clearing of the woodlands and the importance of mining operations are especially noticeable in the Silver Mines and Owney and Arra, where there is also some leasing of farmland to New English tenants of 'husbandman' status. The establishment of state-sponsored garrisons at Cullen, Golden and Farneybridge also brought in new people, as did the rapid growth in urban functions in the frontier towns of Nenagh, Roscrea and Clogheen, with higher proportions of New English settlers than found at Fethard, Tipperary town and the old Butler towns of Carrick and Thurles.

Cashel's central position in the new episcopal order also provided a fulcrum for immigration into, and expansion out from, this old metropolitan axis – a process also reflected in new leasing patterns on episcopal lands at Emly and elsewhere. The power of the new colonial Church was exemplified in Clonmel, where Dean Hugh Gore and Pastor Hough occupied mansions with ten and eight hearths respectively.[42] Clonmel also contained the urban residences of leading landowner-developers such as Martin, Batty and Lawrence – emphasizing the central role that the instruments of the state in the county capital played in protecting the new landed order in the countryside. This feature is nowhere better highlighted than in the Civil Survey's description of the garrisons and castles rebuilt or repaired at the Commonwealth's charge,[43] as at Castlegrace, Ardfinnan, Castlejohn, Killaghy, Longfordpass, Curraguneen, Portland and Grenane – garrisons established to wipe out the remaining pockets of resistance that survived into the mid and late 1650s amongst the woodlands, boglands, and the hills.

By 1667 the triple alliance between the new military/political order, the landed/commercial system and the Established Church had stabilized and consolidated its geographical bases. Figure 9.7 reveals the distribution of the New English in 1667, highlighting, amongst other things, the central role of the towns, the fanning out of settlers along the major routeways and the still residual importance of the many garrison centres. The hearth-money records also reveal the new military/landed order in town and countryside, now dotted with majors, colonels and captains, as well as a host of traders and adventurers. By 1667 the new elites had been installed in well over a hundred of the key settlement units described above. For example, Major John Godfrey ruled at Knockgraffon and thus became the representative of the third military elite that came to dominate this ancient hearthland over the previous 1,500 years. On the same site had ruled both a Celtic and a Norman overlord. A similar pattern was repeating itself across the county and families with names like Hutchinson, Finch, Otway, Langley, Sheldon, Green, Prittie, Sadleir, Armstrong, Harrison, Parker, Minchin and Maude entered into the mainstream of the county's life and, in the process, occupied some of its oldest and most prestigious sites.

It was nevertheless an uneven pattern of settlement and the lines of future conflict and tension were already being laid down in 1667. A parish-by-parish analysis reveals the pre-eminence of the new landowning elites (with their kinsmen and women and sometimes newly introduced tenants) along a line from Roscrea, through Rathnaveoge through Barnane and Killoskehan and along the Suir to Cashel, fanning east and west to dominate much of Clanwilliam to the west, the Graystown/Peppardstown/Modeshill zone to the east, and reaching southwards through Kiltinan to dominate Clonmel, Ardfinnan and Clogheen. In northwest Tipperary earlier incursions had been augmented in both Lower Ormond and the Shannon-side segment of Owney and Arra. The new elites were also solidly established in the lowland core of Upper Ormond.

The old landowners were required to make themselves, their families and their retinue of stock known to the Revenue Commissioners at Limerick or Clonmel, before trekking to their new allocations in Connacht. In Co. Tipperary 221 former landowners complied with these instructions and supplied the commissioners with the relevant details.[44] Included in this group were Lord Dunboyne, Viscount Ikerrin, Baron Purcell of Loughmoe, Lady Mary Hamilton (Roscrea) and O'Meagher of Clonakenny – in short, the majority of the major landowners, with the exception of Ormond, his closest kinsmen and allies.

A striking feature of these Transplantion Certificates for Co. Tipperary is the large number of retainers (second only to Co. Kerry) who are named as travelling to Connacht with their banished landlords. The average number of retainers per transplanting landowner was 20.5 but Co. Tipperary returned 39.1 per landowner. For example, Corr of Tubberhany (Kilgrant) is recorded as being accompanied by 144 persons. While it is not certain how many of these actually travelled to and settled in Connacht, it is instructive to note that the old Corr stronghold is one of the least populated centres in the lower Suir valley in 1667. The 1664 Ormond list of dispossessed Co. Tipperary landowners identifies over 200 of the former elite families which were still hoping that, with the newly restored duke of Ormond's

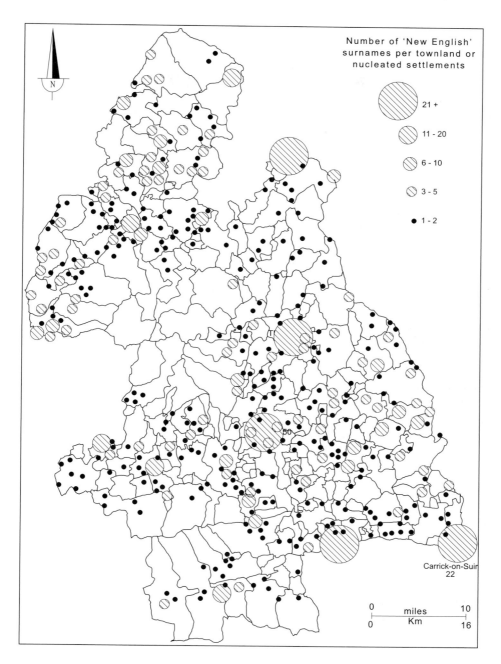

9.7 Distribution of New English immigrant population in Co. Tipperary in 1667

help, they would retrieve at least part of their old properties.[45] Some few families were to be restored to their land. With the others went much of the patronage, not only of the poets and the harpers, as the Gaelic literature attests to, but also of many of the older settlements and their populations. The Reformation weakened the old village geographies but it was the uprooting of the old landownership structure in conjunction with the new economic forces that finally shattered them.

Thomas W. Freeman has mapped the many demesnes of Co. Tipperary for 1841.[46] Future research will likely reveal that buried under those geometric landscapes are the remnants of the old settlement and social order. Practically every demesne in Lower Ormond was built on a former focal point and it is also clear that a similar pattern developed elsewhere. In place of village communities, neighbourhoods and kinship networks, parklands and high walls were built, enclosing forever the vanished worlds of the seventeenth century. The fate of tower-houses by 1654 is already indicative of future patterns of village/hamlet survival or desertion. The heavily planted baronies of the former Gaelic lords of Lower and Upper Ormond reveal that 93.6 per cent and 86.2 per cent respectively of their tower-houses are already in ruins. A middle bandolier of territory, running from Ikerrin, through Kilnamanagh and Clanwilliam shows a 50–70 per cent ruination of the tower-houses. In contrast, the southeastern core of Tipperary displays the lowest discontinuities in tower-house occupation. Middlethird and Slieveardagh baronies, in particular, reveal a remarkable stability, with only 13.3 per cent and 21.3 per cent of their respective tower-houses uninhabited. Thus, even within one county, levels of continuity and change in settlement and social geographies are quite varied and uneven (see Fig. 4.10, p. 164).

The reverberations of such change in patronage and economic structures were to echo into the nineteenth century. The centres of Kilsheelan, Kilfeakle and Ardmayle were already only pale shadows of their former greatness and in subsequent decades Castletown-arra, Buolick, Kilcooly, Knockgraffon, Ballyclerihan, Solloghodmore, Lattin, Derryluskan, Clonakenny and a host of smaller nuclei were also to shrink or disappear. The changing distribution of the county's population between 1650 and 1850 has been examined elsewhere, highlighting the depopulation of the lowlands and the massive expansion of settlement in the boglands/upland regions, but it is likely that the pattern was already an established one in the 1660s and 1670s.[47] This dispersal of the population was linked to the disappearance of the old landowning patrons – some of these old elites were already scattering across Europe and the New World, others to Connacht and others were deflected locally. The material basis for the old order had been appropriated and with it often went the associated settlement infrastructure.

But not everywhere. There were a number of areas where the Cromwellian impact was much weaker. In southeast Tipperary under the shadow of the Ormond Butlers of Carrick-on-Suir and the Butlers of Kilcash, a network of families, including quite a number of 'smaller' Butlers, Mandevilles, Neales and others, had survived. Similarly, in western Iffa and Offa, around Newcastle and the extensive Caher Butler estate, complex meshes of old kinship networks survived, involving mainly Old English families in the Newcastle area but incorporating a more hybrid group in the western half of the Caher estate. This resilient belt extended from the Glen of Aherlow across the southern and eastern parishes of Middlethird to include such fulcrums of the old order as Drangan and Magorban. Likewise, the whole eastern flank of Eliogarty, the adjacent Fennor parish and (for a while) Kilcooly parish were little disturbed by New English settlements. Practically all the core areas of Kilnamanagh had been stripped of their old elites but the hills remained free from the new overlords, as did equivalent areas in inland Owney and Arra and southern Upper Ormond. Butler land patronage also shows up in Lorrha, Dorrha and Aglish, which emerge as pockets of survival, as do the parishes of Dromineer, Knigh and Killodiernan in the heavily planted barony of Lower Ormond.

A comparison of the 1659 and 1667 patterns indicates than an uneasy equilibrium was gradually being forged. In quite a number of instances, the descendants of old families saw not a total displacement but rather a deflection away from the core centres of control. Time and time again, if one searches the hearth-money records, one finds representatives of the old landed families in adjacent townlands – the Tobins had lost out at Killaghy but the head of this family had returned from Connacht and established himself up the road at Clonagoose.[48] The Neales had finally yielded at Ballyneal but they survived in the immediate neighbourhood, as did the Ormond-patronized Walshes of Rathronan – similarly, the Stokes at Coolquill, the O'Dwyers of Kilnamanagh, the Burkes of Borrisoleigh, and further north, the O'Meaghers, the Ryans, the Stapletons and many others.[49] Co. Tipperary's mosaic of families and kinship networks was fragmented but not eradicated.

The Mandevilles and the O'Mearas of Lissinskey held on to their lands by various strategems. After the Restoration, the Morrises were to be reinstated at Latteragh, Knockagh and Castleiney, as were the Walshes of Carrigtoher and the Purcells at Loughmoe. The indirectly administered Butler control of Thurles also persisted. The Caher Butler estates and some other Butler lands survived and later on the Ikerrin Butlers were restored to some of their lands. However, the major beneficiary of the Restoration was the agile duke of Ormonde, who now increased his share of the real estate of Tipperary to a massive 130,000 acres, not only regaining most of his old lands but, as in the two Ormond baronies, acquiring the lands of some of his kinsmen and allies at Dromineer, Killownine and Ballingarry. He was also to ensure that his brother was restored at Kilcash, which, in turn, became the fulcrum of the Catholic Butler dynasty of Co. Tipperary. Such restorations also meant a shift in location for some of the new elites. Minchin moved from the old Morris stronghold at Knockagh to Ballinakill, taking his newly introduced tenants with him; John Shaw shifted from Lisronagh to Ballyneale. Colonel James Hutchinson moved from Youghalarra to open a new settler focus in Knockballymeagher, while Otway moved from another Morris stronghold at Latteragh to the new 'Castleotway' at Cloghonan, while a Captain John Pecke likewise yielded to Oliver Morris in Templeree/Castleiney.[50]

The 1659 Census shows the still surviving old gentry areas in southeast and southwest Iffa and Offa, in east Middlethird, over much of Eliogarty and Ikerrin and in pockets elsewhere.[51] But the most crucial continuities were beneath the elite layer. Here the evidence suggests that Co. Tipperary was, at best, only half-conquered. The hearth-money records point up the continuing strength of both the middle and lower levels of the old society and also pinpoint how sharp were the contrasting patterns of settlement in the late 1660s. The descendants of the old Irish represented around 70 per cent of the population and still retained 40 per cent of the more substantial two-hearth houses. The descendants of the Old English, comprising 25 per cent of population, actually commanded an impressive 48 per cent of the better houses. The New English, while only representing about 5 per cent of the population, had come to occupy 12 per cent of the total number of houses with more than one hearth, but 70 per cent of the houses with five or more hearths. The great phase of their rule was to last only 150 years; but within this period they were to direct the transformation of the landscapes and social structures of at least half the parishes in Co. Tipperary.[52]

However, both beneath and beside these transformed worlds went a host of survivals and forces that were eventually to coalesce and destroy this superstructure. Hidden outside the high walls of the geometric landscape was an evolving world of kinsmen, chapel communities and 'agrarian combinations'. And if one can regard the survival of the same placenames for townlands between 1650 and 1850 as an indirect measure of stability and resilience, one can identify a number of core areas where the older societies were to persist and to modernize more on their own terms. Such a zone was that of the richest of all Tipperary regions, which stretched south of Slievenamon between Carrick and Clonmel; another core area straddled the Suir valley from Inishlounaght to Caher; likewise, with some exceptions, the wealthiest areas of Clanwilliam. Middlethird, as always, was more of a mosaic – but old hearthland areas emerge in an axis extending southeast of Cashel to the edge of the Slieveardagh hills. Eliogarty was another core area of townland survivals, as was the rich lowlands of Ikerrin and Arra, while the new culture areas in the county were clearly being created in the Slieveardagh hills/Keeper Hill zone and, above all, in Lower Ormond. Yet even in this latter zone of greatest discontinuity, older social and landscape structures persisted on the outlying edges in the parishes of Modreeny and Cloghprior and in much of Ardcrony, Lorrha and Dromineer.

Property and patronage still remained critical; and the survival of the duke of Ormond lands and those of his closest allies provided some kind of shield, nowhere better epitomized than in the barony of Eliogarty and the town of Thurles. This Butler shield was to provide three Catholic archbishops of Cashel, who helped reshape the Catholic Church in this region from their cathedral town of Thurles. It was also the town of Thurles that provided the venue for the foundation of the Gaelic Athletic Association in the mid-1880s. With it came to power more than a century of Tipperary hurling teams. They belong to a different age but their names read off like lists from the hearth-money records of 1665–7.[53]

III

A World Turned Upside Down

10

Revolutionary Changes in the Territorial Organization of Irish Society, 1530–1750

Territoriality in humans is best understood as a spatial strategy to affect, influence or control resources and people, by controlling area; and, as a strategy, territoriality can be turned on and off.

Robert D. Sack[1]

After Columbus, the struggle by European powers to control the Atlantic and the New World brought Ireland's geopolitical location into sharp focus. After 1530, Ireland is progressively redefined as a crucial and strategic springboard for colonization and provisioning of migration to and trade with the New World.[2] The island also becomes one of the epic battlegrounds in the struggle between Reformation and Counter-Reformation Europe and, in the process, is transformed by England from a 'kingdom' to a fully-fledged colony. A social revolution also takes place in Ireland, which seeks to replace the variety of social, economic and political structures of late medieval sixteenth-century Ireland with a single territorial and social system modelled on early modern England.[3] Thus, Ireland, in the period 1530–1750, deepens its European engagement, becomes an integral part of the European-controlled Atlantic world, yet – uniquely amongst western European countries – becomes a colonized rather than a colonizing country.

From the beginning, it is important to emphasize that the English (and Scottish) colonial settlement in Ireland was structurally uneven and varied regionally in its impact.[4] The entire process involved a series of complex social and cultural changes at all levels, which are still only partly understood. For example, it is still not clear what interests in the local societies were best served by the new colonial order: how such external pressures were mediated in the localities, and what kinds of class changes resulted from the encounters. As ever, we need to be sensitive here to the law of unintended effects – and so keep a necessary distinction between the intent of certain strategies of colonization and the rather different effects of such strategies. Another major imponderable remains as to how Irish society and settlement would have evolved if a political and economic conquest had not taken place. How different would Ireland have been to what it eventually became under the new order of things?

In this chapter, the notion of 'settlement' is not confined to the structure and morphology of settlements *per se* but addresses the wider questions of the

345

remaking and settling of early modern Ireland and its regions from the mid-sixteenth century onwards. The main focus is on the radical changes in political, economic and social structures that followed from military conquest and how settlement transformations are woven into this complex story. The period is of enormous importance and is full of discontinuities, dislocations and traumata. Geographers have not as yet carried out sufficient research on a whole series of issues and, therefore, the picture remains very unclear.[5] The speed, scale and depth of a whole range of regional transformations makes it even more difficult to bring order to the story.

The strategy adopted here is to look at the critical parameters of territorial organization – the 'enclosures' for living at a variety of scales – and to seek to understand social and settlement changes within these territorial frames of reference and transformation.

Impact of the 'New State'

In an era of centralizing and absolutist state policy, Ireland's political status and its systems of territorial organization (by land and by sea) were radically reformed to serve new ends. Rolf Loeber has carefully documented the march of the English military and settlement frontier in sixteenth- and early seventeenth-century Ireland.[6] Figure 10.1, which summarizes these processes, pinpoints both the extension of the old Pale step by step westwards in the 1550s and 1560s and the parallel foundation of strategic military fortifications southwards along the River Barrow and northwards to front the still hidden world of Gaelic Ulster. The vulnerability of Dublin city is reduced by the consolidation of both the series of fortified settlements across north Wicklow and the Barrow and of a north–south shield against the resilient Gaelic hearthlands of Laois-Offaly to the west. Bridgeheads are built northwards as far as Newry, westwards as far as Athlone and southwards to Waterford city. As a result, areas of Irish resistance and of strong Irish septs are systematically isolated and cut off from one another: for example, the O'Tooles and O'Byrnes of Wicklow from the O'Connors and the O'Mores of the Midlands. This process of strategic fragmentation was to be further intensified in the conquest and subsequent plantation of Ulster.

A central feature of this early extension of the Pale was the utilization of the now dissolved monasteries as key strong points in the reconquest; also, the use made of their extensive Church lands to reward some of the Old English lords and, more particularly, the New English officials and soldiers who were pushed out to colonize the edges of this centralizing state's expanding world.[7] These early thrusts (1550–70) should not be underestimated in settlement terms, for these confiscated Church lands became the first anchors of New English settlement and colonization on the island. The 1570s and 1580s saw the completion of this strategic absorption of the former Church lands.

The crushing of the Desmond rising/rebellion opened up much of the lordships of south Munster to formal state plantation. For the first time, the Old English, even if 'degenerate', were themselves treated no differently than the

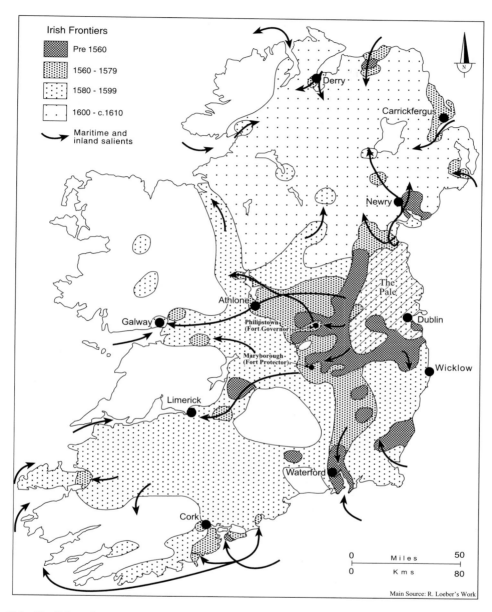

10.1   English settlement and frontier expansion in Ireland between c.1530 and c.1610 (adapted from the Rolf Loeber's maps of English settlement 1534–1609; see reference 6)

Gaelic Irish. Their estates too were now open to confiscation. The balance of power in the Dublin administration was likewise shifting, and as Nicholas Canny has noted, English colonial policy – for some time oscillating between strategies of assimilation and coercion – now hardened in favour of the latter approach.[8] MacCarthy-Morrogh has detailed the fretted, piecemeal character of the areas eventually planted in south Munster.[9] He has also shown that this important south Munster expansion of the gentry from the West Country and further afield in England was not perhaps such a radical change for these settlers as later planters were to experience elsewhere. Munster was already a deeply humanized world of towns, markets, road networks and castles. The immigrants here accelerated rather than initiated the processes of economic development, as well as new house-building and the ornamentation of the landscapes in this region.

Munster, at least at the elite level, was a bilingual world, although one suspects that the linguistic/cultural frontier was still a very important variable here in terms of the content and meaning of social interactions and transactions. The key differences between old and new landowners, however, were increasingly of a political and religious nature. In the new colonial and European order, religious affiliation was to be the essential ethnic marker, thus sharply distinguishing in Ireland the more privileged New English Protestant elites from their long- or not-so-long-established Catholic neighbours, whose powers were on the wane. These ethno-political and status distinctions were to explode at a whole series of social levels in 1641.

Elsewhere, English military expansion had extended salients of control to the west and north – westwards towards Galway city and northwards along the old normanized coastlands of east Ulster to reach Derry and further west along another old medieval corridor that ran from Roscommon into Sligo (see Fig. 10.1). The creation of the provincial presidencies of Munster and Connacht in the 1580s also represented a stepping stone on the way to full administrative integration of these regions into the wider state polity. In the process, key lordship families, such as the O'Briens of Thomond and the Clanricard Burkes of Galway, steered their respective regions away from the path of confrontation to one of strategic accommodation. In the long term, these decisions and the kinds of administration that followed from them were to help conserve much of the settlement structure and culture of both these regions.[10]

By the 1590s the platforms for the final assault by sea and by land on the last frontier of Gaelic Ireland – that of Ulster – had been put in place. Bartlett's maps and sketches help us to understand from an English point of view the literal opening up of the O'Neill countryside:[11] his eye and pen tracks outwards from the Pale through the Gap of the North to reveal the Blackwater river and Charlemont Fort; and the final penetration to the O'Neill capital at Dungannon is depicted, its old castle now capped by the flag of St George. Bartlett is not only recording the military victories and the march of the frontier, but is also very aware of the symbolic inversions as he sketches the deliberately broken inauguration stone of the O'Neills at Tullyhoge. The power and ritual of the last regional lordship had finally yielded to the hammer of the centralizing state.

Bartlett's maps also underwrite the procession of the governors, commanders, lesser officers and officials of the now coercive colonial power as it penetrates and dominates a world that had defeated the Normans. He notes the positions of the military forts at strategic points within the areas to be controlled. These garrisons were almost invariably to be key settlement foci in the future. Documented too are the evolving networks of roads linking these embryonic nuclei back through the Pale to Dublin and onwards to the core of metropolitan power at London. Hidden beneath the surface text of the map is the routine movement of personnel, goods, information and directives that moved up and down the newly constituted state network. By 1603, Ireland as a whole had been welded to the larger island to constitute a shaky, yet unified territorial system.

Crucially, this single geographical system involved a relatively new player, that of Scotland, which, through James I of England (James VI of Scotland), was now part of the Union and also part of this process of aggressive colonization. By 1606, James had come round to the view that the most effective and cheapest way to control Ireland, and in particular Ulster, was to plant it with loyal Protestant settlers and tenants who could act as a garrison in times of crisis.[12] Clearly, the Ulster plantation and the more informal processes of colonization and settlement, put in place both before and after the formal plantation, were to have momentous consequences for the settlement history of Ireland.

Informal Scottish settlements were on the increase from the mid-sixteenth century onwards. Much of this was concentrated in the expanding MacDonnell domain of 'the Route' (between Coleraine and Ballycastle), and the Glens of Antrim, where Highland and island soldiers eventually put down roots. Further south, Co. Down saw significant infiltration from the mid-century by Lowlands Scots. There were also a number of abortive attempts to formally plant these northeastern coastal peninsulas.[13] However, by 1603, the notion of a seemingly underpopulated land had caught the imagination of people in Scotland and England and Ulster became part of a wider Atlantic frontier that stretched from Newfoundland to Virginia and on to Bermuda and Guiana.[14] The propaganda in relation to the fruitfulness of Ulster land was complemented by the vacuum that followed the Nine Years War. All of Ireland had suffered under the Elizabethan–Irish wars, but Ulster suffered the most. The exact scale and extent of the depopulation in Ulster by 1607 is now impossible to measure – some estimates suggest that its population may have been halved in this devastating period.[15] And unlike Munster, Ulster was to be planted and settled in an era of rising tensions between the established Anglican Church, the embryonic Presbyterian Church and a Catholic Church in the process of reconstruction.

The earliest Scottish settlements were dictated by two main forces – geographical proximity and state strategy. Under the patronage of James I, Hugh Montgomery and James Hamilton became key figures in laying down the anchors for settlement in east Down, Phillips was important at Coleraine, and early infiltration also occurred around Derry.[16] These coastal areas nearest to Scotland were the earliest and most intensively settled. This was also crucial from a strategic point of view, for these early Scottish footholds acted as both a defence for the ever-expanding state world of the king and also as a series of funnelling points for later inland colonization. This came with the plantation proper of the six escheated counties, according as O'Neill, O'Donnell and others finally yielded to the incessant campaign of nibbling at, and quarrelling about, their local privileges and residual estates, a campaign which was carried on relentlessly by competent, acquisitive and aggressive incomers.

The centralizing metropolitan state now moved to formally and literally put in place a more carefully planned and mature plantation, which would see a full panoply of settlers – from lords to artisans – brought in to govern and build the towns, seigniories, bawns, mills and ironworks. Attempts at village concentration of farmers and artisans yielded to both existing territorial arrangements and a pastoral economy.[17] And so, the rural immigrant settlement pattern became embedded in ancient townlands. A very complicated amalgam of both old and new worlds was thus grafted on to one of the oldest corners of Europe.

New colonists moved in from both Scotland and England and, as Philip Robinson has noted, a significant sorting-out process ensued, which saw a consolidation of settlement in the coastal lands to the east and north and substantial and permanent penetration in along the richest river valleys nearest these key coastlands.[18] As R. J. Hunter points out, the residual Irish lands were strategically fragmented one by one and closely supervised by the servitor estates.[19] Segregation on planter estates intensified and, as Robinson has highlighted for Co. Tyrone, this process was legalized after 1628, with the Irish tenants confined to one-quarter of the area of such estates.[20] Such 'Irish' lands were almost invariably in the upland and poorest townlands. As early as 1660, levels of segregation, as measured by the number of rural townlands without any 'Irish', ranged between 5 and 10 per cent of all townlands in the Ulster borderlands to a peak of over 20 per cent in the core area of planter settlement in north Armagh, south Antrim and east Londonderry.

Perceval-Maxwell carefully summarizes the consequences of this pattern of settlement, displacement and subordination: 'Deprived of the land they loved and defended for so long, often uprooted from their homes and always under pressure to change their customs and way of life, the Irish deeply resented the intrusion of the newcomers.'[21] He also rightly notes that since the Ulster Irish had become a subject people between 1610 and 1641, 'their voice has almost entirely perished with the passage of time' and 'we are forced to use the barest scraps of evidence that have survived'.[22] Petty's barony maps of the late 1650s confirm the equally scrappy and fragmented character of the Irish estates and their associated settlements. (see Figs. 6.5a and 6.5b)

The 1641 rising/rebellion in Ulster was prompted by a range of issues, relating to lordly status, Church revenues, problems of landed indebtednesses, the battle between the king and parliament in England and the clearly uneven consequences of a rapid agrarian and market revolution.[23] But the scale and power of the immigrant thrusts into the region must have been a central factor in itself. It may well be that the levels of immigration in the 1630s were also rising above the already very high levels in the early years of plantation. The marginalization of both the Irish elites and the country people generally had probably reached a critical new threshold in the late 1630s. The dynamism of the settler frontier at this time is also suggested by immigrant expansion in the borders of Longford, north Sligo and Mayo, where two Scottish-born bishops were established in the 1630s.[24] Immigrant settlement in Ulster and its borderlands was also being consolidated at a time when religious conflict raged across Europe and when identities were being forged locally around either a Protestant colonial or a Counter-Reformation

Catholic Irish ethos. The bitterness of 1641 and its aftermath arose, in part at least, from these deep, structural tensions.

Yet the effective conquest of Ireland was a consequence rather than the achievement of the military and plantation processes *per se*. This conquest was also profoundly administrative, legal and economic in character and took root in the years between 1603 and 1641. Hans Pawlisch in his work on Sir John Davies has itemized the judge-made laws that transformed definitions of property and territory in Ireland: as he shrewdly notes, in previous centuries it was the old Irish population that was put outside the law; now it was Irish notions of territory and systems of property that were outlawed.[25] The extension of the English common law system of property rights turned land into a marketable commodity, with powerfully standardized land measures and landholding arrangements island-wide; and made central the concept of private property. As an integral part of the new estate system, the leasing contract became a powerful instrument for regularizing and reordering life and land use in the townlands. A whole series of key legal decisions were made, not least with regard to the reappropriation of the Bann fisheries, in favour of the new government and its agents.[26] Thus, new law had become a central instrument of colonization and state expansion. In the same way, the introduction of new laws undermined the legal titles to land held by the old elites and saw new estates vastly augmented by enterprising and ruthless colonists such as Boyle and St Leger in Munster, the Hamiltons, Chichesters and Montgomerys in Ulster, the Parsons in Dublin and the Midlands.[27]

Furthermore, it is clear that the final clearance of many woodlands and scrub-lands for strategic, industrial and settlement purposes was one of the most significant environmental changes wrought in late sixteenth- and early seventeenth-century Ireland. Woodlands were seen as the last bastions of resistance and were, therefore, military targets. The woods also fuelled the wide distribution of forges, tanneries and, in some cases, glassworks. Their disappearance opened up about a further one-eighth of the land of Ireland for primary colonization and the construction of new farmlands. The settlement of the former woodlands has not yet received a proper assessment by historical geographers. This clearance and settlement of woodland also highlighted the frontier characteristics of the Irish experience – the wolf retreated in the face of this onslaught, as did the woodkern. Both were treated similarly. Later on, the felling of the trees was to become a central metaphor for the destruction of the old aristocracy.

One of the most enduring administrative achievements – with the most significant settlement consequences – was the solidification of the county shiring system (see Fig. 10.2). The administrative experiences of the southern and eastern counties were older and more enduring – witness the social depth and routine character of this type of administrative structure as revealed in the sheriff's returns for Co. Kilkenny in 1637.[28] The real revolution in county administration was taking place in the Midlands, the west and north. Yet it was the mountainous lands of Wicklow in the east that became the final county area to be carved out and officially bounded by 1606.

A whole series of consequences flowed from the completion of this shiring

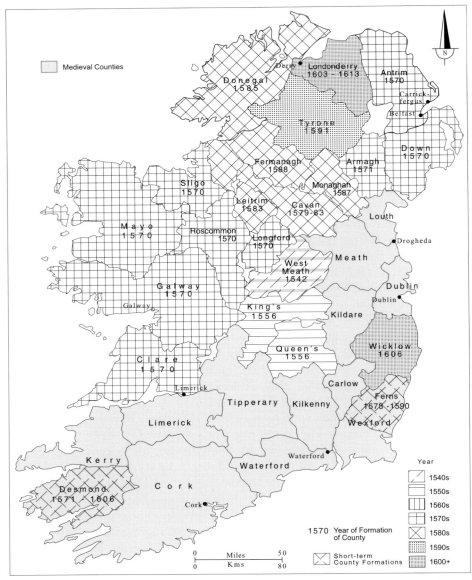

Legend:
Medieval Counties

Londonderry 1603–1613
Derry
Donegal 1585
Antrim 1570
Carrick-fergus
Belfast
Tyrone 1591
Down 1570
Fermanagh 1588
Armagh 1571
Sligo 1570
Monaghan 1587
Leitrim 1583
Cavan 1579–83
Louth
Mayo 1570
Roscommon 1570
Longford 1570
Drogheda
West Meath 1542
Meath
Galway 1570
Galway
King's 1556
Kildare
Dublin
Dublin
Queen's 1556
Wicklow 1606
Clare 1570
Limerick
Carlow
Ferns 1578–1590
Tipperary
Kilkenny
Wexford
Limerick
Waterford
Kerry
Waterford
Year
Cork
1540s
Desmond 1571–1606
1550s
Cork
1560s
1570s
1570 Year of Formation of County
1580s
1590s
Short-term County Formations
1600+

0   Miles   50
0   Kms   80

10.2   Geographical spread of county formation in Ireland from the medieval era to the early seventeenth century. (adapted from K. W. Nicholls, Map 45 in *A New History of Ireland*, 1984 and William Nolan, Map 23 in *The Shaping of Ireland*, 1986)

process. First, units of local government and administration were now firmly bounded and focused on a specific central place – the county town. Many of the new county towns were built on the foundation of the focal points of the old lordships: Monaghan on the MacMahons; Tyrone around O'Neill's Dungannon; Fermanagh on Maguire's Enniskillen; and Cavan around O'Reilly's earlier urban foundation. But there was a further crucial difference in administrative terms. 'Lordship' largely pivoted around strong individual personalities and shifting kin

10.3 Distribution of baronies in Ireland (created mainly in the Tudor and Jacobean eras). Ordnance Survey Ireland Permit No. MP005305. © Ordnance Survey Ireland/Government of Ireland.

and family alliances. County administration was now in the hands of a regular, uniform group of state officials, bureaucrats who answered to Dublin and ultimately to London. The county towns became the centres of the garrison, assize courts and local administration generally, their status boosted by the acquisition of gaol houses, sessions-houses, schools and churches and, particularly, by grants for fairs and markets.

At the next level beneath the county, the barony structures came to gradually displace the rule of the subchiefs. It is significant that the barony remains a central territorial entity in Petty's comprehensive mapping of the counties in the later 1650s (see Fig. 10.3). The baronies are, for the most part, creations of the Eliza-bethan era. As county formation was completed in the south and east and initiated in Connacht, the Midlands and later in Ulster, the new baronies are bounded and defined. For example, in Co. Fermanagh and Co. Monaghan the baronies incorpo-rate the long-established territories of the Maguire and MacMahon lords and sublords (*uirríthe*). Under the Elizabethans, the baronies became essential units of both assessment and legal administration, with the baronial cess collectors and constables key figures. The so-called 'exactions' of the *uirríthe* are now converted into government taxes (see, for example, the Composition Book of Connacht) and are transferred from the localities to the central Exchequer. Slowly, the old lord-ships are drained of their jurisdictional and taxation powers.

Within the barony, a rudimentary system of parish administration was slowly being reconstituted. We are still not clear about the extent and effectiveness of old and new manor courts, but these were likely to have been more influential at the critical local level than has hitherto been allowed for in the literature. Certainly, the figure of the parish constable gains in stature and functions as the seventeenth century progresses.

Transformation of the Cities and Towns

Equally fundamental to the shape of Irish society and settlement was the trans-formation that took place in the distribution, ranking and functions of its cities and towns. As late as the 1570s, the well-being of what Sidney called 'the commonwealth' in Ireland was seen to depend on the old towns.[29] Municipal privileges were augmented until, by the late sixteenth century, the Irish port-towns were largely self-sufficient. Each commanded its own limited hinterland and conducted its own foreign trade. Each of the towns, and especially the ports, looked to different parts of the continental mainland or to England rather than to one another for trade. It was, therefore, far from being an integrated urban system. The merchants of the old towns went out into the countryside, negotiating their rights from local lords, so as to buy and sell amongst the local population.[30] Almost all the towns were walled, chartered institutions, striking in their degree of separateness from a profoundly rural culture all round them. Robin Butlin's description is apt:

> Irish towns . . . were generally peripherally distributed, with the port towns [as along the Boyne and the three 'sister' rivers of the southeast] being related to groups of satellite towns in the interior. The port towns were the largest towns, and were part of a Western European trading system, but they also maintained a high degree of autonomy notwithstanding the necessity for trading with the Irish inhab-itants in their immediate hinterlands.[31]

The towns' walled exteriors were matched by the relatively closed nature of municipal life; each, like the merchant tribes of Galway city and the Tirrys,

Galweys and Roches in Cork city, were characterized by a closed circuit of powerful elite families.[32] Dublin was the pre-eminent city, well ahead of Galway, the
second city. Linked with Bristol and facing west to the great opportunities of the
Iberian peninsula and the Atlantic, Galway had a population of c.4,000 in 1600. As
I have noted elsewhere, there is still in 1570 a striking correspondence between the
hinterlands of the great ports and the distribution of the great lordships – a forging
of a necessary alliance between the lordship as a political/administrative system
and that of the port-city and its hinterland as a commercial trading system.[33]

   All of this was to change after 1580 with new political conditions laid down for
urban officeholders. Both the emerging requirement of the taking of the Oath of
Supremacy by government officials and the growth of Counter-Reformation
culture in urban life drove a wedge between the New and Old English urban
elites. Change was also coming in the area of state revenues, where only the duty
of wine imports (established in 1569) provided any income for the state from the
towns. The reformation was not only religious but social, cultural and economic;
it was now vigorously applied to towns, trade, customs, revenue, manners and
language. Late sixteenth- and early seventeenth-century regional conflicts further
suggested to the English their need to regulate and control the towns. Not surprisingly then, the old urban edges were to be surrounded by great Elizabethan forts,
symbolizing England's intention to regain control not only in the lordships but
crucially in the towns themselves.

   As Anthony Sheehan has demonstrated, urban recusant protests in the early
1600s, although primarily religious in character, were also concerned with the
defence of charter liberties. Mountjoy's response to Waterford Corporation when
it claimed certain rights by charter was chilling in its impact; he told the city
fathers that 'he would cut King John's charter in pieces with King James's sword'
if he was not admitted to the city.[34] Old corporate privileges were thus disposed
of. A new absolutist order was being written into the urban fabric. Likewise, the
garrisoning of the old and new towns continued apace throughout the seventeenth century; after the Cromwellian conquest, no part of Ireland was without its
garrison. No part of Ireland was left outside the new state's surveillance systems.

   Further centralization of control came in 1611 when all grants of tolls and
customs were removed from the cities to the crown. In 1607–8 customs dues
yielded only around 1.2 per cent of the total Irish revenue; by 1623, it comprised
about one-quarter of state income; and by 1637–8 customs receipts were at least
six times that of 1623 – a measure both of further state control and a buoyant
economic order.[35] The new Jacobean state, therefore, proceeded in systematic
fashion to break the grip of the towns on trade and customs. As V. W. Treadwell
notes: 'From being cosseted, quasi-autonomous allies of the Crown, Anglo-Irish
merchant communities found themselves reduced to the unfamiliar and unpalat-
able role of regular taxpayers, their cosy municipal monopolies constantly
challenged by the customs farmers' interest in expanding the volume of taxable
trade of all merchants.'[36]

   A profound geographical transformation was therefore in process – instead of
relatively clearly defined and isolated port-cities, characterized by autonomous

10.4   Revenue districts and town and village distribution in Ireland by the mid-eighteenth century (settlements identified from Figure 6.1 [p. 161] and Figure 7.4 [p. 198] in J.H. Andrews's *Shapes of Ireland* (Dublin, 1997)

circuits of trade and local control of surpluses, a national state system in the management of an integrated urban hierarchy was being put in place. The towns were made subject to the state's coffers and, in the process, linked together in a loose but still single unit. This pattern was further accentuated and extended geographically with the great rush of urban foundations between 1600 and 1641, especially those in Ulster. These new urban foundations and the creation of a large number of parliamentary boroughs culminated in the engineering of a Protestant majority in the Irish parliament. This was achieved as early as 1613, and apart from very short periods, was never to be interrupted until the Act of Union abolished that Irish parliament in 1801.

However, Irish cities and towns still retained some privileges up until the 1641 rising/rebellion. The Cromwellian conquest and settlement was to see a radical revolution in the character of the larger towns. Cromwellian policy with regard to Irish urban centres during the Commonwealth had three objectives: strategic, political and economic.[37] Cromwellian strategy was not only to debar Catholics from membership of civil government and from juries but also set about expelling the old merchant families from within the walls. The Cromwellians, therefore, set about consolidating and reconstructing both the social and political components of port-city and county towns rather than creating new corporations. In the political arena, these processes were to be geared to encouraging the election of safe mayors and aldermen. Finally and equally important, towns were seen as the key hinges in Ireland's economic development, for government revenues depended on urban prosperity. Yet outside of Dublin, the expulsion of Catholic merchants was to retard economic recovery, for the loss of the old Catholic families meant a reduction in key shipping and infrastructural wealth and, above all, in the overseas contacts for trade. However, this proved to be only a temporary slowing of the economy.

The removal of Catholic property owners from the towns was of equal importance to the uprooting of Catholic landed proprietors.[38] Yet this process has received scant attention in the literature. This policy was pursued vigorously in Dublin, and as early as 1643 the cities of Limerick, Waterford and Wexford were offered for sale by the government at £30,000, £25,000 and £7,500 respectively. No sales resulted but this was the start of the policy to take these key towns out from under Catholic control. Indeed, in 1653 half the houses in the cities of Limerick, Waterford and Cork were reserved for sale. Still in the mid-1650s much property stood empty, especially in Cork, Galway, Limerick and Waterford, a symbol of the traumas and dislocation of the previous decade, as well as the utterly transformed character of Irish urban life after the Cromwellian settlement.

Dublin was the single greatest beneficiary of all these transformations (see Fig. 10.4). In the first half of the seventeenth century, Dublin was the seat of parliament, of the law courts, of the university, and had two cathedral chapters. Even though it had suffered heavy depopulation during the plague of the early 1650s, the Cromwellian policy of expulsion of Catholic merchants was still vigorously pursued in the city, so that by 1660, English settlers outnumbered the Irish by three to one in the city core. The Irish were marginalized to the suburbs. Unlike other cities, these expulsions did not have a dramatic effect on Dublin's trade, because from the first decades of the seventeenth century Protestant merchants were gaining a firm hold on Dublin's growing trade; and during the Commonwealth this hold became a monopoly. They were the beneficiaries of Dublin's increasingly pivotal role as Ireland's nerve centre of administration and trade in the 1650s.

The most critical effects of Cromwellian rule in Dublin were religious and economic: the Protestant community in Dublin was consolidated into a very powerful body, including many influential people of a Nonconformist persuasion; and Dublin was also the great beneficiary of economic centralization under Cromwell's rule.[39] Dublin too benefited from the enormous centralization of administration and law, and its established role as an educational, medical and social focus of immigrant life also expanded. According to Petty, over one-fifth of all the Big Houses in Ireland were located in Dublin in 1672, as well as 85 per cent of all houses with more than ten chimneys. Overall, the city had grown dramatically, from a population of c.10,000 in 1600 to 30,000 in 1660, and c.50,000 in 1685 to reach close on 100,000 by 1730, when it became one of the largest cities in Europe (see Fig. 12.8b [Pl. 2p]).

By the early 1660s the fruits of Cromwellian expulsion policies were also clear in other cities. The old city of Waterford had been stripped of its Catholic majority – within its three central wards Protestants now formed a majority. Cork city exhibited a similar pattern, as did the older inland cities like Clonmel and Kilkenny.[40] Galway, given its strategic importance in the west and its strong continental links, was given special treatment. In 1655, its long-established Catholic merchant families were expelled from the city. The Protestant inhabitants who settled there were much poorer than the old Catholic merchants and had little experience of trade. The wars, plagues and expulsions had long-lasting effects on the status of Galway, and its long-term decline began in the 1650s. The old ties with the Continent were severed and the new settlers did not have the skills and resources to create a new trading network.[41] This gaining of urban control, as well as the demographic transformation achieved in key ports and county towns, was to be one of the most powerful and permanent legacies of Cromwellian rule in Ireland.

Figure 6.7 (see Pl. 2j) summarizes the size, distribution and ethnic structure of towns and cities in 1660: there are basically three types of region with rather different urban structures and lifestyles. An elaborate urban hierarchy characterizes the east, southeast and, increasingly, the northeast of Ireland. The Midlands and the border areas of the old feudalized world generally are characterized by a still developing urban hierarchy. In the remoter, mainly western regions, urban settlement hierarchies and lifestyles were still only in their infancy. A striking feature of the map is the almost exclusive dominance of the settler population in the newly planted towns of Ulster. Beyond this region, the towns with a 20-40 per cent planter population form a significant buffer zone stretching from Sligo, through Roscommon on to south Down. A more hidden urban Ireland appears in the south and east; here, the often smaller but deeply stratified borough towns are still overwhelmingly dominated by Irish and Old English Catholic town dwellers.[42] It is clear that these old, enduring and adaptive urban societies are the ones that underpin the higher population densities and complex rural settlement hierarchies of late medieval Ireland. Figure 6.7 thus provides a graphic illustration of the coexistence on this small island of very different urban cultures in the mid-seventeenth century.

Twelve revenue precincts were also established during the Cromwellian period. By 1700, the number had increased to thirty (see Fig. 10.4). These urban-centred functional precincts represented a new ordering of economic space in the service of the state and the government. As Raymond Gillespie has outlined, 'trade was, of course, regulated by law, whether grants of market rights, control of customs or regulation of property rights'.[43] Gradually, also, the standardization of weights and measures spread, as did uniform mechanisms of exchange generally. Likewise, an urban network – as shown in Fig. 10.4 – was extended over most of the island.

The distribution of the permanent barracks of horse and foot soldiers also symbolized the consolidation of other spatial orders – significantly, the greatest density of such garrisons ran through the middle of the country from Derry to Cork (see Fig. 10.5). Dublin was the key army base with new barracks provision for troops of 2 horse and 33 foot in 1704. It thus contained over half of the Leinster contingents and effectively commanded the New Pale. A strategic ring of barracks then curves from Drogheda, through Maryborough to Carlow. However, it is the province of Munster that commands the greatest concentration (36 per cent) of troops. Kinsale and Limerick each contained barracks for 22 troops of foot, while Cork (11 foot) and Waterford (8 foot) also contained large army concentrations. Connacht required one-fifth of the total number of troops, with Galway (22 foot) the key focus. Ulster requires the least concentration (17 per cent) with only Carrickfergus (6 foot) and Derry (6 foot) hosting significant concentrations.

In summary, a hour-glass shape to the army distribution can be discerned, with a strong concentration in the southwest Ulster/east Connacht borderlands, then a narrowing of the army barracks distribution to the west Midlands and ending with a second broad and dense concentration of barracks across Munster and south Leinster, enclosed by a line from Limerick to Bantry to the west and Kilkenny to Wexford on the east. Here it is noticeable that many small outlying places where garrisons were established in Cromwellian times on the edges of mountains and boglands – as at Abbeyowney, Fourmilewater, Galbally, Kilmacthomas, Killenaule and Longfordpass – are still provided with new barracks facilities.

By the late 1750s the number of army barracks had been reduced by almost one-third. Most of the closures (14) were in Ulster, with only 6 barracks still in use in that province. The bordering territory of northeast Connacht and northwest Leinster saw a further 5 barrack closures. More emphatically than ever, the inland territory that needed closest surveillance, control (and pacification, if necessary) comprised a large triangular region with its apex at Carrick-on-Shannon and a very wide Munster/south Leinster base running from Bantry to Wexford. There was also a secondary band of inland barracks in mid-Connacht, stretching from Galway north to Foxford and Belleek. These half-conquered regions regularly recur on a host of distribution maps. In contrast, three regions required the least army presence – Ulster (as we have seen), north and east Leinster, and the remote western halves of the Irish-speaking, and still underpopulated, baronies of Donegal, Mayo, Galway, Clare, Limerick and Kerry.

Overall, the contrasts with the 1570s could not have been greater. Instead of semi-autonomous and independent trading regions controlling most of their own

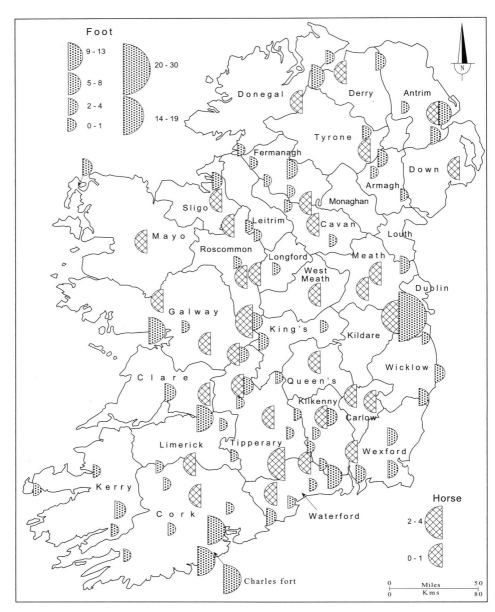

10.5   Distribution of barracks for foot and horse in Ireland, 1708

surpluses, we now have an integrated system of functional urban regions, acting as the collectors of revenue, which are funnelled through to Dublin and London. And instead of small or large local lordships with their own militia, we have a network of colonial garrisons under a single command and a county system of government that is powerfully anchored on Dublin.

Ecclesiastical 'Reformations'

The story of the parish in seventeenth-century Ireland is at the heart of under-standing not just the settlement history of that period but later settlement and social history as well. Running parallel to this secular, territorial and settlement reorganization by the state, Ireland saw the radical transformation of many eccle-siastical functions, their territorial structures and settlements – for example, the creation of a state Church, which, like that of the Anglican Church of England, involved the use of the vernacular language (English) in its ritual and administra-tion.[44] Such a process led to the creation of new linguistic/religious spaces across western Europe, which were characterized by sharp confessional boundaries. The centralizing nation-state, if Protestant, operated a closed style of recruitment and control of its clergy within its own linguistic space. By contrast, the Counter-Reformation Catholic countries still operated a supranational multilingual network of religious personnel and exchanges. In Ireland, these two competing ecclesiastical systems clashed head on. And unique in western Europe, two paral-lel and competing Church systems became deeply embedded in the landscape, as well as in systems of parochial administration and in people's minds.

As we have seen, the expansion of the early English military frontier was often literally built on the ruined foundations of the dissolved monasteries. Likewise, there is an interlocking geographical and temporal synthesis between the (re)estab-lishment of the county administrative system and effective transfer of diocesan and parochial facilities – including the crucial question of tithe collection – from the old Church to the colonial state Church which inherited these long-established territorial structures and functions (see Fig. 10.2, p. 352, and Fig. 10.6). Figure 10.6 summarizes the geographical extension of both the English crown's capacity to tax and the Anglican Church's ability to generate income from its newly acquired benefices across the island.[45] Indirectly, this map also documents the extension of English administrative control in Ireland. The older zone of control and Church taxation is the Pale (and the outlier of Carrickfergus). A rapid expansion of crown and Church control by 1538 includes segments of the northern and western borderlands of the Pale, as well as a broad swathe through south Leinster and eastern Munster (Cashel and Waterford dioceses), with a further pocket of inter-mittent control located in part of the diocese of Limerick.[46] Apart from the earlier 1550s integration of the Queen's County and its benefices, the struggle to gain control of the rest of Munster and the west Midlands is highlighted by a full half-century delay before these regions, as well as much of the province of Connacht, come under official crown and Anglican control by 1584–91. The last frontier of Anglican and crown expansion takes in north Munster (parts of Killaloe), south Galway (remainder of Clonfert), residual pockets from the formerly Gaelic parishes of the Dublin and Kildare dioceses, the northern edges of the Connacht (Tuam) dioceses, as well as most of Ulster. A number of cultural frontiers are revealed on the map – along the Shannon estuary, between anglicizing Limerick and the more Gaelic Clare, the numerous borderlands on the western edges of the Pale, and most particularly and most permanently, the frontier between Gaelic Ulster and north Leinster.

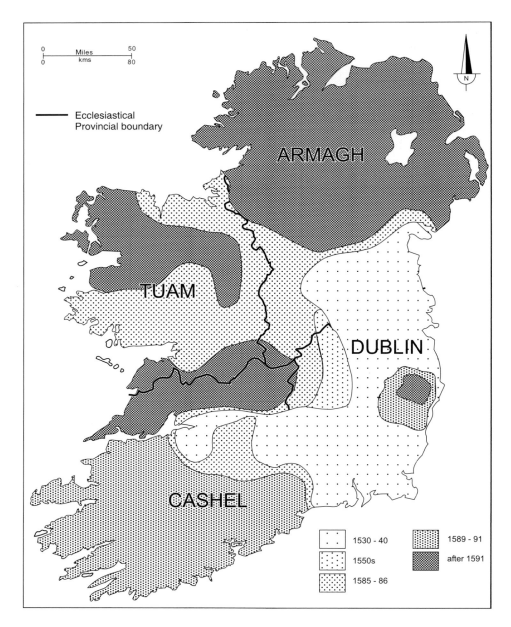

10.6   Geographical expansion of government taxation of Anglican/Church of Ireland parish incomes (after the work of Steven Ellis: see reference 46)

As Alan Ford has documented, the sixteenth-century Reformation Church, while not without its successes in the towns, amongst a minority of the Old English elite, and in parts of the Gaelic world, was, on the whole, bedevilled by poorly trained clergy, low incomes, absenteeism and rampant pluralism in the management of parishes.[47] However, the great failure of the Reformation/Anglican

Church in Ireland was the failure to assimilate and control the population of the Pale region and the older towns. The progressive alienation and growing Catholic self-consciousness of the Old English from the 1570s onwards and their eventual exclusion from office and political influence was one key factor here. A second key factor was the long-standing importance of extra-territorial links between both strands of the Irish Catholic tradition – Gaelic and Old English – with the Continent and especially Spain and France. The critical decade of decision may have been the 1580s, but the crucial reorientation developed in the 1590s, according as Irish seminaries were established in Spain and the Spanish Netherlands. By 1607, as many as one-third of all Irish colleges abroad were established and as many as 73 per cent of all the continental seminaries were founded before 1630.[48] A confident European-centred Counter-Reformation culture was thus being put in place.

Between the 1570s and the 1620s the battle lines were drawn. Two parallel and bitterly opposed systems of Church administration and ritual were crystallized. Critical to the geography of religion and settlement was the fact that the core region of the country (centred on the Pale and the wealthier towns of the south-east, key Old English cities of power, status and extensive information networks) had now become emphatically Catholic in ethos and became the centres of what came to be termed the 'recusant Church'. If the Anglican Church had been successful in this core area at this early crucial stage, then the cultural and settlement geography of Ireland could have been very different.

By the first decades of the seventeenth century, however, the Anglican Church in Ireland had become an establishment Church of officers and administrators, manned by English-born bishops and catering essentially for a New English and sometimes Scottish (as in Fermanagh) immigrant population. It was generally, but not invariably, imbued with an elitist and exclusivist ideology, which had its roots not only in a specific theology but also in the colonial status of its practitioners.[49]

The nature of the settlement and cultural consequences of these mutations were immense. Because of the weaknesses of the Anglican Church, or Church of Ireland, in so many regions, many of the old parish churches – ancient foci of settlement – ended up in ruins (see chapters 7, 8 and 9). Take the Dublin diocese, for example, where there is a striking regional gradation in the ruination of old parish churches. In 1615, in Dublin city and its immediate environs most of the parish churches were still in good repair; by way of contrast, only half the parish churches along the edges of Dublin county were in good condition and on the southern fringes of the diocese most were already in ruins. While the 1615 report may have been a little overcritical of the state of church buildings generally, it is still striking to note that a further seventy-nine parish churches in the diocese are classified as 'being in ruins' by 1630. Whatever the specific merits of the evidence, there is no doubt that a radical transformation of the ecclesiastical landscape of the diocese of Dublin had already taken place by 1630.

This pattern was replicated across most of the island. In 1615, Anglican Church dioceses with above average scores relating to the condition of parish churches were all located in Leinster, with Ferns boasting the highest percentage (78) of churches in good repair. Only Ross/west Cork and Lismore/Waterford displayed an above average level of church maintenance in Munster, a pattern partially coincident with significant immigrant settlement. In contrast, a key axis of church decline and dereliction stretched from Waterford city via Cashel and Limerick to Killaloe. This Anglican weakness – the woeful condition of its churches – reached its peak in Kilfenora, where no church was in good repair and in Ardfert where only three of the parish churches were still viable. On the other hand, above average maintenance of church buildings characterized west and north Connacht. The dioceses of Kilmacduagh, Killala, Achonry and Elphin all show above 50 per cent maintenance of parish churches, a pattern much more characteristic, one assumes (given the absence of survey data), of the northern dioceses.

The situation in the southern half of the country reveals further Anglican decline between 1615 and 1622. While recognizing that the 1622 figures are likely to be more accurate, the comparative materials show for Kildare and Meath a drastic deterioration (–50 per cent) in the condition of church buildings in this short seven-year period, thus confirming 'other accounts of the appalling state of church fabric in the Pale area'.[50] In contrast and possibly due to the earl of Ormond's patronage, the diocese of Ossory shows a slight improvement (+17 per cent) in the number of churches deemed to be in repair by 1622. Yet overall, the Catholic Church had no competitor in many of the parishes of the Pale and in Munster by 1622.

The decay of so many churches in so many places was a symbol of the particular failure of the Anglican Church in Ireland by the early seventeenth century. The Catholic population's resistance is, perhaps, best explained not only by its failure to support the local church but also in the deliberate strategies taken to ruin these churches and their livings once they had been appropriated to what was perceived as 'the heretic Church'. A very significant spoliation of Church property was a distinctive feature of the period 1539–1604.[51] This resistance pivoted around the power bases of the old resident noble and gentry families and likewise on the survival of a significant number of Catholic tithe farmers who withheld this source of material support from the local vicars.

Ulster dioceses were relatively free from the often crippling effects of impropriate rectories (that is, where parish property and/or tithes were held by lay proprietors). Indeed, following on from the plantation, Anglican bishops in Ulster carefully ensured that their Church would be generously endowed with both land and incomes.[52] Not surprisingly, therefore, the density of clergy was greatest in the richer northern dioceses, particularly in the lowland areas dominated by the settlers. The upland and marginal areas, mainly inhabited by the Irish, were more likely to be manned in a pluralist and absentee fashion.

Outside of Ulster, the number of impropriate rectories continued to rise between 1615 and 1634. Already in 1615, about 60 per cent of the recorded parishes for non-Ulster dioceses were impropriate – the proportion reached close to 70 per cent by 1622 and was well over this percentage by 1634. Lay encroachment on Church property thus weakened severely the mission of the Reformation Church. Here again regional variations are significant and have long-term settlement implications. The Pale region had a higher than average level of impropriate parishes and this proportion was still rising in dioceses like Kildare between 1615 and 1634. On the other hand, the dioceses of south Leinster exhibited levels of impropriation 10 per cent below the norm. Munster exhibits a highly varied pattern, with Ardfert, Emly, Cashel and Cloyne similar to the Pale region. Indeed, the level of impropriation rose by a further 33 per cent in the diocese of Emly between 1615 and 1634. However, Thomond's Killaloe and the relatively well-planted dioceses of Cork and Ross had under 50 per cent of their parishes in an impropriate condition. With the notable exception of Tuam, in all the other Connacht dioceses at least 85 per cent of rectories were impropriate, a product of long-established gentry encroachment on Church revenues, a process accentuated by the vacuum after the Reformation. This was the region where 'respect for the Church of Ireland' was clearly at its lowest. The Catholic Church would not have to face a difficult path of reconstruction in that province.[53]

The zones of weaknesses for the Anglican Church, whether described in terms of decayed church fabric, absentee clergy and/or high levels of impropriate rectories, were conversely the regions of greatest Counter-Reformation resistance and Catholic reconstruction. And it was this resistance – domestic and episcopal, and complex and multilayered in its territorial expressions – that made Ireland an exceptional place on the seventeenth-century west European stage. It was the only country where the Counter-Reformation succeeded against the will of the head of state and the instruments of government.[54]

Post-Reformation Ireland inherited an untidy medieval parish system.[55] The normanized areas were characterized by small, sometimes compact, parishes, where lay lords had rights of clerical nomination. In the Gaelic areas, powerful local kin-groups controlled the coarbial and erenagh rights to Church land and wealth in regions where the observant friars played key ritual and circulation functions. In addition, the diocesan parochial system had been seriously weakened in non-Gaelic areas by the earlier widespread appropriation of parishes by the now dissolved religious orders. Such parishes had already suffered from problems of absenteeism and amalgamation before the Reformation era.

Figure 10.7 summarizes the territorial lattice of civil (medieval) parishes islandwide, which, with their churches, tithes (unevenly) and ecclesiastical property, generally came to be appropriated in the early seventeenth century by an Anglican Church which was increasingly 'colonial' in character and personnel. However, this medieval territorial inheritance may well have been an impediment to an effective Anglican mission; in contrast, the underground, if resurgent, Catholic Church, now 'liberated' from the constraints of these untidy and often very small parish arrangements, was free to construct a new parish system that could swiftly adapt and adjust to the often rapidly changing distribution of populations, communication networks and settlements over the latter half of the seventeenth century and the eighteenth century.

Besides this complex mosaic of official Church territories, however, the Counter-Reformation Church had other strengths to build on and other difficulties to overcome. The localized nature of religious traditions meant that its liturgy primarily was centred around domestic rituals of birth, marriage and

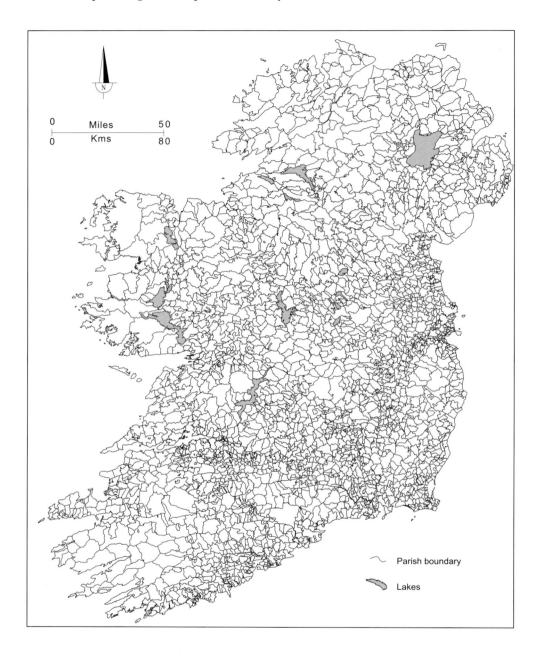

10.7   Distribution of civil parishes in Ireland *c.*1850, effectively the same as the distribution of late medieval parishes, as inherited by the Anglican Church / Church of Ireland. Ordnance Survey Ireland Permit No. MP005305. © Ordnance Survey Ireland/Government of Ireland death. The great importance of patron days, holy wells and pilgrimage-going all gave a specific kind of richness and social vitality to religious life. However, from the Tridentine Church's point of view, the failure of the medieval Church to fully Christianize a number of these rituals – and particularly those relating to the wake and the funeral – was to remain a long-standing problem. So also was the need to re-educate much of the population in the basic tenets of Christianity. Powerful kin-groups involved in ecclesiastical affairs – while giving their own distinctive strength to the local church – also constituted an enduring problematic feature.

Between the 1580s and the 1620s, the Counter-Reformation Church succeeded in building up a sufficient cadre of newly trained priests to lay the foundations for a resurgent Church. In 1622–3, it is estimated that the Catholic Church was being served by c.1,100 priests. This represented a ratio of priests to parishioners of around 1:1,360.[56] By the early 1630s, in dioceses as far apart as Elphin, Cloyne, Waterford, Tuam, Kerry, Killaloe and Kildare, the number of parish priests comes close to matching the total number of known reconstituted Catholic parishes by the early eighteenth century. Of these dioceses, Ferns seems less well favoured than its western counterparts, which stretched from Kerry, through Tuam to Elphin. Overall, a genuinely public Catholic Church had emerged by the 1630s – 'fitting awkwardly into the Commonwealth', yet tolerated.[57] Communal attendance at Sunday mass became a central symbol of this reinvigorated Church, as well as a powerful political statement about the identity of its parishoners.

Despite the major gaps in the evidence (due either to the complete absence of data or the failure to return population details at the parish level), Fig. 10.8 attempts to illustrate the strong regional variations in the extent to which the old parish centres acted as foci of the largest settlements across the townlands of that parish. One can distinguish three broad regions. First, in the extensive Pale region, stretching from the Cooley peninsula into the middle of Co. Westmeath, the eastern edges of Co. Offaly and curving eastwards to include all of Co. Dublin, more than half the parish centres are the foci of the largest populations. Indeed, in the coastal baronies from Dublin northwards, the vast majority of parish centres still constituted the most dominant settlement in the parish as a whole. It is most likely that the Barrow valley (no data) would link this north Leinster region with a second mainly Munster zone, where a majority of parish centres act as the most important nucleating forces in their respective parish territories. All of Co. Limerick, east and south Tipperary, much of east Cork, Co. Kilkenny, and mid Co. Tipperary, mid Co. Wexford complement the Pale region – as does mid-Roscommon and the Ards peninsula in Co. Down.

Second, east Donegal, east Ulster generally, the west Midlands, and significantly, Gaelic north Tipperary and east Clare, southwest Cork and most of counties Kerry and Waterford contain a sizeable minority (25 per cent or more) of parish centres which host the largest townland populations in their respective parishes. Third, in what generally appears to be the most Gaelic regions – in mid and west Ulster, all of Leitrim and most of Sligo, as well as pockets elsewhere, as in north Kerry – it is clear that the townland carrying the parish name is either a

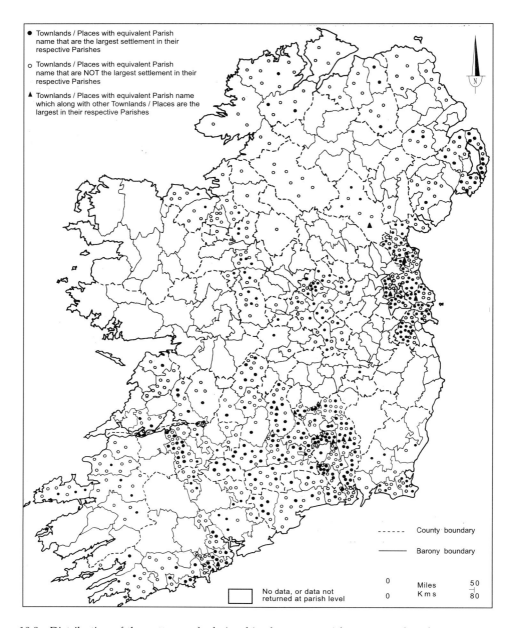

10.8   Distribution of the patterns of relationships between parish centres and settlement size in Ireland *c.*1660

very weak or non-existent force for population concentration or nucleation.

These island-wide patterns reinforce the conclusions already reached in relation to counties Dublin, Kilkenny and Tipperary. The more well-to-do, arable or mixed-farming parishes, dominated by single property ownership patterns, are most likely to be characterized by vital, highly populated, parish centres. On the

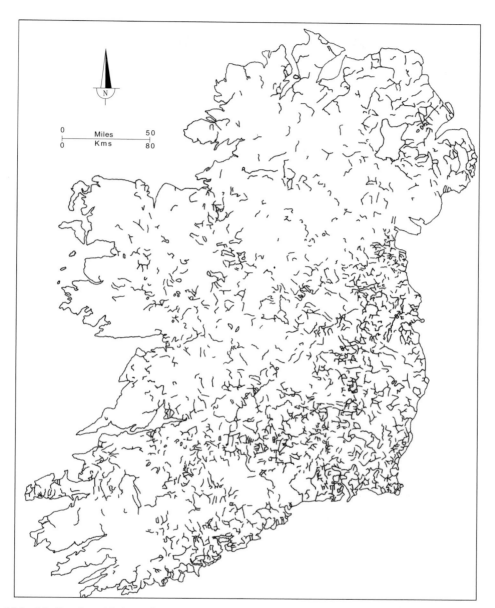

10.9   Medieval parish boundaries lost in the creation of Catholic parish network from c.1650 onwards (based on an island-wide comparison of civil/medieval parishes and later Catholic parish boundaries)

other hand, the more marginal, the more pastoral and the more Gaelic these regions, the less likely that townlands carrying the parish names is a significant force for population concentrations or nucleations. However, all these patterns were in a state of flux by 1660, and were to be subject to further radical changes, as the Catholic community sought to reconstruct its territorial structures as the Church of the disenfranchised majority.

Figure 10.9 attempts to summarize the long-term amalgamation of medieval parishes into new parochial units by the resurgent Catholic Church. The greatest rationalization of old medieval parishes and, one presumes, the greatest desertion of many old parish centres was to occur in this well-developed region of the Pale, along the Barrow valley and on into the core axis of late medieval power that stretched from Wexford, through Kilkenny, Waterford and south Tipperary, on to Limerick and north Kerry, with a salient southwards into east and coastal Cork and northwards through the great middle hearthland of Co. Clare. The old north–south corridor of east Connacht also saw a significant restructuring of parish boundaries, as did the long-settled region of east Down and south Antrim. In the remainder of the country, the older, coarser network of medieval parishes still constituted, for the most part, suitable 'enclosures' to meet the demands of a Church rebuilding along Tridentine lines.

Over the whole period under review, however, the resurgent Catholic Church underwent periods of massive trauma before the rudimentary framework of new parishes would begin to solidify by the early eighteenth century. During the Commonwealth period, Catholicism was deemed not to exist. Intensive religious persecution followed and a majority of priests were either executed or deported. Nuns too were victims of Cromwellian persecution. Dublin was hardest hit by these legislative measures, set up for the 'discovering and repressing of Popish recusants',[58] while, on the other hand, the diocese of Meath in the rich lands of the Boyne appears to have sustained its parish structure almost intact.

By c.1660 there were only 500–550 priests in place to begin the process of reconstruction once again. This represented about one priest per 2,300–2,500 Catholic parishioners, half the equivalent ratio reported in 1622.[59] The parish system had again fallen into disarray. In this case, a greater tendency for survival was shown in Connacht, a poorer situation in Ulster and in Munster, with the Catholic Church under greatest pressure in Leinster. The immediate post-Cromwellian period saw a greater fragmentation not only in religious practice but also in class structures. The old gentry patronage of the Church was often lost or displaced. Irish society generally became fragmented even further, pulled in different directions by old and new landlords, by priest and parson and a schizophrenic parish system. It was out of this period that the mythology of the 'heroic' phase of the history of the Catholic Church in Ireland was forged – culminating in the memory of the implementation of the Penal Laws, which reached their climax in the first two decades of the eighteenth century. Yet in the same period, and especially from the 1670s onwards, key ecclesiastical structures and religious practice were reconstituted along Tridentine lines. Parochial and diocesan organizations were revitalized to begin again the ongoing challenge to a decentralized, kin-based, and increasingly vital folk culture. By 1704–5, around 1,100 priests gave a reasonably satisfactory ratio of one priest to every 1,600 parishioners, given that as many as 424 members of clergy in religious orders (4 out of 10 from the Galway port region) were expelled and shipped to 'foreign parts' in 1698.[60]

The port-cities and towns were to remain the core anchors of the Counter-Reformation Church, characterized by a greater concentration of clergy, both diocesan and regular, patronage and protection offered by wealthy and literate Catholic merchants, by the greater role played by women members and, overall, by more diverse sources of material support for both a still rich liturgical tradition and for the sustenance of religious personnel. For example, the surviving Catholic guilds and chantries in the towns and cities functioned to maintain both Catholic priests and liturgy.[61] The depth and frequency of links with continental Catholicism was also a central factor here. The religious gradations then worked outwards from the cities and towns in a series of circles to the still quasi-Christian communities in the most rural areas. Patrick Corish's regionalization of post-Tridentine religious patterns of vitality by the 1670s is suggestive: in the first rank comes Dublin; next come the provincial towns; third, rural Munster and Leinster, followed by Connacht and finally Ulster.[62] However, the actual density of priests in 1698 – both secular and regular – would suggest that Connacht and Munster, plus counties Kilkenny and Wexford, were in a stronger position than the rest of Leinster. The weakened regions of priestly support were over much of Ulster (except Donegal and Tyrone) and the Dublin/Laois/Wicklow triangle. The north Midlands from Leitrim south to Offaly constituted a transitional region between the well-served west and the less well-provided east.

This picture is confirmed in 1731. In that year the House of Lords compiled a report on 'the state of popery' from returns made by magistrates and Anglican clergy. This report suggests that c.1,445 secular priests and 254 regulars functioned in the country. This is certainly an underestimate – there are no returns for the diocese of Kerry or for a number of parishes in some other dioceses. The returns for secular priests is at best a minimum estimate, while that for the regulars is clearly incomplete;[63] their numbers were certainly double that, and more likely treble the official return, that is, about 760. Overall, one may safely suggest a total number of priests of c.2,360. If we assume the population of Ireland to be 2.5 million in 1732; and that, at most, 1.9 million, or around 73 per cent, were Catholic, this suggests a ratio of priest to parishoner of 1:800. This is an impressive ratio in the context of both earlier and later patterns of priest/people relationships.

The actual material conditions under which the Catholic religion was practised, however, and especially the condition of its churches, varied dramatically across the island. The 1731 report provides descriptions of the conditions under which the population heard mass in most dioceses. The great dichotomy is between those parishes and regions with established mass houses and those dioceses and parishes where mass was said in the open air, on the mountain, or under some sort of shed, built occasionally to shelter the priest from the weather.[64] Figure 10.10 attempts to summarize this evidence, concentrating on the relative significance of such open-air mass sites vis-à-vis formal mass houses and chapels.

Across an extensive region over the middle half of the island, from Meath and Dublin diocese in the east to Ossory, Waterford and Limerick in the south and across to Tuam in the west, mass houses were essentially dominant. However rudimentary some of these buildings were, they point to the already solid position of the Church in these dioceses. Ferns, Leighlin, Cloyne, Cork and Ross (and possibly Kerry) were also characterized by a clear majority of mass houses but still retained

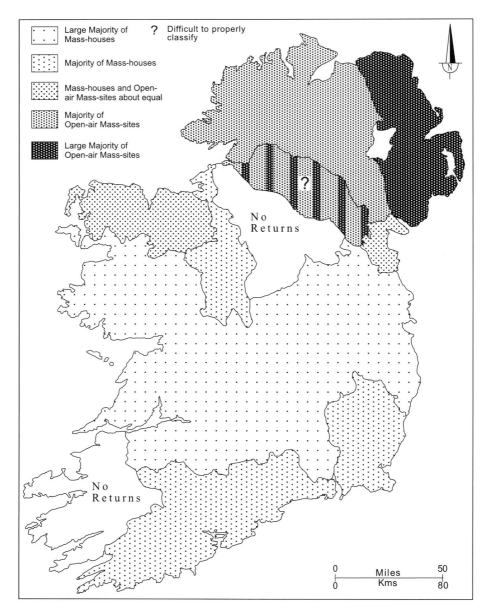

10.10   Conditions for mass attendance in Ireland c.1731 (based on 'State of Popery' report, see reference 64)

a number of movable altars in the fields. In the north Midlands, Elphin and Clonmacnoise appear to be similar in the character of mass provision. The beginnings of
a belt of weakness emerges in the northern part of the diocese of Armagh and
stretches north of a line that goes westwards to embrace the dioceses of Achonry
and Killala in north Connacht. Here a significant number of the centres of Catholic
worship were open-air sites. In Ulster, the situation deteriorates even further in

Raphoe, Clogher,[65] Derry, and the northern half of Armagh, where, in contrast to the southern dioceses, a significant majority of places for Sunday mass were mobile in character and unprotected. Down and Connor and Dromore return the poorest conditions for the Catholic Church, and are also – because of this weakness – the regions most likely to have seen the greatest assimilation of older populations to the new Church denominations. In Down and Connor, it was nine times as likely that a Catholic would attend mass in the open air rather than in a proper chapel in 1731 and this ratio was six to one in Dromore. Corish's model of the geographical distribution of Church vitality in 1670 is strongly supported (with minor modifications) by the evidence of the 1731 report.

S. J. Connolly's survey of 'the state of popery' is succinct and apt:

> Two things are immediately evident from the resulting reports. The first is the scale and level of Catholic ecclesiastical organisation; a generous ratio of clergy to people; an uneven, but still extensive, provision of places of worship; a network of both elementary and more advanced schools; and large numbers of regular clergy, some of them living in settled communities.
>
> The second is the general absence of concealment. The Anglican clergy and lay officials charged with making the returns were all clearly informed as to the location of mass houses, schools, and communities of religious as well as the identity not just of parish clergy but of bishops, vicars-general and other dignitaries.[66]

The Catholic Church was still technically an illegal and proscribed Church; it would still be subject to periodic repression, consequent on the political mood of the day, but it is also clear by 1731 that a moral community of enormous power and durability had emerged from the traumas of the later sixteenth and the seventeenth centuries.

Figure 10.11 (Pl. 21) completes the picture of the recovery of the parish life of the Catholic Church in the eighteenth century. Apart from upland and formerly less densely populated regions, where often completely new Catholic parishes were created in the late eighteenth and early nineteenth centuries, and apart from the slower consolidation of parish units in a few dioceses where the Catholic Church was very much in a minority, the parish boundaries and territories as shown here were already being put in place in the first decades of the eighteenth century. For example, in the admittedly precocious diocese of Ossory (mainly Co. Kilkenny) the 147 civil parishes were reorganized as early as 1635, where new Catholic parishes were created out of unions of three to ten complete civil parishes; on average, an amalgamation of five to six civil parishes. 'Population patterns, baronial boundaries, the townland entities, convenience and accessibility and the wishes of individual landowners were all factors in the division'[67] and construction of these Catholic parishes. Such reorganized parishes were to remain stable well into the early nineteenth century, and subsequent changes were, for the most part, minor modifications. The same applied in the diocese of Ferns (Co. Wexford), where by 1722 'the parish organisation that was to prove permanent was well on the way to being stabilised'.[68] The same can be said of the archdiocese of Cashel, where it should be noted that, despite all the amalgamations of small civil parishes, over three-quarters of the total length of Catholic parish boundaries added together still maintained an old medieval boundary. Both continuity and change went hand in hand. Thus, one of the most extraordinary revolutions in the territorial organization of Irish society was achieved. Having lost its suite of parishes, churches, monasteries and nunneries to the Anglican Church, the Catholic Church set up both new and competing parish and ecclesiastical systems. These parishes, in turn, were to generate 400 settlements, which Kevin Whelan has christened 'chapel-villages'.[69]

A third critical element in the geography of religious institutions and settlements in seventeenth-century Ireland is the Scots Presbyterian Church. Figure 10.12 seeks to summarize Alan Gailey's detailed work on the establishment of Presbyterian congregations in the north. It is difficult to pinpoint the very earliest congregations, 'for they depend on recognition of presbyterial forms of church government and worship within an essentially episcopalian setting'.[70] Gailey has identified 148 foundations between 1611 and 1720 (a further 6 were added before 1735). In the first originating phase in the dissemination of Presbyterianism between 1611 and 1640, early foci emerge in east Tyrone, in two parts of Co. Antrim – in the east between Larne and Islandmagee and to the west around Lough Neagh – and in northeast Down and Strangford Lough. At least 13 such congregations were established by 1641, representing around 9 per cent of all those established up to 1720.

The critical diffusion stage in the spread of Presbyterianism occurred from 1641 to 1660. As Gailey notes: 'equivocation between Presbyterian and Protestant episcopal forms of government continued until c.1638'.[71] However, formal presbyterial ecclesiastical structures in the north of Ireland originated with the army presbyteries formed by chaplains who accompanied the Scots army, which crossed over to Ulster to help defeat the rising/rebellion of 1641. Close on 40 per cent of the 57 new Presbyterian congregations established between 1641 and 1660 were actually established in the bitter and traumatic 1640s. In this context, consolidation of the early Scots areas of settlement in east Down and south Antrim appears most pronounced during these difficult years. Dundonald was one such place, 'where a whole society transplanted itself and brought to Dundonald the speech and manners of the Scottish lowlands'.[72] Likewise, in the early 1650s key new areas of development of Presbyterian congregations took place in the Lower Bann valley, down the Louth Foyle basin and along Lough Swilly in northeast Donegal, reflecting, in part, the massive influx of new Scots in this period.

The period 1641–60 was therefore crucial both for the consolidation of original foci and the development of a number of new core areas. Of all congregations established up until 1720, at least 39 per cent were constituted in this brief critical period. Over the next three decades – between 1661 and 1690 – a further 34 congregations (23 per cent of the total) were established, especially in northwest Antrim, east Co. Londonderry and east Tyrone. Equally important former nuclei were now being linked together, as along the Bann valley into east Tyrone and from mid-Armagh into mid and south Down. In the fourth phase, between 1691 and 1715, a further 44 congregations (29 per cent) were added. This is also a critical consolidation phase, with both an intensification and expansion of key areas of

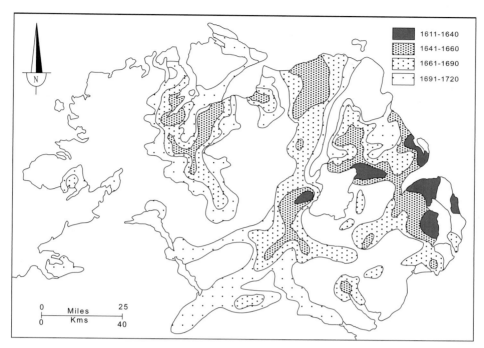

10.12   Geographic expansion of Presbyterian congregations from c.1611 to 1720 (based on the work of Alan Gailey: see reference 70)

Scots Presbyterian settlement between the Lough Swilly and Lough Foyle basins, a merging of Bann valley and south Antrim cores to extend deep inland into Fermanagh and, more particularly, mid-Monaghan and Cavan. The powerful intervening vector of English Anglican settlement extending south from Belfast Lough along the Lagan valley into north Armagh still remains on the map, while strong links have been forged between Presbyterian communities in mid-Armagh and those in much of north and east Down. New outlying foci were also emerging in south Donegal and Sligo. These latter areas, as well as west Down, much of south Armagh, Cavan, Monaghan and Louth, were to see continued Presbyterian expansion well into the mid-eighteenth century.

    The apparent rapid decline in the vitality and expansiveness of the Presbyterian Church, as evidenced in the few foundations after c.1715, is, however, somewhat misleading. From 1672, with modifications in 1689 and 1719, the ministers of what was technically an illegal Church received a fixed royal grant – the *regium donum*. Ministers, therefore, after 1715 sensibly resisted the setting up of new congregations, which would have diminished their share of the grant. However, apart from Dublin (and the small yet vital Quaker establishments in the Midlands and the south), it was Ulster Scots Presbyterians who constituted the core body of the dissenting Church in Ireland. For complex political and religious reasons, Presbyterianism remained subject to harassment in certain religious matters, such as those relating to marriages solemnized in Presbyterian meeting houses, as well as to a number of civil disabilities. Their members, therefore, occupied a middle position between the favoured established Church of Ireland and that of the Catholic Church, in terms of their status and disabilities.

Unlike the often-sponsored English Anglican settlers in Ulster who came to occupy mainly positions of economic dependence, Scots Presbyterians – 'lusty, able-bodied, hardy and stout' – were much more likely to be independent migrants with capital reserves of their own.[73] They thus fostered a dynamic, youthful frontier of expansion not only in the more sparsely populated border-lands of Ulster but also by competing vigorously and displacing both Irish Catholics and English Anglican settlers in the rich lowlands of the Foyle, east Donegal, and of Tyrone. This dynamism was also, in part, a product of the highly disciplined and cohesive structure of Presbyterian ecclesiastical congregations. After the creation of the Synod of Ulster in 1691, Presbyterianism 'was an autonomous and highly organised ecclesiastical polity. The discipline which the kirk session exercised over its members was both strict and broadly defined.'[74] Presbyterian members and lay elders exercised social control not only in matters broadly religious and moral, but also in relation to a whole series of economic transactions, including landlord–tenant relationships. A description of 1716 graphically identifies the specific ethos and strengths of Irish/Ulster Presbyterianism:

> They are a people embodied under their own lay elders, presbyteries and synods and come to their sacraments in crowds of three or four thousand from 20 to 40 miles about, and they make laws for themselves and allow not that the civil magis-trate has any right to control them and will be just so far the King's subjects as their lay elders and Presbyters will allow them.[75]

They also retained echoes of a radical civic – not to say, republican – tradition. A further strength, and a worry for the Anglican Church, was their constant interac-tion with Scotland proper. Their long settlement in Ireland, however, lead gradually to their greater cultural assimilation along quite a number of fronts with the other peoples of the north of Ireland.[76]

Apart from the general and regional dimensions of the settlement implications of all these ecclesiastical transformations, there was also profoundly important specific settlement consequences as well. First, Ireland developed a dual diocesan system, which – with the amalgamation of Anglican dioceses, on the one hand, and displacement of the Catholic bishops from old diocesan foci, on the other – led to the fossilization of a large number of ancient centres of ecclesiastical power: Killaloe, Ferns, Elphin, Cashel and Clogher spring immediately to mind. Equally important, new centres of Catholic diocesan power were to emerge – for example, at Enniscorthy, Thurles, Ennis, Sligo, and Monaghan. Finally, the importance of most of the old monasteries, convents and abbeys vanished forever – never to be restored as either focal points of settlement or of formal ritual.[77]

Even more crucial transformations took place at the parochial scale. We have already delineated the geography of the transformation of parish size and bound-ary structures. Within the older medieval parishes, therefore, many ancient parish foci were abandoned. Since these centres ceased to have any meaning for the great majority of the local population, their small parish hamlets and villages also died.[78] We are still unclear about the total number and distribution of hamlet/village desertion or shrinkage but Fig. 10.13 provides a useful reference point for their geographical distribution (see also chapter 11). Equally important, the now footloose Catholic Church was establishing new centres of community worship and power scattered throughout a newly reconstructed countryside. Embryonic chapel villages were already beginning to emerge by 1731 (see Fig. 10.11, Pl.21). Presbyterian communities were likewise building a new settlement structure across the northern half of the country. Where the Anglican Church remained strong (as in midland, east and southeast Leinster and in Ulster), it either helped to sustain older village life or became a central element in the newly established estate villages.[79]

Property and Settlement Changes

The ownership and control of property was the central anchor of economic and political power in seventeenth-century Ireland. Property units were powerful territorial frameworks for regulating the location and character of most human activities. Paralleling the dislocation and reconstruction of old urban and ecclesiastical centres and their merchant and clerical classes went the dislocation of the old property owners in the countryside. The central features of the vast landownership upheaval in seventeenth-century Ireland are now easily rehearsed: in 1600, more than 80 per cent of Irish land was held by Catholic owners; by 1641, this figure had been reduced to 59 per cent by plantation, purchase and intrigue; by 1688, after the devastating Cromwellian Wars and settlement, Catholic ownership declined drastically to 22 per cent; and by 1703, only 14 per cent of the land remained in the hands of the old owners. Put another way, in the 100 years from 1600 to 1700 the Protestant share of Irish lands rose from under 20 per cent to 86 per cent. No other European country of the period was to witness such an upheaval in the composition of its landowning elites and the consequent restructuring of rural settlement and society. Louis Cullen calls it 'a revolution in its [Ireland's] whole being which is not only unparalleled in its extent in Europe of the period but can find few parallels in other centuries'.[80] T. W. Moody describes the Cromwellian settlement as 'the most catastrophic land confiscation and social upheaval in Irish history'.[81] All this produced a ragged and uneven landscape of pure desolation at the one end of the spectrum, subtle and resilient adaptations in the middle, and vigorous reconstruction and wealth creation at the other end.

The sixteenth and seventeenth centuries in England witnessed the gradual and often bitter transformation of that society from a late feudal to a mercantile capitalist social order. In the new dispensation, property owners, released from the social obligations of lordship, came to see land as a commodity for sale and profit-making, linked to a wider economic system where well-to-do merchants in the towns and cities were playing powerful economic and political roles. It was out of this highly charged cultural, political, economic and social environment that the

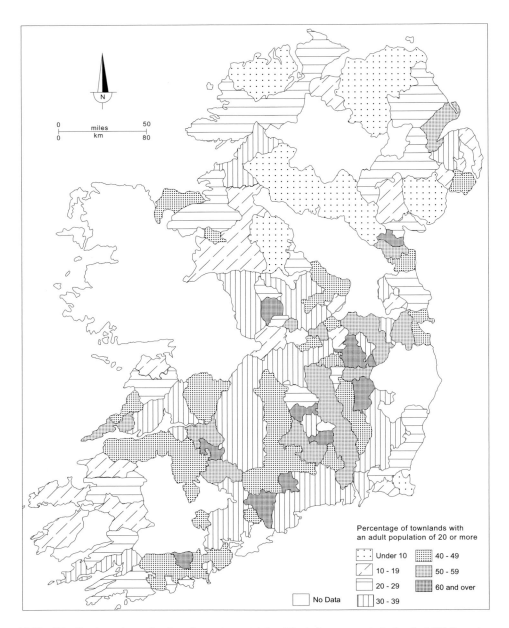

10.13   Distribution of townland settlements containing 20 adults or more in Ireland *c*.1660 (based on materials in the 1659 Census)

often younger sons and daughters of English, Welsh and Scottish gentry, adventurers, soldiers and settlers generally came to Ireland to dominate the property and economic scene.[82]

Because of the scale and depth of the transformation in property ownership and the centralizing role of the state in this process, it is not surprising that seventeenth-century Ireland is a century of mapping, surveying and itemizing. Precise mapping was part of this new rationalist era, culminating in Petty's Down Survey for the Cromwellian settlement, in itself one of the greatest attempts at social engineering ever attempted in any European country before the twentieth century. Petty, in his inimitable style, summarizes the consequences of the Cromwellian settlement as follows: by 1672, he notes, British Protestants controlled three-quarters of all the lands, five-sixths of the best houses, almost all of the houses in walled towns and places of strength, at least two-thirds of all foreign trade, and apart from the inland garrisons, completely dominated all coastal locations.[83] It was a transformation of revolutionary proportions in landscape, settlement, and society and in the distribution of wealth, status and power. But like all revolutions, there were significant regional variations in the extent and depth of its impact (see Fig. 5.6, p. 180).

The long-term cultural impact of these property transformations was probably least disruptive in the long-established and urbanized cultures of the east and the southeast. Outside of the deliberately planted areas, such as Wicklow, north Wexford, and the Desmond lands in Munster, the remainder of Munster and Leinster emerges as a battleground of interests, areas where often the planters' more narrow political Ascendancy is matched by both the residual class power and greater population size of the older society.[84] As illustrated for counties Dublin, Kilkenny and Tipperary, over much of this southern half of the island surviving territorial and social structures were often orchestrated to blunt and deflect the full brunt of colonial rule.[85] Stability in the local distribution of key family names is one indicator of the durability of such rural cultures. And it is likely that many of the strong local farmers took advantage of the chaotic conditions of the mid-seventeenth century to further strengthen their own grip on local resources and power structures in these long settled regions.

Apart from the already commercialized character of these mixed-farming regions and their social and cultural resilience, adaptation was also facilitated by earlier processes tending towards a private property structure. However, if these were regions of significant social and cultural continuities, apart from some striking exceptions, they were not regions of profound continuity in rural settlement forms in the long run. The most populated rural regions of mid-seventeenth-century Ireland were in the Pale, along the Barrow valley and the wider hinterland regions of Waterford, Cork, and Limerick ports. In 1660 these well-populated regions were dominated by church-centred hamlets, settlements then described as typical 'Irish towns', with a straggling street adjacent to a tower-house, as well as larger, manorial-type villages, where church and manor house/tower-house acted as twin pivots of settlement with the grain mill close by on the nearest river or stream.[86] The tower-houses and associated bawns were the anchor points for storing grain in winter, as well as for the capital investment in buildings and machinery needed for a developed mixed-farming economy and to house a complex array of labourers, artisans, and tenants under the patronage of the local lord, who in return extracted heavy labour services and a significant share of the agricultural surplus. Surrounding these focal settlements were an array of townlands, characterized (depending on the region) by scattered big farms, but mainly clustered settlements of kin-groups, or partnership farmers, or big farmers and their labourers and sometimes serf-like labouring families. Elsewhere, especially along the coasts, lakes and rivers, fishermen, artisans and millers were also likely to constitute key social elements in clustered settlements.

The upheaval in landownership and the military conquest shattered many of these pivotal settlements. At the heart of the transformation of early modern Ireland was the undermining of the power bases of these local lords. Lords and trees were felled and castles and villages disappeared. The returns of the Civil Survey are full of descriptions of castles 'unrepaired, ruinous, decayed, broken, derelict'; 40 per cent of Co. Limerick's castle tower-houses were in such a state by 1654 and in Co. Tipperary the proportion was closer to 50 per cent.[87] More detailed research is likely to reveal a great swathe of deserted or shrunken agricultural villages stretching from the Pale along the Barrow into the rich mixed-farming lands of much of Munster and south Leinster. Figure 10.13 (p. 378) may be helpful in providing a general distribution map of the agricultural village world of the mid-seventeenth century, which was centred on churches, tower-houses, and also the houses of the big farmers.

The decline of some of these villages was obviously a much more drawn-out process. As late as 1729 the south Wexford area was still characterized by castle clusters – the dispersion of their occupants into nearby farms and mills and towns, and sometimes their declassing into day labourers, had yet to begin.[88] Likewise, in mid and south Kilkenny, in east Galway and parts of lowland Mayo, in the Dingle peninsula, as well as north Co. Dublin, Louth and parts of Meath and east Down, specific conditions such as old landlord patronage, conservative 'middlemen' administration, maritime and riverine enterprises and proximity to nearby towns/cities, providing outlets for surplus sons and daughters, all allowed for the sustaining of these commercialized agricultural villages well into the eighteenth century and in some cases (such as west of Dingle and in south Kilkenny) into the twenty-first century. However, in much of the rest of these old normanized lands, settlement discontinuity and dislocation were very characteristic in a situation where the Cromwellian and later Williamite land settlement lotteries were to fragment dramatically the old territorial ordering of properties and their associated settlement frameworks. Absenteeism and lack of patronage by new owners all added to the flux and change in settlement reorganization.[89]

Ironically, greater continuity in settlement styles and a much deeper social, economic and cultural discontinuity was to characterize the old Gaelic lordships of Ulster, northeast Connacht, the Midlands and southwest Munster that underwent formal plantations. In these regions, the late sixteenth- and early seventeenth-century evidence points to a close dovetailing between the secular and ecclesiastical ordering of property, people and possessions. Patrick Duffy has meticulously outlined how the old parish system and its basic building block of townlands was locked into 'the *baile biatach*', the landed territory of the local corporate kin-groups, which were, in turn, powerfully integrated in a neat hierarchical fashion into the larger political and property structure of the lordships, such as that of the McMahons of Airghialla in Monaghan.[90] Thomas McErlean's work confirms this hierarchy of shared Gaelic property units throughout most of Ulster and much of Connacht and Clare, with the *baile biatach* or its equivalent – still called the *tuath* in Co. Clare as late as 1585 – occupying a central position in the structure.[91] The *tuath* represented a relatively self-sufficient resource and settlement unit, encompassing arable, meadow, bogland, mountainland and, if possible, access to sea, lake, or river resources. The '16 townland' *baile biatach* or a specific fraction thereof – usually *the quarter*, containing four townlands – constituted key building blocks in a coherent kin-based estate system within the Gaelic world.

The associated rural settlement pattern in such Gaelic or gaelicized regions led to a far greater scattering of houses and institutions across the townlands than the far more centralized single-ownership properties of the more feudalized, more stratified mixed-farming parishes of the east and southeast. Such is the pattern for the gaelicized areas of north Tipperary in 1654; such is the pattern revealed by Raven's maps for south Monaghan as late as 1634 with the newly intrusive Carrickmacross and a few two-storeyed slated houses of planters awkwardly juxtapositioned with an old settlement layer of small clusters of two, three or four cabins and quite a number of single, scattered farmsteads.[92] Although for a rather later period when other economic processes were encouraging greater dispersion, Henry Pratt's maps for north Kerry in 1697 also show a situation where 34 per cent of the settlements were single houses and only 35 per cent of the settlements contained three or more houses.[93]

Although the ghosts of many of the old corporate estates of the Gaelic world still survive in the shape of later landlord estates, the essential aspects of these long-established ecological, territorial and social units were rapidly dismantled and radically reconstructed and defined as discrete private property units. This was done firstly by the plantations themselves but equally by the transformation in economy and property values that followed on the opening up and integration of these regions with the wider Irish/English and Atlantic economies. The failure of local Gaelic lords to adapt to the new economic pressures led to much indebtedness, mortgaging and eventual piecemeal sale of ancestral lands.[94]

The central processes associated with the privatization of property and the carving out of new domains of agricultural production acted as catalysts for local migration and settlement changes. The old extensive systems of farming within kin-centred units were rudely disrupted. New compact individual farms were often created in the better lowland and former woodland areas and increasingly the former common grazing lands were opened up to permanent colonization and the creation of either a new tier of smaller farms or permanent clustered settlements high up the hill slopes or on bog edges or along the coastal *machair* (plain). In some regions, as in north Co. Clare and upland Co. Cork, the older territorial connections between the permanent settled lowland townland and the upland grazing grounds may have been manipulated and modernized to allow for the intensification of cattle-raising and the creation of dairying farms.[95] Much research still needs to be done to understand the transitional arrangements put in place to manage these new commercialized land uses as the older, more *social* definition of townland resources yielded to a primarily *economic* definition of territory and property, which came with this highly market-oriented farming.

In all of this, as the seventeenth and early eighteenth centuries progressed, the tower-house and the lord's stone house came to take on an old-fashioned, archaic look. The fashion of Big House mansion-building (as opposed to essentially fortified houses) was already developing before 1641 and spread rapidly after the Restoration. By the 1730s, this pivotal new settlement form was beginning to dominate this landscape just as its occupants found a new sense of self-confidence and security in their right to rule.

The critical privatization of the Irish landscape, both socially and economically, begins *within* the Big House, with its own complex of elaborate interior spaces with highly differentiated functions. This powerful expression of individualism, privacy and high social status further required a distancing and a shielding of the Big House from the mundane world of commerce and agriculture outside the gates and the widespread poverty developing both along the roadside edges and the margins of the estate. Hence, the creation of still relatively small demesnes and their new geometric landscapes of avenues, lawns and treescapes and well-trimmed, high hedges, walls, estate cottages and model home farms. If the estate was big enough, the world outside of the gates of the demesne was also manipulated to create one of the many estate villages – the specifically designed geometric estate nuclei with their servile and artisan classes ministering to the needs of the Big House, and their market house and few shops emphasizing the greater commercialization of the rural economy.[96]

The Big House was also the centre for a whole series of other fashions, ideas and innovations. The central operative concept in all of this was that of improvement, a key idea in the literature on agricultural development then circulating in Britain, Ireland and elsewhere.[97] The landlord's goal is centred on 'making improvements': improving the road networks via private turnpike trusts; improving farming methods; the establishment of enclosures, better ditches, better systems of manuring, draining and rotations; the building of slated farmhouses; the encouragement of better breeds of cattle and sheep; and, above all, the improvement of the landlord's own income. Landlords were also concerned with sponsoring new immigrants, especially those at the middle capitalist level who were intended to improve the towns and develop industry. The main instruments in achieving these landlord goals were the head-tenants or middlemen, that is, those tenants holding long, favourable leases of a number of townlands. These central figures (that is, resident, 'improving', industrious and, if possible, Protestant leaseholders) were seen as key developers. They were required to reorganize their own large farms, to build slated houses, to plant orchards, to enclose their fields, as well as ensuring that the often mainly Irish subtenants within their townlands carried out the same improvements to meet the new needs of the market and the demands of the Big House.[98]

From the 1690s on, the middlemen were to play an increasingly vital economic and cultural role. They were to be brokers between the Big House and the townland populations, mediators of market trends, of improvement strategies and fashions in building, hedging and draining, as well as a whole range of subtle cultural changes in speech, dress, dance, behaviour and attitude. Again, like the Big House and the estate village distribution, middlemen (and women) were not a uniform breed. They came from different social backgrounds and came to play a diversity of regional roles. There was the Protestant chief tenant (in Ulster and parts of Leinster and Munster); the Catholic ex-freeholder (most strongly in Munster but also elsewhere); the lease speculator, or land-jobber (developing strongly by the mid-eighteenth century); and the perpetuity tenant or holder of leases for three lives renewable forever (the anchor tenant of early eighteenth-century landlordism).[99]

The shake up in these traditional rural forms of settlement was accompanied at the townland level by often rapid transformations of the local social structure. Some local families were privileged in these processes of reform and were allocated bigger townland farms; others slipped down the scale to become smaller farmers within the townland or were encouraged by the estate to create new 'colonial' farms on the moorland or bogland edges;[100] others again were marginalized onto roadside patches or onto 'wasteland', where by the 1720s 'potato cultivation in small patches for domestic subsistence seems to have become commonplace'.[101] Expanding road connections also became a solvent of older communal structures, while social differentiation proceeded apace both within the townland and island-wide. Again, these general processes varied regionally and temporally.

The upheaval in the composition of landowning elites resulted in the restructuring of settlement and society across the island – but with strikingly uneven regional effects. In contrast, the geography of ecclesiastical settlements had been turned upside down with displacement, innovation and reconstruction the central processes involved in this dramatic transformation. In all of this, the towns and port-cities remained the central anchors of immigrant settlement and economic control. Dublin, as the capital of this colonial state, was the great gainer across a whole range of activities, just as London remained the ultimate arbiter and beneficiary of colonial/imperial rule in Ireland.

11

Upheavals in Economy, Family
Naming Patterns and Language,
1530–1750

To slur and stumble

In shame
the altered syllables
of your own name:
to stray sadly home

And find
the turf-curved width
of your parents' hearth
growing slowly alien.

John Montague[1]

. . . a bare face of nature, without houses or plantations; filthy cabins, miserable,
tattered half-starved creatures, scarce in human shape; one insolent ignorant
oppressive squire to be found in twenty miles riding: a parish church to be found
only in a summer's day journey, in comparison of which, an English farmer's barn
is a cathedral: a bog of fifteen miles round; every meadow a slough, and every hill
a mixture of rock, heath, and marsh: and every male and female, from the farmer,
inclusive to the day labourer, infallibly a thief, and consequently a beggar, which in
this land are terms convertible.

Jonathan Swift[2]

In the previous chapter, I addressed the role of a hierarchy of powerful territorial
entities (from the state to the estate) in radically transforming the structure of Irish
society. By way of contrast, this chapter examines how a great variety of transactions across territories culminated in significant cultural changes. The focus here
is on patterns of exchange, family naming patterns and language use. But the
consequences of massive population mobility need also to be addressed.

From 1530 to 1750, Ireland's population increased from over 1 million in 1600
to around 2.4 million by 1750. But these figures do not encompass the dramatic
population declines in Munster and Ulster in the later sixteenth century and
obscure the phenomenal population changes between 1641 and 1660, as well as
the severe consequences of the 1741–2 famine, when around one-eighth of the
population died.[3] These bald figures also neither address the high levels of
immigration into Ireland over the period nor the scale of internal population
mobility within the island, generated by conquest, plantation, economic development and dislocation.

The key lineaments of immigrant settlement in Ireland had been solidly established by 1641. Then a global total of over 300,000 immigrants (including their
offspring) saw 45 per cent located in Ulster, 30 per cent in Leinster, 20 per cent in
Munster and only 4 per cent in Connacht.[4] As noted above, the explosive and bitter
reaction of local populations in the Confederate Wars represented, amongst other
things, a powerful response both to the intrusive scale and the successful character
of many new immigrant settlements. Subsequently, the 1650s saw a second wave of
significant immigration, as did the late 1670s, but these were not to profoundly
alter the map of the distribution of immigrant settlement. They were, however, to
add significantly to the occupational, social and religious diversity of Ireland. One
list of immigrants over the period 1662–72 shows an early peaking of immigration
in 1665 and a more pronounced peaking in 1670.[5] A striking feature of the list is
the high proportion (38.5 per cent) of migrant merchants and butchers, as well as
very significant proportions of both mainstream and specialist artisans. Close on 20
per cent of the group were from mainland Europe – primarily from the French,
Dutch, and German territories – with English migrants generally moving along an
axis from London to Lancashire, with strong outliers in the West Country, Yorkshire
and Leicestershire. Later, the great wave of Scottish immigration into the north of
Ireland in the 1690s, and especially after 1695, was to add further social depth and
geographical dynamism to the immigrant settlements of Ulster and its borderlands.

By 1730, the three key immigrant regions in Ulster, Leinster and Munster
respectively had changed both in the overall distribution and intensity of immigrant settlement.[6] The picture in the northern region – whose southern boundary
extends from north Co. Louth, through Longford to Killala Bay – is one of both
further solidification of the core areas and dynamic expansion into a number of
outer frontier regions. The picture in the Midlands/New Pale region is more
complex. The pattern here is one of significant internal migration and careful
consolidation of key Protestant settlement foci. The Cork/Munster region is
clearly the most volatile and most vulnerable of the immigrant settlement regions,
giving rise to significant contractions in these distributions between 1660 and
1730. A north–south dialectic had already crystallized and entered deeply into the
cultural geography and life of Ireland by 1640–60. By 1732, this pattern is powerfully confirmed (see Fig. 11.7, p. 409).

Colonial/imperial expansion thus created very divergent cultural regions
within Ireland. Equally, however, this process of imperial expansion unified the
island into a single economic entity. Economic integration was helped by the
expansion of both the communications networks and a hierarchy of trading
centres that stretched from the roadside fairs to the busy port-cities.

Economic Transformations

The radical changes in settlement structures following on from the destruction of
so many old landed patronage systems were accelerated and sustained by one of
the most profound single changes in seventeenth-century Ireland – the transformation in systems of land use and production through the creation of a

commodity-based market economy. This market economy was built on the regional spread of fairs and markets,[7] funnelled through the now widespread distribution of towns and villages and orchestrated and managed by the increasingly hegemonic role of the great ports such as Dublin and Cork, with Waterford, Limerick, Drogheda, Belfast, Derry and Sligo playing important regional roles. Ireland's agricultural surpluses were no longer consumed locally. Rather, a dramatically increased share of a vastly increased total production was to reach the fairs and markets and through them transferred on to Cork, Dublin and London, to French and Spanish ports, and, among other places, the West Indian plantations.

Clearly, a more commercially oriented market economy was already a feature of the long-urbanized lands of the south and east. However, the outward expansion of the British Empire and Ireland's incorporation into a wider imperial and Atlantic economy was central to this intensification of market processes. In conjunction with the new innovative forces unleashed in Ireland via a reconstituted property elite and a new immigrant community anxious to make both quick profits and better lives for themselves, a rapid monetization and commercialization of the now island-wide economy took place in seventeenth-century Ireland (and was accentuated in the eighteenth century). In the mid-sixteenth century much of the surplus from the land was still being returned to the local lords in kind. By the 1660s it would appear that most rents were now being paid in cash by a tenantry who were now locked into a new landowning culture, which became solidly based on written contractual leaseholding arrangements.[8]

One critical indicator of this nexus of trade and commerce was the rapid spread of the fairs and markets throughout the more accessible fertile lands of the whole island in the seventeenth century, with the further filling-in of the fair network in more uphill, interstitial and marginal locations in the first half of the eighteenth century. Of the total number of fairs patented between 1600 and 1750 that were still active by the mid-nineteenth century, 62 per cent had been established in the extraordinary expansive decades of the first half of the seventeenth century – 33 per cent in Leinster, 25.5 per cent in Munster, 24.8 per cent in Ulster and 16.4 per cent in Connacht. The half centuries from 1650 to 1700 and from 1700 to 1750 contributed just under 20 per cent each to these enduring fair foundations.[9] However, sharp regional differences in rates of economic development and market intensification are suggested in a breakdown of these figures. Leinster – with the growing capital city of Dublin playing a powerful propulsive role – dominates the second half of the seventeenth century with 48 per cent of all new fair foundations. Munster had 20.2 per cent, Ulster 19.1 per cent and Connacht 12.8 per cent. By way of contrast, between 1700 and 1750, Munster, with almost half the new fairs patented, outstrips Leinster (22.1 per cent), Ulster (14.7 per cent) and Connacht (13.7 per cent). Clearly, Munster's deepening role (centred on Cork city) in the dairying and provision trades was a crucial factor here.

At the centre of all these transformations were the towns and landlord villages, either reconstructed or, more often, newly built. These must have given much of the seventeenth-century Irish landscape a dramatically novel appearance, especially in those regions so long dominated by essentially rural cultures. This was certainly the case over most of Ulster, the Midlands, much of Connacht and west Munster and indeed pockets elsewhere, as in Wicklow/north Wexford (see Fig. 11.1). Over 200 new towns were created, making Ireland a very different place to England or France, where the great majority of towns or villages were medieval in origin.[10] In Ireland the majority of urban foundations belonged to the expansive period between 1550 and 1700; the closest parallels were in the New World with the creation of new colonial towns across the newly conquered lands of Anglo-America and Latin-America.

This greater economic integration (through cities, towns, villages, fairs and markets) also meant a growing regional specialization in economic activities, according as the Irish economy became more and more subservient to the changing demands of the British and Atlantic economies. Grain production remained solidly rooted in the old medieval arable cores of east and south Leinster and south and east Munster, with another core area in north Armagh and the Lagan valley. Cattle farming, while widespread, became most strongly associated with the west Midlands, north and mid-Munster and east Connacht, where sheep farming also became conspicuous. South and west Munster was the hearthland of the growing dairying and provisions industry, with parts of Ulster and Connacht also playing a significant role in this sector. Ulster also underpinned and acted as the diffusion centre for the now rapidly expanding, rural-based flax and linen industry of the early eighteenth century.[11]

In rural settlement terms, the tillage regions best conserved the old townland village structures – at least over this period of review. On the other hand, the growing flax/linen industry was an additional force in the scattering of settlement and the fragmentation of smallholdings in the countryside. It also formed new linen villages and enriched the market towns, which acted as key gathering points in the trade. That apart, it was the massive commercial expansion of cattle, dairying and sheep trades that was most influential in reshaping rural settlement structures and population densities. Combined with the demise of the old church centres and the patronage of old landowners and the role of their houses as focal points for local societies, this 'age of pastoralism' was most critical for the desertion of many agricultural villages across the middle half of the country – particularly on a broad sweep of territory that had at its core counties Roscommon and Westmeath to the north, Clare, east Galway and Tipperary in the middle and east Limerick and north Cork to the south.

David Dickson has identified the critical period 1690–1750 as characterized by a concentration of economic power: 'geographically on the larger ports' and 'socially in the hands of the big graziers and dairymen'.[12] Ingeborg Leister had documented the geographical expansion of large grazier farms for sheep and bullocks in middle Tipperary from the 1660s, and especially from the 1690s, onwards.[13] The houghing 'outrages' in east Galway at the beginning of the second decade of the eighteenth century points to a sufficiently formal and widespread resistance to the process of privatization, enclosures and social reconstruction to make it into the contemporary newspapers and, later, into the history books.[14] How many local and regional

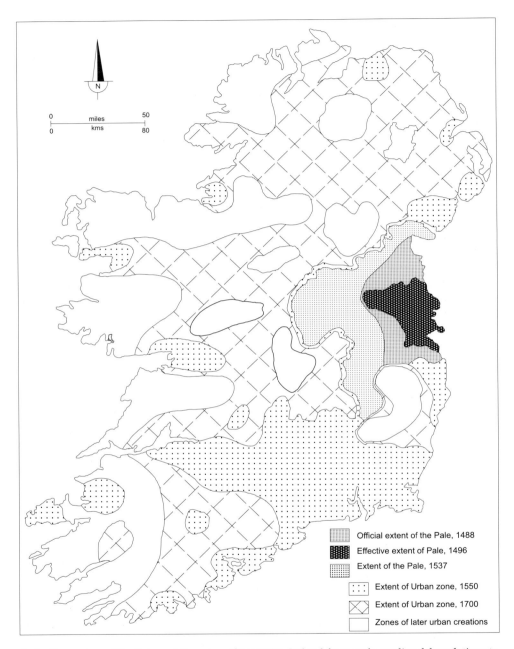

0   miles   50
0   kms   80

Official extent of the Pale, 1488
Effective extent of Pale, 1496
Extent of the Pale, 1537
Extent of Urban zone, 1550
Extent of Urban zone, 1700
Zones of later urban creations

11.1   Expansion of the Pale and the urban 'frontier' in Ireland from early medieval foundations to the middle of the eighteenth century

expressions of resistance in the seventeenth and early eighteenth centuries to this process of enclosure, social engineering and marginalization have gone unnoticed and unacknowledged in the written record? This kind of resistance was, however, noted for Tipperary and Roscommon in the 1720s. Using Charles O'Hara's survey,

Dickson highlights related processes for store-cattle breeding areas in Sligo, where by the year 1720, 'many villagers were turned off and the lands which they occupied stocked with cattle. Some of these took mountain farms but many more went off.'[15] The exceptional population declines shown for this middle part of Ireland on Dickson, Ó Gráda and Daultrey's map of population change in the late seventeenth and early eighteenth centuries is, therefore, highly suggestive of a widespread reconstruction of economies, societies and landscapes in a Midland region that was rapidly becoming classic 'cattle and sheep-walk' country.[16] Sharp regional variations in population growth and class transformations are therefore central themes in these revolutionary times.

Some Irish poetry of the seventeenth century is revealing about the reality of changing demographies, naming patterns, class structures and lifestyles. The best-known work in this genre is *Pairlement Chloinne Tomáis*, which, from an aristocratic vantage point, laments the disdain of the ordinary people for the old ways and their attraction to English forms of dress, speech and behaviour, including what became a universal habit, tobacco-smoking.[17] More critical are the poetic insights which stress that to get on in the world the best activities were tenant-farming and craftwork such as weaving and building.[18] The acceleration and the commercialization of the Irish economy was providing new job opportunities, new ways of earning a better living, even for the poets.

William Petty offers further insights into changing class structures that had occurred by 1672.[19] He produces useful summaries on occupations, some of which may have been based on the returns of the poll-tax. In this exercise, however, Petty clearly underestimates the importance of the servant class in mid-seventeenth-century Ireland. Other contemporary and reliable evidence for south Co. Dublin suggests that servants of various types constituted around 53 per cent of the working population in that region.[20] Petty also underestimates the percentages of the population actively involved in farming, whether as husbandmen/small farmers, labourers or servants. There are, likewise, small key groups missing from his list of occupations, including bakers, basket-makers, carters, coopers and turf/furze-cutters. Allowing for these underestimates and omissions, Petty still highlights the key structural position of the artisan class in this changing society. (In south Co. Dublin artisans account for 10–11 per cent of the working population.) Smiths, carpenters, masons, tailors, shoe/brogue-makers were key figures in the landscape, as well as weavers, glove-makers, dressmakers, knitters and crib-makers. He also notes the growing significance of the shopkeeping trade in providing new opportunities, including the sale of tobacco, salt and iron. And while his estimate of the number of ale houses and breweries seems excessive, his assertion that these key institutions employed at least the same number of workers as all other kinds of shops points to the centrality both of the innkeeper and alcoholic drink in seventeenth-century Irish life.[21]

Apart from these occupational groups there were vagrants and the wandering poor, as well as the people Petty describes as the 'cosherers' (local lords who still sought to maintain their old ways of ruling via food rents and labour services),[22] who, in his view, were failing to adapt to the new order of trade and commerce, caught in a time warp and unable to recognize that their late medieval Ireland was suddenly modern in tone and activity.[23] In the 1730s the number of strolling beggars in Ireland is estimated to have been over 34,000; and Dublin was the great magnet for these wanderers, who, amongst other things, symbolized the levels of dislocation that accompanied Ireland's 'modernization'. The hearth-money and the later poll-tax records also highlight the high levels of local mobility, as families and individuals shifted their locations from townland to townland and from parish to parish in search of a better home.[24]

Naming Transformations

There were other less tangible, less easily measured yet crucial frontiers arising from these levels of colonization, settlement and rapid economic development. In a world turned upside down, the pressures on language and family naming patterns were immense. Even the names of the people were being flattened, transformed and eroded.

The geography of first names and surnames in Ireland provides very important clues to questions of colonization, conflict, conquest, accommodation and assimilation. Excavating such a memory bank of family names allows the scholar to explore hidden and often undocumented social and cultural processes that escape the net of official history. Since the Middle Ages, and particularly in this colonial /early modern era, the forging of Ireland's symbolic/naming universe saw an increasingly uneven battle conducted between the powerful hegemonic forces – that of the Celtic/Gaelic/Irish and that of the Germanic/British/English-speaking/writing traditions. The former was now on the defensive; the latter increasingly in the ascendant.

The 1659 Census does not provide so rich a databank on first names as it does on surnames. Yet its detailed listing of the first and second names of the highest poll-tax payers, the *tituladoes*, is also highly instructive. It is not difficult to distinguish the old Irish gentry names from those of the Old English and one can map, as in Fig. 11.2 (Pl.2m), the extent to which the old Gaelic elites retain their ancient first names or have adopted European-wide forms of Christian names. One can test also the reliability of the results by looking at a comparison of the Tipperary patterns based in the first instance on the very detailed naming evidence from its hearth-money records (1665–7), and second, on the less comprehensive gentry/*tituladoe* naming patterns in the 1659 Census. A very high correlation between the two sources is evident in the three naming regimes revealed for Co. Tipperary (see Fig. 11.3). In its more Gaelic north and west, traditional Irish first name patterns prevail, there is a hybrid middle belt, whereas the very feudalized southeastern zone of the county is dominated by European-style first name forms even amongst the old Irish elite families. This last region is seen in Fig. 11.2 to extend over much of lowland Leinster, presents a sharp frontier to the Gaelic world of Ulster and its borderlands in Leinster and Connacht, extends into normanized Roscommon and swings south to reveal the cultural zones of high assimilation to medieval naming patterns amongst the Gaelic families of both east and north Cork

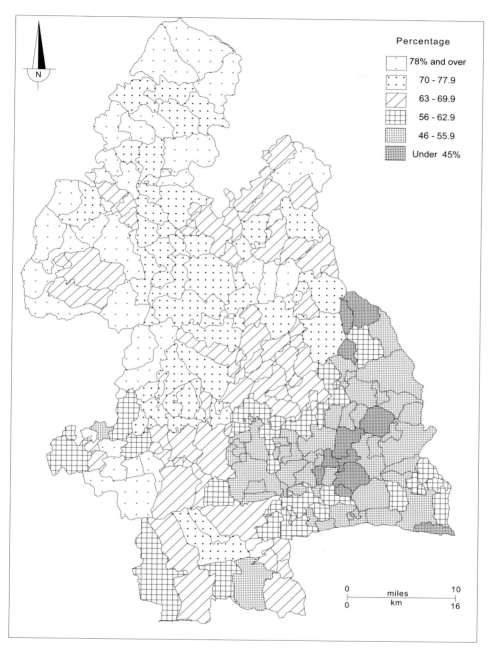

11.3   Percentage distribution of the retention of ancient Gaelic first names amongst Co. Tipperary's Gaelic population 1665–7

and north Kerry. The long-recognized frontier zone between Desmond north Kerry and Gaelic south Kerry is replicated on this map – a Gaelic zone of continuity that extends into west and southwest Cork, with again (as in Tipperary) a classic hybrid marchland zone running north–south in mid-Cork from Liscarroll to Kinsale.

Likewise, pockets of greater 'resistance' to European naming patterns are revealed in parts of the Midlands, the Decies in Waterford and in north Wexford (and probably much of Wicklow). Co. Clare reveals mixed, if more Gaelic-naming patterns, which probably weakened as this zone extended into lowland Galway and Mayo. However, the most striking feature of this map is the emphatic regional distinctiveness of Ulster and adjacent borderlands. Nowhere else does the pattern of first names remain so faithful to its ancestral roots. Nowhere else in Ireland was Gaelic culture more coherent, more conserving, more enduring.

Overall, therefore, the first name evidence from mid-seventeenth-century Ireland as a whole reveals how diverse and regionalized Irish cultural expressions had been at this time. And it is clear that over the greater part of the island (excluding Ulster) medieval first naming patterns had taken a deep hold – a feature even more pronounced amongst women, where first names reveal a greater shift towards the more fashionable European first names than even those of the men. For example, in Co. Tipperary of the mid-1660s fewer than 20 per cent of the women's first names belong to the older Gaelic naming tradition. The Anglo-Norman/Old English settlement and the associated great increase in continental religious foundations had clearly a profound long-term transformational effect on culture and naming patterns.

MacLysaght has provided one measure of these transformations in first names from his analysis of sources such as the Civil Survey, the Books of Survey and Distribution and the Cromwellian Transplantation Certificates. In the mid-seventeenth century, John was the most popular male first name, accounting for approximately 9 per cent of the sample. Thomas, William, James and Edmund followed, each accounting for about 5 per cent. The break with the naming patterns of the earlier medieval period is, therefore, quite sharp. The old Gaelic names Connor, Dermot, Donough, Rory and Teig only occupy a third category, each accounting, in turn, for nearly 3 per cent 'of the Catholic population'.[25] Equally popular were Hugh or Ee (Aedh) and Daniel (or Donell). A little less prolific were Patrick, Richard and Nicholas. There follows Maurice, Edward and Robert, which were each about equal to the Gaelic Brian and Murrough. MacLysaght concludes that the list of these first names, which each reach at least 1 per cent of the total, includes Andrew, Christopher, Francis, Garrett, Henry, Loughlin, Mahon, Peter, Piers and Terlagh. By the mid-seventeenth century, these figures suggest a ratio of at least two to one in favour of the Old English-derived first names for men as against the older Gaelic forms.

The enumerated *tituladoes* of the 1659 Census allows some regional breakdown of this island-wide pattern. Amongst the enumerated old Irish gentry for Ulster, Donall and Patrick come joint second to John, while Hugh, Phelim, Connor, Brian, Terlagh, Cahir, Rory and Niall are also strongly represented. In fact, of the top ten first names of the old Gaelic elites of Ulster, seven were from the Gaelic tradition and only three (John, Edmund and Thomas) from the medieval. In contrast, amongst the Irish gentry of Connacht only Bryen and Patrick figure in the top ten, with John and Thomas dominant (9 per cent each of the total), followed by William, Edmund, Nicholas, Robert and Richard.

The situation was very different amongst the new settler gentry of Ulster. John (21.3 per cent) remains the dominant first name, followed strongly by William (11.9 per cent), James (10.5 per cent), Robert (8.0 per cent) and Thomas (7.0 per cent). Richard, George, Henry, the striking name Alexander (Alasdair) and equally fashionable Irish/Scottish/Gaelic name of Hugh complete the ten most popular names and together constitute a further 20 per cent. Apart from Hugh, Thomas and the ever popular John, no other first name is shared with the top ten names of the old Irish gentry, while names such as Archbald, Arthur, Charles, Cromwell, Gustavus, Jason, Jacob and Joshua, through to Samuel, Theophilius and Tobias bespeak the new political and religious order.

A sample inspection of settler names amongst the 1641 Depositions from the counties of Armagh, Queen's County and Waterford shows that seven first names accounted for almost two-thirds of the total record.[26] John leads with 21 per cent, followed by Thomas (12 per cent) and William (10 per cent) and the following four names – Richard, James, Henry and Robert – combine to make a further 20 per cent. Another twelve names, headed by Nicholas and concluded by David, add a further 18 per cent. The remainder, which occur four times or less, include such wonderful names as Isaak, Jasper, Job, Marmaduke, Rowland, Tristan and Zelopheled. At the urban settler level, very little difference is to be noted. For example, in Cork city, John and Thomas lead the way, followed by Richard and William, with George, Edmund, James and Robert also very popular amongst the new urban elite.

The 1659 Census has little to tell us about incoming women's first names. Only southwest Cork yields a sample of its secrets with Mary (6), Anne (6) and Elizabeth (4) the most popular, with names such as Sophia, Hester, Abigail, Charity, Susan and Grace also represented. The 1641 Depositions – given the much greater sample of women's names – is a more fruitful source. Again, taking the women settlers from Co. Armagh, Queen's County and Waterford, the name Elizabeth is the clear first with 21 per cent, followed by Margaret (11 per cent), Mary (10 per cent), Ann(e) (9 per cent), Jane (8 per cent), Joanne (7.6 per cent) and Alice (6.5 per cent). Katherine and Ellinor score at 5 per cent, while Dorothy, Ellen, Grace and Isabel are each returned 2–3 per cent of the time. Names such as Charity, Eliza, Judith, Madeleine and Joyce speak to new cultural impulses, as both the reality and perception of 'Protestant' Christian names as opposed to 'Catholic' forms take deep root. Two very separate symbolic universes are thus created, mirroring the deep divisions in the society between the two ethno-religious traditions.

The hearth-money records for Co. Tipperary offers a contrasting picture of women's first names amongst the old Irish and the Old English. The leading name by far is Margaret (23.5 per cent), followed by Joan (12.8 per cent), Katherine (10.5 per cent) and Ellen (9 per cent), with Mary and Honor joint fifth. Eilís, More (Mór), Sheila (Síle) and Ellinor complete the top ten first names for women. Elizabeth, first among settler names, is joint twelfth with the strong ancient Irish name Úna. And within Co. Tipperary the Gaelic first names such as Mór, Síle and Úna are more strongly represented in northwest Tipperary amongst key families such as the Kennedys, Gleesons, Ryans and O'Dwyers. The pattern of pre-planter first names amongst the women of mid-seventeenth-century Co. Dublin, while very similar to Tipperary, does reveal subtle regional differences as well.[27] Margaret still heads the list but is followed strongly by Katherine. Mary (third) is in a much stronger position. Elizabeth is also more fashionable, as are Anastasia and Sarah. Distinctive Pale first names include Rose, Marie, Dorothy and Alison. There are very few Gaelic first names left amongst the women of south Co. Dublin. Owney (the anglicized version of Úna) occurs; Brigid is rare, while Finola also makes an appearance. By 1652, the universal saints' names introduced in the medieval period are dominant in the Pale and the old Gaelic first names have been eroded dramatically from this symbolic landscape.

The extent to which the intensification of Scots Presbyterian colonization and settlement in the second half of the seventeenth century and earlier part of the eighteenth century (and the later eighteenth- and especially nineteenth-century evangelical revivals) strengthened as well as narrowed the range of Old Testament-type first names amongst the descendants of this settler community still needs to be thoroughly researched. Likewise, the degree to which these naming patterns were gaelicized – if at all – needs further exploration. At the surname level, we do know that some Johnstons become MacShanes, but this appears to be a relatively rare process.

Irish surnames, as a consequence of conquest and anglicization, are diverse in number and form and the linguistic heritage of English colonization means that most surnames – like the placenames – have at the very minimum two forms: one in Irish and one in English. A name like Mac Con Aonaigh, 'son of the hound/warrior of the fair', ended up by the late nineteenth century as McEnanny, McNeany, McAneany, MacAneeny, MacAneny, MacEneany, MacNeney, MacNeany, Conhenny, Cunneeny, and twenty-seven other versions, including being (mis)translated as Bird in Ulster and Rabbitt in Connacht.[28] The story of early modern Irish surnames is therefore a story of diversities, pluralities, multiplicities, ambiguities, fluidities – a story of the wearing of many masks and the use of many forms of dress and address.

In 1500, Gaelic and gaelicized Ireland was still an expansive confident world and both the Irish language and Irish surname forms predominated in most regions. English speech and English name forms were then concentrated on the enclave of the Pale and Dublin, a few other key port-cities and regional pockets elsewhere. By the early eighteenth century, in contrast, the tide had turned dramatically in favour of the English language and British culture and in favour of anglicized surname forms. The Tudor, Cromwellian and Williamite conquests had oppressed Gaelic Ireland and the story of the beginnings of a linguistic conquest is chronicled with ever-increasing geographical precision between the 1530s and the 1660s in a large number of documents written in English. These begin with the fiants of Henry VIII and of Elizabeth, which provide in extraordinary detail the name forms of many in the Irish population over the sixteenth century.[29] The data on first names and surnames grow stronger in the seventeenth century via sources such as the 1641 Depositions and the hearth-money records and culminate in the key source for this book – the 1659 Census. The increasingly detailed manuscript maps of sixteenth- and seventeenth-century Ireland likewise rendered key Irish family names and their territories in English forms as the rechristening of people and landscapes gathered pace. Recognition of the significance of these English-language-based sources signals that the power to narrate Ireland's story and its naming systems had shifted dramatically by the seventeenth century.

Results from the mapping of the principal Irish surnames enumerated in the 1659 Census indicate that over one-third of these family names were rooted in a single barony and were not prevalent elsewhere in Ireland. Another 16 per cent of these surnames were particular to two or three adjacent baronies. Thus, close on one half of the large sample of principal Irish family names recorded in the 1659 Census were highly localized in distribution. MacLysaght has identified at least 350 surnames of this type, including, for example, MacAteer for Tyrone, Culkin for Galway, Daffey and Normoyle for Clare and Verling for Cork.[30] So despite more than a century of wars and plantations, most of the ancient Irish names and their family bearers persisted strongly in their ancestral localities. This evidence of powerful continuities and deep attachment to local worlds needs emphasizing to counter a possible overemphasis on drastic change and discontinuity.

Similarly, there are also the great regional names, still located in a single province and usually occupying two or three adjacent counties. The O'Sullivans and MacCarthys in southwest Munster and the O'Dohertys and O'Gallaghers of northwest Ulster are examples in this category which comprises a further 12 per cent of the 1659 Census total. Close on one-third of the mapped surnames are located over two or three provinces – names such as Butler, Dillon, Dalton, Fitzpatrick, Fitzgerald, Gormley, Fahey, Fallon, Donnelly, Doyle, Cantwell, Crotty, Cullen, Egan, Healy, O'Hara, O'Rourke, O'Toole and Russell. Finally, we come to the universal names found in all four provinces – including Brennan, (O) Brien, Daly, Kearney, Moore and Smith, as well as other great patronymic family names such as O'Connor, O'Kelly and Martin.

As early as 1659, not only the anglicization but also the fragmentation of Irish surname forms was well on its way. Three surnames – that of Fitzmorris, O'Brien and Morrogh (Murphy) – are each rendered in at least twelve different ways in the Census. A further 19 names – from Byrne and Clarke, through Curran and Nolan to Ryan and O'Sullivan – are all rendered in at least eight, and often up to eleven, variations. A further 41 names, from Duffy and Brennan to Crowley and McDonagh, are rendered in five to seven ways, while an additional 24 names, including Brannagh and Cahill, O'Riordan and O'Rourke, are returned in at least four variant forms. The splintering of Irish cultural and political formations is symbolized in the fracturing of its surname forms, as is the internal differentiation of naming patterns within one linguistic community.

The Census also allows us to map the precise distribution of English and Scottish settler names in the mid-seventeenth century. We are still not fully certain how Petty managed to instruct his clerks to make the crucial ethnic classification that allowed them to distinguish between the 'English' (and Scots) surnames and those of the 'Irish'. The likely process was that Petty's clerks – under the strict supervision of Petty's two most loyal and efficient lieutenants, his cousin John Pettie and the tireless assistant Thomas Taylor – were instructed to abstract and add up the total of Irish family names townland by townland from the parish poll-tax lists.[31] Alternatively, the clerks were also instructed to identify the settlers by their distinctive family names. The evidence for Co. Fermanagh suggests the latter strategy, since, alone for this county, not only are the principal Irish names of specific districts recorded but so are the 'principal Scots and English and their number'. As it happens, the Armstrongs head the list with 47 adults, the John-stons follow with 34, the Eliots 28, the Grahams 21, the Nixons 14, while the Cathcarts, Belfores, Croziers, Irwins, Montgomerys, Nobles and Scotts each recorded from 5 to 10 adults. It is also clear that Co. Down and particularly Co. Antrim presented special problems to the clerks in distinguishing between the local Irish, Scots Gaelic settlers and other planters with 'Mac' prefixes.

Nevertheless, the picture portrayed in Fig. 11.4 is as reliable a guide as we are ever likely to get of the relative distribution of English/Scots names *vis-à-vis* those of the Irish for the mid-seventeenth century. Figure 11.4 summarizes at the barony scale the level of immigrant penetration in Antrim, most of Down, north Armagh, much of the county of Londonderry, east Donegal, and a core around the lakes of Fermanagh. Key settler names include Smith, Brown, Murray, Wilson, Clarke, Johnston, Thompson, Robinson, Reid and Graham. This map illuminates the cutting edge of a southwestward frontier as it advanced into the less densely populated edges of Connacht and the northwest Midlands generally. This advancing front of settler names was marching against an existing Gaelic world and in this encounter some of the older populations were pushed further south into Omeath in the Cooley peninsula to the east, and the Galway/Clare borderlands and islands in the west.

The second most powerful core of planter surnames pivoted around the Pale region and Dublin city. Apart from a strategic northern salient, planter family names are only weakly represented in the rich hearthlands of north Leinster. But to the south and west, a new wide band of significant minorities bearing a great diversity of planter names stretched right across Queen's County, King's County and the edges of north Tipperary to reach the Shannon and Limerick. On the other flank, these settler names curved southwards to colonize the west Wicklow/north Wexford borderlands. Third, there was a southwestern core of a great variety of planter names pivoting around Cork city and the Munster plantation precincts. Beyond these three cores, Irish family names predominated.

The 1641 Depositions, and particularly the far greater survival rate of records of the hearth monies for many of the Ulster counties, provide further insights into the distribution and character of settler names as they were carried into the northern half of Ireland. Philip Robinson has made a major contribution here with his impressive maps of Scottish and English settlement zones, based, amongst other criteria, on surname analysis.[32] Using surname analysis from the seventeenth and eighteenth centuries, Bill Macafee has also pinpointed planter *vis-à-vis* Gaelic Irish sectors for the Maghera region of south Londonderry,[33] while Brian Turner and the late Brendan Adams have furthered our understanding of what they term 'the

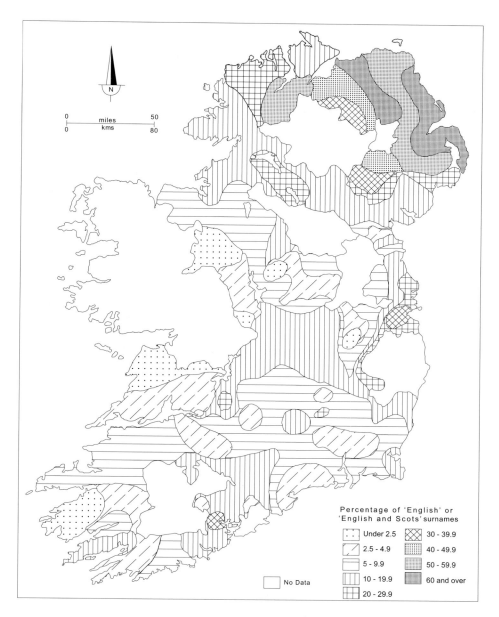

11.4   Relative distribution of immigrant New English and Scottish surnames, 1660

surname landscapes' of Fermanagh and Leitrim.[34] Further south it has likewise
been possible to pinpoint the spread of English settlers in Tipperary using its
hearth-money records (see Fig. 9.7, p. 339). As in Ulster, one notes the key role of
the towns as gathering points and as springboards for funnelling settlers into the
countryside. This surname analysis allows us to track these families and individuals as they spread out along the existing roads into the villages, farms, castles and
Big Houses.

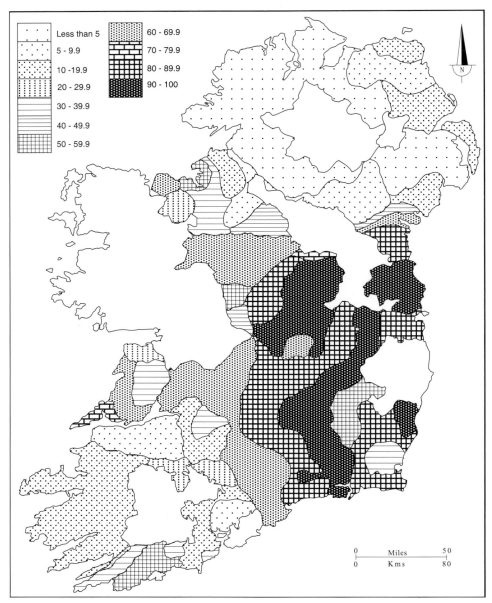

11.5   Percentage distribution of the non-retention of 'O' and 'Mac' forms in Irish family surnames
c.1660 (based on barony summaries of 'Principal Irish names' in 1659 Census)

These detailed seventeenth-century surname distributions also indicate the
fissures along which the English language spread at the expense of the Irish
language. Along these linguistic interfaces, compromises, confusions, ambiguities and pluralities abounded. My own name Smyth/Smith (it has already
splintered!) is the commonest surname in England and the fifth most common
name in Ireland. As MacLysaght explains: 'some of the Smiths are descendants of

settlers and traders but equally probably at least 80 per cent of the Smiths of Cavan are of the stock of Mac Gowans or Gowans who, under pressure of alien legislation and/or social influence, accepted the translated form and used it ever since'.[35] And where I come from in north Tipperary, the ancestors of the present-day Smiths are remembered in the mid-seventeenth-century hearth-money records as the 'Macingownes'.

Yet a brief survey of the fiants of the second half of the sixteenth century shows that both Gaelic first names and surnames were still rendered in their older forms. The seventeenth century is absolutely decisive for the transformation and anglicization of surnames. As MacLysaght notes, this was the period 'during which our surnames assumed approximately the forms ordinarily in use in Ireland today'.[36] The seventeenth century thus marks the great divide between late medieval and modern Ireland and its transformations in surname forms. (Mis)translations, abbreviations, elisions, excisions, misunderstandings abound, a process accelerated further with the later exodus to America.

Finally, the 1659 Census list of 'principal Irish family names' is also of immense value in reconstructing both the late medieval attrition of the 'O' and 'Mac' prefixes in family surnames by the mid-seventeenth century, as well as providing an essential benchmark for an analysis of the later processes of regaelicization and regional expressions of such processes as surname renaissance and symbolic decolonization. Figure 11.5 outlines regional variations in the percentage of the principal Irish family names which displayed *neither* an 'O' nor a 'Mac' form in the mid-seventeenth century. One has to allow that Irish family names in the 1659 enumeration include a number of Old English names that had not been gaelicized. This therefore affects the distribution pattern, especially in Leinster.

Nevertheless, one can clearly identify four cultural regions. First, much of Leinster, with a core in the Pale that expands westwards into the Midlands and southwards down the Barrow valley to Waterford, is seen to be already a strongly anglicized zone. In this region, powerful pressures linked to the Anglo-Norman colonization, the deliberate propagation of the English language as a general policy dating back to legislation such as that of 1465, which required every Irishman living within the Pale to take an English second name,[37] all whittled back the distribution of 'O' and 'Mac' names. The impact of Dublin's anglicizing influences, as well as the early Queen's County/King's County and Wicklow/Wexford plantations, is already evident by the mid-seventeenth century, accelerating this pattern of name modification and transformation. As with the first names, a sharp linguistic and cultural frontier is reproduced by the distribution of 'O' and 'Mac' forms along the Leinster/Ulster borderlands.

The second major cultural region expands from this northern frontier zone into northwest Leinster and east Connacht and stretches south through east Clare and much of Tipperary and Waterford towards an outlet in southwest Cork. This is the great hybrid cultural region that emerges on a number of maps of this later medieval/early modern world. Here, powerful cultural influences from both gaelicizing and anglicizing forces met, clashed and fused. By the mid-seventeenth century, however, the cultural and linguistic balance – as evidenced by the 50–70 per cent attrition of 'O' and 'Mac' name forms – had already swung in favour of an anglicizing model. It also suggests that in these regions families were adapting to the demands of the new economic and political regime.

Parts of counties Galway and Mayo may have also belonged to this transitional/hybrid cultural region but it is also likely that their most western baronies showed many affinities with Clare, which displays a complicated mosaic of naming adaptations. And southwest Clare points the way towards the third major cultural region, comprising most of south and west Munster. Indeed, a relatively sharp frontier extends from mid-Clare into the hills of Tipperary and southwards into the west Waterford coastlands. South and west of this line, a far greater resistance to the anglicization of surnames is revealed for the mid-seventeenth century. A much more intact Gaelic linguistic and naming structure is suggested here, with significant local core areas of strength in both the east Cork and the north Kerry/Limerick hearthlands. These distinctive naming patterns may also confirm the location of traditional clan structures, still conserving old ways of living and naming.

Ulster is again the most outstanding cultural region in its stubborn retention of its 'O' and 'Mac' name forms. Over much of this northern province – from Lecale in Co. Down to the peninsulas of Donegal – less than 5 per cent of the principal Irish names have lost the 'O' or 'Mac' forms. This region of great continuity extends over much of Co. Leitrim (and probably Co. Cavan) as well. And as seen with the regional variations in Gaelic first name patterns, south Ulster presents a very sharp frontier to the anglicizing world of north Leinster.

The processes of surname transformation in the eighteenth century – the mistranslations, the admixture of forms, the attritions – need much further study. For example, MacLysaght notes that the great variety of very specific surnames as revealed in the Elphin diocesan survey of 1766 has been much reduced by the nineteenth century.[38] A summary of the status of family names as rendered in the English language in the 1766 survey of Cloyne diocese provides other clues to the deepening of the anglicization process by the mid-eighteenth century and the forces undermining the 'O' and 'Mac' forms.[39] Only 3 per cent of 'Irish Papist' surnames for this region of north and east Cork are recorded (or transcribed) as retaining the 'O' and 'Mac' forms by 1766. The list of surviving 'O' and 'Mac' names is as follows: MacAuliffe (63), MacCarthy (50), McGrath (48), McNamee (33), McDaniel (27), McDonnell (22), Maguire (8), O/McBrian (7), O'Callaghan (6), O'Connor (3). Five other 'O' or 'Mac' names are each recorded twice and 18 other surnames retain the 'O' or 'Mac' form at least once. And one of the most telling statistics is that the MacCarthy surname form is outnumbered by three to one by the diminished 'Cartie/Carthy' form. By the mid-eighteenth century, the flattening and erosion of the Gaelic name forms appears to be astonishing.

However, it should be remembered that the evidence for the 1766 census was recorded by mainly English-speaking Church of Ireland clergymen. Their rendering of family names may have diverged significantly from local usage in the Irish language, which was then dominant in most of the diocese of Cloyne. The linguistic frontier was a complex one.

The Geography of Language Change

In this turbulent world the pressures on the Irish language were both persistent and many-sided. The poems of the dispossessed fleetingly captured the dark night and despair of the old aristocrats and their praise poets, whatever about the feelings of the occupying tenants.[40] It is striking that the first English words to gain currency in the Irish language move in along the fissures that the new political and cultural hegemony had created and consolidated. Words such as 'execution', 'húda' (hood), 'transplantation' and 'tax' reflect the military and legal conquest and the resultant displacement, and the growth of effective government administration. 'Precept', 'sect' and 'pópaireacht' (popery) are symbols of the new ethnic-religious divisions and stratifications in the society. The symbols of economic change and state control are encompassed by the intrusion of 'ionncam' (income), 'sínéireacht' (act of signing) and 'proinnta' (printed) into the Irish texts and poetry. The new order of a centralizing state, regulating the economy and issuing edicts, and an estate system based on written leases as opposed to the local lordship with its oral contracts and agreements, are all symbolized in these early linguistic fissures. Terms like 'rogue' and 'gaffer' also call attention to the new systems of social stratification, subordination, shaming and marginalization that are being put in place.[41]

An unequal relationship had begun between an imperial, urbanizing, print-based and aggressively expansive English culture and language and an Irish language and culture that was more rural-based, more oral/aural in style and far more manuscript dependent. The 1465 legislation, as well as requiring Irishmen to take English surnames, also required those 'dwelling in the counties of Dublin, Meath, Uriel [Louth] and Kildare' to dress and wear beards like Englishmen and swear allegiance to the crown. The famous 1366 Statutes of Kilkenny were confirmed in 1495, forbidding the Old English to practise the Irish language, or take part in the Irish pastimes of hurling and dancing, as well as fosterage amongst or intermarriage with the Irish. Degaelicizing was, therefore, very much a part of the policy pursued by the centralizing state administrators under the Tudors. An Act for English Order, Habits and Language, passed as early as 1537 by the Dublin parliament, planned to make use of various strategies, including teaching in schools to propagate the English language. Earlier still, in 1531 Henry VIII was requiring of all his true Irish subjects 'to use and speak commonly the English language'.[42]

Pressures to conform and adopt English order, habits and language intensified from the middle decades of the sixteenth century and culminated in its second half with a series of additional Acts, ordinances and instructions to ensure the spread of both the English language and the English Reformation Church. Here, Ireland's complex linguistic story is further complicated by the Elizabethans' attempts to use the Irish language as a proslytizing tool. It was Elizabeth I who sent a Gaelic fount to Ireland to facilitate the printing of a translation of the Bible. The first ever book printed in Irish (in 1570) was a Protestant catechism, which contained a brief introduction to the spelling and sounds of the Irish language.

Subsequently, the whole of the New Testament was translated into Irish and printed in Dublin in 1602–3.[43]

Yet Irish language and culture was continuously assailed and ridiculed across the same period. The recognition of the centrality of language in shaping cultural and political identities was a cornerstone of both Tudor reforms within England and of their expansionist policies in Ireland: the Irish must be enclosed within the frame of the English language. Language was seen to be part of the armoury of the state – a loaded weapon with which to attack the foundations of Irish culture. Hence the legislation against the use of Irish in areas of English rule. Hence Sidney's reformation policies to abolish the Irish language and use of martial law to execute the key adherents of the Irish cultural order, whether monks, priests, brehons, poets or lords.[44] Hence the English chroniclers' cumulative assaults, led by Spenser and Moryson, which ridiculed Irish culture, its history, character and language.[45]

The legislative, propagandist and infrastructural drive for the adoption and spread of the English language further intensifies over the first half of the seventeenth century. Catholic schools are prohibited. The expansion of English common law across the whole country at the expense of Irish brehon law is crucial here. Sir John Davies's observations are instructive:

> Civil assemblies and assizes and sessions have reclaimed the Irish from their wildness, caused them to cut off their glibs and long hair, to convert their mantles into cloaks, to conform themselves to the manner of England in all their behaviour and outward forms. And because they find a great inconvenience in moving their suits by an interpreter, they do for the most part send their children to schools, especially to learn the English language. . . . For heretofore, the neglect of law made the English degenerate and become Irish: and now, on the other side, the execution of the law doth make the Irish grow civil and become English.[46]

Although Davies was more than a little premature in his predictions about the levels of Irish conformity, this statement indicates the processes that put the Irish under linguistic pressure; it also identifies a recurring theme in the wider literature – not only conformity of language was required but also of dress. The mantle and trousers must yield to breeches, stockings and jerkin. In short, total anglicization.

It was the first half of the seventeenth century 'which saw the beginning of the real decline of the Irish language'.[47] Like the Spanish conquest of the Aztecs and Incas, poets, priests, brehons, scribes and schoolteachers were key targets in this programme of cultural destruction and transformation: and, as in Mexico, Peru and elsewhere,[48] the memory of the older culture was assaulted by the extensive destruction of books, manuscripts, repositories and buildings that had been produced, stored and built by the Irish monks, lay scholars and their patrons. Ireland was seen as a 'New England'. Its poets record the radical transformation of landscape, the new methods of fortification and intensive cultivation – 'tilling the land in the English style' – that followed on from the marginalization of many Irish by English and Scottish settlers.

The recognition by Irish-speaking literati of the depth of the cultural and political crisis facing Irish civilization seems a rather belated one. That recognition comes in the first instance from émigrés on the European mainland.[49] The older patterns of domestic life were being broken down by the early seventeenth century as new powerful migration links with a large number of European cities (see Fig. 3.1, p. 57) deepened both the education and outlook of many Irish men and women. Seathrún Céitinn was a central figure here, not only important for his writing of the highly influential *Foras Feasa ar Éirinn* but also because he wrote the text in a modernized, more accessible style.[50] He not only recognized the need to forge together the strengths of both the Gaelic and Old English Catholic traditions, he also saw the need to modernize Irish grammar and spelling so as to be a more effective communicator. The great irony is that this highly influential text only circulated in manuscript. It was not printed in full until the twentieth century, a very different story to the number and diversity of printed books in English that appeared in Irish libraries and bookshops in the seventeenth century,[51] and which increased rapidly in number over the first decades of the eighteenth century. Céitinn also wrote a number of important devotional works – again part of that early to mid-seventeenth-century continental response to the need for Catholic religious literature. A number of such religious texts were printed at Brussels, Louvain and Rome.

However, the linguistic interface was altogether more complicated, confusing and contradictory than the above descriptions suggest. *Pairlement Chloinne Tomáis* points up other dimensions of the language dialectic by the middle decades of the seventeenth century.[52] The use of the model of the parliament (as indeed the extensive use of the form and language of the English court system) in Irish poetry and commentaries is very instructive. The poem presents a biting satire, written from an Irish aristocratic viewpoint, on the newly acquired manners, behaviours and pretensions of a rising/opportunistic Irish tenant-farmer class. It therefore reflects not only change at the upper levels of Irish society, where a New English landlord class is replacing the old aristocratic landowners, it also announces class and cultural transformations beneath that level. This emergent tenant-farming class is seen to be anxious to acquire a facility in the English language – hence their admiration for the stuttering, broken English already acquired by Tomás. This concern also applies to their ambition to school their children in English, to adapt to English legal and dress norms, as well as adjust more fully to a market economy. A striking image from the poem is the dialogue between the New English trader and Tomás (in his broken English) about the purchase of some tobacco. Ireland's place in the Atlantic/American trading networks is here integrated with the acquisition of English speech and the now very popular consumption of tobacco. Clearly, certain emergent categories in Irish society are moving with the fashions of the day – much to the disgust of the old aristocratic patrons and their client poets.

When we look at crucial domains of language for Irish and English by, say, the early 1660s, the following picture emerges. At the military/political/administrative level a whole array of New English officials and agents have become established in Dublin, with all its key ruling institutions, in the county/shires, in town government, as well as in other customs functions in the port-cities. Backing up this new official 'civil service' world were close on 300 'officered' garrisons of various sizes, ready to defend and uphold the rule of English law by physical coercion. Judges and lawyers exercised that law through the courts – a crucial domain for land litigation and ironically parodied, imitated and admired in Irish literature, as revealed, for example, in the activities of the courts of poetry.[53] This island-wide spread of colonial courts and garrisons was dominated by English-speakers, as were the administrative arms of county and town government. Likewise, the landlord estate system, established across the island, printed its leases, managed its rental books and, where necessary, used writs and summonses in the English language only. At the level of the barony and the parish, the Protestant constable or subconstable – outside of Connacht and Clare – were almost invariably English-speakers. This prestigious ruling caste of landlords, judges, barristers and attorneys, officers, officials and agents came to constitute the ruling Protestant Ascendancy – the apex of the English language and cultural system in Ireland.[54]

Economic development and differentiation had seen the penetration into most regions of new commodities and services, as well as the collection from them of a greatly increased agricultural surplus. Mediums varied between barter, exchange and, most particularly, the soon-to-be-dominant currency – money. Central places for these transactions and the language exchanges that went with them were the port-cities, towns, villages and fair sites. By 1660, the leading port-cities were dominated in their core export/import functions by English-speakers of English or Scottish descent. Outside of the Old Pale and the south, most of the towns were newly planted, again ruled by English-speaking traders and artisans, as well as the officials in institutions such as free schools, sessions-houses and market-houses and gaols. A new bourgeoisie had emerged in these towns. Their main streets, their market places and fair days had emerged as the great meeting-places for linguistic encounters – great forgers of new speechways and identities.

In what we may define as the more narrowly linguistic dimension of this cultural encounter, England sought to penetrate and spread the English language into all Irish-speaking territories and localities. As it happened, in this battle between a Germanic and a Celtic language, English is characterized by a weakly synthetic form, far more flexible and simplified in structure as compared with a language such as Irish (or, for example, Arabic). These languages are characterized by great formal complexity, 'in which classificatory ideas such as gender, number, case, relative tense and mood are expressed with considerable nicety and in a great variety of ways'.[55] The key cultural institutions that empires normally use in the diffusion of their language are churches and schools. In Ireland such institutions, therefore, were the Anglican churches and schools, diocesan cathedrals and schools, and Trinity College, as well as the more secular printing houses, bookshops and scholarly/scientific societies.

Here, however, the geographical analysis of imperial expansion and language domains falters. The battle between the Reformation and Counter-Reformation Churches in Ireland had created a bifurcated, or should one say, a trifurcated, territorial system between Anglican, Catholic and Presbyterian Churches. The outlawing of Catholic schools, monasteries and colleges highlighted the Tudor drive to establish uniformity of belief and language in Ireland. However, Catholic chapels and illegal/underground schools (later called hedge schools), as well as Presbyterian meeting-houses-cum-schools, signalled the failure of English religious policy.[56] In the mid-seventeenth century, schools and chapels catering for the disenfranchised Catholic majority were not likely to be agents for the spread of the English language. However, by the early eighteenth century the language used in Catholic institutions varied widely – hybridity and complexity ruled.

In the domain of communications, the New English state in Ireland had engineered a road and sea network, complete with bridges, urban and village nodes, post-stations, naval bases and merchant shipping facilities. This evolving network carried government edicts, books, newspapers, letters and leases between different places. By the 1660s, such a network of communications (see Fig. 11.6) was still only partially developed. Yet practically all the messages carried on this network were written or printed in English. Even the fluent and literate Irish-speaker wrote his/her letter in English.

We are now in a position to assess the overall geography of the dialectic between the English and Irish languages up to the mid-seventeenth century. Kenneth Nicholls's map of the area of common law, the area of brehon law and the area of 'mixed customs' provides a benchmark for understanding the trajectory of the languages from 1500.[57] The Old Pale area and south Wexford, where common law still prevailed, can be assumed to be bilingual areas, with English dominant in the public spheres of law, government and administration. Until the end of the sixteenth century this situation did not change dramatically in these regions. Indeed, there was a further strengthening of Irish within the Pale, consequent on migration from the marchlands into the Pale. On the other hand, the Indian summer of Old English territorial expansions into these borderlands from 1540 onwards, the intrusion island-wide of New English settlers into former Church lands and the creation of pockets of settlers after the Queen's County/King's County and Munster plantations clearly affected the linguistic balance in these areas.

In the second zone of 'mixed customs', involving parts of east Down and Antrim, the borderlands of the Pale, mid-Wexford and an extensive zone stretching from Kilkenny into east and mid-Munster but excluding the two Gaelic regions of southwest Munster (south Kerry and west Cork) and Thomond (Clare and north Tipperary), English was known in the towns and port-cities and sometimes used in drawing up regional ordinances, as in the Ormond lordship.[58] Throughout this zone, however, Irish was dominant.

Over the vast territories of Ulster, all of Connacht, the west Midlands and upland south Leinster, the Irish language and the brehon laws prevailed absolutely after a century and a half of expansion eastwards at the expense of English and the common law. Richard Stanihurst summarizes the situation by 1577: 'all the cities and towns in Ireland with Fingal, the Kingsland (Dublin county), Meath, the counties of Kildare, Louth, Wexford [south] speak to this day English'; in all other places 'the native language is Irish'.[59] He concludes that both

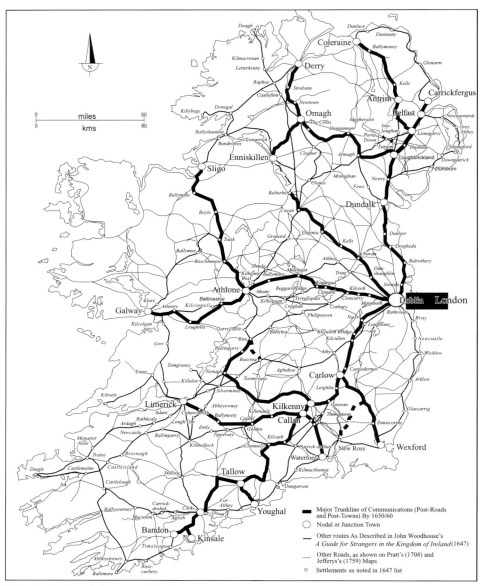

11.6   Evolution of the networks of communications in Ireland, 1650–1750 (based on Figures 5.9, 5.10, and 7.4 [p. 143, p. 144 and p. 198] in J.H. Andrews's *Shapes of Ireland*, Dublin, 1997)

the four provinces and every other region 'differs in the Irish tongue, every county having its dialect or peculiar manner in speaking the language'.[60]

By the late sixteenth/early seventeenth century this picture is beginning to change. The challenge to land titles and the complex and lengthy negotiations-cum-attritions, involved in the tortuous changeover from brehon law to common law, required that the old landowners – both Old English as well as Gaelic – should endeavour to educate their sons in the English law and language. These changes were dwarfed, however, by the impact of large scale migrations by English-speakers following on from the plantations, formal and informal, of the seventeenth century. The admittedly limited evidence of the 1641 Depositions (limited particularly for the northwestern and northeastern parts of Ulster) already confirms the widespread extent of English and Scots settlement. Only four of Munster's baronies reveal no settler presence; there were only sixteen such baronies in Leinster, concentrated in Co. Meath to the north and mid and south Co. Kilkenny in the south. South, mid and west Connacht were least disturbed by settler and English speech incursions: only east Roscommon, south Leitrim and coastal Sligo reveal New English expansion and the reinforcing of English speech in such regions. Otherwise, the 1641 evidence confirms a powerful axis of English speech moving down the Bann and Lagan corridors and curving westwards into Fermanagh and southwestwards into the borders of Connacht and Leinster. There is a second core zone of English speech extending southwards from Dublin to Wexford and westwards into Queen's County/King's County. Finally, the distribution of English speech and settlement over much of south and mid-Munster is very striking, with Cork and west Waterford the fulcrums of the new language (see Fig. 4.4, p. 125).

Equally striking in 1641 is the levels of bilingualism shown on each side of the political-cum-ethnic/religious divide. Quite a number of settlers – including a significant number of women witnesses – infer a knowledge of spoken Irish. Likewise, the evidence shows quite a number of the Irish insurgents reported as alternating between English and Irish, depending on context and audience.[61] In Munster, for example, it is clear that levels of bilingualism are significant on each side of the frontier/contact zone.[62]

Petty's poll-tax evidence for 1660, which some scholars have wrongly interpreted as a *specific* measure of Irish and English languages,[63] is still most helpful here. The depth of both the migration of settlers and new languages into all of Ulster is confirmed, as is the frontier of expansion into east Connacht and north Leinster. Likewise, the south and middle Leinster core of English speech is revealed, now spilling over into Lower Ormond in Tipperary and reaching southwestwards to Limerick city. Furthermore, a strong core of English settlement and speechways is revealed across mid-Munster. Petty's poll-tax also reveals the overwhelming dominance of New English and Scottish settlers and their cultures in the new towns of Ulster, while elsewhere New English settlers and speech are well established in the port-cities, the county and episcopal towns, as well as the new inland plantation towns (see Fig. 11.4, p. 397).

If we assume that only settler families and their offspring spoke English or Ulster English, these 1660 patterns confirm that at the very least 22 per cent of the population knew and spoke these languages. However, if we add the many families of Old English descent who knew and spoke the English language, as well as the increasing number of Irish-speakers who for reasons of proximity to large settler speech-regions, for reasons of trade, social advancement and/or dealing with the writ-governed world of the courts and landlordism and/or assimilation to the Established or Nonconformist Churches, it is likely that the number of English-speakers in the country in 1660 constituted, at the minimum, one-third of the total population. Likewise, assuming a minimum level of bilingualism amongst the families of settlers or settler descendants, the total number on the island who understood and spoke Irish constituted well over four-fifths of the population.

We therefore have two great blocks of Irish- and English-speakers: Irish is still massively dominant both in numbers and distribution – especially over the west and south – but very significant regional clusters of English speech have also emerged. We have identified three critical cores of English speech expansion: in the north; in Dublin and the New Pale of Leinster; and a mid/south Munster region anchored on Bandon/Cork/Kinsale/Youghal. Outliers of English speech are scattered across the island in new plantation towns, estate villages and landlord quarters. Likewise, a whole series of contact zones of interpenetration between Irish and English speech can also be inferred from the 1660 map. A hybrid linguistic group has emerged in these middle spaces, which include the old port-cities. In 1660 it is likely that this mediator group, which understood if not spoke both English and Irish, constituted at least one-fifth of the population. This group of middlemen/women, agents, innkeepers, shopkeepers, pedlars, carters, artisans, midwives, seasonal migrants and servants, and other more mobile classes in the population occupied key cultural hinge positions, facilitating and lubricating the workings of the deeply divided society. At this language interface, ambivalence, hybridity, opportunism and, indeed, sadness and shame were often intermingled.

By the early 1730s, the Protestant population constituted around 27 per cent of the total population of the island. For the greater part, one can assume that this is an English-speaking population. Between 1660 and 1730, Ulster English had clearly gained significant ground.[64] Ulster Protestants then constituted nearly 60 per cent of the population of the province, utterly triumphant in the northeast, where it is likely that some Irish-speaking populations had been assimilated (see Fig. 11.7). But there was also a dramatic and aggressive pushing southwards of settlement and speechways into south Armagh and Cavan, and the establishment of secondary cores for expansion in Longford and coastal Sligo. Nevertheless, it is noticeable how few settler descendants occupy the north Leinster lowlands, where the strong Catholic, Irish-speaking farmers of both Meath and the village county north of the Boyne in Louth represent a zone of stiff resistance.[65] Another core of English speech extends out of Dublin in a narrow salient to create a secondary if dynamic core of expansion over much of King's County and Queen's County. This latter core is extending English speech into the adjacent baronies in north Tipperary and north Kilkenny. Co. Wicklow then constitutes a powerful centre of Elizabethan English speech, extending into the adjacent western borderlands. Louis Cullen concludes that the Irish language had virtually disappeared from counties Wicklow, Westmeath, Laois, and possibly north Wexford by the end of the seventeenth century.[66]

However, the most striking feature of the 1732 'Protestant/Papist' distribution is the significant weakening of the Protestant presence in Munster. Pockets of

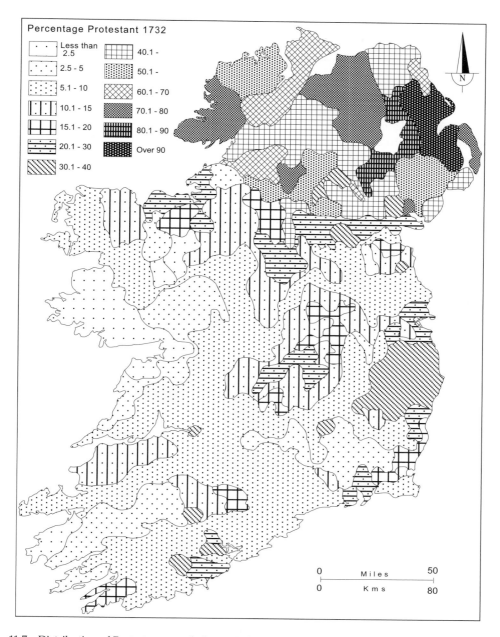

11.7   Distribution of Protestant population in Ireland in 1732 (based on MS. 1742, Lambeth Palace Library, London)

strength extended from Cork city and harbour region to Bandon and along some southern coastal parishes, and in parts of the Blackwater valley, with an outlier of English speech along the Mizen peninsula. In Munster, settler assimilation to both Irish speech and Catholicism may have been the highest in the country. The complex corrugated topography of Munster – its interweaving of hills and valleys

– may have been a factor here. The Munster plantation had taken place before ethno-religious divisions had deepened and soured relationships; indeed, a number of the original planter landowners and, one assumes, some of their tenants were of the Catholic tradition. It is also clear that a number of planter families were Catholic and probably bilingual by the time of the 1641 rising/rebellion, including, for example, the grandson of Edmund Spenser.[67] It is also relevant to note that the Munster plantation precincts did not constitute a compact, contiguous region of settlement and English speech. Rather, they consisted of a scattered series of large estates/islands across mid-Munster, surrounded by a very vibrant and deeply distinctive Irish-speaking culture, headed by still powerful landowners and patrons living in their tower-houses and town houses. Assimilation pressures in this region, therefore, bore more heavily on the Protestant English-speaking communities. The long-term effects of the 1641 rising/rebellion were also severe. The 1732 distribution map likely reflects the consequences of these pressures: at the very least a higher level of bilingualism must have characterized this planter class.

Nationally, however, it is even more likely that the assimilation of many Irish to an English-speaking world had accelerated at an even faster pace between the 1660s and the mid-eighteenth century. In Co. Dublin the Irish language was on the retreat in the 1720s and 1730s. Poet and scribe Tadgh Ó Neachtáin then complained that the Irish language was being forsaken by the nobles, who were changing their names and 'going to the Parliament speaking English'.[68] Increasingly pessimistic views about the Irish language is evidenced by the 1730s – particularly in relation to the decline of its associated high culture and the disappearance of the patrons who had supported it. The desire for social inclusion and economic advancement amongst the aristocracy and the upper middle classes accelerated this process of language change. The massive commercialization of the economy as the eighteenth century progressed saw both the Irish gentry and a growing merchant middle class obsessed with the need for educating their children in English – including for example, in the Sligo city hinterland.[69] By the mid-eighteenth century bilingualism was solidly established in most rural counties in Ulster and Leinster.[70]

As Niall Ó Cíosaín has pointed out, the longer term response of the Catholic Church to the need for religious materials written/printed in the Irish language was very different to its Breton counterpart and indeed to the Nonconformist Churches in Wales.[71] In both these Celtic-speaking countries, either printed Catholic religious texts or Reformation materials and hymns were produced in great numbers to serve the needs of their respective religious communities. It is true that a number of Catholic catechism and sermon books were printed in the early decades of the eighteenth century. Yet the script for these religious materials is in the Roman fount and renders the Irish language phonetically. Such texts clearly reflect a society of Catholic clergy that was already literate in English. In this bilingual situation, where imperial English holds the upper hand in all other public domains of language, it was imperative that Catholic religious materials should be produced in the vernacular, that is, in the Irish language.[72] Such was not the case, despite the patronage offered by some bishops and priests to the poets and scribes of the Irish manuscript tradition.

Irish scholars and schoolmasters, deeply immersed in the business of Irish manuscript transcription, were equally at home with the English language. The marginalia of their manuscripts indicates this, as does their involvement in training their students in modes of legal writing in English, dealing with issues like distraints, leases, receipts, parish summonses to repair roads, claiming non-liability for the payment of hearth-tax – and in a deepening monetized economy – the writing of promissory notes.[73] The teaching of mathematics and arithmetic – addition, subtraction, multiplication, geometry – were all taught and learned in English. As Cullen notes, this world of commerce and law gave enormous prestige to the English language and emphasized its practical value.[74] This imperial language and culture carried high prestige, and where proficiency in speaking and reading English was accomplished before literacy in Irish was achieved, there was no going back.

Between 1660 and 1750, the number of both English-speakers and bilingual speakers increased significantly. By the early 1750s, it is likely that at least half the Irish population knew and understood English. Equally, it is likely that well over half were still primarily Irish-speakers. There were great swathes of territory where Irish still reigned supreme – in north Leinster, in a core area of Irish speech in south Leinster centred on south Kilkenny and across much of Munster and most of Connacht. It was in the poorer lands of Munster, Connacht and west Ulster that the most dramatic increases in the number of Irish-speakers occurred in the late eighteenth and early nineteenth centuries. On the other hand, the eastern half of Ireland was already an English-speaking world and elsewhere English had become the language of the powerful and the socially ambitious.[75] The mid-eighteenth century, therefore, marks a fundamental watershed in the fate of both languages.

In Ireland in the eighteenth century, high levels of illiteracy were associated with regions of Irish speech; conversely high levels of literacy presumed a prior capacity to know and speak English (see Fig. 11.8). Using projections of the oldest age groups from the 1841 Census, one can make guesstimates of levels of literacy for the 1750s and 1760s.[76] It is clear that the highest levels of literacy and English speech are located in the northeastern counties of Down, Antrim and Armagh. Here, it is also clear that literacy levels were highest amongst the mainly middle-class Presbyterians, somewhat lower in the more broadly based Anglican communities and substantially less in the Catholic community.[77] The Catholic group was dominated by the poorest classes, who often lived in more remote upland localities, faraway from the facilities of towns and villages and who could not afford to pay for a travelling schoolmaster. It is also clear that there is a significant transition zone of advancing literacy in English in a wide area that stretched from east Donegal and swung across through all of south Ulster. A frontier of resistance occurs in Oriel, where high levels of illiteracy characterized a core of Irish-speakers resident in north Meath, Louth and southern baronies of Armagh, Monaghan and Cavan. This resilient Irish-speaking region benefited from a strong

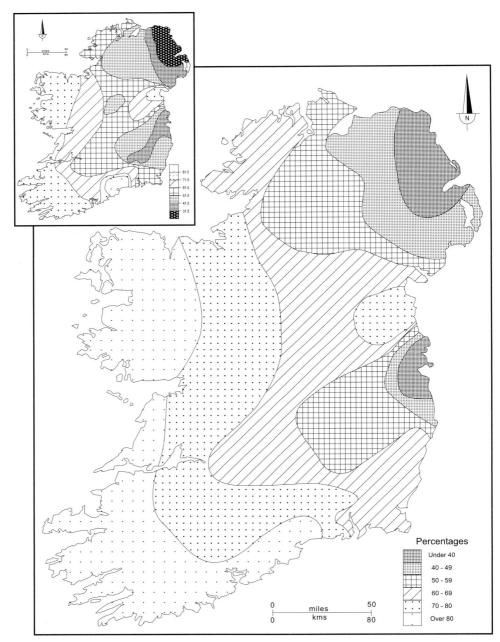

11.8   Generalized map of overall levels of illiteracy in the English language in Ireland by the mid-eighteenth century; inset: male illiteracy levels *c.*1750 (based on materials in the Introduction, 1841 Census)

literate tradition in Irish amongst poets, such as Peadar Ó Doirnín and Aodh MacGiolla Ghunna.[78]

In contrast, the zone of higher literacy in southwest Ulster had carved out a bridgehead into the western Midlands via Longford and Westmeath, in particular, to connect up with the large Leinster zone of higher literacy and English speech. The northern boundary of this latter region stretched from Westmeath to Dublin and extended southwards from Westmeath into Queen's County, King's County, Carlow, on to Wexford and back up to Wicklow. Another major transitional zone of expanding literacy extended out of the south Midlands into the lower Shannon region, north Tipperary and north Kilkenny.

The rapid advance of English over much of Leinster relates to a combination of powerful factors, in addition to the impact of settler concentrations. Dublin city's ascendancy as the centre of the state, law, and commerce, including publishing, printing and book distribution, meant that early corridors or vectors of English speech flowed out from the burgeoning capital city. The density of new turnpike roads radiating out of Dublin intensified from the late 1720s and early 1730s onwards. These drove southwestwards across the Midlands along at least seven axes: through Carlow, Athy and Castlecomer; from Timahoe (Queen's County) to Cashel; from Naas and Monasterevan to Nenagh and Limerick, with a branch to Birr; from Clane to Ballingare; and forking off from Kinnegad to Athlone; to Lanesborough and Roscommon; and to Longford.[79] These roads symbolized the intensification of trade, traffic and English texts and speechways throughout these inland regions. In addition, new turnpike roads drove northwestwards to Athboy and to Kells, as well as linking up via Dundalk with the east Ulster routes from Newry to Armagh and Coleraine, with Belfast acting as a secondary node to this north-centred network (see Fig. 11.6, p. 406).

Parallel to this, a country trade in books, supplied by travelling pedlars, was centred on Dublin in the late seventeenth century. By the 1720s a substantial book-peddling trade had developed. The number of pedlars then probably exceeded 1,500. By 1750 as many as 1,800 pedlars were on the roads, giving Ireland a travelling book sales pattern at least on par with equivalent densities in England and Wales,[80] but still heavily concentrated in the Dublin/Leinster region. Apart from popular romances and stories of Irish highwaymen, these small and relatively cheap printed texts (called chapbooks) saw H. Reily's *Impartial History of Ireland* (first published 1690) compete with N. Crouch's establishment *History of Ireland* (1693). Other texts, like *The Siege of Londonderry*, clashed with *The Battle of Aughrim*.[81] Printed popular texts in English, therefore, worked their way into communities that had only recently become English-speaking or may have still been partly Irish-speaking. The number of printed books in Irish was miniscule by comparison – even then, whether Irish Catholic sermons or catechisms, they came 'clothed in English dress' (Roman script). With Dublin Catholic printers to the fore from the early eighteenth century onwards, book distribution to the rest of the country, and Leinster in particular, was both 'culturally anglicising and politically Catholicising'.[82]

The more rapid spread of English throughout much of Leinster may also reflect the dominance of an extensive yet highly commercial pastoral economy throughout much of this region. Landlord-inspired enclosures across the Midlands led to the creation of a highly regulated parkland and large field system – did the march of these enclosures match the spread of English, slated houses and a whole host of other material and cultural changes that signified transformed attitudes and world views amongst the pre-plantation populations? Unlike Munster, did the absence of significant Catholic-cum-Irish-speaking middle-class patronage in this grazier cattle zone also facilitate the earlier erosion of the language? Finally, mid-Leinster's propensity to assimilate English speech may also reflect a deeper stratum of responsiveness with its foundations in the late medieval period. The earlier analysis (see Fig. 11.2, Pl.2m, and Fig. 11.5, p. 398) of sharp regional variations in the anglicization of first and second names by the mid-seventeenth century has demonstrated how Leinster was most deeply affected by these long-standing processes. The extent of continuing bilingualism amongst its Old English population must also be added to the equation.

Equally striking is the weakness of literacy and English-speaking, or more correctly the strength of an Irish-speaking culture, in much of Munster. The rich lands and older towns of Munster sustained a vibrant, multilayered, socially diverse Irish-speaking culture, epitomized, above all, in the courts of poetry that linked up the poets, scribes and teachers of west Waterford, north and east Cork, much of Limerick, and north Kerry and Clare.[83] Munster and its south Leinster extension to the village world of south Kilkenny had retained thriving Catholic gentry and middle-class components in town and countryside. Levels of literacy in Irish in these regions were higher than in the rest of the country and Irish literature and poetry were held in high esteem. Indeed, it is possible that the courts of poetry and, more particularly, the well-established tradition of issuing poetic and prose warrants (barántaisí) in Irish functioned as part of an alternative system of social control in these Irish-speaking regions. As we have seen, it is likely that some descendants of the plantation settler communities had been at least partially assimilated into this confident bilingual world. It is also significant that by 1732 Munster contained only 12.5 per cent of the island-wide Protestant population.[84] What is particularly noticeable about Munster is the strength of Irish-speaking traditions in the three key cities of Limerick, Cork and Waterford. One of the key factors here is that regular inmigration from the countryside – so characteristic of the dynamic eighteenth century – regularly replenished Irish-speaking and writing traditions in these cities. It is recognized that both levels of literacy and proportions of English-speakers were much higher in the cities: on average about twice the ratio as the surrounding countrysides. For example, in the city of Limerick, c.1750, there was around 30 per cent male illiteracy compared with 62 per cent in Co. Clare and 66 per cent in rural Limerick[85] (see Fig. 11.8 [inset]). Yet, as Neil Buttimer and others have confirmed, Irish poetic and manuscript production were still sustained in these cities, in what were admittedly less hospitable urban environs for the Irish language.[86]

It should also be noted that the intensification of the density of fairs and markets in the province over the first half of the eighteenth century does not appear to have impinged dramatically on patterns of speechways. Nevertheless, by the 1750s, as turnpike roads spread in mid-Munster, a linguistic fissure is beginning to open up along a line from Limerick city through mid-Cork on to the great provisioning port of Cork.[87] English was then spreading along this powerful commercial axis, possibly a factor in the decline of the Maigue courts of poetry around Croom and Ráth (Charleville). The advance of English was probably connected with both the survival and the vitality of Irish scribal activity along this transitional axis, where active bilingual Irish scholars were alert to the severe pressures that the Irish language was now coming under.[88]

The earliest printing of Catholic devotional works in Irish also emanate from Munster – much of this was to come later than 1750, yet it may hint at the some-what different role the Catholic clergy played in this wider cultural region.[89] In contrast, in the southwest and northeastern edges of this core Munster cultural zone, two bitter frontiers between settler and Irish societies had emerged – in southwest Munster, on the one hand, and along to the south Tipperary/Kilkenny borderlands, on the other.

West and north Clare formed a bridgehead of Irish speechways into Connacht. In the mid-eighteenth century this province presented the greatest bulwark to the expansion of English speech. In part, Irish gentry survival and patronage was a factor here – not only among the Dalys and Brownes of east Galway but also among the Mac Dermots, O'Connors and O'Hartes along the Sligo/Mayo/Roscommon borderlands.[90] More particularly, this linguistic bulwark (levels of illiteracy in English were often over 80 per cent) reflects both the slower integration of Connacht into the wider agenda of landlord improvements and the weaker inte-gration of its many small producers into the commercial cattle economy. The cattle trade was dominated by the gentry families themselves. Both road and urban development also lagged behind. The strength of a dominantly subsistent, more introverted cultural and linguistic pattern is best epitomized by the extraordinary geographical extent of an agricultural village world that covered much of Galway, Mayo and Roscommon. In these highly localized worlds, not only did Irish survive in great strength but variations in its dialects were characteristic not only between counties and baronies but even closely adjacent village communities.

Clearly, a city like Galway had higher levels of English speech. Yet in the 1750s levels of literacy in the city are only half that of Cork city. Connacht was also char-acterized by the strongest gender distinctions in levels of literacy acquisition. Only a tiny fraction of Connacht women were literate by the mid-eighteenth century. Their menfolk showed lower levels of literacy than the women of Lein-ster, who, in turn, lagged behind those of Ulster. In Ulster the gender gap in literacy levels was lowest. Greater gender differences in literacy levels in part reflected the lack of religious literature in the Catholic tradition,[91] as well as more highly defined public roles for men *vis-à-vis* predominantly domestic roles for women. The two domains of language where Irish prevailed longest were the home and the townland/neighbourhood.

All of the above analysis suggests a society literally on the move – a society that Cullen has described as in swift transition from one of the last medieval cultures of western Europe to one that was rapidly modernizing in many spheres of life.[92]

The scale of immigration and economic transformation, and the range of dislocation (property-wise and job-wise), inevitably transformed Ireland's stories, its
memories, even its styles of dress.[93] There were equally powerful changes in the
landscape, in settlement, and in the people's ways of working and speaking:
witness the spread of English speechways into Irish life. Alan Bliss suggests that
the divergence between mainland English speech and Irish speechways in English
begins after 1650, and he concludes that at a surprisingly early date (c.1700) 'the
planter's English had become influenced by Irish, as a result of daily interactions
with the Irish servants and tenants'.[94] Similar local interactions with Irish was
likewise to set Scots speech in the north on a new trajectory. Changes in the seventeenth-century Anglo-Irish dialects presupposes a continuous and significant
degree of contact between Irish speech and English speech and a fair degree of
linguistic interpenetration.

The grammar of the settled landscape also revealed some profound shifts in its
architecture and power structures. Back in 1672, Petty, reflecting on the apparent
lack of employment in the country, outlined how his dream landscape could be
constructed to ensure full employment: first, Dublin as the capital city should be
properly fortified and a new palace for the chief governor built there to symbolize
the level of achievement of the new order; second, and more strikingly, he wished
the chimney-less cabins of the ubiquitous poor to be replaced by the building of
168,000 small stone-walled houses, complete with chimneys, doors, windows,
gardens and orchards properly quicksetted; third, he wanted to see 5 million fruit
trees and 3 million timber trees planted on the boundary of every denomination of
land; and to this he would add millions of interior enclosures, complete with
quicksets; fourth, he would also build a shipyard in Dublin, make several rivers
navigable and mend all the highways. In a delicate and diplomatic final touch, he
would build an additional 100 Anglican churches. Petty also stressed the need to
make investments in the building of tan yards, fisheries, glassworks, rape mills,
copperworks, lead and salt works. He would make capital investments in a
10,000-ton shipping fleet, develop the wool, hemp, flax, and rawhide industries
and thus employ an assumed 340,000 'spare' hands in such ventures.[95]

By 1730, Petty's dream landscape had not quite been achieved, but a goodly
part of his vision had been realized. The building and opening of the new Irish
parliament on College Green in 1729 was a powerful symbol of the new-found
self-confidence of both Dublin and Anglo-Ireland. The quality of this building, the
completion of Trinity Library, the building of Castletown House and many other
Big Houses like it, represented a decisive shift in upper-class housing, lifestyles
and attitudes. The writings of Berkeley, Swift and others created a space for a real,
if still narrow, forum of public opinion as a corporate sense of identity was developing in the Irish Protestant settler society; while the foundation of the Royal
Dublin Society in 1731 anticipated the key innovative role of the most influential
members of the Irish gentry in science, technology and agriculture over the rest of
the century.[96] Dublin, Cork and other, smaller cities were breaking free from their
medieval frameworks to expand dramatically beyond their walls and set up new
regularly designed and confident streetscapes. Many Anglican churches were

newly built or rebuilt. The initiation of the Charter School movement in 1733 represented a renewed drive to protestantize, anglicize and develop new industrial skills among the poorer sections of the Irish population. In the countryside, the Big Houses were still scattered islands of power and privilege in a world of growing social extremes. There is no doubt that the regulation and regimentation of both the landscape and its many occupants had deepened considerably. A more stable and stratified society was crystallizing. Rural houses were again becoming more fixed and permanent, except those on the edges of roads, and in parishes and baronies where the hungry poor were beginning to proliferate.

Behind the façade of the landscape, however, legislation, language and life paths spoke to a deeply repressive social order. The year 1729 marked the completion of the series of enactments (from 1695 onwards) known to contemporaries as the Popery laws. The purpose of these laws was to secure a permanent Protestant Ascendancy in the government of Ireland, central and local, and to obviate, or at least minimize, the threat that Roman Catholicism seemed to present to English and Irish Protestants in their religious and political freedom. These laws deprived Catholics of both political power and the means of attaining such power – principally through the ownership of land or the profession of the law.[97] Aogáin Ó Rathaille's bitter poetic vision of a defeated and despairing people, with their friars banished overseas and the old houses lifeless, is matched in its ferocity and imagery on the other side of the frontier only by Jonathan Swift, who then described old Ireland as a lion with its teeth drawn and its claws pared to the quick.[98] Both writers provide powerful images of subjugation and subjection.

Life in Ireland was, however, more complicated than these powerful images would suggest. By 1730 the Catholic Church in Ireland was beginning to experience a reasonable degree of toleration, and almost every diocese had its own bishop. There was also a significant regional variation in the strength of the old gentry families and of long-settled, durable rural and urban societies. The tower-houses might be on the way out, but their old occupants, along with their kinship and neighbourhood networks, did not yield ground so easily. There was also a revitalization of country life in many forms; this life was characterized by a growing liveliness and energy in music and dancing at fairs, weddings, wakes and funerals, which contrasted with the new Puritanism, spreading out from the towns, and which, amongst other things, was to domesticate and fetishize the place and image of women in Irish society. The public house/inn and the mass house were also emerging as key meeting-places in this transitional period, which saw the hedge schools increasingly geared to English-language training.

While Petty's dream of widespread industrialization had not been fully realized, there had been a dramatic expansion of linen production in the northern half of the island and of woollens in the south, while many port industries had developed and flourished. A radical Presbyterian tradition still survived in places but was no longer seen as threatening to the ruling Anglican Ascendancy. In fact, Presbyterian weavers and textile workers generally were now deliberately introduced into the new industrial villages of the Midlands and further south. However, the dynamism of the Presbyterian frontier was on the wane, as North America beckoned more and more young emigrants.[99]

By the 1750s Ireland was in the middle of a revolution in transport, estate management, urban planning and architecture. Yet the resilient placenames and the rooted family names, as well as the embryonic new parish units and centres, spoke of other worlds and other vitalities. The possibilities for many future geographies and histories of Ireland and its regions were therefore unfolding.

The decades of the mid-eighteenth century are a time of great transition in Irish life. Landlord intervention in shaping the economy and designing the landscape reach a peak in the 1740s and 1750s. Levels of economic development accelerate dramatically as exports soar. The balance between the Irish and English languages has shifted decisively in favour of the latter: future political opposition to the ruling Protestant establishment would be expressed more and more in English-language forms, though still often rooted in an Irish poetic tradition that sustained both a strong sense of Irish nationality and a sharp awareness of the levels of oppression associated with the English-speaking Protestant regime. The political leadership of Catholic Ireland was also passing from the remnants of the old aristocratic class into the hands of a less conservative, more urban-based middle-class group. Elsewhere, agrarian movements resisting the final phases in the enclosure and privatization of the land (as well as heavier tithe impositions) began to assume regional rather than local forms and levels of organization. By the 1770s, growing tenant-farmer power was being expressed in even more sophisticated, and geographically more extensive, agrarian movements. The concurrent peaking of Ascendancy power (and taste) in the landscapes of city and country ironically marks the beginning of its slow decline. New worlds were in the making.

IV

A GLOBAL CONTEXT

12

Ireland and America – England's First Frontiers

> . . . And Virginia should be called Aghanure again.
> 1641 Depositions (Co. Cavan)[1]

'Not to meddle with the state of Ireland, nor that of Guiana, there is under our noses the great and ample country of Virginia.' So declared Richard Hakluyt, propagandist and historian of English overseas expansion, when discussing the problem of where to locate England's perceived surplus population of 1599.[2] In contrast, an English government official writing about the same time noted that 'if the princes of England knew what a jewel Ireland were, they would not seek the discovery of foreign lands to settle in'.[3] In another contemporaneous account, Ireland's location is given a dramatic new dimension when it is described as 'this famous island set in a Virginian [that is, American] sea'.[4] These observations highlight how, for the first time in history, people sensed the geographical contiguity between this western isle and the eastern seaboard of America. They also suggest the association of both Ireland and America in the minds of the colonizing English at the close of the sixteenth century.

The object of this chapter is to analyse if there were any parallels in the origins and expressions of English colonial strategy in Ireland and America. Given the general development of English colonial schemes first for Ireland and then for America, and since a number of participants were involved in both Irish and American enterprises, it is only logical to assume that some of the experiences gained and ideas and attitudes generated in Ireland would find some application on the larger American canvas. The major part of this exercise will therefore explore similarities and differences in the processes and patterns of colonization in both lands. By way of conclusion, some comparison will be made between the cultural geographical consequences of these two colonial endeavours for both areas by the late eighteenth century.

The Setting in Time and Space

The story begins midway through the sixteenth century, quickens over the first half of the seventeenth century and ends about 1801, when the Act of Union made Ireland an integral part of the United Kingdom, and when the recently established

United States of America moved forward to organize its newly colonized western lands. Both in terms of time and space, I am working on a large canvas, so all the disclaimers must come very early indeed. The American component of this interpretation is based almost solely on second-hand source-materials and attempts only to sketch in some of the more obvious differences and similarities between the two areas. This field of comparative colonial studies is still a mainly uncharted one, yet it is of crucial significance to geographers, since such rapid and revolutionary geographical changes were occurring contemporaneously over so much of the globe as the Europeans established a cultural hegemony that lasted at least two centuries.

Before embarking on this comparative colonial study, some essential differences in the location, size and environments of the two areas prior to colonization must be illustrated. Ireland is a relatively small island, lying west of both the continental expanse of Europe and the adjacent larger island of Britain. In contrast, the eastern seaboard of America was part of a vast continental territory, lying 3,000 miles or more from the colonizing homeland with the great and violent Atlantic Ocean lying in between. These facts of size and nearness to or distance from Britain have had a profound influence on the history and human geography of both areas under consideration. In terms of environmental characteristics, colonists were initially impressed with the fortuitous similarities between the climate, vegetation, land and sea resources of the homeland and the New World. Leading American cultural geographer Carl Sauer remarks that 'it would be impossible indeed to cross the ocean anywhere else in the world and find so little that was unfamiliar on the other side'.[5] True, both areas were in similar latitudes, with a general correspondence in seasonal rhythms and vegetation patterns. But later on, the American colonist, sobered by the experience of wresting a livelihood from a hostile environment, became aware of the more continental nature of American climates. Here was a great laboratory for exploring societal/environmental relationships: initial, immediate and intimate. Experience also soon revealed the greater extremes in the natural landscape, from the expanse of swamp, marsh and sandy barrens in the south to the extent of rocky hills, granites and poor soils in the north. And behind everything lay the massive barrier of the timbered Allegheny mountains (see Fig. 12.1, Pl.2n). So from the beginning one must emphasize that Ireland and America were very different entities – one, a relatively small insular world and part of the European cultural realm, and the other, a truly continental arena separated from the old European hearth by great cultural and physical distances.

One might be surprised to find both Ireland and America described as 'woodland' societies in the early seventeenth century.[6] The Indians had cleared, burned, reduced and grazed much of the wooded lands of the eastern seaboard, but the first Europeans, and subsequent visitors, were invariably struck by the dominance of the woodland and forest. It is estimated that in 1600 about one-eighth of Ireland was forested.[7] These wooded areas were to be colonized or recolonized during this early modern phase.[8] Both regions were still lightly populated and underdeveloped economically, America much more so than Ireland. In 1600 there may have been anything from 125,000 to 200,000 Indians living along the eastern seaboard,[9] whereas Ireland's population at the same time seems to have been between 1 million and 1.5 million.[10] Given the great difference in the size of the two areas, this suggests an overall population density (and presumably a some-what related level of development) in a still lightly populated Ireland 30 to 40 times as great as that of pre-colonial America. However, it is also relevant to note that the eastern and southern parts of Ireland were more densely populated and more developed economically than the clan-based, more pastoral regions in the remainder of the island.

The rediscovery of the New World led to the emergence of far-flung Spanish and Portuguese empires, with the French, the Dutch, and the English later joining in the race for new lands. In the process, the relative positions of both Ireland and North America were radically transformed. Ireland was no longer regarded as just a rugged outpost on the outer edge of the known world; it was now a key player, lying astride the main routes to and from the colonies in North and Middle America. Earlier still it had become an active participant in the Newfoundland fisheries trade. North America, in turn, was now to become an outer rim of Euro-pean settlement and culture – the recipient of the most thoroughgoing translation of European society to a new land anywhere in the world.[11] Strangely enough, it could be argued that Ireland was now also 'rediscovered' by the English at a time when English colonists were beginning to attempt to establish footholds along the Atlantic seaboard of America. All around the Atlantic basin, it was a time of extra-ordinary movement, encounter, change and development.

Similarities in Colonial Strategies

A number of impulses fundamentally affected the evolution of English colonial strategy. The pioneering role of the Spaniards, Renaissance thinking on colonies as state policy, and earlier examples of Norman and Roman colonial endeavours may all have provided relevant models.[12] We have to recognize how restive, ambi-tious and aggressive these Renaissance men and women of Elizabethan England were. With the New World discoveries, came both a physical and mental libera-tion from the territorial constraints and institutional shackles of the Old World – a releasing of immense intellectual and physical energies. Donald Meinig places a special emphasis on the diffusion of seafaring, cartographic, and colonial ideas in general from the Mediterranean via the Iberian peninsula, through France and into England and suggests that the Anglo-French Channel community of French Huguenots and Westcountrymen may have acted as a particularly critical focus for colonial aspirations and enterprises (see Fig. 12.2).[13] From Bristol to Waterford and Cork is but a short and oft-travelled journey; and south Munster was to be from the beginning a crucial base for the elaboration of English experiences in piracy, naval training and, above all, in full-blooded colonial settlement – an early core area where colonial endeavours and aspirations could be tested and a kind of stepping stone to America (see chapter 2).

It can be argued that in a very real sense it was Ireland – particularly Munster –

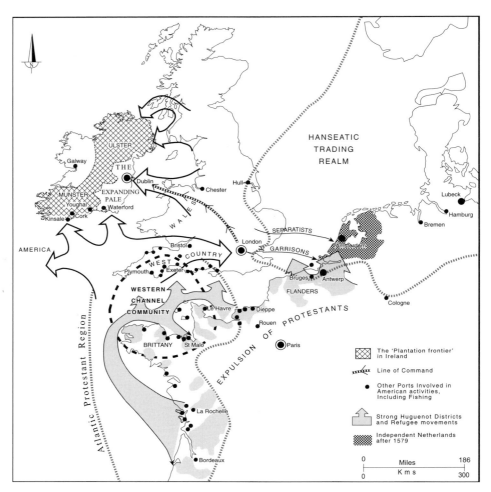

12.2   Ireland and the northwest European culture hearth (adapted, in part from Figure 7 in D.W. Meinig's *Atlantic America, 1492–1800*, p. 47: see reference 13)

that turned English minds towards America.[14] Likewise, early experiences in America prompted many Englishmen to think of Ireland as a real alternative to colonial settlements overseas. And once English colonization had begun, Ireland's strategic location, its agricultural surplus, and its close ties with the colonizing power meant that it came to provide additional energy in the form of capital, goods and settlers for the great leap across the Atlantic. Both America and Ireland were to witness initial probings and attempts at settlement by private entrepreneurs. Queen Elizabeth's patent of 1578 to the Westcountryman Humphrey Gilbert to occupy with English settlers lands 'not actually possessed by any Christian prince or people'[15] in North America actually followed Gilbert's own frustrations in not being able to implement plans for colonizing, firstly parts of east Ulster and later parts of south Munster.[16] His half-brother Walter Raleigh – who attempted to set up the ill-fated American colony on the Roanoke islands – was, on the other hand, probably one of the chief architects, and certainly one of the chief beneficiaries, of the Munster plantation in the late 1580s.[17]

Leaving aside lesser planters who were involved on both sides of the Atlantic, as many as five of the eight main architects of English settlements and colonization in Munster had connections with English overseas enterprises in America and Asia, representing that coalition of government, gentry, and mercantile interests which laid the foundations of the early British Empire.[18] And part of the reason for early settlements in Munster, Virginia and the Caribbean involved a range of related strategic and commercial considerations. In the developing global struggle for land, raw materials and markets, the English feared both Spanish intervention in southern Ireland, as well as Spanish dominance in the New World. Early English voyagers to America invariably stressed the need for 'friendly coasts' and 'well-stored goodly harbours' on the outward and homeward journey.[19] The ports of Kinsale, Cork, Youghal, Dungarvan, Waterford and New Ross were all boosted by the opening up of the Atlantic for fishing, trade, naval and emigrant transactions. The Munster plantation safeguarded this route and opened the way for the conquest of America. The Munster settlement may also have provided some kind of seigniorial model for later land grants in Newfoundland, Nova Scotia, Maryland, Virginia and the Carolinas.[20] It also stimulated the development of the southern Irish/American colonial salted provision trade, which in turn was to shape Irish migrations to both North and Middle America.[21] Above all, the Munster plantation of the later sixteenth century was especially important since it was the first state enterprise on such a scale that was at least a partial success.

It was in Ireland that the English moved first from ideas of an exclusively military conquest (which they found to be expensive and not at all successful) to the need for administrative and legal reorganization, which was partially successful, and to the notion of plantation (that is, the full-blooded colonization of a newly conquered land by loyal subjects under state direction and control).[22] Such state schemes involved the complex problem of funding, transporting, and settling in the new land a wide cross-section of its own population. The seeds of the idea of such self-sufficient colonial settlements may well have been fertilized in Munster soil. Here we have a major plan aimed at massive social engineering – involving ledger books and maps, drawing lines on paper to alienate land from old proprietors to new ones. This rather novel strategy was also to be adopted in the New World.[23] Likewise, initial failures and successes in both areas were to add to the officials' experience in the better planning of later colonial ventures.[24] These setbacks emphasized the need for greater capital investment; the need for better back-up services, especially in the areas of surveying and transportation; the need for larger numbers of more permanent, garrisoned centres; the need for more central state involvement in what were largely private entrepreneurial efforts; and, above all, the need for regional authorities to supervise the organization and monitoring of colonization and settlement in the new land.

So by the beginning of the seventeenth century the stage was set for new endeavours, according as colonization became big business, involving large investments of capital, goods, people, livestock and ideas. The sequence was as follows:

the Munster plantation (second stage), Virginia, Maine, Ulster, Newfoundland, and the Bermuda colonies, then Wexford, Longford, and later the Barbados, the Pilgrim Fathers' and the Massachusetts Bay colonies.[25] Earlier on, in the sixteenth century, Ireland had been England's laboratory for the development of colonial corpora-tions and the use of the joint stock principle in a colonization project.[26] Now specific colonial development companies, such as the London Company, became involved on both sides of the Atlantic. As many as 35 per cent of all merchants investing in the Irish plantations from 1586 to *c.*1620 had investments in other overseas companies and there was a particularly large cross-membership between these Irish investors and those of the Virginia Companies.[27] So on both sides of the Atlantic the burden of early colonial ventures – especially the investment of the necessary organizational skills – fell on the shoulders of ambitious English or Scot-tish adventurers. Later on, some settlers and others in Ireland were to join in the process, transferring servants and tenants from their own estates in Ireland to the American plantations, while the founders of Maryland and Pennsylvania, Lord Baltimore and William Penn, also had Irish properties and connections. And on both sides of the Atlantic we encounter the same kind of mentality at work – a measured, ambitious attempt to take over and settle large well-defined areas in a planned fashion (see Fig. 3.2, p. 60).

There were also other early parallels. In terms of the initial conquest of a people and a territory, what was called the 'method of the frontiers' was applied in both areas. One thinks of the cutting of military roads and passes through woods and boglands in Ireland, the encircling of the so-called rebels, and the establishment of permanent garrisons later supported by an adjacent settler colony.[28] Such processes were to be repeated in the newly discovered territories of North America. Ireland also had its own earlier westward-moving frontier. The Old English area of admin-istration in the Pale was a static frontier – fenced in with a large bank and ditch. But in the expansionist phase of the late sixteenth century, one could see the Pale as a dynamic westward-moving frontier, eventually linking up with successfully established footholds in the strategic northeast and southern coastal areas; this method of the frontiers meant 'a constant hurrying move forward, fragmented, uneven but forever moving, confronting, outflanking, aggressive, unpredictable'.[29] The expanding military frontier, along with its associated English legal system, gradually enveloped the greater part of the island by the latter half of the seven-teenth century.

The main centres of colonial settlement, however, came to be concentrated in some of the more lightly populated parts of pre-colonial Ireland – in Ulster and the northwest generally, also in the Wicklow/north Wexford and Queen's County/King's County regions of Leinster; and in smaller more densely popu-lated pockets in Munster – in parts of Limerick, north Cork and, particularly, in the lower Blackwater and Bandon valleys. Here comparisons with the American situation are most apt. On the other hand, colonial immigrant groups were much less in evidence in the long-settled, well-developed urbanized coastal and river valley zones of the southeast and east.[30] It should also be noted that the extreme recesses of the western parts of Ireland were only opened up by the colonists for the first time in the late eighteenth century and early nineteenth century with the cutting of new roads westwards,[31] and the creation of rudimentary urban foundations, as at Belmullet, Clifden and Cahirciveen. In one sense, this represents the final reach of the colonial frontier in Ireland.

David Quinn, and particularly Nicholas Canny, have noted how the English colonial mind made early anthropological comparisons between the levels of civilization existing among the Irish and the Indians.[32] Point for point, Elizabethan and later English descriptions of the 'wild Irish' are paralleled in writings about the Indians to justify the conquests and the devastating implications for the original populations of these political, economic and social intrusions. Comparison of such items as their levels of agricultural technology, forms of dress, settlement and house types was a feature that was used to defend the often brutal military conquest and either the subsequent economic and political subjugation or displacement of the 'natives'.

Both Indian alliances and Irish lordships and coalitions were broken to clear the way for the colonist and in both conquests English military commanders destroyed the food supplies to defeat resistance by starvation. In both cases, too, the ideology and discourse of English conquest obscured the fact that these colonial encounters were not with simple but with complex civilizations and fellow human beings. Both medieval and particularly Elizabethan Ireland were fertile seedbeds for the elaboration of such an ideology and for its application overseas.

Again, it was in Ireland that printed propaganda tracts were first introduced to encourage immigrants from Britain to colonize newly conquered lands. And there was a striking correspondence between the arguments put forward for colonizing Ireland and those used in promoting settlement in America. Even the images of Ireland and America, as portrayed to potential colonists, bore a striking similarity. Whereas the Elizabethans and their successors might be scathing about Irish and Indian cultures, they waxed eloquent about the equable climate, the availability and richness of the land, the fruitfulness of the rivers and seas, the abundant woodlands. In short, 'a promised land' lay awaiting the settlers across both the Irish and Atlantic seas. So it may be useful to see Ireland in terms of 'colonial space', lying not directly off the European mainland but halfway to the New World. Such a mental map would help to explain Quinn's observation that some of the propaganda encouraging migration to Ireland 'seemed more appropriate to lands far outside Europe'.[33]

The colonization of Ulster from the early part of the seventeenth century onwards seems particularly relevant to this comparison. The planned colonization of Ulster placed greater emphasis than previously on the exclusion of 'natives' from the forfeited lands; on the creation of smaller and more manageable estates; on the establishment of a network of new towns and garrisons; on the use of more speedy though still rudimentary surveying methods; and on the introduction of a major colonial development company to act as an innovator in a county that was henceforth called Londonderry.[34] This northern settlement saw the building of twenty-three new towns – frontier outposts created to dominate and reorganize hitherto hostile territories. Some of the new towns were planned

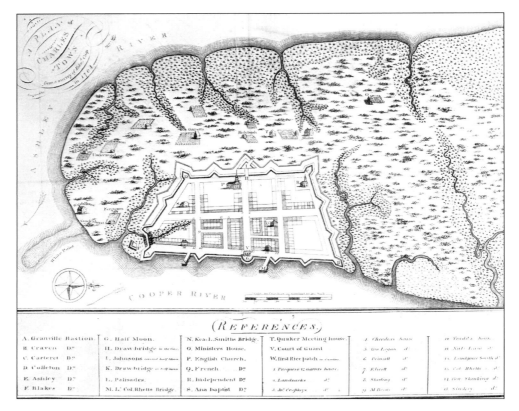

A. Granville Bastion.	G. Half Moon.	N. Kea: L.Smiths Bridge.	T. Quaker Meeting house.	1. Cheedars house	10. Tradd s hous.
B. Craven Dº	H. Draw bridge in the line.	O. Ministers House.	V. Court of Guard	2. Rice Logan ᵈ:	11. Nat: Law ᵈ:
C. Carteret Dº	I. Johnsons recont half down	P. English Church.	W. first Rice patch in cantona.	6. Tynist ᵈ:	12. Landipore Smith d:
D. Colleton Dº	K. Draw bridge in half town	Q. French Dº	1 Pasquere 12 barrets house.	7. Eliot ᵈ:	13. Col Rhetts ᵈ:
E. Ashley Dº	L. Palisades.	R. Independent Dº	2. Landaukes d:	8. Sterling ᵈ:	11 Hon Skenking d:
F. Blakes Dº	M. Lᵗ Col.Rhetts Bridge.	S. Ana baptist Dº	3. Jnᵗ Crofloys d: :	9. M Beins ᵈ:	15. Simley d:

(REFERENCES.)

12.4a   Townplan of: Colonial Charleston (South Carolina); reproduced with the permission of the author John Reps

under influences emanating from Renaissance Europe, with their carefully designed grid-iron street plans and central squares or diamonds enclosed by market-houses, townhalls and gaols – for example, Coleraine, Derry and Monaghan (see Fig. 12.3a and Fig. 12.3b and Fig. 12.3c, Pl.2o). These Renaissance ideas meant the establishing of new standards of living, new tastes, a greater consciousness of new fashions, of keeping up to date and so clearing away the less salubrious, haphazard, chaotic settlement survivals from the Middle Ages to create functional, well-planned frontier towns instead.

As Estyn Evans and others have noted,[35] similar urban forms were to appear within a few years in both tidewater Virginia and New England. There is also some evidence to suggest that such towns as Charleston (South Carolina) and Frederica (Georgia) were influenced by Ulster town plans (see Fig. 12.4a and Fig. 12.4b).[36] The link between the frontier colonial societies of Ulster and America is sometimes explicitly referred to also in official documents requesting money and settlers for 'our plantations in Virginia and Ulster'.[37] Indeed, both Virginia and Ulster represented the first really successful overseas transportation of the full range of a British colonial society. We have to recognize how successful these colonists were, to recognize their drive, initiative and ability, however painful the

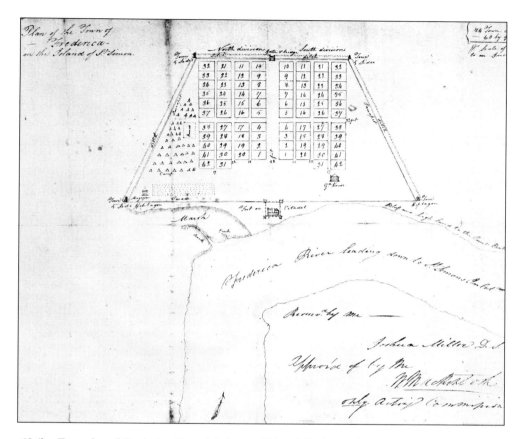

12.4b   Townplan of: Frederica (Georgia), figures 104 and 116 from John Reps, *The Making of Urban America* (1965); reproduced with the permission of the author

cultural consequences. There are broad similarities in the timing and diffusion of initial waves of settlers into both these areas, with a more or less continuous migration from 1607 to 1609, which weakened in areal strength as it rolled westwards and southwestwards; in both areas there was an initial peaking of population in the early 1620s and a process of consolidation and expansion over the latter half of the seventeenth century and the early eighteenth century.[38] On both frontiers there existed the typically fluid colonial situation involving changing settlement strategies and patterns as a mobile tenantry probed and searched for a better home. The close links between the two areas in this early formative phase even found expression in the Irish landscape when a newly planted town in Cavan was christened Virginia in honour of the Virgin Queen, Elizabeth I.

These earlier, more tenuous, links were later considerably strengthened with the migration of perhaps 100,000 Ulster Irish to the American colonies during the eighteenth century.[39] The beginnings of this migratory movement heralds the end of the active phase of immigration into Ireland and the initiation of a second major wave of west European migration to the American colonies. This migration also added a new and very significant component to American colonial society, by bringing experiences of frontier Ulster to bear on the expanding western edges of American settlement. The Ulster Irish settled early in New England; but concentrated especially in the Middle Colonies and also moved south and west of the tidewater into the backcountry of the Carolinas and Georgia. Shaped by the hardy environments of Scotland and then Ulster, they earned a reputation as frontiersmen. The English Puritans of New England and the Quakers of Philadelphia were happy to settle the Ulster Presbyterians well away from their own sects and along the edge of the hostile Indian territories to the west.[40] The Ulster experience may have been relevant to this process, although Evans would see their capacity to adopt Indian ways as more important than their proven ability to adjust to the raw American frontier.[41] Given that they were early on the expanding edge of settlement, they naturally had a formative influence on settlement and adaptation processes generally,[42] and they were to reinforce strongly the importance of the single family farm just then diffusing out from the Middle Atlantic core.[43] If we wish to recognize one item of Irish culture of the greatest significance in making these settlements successful and durable, it was the family farm. The key to successful colonization were these tight-knit families – wives and children, as well as young men – cohesive enough to colonize and work the land and face up to the insecurities and terrors of the frontier.

In Munster, Ulster, and elsewhere in Ireland, the colonial plans favoured nucleated or concentrated arrangements of farming settlements, but individual aspirations, probably combined with pre-existing settlement and landholding systems, led to the rapid dispersal of settlement centred on the vital organizing instrument of the family farm – a flexible, humble and, if necessary, mobile institution.[44] Similarly, William Penn's plans for compact Quaker village settlement in Pennsylvania were frustrated by the Quaker farmers themselves, by Irish, by German and by other immigrants, who scattered throughout this state and adjoining colonies also.[45] So, in America, too, one finds the classical plantation emphasis on an urban or village centre and a hinterland. Between Georgia and Munster, for example, one finds general similarities in settlement aimed at ingenious compromises between nucleation and dispersion. (see Fig. 2.15 [Pl. 1j])[46] Concessions of the lord proprietors of Carolina to certain Irish grantees in 1672 also echoed similar recommendations made in Ulster and elsewhere in Ireland. These grantees were told that they should 'plant in towns and not build their houses stragglingly – such solitary dwellings being incapable of that benefit of trade, the comfort of society and mutual assistance which men dwelling together in towns are capable of one to another'.[47] But these settlers and others elsewhere were imbued with ideas of individual freedom and profit-making and so established the classic American pattern of dispersed family farms and plantations.

It is instructive to note the overall scale of migration into the Irish and the American colonies between 1580 and 1800. By 1622 there were, at the very least, 12,000–15,000 settlers in Munster and 25,000–35,000 in Ulster, and probably many more who were never caught in the official net and documented. In addition, smaller groups of colonists settled on other plantations and in the developing cities and towns. The immigrant population of mainland colonial America at this time was only a few thousand, although it was to increase to 40,000–50,000 by 1650.[48] It has been estimated that between 1586 and 1700 Ireland had received at the very minimum 150,000 immigrant settlers – possibly as many as 250,000 – far more than had moved from Spain and Portugal from 1500 to 1650 to establish their vast imperial domains in Latin America.[49] So, in a comparative colonial sense, this population movement into Ireland represented one of the earliest and largest European migrations of the period – a forerunner to and a later contributor to the ever greater American migrations of the eighteenth and nineteenth centuries. In the demographic vitality and fertility of its populations, Ireland occupied a halfway stage between a more stable, if not static, western European pattern and the phenomenal rates of reproduction experienced in colonial America, especially in its Chesapeake culture hearth. The competing settlement attractions of Ireland and America actually continued over much of the seventeenth century. Even as late as 1680, as eminent an authority as Sir William Petty was still unsure which was the better prospect.[50] There is also no doubt that, according as America developed and prospered, it siphoned off settlers who would otherwise have come to Ireland. Ultimately, of course, America was to prove by far the more attractive and accommodating of the two colonies.

Immigrant links between Ireland and America were forged well before the mid-seventeenth century, with the emergence of the seasonal migration of Irish fisherman to the Newfoundland banks (some of whom drifted into the northern American colonies as permanent migrants). More importantly, the deepening of the harsh indentured servant trade from Ireland to America and the associated rough business of transporting both common and political prisoners to the colonies was to provide colonial America south of New England with from one-fifth to one-third of all its white immigrants. The lowest estimate of net migration from Ireland to British North America and the West Indies gives a total of 165,000 migrants between the years 1630 and 1775.[51] In contrast, Seamus Smyth has argued that 100,000 migrants left Ireland for the thirteen American colonies in the seventeenth century alone and that as many as a further 250,000–400,000 left between 1700 and 1776.[52] Whatever the precise figures, all commentators are agreed that the Irish of all persuasions constituted the most constant and probably the largest emigrant group to the colonies (see Fig. 12.6, p. 443).[53]

Already in the first half of the seventeenth century – and given the level of social disorganization that followed conquest and plantation in Ireland – the island had become a prime source for the supply of indentured servants to the colonies. There they were eagerly welcomed by planters and farmers who wanted cheap labour, by speculators who needed more settlers to validate their grants and by colonial proprietors who wished to build up their populations. This form of migration was closely tied to the Irish provisions trade with the West Indies and the southern colonies, in particular, thus representing one strand in a web of shipping that also brought the first black African slaves to the Caribbean. By the mid-seventeenth century 'the Irish already accounted for roughly half of the entire population of the English West Indies'.[54] By the early eighteenth century a further 40,000 Irish had moved there. They were not only strongly represented amongst the lower class white population, but were also represented as slave-holding plantation owners, merchants and overseers on a number of islands.[55] Some of these later moved on to the mainland.

The deepening of trade connections with the thirteen colonies from the early eighteenth century further strengthened these transatlantic links. More than two-thirds of the Irish migrants to the eastern seaboard before 1775 were of Protestant, mainly Ulster Presbyterian, stock. The other major component of the migrant stream to pre-revolutionary America were of Catholic background from the south of Ireland. However, given frontier conditions and the absence of priests and chapels in the southern colonies in particular, some of these migrants joined the burgeoning Protestant congregations and eventually merged with the wider Presbyterian/Baptist and later Methodist populations.[56] A similar process may have also occurred in pockets of counties Antrim and Down in the most difficult decades of the seventeenth century.

There was also a replication of administrative systems on both sides of the Atlantic, as the English sought to establish not just political but also linguistic, cultural and legal control. The administrative entity known as the county was a fundamental unit in this process; already well developed in sixteenth-century England, the shiring process was completed in Ireland by the early seventeenth century, thus providing a definitive framework within which English law and language should be seen to prevail throughout the society. The county model was likewise transferred to colonial America and – apart from New England, with its distinctive township system of government – the county became a deeply rooted instrument of government even in colonies like New York (originally the Dutch New Amsterdam) that were not originally settled by the English. Although in some parts of Ireland, and particularly in Ulster, there may have been some association between estate areas and parochial units, over much of the country there was no such neat dovetailing of these administrative areas.[57] Moreover, Ireland saw the creation of a dual parish system – one Anglican, the other Catholic – which led to the erosion of so many old parish centres. Apart from 'plantation' Virginia, a correspondence between estate and parish never really emerged in the much more spacious, more chaotic and ethnically and religiously more diverse American colonies.

At the state level, British mercantile thinking regarded both the Irish and American colonies as part of, and tributary to, its own colonial system. Neither colony was given much autonomy to develop enterprises directly in competition with the metropolitan colonial power. The administrative machineries of such colonies were thus very similar in so far as they were required to ensure that their territories acted as sources of raw materials and outlets for finished British goods. Ireland and the American plantations thus shared a common colonial status. Yet the geographical forerunners of the future federal American state pattern, and the basic framework of a modern state centred on Dublin, underlay this grand imperial design.

Finally, in both cases we are dealing with the rough and tumble of a ruthless colonial society in a frontier situation – with the clash of two traditions and the cultural fragmentation and social disorganization that follow such encounters. In both areas it was a tough world of energetic adventurers, ruthless land-grabbers, and a highly speculative, grasping, rural middle class, which often led to a violent clash between the existing and new society. The effect on the economic geography of both areas was the rapid exploitation of timber resources and an early emphasis on an extensive pastoralist or 'plantation' agriculture. In Ireland, the commercialization of sheep- and cattle-rearing produced an untidy and unkempt landscape across large swathes of the Midlands and in parts of Ulster and Munster. Tobacco, sugar, and later cotton plantations in America produced even more extreme exploitative economies and dishevelled landscapes.

In terms of landholding patterns, the activities of such colonists in Ireland led in some cases to the consolidation of fragmented medieval holdings.[58] But overall, given the highly varied mechanisms for allotting land, subsequent official modifications of such land grants and, above all, the cumulative effects of frequent private transactions of land in this mobile colonial setting, 'the new proprietorial geography was not demonstrably simpler or more rational than the old'.[59] The American land system, with its greater emphasis on, and greater facility for, the use of geometric boundaries, was superficially more simple, but underneath was the generally uncontrollable, often chaotic, carving, recarving and reallocating of blocks of land in varying sized estates.[60] This was essentially true of the Old South, it was also very characteristic of much of the Middle Colonies, and was less characteristic but by no means absent in the more tightly controlled New England township landholding systems. In both Ireland and America, the colonial elites, beyond the reach of the central power, acted strictly and often violently in terms of their own interests and not that of the wider society. V. S. Pritchett has summarized the Irish colonial situation well: 'Immigrants, who had they stayed in England would have behaved like honest Englishmen, found in Ireland an almost rootless society of speculators and go-getters.'[61] They quickly adapted – as their counterparts in America did to an even greater extent – to the more violent, more mobile and generally more insecure environments characteristic of frontier situations. In Ireland, the colonial system culminated in the excesses of landlordism; in the thirteen colonies it laid the foundations for rampant free-enterprise capitalism.

Figure 12.5 summarizes Donald Meinig's arguments about the structure of the British Atlantic empire in the mid-1760s, which he sees as consisting of two major components divided by an ocean and bound together around the great city node of London and its surrounding wealthy imperial core. Aggressive expansion against the other peoples of the islands had seen the English dominate the plains, encircle the uplands and control the use of the vital Atlantic approaches both to the north and south of Ireland and so on to America. The common culture of the core English homeland was considered as representative of the society's norms which, in turn, were to be transmitted throughout this Atlantic empire – both to the rest of Britain and Ireland and across the seas to America. Meinig therefore envisions this first British Empire as 'two great sectors of concentric patterns, a radiating set of provinces – anchored on a single point – ringing much of the North Atlantic'.[62] Equally for Meinig, 'the essence of empire lies in the coercive dominance of one people by another in a territorially structured relationship'.[63] In such a context the

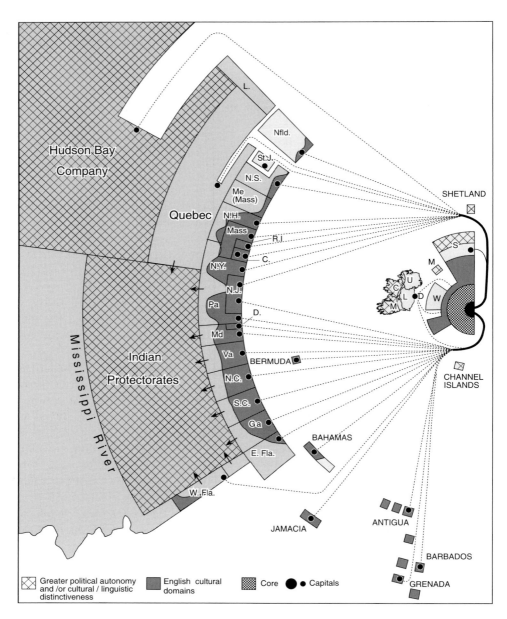

12.5 Ireland and the British Atlantic Empire *c.1750* (adapted from Figure 65, p. 376 in D.W. Meinig's *Atlantic America, 1492–1800*; see reference 13)

conquered territory will be characterized by a provincial capital – the local head-quarters of imperial authority and cultural diffusion. It may contain three kinds of imperial/colonial territories: (i) areas of conquered people under direct rule; (ii) areas colonized by migrants from the conquering state; and (iii) marginal areas under indirect rule and/or characterized by greater cultural autonomy.

Meinig recognizes examples of these three types of territories on both sides of the Atlantic. The complexity of the American imperial provinces in the mid-1760s is thus revealed (i) in the conquered provinces of Quebec, west Florida and the (now long-assimilated Dutch of the) Hudson valley, (ii) by the great eastern seaboard and associated northern and southern inland seaways characterized by in-depth colonization (and Indian displacement) by peoples drawn mainly, but by no means exclusively, from Britain and Ireland, and (iii) the vast territories of the transappalachian interior that had come under the force of imperial rule and which, for the moment, were protected by treaties recognizing the cultural and political autonomy of the various Indian nations.

Figure 12.5 also summarizes Ireland's complex status in the British Atlantic empire. Given Meinig's overall characterization and the varying regional expressions and experiences of imperial realms, he sees Ireland as likewise providing examples of the three kinds of colonial societies. Ulster is seen as 'the archetype of an imperial plantation',[64] a classic settler society where a newly planted English and Scottish landlord class and its associated immigrant tenant farmers, traders and artisans have acquired dominant positions and locations. Here, in contrast, the conquered Irish have been either marginalized locally or expelled from their homelands. Similarly, Meinig sees the complex and deeply rooted societies of much of Leinster (and east Munster) as showing evidence by the mid-eighteenth century of at least partial assimilation to the then dominant Anglo-Irish cultural norms illustrated most particularly by the more widespread use of the English language in this eastern half of the island. In this region he sees the provincial capital, Dublin, and its expanding hinterland (as well as those of the southern port-cities) as forming the core of a dominant Anglo-Irish society that exerted powerful pressures of acculturation. In contrast, the rest of Munster and all of Connacht (plus west Donegal) are seen as regions of less effective assimilation, where the Irish language and Irish cultural forms generally have retained a striking vitality. Meinig also recognizes that, technically, Ireland was a separate kingdom with its own parliament, but nevertheless, 'all of it was demonstrably under the ultimate control of coercive imperial force'.[65]

Enough has now been said to suggest the reality of the intertwining of American and Irish experiences and to support the notion that Ireland can be regarded as very much a colony in this era. As F. G. James has observed, it was a colony in the sense that it became a new home for colonials, that is, a land of opportunity for ambitious Englishmen,[66] colonial in the sense of a movement into a generally less well-developed economic region over which the English established first military and then political, social and economic domination; and colonial in the sense of the imposition of a hierarchical cultural system that was supported by, yet exploited, that majority population which was itself recognized as being subservient and resistant to assimilation. Such distinctions, as Jones Hughes has pointed out, actually led, in areas of the most effective colonial settlement, to the segregation of planter and local in both town and countryside.[67]

The Irish social landscape was therefore a dual and fragmented one. A generally alien minority established an impressively designed landscape façade. But underlying this relatively thin layer of colonial accretions was another much older cultural and social world. This latter landscape was characterized by a long-established rapport between ordinary country men and women and their local environments, and was expressed in regional variants of traditional house types, field-systems, farming technologies, religious and commercial traditions, and in a thousand old ways of doing and saying things, the last often expressed in the Irish language and enshrined in traditional stories, sporting activities, music, poetry and song.[68] The language barrier and associated cultural traits were to remain for much of the eighteenth century, although it is now certain that this same century witnessed the gradual diffusion of the English language throughout the more commercialized farming regions. English (and west European) colonization in North America involved an in-depth filling-in of the land in a reasonably compact line of settlements expanding westwards from the coast. In Ireland, in contrast, even in mid-seventeenth-century Ulster, planters and settlers often still represented islands of settlement in the still densely populated Irish areas. In addition, Ireland, as Evans has often noted, with its complex and varied topography, was much more conducive to localized, cultural fragmentation.[69] The more clear-cut pattern of American settlement and the greater absence of a dichotomy in its cultural expressions (apart, that is, from the plantation South) was facilitated not only by the ultimate weakness of the Indian resistance and its cultural imprint but also by the physical openness of the extensive coastal lowlands of the eastern seaboard. These varying landscape expressions, however relevant the parallels discussed above, suggest that we are dealing with two very different colonial societies and two very different colonial landscapes.

Differences in Settlement Patterns and Processes

To English men and women, America was a newly discovered, shadowy and strange land. Yet some parts of Ireland also appeared to them in this light. This was especially true of Ulster and the north west generally, which as late as 1609 Sir John Davies believed was as strange to the English as the most interior parts of America.[70] That said, the English conquest and colonization in Ireland had begun in the Middle Ages and while the area of effective English control in 1500 – the Pale around Dublin – had contracted very considerably, it provided an already established springboard for extending colonization inland. The machinery for government centred in Dublin was, thus, 'still quite elaborate and so designed that, in theory at least, it could comprehend the whole of the island'.[71] In addition, the rudiments of an English administrative, legal and military system survived in the semi-feudal eastern and southeastern parts of the country – areas whose physical and social geography were already fairly well known to English officials.[72] They had no such prior knowledge or skeletal administration on which to build in the new American colonies.

There were also significant differences between the initial experiences of colonials on either side of the Atlantic. Apart from the west Midlands and much of Ulster, most of the remainder of Ireland represented a very different landing stage from that of the eastern seaboard of America.[73] Ireland, east and south, already possessed seaports, harbours, some inland towns and an inland communications network that facilitated the bringing in of soldiers and settlers, their livestock and other paraphernalia. Besides, there already existed a basic marketing system, however localized in structure, over much of the country. This smoothed the way for a much quicker economic takeoff for the colonists in Ireland. The overall economy and society of Elizabethan Ireland (with the exception of the remoter lightly populated areas) was closer to that of England than the British economic system was to that of the Indian.

Early settlers in America had a more difficult time trying to establish footholds and gain a livelihood. American colonists were often to select initial sites in already well-developed Indian areas and were to learn a lot from the Indians about the best lands and the better routeways.[74] Most importantly, the numerous Indian groups taught the colonists how to plant and cultivate the great variety of domesticated crops in the New World, including the all-important maize, squash, beans, and tobacco. They thus helped to fuse together Old World and New World agricultural systems, one of the major achievements of this colonial region.[75] They also provided a humanized landscape of settlement sites and routeways. Nevertheless, the overall impact of the Indian cultures on the emerging American societies and landscapes was rather slight, since their populations were decimated by epidemic diseases, demoralization and war. In the rediscovery and resettlement of the eastern seaboard, the English colonist, inadvertently in part, had created a depopulated wasteland, ready for a new forging, a new imprint.

In contrast, colonists in Ireland not only had to adjust to older proven methods of dealing with local natural environments but also had to adjust even more to the long-established social institutions, landholding and settlement patterns of the more resistant and deeply rooted Irish populations. There appear, for example, to have been some continuities in the Irish economic system, although it was now characterized by a greater specialization in and commercialization of the older pastoral and tillage traditions. America was more of a *tabula rasa* at the outset of its European settlement, offering much more opportunity for testing a wide range of settlement, land-use schemes, and crop combinations.[76] The American experience was, in short, a more straightforward dialogue between a new society and a strange environment; there were fewer existing local and regional institutions to filter and reshape the process of adjustment.[77]

One finds that in spite of the geometry of the colonial blueprints for Ireland, the necessary adjustment between the new society and the older settled communities and the eternal influences of the local topography often resulted in many compromises. True, Ireland was less encumbered with long-established institutions than was the English homeland in this era of rural reconstruction; true also that the colonists did impose a general uniformity in the layout of Irish towns, estate villages and demesnes.[78] From Donegal to Wexford and from Dublin's Fitzwilliam Square to Limerick's Pery Square, similarities in the creators' goals and designs produced an outstanding homogeneity in Ireland's colonial heritage. The climax colonial landscape of great town houses and rural mansions constituted an upper fragile crust, overlying very old, deep and stable cultural strata. Given this type of colonial landscape, so unrepresentative of the feelings, motivations and life of most of the population, many compromises were necessary between the long-established Irish populations and the colonial incomers, between old and new ways of doing things.

So apart from the northeast, there developed a striking correspondence between the wealthier colonial areas and the more well-to-do regions of the medieval period. The new elites also adopted the older (and initially strange) landholding units, particularly the smallest landholding building block, later generally known as the 'townland'. Some new manors and estates did correspond to older landholding entities, while there was a striking continuity between the newly constituted baronies and counties and the older territories of major families. Co. Tyrone, for example, was to encompass the lands held by the O'Neills, and Co. Monaghan that of the MacMahons. Likewise, many new towns and county capitals were built on the sites of older settlements beside churches, monasteries, castles and forts. In terms of territorial and locational strategies, the new colonial elite were not so revolutionary as their American counterparts, as they took over both pre-existing forms of territorial organizations – the townland, the parish, and the reconstituted baronies – and utilized older sites, including medieval parish centres, for their new settlement creations. Locational conservatism was the rule, with the existing settlement and economic patterns acting as powerful guides to later developments.[79]

There was, therefore, a greater mixing together of the two traditions in Ireland, particularly in the south, southeast and east. Although the English language and legal system were to prevail, the adapting planter was also gradually and unconsciously absorbing at least some of the traditions and attitudes of the Irish countryside. Assimilation and a growing away from England were later reflected in a greater striving for political independence, in Anglo-Irish literature, in regional dialects of English, and in the musical, sporting, and hospitable traditions of the gentry families. This process was to leave many of the long-settled Irish colonial groups with an ambivalent, even dual identity. It was not all one-way traffic: the influence of the colonial Big House percolated down to the Irish rural population and was expressed at the linguistic and institutional level even in a brand of Catholicism that had to survive, grow up in and adapt to a privileged Protestant world, and also in activities like horse-racing, courtly music and dances, house design, and forms of dress, down to the wearing of bowler hats at funerals. The descendants of the local populations too inherited a fragmented and ambivalent identity.

The difference in the 'native' population densities of both areas also had further profound consequences. The English and Scottish planters availed of the ready supply of cheap and abundant Irish labour to develop their estates and towns. In America the Indians, already decimated by disease, had retreated or had been eradicated, and were rarely retained by the planters. Equally important, colonists in Ireland quickly came to accept the Irish as tenant farmers, although such an arrangement was often prohibited in the original land grants. Given the relative size and density of the ancestral *vis-à-vis* the colonial populations, such adjustments were both necessary and to the economic advantage of the settler. There may have been a scarcity of labourers and prospective tenants in some parts of mid-seventeenth-century Ireland, particularly in Ulster; the original landowning elite were uprooted over much of Ireland and local communities were eradicated or displaced in some areas. Yet, apart from areas of northeastern Ulster, where the second wave of Scottish migrants, especially in the mid- and later seventeenth century, did lead to the displacement of existing populations onto more marginal lands,[80] both the general retention and rootedness of the ordinary tenants elsewhere helps partly to explain the durability of rural structures in so many areas of Ireland. We may note, in particular, the regular recurrence in localized and adjacent situations of particular family names, such as Ryan, O'Dwyer and O'Meagher in Co. Tipperary. Such localized patterns strongly suggest the active operation of the support mechanisms of the extended family and provide firm evidence of stability and continuity in these rural cultures.

In the American colonies, by contrast, shortage of labour was always a chronic problem. Hence the perceived necessity for the indentured servant and the slave trade. The governor of New York noted in 1698 that 'hemp and flax are better for production in the soil of Ireland and to be manufactured there where labour is cheaper by three-fourths than here in New York or New Hampshire'.[81] The proliferation and exponential increase in the numbers of landless labourer families in Ireland points to a very different social system. With the availability of free land for clearing in America, there were few reasons why one hard-working, able and ambitious white man should have to work for another. Thus, the seemingly endless stretches of unused land in America made redundant many of the traditional European ground rules about land-use and occupation. Despite a catalogue of speculation, inequity and fraud, land was easier to acquire, to work, to sell and to inherit in the American colonies than in any other place in the Atlantic world.[82] It was, in short, a world dominated by farmer proprietors, not by landlords and tenants. And the problem of labour in colonial America was solved in the large plantations of the South by the introduction of the deeply divisive and degrading black slave system. It was made increasingly redundant in the other colonies with the emerging dominance of the family farm as the unit of agricultural production. In Ireland, especially in the more commercialized farming regions, there existed a variety of tenant layers, underpinned, in turn, by a large landless class whose great diversity of surnames reflected high levels of mobility and dislocation.

The greater availability of free land in America, and the associated traditions of owner-occupancy, squatting, and the extensive (often careless use) of land, brings us to another fundamental contrast between the two colonial regions – landholding. Indian property rights in land were not well-developed in a European legal sense and they were easily ignored and discarded. Likewise, the newly established proprietors of large blocks of land generally exerted only a slight influence on the development of settlement and landholding patterns. They and their surveyors often 'had to give way in their geometric ideas to the evolved haphazard irregular arrangement of holdings'.[83]

In much of Ireland the new colonists had to face a long-established and complex landholding system where every inch of the ground had been appropriated, thus necessitating careful landholding surveys. Property boundaries were more deeply embedded both in the Irish landscape and in Irish mentalities and often came to represent sharp frontiers in relation to the shape of settlement and land use. The seventeenth-century dismantling and reorganization of the older landowning pattern, and its institutionalization in a penal legal system, was at the heart of tensions, contradictions and conflicts in eighteenth- and nineteenth-century Ireland. Whatever the status of the bulk of the population in pre-plantation Ireland, from the seventeenth century onwards practically a whole nation was reduced to the status of labourers or tenants in their own land by an alien colonial elite. It would be difficult to find any other nation in Europe that underwent this intensity of experience. Tensions and conflicts also erupted at ground level, according as the modernization of agriculture, the creation of compact individual holdings, of new settlements and of roads all cut into the older, more communally organized settlement and landholding patterns.

All of these transformations were achieved by, based on and backed up by superior military power. As James has noted, in a far more fundamental sense than the conquered colonies of New York or Jamaica or wherever in America, the Irish colonial administration and elite 'rested on conquest and could not easily escape its military, i.e. its violent origins'.[84] The garrison towns – the Athlones and Templemores of Ireland – gave geographical expression to this fundamental aspect of Irish colonial life.

Another crucial difference was the contiguity factor. England's sheer proximity to Ireland made for an 'older, deeper, more intimate, more quarrelsome relation-ship between the metropolitan colonial power and the adjoining dependent colony'.[85] In Ireland's case, closer administrative and institutional links were strongly reinforced by the obvious facility for maintaining stronger social, economic and cultural links between the two islands. North America, by contrast, protected by the great buffer of the Atlantic Ocean, had more room to develop its own ways from the beginning. This greater freedom from centralized government controls released and cultivated an emphasis on individual freedom, greater social mobility, and greater self-government. It also facilitated the emergence of a more literate population and paved the way for a more democratic society.

Finally, any comparison could not ignore the far greater variety of land grants, settlement schemes, types of proprietors, social origins of colonists and the numerous ethnic groups involved in settling the American environment.[86] The great social and ethnic diversity of America may well be the most fundamental difference. The majority of the colonists were of English origin, but the Irish, Scots, and Welsh were prominent, as were the Germans. A smaller number of French Huguenots, Dutch, Swedes, Swiss and Italians were also present, while nearly a half million black Afro-Americans were represented at the time of the revolution. The European groups were not very representative of their home cultures, for selective migration had reduced the range of the social structure and made for a society dominated by middle and lower class strata. The picture was further complicated by the even greater religious variety of the population, although composed mainly of a wide range of intense and highly competitive Protestant denominations. Indeed, the religious refugee searching for a new paradise was a conspicuous figure in the American landscape.[87] Colonial America was a complicated mosaic of peoples and places.

Ireland was by no means mono-ethnic. It was more varied than one might expect, but the encounter there was confined essentially to the peoples of the two islands: there were Irish, Old English, the New English and the Ulster Scots. There was also a small number of French Huguenot and German Palatine settlements, for Ireland was also to receive its share of religious refugees. In 1732, although the population was predominantly (73 per cent) Catholic in religion, at least 10 per cent belonged to the highly self-conscious independent Presbyterian communities; another 16 per cent belonged to the Anglican communion; small but significant groups belonged to the Society of Friends, Baptists, Independents and later on Wesleyan Methodism was to develop. It may well be that in the rapidly developing economy of eighteenth-century Ireland – opening up, as it did, a far wider range of opportunities for the pursuit of human happiness – it was found more essential to slowly tolerate the exercise of such different forms of religion and culture. This was certainly the case in a still Protestant-dominated colonial America and one suspects that there are echoes of this feeling in late eighteenth-century Ireland. It is to the societies and landscapes of this later more creative phase that we now turn to conclude our story.

How Similar the Evolved Colonial Societies and Landscapes?

Surprisingly, a comparison of the consequences of colonization for the societies and cultural landscapes of Ireland and America is still manageable and, I think, fruitful up to 1780–1800. First, a few general comments will set the scene for a more detailed analysis of the regional societies of late eighteenth-century Ireland and America. By the time of the American Revolution (1775–83), Ireland was still second only to Britain in the empire in terms of population size, public revenue and expenditure, and in volume of trade.[88] The population of the newly created United States of America surpassed that of Ireland only in the early nineteenth century; in 1800 both areas contained a population of just over 5 million people; and the cities of Cork and Dublin were far larger than any of the American colonial cities. Cork then had a population of 65,000–70,000. Dublin's population in 1800 exceeded 200,000 – making it one of the great cities of Europe at the end of the triumphant eighteenth century. At that time Philadelphia was the largest colonial city of America, with a population of about 40,000; New York contained 25,000; Boston 16,000 and Charleston 12,000.[89] Given the enormous difference in the size of the two settled areas, Ireland's population density was still about ten times as great as that of North America. Both societies were predominantly rural and agrarian, working on a mainly pre-industrial technological base. Both colonial societies had a rural cast, the leisure pursuits of its elites dominated by the fishing rod, the gun and the horse. By the end of the eighteenth century only 5 per cent of Americans lived in 24 urban places with a population of 2,500 or more,[90] while 10 per cent of

Ireland's population lived in 23 borough towns, each with a population in excess of 4,000.[91] In both countries, large cities were almost invariably seaports; these were also the only major industrial centres, their morphologies reflecting the over-whelming importance of long-distance overseas trade in the economies of both areas. This was as true for Boston, Philadelphia and the Chesapeake Bay area as it was for the ports of southern and eastern Ireland. At this same time, Ireland's exports and imports were roughly equal to those of the thirteen rebelling American colonies combined, emphasizing the importance of Ireland's economic position in the 'old empire'. It is also useful at this time to see the embryonic United States of America as still an ocean-fronted 'island' hemmed in to the west by topographical barriers, hostile Indians and other colonial powers.

Both Ireland and America witnessed a staggering phase of economic growth in the eighteenth century. Ireland's exports quadrupled between 1700 and 1765 and doubled again by 1800,[92] while the American colonies' trade with the rest of the empire likewise quadrupled between 1705 and 1765.[93] In both cases economic development was closely linked with Britain's own growth and that of the wider Atlantic economy, and in both examples Britain's position as the major trading partner was enhanced over the century. In 1683 only 38 per cent of Irish exports went to England, while scarcely a century later, in 1774, this figure was as high as 74 per cent.[94] Similarly, American colonial trade with Britain amounted to only one-sixth of its total in 1700 but this proportion had doubled by 1770.[95] Overall, what needs to be stressed is that the economic and cultural development of both regions was very much related to the transformation of the economic geography of the whole Western world. The peoples on both sides of the Atlantic had immense drive and initiative and, in their magnificent houses, towns and villages, have left many beautiful legacies from the eighteenth century.

These general comparisons confined to one point in time may be more than a little misleading unless one compares the timing, the scale, and the diffusion of social and economic change in both areas during the whole colonial period. The military conquest of Ireland was effectively completed by the late-seventeenth century, while Americans were still involved in this process long after securing independence. Large immigrations into Ireland ceased around 1715, just when America was witnessing a massive increase in its migrant populations. The landholding patterns in Ireland had been effectively transformed by 1700, whereas this remained an ongoing process in America. Likewise, the major phases of administrative and territorial reorganization had been completed in Ireland by the late seventeenth century, whereas colonial America was to witness a phenom-enal expansion in the number of counties in the mid-eighteenth century as migrants poured westwards and southwards into the interior. Similarly, while the seventeenth century marked the most important phase for urban foundations (if not urban growth) in Ireland, America was to witness a further major burst of town-building from the 1730s onwards. Ireland's population quadrupled from about 1.2 million in 1650 to 5 million in 1800. The American colonial population expanded even more dramatically – by, say, 600 per cent between 1700 and 1760 (from 0.3 million to 1.5 million) and was to increase again by over 300 per cent between 1760 and 1800.[96] Ireland was to witness an inversion of its east–west population densities in the late eighteenth and early nineteenth centuries as marginal subsistence farming and rapid population growth spread rapidly westwards, linked to, as yet, such poorly documented processes as smallpox inoculation and the final phase in the diffusion of the potato as a staple food.[97] By contrast, America was to retain its densely settled coastal versus lightly populated interior areas until well into the nineteenth century – a pattern more reminiscent of late seventeenth- early eighteenth-century Ireland (see Fig. 12.6). In terms of the elaboration of communications, Ireland had witnessed a very significant expansion in an already well-developed road and waterway network from the 1730s on,[98] whereas American developments in this sphere (and in canal-building) came a half-century later, because of both the overwhelming importance of coastal and riverine traffic and the high labour costs involved in road-building.[99] On the other hand, it would appear that the diffusion of better agricultural techniques, linked with the enclosure movement and the expansion of the manufacturing frontier, all proceeded at about the same time in both areas. The general timing of the

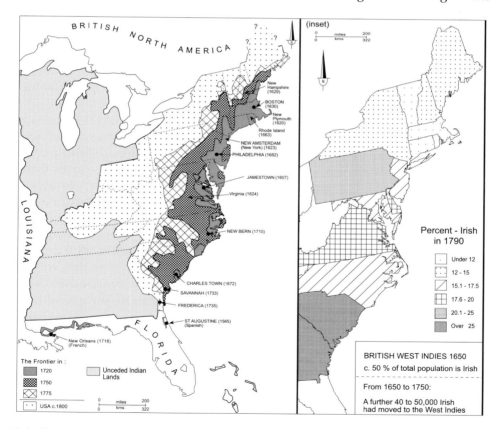

12.6   The expansion of European settlement in eastern North America, 1607–1800; (adapted in part from R.H. Brown's *Historical Geography of the United States* and D.W. Meinig's *Atlantic America, 1492–1800*: see references 5 and 13) (inset: distribution of Irish migrants as a proportion of the European population per state in 1790, after work of David Doyle: see reference 56)

Georgian embellishment of the cultural landscape also overlapped in both regions.

These overall differences would suggest that economic takeoff occurred earlier in Ireland; one might suggest a shift to a 'post-pioneer' phase in colonial Ireland by at least 1660, whereas this phase was not initiated in coastal America until about 1720. What this means is that, allowing for variations over time and space between and within the two areas, one could document similar stages of development in the spatial organization of the economies of both regions.[100] Over the eighteenth century both societies were to witness greater regional specialization in agricultural production, an increased diversification of manufacturing and services, the greater elaboration of smaller lower-order central places, and more frequent and sustained contacts and exchanges between rural populations and larger market centres. These developments ushered in major changes in styles of living across both territories. In Ireland, the most striking element is the floresence of village and small town lifestyles, uncomfortably juxtapositioned with and superimposed upon the rhythms of very old and scattered settlements and communities.

Underpinning these trends was the development of a sophisticated provincial mercantile capitalism and associated retailing strategies that led first to an expansion in the effective hinterlands of major seaports and later on to a much fuller utilization of the whole central place hierarchy in the marketing of produce and the distribution of finished goods. And in both areas, there were wealthy core areas and poorer peripheries, both within the cities and between more commercialized and more subsistence-type farming regions.

Regional variations in economic and cultural development in the American colonies were to produce extremes in the landscape and social structure but never so pronounced or so deep as in the Irish scene. One can distinguish three particular areas in mainland America: New England, with its relatively small farms, Puritan culture and far-ranging commerce; the 'plantation' South, an area devoted to the commercial production of staples such as tobacco, rice and indigo for export to England; and the Middle Colonies, an area of more conspicuous social and settlement diversity than either of the other regions. Here (in Pennsylvania, Maryland, New Jersey and New York) were combined trading skills with a mixed commercialized agricultural system. It was also at Philadelphia that colonial manufacturing reached its peak of development. But by the end of the colonial era the practices of the British industrial revolution had begun to reach not just the Middle Colonies, but also New England.[101]

In Ireland, the commercialization of cattle, sheep and dairying regions, as well as urban and industrial growth, were also features of the developing landscape. Whereas the linen town of Lisburn was the eighth largest urban centre in 1725, with a population of over 4,000, by 1798 there were 23 towns with populations greater than this.[102] In the later decades of that dynamic century, large scale grain-milling had become a feature of both town and countryside, while earlier in the century the woollen industry had expanded rapidly – actually equalling one-third of the volume of exports in the linen industry. The story of the linen industry was one of phenomenal growth, zooming from an export rate of 0.5 million yards in the 1680s to over 40 million yards in the 1790s.[103] Unlike the woollen industry – more strongly urban-based and concentrated in the southern parts of the island – the linen industry, long established, domestic and rural in character, helped to make for a better overall standard of living, revolutionized the Ulster economy by the late seventeenth century and subsequently intensified in north Leinster, Connacht, and parts of west Munster. But its major long-lasting impact was in Ulster, transforming a relatively self-sufficient economic region into a position of industrial strength, boosting Belfast into fourth place among Irish ports by the 1690s and making for one of the most densely populated regions in Europe.

There are some parallels (and indeed strong cultural links) between Ulster and Puritan New England. The latter region was a poorer agricultural area of small live-stock farms, which prospered through provisions, furs, fish and mercantile capitalism and played a key role in the development of a far-flung British economy in the North Atlantic. All of this was born out of the certainties of an exclusive reli-gious tradition and the evolution of tightly knit and spiritually intense congregational communities and busy commercial and manufacturing centres, which focused on the port-city of Boston – then a city with a touch of the seriousness of the Scot about it.[104] And like the more well-to-do parts of Antrim, north Down and north Armagh, New England had its more wealthy rural areas such as the Connecticut valley, whose eighteenth-century wheat fields, elms and orchards are described as taking on the aspect of the peaceful English countryside.[105] North and east Ulster was also dominated by cohesive settler communities, often of a strongly Nonconformist religious persuasion, which, in turn, were also to play a powerful role in the shaping of the geography of settlement in their region. Here again, in a generally poorer agricultural area, segments of the colonial society grew wealthy and popu-lous through the rapid expansion of the linen, the provisions, and the colonial shipping trade. Belfast in this case was the economic and cultural centre, with its strong economic ties with Glasgow and overseas shipping in general and, of course, close emigrant links with the New World.

In America the maturing of the colonial landscape of the Middle Colonies centred on Pennsylvania is also reflected in various travellers' descriptions in the second half of the eighteenth century. Much emphasis is placed on the succession of individual dispersed farms, meadows, gardens and dwellings. One traveller comments that if hedges were substituted for rail fences, these states would very much resemble those of some of the English or, for that matter, some of the more prosperous Irish counties.[106] Just as in the more commercialized farming regions of Ireland, a rationalized inheritance pattern emerged on the mainly owner-occupier Middle Atlantic farms; subdivision was generally prohibited beyond a viable farm size that averaged about 100 acres.[107] And there was always the safety valve of the expanding frontier, plus a growing number of non-farming occupa-tions to cater for other sons. Although characterized by a complex landholding structure with quite a proportion of tenant farmers and labourers, the Middle Colonies were, above all, distinguished by family farms geared to cattle, pig and especially grain production. This trade was centred along the many fine harbours that sheltered the thriving cosmopolitan mercantile seaports of Philadelphia, New

York and Baltimore. This middle zone – and particularly these ports – was the meeting-place of all immigrant groups and contained the highest proportion of southern Irish immigrants at this time in all of America.

The Middle Colonies were in many ways the most diverse and most representative, and certainly the most tolerant and most geographically influential, of the whole American colonial world. On a different scale, one notes some similarities, however superficial, with the Munster/south Leinster area, another zone of mixed cultural heritage and of a fractured hill-valley topography. Again, this region was centred on the thriving Atlantic European city of Cork and the smaller ports of Waterford and Limerick, all three seaports dominating the best harbours of the south and all gathering in the beef and pork trade, the butter and the grain of this strong tillage/dairying area. In both regions, rural communities were connected by a chain of credit, linking marketing towns and villages through the provincial cities of Cork, Waterford, Philadelphia and New York with the London merchants and moneylenders who enjoyed access to more highly developed credit institutions.[108] Like Pennsylvania and the other Middle Colonies, much of Munster and south Leinster was a zone of relatively rich agricultural lands, wealthy market towns and a complex, stratified society. In this colonial period it was to see a greater accommodation between a minority of widely dispersed farmers, well-to-do millers and merchants of New English descent, and the overwhelming majority of Catholic Irish, quite a proportion of whom were substantial farmers, millers, comfortable dairymen, small tenants, artisans, or well-to-do shopkeepers, bakers and brewers. Finally, there were powerful shipping and immigrant links between the two areas. In the late 1760s, 84 per cent of all Irish flaxseed was imported from the American colonies, through New York and, particularly, Philadelphia. There was probably a three-cornered shipping trade involved in these links: many of the ships bound from southern Ireland, in particular, went with servants and provisions to the West Indies, then to Philadelphia and New York with servants, sugar, molasses and rum, and returned back again to Ireland. Flaxseed was the most important commodity on the final passage from North America to Ireland. So, in a curious way the export of the provisions of the south was linked with the growing linen industry in the north.[109]

As regards the owners of feudal-like estates, tenant farms and Big Houses of the Hudson valley, parts of Maryland, and the plantation economy of the Old South all are reminiscent of the privileged ruling landed elite in Ireland; both were to dominate their respective governmental machineries with an eye to their own interests. Both kinds of estate system were expanding in size through economies of scale: in America at the expense of the smaller yeoman farmers who ended up as 'poor whites' in the Appalachian hills and valleys;[110] and in Ireland at the expense of subsistence farming communities, which were often squeezed out to the edges of the estate and pushed on to more marginal lands near the boglands, wetlands and uplands. There were thus broad similarities in the role of the plantation overseer in the American south and the role of the landlord agent in Ireland. Both societies were also essentially agrarian; both belonged to the Established Anglican Church and dominated the vestry of the local community; both catered for the stables and the horse. And the consequences of their wealth and power were expressed in such things as the well-furnished, elaborately decorated Big House and expressed socially in a patriarchal and leisurely style of life. Thus, both the Big House in Ireland and the plantation mansion in America came to be the symbol of the power and prestige of the ruling elite and a model of exploitation. But there was a great difference between the temperate, healthy climate of Ireland and the torrid subtropical conditions of the deep South. Another great difference was that the American elites were in the long run of the same stock as the majority of the population, resided on their estates, and were more involved in the actual day-to-day running of their local and regional economies. In Ireland, cultural alienation loaded on to economic exploitation, as rents to absentee landlords, charges on English shipping and merchant commissions exported so much of the hard-won surplus to the metropolitan core.

Urban landscapes were also a common bond between the two colonial areas. (see Fig. 12.7a and Fig. 12.7b) After the defensive, huddled urban phase of the seventeenth century, newly designed towns of brick and paint, with right-angled, tree-lined streets and steepled skylines, became the norm in early eighteenth-century America. Again, as in wealthier parts of Ireland, the influence of elegant French and Italian garden, house, and urban designs emerge, with American buildings replicating in brick and wood their European equivalents in stone. The exotic gardens of the bigger mansions or mercantile villas display the typical French pattern of terraces, avenues and oak trees, complete with the elaborate wrought-iron gate entrances. And cities like Georgian Dublin, Penn's Philadelphia, and new colonial capitals like Williamsburg, were laid out or redesigned with wide, open streets, created to display the well-proportioned town houses and public buildings. Ideas of urban planning also extended into smaller market towns and villages; Ireland has numerous examples of superbly planned landlord towns (for example, Stokestown, Stradbally, (Fig. 12.8a [Pl. 2p]) and Mitchelstown), while in America newly planned county seats with characteristic court-house squares and other newly designed urban centres dotted the landscapes of Virginia, Pennsylvania and elsewhere. Thus, European and, more particularly, English metropolitan fashions in the design of the Big House, demesne, garden, small town and city were echoed on both sides of the Atlantic, reflecting the emergence of a more integrated transatlantic world as the eighteenth century progressed.[111]

In sharp contrast to Georgian Dublin and the mercantile cities of the American eastern seaboard, however, were conditions in both the western parts of Irish-speaking Ireland and in the western Indian territories in America. In the later eighteenth century the American frontier was spreading westwards from the uplands of Maine in the north to beyond the pine belt of the Carolinas in the south. Ireland's land frontiers in the later eighteenth and early nineteenth centuries were, as always, the bogs, mountains, and river marshes throughout the country and particularly those in some of the formerly most sparsely populated areas in the west and northwest. But there were vast differences here between the extreme scarcity of good land in Ireland and – after the Indian conquests – its availability on the American frontier; between family farms held in fee simple and

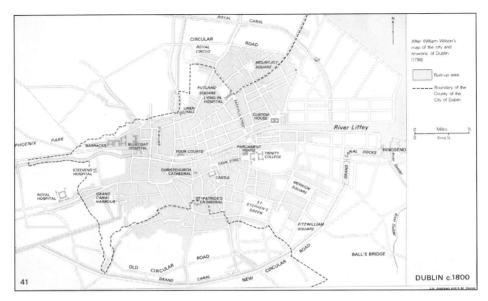

12.7a   Map of Dublin city's expansion by c.1800 (Figure 41 reproduced with the permission of its authors J.H. Andrews and K.M. Davies in *A New History of Ireland IX*, p. 39)

occupied by opportunistic settlers and the still feudal-like Irish tenant system; and between the small percentage of landless poor in America and their proliferation in Ireland.

Another crucial difference relates to the relatively autonomous and growing maritime power of the American colonies, as compared with Ireland's deepening dependency on Britain's shipping and economy. From the beginning, the American colonies had to build their own shipping fleets and merchant communities all along the eastern seaboard, with Boston and Philadelphia the two great foci. By the middle of the eighteenth century, it is very relevant to note that coast-wise intercolonial trading between the more developed American colonies had actually come to equal the importance of transoceanic commerce. Its key ports and merchants then built and sold their own ships and provided much valuable shipping and commercial services to others.[112] By contrast, as early as the late seventeenth century two-thirds of Irish trade to England was carried in English-owned ships.[113] As the eighteenth century moved on, Irish shipping and its export economy came to be more and more dominated by English shipping and credit facilities, with each Irish port in a dependent relationship with the hub-ports of Britain. In contrast to America, therefore, Ireland's economic structure was both deeply disarticulated and dominated.

And finally we come to a profound political difference. The ongoing elaboration of the cultural, economic and political worlds of the mature American colonies saw what Jack Greene has described as 'the conjoint processes of creolisation – adaptation to local conditions – and metropolitanisation – successful cultivation of the principal values and forms of the parent culture'[114] converge to underpin a loose political confederation all along the eastern seaboard. Denied equal rights

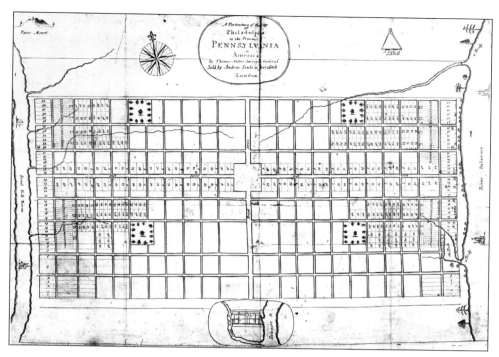

12.7b   Map of William Penn's plans for Philadelphia, (1682) figure 97 in John Reps, *The Making of Urban America* (1965). Reproduced with permission of the author.

with the parent state, this confederation proceeded to rupture the overarching imperial superstructure to establish an independent republic and put in place one of the most democratic and most influential constitutions ever written.

Ireland (as were many of the other British colonies) was deeply affected by this revolutionary movement and the ideas that underpinned it. But the conditions for revolution in America and Ireland were very different. America saw a revolution carried out by its own mainstream governing elites, who used the existing law to fight for their independence and their interests. In contrast, the United Irishmen – representing the educated, urban elite of the excluded classes in Irish political life – had the laws of the ruling minority to fight against.[115] America's revolution was led by its learned elites. In Ireland the ruling Anglo-Irish Anglican elite ultimately had to depend upon the power of the metropolitan government in London to keep the excluded majority Catholics – and the radical Presbyterians – in line. And a final ironic difference. It was Lord Cornwallis who presided over the series of British defeats that led to the loss of the thirteen colonies. Fifteen years later, as the king's viceroy in Ireland, he made sure he succeeded in preventing the loss of another large British possession – Ireland – then in the throes of the 1798 rising/rebellion.[116]

Thus, at the end of the eighteenth century, the political destinies of Ireland and the fledging United States of America diverged in the most dramatic and, for Ireland, in the most tragic way. Among other things, the Act of Union represented the British government's loss of faith in the capacity of the privileged Anglo-Irish elite to rule and hold down Ireland. More poignantly, the abolition of the Irish parliament eliminated the potential for greater self-government until 1921 – so depriving the majority of the Irish people of the ability to determine their own national priorities and to care for their own particular needs.

And so, as we move into the first decades of the nineteenth century we note that the United States – having solved most of its international boundary problems and witnessing a new wave of immigration from northwestern Europe – accelerates its urban and industrial expansion as it pushes deeper and deeper west to reach the Pacific by mid-century. On the other hand, Ireland – given the collapse in agricultural prices following the end of the Napoleonic War and with a still exploding population confined within a small cramped space – sees the initiation of processes of rural conflict associated with farm consolidation, evictions and emigration, processes that were to be accelerated after the Great Famine (in which Ireland lost over 2 million of its population either through death by starvation and disease or through emigration).

Thus, by 1820 the wheel had come full circle, and the descendants of the Irish who had in the previous centuries witnessed the colonization of their own country now, more than ever before, became one of the most significant national groups in the expansion of settlement throughout much of the New World and in the United States in particular. The safety valve of the American frontier had also become Ireland's safety valve and America itself had truly become Ireland's western frontier.

Conclusion

Only the dispossessed people know their lands in the dark.

Elizabeth Bowen[1]

The prismatic view of Ireland presented here is book-ended by the Tudor Revolution on the one hand and by the American and French Revolutions on the other. The first revolution saw the creation of the English nation; the second that of the American nation;[2] and the third 'the beginning of the modern world and the end of the old one'.[3] Located between these revolutionary places and periods is a distinctive European country, Ireland – which, uniquely in western Europe, had experienced a colonial conquest that in truth was never more than a half-conquest. It experienced the attempted destruction of an old civilization that almost succeeded, yet saw the creation of a number of new regional societies. By the 1770s and 1780s, Ireland is a place full of hyphenated identities, including the Anglo-Irish Protestant Ascendancy, the English-speaking Catholic Irish, the Scots Presbyterian Irish, the Irish-speaking Irish and a whole series of other often twilight identities.

What Ireland would have been like without this conquest can never be known. But given the experience of other smaller countries of Atlantic Europe – from Denmark through the Netherlands to Portugal – it could be argued that Ireland would have 'modernized' on its own terms and could have seen the creation of a more integrated and stable society which would have evolved out of existing territorial frameworks and cultural institutions. It would have almost certainly been characterized by a single language (Irish) and a single religious tradition. It would have developed commercially; apart from the nascent commercializing worlds of the south and east, new Gaelic urban-cum-trading centres would have emerged, as had already happened at places such as Aghaboe, Armagh, Cashel, Cavan, Durrow, Ennis, Kells, Kildare, Lismore and Longford.

The creation of a unified political entity would have been the greatest challenge. Given existing provincial power structures, it is more likely that a federal rather than a unitary state would have emerged. One of the great regional lordships and magnates would have had to assume a dominant leadership role, such as the House of Orange was to assume in the unification of the Netherlands. The Ormond Butlers with a capital city of Kilkenny? Or the O'Neills with a capital city at

451

Armagh? The most likely candidates would have been the most strategically located Leinster Fitzgeralds, who, if they had been successful in their continued building up of coalitions beyond Leinster and in hammering out a consensus island-wide, could have come to command a greatly expanded power base centred on their capital city Dublin. But here my counterfactual historical geography immediately flounders because the vital interests of the early modernizing English nation-state would not have allowed such a development on its western flank. The very first phase of what turned out to be the New English conquest was the literal decapitation of the dynamic potential of the Fitzgerald challenge in east Leinster.

As we have seen (chapters 2 and 3), maps were deeply implicated in the military conquest of Ireland. England would have preferred – it would have been far less costly – a peaceful assimilation of the Irish populations to New English economic, legal, political and religious norms. The 'reformation' of Ireland assumed the greater superiority of English ways of living over Irish ways. For the peoples of Ireland, 'reformation', 'anglicization' and 'evangelization' saw the imposition of legal and other penalties for refusing to conform, so exercising real social and psychological violence. The great majority of Irish people – of whatever traditions – saw little need for, and in time came to resent this reformation.

Many of the poets and literati came to oppose the ideology of the 'map-makers'. Gradually innovative strands within the generally conservative bardic traditions – as well as amongst the Irish clergy and other intellectuals – came to stress and articulate a newly awakened, more inclusive, national consciousness. This new national awareness synthesized allegiance to Tridentine Catholicism, loyalty to Gaelic and gaelicized cultural norms and a consciousness of the territorial integrity of the island of Ireland.[4] Catholic Irish exiles played a key role in this synthesis.

Map-maker Robert Lythe's life and career overlaps with that of the bardic poet Tadhg Dall Ó hUiginn (1550–91). The dialectic between their two worlds and their two functions is neatly brought out in the parallel dangers they encountered in carrying out their professional occupations. Lythe needed not only the protection of Sir Henry Sidney but also that of the local lords as he attempted to map the south of Ireland. Equally, Ó hUiginn needed the protection of one of his overlords and patrons, Cormac O'Hara of Leyney (Co. Sligo), as well as the other lords of north Connacht. From the time of Henry VIII onwards, the New English authorities had been adamant in their hostility to the Irish learned classes: anti-bardic measures had been promulgated and Irish manuscripts destroyed. Poets such as Ó hUiginn were constantly in fear of the new laws being used against them. As he stated in one of his poems: 'A-tú a mbeol ghuasi do ghnáth' (I am continually in the jaws of danger).[5] In a famous poem, 'Fearann cloidhimh críoch Bhanbha', which Ó hUiginn composed about the time Lythe was finishing his map-surveying in Ireland, he argues 'that Ireland is effectively swordland (fearann cloidhimh) and this means that the island will inevitably be in the possession of the strongest contender for its domination'.[6] Here Ó hUiginn shows the forward-thinking ability of his class by recognizing the gaelicized descendants of the Anglo-Normans – such as the Lower MacWilliam Burkes of north Connacht – as equally Irish ('Éireannaigh'). While Ó hUiginn may provide a sophisticated poetic legitimation for the Connacht lords in their complex accommodations with the Tudor state, in the end the message of this poet to his patrons is to resist the Tudor invasion by force.[7]

Sir Henry Sidney, a pivotal English figure in 'Tudor' Ireland, while respectful of the persons of the Irish lords with whom he negotiated, is a classic product of Renaissance nationalizing England – utterly convinced of the superiority of English ways of living and ways of doing things, including the strategic use of map-making and map-makers like Robert Lythe. Sidney makes three great geographical circuits of Ireland – rather in the manner of the Irish high-kings – staking out his control of the island by moving from lordship to lordship and receiving the submissions and promises of obedience from the local lords.[8] Often, however, it is his impressive show of force that acts as the catalyst for the submissions. Because of Sidney's (and other viceroys') determined drive to extend the power of provincial and shire governments – and so bring the recalcitrant Irish into a writ-governed constitutional relationship with the crown via new forms of taxation – Ireland becomes a war zone.[9]

Maps were integral to what became a military conquest of Ireland, as well as to the seizure, delineation, reallocation and administration of the lands of the plantations. The mapping created a new construct, revealing a new Ireland as viewed through English lenses, assumptions and intentions. But in this process, other Irelands are obscured or made invisible. The language of the map is English; and the ubiquity of the Irish language and Irish language placenames are airbrushed from such maps of Ireland or its regions. The original maps are only a small part of the much wider process of silencing: I have also explored and mapped in great detail the many narrative surveys commissioned, implemented and completed during the sixteenth/seventeenth centuries. The actual carrying out of these narratives (usually judicial surveys) are in themselves a measure of England's growing territorial power, even before the results of these surveys are used to implement either new tax assessments or plantations.[10]

Writing as well as mapping is deeply implicated in the colonization of space. Elizabethan and later colonial texts effaced Irish, silenced the language, deemed it not to exist: 'English writers consistently erased the majority language, reducing Irish language utterances to English paraphrases.'[11] Such behaviour was underpinned by Henry VIII's imperial claim in his proclamation of 1541, then ratified by a deferential Irish parliament, that he was now king of Ireland. English officials and colonists in Ireland could now view themselves as operating within a 'homeland territory' where only one language should legitimately prevail. The expansion of English power intersected with the burgeoning use of the English language and its legitimizing regime of truth.

That is not to say that the Irish language and its speakers did not have their uses for the colonizer. In all the surveys and inquisitions, they must be first made to yield their understandings of territorial structure and systems of land tenure. Once the crucial evidence of land titles and rents due are extracted from such specialists as the brehons and the poets, and once the details from Irish language parchment rolls are translated into English modes of understanding and measurement, the same parchments – sacred to their brehon custodians – are discarded as trifles.[12]

The Irish brehons, poets and *seanchaithe* were well aware of the implications of these transformations. The translations of Irish territories and land measures into imperial units signalled territorial dispossession and the dismantling of the intimate relationship between their knowledge/power and the surrounding society and landscape. There are frequent examples of gaps between verbal and mapping representations of space and the realities on the ground – as in the severe underestimation of the extent of the confiscated lands in the Ulster plantation surveys. Such gaps highlight the damaging incomprehension between the two language communities – one in the process of assuming control of an island people it could (or would) not understand and the other losing its control of a land it knew so intimately.

A function of section I, 'Making the Documents of Conquest Speak', is to highlight the power of the early modernizing New English in conquering, itemizing and reorganizing the territorial structures of Ireland. Another specific objective is to excavate Irish world views which were buried under this avalanche of English language documents. The profound English language bias in the documentary records requires that we see the people and the landscape as texts, see human beings as shapers and dreamers and the landscape as a key repository of human efforts and values. With this in mind, one can also map and explore regional patterns of first names, family names, sporting and language traditions, as well as interrogating folklore and poetry.

Maps and surveys were useful to the early modernizing, capitalist New English in 'emptying' Irish spaces and making them amenable to new resource uses and management techniques. Old centres of power were eroded by the classical imperial strategy of building fortifications and plantation towns on the sites of the old ruling places. These old sources of power – including their territorial expressions – were further obscured by the multiplication of bureaucratic techniques for ruling the country: counties, baronies, revenue districts, military districts, market hinterlands, law circuits and landlord estates all fragmented the old patterns of power. Men of letters like Spenser and Moryson articulated the intellectual legitimization for the military conquest; then came the bureaucrats and legal experts who dominated policy-making and execution. Sir John Davies, for example, came to play a key role in the strategic use and island-wide extension of English common law, which sanctified an individualistic, profit-making property system.

The 1641 Depositions produce an extraordinary example of Irish animosity towards the imposition of English law and language, as well as towards the imposition of English cultural norms. One witness, a Thomas Johnson, reports from Co. Mayo that the local Irish brought bills of indictment against the English breeds of cattle and tried them in a court situation:

> Having on their fashion arraigned those cattle . . . their scornful judge then sitting amongst them would say they looks as if they could speak English, give them the book and see if they can read, pronouncing the words *legit anon* [does it read, or not?] to the jury. And then, because they stood mute and could not read, would and

did pronounce judgement and sentence of death against them and so they [the cattle] were committed and put to slaughter.[13]

The playing out of mock justice in this courtroom scene tells us much about the depth of Irish animosity toward the cynical behaviour of English judges and officers, specifically their feelings about how they themselves, as monoglot Irish-speakers, were treated in English legal proceedings. But the symbolic import of the inversion of English cultural and legal superiorities goes even deeper: it reflects the feeling that the Irish and their normal means of discourse have been silenced by the new regime; they are made to feel *mute* in the new environment. The mock-justice scene speaks to a classic colonial situation – the conquered no longer have a voice in their own affairs, can no longer speak up for or defend themselves in judicial proceedings:[14]

> Atáid ó shoin 'na dtocht faoi gheársmacht
> Nach míne tréad le taobh na faolchon.
>
> Ever since they are mute in dire oppression
> Treated no more kindly than the flock ruled
> by the wolf.[15]

England's representatives in Ireland – like Davies, Gilbert, Raleigh and Spenser – were highly educated, reflective, and courteous people, yet they were absolutely ruthless in their dealings with the Irish. Historical and cultural geographers have long commented on the problematic impact of European-centred modernity drives outside of Europe – a dark side that involved 'violent, coercive and insidious cultural practices' against so-called traditional societies in the New World.[16] This too was Ireland's experience.

Ireland also saw the commodification of its lands – valued places were transformed into geometric chess pieces to be traded like stocks and shares. It too saw the erosion of existing complex ecologies, not least in the destruction and asset-stripping of its extensive woodlands; and the growth of vulnerable forms of monoculture. One may ask, for example, whether the massive clearances of space between the 1690s and late 1730s and the associated marginalization and impoverishment of so many former village dwellers to make way for vast cattle- and sheep-walks across the middle of Ireland (from Roscommon south to Cork) exacerbated the specific mortal impact of the great frost and famine of 1740–1.[17] Whatever about the effects of a commercializing pastoral monoculture then, it is clear what the tragic effects were to be of the massive dependence of so many of the Irish poor on the single food crop of the potato by the 1840s. Likewise, early modernity, in the specific form that landlordism assumed in Ireland, promoted new and punishing divisions of labour where the number of annual workdays required for the cottier or smallholder to ensure his/her family's bare subsistence exceeded that of any other economic regime in western Europe and seemed unimaginable amongst the hard-working settlers along the American frontier.[18] In short, early modernity and colonial conquest went hand in hand in Ireland.

It is still salutary to be reminded of just how central military matters were to the Irish experience. At the peak of the power of Gaelic and gaelicized lordships in the 1560s, the accumulated totals of their military came to close on 4,000 horse, over 15,000 kern and about 47 batallions [each of 60 to 80 men] of gallowglasses. These figures do not include the back-up servants and boys who served these soldiers.[19] It was a highly militarized society. The Catholic Confederate army at its peak in 1646–7 amounted to over 20,000 men. In the 1640s, the Scots fed an army of 16,000 men in Ulster alone; Cromwell's New Model Army had 12,000 men. After 1699, a standing army of 12,000 men were maintained in the country, which after 1769 increased to over 15,000. Between the 1550s and the 1700s, military conquest, followed by plantations, more risings/rebellions and more plantations required far larger investments of money, men and materials than hitherto allocated. Historian Tom Bartlett is struck by the numbing ferocity with which Irish wars were conducted from the 1560s on, characterized by more than a whiff of the frontier and the regular resort to martial law. A colonialist model of war was exercised in these encounters, whether in Ireland or America. England's enemies, Irish or Indian, were generally regarded and accordingly treated as 'savages'. For Bartlett, the battle of Kinsale 'deserves comparison with the victories of Cortez and Pizarro in the "New World"'.[20]

The particular nature and development of English government in Ireland was thus influenced profoundly by a military establishment that cost three to twenty times that of the civil administration: it is estimated that over the period 1550 to 1800, the government's main function was to pay, clothe, feed and administer the English military establishment distributed across Ireland – a government acting as a kind of revenue wing to the military.[21] The military arm was central to the maintenance of new territorial systems of rule, administration and exploitation.

However, the break-up and fragmentation of the old power structures did not mean that they all disappeared; or that new hybrid territorial institutions did not emerge in the colonial period proper. Like many colonized peoples, the Irish felt that their own territories and lands remained but were now occupied by strangers/foreigners. This feeling is best exemplified by the evidence of the 1641 Depositions where new estate owners in their castle-mansions (supported by their refugee settler tenants) were almost invariably besieged by local Irish leaders and kin-groups who regarded themselves as the 'real' owners of these properties. Both the diocesan and regular clergy of the Catholic Church sought to regain control of churches and monasteries as well as former ecclesiastical territories and incomes.

The elimination or assimilation of some members of the professional classes – the brehons, *seanchaithe*, the bardic poets and their associated high culture – did not mean the disappearance of the culture as a whole and its specific constructions of territoriality. By the 1650s, with the bardic schools destroyed, Irish poetry was in the hands of well-educated, often clerical, practitioners who, however, spoke not only in the highly sophisticated language of a bardic and aristocratic elite only but in a language that embraced the whole community.[22]

Very different voices can be heard in the turbulent 1640s and 1650s. The detailed analysis of the 1641 Depositions in chapter 4 pointed to the construction of what may be called a mythico-history of the sufferings, travails and destiny of the

Protestant Irish settlers.[23] As regards the parallel mythico-historical outlook of the Catholic Irish at the time, the closest approximation to an elucidation of their feelings and experiences is articulated in the political poetry produced in the Irish language over the same period as the 1641 Depositions and the later Cromwellian examinations in the 1650s.[24] Images and phrases are newly minted out of the traumas and depth of feeling that arose out of the Confederate Wars, the Cromwellian conquest and its aftermath: 'Hence the language of the poems is . . . simple, vigorous, full of dialect forms and borrowed English words already current in that speech.'[25] This poetry was written in a more modern mode that better reflected contemporary reality. Here is the centrality of the artistic visionary 'voice' in the Irish tradition which later transcends the linguistic divide to speak in English. The poets agree in their disdain and contempt for what they see as the low-born rabble of Cromwellian planters and settlers; and they stress the chicanery of the laws that deprived the Irish of their lands. Some also provide chilling images of the political and religious persecution under the Cromwellian administration.[26]

Emphasizing the deep impact of English law in Ireland, these poets break their Irish rhythms with the names of powerful English legal institutions and processes: their poems are peppered with terms such as 'Court of Wards', 'Exchequer', 'Star Chamber', 'King's Bench', 'Bishop's Court', 'Assizes', 'writ', 'provost', 'sheriff', 'receiver', 'cess' and 'tax' – a litany that recalled their respective functions in proslytizing, increasing crown revenue, in outlawing and sweeping away Irish systems of law and land tenure (1603–5), in punishing 'recusants', and imprisoning and banishing 'popish priests and school teachers'. Not forgotten is one other little legal stratagem: 'Surrender and Regrant':

> Dlí beag eile do rinneadh do Gaeulaibh,
> surrender ar a gceart do dhéanamh.
> Do chuir sin Leath Chuinn trí na chéile . . .
>
> Yet another small law which was imposed on the Gaels;
> To make surrender of what was theirs by right.
> This put Leath Chuinn into turmoil . . .[27]

A striking theme of much of the 1640s and 1650s Irish poetry is the celebration of both the prowess and heroism of the great Irish families – both Gaelic and Old English. Yet the overwhelming impression is one of grief-stricken poets [see titles of poems, ref. 24 above], describing a devastated culture and ravaged landscapes that would long struggle to recover. They were only too well aware of the pain that followed the rupturing of a society's psychic moorings, the undermining of a people's sense of place and identity. In the 1750s, a century after the composition of Seán Ó Conaill's extraordinarily popular *Tuireamh na hÉireann*, this poem 'was repeated and kept in memory on account of the great knowledge of antiquity comprehended in it'.[28] Thus, the poets of the 1640s and 1650s came to perpetuate the memories of the cataclysm and trauma of conquest from a Catholic Irish perspective.

Levels of repression, shaming and humiliation invariably shaped a range of long-lasting cultural responses. The oppressive environment that came with military and legal rule brought with it the life-saving need of not speaking up, the fear of confrontation, the dread of persecution from a whole panoply of laws that remained on the statute books and could be brought back into play at very short notice. For safety's sake came the need to remain silent, to suppress true feelings, to speak in code or sideways; also the need to develop secretive ways of doing and saying things – for example, priests disguising themselves as servants or harpers in Big Houses in order to sustain their mission – or the need to develop secret organizations like the Houghers and the Whiteboys. One could not be too demonstrative either in one's actions or in the display of one's by now limited material wealth. Keeping such a low profile also meant that the traveller, viewing this world from a coach window, saw only a dishevelled and disordered landscape, which was in many ways still quite a nuanced and well understood-world – not least the landscape of a very discreet yet well organized Catholic Church. The colonial state's instruments of surveillance ran up against sophisticated cultural techniques for ensuring invisibility and impenetrability.[29]

The repression of so many negative feelings also had their dark expressions: the response to violence produced, for example, the vicious, explosive retaliations of the early months and years of the 1641 rising/rebellion; a patriarchal land-law worked its way throughout the whole social system and reinforced male dominance; levels of sexual violence were exacerbated due to the trauma and effects of conquest. Likewise, levels of alcoholism, vagrancy and begging all rose after the conquest. A reverence for family land, its retention and transmission is reinforced – sometimes to pathological levels – as a by-product of this era.

One final and inevitable product of the trauma of conquest and plantation is a widespread confusion about issues of identity. As I have argued in chapter 4, one hitherto unrecognized factor adding to the explosiveness of the 1641 rising/rebellion was the threats to identities that followed on from military, religious and linguistic repression, the rapidity of social changes, the attempts to anglicize family names, the elimination of 'O' and 'Mac' prefixes and the anglicization of placenames. Yet, as revealed in a series of detailed maps in Chapters 6, 10 and 11, there were striking regional variations in levels of adaptation and resistance to these pressures.

Given the depth of the trauma associated with such a devastating conquest, the classic response of some bardic poets was one of denial – denial that the world had changed so radically, denial of events too painful to articulate.[30] Yet the preponderance of vernacular poetic voices that have survived are interrogating not only the dislocations but, more particularly, the imposition of a radically new social and cultural framework. Irish communities were not passive receivers of knowledge transmitted downwards from an outsider conquering group – they were constantly engaged in trying to make sense of, interpret and give meaning to their own often rapidly changing experiences and worlds. Their storytellers, local historians, poets and musicians continued to present to the parish, church or townland community its significant 'texts'.

It is clear that in late medieval Irish society, the parish, in conjunction with its key landowner(s), occupied dominant positions in shaping both community norms and settlement structures. As the regional case-studies (chapters 7, 8 and 9) and later chapters demonstrate, the reconstructed Catholic parish of the seventeenth and eighteenth centuries was one of the most vital territorial institutions in the shaping of that society. It had the latent power to evade, resist or accommodate the prevailing political authorities. Jolted free from the constraints of the untidy and fragmented patterns of medieval parishes, the Catholic Church constructed a more flexible system of parishes which could more rapidly adapt to the changing distribution of priests, central-places and the population as a whole. In this process, the Church sought to incorporate as much of the territorial frames of the medieval parish networks as was possible. Likewise, the construction of rudimentary mass houses demonstrated the resourcefulness of congregations in harnessing their often limited resources. Since the colonial state neither granted recognition to or catered for the needs of its Catholic subjects, it could be argued that the revamped Catholic parish assumed some of the functions of local government – a unit of social control and later, despite official Church disapproval, a unit in the mobilization of often aggressive agrarian resistance movements. A dynamic territorial institution – partly ancient, partly hybrid and very adaptive – had been created.

Colonial Ireland is unique in western Europe in the development of two major parallel ecclesiastical territorial structures over the whole political space – that of the Established Anglican Church and that of the Catholic Church, one a state church system, the other that of a disenfranchised majority population. Unlike colonial Latin America, where the territorial systems of the Catholic Church and the imperial government reinforced one another, in Ireland the failure of the Anglican Reformation saw a dual parish and ecclesiastical system established. As can be seen in chapter 10, the English-speaking Anglican Church of Ireland inherited all the old parish and diocesan centres, territories and resources. The territorial system of the state Anglican Church was countered in the landscape and in many people's minds by the piecemeal construction of a competing, if necessarily 'underground', Catholic parish system: 'there was not supposed to be a clandestine, parallel counter-church' in the seventeenth century, yet by the 1630s 'it was ubiquitous, and seemingly uneradicable'.[31] The colonial state's forms of government – which sought to appropriate and dominate the spheres of activity of a subject people – was failing in the areas of religion, education and recreation.

Where the Catholic Irish remained demographically dominant and especially as long as Catholic gentry leadership survived, this dialectic led to the impoverishment and ruination of the Anglican parish church. Such deliberate emptying and destruction of the old parish centres was carried out to symbolize the old community's sense of an invalid, alienating territoriality – the occupation of old sacred sites by 'foreigners/heretics'. Hence, outside core areas of English Anglican settlement and parochial vitality in middle Ulster and parts of east Leinster, we often find the juxtaposition of a deserted parish centre or shrunken Anglican village community, with an embryonic but increasingly vibrant Catholic chapel community. The centres of community life, therefore, often shifted either towards the dispersed chapel or embryonic village/hamlet where the chapel, public houses(s), forge and other artisan houses acted as a new focus for anchoring community solidarity. Parallel to this, the pattern days of the local saint, pilgrimage to the local holy wells and reverence for prehistoric 'sacred sites' constituted further examples of cultural continuity. These liminal spaces – not at all central in the daily round of work – retained a potent symbolic centrality to the community, as did funeral ceremonies. Equally powerful for cultural continuity and adaptation was the survival of lineage-type kinship structures amongst key local families whose names were perpetuated in so many specific locales and regions.

Beyond the parishes, colonial Ireland was characterized by a fragmentation of territories and energies at both the diocesan and urban levels. The Catholic Church managed to retain an episcopal footing in most of the key port-cities – in Cork, Dublin, Derry, Limerick, Waterford and later Galway. Interestingly only three inland diocesan centres – at Armagh, Tuam and Kilkenny – kept this footing. Yet within those urban centres – especially in Cork and Dublin – the dialectic between the two traditions is epitomized in the less prestigious sidestreet locations for the Catholic facilities versus the more elaborate and privileged Anglican foci to the south of each city. In Derry and Belfast the dialectic was between an eastern privileged core and a western Gaelic periphery.

Elsewhere, whereas the Anglican Church either clung to old medieval diocesan centres or saw a number of diocesan amalgamations, the more footloose Catholic Church eventually moved to new and more dynamic urban foci, from Raphoe to Letterkenny in the northwest through to Ferns and Enniscorthy in the south-east. Ethnic, social, territorial and settlement bifurcation was also symbolically embedded in the fabric of many of the plantation and landlord towns.[32]

Yet a whole series of contact zones, hybrid cultural forms and hybrid identities are also inevitable outcomes of the colonial engagement. Cultural exchanges, however uneven, required shared meeting-places. The Main Street was one such meeting-place, characterized by many exchanges, as were the fairs, markets, shops, inns/public houses, courthouses, the pedlars' circuits and the hurling matches and race-meetings. The Catholic Church learned to speak in English, to print its Irish language religious texts in the English/Roman form and to accommodate, if not acculturate, itself to the structures and contours of the ruling Protestant Ascendancy. Indeed, given the forced simplicity of its liturgy and the centrality of the sermon at mass, it could be argued that the Catholic Church in Ireland was one of the most 'puritanical' in Europe.

Similarly, while general cultural resistance to the English language was sustained over a very long period in many regions, the necessarily lengthy phases of bilingualism allowed room for both the transfer and reappropriation of 'memory' in the English language, as well as the carriage of new ideas, music and dance forms, dress styles and other material cultural elements into the Irish-speaking communities. Both the symbolism and functions of the English court system and the legal instrument of the summons carried over into the Irish courts of poetry and the prose *barántas* respectively, as well as in their joint functions as instruments of social control. From the mid-sixteenth century onwards, Irish landowners had seen the need to have their sons or indeed their brehon specialists trained in English common law so as to be able to deal with the increasing pressures on Irish titles to lands. By the early seventeenth century, not only the sons of Old English landowners and merchants but increasingly those of Gaelic/gaelicized stock were sent to the London inns of court to be trained in English law.[33] It is striking how the Irish [counter-?] revolutionaries of the Confederate Wars utilized the English-derived institutions of the barony and the county for their own ends. After the seventeenth century, it is clear that the Irish populations learned to transfer their loyalties from the lordship to county identities, not least in terms of sporting allegiances to county hurling teams.[34] Likewise, it is clear that apart from the acculturating brehon-lawyers, at least some of the sergeants and stewards of the Gaelic/gaelicized tradition managed to make the transition as middlemen administrators for the new landlords. In the regions where Catholic tenant farmers and the Catholic population remained demographically dominant, landlordism could not have functioned without the facilitating role of key local middlemen families.

Landlordism was most subdued in the strong farmer, grain-producing and mixed-farming counties of east Leinster and Munster, and in their thriving port-cities and inland towns, as well as in the Galway city hinterland. The regional case-studies for Dublin, Tipperary and particularly Kilkenny confirm these patterns. In such regions, a residual Catholic gentry class, a substantial number of Catholic middlemen, strong tenant farmers and mill-owners, as well as the significant and expanding merchant wealth of their entrepreneurial cousins in the main towns and port-cities, ensured greater cultural continuities as well as strategic adaptations.[35] These can be measured in terms of striking continuities in family name distributions, farmhouse types and styles and the solidity of Catholic merchant wealth in town and port-city. Their more substantive support structures for post-Tridentine Catholicism in turn reflected significant overseas networks.[36] This wider southern/southeastern region also led in the construction of regional agrarian movements opposed to the excesses of the enclosure movement, the 'canting' or auctioneering of tenant-farm leases, and the deepening oppressiveness of the tithe system and clerical dues generally.

Perhaps the most striking hybrid institution to emerge out of this encounter was the townland, bearing for the most part an ancient Irish name which over time has fossilized into an accepted anglicized form. The origins of some of these townlands, 62,000 of them, clearly bounded and averaging 350 acres in size, echo back to the Iron Age, some to the sixth and eighth centuries and others to later phases. Once constituted as units of land management, military mobilization and taxation in the Gaelic/gaelicized worlds, they now came to be transformed into rent-yielding, market-driven leaseholding units or 'farms' under the landlord-tenant system. Continuity in the territorial form of the townland was now complemented by a radical transformation in functions and class composition. In many cases, their settlement structures were transformed by landlordism: hamlets disappear in the face of large sheep and cattle grazier farms and either large clustered settlements or the proliferation of dispersed small farms emerge in areas of labyrinthine middlemen layers. Whatever the settlement or social forms, the townland generally survived as a focal point of local opinions and identities, as a unit of co-operation and conflict as well as of civil, ecclesiastical and estate administration.

The great majority of these thousands of townlands carried Irish language names, albeit in often severely modified forms. In the early maps and writings, when Ireland is often being represented as a kind of empty space, the dense plethora of impenetrable placenames resist appropriation. Such names are extant guides to understanding the genealogical and territorial depth of the old society. William Petty sought to initiate a major programme to provide English names for all the units mapped in the Down Survey and ended up with the compromise solution of an anglicized, phonetic rendering of each name. The ongoing battle between the English and Irish languages left placename formations in a state of flux. Nevertheless, Petty's own Down Survey renderings endured to stabilize many English language placenames, given the continued high status of Down Survey maps as legal documents and the passage of such name-forms into the rent-roll lists. In addition, phonetic rendering of townland names remained faithful to the local Irish pronunciation, whatever the speaker's background. The townland and its name thus became part of a shared heritage.

Colonial encounters also generate hybrid identities. The New English conquest set off explosive charges that scattered Irish populations locally and globally. Old elites, now eliminated or shunted sideways, make way for the newly installed 'commanders' of labour, landscapes and properties. The greater commercialization of the Irish economy – especially the creation of vast grazing farms across the middle of the country – broke up many former subsistence tillage farms and scattered their occupants onto roadsides or bog and mountain edges, to survive by cultivating the potato and becoming hired, often migrant, labourers. Local dislocations were matched by regional and provincial migrations. The broken 'septs of Leix' are eventually relocated in Co. Kerry. Both before and after the 1641 rising/rebellion, the ancient inhabitants of Ulster were obliged to move by dictat, by force, by economic pressures, as a consequence of reprisals, or famine. Co. Leitrim was one such refuge region, as was the Cooley peninsula. The fury of the Irish in 1641 drove out many Protestant settlers: some never returned, although in many cases new settlers gravitated into their places. The most epic transplantation was to Connacht – and this trek is matched at the global scale by the westward transportation of many Irish to the West Indies and Virginia and the eastward migration of the remnants of the Irish armies and other emigrants to the Continent of Europe. Their places in Ireland were, in turn, taken up by members of a massive immigration from both England and Scotland, as well as some migrants from the European mainland (chapters 5 and 6).

When we try, then, to map Irish identities for, say, the 1730s we encounter: the emigrant Irish in exile in Catholic Europe; and a minority of the colonized Irish at home involved in agrarian and other resistance movements. The majority of colonized Irish lowered their heads, adapted to the new realities, took good care of their cows, cattle, pigs and/or crops to pay the rent, became servants and workers on the estates and big farms or survived in the burgeoning Irishtowns and cabin suburbs. There were others – not only of aristocratic background but also some in an upwardly mobile entrepreneurial class – who in culture and speech crossed over into an English ambience. Across the Atlantic, many Irish were indentured servants, a few were plantation owners and some – especially the Scots Irish – were emigrants seeking new freedoms on the American frontier.

On the other side of the divide at home in Ireland were long settled planter families, some of whom were now Catholic; many others were now known as the 'Old Protestants'; there were the more recently established Protestant settlers – whether of Anglican, Presbyterian or other Nonconformist congregations – with the Lowland Scots occupying key economic positions in the north of the country, as the leaders in the geographic expansion of the linen industry.

As I argue in the final chapters, political divisions ran deep in Ireland but cultural transfers were more common than are allowed for in the literature. As the eighteenth-century progressed, 'homeland' English commentators saw the Anglo-Irish as becoming more like the old Irish inhabitants – or rather more like their images of the old Irish. The Anglo-Irish were perceived to be as proud and inso-lent, given to drinking and to music, dancing and sporting; they were deemed to have a propensity to violence; seemed obsessively concerned with finding wealthy marriage partners; and loved horses, houses and talking.[37] Yet intermar-riage between members of the two major traditions remained rare and levels of assimilation low. The 1766 Census reveals that only about one-tenth of the Protes-tants in their core settlements in the diocese of Cashel and Emly bear Gaelic or Old English names.[38] With some local exceptions the ethno-religious boundary, firmly established after 1641, remained intact.

This generalization carries, however, less weight in the regions of Presbyterian dominance. It is true that the Scottish tenant-farming settlers in the north of Ireland did not find it difficult to adapt to a townland framework, a dispersed settlement system and a mixed-farming, if dominantly pastoral, tradition. These patterns were already part of their cultural experience back in Scotland. What was new was the ongoing battle to extend control into the best lands against a deeply rooted prior population who greatly resented these intrusions. As we have seen, members of Presbyterian communities were killed or died of hunger or exposure during the first months of the 1641 rising/rebellion while others sought refuge with their relatives in Scotland. Yet the earliest, stiffest and best organized resis-tance to Irish attacks and incursions was primarily a feature of the already cohesive and strongly rooted Scottish Presbyterian communities. Brutal methods were used by Monro's Scottish army as he put down the rising/rebellion and cleared the way in east Ulster, slaughtering his captives at Kilwarlin Wood, Loughbrickland and Newry: 'marching north again he seized the cattle and slaughtered any Irish men, women and children that he found'.[39] As late as 1714, Bishop McMahon of Clogher reports that, though all of Ireland was suffering at this time, Ulster was worse off because Scottish 'Calvinists [Presbyterians] are coming over here daily in large groups of families, occupying the towns and villages, seizing the farms in the richer parts of the country and expelling the natives'.[40] Ulster and its borders saw the creation of many sharp frontiers.

This Presbyterian Church in Ireland was the first regional outgrowth of the Church of Scotland. With the geographic spread of Scots Presbyterian settlers, this austere, direct and hard-working community – which retained a deep suspicion of centralized power, whether secular or ecclesiastical, and remained strongly committed to local involvement in decision-making – established new congregations, kirk sessions and presbyteries. By 1659 five presbyteries – characterized by that rooted emphasis on equality of representation by ministers and lay elders – had been established from Down to the Laggan in east Donegal.[41] As discussed in chapter 10, new frontier Presbyterian congregations were being established after the Williamite Wars (1688–91) by incoming migrants as far south as Cavan, Longford and Monaghan. This eventually gave rise to the Presbyterian equivalent of the chapel village, characterized by austere, vernacular meeting houses. By the early eighteenth century, the number of presbyteries had more than doubled. The first General Assembly was held in 1740, completing a clear territorial structure of Church government that stretched from the local kirk sessions, through the deliberations of the presbyteries and synods, on up to the General Assembly.

Strong links were maintained with Scotland, most particularly in the training of its preachers in the theological colleges of the ancient Scottish universities. As in Scotland, this Ulster community was also subject to theological rifts and splits. However, in Ireland the Presbyterians were also subject to legal restrictions. Following the 1704 Sacramental Test Act, conscientious Presbyterians would or could not serve as state officials or sit on corporations. They too had to pay tithes to the Established Church; sometimes they were brought before the Bishop's court, their preachers gaoled and meeting houses levelled. In fact, for most of the eighteenth century, Presbyterians were second-class citizens in Ulster.[42]

Scots Presbyterians were by far the largest group of Irish migrants to North America in the eighteenth century. With the forging of these new Atlantic links and influenced by the American War of Independence and the writings of people like Thomas Paine, some Presbyterians – including key thinkers and leaders like William Drennan, Henry Joy McCracken and Samuel Neilson – joined the United Irishmen. If it was the dream of these Presbyterians – with a dual heritage of colonizer and colonized – to build a lasting bridge between the Catholic and the Protestant Irish, it was not to be. Unlike the earlier blending that took place between the old Irish and the Old English and despite the growth in shared values and levels of interdependence, there was to be no such fusion between the Catholic Irish and Anglo-Irish populations.

The basis for the rise of an exclusive Anglo-Irish Protestant Ascendancy class was established back in the 1640s and 1650s when much of the discriminatory code against Catholics was put in place. It was then that the notion of 'the Protestant interest' was fully formulated.[43] The capture of urban properties and government, as well as the skilful mobilization of regional militias to defend 'the Protestant interest', were legacies of this most formative period. The business of establishing hegemonic spaces continued after the Restoration.[44] However, the full realization of the power of the Protestant Ascendancy in the landscape began after the 1690s. Following 'deliverances' from the Catholic threat during the Glorious

Revolution, the Williamite Wars and the Williamite confiscations, Protestant power was made to appear permanent, as a series of penal laws deprived Catholics of most of their rights as subjects.

Most specifically aimed at reducing the political and propertied power of the now residual Catholic Irish landowners, the penal laws reveal much about the mindsets and identities of the Protestant Irish. They saw themselves as an exposed, yet superior, ruling class. Their aggressiveness and insecurities were manifested in the ferocity with which the local gentry-led militias behaved in crisis periods both in the mid and latter half of the seventeenth century and throughout much of the eighteenth century. Insecurities were exacerbated by the archipelagic nature of so much of the original settler distribution. Unlike America, with its single, integrated compact settlement frontier stretching east–west across the whole of the land, settler concentrations in Ireland were highly regionalized and localized. Outside of a northeastern core, a whole series of multiple and complex frontiers had emerged in regional clusters across the island. In those areas where the Protestant Irish population constituted islands of minority settlement, their sense of isolation must have always been severe and felt with even greater intensity in times fraught with political danger.

Yet the notion of a more self-confident Protestant 'colonial nation' was being forged by Anglo-Irish intellectuals who sought to imagine and distinguish themselves from both the 'othered' Catholic Irish and the English of metropolitan England.[45] The growing patriotism of the Protestant Anglo-Irish made them increasingly see Ireland as their home. Like other colonial elites, whether in Mexico, Peru, Virginia or Carolina, they strengthened their special sense of cohesion and identity by imagining themselves as agents of a 'civilizing mission' in their new country. The most central and enduring feature of this identity was the memory of their specific historical experiences in Ireland. Their victories after the disaster of 1641 and their 'deliverance' in 1688 were seen as providential, indeed miraculous.

Given their establishment status, the Protestant communities did not only remember and celebrate their moments of crisis and deliverance in their informal domestic story-tellings and more formal readings of regularly reprinted texts like Temple's *The Irish Rebellion* and King's *State of the Protestants in Ireland under King James*.[46] They could attend formal memorials of these key events, both at the Anglican church with its anniversary sermons and in the capital city and county towns with their corporate fostering of ceremonies and official processions. These were held on key dates such as the king's birthday, and more particularly on both 23 October (the discovery and foiling of the attempted capture of Dublin Castle by Irish insurgents on this day in 1641) and 5 November (the discovery of the so-called Gunpowder Plot by extremist Catholics against the crown in London on this day in 1605). A triumphalist mentality was routinely built into the ritual fabric of the seasonal round of Church and State as Protestants regularly assembled to assert their own Ascendancy and, as Toby Barnard notes, in the process mock the Catholics, driving home the latter's feelings of humiliation and defeat.[47]

One could expect contrasting responses to the contemporary landscape creations when so much of all rural wealth went to the landlords and rents rose tenfold between 1600 and 1800. For the colonial nation, landscape transformations and innovative engineering works came to legitimize their rule, as well as to signify and encode both their feelings of supremacy and their 'civilizing' modernizing role as champions of an anglicizing/Anglican order. Their sense of supremacy facilitated a particular aesthetic sensitivity, further refined by the European Grand Tour and the exchange of design ideas between Britain and Ireland. The building of magnificent and expansive Georgian houses, the spread of elaborately designed and enclosed walled gardens and demesnes, the great fashions of road-building and extending enclosures to the mountain and bog edges, as well as either the creation or refurbishment of towns and villages, all speak to this ideology.[48] Indeed, there is no contemporary parallel in the rest of Europe for the creation on this scale of so many landlord-led planned villages and towns. (Fig. 12.8a [Pl.2p]).

Dublin continued to be embellished as a powerful primate city, the 'second city of the empire'. Its legacy of fine Georgian streets and squares owes much to the demand of the landed aristocracy for town houses during sessions of the Irish parliament. This was part of that pattern of European involvement in the planning and development of key colonial cities, with their magnificent squares and architecture designed as signifiers of both achievement and authority.[49] Outside the glittering life of Dublin and Dublin Castle, so brilliantly captured in van der Hagen's 1730s painting (Fig. 12.8b Pl.2p),[50] this elaborately revamped landscape was complemented by a social geography of friendship networks established at the assizes, the vestry, in civic celebrations, in the clubs and Masonic lodges. Ascendancy life also swirled around the hunt and the seasonal balls, in the mustering and 'security' drives of the militia, as well as in the excitement of contesting municipal and parliamentary elections.[51] And in the necessary symbiosis between the officers of the garrison and the landlord class. The Big House of the landlord families acted as the nerve-centre of a web of social and political alliances which linked related interest groups, all depending on the ownership or management of land for incomes and positions.

Surviving Catholic Irish gentry might seek to emulate these landscape achievements. Many Irish artisans were involved in building this landscape of enclosures, roads and mansions: and many enjoyed the colour and passion of the race meetings and hurling matches. But for some these new triumphant landscape expressions were seen as eroding memory and blocking out older sacred centres and ancestral places.[52] Woodland territories had become thoroughfares: the mountain edges were all fenced with hedges and many former village greens were now crossed by demesne gardens and 'girdles of twisting fields'. There was the feeling of not being at home in one's own country. Responses were predictably varied – no doubt the new Big House and its trappings inspired awe and deference, if not reverence. Loyal estate communities were often created. But other kinds of responses were being articulated by agrarian combinations, which, right through the eighteenth century and particularly after the 1760s, challenged this extreme privatization of former public/common lands, as well as the tithe system of the Established Church and the excesses of landlordism generally.

The legacy of the Anglo-Irish colonial nation was complex and ambiguous. As Bartlett points out, Protestant nationalism evolved slowly from the late 1690s, matured in the middle decades of the eighteenth century, 'reaching a high point in 1782 [with the establishment of Grattan's parliament], and finally expired some time in the 1790s'.[53] It was an uncertain, conditional and very flawed nationalism. Yet it was to inspire later nationalists by its writings, its objectives and achievements. It provided role models in the somewhat unlikely figure of Jonathan Swift and, later, Henry Grattan and Henry Flood. More particularly, some of its members helped lay the English language foundations for a reawakening of interest in Ireland's Gaelic past. By the 1770s and 1780s, this fruitful dialogue had led to a convergence of Anglo-Irish and Gaelic scholarly endeavours.

The patriot Protestants at their most confident rejected England's claim to legislate for Ireland; they were adamant that Ireland was not just a colony and talked up the ancestry and autonomy of the Irish parliament. Rather, they saw Ireland as a 'sister kingdom' to England. By contrast, given England's trade restrictions on Irish commerce, its retention of all the top positions and perks in government, in revenue, in the military, in law and in the Church of Ireland for English-born, it continued to see and treat Ireland as a colony. In the end, it was Anglo-Irish anxiety and fear about both the growing demographic and political power of the Catholic Irish that pointed up the fatal flaw in this brand of exclusive nationalism. From the 1760s on, and growing strongly in the 1780s, the drive to restore full equality to the Catholic Irish gathered momentum, just as the needs of an expanding complex British state and empire also grew.[54]

Petty is worth a hearing on this question of Catholic demographic power. He feared this threat right from the beginning of his reflections on Ireland. As James II came to the throne (1685) and as Catholic power was progressively restored in Ireland, Petty dreaded the erosion of 'the Protestant interest', as well as his own vested interests. In a feverish bout of writing in the summer of 1687, he penned his final political treatise on the resolution of England's Irish problem and the possibility of establishing some kind of union between the peoples of both islands. Out of Ireland's total population of 1.3 million, he proposes that one million people (without distinction of religion or affiliation) be transplanted to England, leaving 150,000 herdsmen and 150,000 dairywomen to manage the rearing and trading of a herd of 6 million cattle for export to England. These herdsmen and women were to live simply and only imports of salt and iron would be allowed. The people remaining in Ireland would be servants to those who lived in England; they would hold no property in land or stock; they would wear standard uniforms; the 267,000 Catholics among them would speak English, take English names; and the townlands would have English names. And since there would be no freeholders on the island, there would be no need for a parliament.[55]

In answering a series of objections that might be made against such proposals, Petty argues that the transportation of a million people – although apparently impractical and utopian – would easily be paid for both from the profits of the cattle trade and the increase in England's wealth consequent on such a population increase. He recognises that such a transplantation and change in trade would amount to the abolition of the Irish nation 'which will be [both] odious to them'[56] and not be compensated for by the benefits he had outlined. He counters by stressing that union of the two nations will prevent all future civil wars, the assimilated and anglicized Irish would be safe from any reconquest 'and will be ingrafted and incorporated into a Nation more Rich, Populous, Splendid and Renowned than themselves for Letters, Arms and other Atchievements'.[57]

American historian William H. McNeill is also convinced of the effects of Catholic demographic power. Adopting a global, comparative perspective, he notes that English overseas settlement met with very imperfect success in one notable case – the colonization of Ireland by Cromwell and his predecessors, which he interprets as failing to extend English society across the Irish Sea. Driven to subsist mainly on the potato, he sees the Irish as willing to work more cheaply for their new landlords than English or even Scottish settlers were willing to do: 'hence they prevailed demographically but at the price of miserable economic bondage to a culturally alien aristocracy'.[58] He interprets the social patterns of eighteenth-century Ireland as resembling those of the southern colonies of North America and eastern Europe 'in being sharply polarised between a privileged body of landowners who shared in a European civilisation, and a culturally deprived, psychologically alienated mass of agricultural labourers'.[59] If we add tenant farmers, tradesmen and townspeople to his agricultural labourers, McNeill's generalization rings true. The regime of the Anglo-Irish Ascendancy can be seen as a kind of foreign rule, which, as Edmund Burke argued, neither commanded the assent nor the affection of the people whom it dominated and made 'a virtue of the lack of affection, or the lack of those ties that would give a political system intimacy' and legitimacy.[60]

Ireland in the 1530s was described as a strange country when viewed from the perspective of both the English and the mainland Europeans. By the 1780s it was still a very distinctive country but for different reasons. A cultural geographer might identify at least four constellation of forces that Ireland and the Irish had to negotiate by this time. First, Ireland – deeply European in its ethos – remained exposed to ideas and currents, whether revolutionary or counter-revolutionary – flowing from continental Europe. Nearer to hand, Ireland was most deeply exposed to, involved with and shaped by a British imperial world which could be broken into its mainly English/Anglican and Scottish/Presbyterian components. Third, as we saw in the previous chapter, Ireland lay astride the numerous pathways, migration fields and exchanges that had long linked this part of Atlantic Europe with the Americas – and particularly North America. This American world was to become more significant in the shaping of Ireland. Finally, Ireland's experiences under British imperial, colonial rule had exposed it to the stresses and indignities of a 'colonized' Third World country.

These overlapping constellation of forces made their own particular arcs across the island. Eastern and southern Ireland, in particular, had long been most exposed to direct continental European influences. All of Ireland, but most particularly its eastern and northern societies, equally had long been intertwined with English and Scottish worlds. Likewise, all of Ireland had developed American links but these were perhaps most pronounced and deepest in the northeastern and southern parts of the country. The western half of Ireland – in particular the Irish-speaking part – was by the 1780s undergoing a population explosion, the further parcelling out of small kin-based properties and a consequential reduction in 'food entitlements', which would eventually culminate in the tragedy of the Great Famine. At the meeting-point of all these forces, mediating, negotiating and struggling to define its place in the world, was this very particular country – Ireland and its peoples.

This book is one historical geographer's interpretation of an Ireland that, I argue, was at once both colonial and early modern. Maps – mainly tabulated and constructed from the immense data-sources of the seventeenth century – have been central to this interpretation. Equally, the maps reveal that colonialism and modernity varied greatly in their regional and temporal impacts. The quality of regional leadership provided and the levels of resistance or accommodation accorded to these transformational forces varied widely. The experiences, memories, attitudes and aptitudes of regional communities, located at very different positions along the colonial/early modernizing axis, consequently diverged strongly. Yet the overall effect was a radically transformed Ireland in its economic, political and landscape expressions and most particularly in its now greatly differentiated cultural geographies.

Notes and References

List of Abbreviations

BL	British Library
NLI	National Library of Ireland
NMI	National Museum of Ireland
NMM	National Maritime Museum, Greenwich
OS	Ordnance Survey
PRO	Public Record Office, London
PROI	Public Record Office of Ireland
PRONI	Public Record Office of Northern Ireland
RIA	Royal Irish Academy
TCD	Trinity College Dublin
TCL	Trinity College Library
UCD	University College Dublin

Introduction

1 E. Boland, 'The Poets', *Selected Poems* (Manchester: Carcanet Press, 1989), p. 9
2 E. W. Said, *Culture and Imperialism* (London: Vintage, Chatto and Windus, 1993)

1 Marking Out the Terrain

1 S. Heaney, 'Markings', *Seeing Things* (London: Faber and Faber, 1991), p. 8
2 *Lebar Gabála Érenn: The Book of the Taking of Ireland,* ed. R. A. S. Macalister (Dublin: Irish Texts Society, 1938)
3 S. Céitinn, *Foras Feasa ar Éirinn: The History of Ireland,* ed. P. S. Dineen (Dublin: Irish Texts Society, 1914); see also, Bernadette Cunningham, *The World of Geoffrey Keating: History, Myth and Religion in Seventeenth-Century Ireland* (Dublin: Four Courts Press, 2000)
4 The descendants of the (Anglo-)Normans were known as the Old English by the late sixteenth century. See A. Clarke, *The Old English in Ireland 1625–1642* (London: Macgibbon and Kee, 1966).
5 F. Mitchell, *The Irish Landscape* (London: Collins, 1976)
6 Raymond Crotty, *Ireland in Crisis: A Study in Capitalist Colonial Underdevelopment* (Dingle: Brandon Books, 1986); see also his *Irish Agricultural Production: Its Volume and Structure* (Cork: Cork University Press, 1966).
7 E. Estyn Evans, *The Personality of Ireland*: *Habitat, Heritage and History*, 2nd edn (Belfast: Blackstaff Press, 1981), pp. 18–41
8 E. Gwynn, *The Metrical Dindshenchas,* Todd Lecture Series X (Dublin: Royal Irish Academy, 1913)
9 See Mitchell, *Irish Landscape*
10 A. Rees and B. Rees, *Celtic Heritage: Ancient Tradition in Ireland and Wales* (London: Thames and Hudson, 1961)
11 W. J. Smyth, 'Excavating, Mapping and Interrogating Ancestral Terrains: Towards a Cultural Geography of First and Second Names in Ireland', in H. Clarke, M. Hennessy and J. Prunty (eds), *Surveying Ireland's Past: Multidisciplinary Essays in Honour of Anngret Simms* (Dublin: Geography Publications, 2004), pp. 243–80

12   Evans, *Personality of Ireland*, pp. 18–24; P. Flatrès, *Géographie Rurale de Quatre Contrées Celtiques* (Rennes: Librairie Universitaire J. Plihon, 1957), pp. 1–8

13   N. Canny, *From Reformation to Restoration: Ireland 1534–1660* (Dublin: Helicon Press, 1987)

14   E. McCracken, *The Irish Woods since Tudor Times: Their Distribution and Exploitation* (Newton Abbot: David and Charles, 1971)

15   R. Gillespie, *The Transformation of the Irish Economy* (Dundalk: Group for the Study of Irish Settlement, 1991), pp. 26–7

16   M. Craig, *The Architecture of Ireland from the Earliest Times to 1880* (Dublin and London: Batsford, 1989), pp. 111–36

17   L. M. Cullen, *The Emergence of Modern Ireland 1600–1900* (London: Batsford, 1981), p. 8

18   D. B. Quinn and K. W. Nicholls, 'Ireland in 1534', in T. W. Moody, F. X. Martin and F. J. Byrne (eds), *A New History of Ireland, III: Early Modern Ireland 1534–1691* (Oxford: Clarendon Press, 1976), pp. 1–38

19   T. Jones Hughes, 'Society and Settlement in Nineteenth-Century Ireland', *Irish Geography*, vol. 5, no. 2, 1965, pp. 79–96. See also, his 'The Estate System of Landholding in Nineteenth-Century Ireland', in W. Nolan (ed.), *The Shaping of Ireland – the Geographical Perspective* (Cork: Mercier Press, 1986), pp. 137–50

20   M. MacCarthy-Morrogh, *The Munster Plantation: English Migration to Southern Ireland, 1583–1641* (Oxford: Oxford University Press, 1986). P. Robinson, *The Plantation of Ulster: British Settlement in an Irish Landscape, 1600–1670*, 2nd edn (Belfast: Ulster Historical Series, 1994); see also, J. M. Hill, 'The Origins of the Scottish Plantations in Ulster in 1625: A Reinterpretation', *Journal of British Studies*, vol. 32, no. 1, 1993, pp. 24–43

21   See, for example, B. Cunningham, 'Native Cultural and Political Change in Ireland, 1580–1640', in C. Brady and R. Gillespie (eds), *Natives and Newcomers: The Making of Irish Colonial Society 1534–1641* (Dublin: Irish Academic Press, 1986); D. Edwards, 'The Mac Giolla Padraigs (Fitzpatricks) of Upper Ossory, 1532–1641', in P. Lane and W. Nolan (eds), *Laois: History and Society* (Dublin: Geography Publications, 1999), pp. 327–75. Queen's County is known later as Co. Laois, and King's County is known as Co. Offaly

22   A. Simms, 'Core and Periphery in Medieval Europe: The Irish Experience in a Wider Context', in W. J. Smyth and K. Whelan (eds), *Common Ground: Essays on the Historical Geography of Ireland* (Cork: Cork University Press, 1988), pp. 22–40

23   C. Carroll, 'Barbarous Slaves and Civil Cannibals: Transplanting Civility in Early Modern Ireland', in C. Carroll and P. King (eds), *Ireland and Postcolonial Theory* (Cork: Cork University Press, 2003), pp. 63–80; Gerald of Wales, *The History and Topography of Ireland*, trans. J. J. O'Meara (London: Penguin, 1982). See also, A. Pagden, *Lords of All the World: Ideologies of Empire in Spain, Britain and France c.1500–c.1800* (New Haven: Yale University Press, 1995). See also, M. Dorrian, 'On Some Spatial Aspects of the Colonial Discourse on Ireland', *Journal of Architecture*, vol. 6, spring 2001, pp. 27–51. Many thanks to colleague Dr Denis Linehan for drawing my attention to this and indeed a number of other articles.

24   A. Hadfield and W. Maley (eds), *Edmund Spenser: A View of the State of Ireland* (Oxford: Oxford University Press, 1997)

25   This argument is more fully developed in W. J. Smyth, 'Semi-Colonial Ireland?', in A. Baker (ed.), *Home and Colonial: Essays in Honour of Robin A. Butlin*, Historical Geography Research Series, No. 39 (Cambridge: Cambridge University Press, 2004), pp. 53–65. For a detailed explanation of my use of 'rising/rebellion' in this work, see chapter 4, p. 105.

26   N. Canny, *Making Ireland British 1580–1650* (Oxford: Oxford University Press, 2001), p. 133

27   Dorrian, 'Spatial Aspects of the Colonial Discourse on Ireland' pp. 35–7

28   D. J. Baker, 'Off the Map: Charting Uncertainty in Renaissance Ireland', in B. Bradshaw, A. Hadfield and W. Maley (eds), *Representing Ireland: Literature and the Origins of Conflict* (Cambridge: Cambridge University Press, 1993), pp. 76–92

29   Hadfield and Maley (eds), *Edmund Spenser: A View*, p. xiv

30   One might note the irony that both Spenser and the bardic poets of Munster had almost identical poetic functions. Spenser's role as poet is to praise, assess and further motivate the crown in its territorial and cultural conquest of Ireland, while that of the Irish and Munster poets is likewise to exhort Irish lords to defend their patrimony and territory

31   R. A. McCabe, 'The Fate of Irena: Spenser and Political Violence', in P. Coughlan (ed.), *Spenser and Ireland: An Interdisciplinary Perspective* (Cork: Cork University Press, 1989), pp. 109–26

32   Hadfield and Maley (eds), *Edmund Spenser:A View* pp. 101–2

33   ibid., pp. xxii–xxiv

34 J. Ruane, 'Colonialism and the Interpretation of Irish Historical Development', in M. Silverman and P. Gulliver (eds), *Approaching the Past: Historical Anthropology through Irish Case–Studies* (New York: Columbia University Press, 1992), pp. 293–323

35 D. W. Meinig, 'Geographical Analysis of Imperial Expansion', in A. Baker and M. Billinge (eds), *Period and Place: Research Methods in Historical Geography* (Cambridge: Cambridge University Press, 1982), p. 71

36 ibid., p. 72. See also, J. Morrissey, *Negotiating Colonialism: Gaelic–Irish Resistance to English Expansion in Early Modern Tipperary* (Cambridge: Cambridge Historical Geography Research Group, 2003).

37 Meinig, 'Geographical Analysis of Imperial Expansion', pp. 72–3

38 T. Jones Hughes, 'Historical Geography of Ireland from circa 1700', in G. Herries–Davies (ed.), *Irish Geography Jubilee Volume* (Dublin: 1984), especially p. 159, with regard to the wide, almost exclusively colonial, residential belt that enveloped the city of Dublin in 1850. This belt was made up of an admixture of the residences of great landowners, the most successful of business and professional families, as well as the more humble homes of the officials and cohorts of the colonial administration. See also, A. Cronin, *Samuel Beckett: The Last Modernist* (London: Harper Collins, 1996), pp. 8–12, with regard to how such patterns, attitudes and behaviours persisted in south Co. Dublin at the turn of the twentieth century.

39 A. R. Orme, 'Segregation as a Feature of Urban Development in Medieval Plantation Ireland', *Geographical Viewpoint*, vol. 2, no. 3, 1971, pp. 193–206

40 In Ulster, towns like Armagh, Carrickfergus and Downpatrick had not only an 'Englishtown/street' and 'Irishtown/street' but also a 'Scotstown/street' or 'Quarter' reflecting the distinctive strength and visibility of the Scots Irish population and its subculture in the seventeenth and eighteenth centuries.

41 Meinig, 'Geographical Analysis of Imperial Expansion', pp. 72–3

42 See, for example, for England, E. Duffy, *The Stripping of the Altars: Traditional Religion in England 1400–1580* (New Haven and London: Yale University Press, 1992), especially Part II, pp. 377–504, and for Ireland, P. J. Corish, *The Catholic Community in the Seventeenth and Eighteenth Centuries* (Dublin: Helicon Press, 1981)

43 J. Brady and P. J. Corish, 'The Church under the Penal Code', in P. J. Corish (ed.), *A History of Irish Catholicism*, 8 vols (Dublin and London: Gill and Macmillan, 1971), IV, pp. 1–88

44 P. J. Dowling, *The Hedge Schools of Ireland* (Dublin: Longmans, Green, 1935). See also, M. Daly and D. Dickson (eds), *The Origins of Popular Literacy in Ireland: Language Change and Educational Development 1700–1920* (Dublin: University College Dublin/Trinity College Dublin, 1990).

45 G. Fitzgerald, 'Estimates for Baronies of Minimum Level of Irish-speaking amongst Successful Decennial Cohorts 1771–1781 to 1861–1871', *Proceedings of Royal Irish Academy*, vol. 84C, 1984, pp. 3–155. See also, B. G. Adams, 'Language in Ulster, 1820–1850', *Ulster Folklife*, vol. 19, 1973, pp. 50–5.

46 See, for example, D. Dickson, C. Ó Gráda and S. Daultrey, 'Hearth tax, Household Size and Irish Population Change 1672–1821', *Proceedings of Royal Irish Academy*, vol. 82C, 1982, pp. 125–81, and W. J. Smyth, 'Wrestling with Petty's Ghost: The Origin, Nature and Relevance of the so–called "1659 Census"', new Introduction to S. Pender (ed.), *A Census of Ireland circa 1659* (Dublin: Irish Manuscript Commission, 2002), pp. v–lxii

47 As, for example, under Cromwell's Commonwealth administration when the key Irish port-cities are put up for sale in the mid-1650s

48 L. M. Cullen, *An Economic History of Ireland since 1660* (London: Batsford, 1972), pp. 7–49

49 See, for example, M. MacCurtain, *Tudor and Stuart Ireland* (Dublin and London: Gill and Macmillan, 1972), especially pp. 39–56

50 Canny, *Making Ireland British*, which examines in great depth all the attempts to anglicize Ireland in the later sixteenth and first half of the seventeenth century, which – in his judgement – had proven to be 'a costly failure'. My thanks also to the novelist James Ryan for stimulating my reflections on this theme.

51 As Cullen points out: 'The cost of conquering Ireland was enormous: more than any other single factor, the cost of Elizabeth's Irish campaigns set parliament and Crown on the course which culminated in civil war in the 1640's', *The Emergence of Modern Ireland*, p. 11

52 See, for example, P. O'Flanagan, 'Markets and Fairs in Ireland, 1600–1800: Index of Economic Development and Regional Growth', *Journal of Historical Geography*, vol. 11, no. 4, 1985, pp. 364–78; P. J. O'Connor, *Fairs and Markets in Ireland: A Cultural Geography* (Midleton: Oireacht na Mumhan Books, 2003), especially pp. 28–63. L. M. Cullen, 'Merchant Communities Overseas, the

Navigation Acts and Irish and Scottish Responses', in L. M. Cullen and T. C. Smout (eds), *Comparative Aspects of Scottish and Irish Economic and Social History* (Edinburgh: John Donald, 1977).

53   Meinig, 'Geographical Analysis of Imperial Expansion', pp. 73–4

54   M. Craig, *Dublin 1660–1860* (Dublin: Allen Figgis, 1952; repr. 1968 and 1980)

55   H. B. Clarke, *Irish Cities* (Cork: Mercier Press, 1995), especially pp. 14–27, 41–62, 96–108 and 204–13, and Jones Hughes, 'Historical Geography', pp. 154–60

56   Jones Hughes, 'Estate System of Landholding'

57   W. J. Smyth, 'Estate Records and the Making of the Irish Landscape', *Irish Geography*, vol. 9, 1976, pp. 26–49

58   See T. Barnard, 'Crisis of Identity among Irish Protestants, 1641–1685', *Past and Present*, vol. 127, May 1990, p. 50. See also, note 99.

59   T. Bartlett and K. Jeffrey (eds), *A Military History of Ireland* (Cambridge: Cambridge University Press, 1996)

60   L. Gibbons, *Transformations in Irish Culture* (Cork: Cork University Press, 1996), especially pp. 3–22. See, for example, K. Whelan, 'The Geography of Hurling', *History Ireland*, vol. 1, 1993, pp. 27–31.

61   W. Nolan, *Fassadinin: Land Settlement and Society in South East Ireland 1600–1850* (Dublin: Geography Publications, 1979). See also, D. Dickson, 'Middlemen', in T. Bartlett and D. W. Hayton (eds), *Penal Era and Golden Age* (Belfast: Ulster Historical Foundation, 1979), pp. 162–85.

62   J. Cleary, 'Misplaced Ideas? Colonialism, Location and Dislocation in Irish Studies', in Carroll and King (eds), *Ireland and Postcolonial Theory*, pp. 16–45

63   ibid., p. 30

64   K. W. Butzer, 'The Americas before and after 1492: An Introduction to Current Geographic Research', *Annals of the Association of American Geographers*, vol. 82, 1992, pp. 345–68. R. C. West, 'Aboriginal and Colonial Geography of Latin America', in B. W. Blouet and O. W. Blouet (eds), *Latin America and the Caribbean* (New York: Wiley, 1997), pp. 45–88

65   C. O. Sauer, *The Early Spanish Main* (Berkeley and Los Angeles: University of California Press, 1966)

66   Crotty, *Ireland in Crisis*, pp. 199–230, especially pp. 204–9

67   ibid., pp. 199–220

68   J. MacLaughlin, *Reimagining the Nation-State: The Contested Terrains of Nation-Building* (London and Sterling, VA. Pluto Press, 2000), especially pp. 43–69

69   See S. Greenblatt, *Renaissance Self–Fashioning: From More to Shakespeare* (Chicago and London: University of Chicago Press, 1980), especially pp. 182–92

70   For Ireland, see A. Crookshank and the Knight of Glin, *Irish Painting 1600–1940* (New Haven and London: Yale University Press, 2002); see also their *The Painters of Ireland c.1660–1920* (London: Barrie and Jenkins, 1978), pp. 16–52, and J. Fenlon, 'Restoring the Butler Heritage', *Irish Arts Review*, autumn 2002, pp. 95–103

71   E. E. Eistenstein, *The Printing Press as an Agent of Change: Communication and Cultural Transformations in Early Modern Europe* (Cambridge: Cambridge University Press, 1979)

72   See, for example, A. L. Rowse, *The England of Elizabeth* (London: Macmillan, 1950), especially chapter 2 'The Elizabethan Discovery of England', pp. 49–86; and D. Livingstone, *The Geographical Tradition* (Oxford: Blackwell, 1992), especially chapter 3, pp. 63–102

73   P. Sidney, *A Defence of Poetry*, ed. J. A. Van Dorstan (Oxford: Oxford University Press, 1966); see also A. Stewart, *Philip Sidney: A Double Life* (London: Chatto and Windus, 2001)

74   N. Machiavelli, *The Prince*, rev. trans., ed. R. M. Adams (New York: Modern Library, 1940)

75   T. More, *Utopia*, vol. IV, *The Yale Edition of the Complete Works of Saint Thomas More*, eds E. Sartz and J. H. Hexter (New Haven: Yale University Press, 1965)

76   C. Nash, 'Historical Geographies of Modernity', in B. Graham and C. Nash (eds), *Modern Historical Geographies* (Harlow: Prentice Hall, 2000), p. 17

77   ibid., p. 13

78   J. Barrington Moore, *The Social Origins of Dictatorship and Democracy* (Boston: Beacon Press, 1966), especially pp. 3–39; Nash, 'Modernity', p. 19; Joan Thirst, *Tudor Enclosures* (London: Routledge and Kegan Paul, 1959)

79   R. A. Butlin, *Historical Geography through the Gates of Space and Time* (London: Edward Arnold, 1993). See also, J. A. Yelling, 'Agriculture 1500–1730', in R. A. Dodgshon and R. A. Butlin (eds), *An Historical Geography of England and Wales* (London: Academic Press, 1978), pp. 151–72

80   B. Klein, *Maps and the Writing of Space in Early Modern England and Ireland* (Basingstoke and New York: Palegrave, 2001), especially pp. 42–60

81 Nash, 'Modernity'. See also, Miles Ogborn, 'Historical Geographies of Globalisation c.1500–1800', in Graham and Nash (eds), *Modern Historical Geographies*, pp. 43–69

82 Nash, 'Modernity' pp. 13–17

83 Cleary, 'Misplaced Ideas?', pp. 31–3. See also, F. A. Yates, *Astraea: The Imperial Theme in the Sixteenth Century* (London and Boston: Ark, 1985), especially Part II, 'The Tudor Imperial Reform', pp. 29–120

84 See, for example, M. Poovey, *A History of the Modern Fact: Problems of Knowledge in the Sciences of Wealth and Society* (Chicago: University of Chicago Press, 1998), especially chapter 3 on William Petty. My thanks to Professor Kevin Whelan for this reference. The founding of Dublin University (Trinity College) is also part of this expansion of the idea of educating the rulers, the clerical and landed elites and the merchant-developers.

85 W. Cronon, 'Modes of Prophecy and Production: Placing Nature in History', *Journal of American History*, vol. 76, 1990, pp. 22–31

86 Nash, 'Modernity' p. 13

87 B. Bailyn, *The Peopling of British North America: An Introduction* (New York: Vintage Books, 1988)

88 Jones Hughes, 'Society and Settlement'

89 See, for example, M. Perceval-Maxwell, *The Outbreak of the Irish Rebellion of 1641* (Dublin: Gill and Macmillan, 1994)

90 For a general analysis of domains of language, see J. A. Fishman, 'Language Maintenance and Language Shift as a Field of Enquiry', *Linguistics*, vol. 9, 1964, pp. 32–70

91 P. Nugent, 'A Historical Geography of the Transformation in the Territorial Organisation of Gaelic Society in County Clare during the Early Modern Period', unpublished Ph.D. thesis, National University of Ireland, Cork, 2002, especially chapter 7, 'Property and Societal Change from 1585 to 1637', pp. 303–62

92 C. O'Mahony, 'The Manor Courts of the Earl of Thomond 1666–1686', *Analecta Hibernica*, vol. 38, 2004, pp. 135–220

93 Crotty, *Ireland in Crisis*, chapters 3 and 4, 'The Evolution of English "Capitalism"', 'Irish Capitalist Colonialism', especially pp. 29–48

94 See Cullen's Introduction to *The Emergence of Modern Ireland*, pp. 11–24. It could be argued that the cumulative consequences of legal and linguistic conquest was to leave the old Irish estranged in, and alienated from, their own land, the ownership, use and naming of which had passed into the hands and voices of an alien elite.

95 Detailed references to all these documentary materials may be found in the relevant chapters below.

96 R. Flatman, 'Some Inhabitants of the Baronies of Uppercross and Newcastle, County Dublin, ca.1650', *Irish Genealogist*, vol. 7, 1989, pp. 496–504, vol. 8, 1990, pp. 3–14, vol. 9, 1991, pp. 162–74. The original 'census' materials are in the National Archives, Ms. 2467.

97 A. Clarke, 'The 1641 Depositions', in Peter Fox (ed.), *Treasures of the Library of Trinity College Dublin* (Dublin: Royal Irish Academy, 1986), pp. 111–22; N. Canny, 'The 1641 Depositions as a Source for the Writing of Social and Economic History: County Cork as a Case Study', in P. O'Flanagan and C. Buttimer (eds), *Cork: History and Society* (Dublin: Geography Publications, 1993), pp. 249–308

98 See, for example, M. McCarthy, 'The Forging of an Atlantic Port City: Socio–Economic and Physical Transformations in Cork 1600–1700', *Urban History*, vol. 28, no. 1, 2001, pp. 25–45

99 Gibbons, *Transformations in Irish Culture*, especially pp. 3–22; T. Barnard, 'The Uses of 23 October 1641 and Irish Protestant Celebrations', *English Historical Review*, vol. 106, 1991, pp. 889–920

100 J. Montague, *The Rough Field* (Oldcastle: Gallery Press, 1989) p. 35

101 W. J. Smyth, *Atlas of Family Names in Ireland: Part I*, CD on *Documents of Ireland*, University College Cork, 2002

102 See, for example, K. Whelan, 'The Bases of Regionalism', in P. Ó Driscéoil (ed.), *Culture in Ireland – Regions, Identity and Power* (Belfast: Institute of Irish Studies, 1993), pp. 5–62

103 Smyth, 'Excavating, Mapping and Interrogating Ancestral Terrains'

2 Making Ireland Visible

1 D. Harvey, *The Condition of Postmodernity: An Enquiry into the Origins of Cultural Change* (Oxford and Cambridge, MA: Blackwell, 1989) pp. 244–5

2 Cotton Collection, MS Augustus I, ii, 21, BL

3 W. Petty, *Hiberniae Delineatio* (London: s.n., 1685)

4   *Portugaliae Monumenta Cartographica*, eds A. Cortesao and A. Teixeira da Mota (Lisboa: Republic of Portugal Government Publications, 1960), vol 1, Plate 17. (The Lopo Homem–Reinels Atlas of 1519.)

5   C. Saxton, *Atlas of England and Wales* (Sp Coll Hunterian Di.1.12, 1579). See also, R. A. Skelton (ed.), *Saxton's Survey of England and Wales* (Amsterdam: Nico Israel, 1974)

6   J. Speed, *The Theatre of the Empire of Great Britaine* (London: Dudbury and Humble, 1611); John Norden's manuscript map of Ireland *c*.1610 (MPF/117) is now held by the PRO, London.

7   T. A. Larcom (ed.), *A History of the Survey of Ireland commonly called the Down Survey by Doctor William Petty, A.D. 1655–6* (Dublin: Irish Archaeological Society, 1851); Y. M. Goblet, *La Transformation de la Géographie Politique de l'Irlande au XVIIeme Siècle dans les Cartes et Essais Anthropogéographiques de Sir William Petty*, 3 vols (Paris: Berger-Levrault, 1930); J. H. Andrews, *Shapes of Ireland: Maps and Their Makers 1564–1839* (Dublin: Geography Publications, 1997), pp. 118–52, and also his *Plantation Acres: An Historical Study of the Irish Land Surveyor and His Maps* (Omagh: Ulster Historical Foundation, 1985), pp. 63–72

8   A. Ortelius, *Theatrum Orbis Terrarum* (London, 1606)

9   J. B. Harley, 'Deconstructing the Map', *Cartographica*, vol. 26, no.2, 1989, pp. 1–20; 'Maps, Knowledge and Power', in D. Cosgrove and S. Daniels (eds), *The Iconography of Landscape* (Cambridge: Cambridge University Press, 1988), pp. 277–312

10 See, for example, reconstruction of Ptolemy's map of Ireland *c.* AD 150 by F. J. Byrne, Fig. 14 in T. W. Moody, F. X. Martin and F. J. Byrne (eds), *A New History of Ireland, IX: Maps, Genealogies, Lists* (Oxford: Oxford University Press, 1984), p. 16

11 J. Brotton, *Trading Territories – Mapping the Early Modern World* (London: Reaktion Books, 1997), p. 32

12 Harvey, *Postmodernity* p. 244

13 ibid., p. 244. However, Alpers is not convinced of the genetic relationship between the earlier Ptolemaic theory of map projections and the Renaissance discovery of linear perspective. She would argue that there is a fundamental difference between perspective paintings and maps in terms of their pictorial conception. See S. Alpers, 'The Mapping Impulse in Dutch Art', in D. Woodward (ed.), *Art and Cartography. Six Historical Essays* (Chicago: University of Chicago Press, 1987), pp. 51–96.

14 Harvey, *Postmodernity*, p. 245

15 ibid

16 Brotton, *Trading Territories*; See also, P. E. James, *All Possible Worlds – A History of Geographical Ideas* (Indianapolis, IN: Bobbs–Merrill, 1972), pp. 50–1

17 D. W. Meinig, *The Shaping of America I – Atlantic America 1492–1800* (New Haven and London: Yale University Press, 1986)

18 Andrews, *Shapes of Ireland*, p. 38

19 ibid., p. 26

20 W. Ivins, *Prints and Visual Communication* (New York: Da Capo Press, 1969), pp. 1–50; E. L. Eisenstein, *The Printing Press as an Agent of Change: Communications and Cultural Transformations in Early Modern Europe* (Cambridge: Cambridge University Press, 1979). See also, N. Crane, *Mercator: The Man Who Mapped the Planet* (London: Weidenfeld and Nicholson, 2002).

21 Andrews, *Shapes of Ireland*, p. 51

22 J. Goghe, 'Hibernia, insula non procul ab Anglia vulgare Hirlandia vocata', 1567, PRO, London, 1/MPF 68; Lawrence Nowell, Ireland, *c*.1564–5, Cotton MS Domitian, XVII, ff. 101, 102, BL

23 P. Barber, 'England I: Pageantry, Defence and Government: Maps at Court to 1550', in D. Buisseret (ed.), *Monarchs, Ministers and Maps* (Chicago and London: University of Chicago Press, 1992), pp. 26–56

24 ibid., pp. 34–9

25 See S. Alpers, *The Art of Describing – Dutch Art in the Seventeenth Century* (Chicago: University of Chicago Press, 1983), especially pp. 119–68 for detailed discussion of these developments

26 J. Dee, *General and Rare Memorials Pertayning to the Perfect Art of Navigation* (London, 1577: facsimile, Amsterdam: Da Capo Press, 1968). On Prince Henry the Navigator, see James, *All Possible Worlds* pp. 85–91

27 Barber, 'England I', pp. 42–5

28 L. B. Cormack, *Charting an Empire – Geography at the English Universities 1580–1620* (Chicago and London: University of Chicago Press, 1997), pp. 1–47; see also, P. Barber, 'England II: Monarchs, Ministers and Maps', in Buisseret (ed.), *Monarchs, Ministers and Maps*, pp. 69–71, 74–5

29 J. H. Andrews, 'Colonial Cartography in a European Setting: The Case of Tudor Ireland', received by the author in manuscript form. See also, J. B. Harley and D. Woodward (eds), *History of Cartography* (Chicago and London: University of Chicago Press)

30   PRO, London, MPF 1/72
31   Barber, 'England II', pp. 57–8
32   ibid., pp. 68–77
33   The front cover enclosing this map contains a handwritten statement that 'Lord Burleigh carried this map always about him', Cotton MS Domitian, BL.
34   B. Klein, *Maps and the Writing of Space in Early Modern England and Ireland* (Basingstoke and New York: Palgrave Press, 2001), pp. 115–16
35   Later on, in 1577, Sir William Gerrard favoured the transformation of Irish countries into counties and so 'by little and little to stretch the Pale further'. See J. H. Andrews, 'Geography and Government in Elizabethan Ireland', in N. Stephens and R. Glasscock (eds), *Irish Geographical Studies in Honour of E. Estyn Evans* (Belfast: Department of Geography, Queen's University Belfast, 1970), p. 182. Much more research is needed to identify Cecil's use (and that of the lord deputies and their officials in Ireland) of geometry and mapping in the planning of Irish fortifications and garrisons. Indeed, much more needs to be done to analyse the role of the English army as a matrix of organization, knowledge and behaviour in sixteenth-century Ireland. We need to know far more about how the garrisons operated locally, their involvement in ongoing war campaigns and their contribution to the carving out and the stabilizing of the spaces of the civil colonies.
36   M. MacCurtain, *Tudor and Stuart Ireland* (Dublin: Gill and Macmillan, 1972), pp. 54–61
37   P. M. Kerrigan, *Castles and Fortifications in Ireland 1485–1945* (Cork: Collins Press, 1995), p. 3
38   ibid., p. 34
39   T. Ó Laidhin (ed.), *Sidney State Papers, 1565–70* (Dublin: Irish Manuscripts Commission, 1962), pp. 30–3, 65–6. See also, Kerrigan, *Castles and Fortifications*, pp. 37–8
40   Kerrigan, *Castles and Fortifications*, pp. 37–41. See also, Barber, 'England II', pp. 65–77
41   Kerrigan, *Castles and Fortifications*, p. 1
42   ibid., pp. 1–2
43   M. Swift, *Historical Maps of Ireland* (London: Parkgate Books, 1999), p. 27. Original of Lythe map of Corkbeg fort is in PRO, London, MPF 1/85
44   Kerrigan, *Castles and Fortifications*, pp. 35–6
45   See M. Maroto Camino, '"Methinks I See an Evil Lurk Unespied" – Visualising Conquest in Spenser's "A View of the State of Ireland"', *Spenser Studies*, vol. 12, 1998, pp. 169–94 and especially 174–8 for a lively discussion with regard to mapping, enclosure and surveillance in the conquest of Ireland.
46   Andrews, 'Geography and Government', pp. 178–80
47   R. A. Skelton and J. Summerson, *A Description of the Maps and Architectural Drawings in the Collection made by William Cecil, Baron Burghley now at Hatfield House* (Oxford: Roxburghe Club, 1971), p. 3. See also, the excellent summary of Lord Burghley's use of maps in government by Barber in 'England II', pp. 68–77.
48   M. J. Blake, 'A Map of the County of Mayo in 1584', *Journal of the Galway Archaeological and Historical Society*, vol. 5, 1907, p. 146; Swift, *Historical Maps of Ireland*, with county map of Sligo, p. 42, and two versions of Co. Monaghan pp. 44 and 46; for Co. Cork see MS 1209/43, TCL, Dublin
49   Barber, 'England II', p. 74
50   Quoted in full by Barber, 'England II', pp. 71–2, 93, from C. Read, *Mr Secretary, Walsingham and the Policy of Queen Elizabeth* (Cambridge: Clarendon Press, 1925), pp. 428–9
51   Andrews, 'Geography and Government', p. 180
52   See N. Canny, *The Elizabethan Conquest of Ireland: A Pattern Established 1565–1576* (Hassocks: Harvester Press, 1976), pp. 46–65
53   Ó Laidhin (ed.), *Sidney State Papers*, p. 70
54   Quoted in Klein, *Maps and the Writing of Space*, p. 62
55   ibid., pp. 62–3
56   ibid., p. 63
57   ibid., p. 64
58   Barber, 'England II', p. 67
59   Andrews, *Shapes of Ireland*, p. 61 and 94–8
60   J. H. Andrews, 'The Mapping of Ireland's Cultural Landscape, 1550–1630', in P. Duffy, D. Edwards and E. Fitzpatrick (eds), *Gaelic Ireland: Land, Lordship and Settlement c.1250–c.1650* (Dublin and Portland: Four Courts Press, 2001), pp. 153–80. Like all researchers writing on early Irish maps, I am greatly indebted to the single–handed reconstruction of the story of Irish maps since the sixteenth century by Professor John Andrews.
61   D. Baker, 'Off the Map: Charting Uncertainty in Renaissance Ireland', in B. Bradshaw, A.

Hadfield and W. Maley (eds), *Representing Ireland – Literature and the Origins of Conflict, 1534–1660* (Cambridge: Cambridge University Press, 1993), pp. 76–92

62   Canny, *The Elizabethan Conquest*, p. 52
63   J. H. Andrews, 'Robert Lythe's Petitions, 1571', *Analecta Hibernica*, vol. 24, 1967, pp. 232–41; see also his 'The Irish Surveys of Robert Lythe', *Imago Mundi*, vol. 19, 1965, pp. 22–31
64   R. Dunlop, 'Sixteenth-Century Maps of Ireland', *English Historical Review*, vol. 20, 1905, p. 333
65   PRO, London, MPF 1/73
66   Canny, *The Elizabethan Conquest*, pp. 95–116
67   Andrews, 'The Irish Surveys of Robert Lythe', pp. 30–1
68   Blake, 'A Map of the County of Mayo in 1584'. See also, Swift's *Historical Maps of Ireland*, p. 40, which reproduces this most interesting map of north Connacht. The later magnificent map of Connacht by the Brownes is located in the TCL Manuscripts Division, MS 1209/68.
69   Andrews, *Shapes of Ireland*, p. 103
70   Canny, *The Elizabethan Conquest*, p. 116
71   Andrews, *Shapes of Ireland*, p. 73
72   Canny, *The Elizabethan Conquest*, pp. 46–75. See also, Ó Laidhin (ed.), *Sidney State Papers*
73   PRO, London, MPF 1/70. Also reproduced in Swift's *Historical Maps of Ireland*, p. 35
74   Nicholas Canny confirms that 'the activities of the map maker Robert Leith [Lythe] were concentrated upon those areas where it was hoped that land would become available for [English] settlement,' p. 67, *The Elizabethan Conquest*
75   Ó Laidhin, *Sidney State Papers*, p. 62
76   Andrews, 'Robert Lythe's Petitions, 1571', pp. 235–41
77   Swift, *Historical Maps of Ireland*, pp. 24–5
78   Andrews, *Shapes of Ireland*, p. 69
79   Swift, *Historical Maps of Ireland*, p. 24
80   Andrews, *Shapes of Ireland*, pp. 61–88
81   Klein, *Maps and the Writing of Space*, p. 117
82   ibid
83   ibid
84   ibid
85   ibid
86   ibid., p. 118
87   G. L. Martin and P. E. James, *All Possible Worlds: A History of Geographical Ideas* (New York: Wiley, 1993), chapter 5
88   M. Kelly, '"We do see the state of that kingdome principally with your eyes": Edmund Spenser, Fynes Moryson, and William Petty and the Imaginative Geographies of Colonialism', unpublished M.Phil. thesis, University College Cork, July 1999, pp. 40–84. See also, J. Breen, 'Spenser's "Imaginative Groundplot: A View of the Present State of Ireland"', *Spenser Studies*, vol. 12, 1998, pp. 151–68
89   Spenser, *A View*, p. 121. This sentence continues, 'for the Irish do strongly hate and abhor all reformation and subjection to the English by reason that having been once subdued by them, they were thrust out of all their possessions'.
90   Quoted in Canny, *The Elizabethan Conquest*, p. 101
91   C. Lennon, *Sixteenth–Century Ireland: The Incomplete Conquest* (Dublin: Gill and Macmillan, 1994), p. 214
92   ibid., p. 215
93   ibid., J. R. Brink, in *Spenser Studies*, vol. 13, 1999, p. 265, reports on another version of this story. In *A General Rehearsal of Warrs* (1579), written by the poet Thomas Churchyard, Sir Humphrey Gilbert's methods of deterring rebellion are vividly described: 'According to a well known anecdote, Gilbert had the heads of the slain foes placed in a circle round his tent and forced the relations of his victims to crawl through the circle.'
94   Lennon, *Sixteenth-Century Ireland*, p. 224
95   ibid., p. 225
96   ibid., p. 227
97   D. Edwards, 'The Demographic Impact of the War in Elizabethan Ireland: A Case-Study of the Desmond Rebellion, 1579–83', paper given at the conference 'Age of Massacres: Violent Death in Ireland c.1547–1650' at Collins Barracks, Dublin, 20 April 2002. My thanks to Dr Edwards for discussions about this paper and to David Butler, Department of Geography, University College Cork, for his notes on the conference

98 Spenser, *A View*, p. 35
99 Klein, *Maps and the Writing of Space*, pp. 184–5
100 ibid., p. 186
101 ibid
102 ibid., p. 187
103 PRO, London, MPF 1/273
104 The most original and stimulating paper on the Munster plantation remains D. B. Quinn's 'The Munster Plantation: Problems and Opportunities', *Journal of Cork Historical and Archaeological Society*, vol. 3, 1943, pp. 60–77.
105 Andrews, 'Geography and Government, pp. 188–9. For the definitive work on this plantation, see M. MacCarthy-Morrogh, *The Munster Plantation: English Migration to Southern Ireland 1583–1641* (Oxford: Oxford University Press, 1986). See also his 'The English Presence in Seventeenth-Century Munster', in C. Brady and R. Gillespie (eds), *Natives and Newcomers: Essays on the Making of Irish Colonial Society 1534–1641* (Dublin: Irish Academic Press, 1986), pp. 171–90.
106 NMM, Greenwich, London, Ms P. 49, 20 and Ms P. 49 and 27
107 Swift, *Historical Maps of Ireland*, p. 39
108 Andrews, 'Geography and Government', pp. 186–8
109 Map of Sir Walter Raleigh's lands in Co. Cork (1589), NLI, 16.L.33(18); Paul Hulton, *America 1585 – The Complete Drawings of John White*. (Chapel Hill, NC: University of North Carolina Press, 1984), p. 15
110 PRO, London, MPF 1/312
111 G. A. Hayes-McCoy (ed.), *Ulster and Other Irish Maps c.1600* (Dublin: Stationery Office for the Irish Manuscripts Commission, 1964), p. 14; NLI, Ms Bartlett VII
112 Kelly, '"We doe see the state of that Kingdome principally with your eyes"', pp. 85–146
113 Hayes-McCoy (ed.), *Ulster and Other Irish Maps*, pp. 8–10; NLI, Ms Bartlett V
114 Lennon, *Sixteenth-Century Ireland*. S. O'Faolain, *The Great O'Neill – A Biography of Hugh O'Neill, Earl of Tyrone 1550–1616* (Cork: Mercier Press; Chester Springs, PA: Dufour Editions, 1997) pp. 268–72.
115 PRO, London, MPF 1/35. See also, Swift, *Historical Maps of Ireland*, p. 49,
116 TCL Manuscripts Division, MS 1209/14
117 PRO, London, MPF 1/36. See also, Swift, *Historical Maps of Ireland*, p. 50
118 Speed, *Theatre of the Empire of Great Britaine*. The editions of Speed's work are detailed in T. Chubb, *The Printed Maps in the Atlases of Great Britain and Ireland: A Bibliography 1579–1870* (London: Burrow, 1927), pp. 23–39
119 In Speed's 1601 map of Ireland, showing major historic battles and events, he notes the battle of Blackwater in 1598 and the subsequent invasion of Ulster by English forces, 'for whose prosperous success,' adds Speed, 'with the overthrow of all treasons and rebellions, let all true-hearted subjects pray' (Andrews, *Shapes of Ireland*, p. 92)
120 Klein, *Maps and the Writing of Space*, p. 23
121 Baker, 'Charting Uncertainty in Renaissance Ireland', p. 90
122 For example, see Michel Foucault, *Surveillir et Punir: Naissance de la Prison* (Paris: Gallimard, 1975), translated as *Discipline and Punish: The Birth of the Prison* by A. Sheridan (London and New York: Tavistock, 1977). See also, Colin Gordon (ed.), *Power/Knowledge: Selected Interviews and Other Writings 1972–1977 by Michel Foucault* (Hassocks: Harvester Press, 1980), especially pp. 63–77
123 At that time, the words 'plot', 'platte', 'plan', 'mappe', 'image', 'peinting', 'chart', 'card' and 'view' invariably overlap in meaning between a graphic mapping and a narrative strategy of knowledge formulation and utilization: for example, in the late 1560s, Robert Lythe was instructed 'to take a view of the Irish terrain' and set his observations down on 'a platte', which in turn combined the lines and images of the map with detailed written descriptions. And 'a plot of land' could then mean a plot or plan *about* the land, as in the Ulster plantation, a plot made *of* the land (i.e. a map of the land), as well as the 'applotment and settlement' of the land. The mapping metaphor is a central and dominant one in this era

3 Maps versus Memory

1 H. Melville, *Moby-Dick; or, The Whale* (1851; repr. New York: Modern Library, 1992), p. 222
2 Quoted in G. A. Hayes-McCoy (ed.), *Ulster and Other Irish Maps* (Dublin: Stationery Office for the Irish Manuscript Commission, 1964), p. xii

3   Quoted in J. H. Andrews, *Shapes of Ireland: Maps and Their Makers 1564–1839* (Dublin: Geography Publications, 1997), p. 104

4   ibid., p. 103

5   J. H. Andrews, 'The Maps of the Escheated Counties of Ulster, 1609–10', *Proceedings of the Royal Irish Academy*, vol. 74 (c), no. 4, 1974, p. 142

6   ibid.

7   E. McCracken, *The Irish Woods since Tudor Times – Their Distribution and Exploitation* (Newton Abbot: David and Charles, 1971), p. 50; see also reference to this event in *Celtic Dimensions of the British Civil Wars*, ed. John R. Young (Edinburgh: John Donald, 1997), p. 146

8   Quoted in Andrews, 'Maps of the Escheated Counties', pp. 140–1

9   The social and intellectual milieu in which Sir John Davies grew up and prospered is enthusiastically described by A. L. Rowse in his chapter 'The Elizabethan Discovery of England', especially pp. 59–86, in *The England of Elizabeth* (London: Macmillan, 1950).

10 J. O'Donovan (ed. and trans.), *Annála Rioghachta Éireann: Annals of the Kingdom of Ireland by the Four Masters from the Earliest Times to the Year 1616*, vol. 5, 3rd edn (Dublin: Edmund Burke, 1998), pp. 1445–9

11 B. Ó Buachalla, 'Annála Rioghtachta Éireann is Foras Feasa ar Éirinn: An Comthéacs Comhaimseartha', *Studia Hibernica*, vols 22–3, 1982–3, pp. 59–105

12 O'Donovan (ed. and trans.), *Annála Rioghachta Éireann: Annals of the Four Masters*, see introductory remarks pp. vii–lxi, especially x–xii

13 Ó Buachalla, 'Annála Rioghtachta Éireann is Foras Feasa ar Éirinn', pp. 70–105. See also, M. Caball, 'Faith, Culture and Sovereignty: Irish Nationality and Its Development, 1558–1625', in B. Bradshaw and P. Roberts (eds), *British Consciousness and Identity: The Nationality of Britain, 1533–1707* (Cambridge: Cambridge University Press, 1998), pp. 132–4

14 E. Boland, *In a Time of Violence* (Manchester: Carcanet, 1994), p. 5

15 J. G. A. Pocock, chapter 7 in *The British Problem c.1534–1707: State Formation in the Atlantic Archipelago* (Basingstoke and London: Macmillan Press, 1996)

16 P. Coughlan, 'Cheap and Common Animals: The English Anatomy of Ireland in the Seventeenth Century', in T. Healy and J. Sawday (eds), *Literature and the English Civil War* (Cambridge: Cambridge University Press, 1990), pp. 205–23

17 See, for example, Ó Buachalla, 'Annála Rioghtachta Éireann is Foras Feasa ar Éirinn'; P. Lenihan, *Confederate Catholics at War 1641–49* (Cork: Cork University Press, 2001), pp. 4–7

18 There were regions of English speech and writing especially in Dublin and the Pale but also in pockets of south Leinster and east Munster and the port-cities generally.

19 E. Estyn Evans, *The Personality of Ireland: Habitat, Heritage and History* (Cambridge: Cambridge University Press, 1973), pp. 50–1

20 S. O'Faolain, *The Great O'Neill – A Biography of Hugh O'Neill, Earl of Tyrone 1550–1616* (Cork: Mercier Press and Chester Springs, PA: Dufour Editions, 1997), p. 10. See also, O'Faolain's highly original *The Irish* (1947: rev. edn. Middlesex: Penguin Books, 1969).

21 Pocock, chapter 7 in *The British Problem*, p. 174

22 'The Present State of that Countrye', TCL Manuscripts Division, G.216 (743), described by R. Dunlop in *English Historical Review*, vol. 20, 1905, p. 313, and by D. B. Quinn in *Irish Historical Studies*, vol. 5, 1947, p. 308, dated between 1586 and 1593, probably 1587–9

23 See, for example, the power of the late medieval lordship of O'Donnell's Tír Chonaill as demonstrated by D. Mac Eiteagáin, 'The Renaissance and the Late Medieval Lordship of Tír Chonaill 1461–1555', in W. Nolan, L. Ronayne and M. Dunlevy (eds), *Donegal: History and Society* (Dublin: Geography Publications, 1995), pp. 203–28

24 G. Henry, *The Irish Military Community in Spanish Flanders, 1586–1621* (Dublin: Irish Academic Press, 1992). See also, T. W. Moody, F. X. Martin and F. J. Byrne (eds), *A New History of Ireland, III: Early Modern Ireland 1534–1691* (Oxford: Clarendon Press, 1976), pp. 509–45, 587–633, especially 612–16

25 See, for example, J. Reinhard Lupton, '"Mapping Mutability" or Spenser's Irish Plot' chapter 6 in B. Bradshaw, A. Hadfield and W. Maley (eds), *Representing Ireland: Literature and the Origins of Conflict, 1534–1660* (Cambridge: Cambridge University Press), pp. 93–115; see also, D. Cosgrove, *Mappings* (London: Reaktion, 1999), especially pp. 1–23

26 M. Foucault, *The Archaeology of Knowledge and the Discourse on Language*, trans. A. Sheridan (London and New York: Tavistock, 1972); see also, C. Philo, 'Foucault's Geography', *Environment and Planning D. Society and Space*, vol. 10, 1992, pp. 137–61; A. Sheridan, *Michel Foucault: The Will to Truth* (London and New York: Tavistock, 1980), especially pp. 89–134, and L. Hunt (ed.), *The*

New Cultural History (Berkeley, Los Angeles and London: University of California Press, 1989), especially the chapter by P. O'Brien, 'Michel Foucault's History of Culture', pp. 25–46

27   C. Gordon (ed.), *Michel Foucault, Power/Knowledge: Selected Interviews and Other Writings 1972–1977* (Brighton: Harvester Press, 1980), pp. 74–7. See also, G. Deleuze, *Foucault*, ed. and trans. S. Hand (Minneapolis and London: University of Minnesota Press, 1986), especially pp. 23–46.

28   J. Woolway, 'Significant Spaces in Spencer's *Vewe of the Present State of Ireland*', *Early Modern Literary Studies*, vol. 4, no. 2, Special Issue 3, 1998, pp. 1–21. See also, G. Hooper, 'Writings and Landscape in Early Modern Ireland', *Literature and History*, vol. 5, no. 2, autumn 1996, pp. 1–18

29   See Deleuze, *Foucault*, especially chapter 2 'A New Cartographer (*Discipline and Punish*)', pp. 23–46

30   See, for example, Sheridan, *Michel Foucault*, especially Part II 'The Genealogy of Power', pp. 113–63; see also, Mary Kelly, '"We doe see the state of that kingdome principally with your eyes": Edmund Spenser, Fynes Moryson and William Petty and the Imaginative Geographies of Colonialism', unpublished M.Phil. thesis, University College Cork, July 1999, especially pp. 9–29 and 194–207, and D. Sopher, 'Notes on the Spatial Patterning of Culture', in L. Scheider and C. M. Bonjean (eds), *The Idea of Culture in the Social Sciences* (Cambridge: Cambridge University Press, 1970), pp. 101–17

31   M. Foucault, *Surveiller et Punir: Naissance de la Prison* (Paris: Gallimard, 1975), translated as *Discipline and Punish: The Birth of the Prison* by A. Sheridan (London and New York: Tavistock, 1977). See also, Sheridan's *The Will to Truth*, pp. 135–63.

32   K. Noonan, '"The Cruell Pressure of an Enraged Barbarous People": Irish and English Identity in Seventeenth-Century Policy and Propaganda', *Historical Journal*, vol. 41, no. 1, 1998, pp. 151–78; D. B. Quinn, *The Elizabethans and the Irish* (Ithaca, NY: Cornell University Press, 1966); C. Maxwell (ed.), *Irish History from Contemporary Sources 1509–1610* (London: Allen and Unwin, 1923); E. Spenser, *A View of the State of Ireland*, ed. W. L. Renwick (Oxford: Clarendon Press, 1970)

33   See, for example, W. Boelhower, 'Inventing America: A Model of Cartographic Semiosis', *Word & Image*, vol. 4, no. 2, April–June 1988, pp. 475–97, especially 489–93

34   O'Faolain, *The Great O'Neill*, pp. 4–5

35   O'Donovan (ed. and trans.), *Annála Rioghachta Éireann*, vol. 6, pp. 2147–65

36   ibid., pp. 2163–5

37   ibid., pp. 2171–7

38   ibid., p. 2363

39   'A booke of the Kings lands founde upon the last generall survey within the province of Ulster anno 1608', MS Rawlinson A. 237, The Bodleian Library, Oxford; printed in *Analecta Hibernica*, vol. 3, 1931, pp. 151–218

40   Andrews, 'Maps of the Escheated Counties', pp. 139–40

41   ibid., p. 139

42   ibid., p. 140

43   ibid., p. 142

44   ibid., p. 146

45   ibid., p. 145

46   ibid., pp. 133–70

47   Applying Professor Waldo R. Tobler's techniques to test the level of agreement between escheated counties maps and one–inch OS maps, John Andrews provides useful statistical data for each barony or part–barony in 'Maps of the Escheated Counties', pp. 148–55, especially 145.

48   ibid., p. 152

49   ibid., p. 160

50   ibid., p. 159

51   ibid., p. 163

52   Hayes-McCoy (ed.), *Ulster and Other Irish Maps*, pp. xi–xv. See also, Andrews, 'Maps of Escheated Counties', p. 135

53   It is likely that it was the Elizabethan scholar and cartographer John Norden, still working in the Jacobean era, who had the skill and ingenuity to actually construct the Cotton summary map of plantation Ulster as a whole from the rather difficult raw materials of the Bodley survey.

54   See Norden's Maps of the Escheated Counties in Ulster *c*.1610 in Cotton Collection, MS Augustus I. ii. 44, BL

55   P. J. Duffy, 'The Territorial Organisation of Gaelic Landownership and Its Transformation in County Monaghan 1591–1640', *Irish Geography*, vol. 14, 1981, pp. 1–26

56   S. Ó Ceallaigh, *Gleanings from Ulster History – Punann ó Chois Bhanna* (Cork: Cork University Press, 1951), p. 26, note 2

57   Andrews, 'Maps of the Escheated Counties', p. 146

58   ibid., p. 147

59   ibid.

60   Ó Ceallaigh, *Gleanings*, pp. 112–13

61   P. S. Robinson, 'The Ulster Plantation and Its Impact on the Settlement Pattern of Co. Tyrone', in C. Dillon and H. A. Jeffries (eds), *Tyrone – History and Society* (Dublin: Geography Publications, 2000), pp. 234–7. See also, P. S. Robinson's *The Plantation of Ulster: British Settlement in an Irish Landscape* (Belfast: Ulster Historical Foundation, 1994).

62   McErlean, Duffy, Nugent and Dodgshon have all helped to elucidate the general principles underlying this dynamic system of territorial and landscape organization. See Thomas McErlean, 'The Irish Townland System of Landscape Organisation', in T. Reeves Smyth and F. Hammond (eds), *Landscape Archaeology in Ireland*, BAR British Series 116 (Oxford: British Archaeological Report, 1983), pp. 315–39; R. A. Dodgshon, *From Chiefs to Landlords: Social and Economic Change in the Western Highlands and Islands c.1493–1820* (Edinburgh: John Donald, 1998); Duffy, 'Territorial Organisation of Gaelic Landownership', pp. 1–26; P. Nugent, 'A Historical Geography of the Transformation in the Territorial Organisation of Gaelic Society in County Clare during the Early Modern Period', unpublished Ph.D. thesis, Department of Geography, University College Cork, 2002.

63   Robinson, 'The Plantation of Ulster/Tyrone', p. 235

64   ibid., pp. 242–5

65   J. M. Graham, 'Rural Society in Connacht, 1600–1640', in N. Stephens and R. E. Glasscock (eds), *Irish Geographical Studies in Honour of E. Estyn Evans* (Belfast: Department of Geography, Queen's University Belfast, 1970), pp. 192–208

66   N. Buttimer, Review of *Gaelic Ireland: Land, Lordship and Settlement c.1250–c.1650* in *Journal of the Cork Historical and Archaeological Society*, 2002, pp. 217–28. My thanks to Dr Buttimer, Department of Modern Irish, University College Cork, for most helpful discussions and pointers in assessing 'modes of mapping' in the Irish tradition.

67   For an earlier period, see F. Kelly, *Early Irish Farming* (Dublin: Dublin Institute for Advanced Studies, 1997), pp. 376–9 and 409 for discussion on field and property fences and boundary markers. My thanks to Professor Kelly for a helpful discussion on 'ways of mapping/understanding the Irish landscape'.

68   R. C. Simington (ed.), *The Civil Survey, A.D. 1654–1656 County of Tipperary, Western and Northern Baronies* (Dublin: Irish Manuscripts Commission, 1934), p. 12

69   P. J. Duffy, 'Social and Spatial Order in the MacMahon Lordship of Airghialla in the Late Sixteenth Century', in P.J. Duffy, D. Edwards and E. Fitzpatrick (eds), *Gaelic Ireland: Land, Lordship and Settlement, c.1250–c.1650* (Dublin: Four Courts Press, 2001), pp. 122–5

70   N. Ó Muraíle, 'Settlement and Place-names', in Duffy, Edwards and Fitzpatrick (eds), *Gaelic Ireland: Land, Lordship and Settlement*, pp. 223–45

71   See E. Eckwall, *Scandinavians and Celts in the North-West of England* (Lund: C. W. K. Gleerup, 1918)

72   Quoted in N. Canny, *The Elizabethan Conquest of Ireland: A Pattern Established 1565–1576* (Hassocks: Harvester Press, 1976), p. 25. See also, his *From Reformation to Restoration: Ireland, 1534–1660* (Dublin: Helicon Press, 1987), especially pp. 70–187.

73   Duffy, 'Social and Spatial Order', pp. 117, 126–8

74   Robinson, 'The Plantation of Ulster/Tyrone', pp. 243–4

75   K. Simms, *From Kings to Warlords: The Changing Political Structure of Gaelic Ireland in the Later Middle Ages* (Woodbridge: Boyell Press, 1987), pp. 129–46, especially 139–40

76   Much research is still needed on the training and skills held by the Irish professional classes, particularly in terms of their 'geographical/mapping' knowledge. See K. W. Nicholls, *Gaelic and Gaelicised Ireland in the Later Middle Ages* (Dublin: Gill and Macmillan, 1972); Simms, *From Kings to Warlords*; B. Cunningham, 'Native Culture and Political Change in Ireland, 1580–1640', in C. Brady and R. Gillespie (eds), *Natives and Newcomers: Essays on the Making of Irish Colonial Society 1534–1641* (Dublin: Academic Press, 1986), pp. 148–70; see also, M. O'Dowd's chapter 'Gaelic Economy and Society' in same volume, pp. 120–47.

77   See, for example, S. A. Meigs, *The Reformations in Ireland: Tradition and Confessionalism, 1400–1690* (Dublin: Gill and Macmillan, 1997), pp. 16–40, 77–89. *Cuius regio, eius religio* (the faith of the sovereign is to be the faith of the nation).

78   P. MacCana, 'The Rise of the Later Schools of Filidheacht', *Ériu*, vol. 25, 1974, pp. 126–47

79 See, for example, B. Cunningham, *The World of Geoffrey Keating: History, Myth and Religion in Seventeenth-Century Ireland* (Dublin: Four Courts Press, 2000) for many stimulating insights into Keating's milieu, his work, his construction of an Irish Catholic perspective on the past and the later dissemination and reception of his work in both Irish and English forms.

80 O'Donovan (ed. and trans.), *Annála Rioghachta Éireann*, vol. 5, pp. 1259–874

81 ibid., vol. 6, pp. 1875–2369; Hugh O'Neill's death in 1616 is remembered, pp. 2372–5

82 See, for example, *Codex Mendoza: Aztec Manuscript* (Fribourg: Liber, 1978–84), with commentaries by Kurt Ross, especially Part II, which is a copy of the 'Tribute Role of Moztezuma', containing a detailed account of the tribute paid by over 400 towns to the last ruler of ancient Mexico (and not dissimilar to the kinds of evidence gathered by the colonial English in surveys such as the Composition Book of Connacht). Large numbers of the Aztec painted books, including their chronicles, annals and other land records were destroyed by Spanish military action when the libraries of the defeated Aztec towns were burnt down. See also, N. Wachtel, *The Vision of the Vanquished: The Spanish Conquest of Peru through Indian Eyes, 1530–1570* (Brighton: Harvester Press, 1977) for the story of the destruction of the Incan civilization.

83 See Duffy 'Territorial Organisation of Gaelic Landownership'; see also his 'Social and Spatial Order' in Duffy, Edwards and Fitzpatrick (eds), *Gaelic Ireland*, pp. 117–28 and the editors' Introduction for this volume, especially pp. 47–53

84 My thanks to Dr John Carey, Department of Old and Middle Irish, University College Cork, for a useful discussion on this point.

85 See note 63 above. In particular, I wish to thank Dr Pat Nugent, Institute of Irish Studies, University of Liverpool, for useful discussions and insights on these points.

86 J. H. Andrews, *Plantation Acres: An Historical Study of the Irish Land Surveyor* (Belfast: Ulster Historical Foundation, 1985), p. 52. In comparing early modern cartography with medieval traditions of cosmography, Bernhard Klein makes the very valid point that there is a significant 'rupture between geographic scales that encode the world as either a space of lived social experience [medieval] or as an object of a clinical scientific quest [early modern] . . . [so] we arrive at a self–proclaimed new scientific world image "conscious of its novelty, confident of its superiority to the ancient geography"', *Maps and the Writing of Space in Early Modern England and Ireland* (Basingstoke and New York: Palgrave Press, 2001), p. 41.

87 Andrews, *Plantation Acres*, p. 57. See also, H. Goff, 'English Conquest of an Irish Barony: The Changing Patterns of Land Ownership in the Barony of Scarawalsh 1540–1640', in K. Whelan (ed.) and W. Nolan (assoc. ed.), *Wexford: History and Society* (Dublin: Geography Publications, 1957), pp. 122–50.

88 S. Heaney, *Preoccupations: Selected Prose 1968–1978* (London: Faber and Faber, 1980), pp. 34–7. Heaney further notes: 'I speak and write in English, but I do not altogether share the preoccupations and perspectives of an Englishman . . . Two Elizabethan poets enforce this realization. Edmund Spenser's view of the state of Ireland, amongst other things, puts me at a distance from him. From his castle in Cork he watched the effects of a campaign designed to settle the Irish question. "Out of every corner of the woods and glens they came creeping forth upon their hands, for their legs could not carry them; they looked like anatomies of death, they spake like ghosts crying out of their graves." At that point I feel closer to the natives, the geniuses of the place. . . . And a little after that, Sir John Davies, that silver poet of the sixteenth century, arrived in Ireland as Queen Elizabeth's Attorney–General with special responsibility for the Plantation of Ulster, playing a forward–looking colon to my backward–looking colonisé.'

89 Irish version of this poem from *An Duanaire 1600–1900: Poems of the Dispossessed*, curtha i láthair ag S. Ó Tuama with translations into English verse by T. Kinsella (Mountrath/Portlaoise: Dolmen Press, 1981), pp. 328–9. This English translation fuses that of Frank O'Connor's and my own

90 In this estimate, I have followed Joyce by only allowing that one–fifth of the 'Kil' names refer not to 'cill/church' but rather to 'coill/wood'. I have also assumed that about a half of 'Ros' names refer not to peninsulas but rather to woods (many peninsulas were, of course, wooded to begin with). P. W. Joyce, *The Origin and History of Irish Names of Places*, 3 vols (repr. 1995, Dublin: Edmund Burke, 1875), vol. 1, pp. 491–522.

91 Joyce, *Origin and History of Irish Names of Places*, p. 491

92 See, for example, Sir John Davies's comments at the beginning of this chapter and those of Spenser in *A View*, p. 49

93 TCL, Manuscripts Division, G215 (743)

94 Much further research is needed to either solidify or qualify McCracken's pioneer work.

Certainly, the determination of the scale and extent of woodland in early modern Ireland remains a difficult question

95 See the impressive reproductions in colour of many of these Bodley barony maps in M. Swift, *Historical Maps of Ireland* (London: Parkgate Books, 1999), pp. 52–63

96 Robinson, 'The Plantation of Ulster/Tyrone', pp. 238–40

97 Paddy Duffy has demonstrated the intricate ways in which townland structures in Co. Monaghan contain a wide range of land-use potentials and his description of the Raven townland maps and associated land-use categories (1634) still shows woodland as an integral element in townland culture.

98 This statement is based on an analysis and mapping of woodland evidence for all Down Survey barony maps across the island.

99 PRO, London, MPF 1/35 and MPF 1/36. These striking Bartlett maps are reproduced in Swift's *Historical Maps of Ireland*, pp. 49–51.

100 This map is constructed by fusing data from Kenneth W. Nicholls's map of Irish lordships *c*.1534 in Moody, Martin and Byrne (eds), *A New History of Ireland, III*, pp. 2–3, with Eileen McCracken's key island-wide map of woodland distribution in *Irish Woods since Tudor Times*, p. 36

101 J. H. Andrews and R. Loeber, 'An Elizabethan Map of Leix and Offaly: Cartography, Topography and Architecture', in W. Nolan and T. P. O'Neill, *Offaly: History and Society* (Dublin: Geography Publications, 1998)

102 O'Donovan (ed. and trans.), *Annála Rioghachta Éireann*, pp. 1546–7

103 ibid., pp. 1548–9

104 J. O'Hanlon, *History of the Queen's County* (Dublin: Sealy, Bryers and Walker, 1914), vol 2, pp. 450–1

105 Quoted in McCracken's *Irish Woods since Tudor Times*, p. 27, from H. F. Hore, 'Woods and Fastnesses in Ancient Ireland', *Ulster Journal of Archaeology*, first series, vol. 6, 1900, p. 154. See also, Rolf Loeber, 'Settlers' Utilisation of the Natural Resources', in K. Hannigan and W. Nolan (eds), *Wicklow: History and Society* (Dublin: Geography Publications, 1994), pp. 267–304.

106 McCracken, *Irish Woods since Tudor Times*, pp. 99–100

107 Personal communication from Dr Alf O'Brien, Department of History, University College Cork, who has carried out detailed research on this theme.

108 K. W. Nicholls, 'Woodland Cover in Pre-Modern Ireland', in Duffy, Edwards and Fitzpatrick (eds), *Gaelic Ireland*, p. 199. See also, McCracken, *Irish Woods since Tudor Times*, and C. Litton Falkiner, *Illustrations of Irish History and Topography mainly on the Seventeenth Century* (London, New York and Bombay: Longmans, 1904), chapter 5 'The Woods of Ireland', pp. 142–56

109 As R. G. Albion has written: 'the first two Stuarts greatly hastened the danger of oak shortage by extending the exploitation of forests commissioned by the Tudors. The practice of deriving revenue at the expense of future oak supply must stand as the real forest policy of England from 1534 to 1660.' And it appears that the civil wars and the Cromwellian Interregnum contribute to deliver the *coup de grâce* to England's forest *surplus*; noted in H. C. Darby (ed.), *An Historical Geography of England before AD 1800* (Cambridge: Cambridge University Press, 1963), pp. 395–6.

110 O. Rackham, *The History of the Countryside* (London: Dent, 1986), p. 115

111 McCracken, *Irish Woods since Tudor Times*, p. 105

112 ibid

113 ibid., p. 106

114 ibid., p. 102

115 ibid., pp. 101–2

116 ibid., pp. 100–1

117 Nicholls, 'Woodland Cover', p. 188

118 McCracken, *Irish Woods since Tudor Times*, p. 100

119 ibid., p. 48

120 ibid

121 See N. Canny, *The Upstart Earl: A Study of the Social and Mental World of Richard Boyle, First Earl of Cork 1566–1643* (Cambridge: Cambridge University Press, 1982)

122 Nicholls, 'Woodland Cover', pp. 188, 199–205

123 ibid., p. 199

124 W. Petty, *Political Anatomy of Ireland* ([1672] 1691: repr. Shannon: Irish University Press, 1970), pp. 25–47

125 McCracken, *Irish Woods since Tudor Times*, p. 45

126 ibid., p. 50. See also, Loeber on settlers' use of natural resources in Co. Wicklow in his 'Settlers' Utilisation of the Natural Resources'
127 Nicholls, 'Woodland Cover', pp. 200–2, and McCracken, *Irish Woods since Tudor Times*, pp. 66–7. See also, J. H. Andrews, 'Notes on the Historical Geography of the Irish Iron Industry', *Irish Geography*, vol. 3, no. 3, 1957, pp. 139–49
128 McCracken, *Irish Woods since Tudor Times*, p. 92
129 L. M. Cullen, *The Emergence of Modern Ireland* (London: Batsford, 1981), p. 25
130 McCracken, *Irish Woods since Tudor Times*, p. 82
131 Petty, *Political Anatomy*, pp. 12–13
132 Nicholls, 'Woodland Cover', pp. 202–6
133 D. Woodward, 'A Comparative Study of the Irish and Scottish Livestock Trades in the Seventeenth Century', in L. M. Cullen and T. C. Smout (eds), *Comparative Aspects of Scottish and Irish Economic and Social History* (Edinburgh: John Donald, 1977), pp. 147–64; see also his 'The Anglo-Irish Livestock Trade in the Seventeenth Century', *Irish Historical Studies*, vol. 17, 1973, pp. 489–523
134 Canny, *The Elizabethan Conquest* pp. 8–9
135 See P. O'Flanagan, 'Markets and Fairs in Ireland 1600–1800: Index of Economic Development and Regional Growth', *Journal of Historical Geography*, vol. 2, no. 3, 1985, pp. 364–78; and A. Sheehan, 'Irish Towns in a Period of Change 1558–1625', in Brady and Gillespie (eds.), *Natives and Newcomers*, pp. 114–19
136 McCracken, *Irish Woods since Tudor Times*, pp. 73–9
137 D. A. Chart (ed.), *Londonderry and the Companies 1609–1629, being a Survey and Other Documents Submitted to King Charles I by Sir Thomas Phillips* (Belfast: HMSO, 1928)
138 McCracken, *Irish Woods since Tudor Times*, p. 78, and Nicholls, 'Woodland Cover', pp. 205–6
139 Nicholls, 'Woodland Cover', p. 197
140 ibid., p. 196
141 ibid., p. 198
142 Cullen, *Emergence of Modern Ireland*, p. 84
143 ibid., p. 84. See also his 'Economic Trends, 1660–91', in Moody, Martin and Byrne (eds), *A New History of Ireland, III*, pp. 388–91; N. Canny, 'Migration and Opportunity: Britain, Ireland and the New World', *Irish Economic and Social History*, vol. 12, 1985, p. 30; see also his 'English Migration into and across the Atlantic during the Seventeenth and Eighteenth Centuries', in N. Canny (ed.), *Europeans on the Move: Studies in European Migration, 1500–1800* (Oxford: Clarendon Press, 1994), p. 62
144 McCracken, *Irish Woods since Tudor Times*, p. 93
145 A major comparative research programme is necessary to investigate and assess the farm landscapes and societies created in the former woodland territories across the island. We need to be able both to itemize and compare the shapes of farms and fields, the forms of enclosure, the kinds of farmhouse architecture and outbuildings, the kinds of social structures, the nature of communications and a host of other variables that characterized these reclaimed woodland regions. We need to be able to compare the Bandon and Blackwater valleys with those of Wicklow and north Wexford, with those of the Lagan and Bann valleys, with the former Kilhuggy woodland region on the Tipperary/Limerick border, the territory of the great wood/Kilmore in north Cork and on into the former wooden fastnesses of Leanmore on the Kerry/Limerick/Cork borderlands. And we also need to look at the new farmlands created among the former woodlands along the Shannon river, including 'the woods of Bryall' in the south of Athlone barony and further west in the mysterious Kilbigher woodland region that Kenneth Nicholls ('Woodland Cover', pp. 190–1) locates on the north Galway border world which straddles the three baronies of Tiaquin, Ballymore and Killian
146 J. Swift, 'A Letter from a Member of the House of Commons of Ireland', in J. McMinn (ed.), *Swift's Irish Pamphlets: An Introductory Selection* (Gerrards Cross: Colin Smythe, 1991), p. 41. Skilled workers in timber and iron-making (mainly English) earned as much as their counterparts in England but 'the fellers, the charcoal burners, and the carters earned considerably less: and it is possible that these latter, the hewers of wood and drawers of water, were Irish' (McCracken, *Irish Woods since Tudor Times*, p. 93).
147 See Austin Clarke's poem 'The Planter's Daughter':
    When night stirred at sea
    And the fire brought a crowd in,
    They say that her beauty

Was music in mouth
And few in the candlelight
Thought her too proud,
For the house of the planter
Is known by the trees

From A. Clarke, *Collected Poems* (London, Oxford and New York: Dolmen and Oxford University Press, 1974), p. 173

148 W. J. Smyth, 'The Greening of Ireland: Tenant Tree-Planting in the Eighteenth and Nineteenth Centuries', *Irish Forestry*, vol. 54, no. 1, 1997, pp. 55–72

4 The Transformation of Ireland 1641–1654

1   Seán Ó Conaill's poem 'Tuireamh na hÉireann', in Cecile O'Rahilly (ed.), *Five Seventeenth-Century Political Poems* (Dublin: Dublin Institute for Advanced Studies, 1952), p. 75, lines 353–4

2   John Hewitt's poem 'The Glens', in Brendan Kenneally (ed.), *The Penguin Book of Irish Verse* (Middlesex and Baltimore: Penguin Books, 1970), p. 346

3   Now housed in the Department of Irish Folklore, UCD. See also, R. F. Foster's assessment: Cromwell 'Trod on Irish soil for only nine months but few men's footprints have been so deeply imprinted upon Irish history and historiography', *Modern Ireland* (London and New York: Penguin Books, 1988), p. 101.

4   TCD Depositions, Co. Tyrone volume, Barony of Dungannon, John Kerdiff, folio 2b

5   R. Walsh, *Fingal and Its Churches* (Dublin, 1888), pp. 151–2

6   T. C. Barnard, 'Crises of Identity among Irish Protestants 1641–1685', *Past and Present*, vol. 127, May 1990, p. 50; see, for example, N. Canny, 'The 1641 Depositions as a Source for the Writing of Social History: County Cork as a Case Study', in P. O'Flanagan and C. G. Buttimer (eds), *Cork: History and Society* (Dublin: Geography Publications, 1993), pp. 249–308

7   N. Canny, *Making Ireland British 1580–1650* (Oxford: Oxford University Press, 2001), especially pp. 461–550; M. Perceval-Maxwell, *The Outbreak of the Irish Rebellion of 1641* (Dublin: Gill and Macmillan, 1994)

8   P. J. Corish, 'The Cromwellian Conquest 1649–53' and 'The Cromwellian Regime, 1650–60', in T. W. Moody, F. X. Martin and F. J. Byrne (eds), *A New History of Ireland, III: Early Modern Ireland 1534–1691* (Oxford: Clarendon Press, 1976), pp. 336–86

9   Perceval-Maxwell, *The Irish Rebellion*, pp. 192–212. See also, for example, Co. Meath volume of Depositions, folio 2, and Co. Mayo volume, folio 145, with regard to reports on planning and preparations for the rising/rebellion

10 TCD Depositions, Co. Kildare volume

11 Perceval-Maxwell, *The Irish Rebellion*, pp. 199–204

12 ibid., p. 231. See numerous references in the TCD Depositions to the activities of the clergy, as, for example, the Co. Meath volume, where examinant Edward Dowdall (folio 49) reports that 'Valentine Browne, a Franciscan Fryer, from Galway [came] to observe how matters went in the countie of Meath, as also with an addresse unto the Lord of Gormanstown . . . thence to the camp at Drogheda.'

13 See, for example, D. Stevenson, *The Scottish Revolution 1637–1644: The Triumph of the Convenanters* (Newton Abbot: Saltire, 1973), and J. Morrill (ed.), *The Scottish National Covenant in Its British Context 1638–51* (Edinburgh: Edinburgh University Press, 1990)

14 This mapping is known as the Strafford survey. Indeed, Connacht was then so well mapped that William Petty would have no need to survey the region again for the later Cromwellian settlement. See also, Canny, *Making Ireland British*, pp. 266–73, 280–6.

15 P. Lenihan, *Confederate Catholics at War 1641–1649* (Cork: Cork University Press, 2001), p. 12

16 ibid., pp. 80–110; see also P. J. Corish, 'The Rising of 1641 and the Catholic Confederacy 1641–5' in Moody, Martin and Byrne (eds), *New History of Ireland, III*, pp. 304–15

17 Perceval-Maxwell, *The Irish Rebellion*

18 ibid., pp. 213–39. For example, in the TCD Depositions, Co. Meath volume, examinant Edward Dowdall (folio 45/45b) reports that Roger Moore said 'that the grounds of their cominge thither and taking up Armes were for the freedom and liberty of their consciences, the maintenance of His Majesty's prerogative in which he understood he [the King] was abridged. And for the making of the Subjects of this kingdom as free as those of England were.'

19 Lenihan, *Confederate Catholics*, pp. 3–12

20 Canny, *Making Ireland British*, pp. 461–578, especially 534–42. We are dealing here with the *longue durée* of hatred, violence and stories amongst the Irish about English injustice which periodically erupted into a volcanic force after simmering below the surface for long periods. In short, the Irish situation in the early modern period was always bordering on violence.

21 Perceval-Maxwell, *The Irish Rebellion*, pp. 213–39, especially maps 3 and 4

22 D. Stevenson, *Scottish Convenanters and Irish Confederates: Scottish-Irish Relations in the Mid-Seventeenth Century* (Belfast: Ulster Historical Foundation, 1981)

23 Canny, *Making Ireland British*, pp. 507–15

24 ibid., pp. 473–7, and Perceval-Maxwell, *The Irish Rebellion*, pp. 227–33

25 Quoted in Canny, *Making Ireland British*, p. 474

26 TCD Depositions, Co. Cavan volume, James Stewart, folio 70

27 Canny, *Making Ireland British*, p. 476. See also, TCD Depositions, Co. Armagh volume, Thomas Jukes, folio 16: 'that after the fight and loss of the Irish at Lisnegarvey in December . . . they began to murder the English everywhere in the counties and in Armagh also'

28 Canny, *Making Ireland British*, p. 483. With regard to the Irish reaction to their defeat at Ardee by the English army, see Co. Monaghan volume, folio 64, which deals with reprisals in Carrickmacross

29 M. Elliott, *The Catholics of Ulster: A History* (London and New York: Penguin Books, 2000), p. 101

30 Canny, *Making Ireland British*, pp. 501–18. The Co. Meath volume of the depositions in the person of Charles Huss, deponent, folio 115, gives an example of these two levels in the uprising: he states that 'they [the local rebels] bound deponent with a rope, and had hanged him had not a gent of good fashion by chance come by'.

31 Canny, *Making Ireland British*, p. 461

32 Perceval-Maxwell, *The Irish Rebellion*, p. 259

33 Lenihan, *Confederate Catholics*, p. 222

34 A. Clarke, 'The 1641 Depositions', in P. Fox (ed.), *Treasures of the Library of Trinity College Dublin* (Dublin: Royal Irish Academy, 1986), especially pp. 111–12. Nicholas Canny in *Making Ireland British*, pp. 461–469, provides a very useful summary of the historiography of the '1641 Depositions', from Sir John Temple's enduring and highly influential *The Irish Rebellion* through to the nineteenth-century work of W. E. H. Lecky and the interpretations of a number of current historians. For a different overview, see Introduction to Mary Hickson's *Ireland in the Seventeenth Century or the Irish Massacres of 1641–42* (London: Longmans and Green, 1884), especially pp. 116–169.

35 Clarke, '1641 Depositions', pp. 112, 120. It is clear that special arrangements had to be made to collect depositions from the Munster region but it should not be assumed that Dublin was the only location for all other commissioner meetings with deponents: for example, one session was held in Athy in April 1642 and another at Maryborough in the same month (see Queen's County volume, Lawrence Wilkinson, deponent, folio 45).

36 Clarke, '1641 Depositions', p. 116

37 ibid

38 ibid., p. 118–19

39 ibid., p. 119

40 ibid., p. 112

41 ibid., p. 120

42 ibid

43 ibid

44 TCD Depositions, Co. Cork, Volume V, Richard Gething, 'before the High Court of Justice', folio 171b

45 Clarke, '1641 Depositions', p. 120

46 Perceval-Maxwell, *The Irish Rebellion*

47 Lenihan, *Confederate Catholics*, p. 42

48 Clarke, '1641 Depositions', pp. 111–12

49 TCD Depositions, Co. Dublin, Volume I, evidence of Robert Maxwell DD, rector of Tynan, Co. Armagh (with regard to the '154,000 slaughtered') and whose brother Lieut. James Maxwell was murdered in the early phase of the rising/rebellion, see folio 8b

50 Clarke, '1641 Depositions', p. 111; J. Temple, *The Irish Rebellion* (London: printed by R. White for Samuel Gellibrand, 1646)

51 Barnard, 'Crises of Identity', pp. 51–8, especially 52

52 ibid., p. 52

53   Canny, *Making Ireland British*, p. 463
54   Clarke, '1641 Depositions', p. 111
55   K. Lindley, 'The Impact of the 1641 Rebellion upon England and Wales, 1641–5', *Irish Historical Studies*, vol. 18, no. 70, 1972, pp. 143–76
56   ibid., p. 151. See also, the highly relevant 'Tracts 1578–1642' in the Royal Irish Academy, Dublin
57   Clarke, '1641 Depositions', p. 117
58   Canny, *Making Ireland British*, p. 464
59   This whole process is somewhat reminiscent of other controversial 'tribunals', such as the battle for memory that has gone on in the past ten to fifteen years about Bloody Sunday in Derry and in the current tribunal (2002–3), which again reveals the complicated interrelationships and layerings between actions, memories and investigations. The Bloody Sunday inquiry was set up to inquire into killings by paratroopers of thirteen unarmed civilians during an illegal civil rights march in Derry city, Sunday, 30 January 1972; a fourteenth died later. At the time of writing (16 May 2003) this inquiry has been sitting for 330 days.
60   Lenihan, *Confederate Catholics*, p. 23
61   D. Butler, 'Competing for Hegemony: The Geography of the Protestant and Roman Catholic Communities of South Tipperary c.1590–c.1841', Ph.D. thesis, University College Cork, 2003, pp. 67–82. See also, Canny, *Making Ireland British*, pp. 526–7.
62   TCD Depositions, Co. Antrim volume, Cromwellian Examinations, folios 137, 138, 139 and folios 155, 156, 160 and from folio 191 to folio 223
63   Co. Antrim volume, Cromwellian Examinations, Elizabeth McOwen, examinant, folio 263
64   Elliott, *Catholics of Ulster*, p. 102
65   ibid.
66   ibid. Likewise, Roger Gill, examinant Co. Antrim volume, Cromwellian Examinations, folio 282, reports that 'the Scotsmen living thereabouts [near Glenarm] pursued them and the rest of the Irish . . . [and] . . . forced [them] to fly for their lives'; see also, Co. Armagh volume, folio 181b, John Bratton, examinant, escaped 'when the Newry was taken and that the Irish were in fear'.
67   A. Mervyn, *An Exact Relation of All Such Occurrences as have Happened in the Several Counties Donegall, London-Derry, in the North of Ireland since the Beginning of this Horrid, Bloody and Unparaleld Rebellion there, Begun in October Last* (London: The Downes and William Bladen, 1642), pp. 1–14
68   TCD Depositions, Co. Antrim volume, Cromwellian Examinations, examinant Fedoragh Magee, folio 35. In folio 29b, Brian O'Cahan reports that 'when the Scottish Army came into the Roote in May 1642 he and all the Irish fled over the Bann'; see also, Co. Antrim volume, Cromwellian Examinations, where Arthur Gore, folio 3, testifies in June 1644 that 'Scottish regiment now in Ulster take as many Irish papists daily as come to them', while Michael Doyne (Dunne) suggests that 'between three and four thousand men (disaffected Papists) taken into Scottish regiments'
69   Co. Antrim volume, Cromwellian Examinations, examinant Coll McAllester, folio 32b
70   Quoted by Lenihan, *Confederate Catholics*, p. 212
71   ibid., p. 48
72   ibid., p. 62
73   ibid., p. 89. See also Dillon, Charles, '*Cín Lae Ní Mhealláin*, Friar O Meallan Journal', *Tyrone: History and Society*, 327–402
74   See, for example, Canny, *Making Ireland British*, pp. 468–9
75   See similar type statement in Co. Longford volume, John Settle, deponent, folio 161; see also, folio 186 and Co. Cork, Volume II, George Davis, folio 223
76   TCD Depositions, King's County volume, Henry Aeyloffe, folio 61b. See also, Co. Cork, Volume II, John Warren, folio 155
77   See Co. Armagh volume, Richard Newberrie, Greenagh, folio 61; see also, King's County volume, Marmaduke Clapham, folio 79
78   Queen's County volume, Samuel Frank, folio 81
79   King's County volume, Grace Smith's evidence, folio 164b
80   G. Ó Crualaoich, 'Non-Sovereignty Queen: Aspects of the Otherworld Female in Irish Hag Legends: The Case of *Cailleach Bhéarra*', *Béaloideas*, 1994–5, pp. 147–62, especially 162. In a personal communication, Gearóid Ó Crualaoich stresses 'the continued allegiance in Irish vernacular traditions to the figure and symbolic potential of the *cailleach*. The realisation of this potential in a political ideology sees a shift from a medieval to an early modern Republican perspective'. This latter theme is explored fully in B. Ó Buachalla's *Aisling Ghéar: Na Stiobhartaigh agus an tAos Léinn* (Baile Átha Cliath: Clóchomhar, 1996)
81   Co. Cavan volume, Henry Baxter, folio 79b. In Co. Armagh volume reports of apparitions by Elizabeth Price in folios 102b and 103

82 Co. Cavan volume, John Hickman, folio 141
83 Likewise, Protestant fears were manifest. See Queen's County volume, Thomas Hynes, folio 38, who reports that 'it was the common voice that the King had forsaken the Protestants of Ireland'.
84 TCD Depositions, Co. Galway volume, Ralph Lambart, folio 174b. In Co. Armagh volume, George Littlefield, folio 72, reports rebel talk 'if Owen McArt should not ere long come out of Spain then they would make Sir Phelim O'Neill their King'
85 TCD Depositions, Co. Limerick volume, William Fytton, folio 310, reporting the views of Robert Freeman
86 TCD Depositions, Co. Cavan volume, Nicholas Michaell, folio 102b
87 Quoted in M. O'Dowd, *Power, Politics and Land: Early Modern Sligo, 1568–1688* (Belfast: Institute of Irish Studies, Queen's University Belfast, 1991), p. 122. See also, Co. Meath volume, John Reade, examinant, folio 5b, where it is stated 'that the Lords and gentry of the Pale had prepared a draught of a petition unto his Majesty the heads whereof were they had soe taken up arms, for the libertie of their religion, the maintenance of his Royall prerogative and the reformation of the present government heere in this Kingdom by a Parliament'.
88 See Corish, 'The Rising of 1641 and the Catholic Confederacy, 1641–5', pp. 298–9, for the details of the oath of association that established the 'Confederate Catholics of Ireland'. The flag of the Confederacy is still preserved in Dominican House in Tallaght. My thanks to Dr Willie Nolan for this information
89 Co. Armagh volume, Ellen Matchett, folio 59
90 Mervyn, *An Exact Relation of All Such Occurrences*, pp. 10, 12
91 Queen's County volume, Thomas Collins, folio 70
92 Queen's County volume, Samuel Frank, folio 80
93 There are numerous references of this kind throughout the depositions. See, for example, Co. Cavan volume, Mary Pignott, folio 81, 'however it pleased God to command and work . . . so as the most imminent danger was prevented'
94 Lenihan, *Confederate Catholics*, p. 202
95 Perceval-Maxwell, *The Irish Rebellion*, p. 23
96 Lenihan, *Confederate Catholics*, p. 203. (See also, Co. Armagh depositions where, folio 62, John Parrie reports that 'the priest said at masse that the bodies of such men as died in that quarrel [rising] should not be cold before their souls should ascend up to Heaven and that they should be free from the pain of purgatory'.)
97 Lenihan, *Confederate Catholics*, p. 203
98 ibid
99 TCD Depositions, Co. Roscommon volume, John Lambert, folio 41b
100 TCD Depositions, Co. Cavan volume, John Wheelright, folio 80b
101 M. Taussig, *The Nervous System* (New York: Routledge, 1991), p. 2. The depositions frequently record the fear of deponents, for example Thomas Robins of Queen's County, folio 73, 'was in bodily fear and danger' and Charles Cosby, folio 74, 'lived in the house with Francis Cosby for fear of his life'
102 See, for example, A. Clarke, 'The 1641 Rebellion and Anti–Popery in Ireland', in B. MacCuarta (ed.), *Ulster 1641: Aspects of the Rising* (Belfast: Institute of Irish Studies, 1993), pp. 139–58; see also chapter 10 by T. C. Barnard, '1641: A Bibliographical Essay', pp. 173–86
103 J. Theibault, 'The Rhetoric of Death and Destruction in the Thirty Years War', *Journal of Social History*, vol. 27, no. 2, 1993, pp. 271–98
104 ibid., pp. 285–6. My thanks to Dr John Crowley for drawing this and other articles to my attention
105 Elliott, *Catholics of Ulster*, pp. 106–7
106 L. H. Malkki, *Purity and Exile: Violence, Memory and National Cosmology among Hutu Refugees in Tanzania* (Chicago and London: University of Chicago Press, 1994); see also, M. Douglas, *Purity and Danger: An Analysis of the Concepts of Pollution and Taboo* (London and New York: Routledge, 1966), and F. Barth (ed.), *Ethnic Groups and Boundaries: The Social Organisation of Cultural Difference* (Bergen-Oslo: Universitets Forlaget, and London: George Allen and Unwin, 1969)
107 Malkki, *Purity and Exile*, especially chapter 2, 'The Mythico-History', pp. 52–104
108 ibid., chapter 3, 'The Use of History in the Refugee Camp', pp. 105–52
109 ibid., chapter 2, pp. 92–5. My thanks to Dr Stephen Jackson (formerly International Famine Centre, University College Cork) for lengthy discussions on these issues, for a draft copy of chapter from his doctoral thesis entitled 'Making Sense: Factsx, Tracts and Secret Knowledge' and for a number of key references.

110 Perceval-Maxwell, *The 1641 Rebellion*, pp. 224–5
111 Over one–fifth of the settler numbers accounted for in the depositions came from Co. Cork alone. It is likely that Bysse's organization and collection of the Munster depositions *in situ* produced this southern bias
112 Lenihan in *Confederate Catholics* notes that François la Gouz, a French traveller to Ireland in 1644, 'found the people whom he questioned called themselves Ayrenake' (Éireannach or Irish), p. 5
113 See Corish, 'The Rising of 1641 and the Catholic Confederacy', 1641–5', pp. 302–3, and 366
114 D. Corkery, *The Hidden Ireland – A Study of Gaelic Munster in the Eighteenth Century* (Dublin: Gill, 1924); see also, L. M. Cullen, *The Hidden Ireland: Reassessment of a Concept* (Mullingar: Lilliput, 1988)
115 There is an insightful book by Henry Reynolds, *The Other Side of the Frontier* (Harmondsworth: Penguin, 1982), where he seeks to re-create the Australians' understandings and responses to the intruding Europeans. Another insightful book by Nathan Wachtel, *The Vision of the Vanquished* (Brighton: Harvester Press, 1977), illuminates how the Peruvian Indians of the Incan culture responded and remembered Spanish imperialism and its devastating effects on their society. The Peruvian Indians remembered what happened mainly through the re-creation of the events in dramatic form in the local theatres: they had no courts in which the story might be written down. So they remembered on stage what happened when the Spanish surged in, colonized and broke their culture, and literally decimated the population. We can learn from these reconstructions how the different local voices represented the experiences and responses of the original Australians and Peruvian Incas to actual conquest.
116 See Canny, *Making Ireland British*, pp. 476–7
117 A. Appadurai, 'Dead Certainty: Violence in the Era of Globalization', in B. Meyer and P. Geschiere (eds), *Globalization and Identity* (Oxford and Malden, MA: Blackwell, 1999), pp. 305–24; see also, R. Hayden, 'Imagined Communities and Real Victims: Self-Determination and Ethnic Cleansing in Yugoslavia', *American Ethnologist*, vol. 23, no. 4, 1996, pp. 783–801; A. Fellman, *Formations of Violence: The Narrative of the Body and Political Terror in Northern Ireland* (Chicago: University of Chicago Press, 1991)
118 See, for example, C. Tilly, *Coercion, Capital and European States, AD 900–1990* (Cambridge, MA: Harvard University Press, 1990), and G. Parker, *The Military Revolution Revisited* (Cambridge: Cambridge University Press, 1988)
119 Lenihan, *Confederate Catholics*, p. 2
120 P. J. Corish, *The Catholic Community in the Seventeenth and Eighteenth Centuries* (Dublin: Helicon Press, 1981), pp. 23–40. See also, J. Bossy, 'The Counter–Reformation and the People of Catholic Ireland, 1596–1641', *Past and Present*, vol. 47, 1970, pp. 51–70.
121 Paddy Duffy quotes one of the undertakers in Farney in Co. Monaghan in 1625 on the practice of issuing proclamations to the tenants at market day and 'at the masse', reflecting a degree of normality to mass-going which some commentators have overlooked, see P. J. Duffy, 'The Territorial Organisation of Gaelic Landownership and Its Transformation in County Monaghan, 1591–1640', *Irish Geography*, vol. 14, 1981, p. 17. Likewise, a deponent from Kinard in Co. Tyrone notes that the singular difference between the communities was that on Sunday 'one side went to Mass and the other to the Protestant church'. The political significance of the mass is signalled in the depositions, Co. Dublin, Volume I, where Robert Maxwell reports, folio 6, that Sir Phelim O'Neill said that they 'would be saying mass in Christchurch, Dublin within 8 weeks', i.e. after a successful rebellion and capturing of Dublin
122 TCD Depositions, Queen's County volume, John Dean, folio 27, and Richard Oliver, folio 37; see also, Co. Meath volume, Thomas Page, folio 128, who names the Protestants who 'are turned to Masse'
123 TCD Depositions, Co. Kilkenny volume, John Watkinson, folio 193b; Co. Limerick volume, John Bradish, folio 262, and James Lylles, folio 273
124 TCD Depositions, Co. Wexford volume, Sir Walsingham Cooke, folio 10b
125 TCD Depositions, Co. Wexford volume, William Whalley, folio 24b; see also, Co. Cork, Volume III, Edmund Cock, folio 152
126 TCD Depositions, Co. Wexford volume, Abell Ram, folio 9, and Thomas Ricroft, folio 27
127 TCD Depositions, Co. Leitrim volume, John Cooke, folio 11
128 TCD Depositions, Co. Mayo volume, Thomas Hewett, folio 162b
129 TCD Depositions, Queen's County volume, Clement Woodroofe, folio 47
130 TCD Depositions, Co. Kildare volume, Joan Brydges, folio 364; see also, Co. Meath volume, William Metcalf, folio 179

131 TCD Depositions/Examinations, Co. Galway volume, Joseph Hampton, examinant, folio 259

132 There are numerous references to the death of Mrs Nicholson in the Queen's County volume. See, for example, Emanuel Beale, folio 26b, John Glasse, folio 60, and James Weld, folio 71b

133 Queen's County volume, Thomas O'Carroll, folio 23, Donogh O'Brennan, folio 24b, and Martha Piggott, examinant, folio 37b. See also, Co. Wexford volume, William Whalley, folio 25

134 TCD Depositions, Co. Armagh volume, John Parrie, folios 63b and 64

135 TCD Depositions, Co. Cavan volume, Richard Parsons, deponent, folio 87

136 TCD Depositions, Co. Kilkenny volume, James Benn, folio 213b; see also, Co. Cork, Volume III, Agnes Tucker, folio 149

137 TCD Depositions, Co. Wexford volume, Henry Palmer, folio 8b; for Co. Armagh volume, see Elizabeth Rolleston, folio 68b; and for Co. Wicklow volume, see Henry Fisher, folio 47: 'Burned the pews and bibles in Powerscourt Church'

138 TCD Depositions, Co. Meath volume, Robert Nicholl, folio 226

139 TCD Depositions, Co. Kilkenny volume, John Moore, folio 197b

140 TCD Depositions, Co. Dublin, Volume II, John Luky, folio 38

141 A. Ford, *The Protestant Reformation in Ireland 1590–1641* (Frankfurt am Main: Verlag Peter Lang, 1985)

142 TCD Depositions, Co. Wexford volume, William Whalley, folio 24b; Queen's County volume, Barnabee Dunne, folio 108; King's County volume, Thomas Lestrange, folio 67. See also, Canny, *Making Ireland British*, p. 515.

143 TCD Depositions, Co. Cavan volume, Jean Stevenson, folio 84b. See also, Simon Grehame, folio 105: 'They were not Christians nor worthy to be buried amongst Christians.'

144 TCD Depositions, Co. Fermanagh volume, Richard Bourk BD, folio 20

145 See, for example, TCD Depositions, Co. Armagh volume, Bridgett Drewrie of Crewcatt, folio 46, and William Duffeild, folio 49

146 See, for example, TCD Depositions, Co. Cavan volume, George Crichtoun, folio 153b; Co. Down volume, William Burley, folio 29; Queen's County volume, David Burke, folio 24

147 See Canny, *Making Ireland British*, p. 490

148 Numerous examples of this form of insult are scattered throughout the depositions

149 TCD Depositions, Co. Kilkenny volume, John Moore, folio 197b

150 See, for example, TCD Depositions, Queen's County volume, John Carpenter, folio 75b; Co. Wicklow volume, James Shane, deponent, folio 51

151 TCD Depositions/Examinations, Queen's County volume, Christopher Goulding, folio 43

152 TCD Depositions, Co. Limerick volume, Elizabeth Martin, folio 330

153 TCD Depositions/Examinations, Queen's County volume, Martha Piggott, examinant, folio 376b. For a detailed county study, see Hilary Simms, 'Violence in County Armagh, 1641', in MacCuarta (ed), *Ulster 1641: Aspects of the Rising*, pp. 123–38

154 Canny, *Making Ireland British*, especially pp. 542–5

155 TCD Depositions, King's County volume, Magdalen Redman, folio 77

156 TCD Depositions, Co. Kilkenny volume, William Parkinson, folio 191

157 TCD Depositions/Examinations, Queen's County volume, Samuel Frank, folio 81 who reports 'rebel talk' that once Dublin is captured 'Owen Roe O'Neill to go to England against the "Puritanical parliament" with forty thousand men to assist the King'; see also, Co. Longford volume, William Stewart, examinant, 'that they [the rebels] would carry over 20,000 soldiers of their own to assist the King there against the Parliament'

158 Lindley, 'Impact of the 1641 Rebellion upon England and Wales', p. 151

159 TCD Depositions, Queen's County volume, Thomas Collins, deponent, folio 70b

160 TCD Depositions/Examinations, Co. Longford volume, William Stewart, examinant, folio 201; with regard to Colmcille's prophecies see, for example, Co. Donegal volume, M. Barr, folio 125

161 Canny, *Making Ireland British*, p. 549. See also, Appadurai, 'Dead Certainty', p. 307

162 Canny, *Making Ireland British*, pp. 497–8. See also, TCD Depositions, Co. Meath volume, deponent Robert Ovington, reporting losses in folio 148, states that his robbers said 'no Englishman should stay in the Kingdom'

163 TCD Depositions, Co. Cavan volume, George Crichton, folio 149b

164 Lenihan, *Confederate Catholics*, p. 22

165 C. Russell, *The Fall of the British Monarchies 1637–1642* (Oxford: Oxford University Press, 1991), p. 79

166 TCD Depositions, Co. Cavan volume, William Hoe, folio 133b

167 Quoted in introduction to chapter 2 in Lenihan, *Confederate Catholics*, p. 73

168 TCD Depositions, Queen's County volume, folio 68b

169 TCD Depositions, Co. Cavan volume, John Cooke, folio 103; see also in Co. Cavan volume, Francis Greham, folio 92b; see, for example, the actions of the O'Farrells in Longford and the O'Rourkes in Leitrim.

170 See, for example, K. J. McKenny, 'British Settler Society in Donegal c.1625–1685', in W. Nolan, L. Ronayne and M. Dunlevy (eds), *Donegal: History and Society* (Dublin: Geography Publications, 1995), especially pp. 329–36

171 TCD Depositions, King's County volume, Ralph Walmisley, folio 108b

172 With regard to treatment of 'renegade' Protestants, see TCD Depositions, Co. Carlow volume, folio 66b, where it is reported that John Hope had 'turned to Masse and accordingly those in the Castle [of Carlow town] would give him no relief'. As for 'renegade' Catholics, Co. Leitrim volume, James Stevenson, reports on the hanging of McGranald: 'notwithstanding he was one of their own nation but he went to the Protestant Church which was without doubt the cause of their quarrel against him'; see, in addition, Co. Wexford, Volume II, Edmund Synnott, examinant, folio 253, who reports that Philip Hill of Glascarrig was hanged 'as a spy'. See Cork, Volume V, Donogh McCormack, examinant, folio 86, 'and this examinant saith that the reason why he [Owen McDermod] was hanged was (as he heard) that they had a law amongst them that if any Irish man did serve in the English party and were taken he should be hanged'

173 Likewise, David Boyes, examinant, reports in the Co. Antrim, Cromwellian Examinations, folio 280, that he was saved 'by a gentlewoman and 3 priests'.

174 TCD Depositions, Co. Armagh volume, John Wisdome, folio 14b

175 See Co. Meath depositions

176 TCD Depositions, Co. Cavan volume, John Seaman, folio 72. Likewise, Co. Cavan deponent Eleanor Reinclas reports that the rebels attempted to murder her husband and father 'but by good fortune the masse priest of the parish lodged that night and threatened them with curses till they promised not to hurt them'.

177 TCD Depositions, Co. Londonderry volume, Andrew Hickson, folio 118

178 See TCD Depositions, Co. Armagh volume, William Todd, folio 40b, and Francis Sachaverrell, who in folio 110 reports a number of priests as saying 'that the priests, Jesuits and friars of England, Ireland and of Spain and other countries beyond the seas were the plotters, prosecutors and contrivers of this rebellion'. See King's County depositions, Ralphe Walmisley, folios 110 and 110b.

179 Barnard, 'Crises of Identity', pp. 55–6

180 TCD Depositions, Co. Kildare volume, folio 285

181 See TCD Depositions, Co. Fermanagh volume, Thomas Knowles, folios 131 and 158

182 TCD Depositions, Co. Meath volume, Joan Talbott, folios 1, 2, 3

183 See, for example, TCD Depositions, Co. Wicklow volume, Thos Tronte, folio 102, where he reports losses to the 'rebels' who argued 'the land was theirs and all that there on was'

184 Such a report occurs in almost every county volume. See amongst numerous examples, Co. Cavan volume, William Jameson, folio 61, 'and that the Irish rebellious women were far worse and more fierce and bloody than the men rebell and carried their skeins'; Co. Fermanagh volume, Robert Cheetom, folio 44; King's County volume, John Robinson, folio 63b; and Queen's County volume, William Hill, folio 64b.

185 See Canny, *Making Ireland British*, especially pp. 548–9, and M. MacCurtain and M. O'Dowd (eds), *Women in Early Modern Ireland* (Dublin: Wolfhound Press, 1991), especially pp. 91–111; see, for example, TCD Depositions, King's County Volume, Henry Aeyloffe, folio 60b

186 Men also lost their clothing. Thomas Giffen, folio 50b of the Co. Antrim Cromwellian Examinations, reports that 'this Examinant's breeches were taken off him by an Irishman unknown'

187 Nevertheless, this sample bias in the depositions as a whole exaggerates the Munster and especially the Co. Cork losses.

188 See, for example, P. Seed, *Ceremonies of Possession in Europe's Conquest of the New World* (Cambridge: Cambridge University Press, 1996), where Seed argues that the colonial powers legitimate their claims to colonize areas of the New World through very specific ceremonial practices – the English laid claim to their territory by building fine houses, gardens and fenced enclosures.

189 Quoted in J. MacLaughlin, *Reimagining the Nation-State: The Contested Terrains of Nation-Building* (London and Virginia: Pluto Press, 2001), p. 480. See also, for example, in TCD Depositions, Co. Wexford, Volume I, Richard Claybrook, folio 59.

190 For example, in TCD Depositions, Co. Fermanagh volume – as in most volumes – there are regular references to the parish of both the deponent and the 'rebel'.

191 See, for example, TCD Depositions, Co. Cavan volume, folios 103 and 108
192 See, for example, TCD Depositions, Co. Wexford volume, Nicholas Rochford, folio 139b; also Robert Browne, folio 81
193 TCD Depositions, Co. Wexford, Volume I, Andrew Sherlock, folio 120; Volume II, Robert Browne, folio 59b. See also, King's County volume, Grace Smith, folio 165b.
194 See Roger Markham in TCD Depositions, Co. Tyrone volume, folio 17, and Co. Antrim, Cromwellian Examinations, Donnell Magowne, folio 62, and Fergus Fullerton, folio 56
195 TCD Depositions, Co. Galway volume, Margaret Powleright, folio 169b
196 Lenihan, *Confederate Catholics*, p. 57
197 ibid., p. 165
198 TCD Depositions/Examinations, Co. Longford volume, Dame Jane Forbes, examinant, folio 187
199 ibid
200 TCD Depositions, King's County volume, Joseph Joice, folio 84
201 TCD Depositions, King's County volume, Henry Bolton, folio 76
202 Lenihan, *Confederate Catholics*, chapter 5
203 TCD Depositions/Examinations, Co. Antrim volume, Thomas Theaker, examinant, folio 7–7b
204 See, TCD Depositions/Examinations, Co. Meath volume, John Talbott, examinant, folios 1, 2, 2b, 3, especially 2b, and Nicholas Dowdall, examinant, folio 34. However, in Co. Antrim, the Cromwellian Examinations for that county report (folio 40b) that 'the chief Irish had every one a precinct'.
205 See, for example, TCD Depositions, Co. Cork, Volume V and the evidence of Richard Cooke (folio 94): 'a soldier ever since he was 18 years of age and first serving under the Earl of Essex . . . Had two sons killed while serving against the Irish and although he, this deponent, was very old he took up arms against the Irish rebels . . .'
206 TCD Depositions/Examinations, Co. Wexford, Volume II, William Stafford, examinant, folios 100, 234, 246, 176, 177, 178, 226–226a, and Richard Rochfort, examinant, folio 218. See also, explicit references to the functioning of the County Council in the depositions of King's County, John Helmstead, folios 99–100.
207 See TCD Depositions/Examinations, Co. Carlow volume, Harry Stokes, examinant, folio 145, 're the raising of Pole-money'.
208 Under Sir John Davies, the geographical expansion of the English court system in each county is a notable feature of the early decades of the seventeenth century. See H. S. Pawlisch, *Sir John Davies and the Conquest of Ireland – A Study in Legal Imperialism* (Cambridge: Cambridge University Press, 1985).
209 Lenihan, *Confederate Catholics*, p. 127
210 ibid., pp. 126–8
211 During the early modern period, the armies of European states expanded in size by ten times between 1530 and 1710.
212 Lenihan, *Confederate Catholics*, pp. 120–5
213 TCD Depositions, King's County volume, Anthony Preston, folio 145
214 Lenihan, *Confederate Catholics*, pp. 38–44
215 The depositions tell us that John Lacey and Pierce Creagh made soldiers out of their tenants in their Co. Limerick estates. In Queen's County Walter Dongan's company was made up of gentlemen, ploughmen, husbandmen, labourers and one carrier, while Capt. James McDonnell's small company in Tinnekilly, Queen's County, comprised one weaver, two husbandmen, two ploughmen, one tanner, two gentlemen and two 'idle vagabonds'.
216 Again, there are numerous references throughout the depositions, especially for the Ulster counties, referring to the leadership role of the Protestant landlords and gentry
217 See, for example, Lenihan, *Confederate Catholics* (and J. R. Young (ed.), *Celtic Dimensions of the British Civil Wars* (Edinburgh: John Donald, 1997).
218 Lenihan, *Confederate Catholics*. See also, TCD Depositions/Examinations, Co. Meath volume, where examinant Edward Dowdall (folios 49b, 50) reports of meetings and 'more plotting' in the counties in mid-February 1642, where papers are presented outlining 'a model for a forme of government which was to bee observed throughout the whole Kingdome during the said troubles . . . [that there] should be a Supreme Counsell and that to them there should be subordinate the Provincial Councells and under them again a select councell in every countie the two latter to receive their power and directions from the former'.
219 Lenihan, *Confederate Catholics*, and J. S. Wheeler, *Cromwell in Ireland* (Dublin: Gill and Macmillan, 1999), and Corish, Cromwellian Conquest', pp. 336–52

220 Lenihan, *Confederate Catholics*, p. 226
221 ibid., pp. 71–2
222 ibid., p. 99
223 Barnard, 'Crises of Identity', p. 57
224 Lenihan, *Confederate Catholics*, pp. 100–1
225 ibid., p. 101
226 ibid., pp. 224–7. See also, M. Ó Siochrú, *Confederate Ireland 1642–1649* (Dublin: Four Courts Press, 1999), pp. 30–86, especially map I
227 TCD Depositions/Examinations, Co. Mayo volume, Walter Bourk, examinant, folio 170
228 TCD Depositions, Co. Armagh volume, Henry Cartaine, folio 27; see, in addition, Co. Meath volume, John Reade, folio 26, who reports that 'father Talbutt a prieste, was sente into Flanders . . . For to procure Armes and munitions'
229 TCD Depositions/Examinations, Co. Mayo volume, Walter Bourk, examinant, folio 170
230 TCD Depositions, Co. Mayo volume, John Goldsmith, folio 145
231 Lindley, 'Impact of 1641 Rebellion upon England and Wales', pp. 150–1; O. P. Grell, *Calvinist Exiles in Tudor and Stuart England* (Aldershot: Scholar Press, 1996), especially chapter 5, pp. 98–119
232 O. P. Grell, 'Godly Charity or Political Aid? – Irish Protestants and International Calvinism 1641–1645', *Historical Journal*, vol. 39, no. 3, 1996, pp. 743–53
233 ibid., p. 744
234 ibid., p. 753. See also, Co. Antrim volume, Cromwellian Examinations, where Capt. Edward Trevor, folio 11, reports that Carrickfergus 'fedd out of provisions from the Loe-Countries'
235 Lenihan, *Confederate Catholics*, p. 221
236 For the wider context, see J. Adamson, 'The British Context of Viscount Lisle's Lieutenancy of Ireland', in J. H. Ohlmeyer's *Ireland: From Independence to Occupation 1641–1600* (Cambridge: Cambridge University Press, 1995), pp. 128–59. See also, Canny, *Making Ireland British*, especially pp. 551–78.
237 Wheeler, *Cromwell in Ireland*, pp. 68, 99
238 ibid., pp. 67–71
239 ibid., p. 68; see also, Lenihan, *Confederate Catholics*, pp. 110–16
240 Wheeler, *Cromwell in Ireland*, pp. 117–20, pp. 160–4
241 ibid., pp. 94–100
242 ibid., p. 106
243 ibid., pp. 103–4
244 ibid., pp. 132–9
245 ibid., p. 191
246 ibid., p. 123
247 Lenihan, *Confederate Catholics*, p. 112
248 Corish, 'Cromwellian Regime', pp. 382–3
249 Wheeler, *Cromwell in Ireland*, p. 5
250 ibid., pp. 197–8
251 Corish, 'Cromwellian Regime', pp. 352–3
252 Éamonn Ó Ciardha, 'Tories and Moss-Troopers: Scotland and Ireland in the Interregnum: A Political Dimension', Young (ed.), *Celtic Dimensions of the British Civil Wars*, p. 152
253 Quoted in ibid., p. 152, with translation
254 ibid
255 ibid., p. 153
256 ibid. See also, Lenihan, *Confederate Catholics*, pp. 221–5
257 Wheeler, *Cromwell in Ireland*, p. 212
258 Ó Ciardha, 'Tories and Moss-Troopers', pp. 144–6. (See also, Wheeler, *Cromwell in Ireland*, pp. 220–4.)
259 Ó Ciardha, 'Tories and Moss-Troopers', pp. 153–4
260 Wheeler, *Cromwell in Ireland*, p. 212
261 ibid., p. 213. See also, R. Dunlop, *Ireland during the Commonwealth* (Manchester: Manchester University Press, 1913), p. 321.
262 J. Morrill, 'Historical Introduction and Overview: The Un-English Civil War', in Young (ed.), *Celtic Dimensions of the British Civil Wars*, p. 7
263 Wheeler, *Cromwell in Ireland*, p. 214
264 'Inhabitants 1650 Uppercross and Newcastle', National Archives, Dublin Ms. 2467. These manuscript details have been edited by Richard Flatman for the *Irish Genealogist* volumes for 1989, 1990, 1991 and 1992

265 R. Gillespie, 'The Irish Economy at War, 1641–52' in Ohlmeyer (ed.), *Ireland: From Independence to Occupation*, p. 170

266 J. P. Prendergast, *The Cromwellian Settlement of Ireland* (Dublin: McGlash and Gill, 2nd edn, enlarged, 1875), p. 79

267 P. Lenihan, 'War and Population, 1649–52', *Irish Economic and Social History*, vol. 24, 1997, pp. 1–21

268 ibid., p. 9

269 ibid., pp. 9–10

270 ibid., p. 10

271 ibid., p. 11

272 ibid., pp. 11–12

273 ibid., pp. 12–18

274 ibid., pp. 19–20

275 Wheeler, *Cromwell in Ireland*, p. 7

276 ibid., pp. 194, 226

277 ibid., p. 227. See also, Foster, *Modern Ireland*, pp. 107–8: 'The losers were more immediately apparent: the inhabitants of a devastated and depopulated land, whose property was now effectively up for sequestration.'

278 R. I. Moore (ed.), *The Hamlyn Historical Atlas* (London, New York, Sydney, Toronto: Hamlyn, 1981), map 47 'The Thirty Years War', p. 95

279 Wheeler argues that 'there is no doubt that the country suffered a demographic disaster at least equal in magnitude to that suffered by Germany during the Thirty Years War', *Cromwell in Ireland*, p. 227

280 Petty, *Political Anatomy* p. 18

281 Wheeler, *Cromwell in Ireland*, p. 226

282 L. M. Cullen, 'Population Trends in Seventeenth Century Ireland', *Economic and Social Review*, vol. 6, 1975, pp. 149–65

283 Petty, *Political Anatomy*, p. 18

284 W. H. Hardinge, 'On Circumstances Attending the Outbreak of the Civil War in Ireland. . . . The Numerical Extent and Manner of the Transplantation of Irish into Connaught and Clare', *Proceedings of the Royal Irish Academy*, vol. 24, 1866, pp. 379–417, especially Appendix H, p. 416

285 ibid., pp. 399–405, and Appendix H, p. 416

286 Corish, 'Cromwellian Regime', p. 370

287 ibid., pp. 382–3

288 Barnard, 'Crises of Identity', pp. 58–72

289 Corish, 'Cromwellian Regime', p. 375

290 Lenihan, 'War and Population', p. 6

291 R. Gillespie, 'The End of an Era: Ulster and the Outbreak of the 1641 Rising', in C. Brady and R. Gillespie (eds), *Natives and Newcomers: Essays on the Making of Irish Colonial Society, 1534–1641* (Dublin: Irish Academic Press, 1986), p. 161

292 ibid., pp. 161–2. See also, J. H. Ohlmeyer, 'The Wars of Religion 1603–1660', in Thomas Bartlett and Keith Jeffrey (eds), *A Military History of Ireland* (Cambridge: Cambridge University Press, 1996), especially pp. 160–87.

293 Petty, *Political Anatomy*, p. 153

294 Gillespie, 'The Irish Economy at War', pp. 175–6

295 Corish, 'Cromwellian Regime', pp. 373–4. (See also, Prendergast, *The Cromwellian Settlement*, pp. 272–306.)

296 Corish, 'Cromwellian Regime', pp. 375–80

297 ibid., p. 376

298 ibid., pp. 378–80

299 Wheeler, 'Cromwell in Ireland', pp. 228–30

300 ibid., p. 227

301 W. H. Hardinge, 'On Manuscript Mapped and other Townland Surveys in Ireland of a Public Character, Embracing the Gross, Civil and Down Surveys from 1640 to 1688', *Proceedings of the Royal Irish Academy*, vol. 24, 1865, pp. 3–115

302 ibid., p. 15

5 William Petty and the Construction of Cromwellian Ireland

1   T. Kinsella, 'Down Survey (1655–1657)', *Collected Poems* (Manchester: Carcanet Press, 2001), p. 351

2   'A Briefe Account of the most Materiall Passages Relatinge to the Survey Managed by Doctor Petty in Ireland, anno 1655 and 1656', in T. A. Larcom (ed.), *The History of the Survey of Ireland commonly called the Down Survey by Doctor William Petty, A.D. 1655–6* (Dublin: Irish Archaeological Society, 1851), pp. xiv–xv. See also, W. Petty, *The Political Anatomy of Ireland, 1672* (London: printed for D. Brown and W. Rogers, 1691), and also P. Coughlan, 'Cheap and Common Animals: The English Anatomy of Ireland in the Seventeenth Century', in T. Healy and J. Sawday (eds), *Literature and the English Civil War* (Cambridge: Cambridge University Press, 1990), pp. 205–23

3   P. J. Corish, 'The Cromwellian Regime, 1650–60', in T. W. Moody, F. X. Martin, F. J. Byrne (eds), *A New History of Ireland, III: Early Modern Ireland 1534–1691* (Oxford: Clarendon Press, 1976), p. 360

4   K. S. Bottigheimer, *English Money and Irish Land: The 'Adventurers' in the Cromwellian Settlement of Ireland* (Oxford: Clarendon Press, 1971), pp. 50–3, 127–9

5   Corish, 'Cromwellian Regime', pp. 359–61, and Bottigheimer, *English Money and Irish Land*, p. 53

6   Corish, 'The Cromwellian Regime', p. 357

7   ibid., p. 359

8   Bottigheimer, *English Money and Irish Land*, pp. 126–33

9   ibid., p. 133. See also, map 9, 'The Cromwellian Land-Confiscation', in Corish, 'The Cromwellian Regime', p. 358

10   Appendix I in Larcom (ed.), *History of the Survey*, pp. 376–7

11   ibid., pp. 377–8

12   W. H. Hardinge, 'On Manuscript Mapped and Other Townland Surveys in Ireland for Public Character, Embracing the Gross, Civil and Down Surveys, from 1640 to 1688', *Proceedings of the Royal Irish Academy*, vol. 24, 1865, pp. 11–12. The rate of payment was forty shillings per every 1,000 plantation acres of land admeasured and no distinctions appear to have been made between profitable and unprofitable acres measured

13   ibid., p. 12

14   ibid., p. 14. Interestingly, records of the Commissions of Surveys for the counties of Cavan and Fermanagh have not been found. It is likely that they were never needed because of the early completion of Cromwellian plantations in these counties.

15   Bottigheimer, *English Money and Irish Land*, p. 49

16   Larcom (ed.), *History of the Survey*, pp. 311–12

17   ibid., pp. 7–9

18   ibid., p. xiv

19   ibid., pp. 311–12

20   ibid., p. 4

21   ibid., p. 8

22   ibid., p. 10

23   ibid., pp. 22–3

24   ibid., p. 12

25   ibid., p. 38

26   Hardinge, 'Mapped Surveys' pp. 95–9

27   Larcom (ed.), *History of the Survey*, pp. xiv–xvii, 17–21. See J. H. Andrews, *Shapes of Ireland: Maps and Their Makers* (Dublin: Geography Publications, 1997), pp. 118–27, and also, his *Plantation Acres: An Historical Study of the Irish Land Surveyor* (Omagh: Ulster Historical Foundation, 1985), chapters 3 and 4.

28   Larcom (ed.), *History of the Survey* pp. 51–2

29   ibid., p. 29, 75

30   See note 2 above. This facility was later to be greatly exploited by Petty in his drive to gather vital statistics on the performance of the Irish economy and state, on questions of taxation and a whole range of other government issues.

31   Larcom (ed.), *History of the Survey* p. 122

32   ibid., pp. 13–14

33   M. Poovey, *A History of the Modern Fact: Problems of Knowledge in the Sciences of Wealth and Society* (Chicago: University of Chicago Press, 1998). See especially chapter 3, 'The Political Anatomy of the Economy: William Petty, Ireland and Economic Matters of Fact'.

34   See, for example, 'The Narration of Lewis Smith [admeasurer of lands] Concerning Kerrey', in Larcom (ed.), *History of the Survey* pp. 93–101. See also, chapter X, pp. 50–92.

35   ibid., p. 50

36   ibid., p. 72

37   ibid., p. 80

38 Hardinge, 'Mapped Surveys' pp. 100–3
39 See in particular, J. P. Prendergast, *The Cromwellian Settlement of Ireland* (Dublin: McGlashan and Gill, 1875), pp. 259–71
40 D. Butler, 'Contesting Hegemony: A Historical Geography of the Protestant and Roman Catholic Communities of South Tipperary *c*.1570–*c*.1841, Ph.D. thesis, National University of Ireland, University College Cork, pp. 191–4
41 Prendergast, *Cromwellian Settlement*, p. 57. See also, R. Dunlop, *Ireland under the Commonwealth* (Manchester: Manchester University Press, 1913), especially vol. II
42 R. C. Simington, *The Transplantation to Connacht 1654–58* (Dublin: Irish University Press, 1970)
43 Simington, *Transplantation to Connacht*; W. H. Hardinge, 'The Numerical Extent and Manner of the Transportation of the Irish into Connaught and Clare', *Proceedings of the Royal Irish Academy*, vol. 24, 1866, pp. 379–417, especially Appendix H, p. 416
44 S. C. O'Mahony, 'Cromwellian Transplantation from Limerick', *North Munster Antiquarian Journal*, vol. 42, 2000, pp. 29–52. My thanks to Dr Chris O'Mahony for a copy of this paper
45 Larcom (ed.), *History of the Survey*, p. 328
46 ibid., p. 338
47 ibid., pp. 85–6
48 ibid., p. 186
49 ibid., p. 207
50 ibid., pp. 207–8
51 ibid., p. 208
52 ibid., p. 337
53 ibid., p. 195
54 ibid., p. 194
55 ibid
56 ibid., p. 195
57 See, for example, D. J. Gleeson, *The Land Lords of Ormond* (London: Sheed and Ward, 1938), and Prendergast, *Cromwellian Settlement*, pp. 187–238
58 Larcom (ed.), *History of the Survey*, p. 325
59 ibid., p. 201
60 Bottigheimer, *English Money and Irish Land*, pp. 143–5
61 ibid., pp. 232–3
62 ibid., pp. 230–1
63 ibid., pp. 233–4
64 ibid., p. 247
65 ibid., p. 246
66 ibid., p. 247
67 ibid., p. 248
68 Bottigheimer, *English Money and Irish Land*, p. 139
69 Hardinge, 'Mapped Surveys', pp. 26–8
70 Bottigheimer, *English Money and Irish Land*, p. 152; Larcom (ed.), *History of the Survey*, pp. 232–3
71 Bottigheimer, *English Money and Irish Land*, p. 142
72 ibid
73 MS Z.2.(1.5), Marsh's Library, Dublin
74 S. Pender (ed.), *A Census of Ireland circa 1659*, with a new Introduction by William J. Smyth (Dublin: Irish Manuscripts Commission, 2002), pp. 519–21
75 ibid
76 Bottigheimer, *English Money and Irish Land*, pp. 158–9, and especially Appendix B, 'Names of Adventurers who drew Irish Land', pp. 198–213; Pender (ed.), *A Census of Ireland*, pp. 149–765
77 Bottigheimer, *English Money and Irish Land*, p. 141. See also, T. C. Barnard, *Cromwellian Ireland: English Government and Reform in Ireland, 1649–60* (Oxford: Oxford University Press, 1975), pp. 60–2.
78 See W. J. Smyth, 'Wrestling with Petty's Ghost: The Origins, Nature and Relevance of the so–called "1659 Census"', in Pender (ed.), *A Census of Ireland*, pp. v–lxii

6 Society, Settlement and Immigration in Mid-Seventeenth-Century Ireland

1 L. Gernon, 'A Discourse of Ireland (1620)', reproduced in C. Litton Falkiner's *Illustrations of Irish History and Topography* (London, New York, Bombay: Longmans, Green, 1904), p. 355

2   T. Jones Hughes, 'Society and Settlement in Nineteenth-Century Ireland', *Irish Geography*, vol. 5, no. 2, 1965, pp. 79–96

3   W. J. Smyth, 'Wrestling with Petty's Ghost: The Origins, Nature and Relevance of the so-called "1659 Census"', new Introduction to S. Pender's *A Census of Ireland circa 1659* (Dublin: Irish Manuscripts Commission, 2002), pp. v–lxii; for details on surviving hearth-money records, see R. ffoliott, 'Irish Census Returns and Census Substitutes', in D. F. Begley (ed.), *Irish Genealogy: A Record Finder* (Dublin: Heraldic Artists, 1981), pp. 51–75

4   For earlier interpretations of the nature of the 1659 Census, see: W. H. Hardinge, 'Observations on the Earliest Known Manuscript Returns of the People in Ireland', *Transactions of the Royal Irish Academy*, vol. 24, 1864, pp. 317–28; S. Pender (ed.), *A Census of Ireland circa 1659 with Supplementary Material from the Poll Money Ordinances 1660–1661* (Dublin: Irish Manuscripts Commission, 1939), pp. i–xix. For further arguments in favour of seeing the document as poll-tax abstracts, see R. C. Simington, 'A "Census" of Ireland, *c.*1659 – the term "Titulado"', *Analecta Hibernica*, vol. 12, 1943, pp. 177–8, and N. J. Pilsworth, 'Census or Poll-Tax', *Journal of the Royal Society of Antiquaries of Ireland*, 1943, pp. 22–4

5   The only surviving *original* returns of the poll-tax are: (i) 'A Return of the Parish of Termon McGoork for the Second Pole Money', Appendix L in Earl of Belmore, *The History of Two Ulster Manors* (London: Longmans, Green, 1881), pp. 305–9; (ii) Poll-tax return Aghlow parish, PRONI, T 1365/3; (iii) Poll-money book of 1660 for parish of Urney, PROI, MS 469; (iv) Poll-money book of Clonmel 1661, South Tipperary Museum, Clonmel

6   W. J. Smyth, 'Society and Settlement in Seventeenth Century Ireland: The Evidence of the "1659 Census"', in W. J. Smyth and K. Whelan (eds), *Common Ground: Essays on the Historical Geography of Ireland* (Cork: Cork University Press, 1988), pp. 55–83

7   Returns for a number of civil parishes are missing: eight parishes in Co. Sligo, two in counties Monaghan, Wexford and Louth, and one each in counties Londonderry and Waterford. There are also major difficulties in the returns for south Antrim, north Down, counties Armagh and Monaghan, the baronies of Loughinsholin in Co. Londonderry and Raphoe in Donegal. The returns for north Wexford and Kerry are also suspect – as they are for a small number of other baronies, including Ferrard in Louth and Longford in Co. Longford. See also, W. Macafee and V. Morgan, 'Population in Ulster 1660–1760', in P. Roebuck (ed.), *Plantation to Partition: Essays on Ulster History in Honour of J. L. McCracken* (Belfast: Blackstaff Press, 1981), where it is suggested that the *total* population of Ulster 'probably numbered somewhere between 217,000 and 260,000' (p. 47)

8   The city of Dublin's adult population also appears to be underestimated by *c.*4,000. See R. A. Butlin, 'The Population of Dublin in the Late Seventeenth Century', *Irish Geography*, vol. 5, no. 2, 1965, pp. 51–66, for estimates of the city's population in the late 1660s

9   On problems of interpreting later poll-tax evidence, see J. H. Andrews, 'Land and People, *c.*1685', in T.W. Moody, F. X. Martin and F. J. Byrne (eds), *A New History of Ireland, III: Early Modern Ireland 1534–1691* (Oxford: Clarendon Press, 1976), p. 458

10   Hearth Money Roll, Co. Tyrone, 1664, NLI, MS 9583 (and also PRONI, T.283.D/2); L. Price, 'The Hearth Money Roll for Co. Wicklow (1668)', *Journal of the Royal Society of Antiquaries of Ireland*, vol. 60, no. 50, 1931, pp. 164–78

11   D. Dickson, C. Ó Gráda and S. Daultrey, 'Hearth Tax Household Size and Irish Population Change 1672–1821', *Proceedings of the Royal Irish Academy*, vol. 82C, no. 6, 1982, Appendix Table II, p. 179. See also, Smyth 'Society and Settlement', for a detailed analysis of the basis for these and earlier estimates

12   B. MacGiolla Choille and R. C. Simington (eds), *Books of Survey and Distribution, Counties Roscommon, Mayo, Galway and Clare*, vols 1–4 (Dublin: Irish Manuscripts Commission, 1949–1962); Books of Survey and Distribution, Co. Cavan, PROI

13   R. C. Simington (ed.), *The Civil Survey A.D. 1654–56, V, County of Meath* (Dublin: Irish Manuscripts Commission, 1940); Books of Survey and Distribution, counties Cork and Meath, PROI; details about the Muskerry (Co. Cork) poll-tax for 1660 in *Journals of the House of Commons of the Kingdom of Ireland*, vol. 2, no. 11, 1796, p. 407

14   Civil Survey volumes for counties Dublin, Kildare, Meath and the barony of Louth, and W. H. Hardinge, 'The Civil War in Ireland 1641–1652', *Transactions of the Royal Irish Academy*, vol. 24, 1866, pp. 379–420

15   Hardinge, 'Civil War in Ireland' Appendix G

16   Gernon, 'A Discourse of Ireland', p. 355

17   T. P. O'Flanagan, 'Markets and Fairs in Ireland 1600–1800: Index of Economic Development and Regional Growth', *Journal of Historical Geography*, vol. 11, no. 4, 1985, p. 367

18 R. C. Simington (ed.), *The Civil Survey A.D. 1654–56, IX, County of Wexford* (Dublin: Irish Manuscripts Commission, 1953), p. x

19 Down Survey barony and parish maps, counties Down, Armagh and Tyrone, PRONI, D.597; R. C. Simington (ed.), *The Civil Survey A.D. 1654–56, III, Cos. Donegal, Derry and Tyrone* (Dublin: Irish Manuscripts Commission, 1937)

20 T. W. Freeman, *Ireland: A General and Regional Geography,* 2nd edn (London: Methuen, 1960), Figure 15, p. 108

21 Jones Hughes, 'Society and Settlement', p. 93

22 R. C. Simington (ed.), *The Civil Survey A.D. 1654–56, IV, County Limerick* (Dublin: Irish Manuscripts Commission, 1938); J. Walton, 'The Hearth Money Rolls of Co. Kilkenny', *Irish Genealogist*, vol. 5, no. 1, 1985, pp. 33–47, and vol. 5, no. 2, pp. 69–79

23 J. M. Graham, 'Rural Society in Connacht, 1600–1640', in N. Stephens and R. E. Glasscock (eds), *Irish Geographical Studies* (Belfast: Department of Geography, Queen's University Belfast, 1970), pp. 192–208, and her 'South-West Donegal in the 17th Century', *Irish Geography*, vol. 2, 1970, pp. 136–53

24 T. Jones Hughes, 'Historical Geography of Ireland from *circa* 1700', in G. L. Herries Davies (ed.), *Irish Geography: The Geographical Society of Ireland Golden Jubilee 1934–1984* (Dublin: Geographical Society of Ireland, 1984), p. 151

25 This analysis of the relative proportion of Old English names amongst the list of 'important Irish names' was tested against the much more comprehensive listing of family names returned in the Tipperary hearth-money records. There was a strong consistency between the evidence of the two records, especially in the percentage range 15–35 per cent, but there was a tendency for the summary 1660 returns to *underestimate* Old English names by around 4–6 per cent in the under 15 per cent range that emerged from the hearth-money records and somewhat *overestimate* by around 4–8 per cent the proportion of such names in the over 40 per cent range as compared with the equivalent hearth-money materials.

26 T. Jones Hughes, 'The Large Farm in Nineteenth Century Ireland', in A. Gailey and D. Ó hÓgáin (eds), *Gold Under the Furze: Studies in Folk Tradition* (Dublin: Glendale Press, 1982), pp. 93–100

27 T. Jones Hughes, 'Town and Baile in Irish Place-Names', in Stephens and Glasscock (eds), *Irish Geographical Studies*, pp. 253–5

28 W. J. Smyth, 'The Long-Term Cultural Impact of the Normans in Ireland', paper read to Cumann Merriman, Lahinch, August 1982

29 D. B. Quinn and K. W. Nicholls, 'Ireland in 1534', in Moody, Martin, Byrne (eds) *A New History of Ireland, III*, pp. 2–3

30 Smyth, 'Cultural impact of Normans'

31 Jones Hughes, 'Town and Baile', pp. 253–5

32 W. J. Smyth, 'Property, Patronage and Population: Reconstructing the Human Geography of Mid-Seventeenth Century County Tipperary', in W. Nolan (ed.), *Tipperary: History and Society* (Dublin: Geography Publications, 1985), pp. 104–38

33 This generalization also holds true at the island-wide scale: counties Donegal, Londonderry, Antrim, Down, Offaly and Kerry have the highest average townland size (400–500 statute acres) in the country but obviously do not exhibit the biggest townland populations in 1660. See T. McErlean, 'The Irish Townland System of Landscape Organisation' in T. Reeves-Smyth and F. Hammond (eds), *Landscape Archaeology in Ireland* (Oxford: British Archaeological Reports, No. 116, 1983), pp. 315–19.

34 Down Survey parish maps for Crannagh barony, Co. Kilkenny, NLI, MS 720

35 W. J. Smyth, 'The Dynamic Quality of Irish "Village" Life – A Reassessment', in J. M. Dewailly and R. Dion (eds), *Campagnes et Littoraux d'Europe (Melanges Offert à Pierre Flatrès)* (Lille: Société de Géographie de Lille, Institut de Géographie de Lille, 1988); J. Burtchaell, 'The South Kilkenny Farm Villages', in Smyth and Whelan (eds), *Common Ground*, pp. 110–23

36 P. J. O'Connor, *Exploring Limerick's Past: An Historical Geography of Urban Development in County and City* (Limerick: Oireacht na Mumhan Books, 1987), p. 23

37 Simington (ed.), *Limerick Civil Survey*, pp. 16–91

38 Simington (ed.), *Meath Civil Survey*, pp. 1–112, 133–62; Down Survey parish maps for Co. Meath, NLI, MS 715; Roberts estate maps, BL, Harley MS 4784

39 Smyth, 'Property, Patronage and Population', pp. 118–37

40 See the composite Down Survey/OS six-inch maps (NLI, 20D) drawn for this barony and county by R. Johnston under the direction of R. C. Simington.

41   Introduction to Down Survey parish maps for Crannagh barony, NLI, MS 720; J. Edwards, 'A Rural Geography of County Louth', unpublished MA thesis, University College Dublin, 1965; B. J. Graham, 'Anglo-Norman Settlement in County Meath', *Proceedings of the Royal Irish Academy*, vol. 75C, no. 11, 1975, pp. 223–48; Down Survey barony and parish maps for Co. Eastmeath, NLI, MS 715

42   Based on evidence of 1650–2 Census of south Co. Dublin, National Archives, MS 2467

43   O'Connor, *Exploring Limerick's Past*, p. 23. See also Luke Gernon's description of Irish villages at the beginning of this chapter.

44   Graham, 'Anglo-Norman Settlement in County Meath'; the Down Survey parish maps for Co. Kilkenny, NLI, MS 720

45   E. Estyn Evans, *The Personality of Ireland*, 2nd edn. (Belfast: Blackstaff Press, 1981)

46   See, for example, Hearth Money Roll, Co. Tyrone, 1664, NLI, MS 9583

47   P. J. Duffy, 'The Territorial Organisation of Gaelic Landownership and Its Transformation in Co. Monaghan 1591–1640', *Irish Geography*, vol. 14, 1980, pp. 1–26; McErlean, 'The Irish Townland System'; see also, P. J. Duffy, 'The Evolution of Estate Properties in South Ulster 1600–1900', in Smyth and Whelan (eds), *Common Ground*, pp. 84–109

48   Down Survey parish maps for Co. Armagh, PRONI, D.597

49   P. J. Duffy, 'Farney in 1634: An Examination of Thomas Raven's Survey of the Essex Estate', *Clogher Record*, vol. 11, no. 2, 1983, pp. 245–56

50   R. C. Simington (ed.), *The Civil Survey A.D. 1654–56, VI, Co. Waterford, Muskerry Barony (Co. Cork) and Kilkenny City* (Dublin: Irish Manuscripts Commission, 1942); Down Survey parish maps for Co. Waterford, NLI, MS 722

51   Thomas Raven's Hamilton maps of 1625 are in the North Down Borough Council office, Bangor (copies in PRONI); R. Gillespie, 'Thomas Raven and the Mapping of the Clandeboye Estates', *Journal of the Bangor Historical Society*, vol. 1, 1980, pp. 7–9

52   J. Walton, 'The Subsidy Roll of Co. Waterford, 1662', *Analecta Hibernica*, vol. 30, 1982, pp. 49–95; C. D. Ó Murchú, 'Land and Society in Seventeenth-Century Clare', unpublished Ph.D. thesis, University College Galway, 1982; L. P. Murray, 'The County Armagh Hearth Money Rolls, A.D. 1664', *Archivium Hibernicum*, vol. 8, 1936, pp. 121–202

53   P. Robinson, *The Plantation of Ulster: British Settlement in an Irish Landscape, 1600–1670* (Dublin: Gill and Macmillan, 1984), pp. 109–28

54   G. Hayes-McCoy (ed.), *Ulster and Other Irish Maps c.1600* (Dublin: Irish Manuscripts Commission, 1964)

55   M. MacCarthy-Morrogh, *The Munster Plantation: English Migration to Southern Ireland 1583–1641* (Oxford: Oxford University Press, 1986)

56   See, for example, Smyth, 'Property, Patronage and Population', pp. 131–28

57   Ó Murchú, 'Land and Society'; also, personal communication from Jack Burtchaell on Co. Kilkenny; see also, Smyth, 'Property, Patronage and Population', pp. 130–1

58   Pender (ed.), *A Census of Ireland circa 1659 with Supplementary Material*, pp. 3–21

59   E. MacLysaght, *The Surnames of Ireland* (Dublin: Irish Academic Press, 1980)

60   R. Gillespie, *Colonial Ulster – The Settlement of East Ulster 1600–1641* (Cork: Cork University Press, 1985), and Robinson, *The Plantation of Ulster*, pp. 109–49

61   T. Jones Hughes, 'The Origin and Growth of Towns in Ireland', *University Review*, vol. 2, no. 7, 1960, pp. 8–15

62   D. Dickson, 'An Economic History of the Cork Region in the Eighteenth Century', Ph.D. thesis, Trinity College Dublin, 1977

63   N. Canny, 'Migration and Opportunity: Britain, Ireland and the New World', *Irish Economic and Social History*, vol. 12, 1985, pp. 7–32

64   Andrews, 'Land and People', p. 477

65   T. Jones Hughes, 'Landlordism in the Mullet of Mayo', *Irish Geography*, vol. 4, no. 1, 1959, pp. 16–34; his 'Landholding and Settlement in the Cooley Peninsula of Louth', *Irish Geography*, vol. 4, no. 3, 1961, pp. 145–74, and his 'Society and Settlement', pp. 79–96

7 Dublin County

1   J. H. Andrews, 'A Geographer's View of Irish History', in T. W. Moody and F. X. Martin (eds), *The Course of Irish History* (Cork: Mercier Press, 1967), p. 21

2   D. B. Quinn and K. Nicholls, 'Ireland in 1534', in T. W. Moody, F. X. Martin and F. J. Byrne (eds), *A New History of Ireland, III: Early Modern Ireland 1534–1691* (Oxford: Clarendon Press, 1976), pp. 20–1

3   The social geography of the early modern city of Dublin has received much attention from a number of writers and will not be directly addressed here. See, for example, R. A. Butlin, 'The Population of Dublin in the Late Seventeenth Century', *Irish Geography*, vol. 5, no. 2, 1965, pp. 51–66; M. Craig, *Dublin 1660–1860* (Dublin: Figgis, 1969); N. T. Burke, 'An Early Modern Dublin Suburb: The Estate of Francis Aungier, Earl of Longford', *Irish Geography*, vol. 6, no. 4, 1972, pp. 365–85; J. H. Martin, 'The Social Geography of Mid-Nineteenth-Century Dublin City', in W. J. Smyth and K. Whelan (eds), *Common Ground: Essays on the Historical Geography of Ireland* (Cork: Cork University Press, 1988), pp. 173–88; C. Manning (ed.), *Dublin and Beyond the Pale* (Bray: Wordwell, 1998); L. M. Cullen, 'The Growth of Dublin 1600–1900', in F. H. A. Aalen and K. Whelan (eds), *Dublin City and County: From Prehistory to the Present* (Dublin: Geography Publications, 1992), pp. 251–78.

4   'List of all seamen, fishermen, watermen, lightermen, galleymen, kielmen, bargemen, boatmen, ferrymen and diverse seafaringmen in Kingdom of Ireland 1697', CA.L.P. 19.3, Royal Society, London

5   S. Pender (ed.), *A Census of Ireland circa 1659* (Dublin: Irish Manuscripts Commission, 2002), with a new Introduction by W. J. Smyth

6   R. C. Simington (ed.), *The Civil Survey A.D. 1654–1656, VII, County of Dublin* (Dublin: Irish Manuscripts Commission, 1945)

7   R. Walsh, *Fingal and Its Churches* (Dublin: McGee, 1888)

8   See T. O'Keefe, 'Medieval Frontiers and Fortifications: The Pale and Its Evolution' and W. Nolan, 'Society and Settlement in the Valley of Glenasmole c.1750–c.1900', in Aalen and Whelan (eds), *Dublin City and County*. See also, T. W. Freeman, *Ireland – A General and Regional Geography* (London: Methuen, 1960), pp. 263–83.

9   E. MacLysaght, *Irish Life in the Seventeenth Century* (Cork: Cork University Press, 1969). See Appendix B (John Dunton's letters), especially p. 373. See also, Walsh, *Fingal*, pp. 1–72; J. Kelly and U. MacGearailt (eds), *Dublin and Dubliners: Essays in the History and Literature of Dublin City* (Dublin: Pelican, 1990), pp. 147–82. The name Fingal – Fine Gall – recalls the lands of the 'fair foreigner', i.e. the Scandinavian-Irish

10   F. E. Ball, *Southern Fingal* (Dublin: Gill and Macmillan, 1920), p. 22

11   ibid., pp. 84–6

12   Simington (ed.), *The Civil Survey*, Dublin; see summary details re. land use at end of each barony entry, pp. 77–8, 159, 213–14, 251–2, and 280–1

13   Abstract of grants of fairs and markets in Ireland in the Chancery Rolls 1293–1773, for County Dublin, pp. 59–62, National Archives, Dublin

14   W. H. Hardinge, 'The Civil War in Ireland 1641–1652', *Transactions of the Royal Irish Academy*, vol. 24, 1866, pp. 379–420, and especially Appendix G for a detailed summary of the Transplantation Certificates

15   Pender (ed.), *A Census of Ireland*; see also, W. J. Smyth, 'Society and Settlement in Seventeenth Century Ireland: The Evidence of the "1659 Census"', in Smyth and Whelan (eds), *Common Ground*, pp. 55–81

16   F. E. Ball, *A History of the County of Dublin*, 8 vols (Dublin: Gill and Macmillan, repr. 1979), vol. 3, p. 6

17   There is a problem with the relative reliability of the poll-tax returns for the barony of Newcastle and Uppercross. There are frequent references to 'chaffe houses' in Simington (ed.), *The Civil Survey*, Dublin, such as the following on p. 19: 'There is upon ye premisses one Chaffe house, one barn, one garden plott with six tenemts and three Backsides'. The 'Chaffe house' was a thatched farmhouse.

18   See 'Principal Irish names and their number' at the end of each barony entry for Co. Dublin in Pender (ed.), *A Census of Ireland*, pp. 380, 384, 387, 390 and 391. See also, range of surnames in 'Inhabitants 1650 Uppercross and Newcastle', National Archives, Ms 2467.

19   Pender (ed.), *A Census of Ireland*, pp. 384, 387, 390, 391, and especially 380, where Petty's clerk notes that a name like 'Williams' is both 'English' and 'Irish' and Welsh.

20   M. V. Ronan, *The Reformation in Dublin 1536–1558* (London: Longmans, Green, 1926), pp. 129–239, and especially appendices, pp. 449–534

21   Dublin's almost island-wide sphere of commercial influences in the mid-seventeenth century is strongly suggested by adding the Catholic merchants' hinterland to Nicholas Canny's mapping of the business links of Dublin Protestant merchants in 1641 in his *Making Ireland British 1580–1650* (Oxford: Oxford University Press, 2001), p. 367.

22   J. Otway-Ruthven, 'The Medieval Church Lands of County Dublin', in J. Watt, J. Morrill and F. X.

Martin (eds), *Medieval Studies Presented to Aubrey Gwynn, S.J.* (Dublin: C. Ó Lochlainn, 1961), pp. 54–73; Colmcille Ó Conbhuidhe, 'The Lands of St Mary's Abbey, Dublin', *Proceedings of the Royal Irish Academy*, vol. 62, 1962, C, pp. 21–84 and excellent accompanying map. See also, C. McNeill, 'The Secular Jurisdiction of the Early Archbishops of Dublin', *Journal of the Royal Society of Antiquaries of Ireland*, vol. 45, 1915, pp. 81–108

23   Ball, *Dublin*, vol. 1, p. 100

24   E. Curtis, 'The Court Book of Esker and Crumlin 1592–1600', *Journal of the Royal Society of Antiquaries of Ireland*, vol. 59, 1929, pp. 45–64, 137–49, and vol. 60, 1930, pp. 38–51, 137–49

25   B. Bradshaw, *The Dissolution of the Religious Orders in Ireland under Henry VIII* (Cambridge: Cambridge University Press, 1974), pp. 181–230

26   I am grateful to Ciaran Brady for drawing attention to ongoing research on this topic

27   Simington (ed.), *The Civil Survey*, Dublin. In the following discussion, use is made of estimated size of estates as returned in the Civil Survey in plantation acres.

28   D. Jackson, *Intermarriage in Ireland 1550–1650* (Montreal and Minneapolis: Cultural and Educational Productions, 1970), pp. 20–1. My thanks to Kenneth Nicholls for helping me avoid some of the genealogical minefields in this area.

29   Ball, *Dublin*, vol. 2, pp. 21–39, 15–32; Moody, Martin and Byrne (eds), *A New History of Ireland, III*, pp. 230–40. Parsons is described by Carte as 'plodding, assiduous and indefatigably greedy', quoted in L. J. Arnold, *The Restoration Land Settlement in County Dublin* (Dublin: Irish Academic Press, 1993), p. 25.

30   Simington (ed.), *The Civil Survey*, Dublin, pp. 156–8

31   ibid., pp. 154–8

32   Books of Survey and Distribution, County Dublin, National Archives

33   Ball, *Dublin*, vol. 4, pp. 114–30

34   ibid., pp. 18–20. See also, Jackson, *Intermarriage*, pp. 20–8.

35   Moody, Martin and Byrne (eds), *A New History of Ireland, III*, pp. vi–vii, ix, xi, 532–85. This total of 44,000 acres of Protestant land also includes all Church, crown, city and college land. Lord Ranelagh held 850 acres. Smaller landowners with less than 500 acres included George Radcliffe in Rathmines, Viscount Moore, William Reeves, Richard Roe, a Sir Robert Dixon, Robert Loftus and a Charles Foster. In addition, the Protestant corporation of the city of Dublin held 1,066 acres.

36   Simington (ed.), *The Civil Survey*, Dublin, p. 54

37   F. E. Ball, *Howth and Its Environs* (Dublin: Gill and Macmillan, repr. 1979), pp. 68–111

38   Simington (ed.), *The Civil Survey*, Dublin, pp. 7–161

39   Jackson, *Intermarriage*, pp. 31–2

40   ibid., p. 32

41   The classic work on this cultural group is A. Clarke, *The Old English in Ireland 1625–42* (London: Macgibbon and Kee, 1966)

42   Jackson, *Intermarriage*, p. 34

43   Ball, *Dublin*, vol. 3, pp. 120–2

44   ibid., vol. 4, pp. 1–21

45   ibid., vol. 2, pp. 1–21, 44–7, 67–9, 80–95

46   ibid., vol. 4, pp. 39–48

47   Bradshaw, *Dissolution*, pp. 67–90, 110–21

48   Ball, *Dublin*, vol. 2, pp. 117–32

49   M. V. Ronan, 'Archbishop Bulkeley's Visitation of Dublin, 1630', *Archivium Hibernicum*, vol. 8, 1941, pp. 75–6

50   Simington (ed.), *The Civil Survey*, Co. Meath

51   ibid., Co. Kildare

52   This map involves the superimposition of the property patterns derived from the Civil Survey onto the superb appendixed map of Church lands (*c*.1540) produced by Otway-Ruthven, 'Medieval Church Lands', pp. 54–73.

53   See chapter 8 this volume, and Arnold, *Restoration Dublin*, especially Appendix A, pp. 149–61

54   G. S. Cary, 'Hearth Money Roll for County Dublin 1664', *Journal of the Kildare Archaeological and Historical Society*, vol. 11, 1940, pp. 245–54, 386–466. Overall, this section is based on a detailed analysis of the Books of Survey and Distribution for County Dublin

55   Arnold, *Restoration Dublin*, p. 36

56   Ball, *Dublin*, vol. 3, pp. 120–2

57   Simington (ed.), *The Civil Survey*, Dublin. See, for example, parishes of Naul, Balscaddan, Holmpatrick, Garristown, Swords, Howth, Rush, Finglas, Castleknock, Balmadun and Grallagh.

58 M. V. Ronan, 'Royal Visitation of Dublin, 1615', *Archivium Hibernicum,* vol. 8, 1941, pp. 7–35; Ball, *Dublin,* vol. 2, pp. 96–7

59 Ball, *Dublin,* vol. 2, pp. 23–42

60 There were chapels dedicated to St Catherine at Fieldstown, Lusk, and at St Catherine's Park, and a Dublin city parish was also dedicated to St Catherine.

61 P. Fagan, 'The Origin and Development of Villages in County Dublin', unpublished MA thesis, University College Dublin, 1987. See also, A. Simms and P. Fagan, 'Villages in County Dublin: Their Origins and Inheritance', in Aalen and Whelan (eds), *Dublin City and County,* pp. 79–119

62 A. Simms, 'Rural Settlement in Medieval Ireland: The Example of the Royal Manors of Newcastle Lyons and Esker in South County Dublin', in B. K. Roberts and R. E. Glasscock (eds), *Village, Fields and Frontiers,* BAR International Series, No. 185 (Oxford: British Archaeological Reports, 1983), pp. 135–52

63 Pender (ed.) *Census of Ireland,* pp. 377–92

64 'Inhabitants 1650 Uppercross and Newcastle', National Archives, MS 2467. These manuscript details have been edited by R. Flatman in 'Some Inhabitants of the Baronies of Uppercross and Newcastle, County Dublin, *ca.* 1650', *Irish Genealogist,* vol. 7, 1989, pp. 496–504, vol. 8, 1990, pp. 3–14, vol. 9, 1991, pp. 162–74,

65 See chapter 9 this volume

66 See Appendix A, 'Book of Reference' to Down Survey Maps; Simington (ed.), *The Civil Survey,* Dublin, pp. 290–1

67 See Appendix B (John Dunton's letters) in MacLysaght, *Irish Life,* pp. 352–4

68 ibid., pp. 353–4

69 ibid., pp. 341–60, 364–8

70 Ronan, 'Visitation 1615' and 'Visitation 1630'

71 'Visitation 1615', p. 63

72 A. Ford, *The Protestant Reformation in Ireland 1590–1641* (Frankfurt am Main:Verlag Peter Lang, 1985), especially pp. 1–18, 98–122, 243–92. (New edn: Dublin: Four Courts Press, 1997)

73 Ronan, 'Visitation 1630'

74 ibid., p. 64

75 ibid., p. 65

76 ibid., p. 57

77 This conclusion is based on an analysis of all the details relating to parish tithes that are returned in Civil Survey, Dublin.

78 Ronan, 'Visitation 1630', p. 57

79 Quoted in ibid., p. 56

80 ibid., p. 68

81 ibid., pp. 77–8

82 ibid., p. 86

83 ibid., p. 63

84 ibid., p. 89

85 ibid., p. 70

86 ibid., p. 71

87 ibid., p. 73

88 Ronan, 'Visitation 1615', p. 21; see also, C. Lennon, 'Civil Life and Religion in Early Seventeenth-Century Dublin', *Archivium Hibernicum,* vol. 38, 1983, pp. 14–25, emphasizing the depth and quality of late medieval forms of piety in Dublin city

89 Ronan, 'Visitation 1630', pp. 57–98

90 ibid

91 'An account of Romish clergy according to a return made April 1698', Pepys Ms vii (1) and vii (2), Royal Society, London. For a detailed analysis of parish reconstruction after the severe disruption of the Cromwellian era, see Conchubhair Ó Fearghail, 'The Evolution of Catholic Parishes in Dublin City from the Sixteenth to the Nineteenth Centuries', in Aalen and Whelan (eds), *Dublin City and County* pp. 229–47.

92 This map is entitled 'To the high and most noble prince John Duke of Bedford . . . This actual survey of the county of Dublin is humbly inscribed by his Grace's most humble and obedient servant J. Rocque', King's Collection, Map Library, British Museum.

93 Ronan, *Reformation in Dublin,* pp. 396–448, and 'Visitation 1630', pp. 57–98

94 'Inhabitants 1650 Uppercross and Newcastle', National Archives, Ms. 2467

95 ibid., p. 20
96 ibid., p. 42
97 ibid.
98 See Simms and Fagan, 'Villages in County Dubin', pp. 96–109
99 Cary, 'Hearth Money Roll for County Dublin', pp. 245, 247, 251, 286, 417, 419, 421, 433, 454, 458, 464
100 D. Dickson, 'No Scythians Here: Women and Marriage in Seventeenth-Century Ireland', in M. MacCurtain and M. O'Dowd (eds), *Women in Early Modern Ireland* (Dublin: Wolfhound Press, 1991), pp. 223–35
101 MacLysaght, *Irish Life*, pp. 54–84
102 Dickson, 'No Scythians Here', pp. 230–5
103 Cary, 'Hearth Money Roll for County Dublin'
104 What is involved here is a detailed analysis of the townland returns for the 1650–2 Census for Uppercross and Newcastle, with the specific returns for the same townland 'places' in the 1659 Census. One can attempt to arrive at a more stringent comparison by excluding from the 1650 settlements all those enumerated between the ages of 11 and 14, so that the comparison is strictly between the adult populations aged 15 and over. However, one must enter the caveat that the 1660 returns for Newcastle and Uppercross may have been somewhat defective.
105 Ball, *Dublin*, vol. 3, pp. 127–39. See also, P. O'Sullivan (ed.), *Newcastle Lyons: A Parish of the Pale* (Dublin: CDVEC, Curriculum Development Unit, 1986).
106 Walsh, *Fingal*, pp. 151–2
107 J. H. Andrews, 'The French School of Irish Land Surveyors', *Irish Geography*, vol. 5, no. 4, 1967, pp. 285–92

8. County Kilkenny

1 S. O'Faolain, *The Irish* (Harmondsworth: Penguin, 1969), pp. 60–2
2 F. O'Connor, *Leinster, Munster and Connaught* (London: R. Hale, 1950), p. 103
3 S. Pender (ed.), *A Census of Ireland circa 1659* (Dublin: Irish Manuscripts Commission, 2002), pp. 413–31
4 Books of Survey and Distribution (Kilkenny), National Archives, Dublin
5 W. Healy's *History and Antiquities of Kilkenny (County and City)* (Kilkenny: Egan, 1893) includes a very useful list of 46 inquisitions relating to Co. Kilkenny from the time of Elizabeth through to the 1620s.
6 *Calendar of Ormond Deeds, 1172–1350,* vol. 1, ed. E. Curtis (Dublin: Irish Manuscripts Commission, 1932) and vol. 2 (1934)
7 W. Carrigan, *The History and Antiquities of the Diocese of Ossory*, 4 vols, new edn (Kilkenny: Roberts, 2000). Originally published in Dublin by Sealy, Bryers and Walker, 1905.
8 O. O'Kelly. *The Place-Names of County Kilkenny* (Kilkenny: Kilkenny Archaeological Society, 1985)
9 Down Survey parish maps, Co. Kilkenny. NLI, MS 720
10 D. Edwards, *The Ormond Lordship in County Kilkenny 1515–1642: The Rise and Fall of Butler Feudal Power* (Dublin: Four Courts Press, 2003), p. 48
11 ibid., p. 49
12 Healy, *History and Antiquities of Kilkenny*, pp. 74–6
13 ibid
14 ibid., p. 76. Over three centuries later, both O'Faolain and O'Connor were to be so impressed by a variety of crafts in this part of Ireland, notably in the Graiguenamanagh region – powerful echoes indeed of the seventeenth-century way of life
15 A. Byrne, 'Kilkenny City from the Civil Survey', unpublished BA dissertation, University College Dublin, 1985
16 Ordnance Survey Mss letters, Co. Kilkenny. RIA, vol. ii, pp. 241–77, 14.D.10
17 'Presentments at the Sheriff's Court in the county Kilkenny Apr.–Jul. 1637', NLI, D. 4052
18 W. H. Hardinge, 'The Civil War in Ireland 1641–1652', *Transactions of the Royal Irish Academy*, vol. 24, no. 7, 1866, pp. 379–420
19 E. St John Brooks, *Knights' Fees in Counties Wexford, Carlow and Kilkenny* (Dublin: Stationery Office, 1950), pp. 65–130. See also, C. A. Empey, 'Medieval Knocktopher', *Old Kilkenny Review*, vol. 2, 1982, pp. 441–52.
20 Ordnance Survey letters, Co. Kilkenny, 14. D. 9 and 14. D. 10

21 'The tythes of the County Kilkenny supposed to belong to the Earl of Ormond and the value in the present year (1619)', NLI, D. 3633

22 C. A. Empey, 'The Butler Lordship', *Journal of the Butler Society*, vol. 3, 1970–1, pp. 174–87

23 My thanks to Kenneth Nicholls for helping to clarify the history of these and other Butler families. See also, W. G. Neely, 'The Ormond Butlers of County Kilkenny 1575–1715', in W. Nolan and K. Whelan (eds), *Kilkenny: History and Society* (Dublin: Geography Publications, 1990).

24 Edwards, *The Ormond Lordship in County Kilkenny*, pp. 44–5

25 W. Nolan, *Fassadinin and Settlement and Society in South–East Ireland* (Dublin: Geography Publications, 1979), pp. 105–48

26 J. Walton, 'The Hearth Money Rolls of County Kilkenny – extracted from the Carrigan MSS', *Irish Genealogist*, vol. 5, nos. 1 and 2, 1985. See also, T. G. Fewer, 'The Hearth Money Roll of 1665 for the City of Kilkenny', *Old Kilkenny Review*, vol. 53, 2001, pp. 89–102.

27 See chapter 9 this volume

28 W. J. Smyth 'Society and Settlement in Seventeenth Century Ireland: The Evidence of the "1659 Census"', in W. Smyth and K. Whelan (eds), *Common Ground: Essays on the Historical Geography of Ireland* (Cork: Cork University Press, 1988), p. 79

29 ibid., p. 65

30 Edwards, *The Ormond Lordship in County Kilkenny*, pp. 17–31

31 ibid., p. 33

32 See chapter 9 this volume

33 'Ida, Igrin and Ibercon barony in the county of Kilkenny, admeasured by John Buckley, 1657', reproduced by OS Office, Southampton (1908), from the original in the Bibliothèque Nationale, Paris

34 Down Survey barony map of Crannagh, NLI, MS 720

35 Edwards, *The Ormond Lordship in County Kilkenny*, p. 36

36 Nolan, *Fassadinin*, pp. 65–6

37 O'Kelly, *Place-Names of County Kilkenny*, pp. 1–192

38 ibid., p. 16

39 ibid., p. 7

40 F. H. A. Aalen, K. Whelan and M. Stout (eds), *Atlas of the Irish Rural Landscape* (Cork: Cork University Press, 1997), p. 183

41 'Presentments at the Sheriff's Court', NLI, D. 4052

42 Pender (ed.), *A Census of Ireland*, pp. 413–32. See also, Walton, 'Hearth Money Rolls'.

43 'Presentments at the Sheriff's Court', NLI, D. 4052

44 Edwards, *The Ormond Lordship in County Kilkenny*, pp. 201–332

45 ibid., p. 6

46 ibid., pp. 264–6

47 ibid., pp. 296–308

48 ibid., p. 7

49 T. Barnard, 'Planters and Policies in Cromwellian Ireland', *Past and Present*, vol. 61, Nov. 1973, p. 66. See also, his *Cromwellian Ireland: English Government and Reform in Ireland 1649–1660* (Oxford: Oxford University Press, 1975).

50 Personal Communication from Jack Burtchaell, based on his map of the 1660 poll-tax. See also, B. Elliott's 'Emigration from South Leinster to Eastern Upper Canada', in K. Whelan and W. Nolan (eds), *Wexford: History and Society* (Dublin: Geography Publications, 1987), especially Figure 5.1, p. 425, of the distribution of the mature Protestant settlement in south Leinster, 1831.

51 T. Ryan 'Persons Transplanted to Connaught from Kilkenny County and City', in his *Mooncoin: Landlords and Tenants 1650–1977* (Mooncoin: Ryan, 1977), pp. 58–60

52 H. Gallwey (ed.), 'The Dispossessed Landowners of Ireland, 1664: Lists Given to the Duke of Ormonde to Select his Nominees for Restoration', *Irish Genealogist*, vol. 4, no. 4, 1971, pp. 285–8

53 See also, W. J. Smyth, 'Land Values, Landownership and Population Patterns in County Tipperary for 1641–60 and 1841–50: Some Comparisons', in L. M. Cullen and F. Furet (eds), *Ireland and France, 17th–20th Centuries: Towards a Comparative Study of Rural History* (Paris: Éditions de L'École des Hautes Études en Sciences Sociales, 1980), pp. 189–94

54 Smyth, 'Society and Settlement', p. 71

55 Jane Fenlon in 'Restoring the Butler Heritage', *Irish Arts Review*, autumn 2002, pp. 95–103, details the remarkable collection of paintings which James Butler, Duke of Ormonde – the leading patron of the arts in his time – had initiated. This collection not only reflects the

aristocratic taste and wealth of the Ormonds: the collection of royal portraits signified royal favour, while others symbolized Ormond's network of powerful political friends, as well as influential marriage alliances.

56 See W. Carrigan, *Diocese of Ossory*, for detailed histories of each of these families.

57 Nolan, *Fassadinin*, pp. 82–3

58 M. Brennan, 'The Making of the Protestant Ascendancy in County Kilkenny', unpublished Ph.D. thesis, State University of New York, 1985; see also her 'The Changing Composition of Kilkenny's Landowners 1641–1700', in Nolan and Whelan (eds), *Kilkenny: History and Society*, pp. 161–96

59 Appendix IV, 'Williamites of the County Kilkenny and Queen's County Outlawed by King James the Second's Irish Parliament, A.D. 1689', and Appendix V, 'Jacobites of the County Kilkenny and Upper Ossory Outlawed by the Williamites, AD, 1690–96', in Carrigan, *Diocese of Ossory*, vol. 4, pp. 396–403

60 J. Burtchaell, 'The South Kilkenny Farm Villages', in Smyth and Whelan (eds), *Common Ground*, pp. 110–23

9 County Tipperary

1 T. Jones Hughes, 'Landholding and Settlement in County Tipperary in the Nineteenth Century', in William Nolan and Thomas G. McGrath (eds), *Tipperary: History and Society* (Dublin: Geography Publications, 1985), p. 339

2 R. C. Simington (ed.), *The Civil Survey A.D. 1654–1656 County of Tipperary*, 2 vols (Dublin: Irish Manuscripts Commission, 1931–4)

3 T. Laffan (ed.), *Tipperary's Families: Being the Hearth Money Records for 1665–6–7* (Dublin: Duffy, 1911). S. Pender (ed.), *A Census of Ireland circa 1659* (Dublin: Irish Manuscripts Commission, 2002), with a new Introduction by W. J. Smyth, pp. v–xi.

4 'Grants of all the fairs and markets which are inrolled in the Office of the rolls of the High Court of Chancery in Ireland', *Records of the Rolls Courts*, vol. 19, National Archives, Dublin. In Upper Ormond at Toomevara, Tyone and Lissinisky, in Clanwilliam at Cullen, Kilfeakle, Knockordan/Lattin and Tipperary, in Eliogarty at Templemore and Moycarkey, in eastern Middlethird at Knockkelly, Kilknockane and Killerk, in western Iffa and Offa at Ballyboy-Clogheen, in southern Kilnamanagh at Kilsenane/Oughterleague and in the Ryan country of Owney at Cragg. See also, W. J. Smyth, 'Towns and Townlife in Mid–17th-Century Co. Tipperary, *Tipperary Historical Journal*, vol. 4, 1991, pp. 163–70.

5 See W. H. Hardinge, 'The Civil War in Ireland 1641–1652', *Transactions of the Royal Irish Academy*, vol. 24, no. 7, 1866, pp 379–420, and especially Appendix G for a detailed breakdown of the Transplantation Certificates

6 Simington (ed.), *The Civil Survey*, vol. 1, p. 43

7 W. J. Smyth, 'Land Values, Landownership and Population Patterns in County Tipperary for 1641–60 and 1841–50: Some Comparisons', in L. M. Cullen and F. Furet (eds), *Ireland and France, 17th–20th Centuries – Towards a Comparative Study of Rural History* (Paris: Éditions de L'École des Hautes Études en Sciences Sociales, 1980), pp. 159–84

8 A. Clarke, 'The Irish Economy, 1600–60', in T. W. Moody, F. X. Martin and F. J. Byrne (eds), *A New History of Ireland, III: Early Modern Ireland, 1534–1691* (Oxford: Clarendon Press, 1976), pp. 170–3

9 C. A. Empey, 'The Butler Lordship', *Journal of the Butler Society* vols 1–3, 1970–1, pp. 174–87. See also, V. T. H. Delany, 'The Palatinate Court of the Liberty of Tipperary', *American Journal of Legal History*, vol. 5, 1961, pp. 95–117.

10 Laffan, *Hearth Money Records*

11 My thanks to Mr Kenneth Nicholls both for assistance in analysing the major elements in the mosaic of Butler territories and indeed for many other insights into late medieval Tipperary. See also, Conleth Manning, 'The Two George Hamiltons and Their Connections with the Castles of Roscrea and Nenagh', *Tipperary Historical Journal*, 2001, pp. 149–54.

12 Other leading families in this zone included Boytons of Ballyclerihan, Walls of Figlass, Archers of Archerstown, Walshes of Rathronan, Mocklers of Mocklerstown, Powers of Powerstown, Hacketts of Ballysheehan, Salls of Garran, Stokes of Coolquill, Brittons of Killusty, Laffans of Graystown and Sauces of Fethard.

13 See D. F. Gleeson, *The Last Lords of Ormond*, new edn (Nenagh: Relay Books, 2001), 1st edn. (London: Sheed and Ward, 1938), for a detailed breakdown of landownership patterns in the two Ormond baronies. The Civil Survey alone reveals thirty instances where members of the

Kennedy septs, especially those of 'McDaniell' and 'Clan Morrish' had sold part of their lands. See also, J. O'Meara, 'The O'Mearas of Lissinisky', *Tipperary Historical Journal*, 1996, pp. 117–35.

14 Other leading families in Lower Ormond included the Hurleys of Annagh, the O'Carrolls on the eastern edges of Modreeny and Loughkeen, while the O'Clearys, Morrisseys, MacGuilfoyles and MacIngownes were all represented among the smaller Irish landowners

15 The composite Down Survey/OS six-inch maps were drawn by R. Johnston under the direction of Robert C. Simington (Dublin, 1955).

16 Down Survey barony maps of Co. Tipperary, NLI, MS 721. Townland named in each case and, in brackets, are the numbers of hearths and parish location.

17 Simington (ed.), *The Civil Survey*, vol. 2, p. 360. See similar type references, for example, for Cloycoile/Cloycoyle in the parish of Kilshane, Clanwilliam, pp. 26–7.

18 ibid., p. 323

19 ibid., pp. 325–6. The specific 'villages' referred to include: the parish centre Tullaghmelan (5), with 'two thatched houses with a double chimney in each of these and some cabbins'; Ballybeg (6), 'a thatched house with a chimney, a gristmill, an orchard, and some cabbins'; Carrigteary (4), 'an orchard, a castle and some cabbins' and headed in 1667 by John Barrett with two hearths; Old Grange, with 'three houses waste' in 1667, and Rathwalter, described as 'waste without improvement' in 1667. The first three settlements named above were each headed by a resident Prendergast owner in 1640.

20 Simington (ed.), *The Civil Survey*, vol. 2. See, for example, description for Boher townland, parish of Templeachally and Kilmastulla, p. 168.

21 The details for 'Lackeen Towne' are not shown on the parish but rather on the Down Survey barony map.

22 Simington (ed.), *The Civil Survey*, vol. 2, p. 367

23 ibid., p. 103

24 ibid., vol. 1, p. 75

25 ibid., p. 100

26 ibid., p. 410

27 Quoted in Sir Michael O'Dwyer, *The O'Dwyers of Kilnamanagh: The History of an Irish Sept* (Herts: Oahspe, 1933), p. 131. See also, John Morrissey, *Negotiating Colonialism: Gaelic–Irish Resistance to English Expansion in Early Modern Tipperary* (Cambridge: Historical Geography Research Group, 2003), for further insights into the historical geography of the O'Dwyer territory.

28 John O'Donovan, Ordnance Survey Letters for County Tipperary, 3 vols, RIA, 14. F. 18, 14. F. 19, 14. F. 20

29 Index to St Joseph aerial photography collection, NMI; Simington (ed.), *The Civil Survey*, vol. 1, description of the Comyn-owned Tullamain settlement is as follows: 'there is on the said lands an old castle, thatched with straw and a thatched house and several other Cottages and Cabbins and a Windmill', p. 206; for Boytonrath, 'an old broken castle, a Mill, a thatcht house with some few cabbins', p. 238; for Barretstown, 'a small castle wanting repair and a few cabbins', p. 208, while Ballyduagh comprised 'a thatcht house and some few cabbins and a parke of ash trees', p. 204

30 There were also over 100 townland units with populations in excess of ten hearths whose settlement structure can only be guessed at. Some, like Upper Dovea and Rathbeg, were clearly large agglomerations. Others may have involved populations scattered over more extensive townlands.

31 W. P. Burke, *History of Clonmel* (Waterford: Harvey, 1907; new edn, Kilkenny: Roberts Books, 1983), pp. 25–35

32 K. Nicholls, 'Continuity and Decay of Late Medieval Urban Settlement in Ireland', paper read to conference on 'Villages and Towns in Ireland 1600–1900', Trinity College Dublin, February 1984

33 K. Whelan, 'The Catholic Parish, the Catholic Chapel and Village Development in Ireland', *Irish Geography*, vol. 16, 1983, pp. 1–15

34 Leading settlements here included, for example, Cloneen (24 – Tobin), Modeshill (25 – old burgage town), Corbally (26 – O'Meagher), Magowry (13 – St John), Colman (12 – Mockler), Moratownkirke (12 – Butler), Uskeane (12 – C. of Ormond), Lattin (*c.* 25 – Heffernan), Kilruane (18 – mixed), Bonocum (12 – Kennedy), Temple-etney (12 – Butler), Kilmore (*c.*20 – mixed), Newtownlennon (17 – old burgage settlement), Grangemockler (17 – Tobin), Borrisofarney (19 – McSweeny), 'Shronell Towne' (21 – Burkes/Heffernans), Youghalarra (12 – mixed), Clonoulty (24 – townland), and Solloghodmore (29 – Ryan), not to speak of the powerful roles of other

ecclesiastical institutions as settlement centrepieces at Holycross (34), Emly (9), Cahir Abbey (18), Abbeyinishlounaght, Lorrha (31), Kilcooly (43), Toomevara (14), and St Patrick's Rock (17) and St Dominick's Abbey at Cashel (17).

35 Among this group of key settlements are the by now Butler-patronized settlements at Drangan (25), Twomileborris (24), Kilcash (27), Moyaliff (22), Kilconnell (9), Kilsheelan (9), Kiltinan (12), Donaskeigh–Rathleyney (28), Tullowmacjames–Templetuohy (12), Rahelty (12), Kilshane (22), Outrath (12), Croaghane (18), Donohill (12), Knockgraffon (38), Lismalin (55), Boytonrath (28), Buolick (36), Barnane (28), Ardmayle (39), Ardfinnan (25), Kilfeakle (19), Loughkeen (*c*. 15), Killenaule (14), Lisronagh (21), Templemore (16) and Castlegrace–Tullaghorton (25). The Butler influence was in the background of the Laffan-controlled Graystown (26), the O'Carrolls at Modreeny (11), the Graces at Cloghprior (30) and the Kennedys at Ballinaclogh (18). Elsewhere, other landowners dominated the patronage of such parish centres as Lisbunny (13 – O'Meara), Latteragh (12 – Morris), Rathronan (11 – Walsh), 'Cordangan Towne' (10 – Ryan), Ballysheehan (16 – Hackett), Kilmastulla (17 – O'Brien), Ballina–Templeachally (13 – O'Brien), Solloghodbeg (16 – Butler/English), Moycarkey (20 – Cantwell), Dromineer (7? – Cantwell), Ballingarry–Ormond (14 – Grace/ Kennedy), Ballygibbon (24 – mixed), Finnoe (16? – mixed) and Castletown–Kilbarron (56? – Kennedys). The merchant family of Wyses owned Rochestown (14), the Neales were at Ballyneal–Kilmurry (16), the Hogans at Ardcrony (18), the Prendergasts at Newcastle (21), the Fannings at Ballingarry (Slieveardagh – 17), the Tobins at Garrangibbon (14), St Johns at St Johnstown (19), Purcells of Loughmoe (30), Comyns at Tullamain (19), McGraths at Ballymackey (19) and the Fogartys/Stapletons at Inch (21).

36 One can thus read off a list of medium to large-sized settlement units, where the gentry landowners seem to have provided both the patronage and the focal points for a village-like settlement. Included in this group are the Butler-patronized settlements of Fithmone (31), Boolynahow (24), Lisatubbrid (22), Clocully (16), Derryluskan (38), Cappagh (29), Killoskehan (24), Ballyquirk (36), Clonbough (15), Bansha (115), Ballykinass (*c*.25?), Kilveligher (16), Bealladrehid (19), Cloghbridy (13), Widdingstown (16), Pallice (31?), Knockananamy (*c*.25), Mullaghneony (27), Knocklofty (12), Rossnaharly (14), Cominstown (18), Gormanstown (20), Grenane (15), Clonamicklon (27) and Ballysheeda (28). Other castle-villages most likely included those of O'Meagher at Clonakenny (39), Ryan at Drombane (34), Tullagh (20), and Cragg (18). Wall at Figlass (15), Mandeville at Ballynarahy (15), Keating at Nicholastown (22), Loughloughery-Keating (12) and Moorstown-Keating (21), Kearney at Ballyduagh (19), O'Brien at Knockane (19) and Ballina (13), Stoke at Coolquill (18), Walsh at Pallisarra (13), Tobin at Killaghy (21) and Castlejohn (21), Cantwell at Ballymackeady (39) and Pointstown (14), Purcell at Cloghraily (17) and Knockanroe (19), Everard at Knockelly (19), Ballyboy (13) and Rathmacarthy (40), O'Kennedy at Ballingarry (20), Lackeen (15), Kilcharin (15), Cloghensy (18), Kilboy (15) and Killownine (20), Archer at Archerstown (29), Mockler at Mocklerstown (26), Meara at Lissinsky (24), Fennell at Ballygriffin (23), Hackett at Kilballyherbery (16), McGrath at Ardavollane (*c*.25), Croke at Mellison (14), Fanning at Farrenrory (19), Burke at Borrisoleigh (19 +), Killawardy (16) and Drisane (15) and O'Dwyer at Dundrum (25) and Clonyharp (27).

37 W. J. Smyth, 'The Long-Term Impact of the Norman Settlement on Ireland's Cultural Geography', paper read to Cumann Merriman, Lahinch, August 1982

38 See I. Leister's *Peasant Openfield Farming and Its Territorial Organisation in County Tipperary* (Marburg: Lahn, 1976) for a detailed analysis of the complex layers of territorial entities in medieval and post–medieval Tipperary.

39 Burke, *Clonmel*, p. 90

40 Simington (ed.), *The Civil Survey*, vol. 2, pp. 413–14

41 County Tipperary 1641 Depositions, TCD, Mss/821

42 Laffan, *Hearth Money Records*, pp. 67–70

43 Simington (ed.), *The Civil Survey*, vol. 1, pp. 371, 142, 136, 49, 8, and vol. 2, pp. 317, 42

44 Hardinge, 'The Civil War in Ireland', p. 415

45 H. Gallwey, 'The Dispossessed Landowners of Ireland, 1664', *Irish Genealogist*, vol. 4, no. 5, 1972, pp. 429–34

46 T. W. Freeman, *Pre–Famine Ireland: A Study in Historical Geography* (Manchester: Manchester University Press, 1957), p. 215. See also, W. J. Smyth, 'Estate Records and the Making of the Irish Landscape: An Example from County Tipperary', *Irish Geography*, vol. 9, 1976, pp. 29–49, for a detailed analysis of landlord–inspired settlement transformations in southwest Tipperary

47 Smyth, 'Land Values'

48 H. Gallwey, 'Tobin of Killaghy – The Line of Descent from 1514 to 1708', *Irish Genealogist,* vol. 5, no. 2, 1975, pp. 190–200

49 O'Dwyer, *The O'Dwyers of Kilnamanagh,* pp. 264–8. See also, W. H. Hardinge, 'List of Innocent Proprietors', *Transactions of the Royal Irish Academy,* vol. 24, no. 3, 1865, Appendix B, pp. 294–303.

50 Laffan, *Hearth Money Records*

51 Pender (ed.), *A Census of Ireland,* pp. 295–327

52 The later transformation of Co. Tipperary under landlordism is comprehensively explored in T. P. Power, *Land, Politics and Society in Eighteenth-Century Tipperary* (Oxford: Clarendon Press, 1993)

53 Other relevant works on Co. Tipperary's story and its people's sense of place include S. J. King, *Tipperary's GAA Story 1935–1984* (Naas: Leinster Leader, 1988): D. O'Grady, *Tipperary* (Galway: Salmon Publishing, 1991); M. Ó Corbuí, *Tipperary* (Dingle: Brandon, 1991); M. Hallinan, *Tipperary County: People and Places: An Anthology of the Evolution of County Tipperary* (Dublin: Kincora Press, 1993). See also, the annual issues of *Tipperary Historical Journal.*

10 Revolutionary Changes in the Territorial Organization of Irish Society, 1530–1750

1 R. D. Sack, *Human Territoriality: Its Theory and History* (Cambridge: Cambridge University Press, 1986), pp. 1–2

2 K. R. Andrews, N. Canny and P. E. H. Hair (eds), *The Westward Enterprise* (Liverpool: Liverpool University Press, 1978); R. Gillespie, 'Explorers, Exploiters and Entrepreneurs, 1500–1700', in B. J. Graham, and L. J. Proudfoot (eds), *A Historical Geography of Ireland* (London and Toronto: Academic Press 1993), pp. 123–57; W. J. Smyth, 'The Western Isle of Ireland and the Eastern Seaboard of America: England's First Frontiers', *Irish Geography,* vol. 11, 1978, pp. 1–22

3 C. Brady and R. Gillespie (eds), *Natives and Newcomers: Essays on the Making of Irish Colonial Society, 1534–1641* (Dublin: Irish Academic Press, 1986); N. P. Canny, *Kingdom and Colony: Ireland in the Atlantic World 1560–1800* (Baltimore and London: John Hopkins University Press, 1988); R. Gillespie, *The Transformation of the Irish Economy 1550–1700,* Studies in Irish Economic and Social History, 6 (Dundalk, 1991)

4 J. Ruane, 'Colonialism and the Interpretation of Irish Historical Development', in M. Silverman and P. H. Gulliver (eds), *Approaching the Past – Historical Anthropology through Irish Case Studies* (New York: Columbia University Press, 1992), pp. 293–323

5 The study of the historical geography of sixteenth- and seventeenth-century Ireland is still only in its infancy – the work of historian Kenneth Nicholls on the sixteenth century highlights the possibilities here for geographers. The seventeenth century is currently receiving more attention by a handful of geographers and a growing cadre of historians (referenced throughout this work) who are bringing new life and insights to this crucial period

6 R. Loeber, *The Geography and Practice of English Colonisation in Ireland 1534 to 1609* (Athlone: The Group for the Study of Irish Historic Settlement, no. 3, 1991)

7 ibid., pp. 11–22; also, B. Bradshaw, *The Dissolution of the Religious Orders in Ireland under Henry VIII* (Cambridge: Cambridge University Press, 1974)

8 N. Canny, 'Early Modern Ireland, *c.*1500–1700', in R. Foster (ed.), *The Oxford Illustrated History of Ireland* (Oxford: Oxford University Press, 1989), pp. 104–60

9 M. MacCarthy-Morrogh, *The Munster Plantation: English Migration to Southern Ireland 1583–1641* (Oxford: Oxford University Press, 1986); see also his excellent chapter in Brady and Gillespie (eds), *Natives and Newcomers,* pp. 171–90

10 B. Cunningham, 'Native Culture and Political Culture, 1580–1640', in Brady and Gillespie (eds), *Natives and Newcomers,* pp. 148–70, and also her work on 'The Composition of Connaught in the Lordships of Clanricard and Thomond 1577–1642', *Irish Historical Studies,* 1984, pp. 1–14

11 G. A. Hayes-McCoy (ed.), *Ulster and Other Irish Maps, c.1600* (Dublin: Irish Manuscripts Commission, 1964)

12 P. S. Robinson, *The Plantation of Ulster: A British Settlement in an Irish Landscape, 1600–1670* (Dublin: Gill and Macmillan, 1984), pp. 43–53

13 M. Perceval-Maxwell, *The Scottish Migration to Ulster in the Reign of James I* (Dublin: Gill and Macmillan, 1973), pp. 5–14, 73–5

14 Smyth, 'England's First Frontiers'; Canny, *Kingdom and Colony;* D. B. Quinn, 'The Munster Plantation: Problems and Opportunities', *Journal of the Cork Historical and Archaeological Society,* vol. 71, 1966, pp. 19–40; Perceval-Maxwell, *Scottish Migration to Ulster,* pp. 12–15

15 Perceval-Maxwell, *Scottish Migration to Ulster*, p. 17
16 Robinson, *The Plantation of Ulster*, chapters 1 and 2; also, Perceval-Maxwell, *Scottish Migration to Ulster*, pp. 52–3
17 Robinson, *The Plantation of Ulster*, pp. 91–108
18 ibid., pp. 109–29; Perceval-Maxwell, *Scottish Migration to Ulster*, pp. 52–60
19 R. J. Hunter, 'Towns in the Ulster Plantation', *Studia Hibernica*, vol. 11, 1971, pp. 40–79
20 Robinson, *The Plantation of Ulster*, pp. 103–4
21 Perceval-Maxwell, *Scottish Migration to Ulster*, p. 152
22 ibid
23 R. Gillespie, 'The End of an Era – Ulster and the Outbreak of the 1641 Rising', in Brady and Gillespie (eds), *Natives and Newcomers*, pp. 191–214; B. MacCuarta (ed.), *Ulster 1641: Aspects of the Rising* (Belfast: Institute of Irish Studies, Queen's University Belfast, 1993)
24 A. Ford, *The Protestant Reformation in Ireland 1590–1641* (Frankfurt am Main: Verlag Peter Lang, 1985), and also his excellent summary 'The Protestant Reformation in Ireland', in Brady and Gillespie (eds), *Natives and Newcomers*, pp. 50–74
25 H. Pawlisch, *Sir John Davies and the Conquest of Ireland: A Study in Legal Imperialism* (Cambridge: Cambridge University Press, 1983)
26 ibid., pp. 33–4
27 W. J. Smyth, 'Exploring the Social and Cultural Topographies of Sixteenth- and Seventeenth-Century County Dublin', in F. H. A. Aalen and K. Whelan (eds), *Dubin City and County: From Prehistory to Present* (Dublin: Geography Publications, 1992), pp. 135–8; see also D. Jackson, *Intermarriage in Ireland 1550–1650* (Montreal and Minneapolis: Cultural and Educational Productions, 1975) and L. M. Cullen, 'Social and Cultural Frontiers', in his *The Emergence of Modern Ireland* (London: Batsford, 1981), pp. 109–39
28 W. J. Smyth, 'Territorial, Social and Settlement Hierarchies in Seventeenth-Century Kilkenny', in W. Nolan and K. Whelan (eds), *Kilkenny: History and Society* (Dublin: Geography Publications, 1990), pp. 125–58
29 A. Sheehan, 'Irish Towns in a Period of Change 1558–1641', in Brady and Gillespie (eds), *Natives and Newcomers*, pp. 93–119
30 N. Canny, *The Elizabethan Conquest of Ireland: A Pattern Established 1565–1576* (Hassocks: Harvester Press, 1976), pp. 4–10
31 R. A. Butlin, 'Irish Towns in the Sixteenth and Seventeenth Centuries', in R. A. Butlin (ed.), *The Development of the Irish Town* (London: Croom Helm, 1977), p. 76. See also, his 'Land and People c.1600' in T. W. Moody, F. X. Martin and F. J. Byrne (eds), *A New History of Ireland, III: Early Modern Ireland 1534–1691* (Oxford: Clarendon Press, 1976), pp. 142–67.
32 L. M. Cullen, 'The Growth of Dublin 1600–1900: Character and Heritage', in Aalen and Whelan (eds), *Dublin City and County*, p. 251; see also, Sheehan, 'Irish Towns'
33 W. J. Smyth, 'Society and Settlement in Seventeenth-Century Ireland – The Evidence of the "1659 Census"', in W. J. Smyth and K. Whelan (eds), *Common Ground*: *Essays on the Historical Geography of Ireland* (Cork: Cork University Press, 1988), pp. 58–60
34 Sheehan, 'Irish Towns', p. 110
35 Gillespie, *Irish Economy 1550–1700*, p. 62
36 V. W. Treadwell, 'The Establishment of the Farm in the Irish Customs, 1603–10', *English Historical Review*, vol. 93, 1978, p. 602
37 T. C. Barnard, *Cromwellian Ireland: English Government and Reform in Ireland 1649–60* (Oxford: Oxford University Press, 1975); see also his 'Planters and Policies in Cromwellian Ireland', *Past and Present*, vol. 61, 1973, pp. 31–69
38 Barnard, *Cromwellian Ireland*, pp. 50–3
39 ibid., pp. 77–89
40 Smyth, 'Society and Settlement', pp. 76–9
41 Cullen, *The Emergence of Modern Ireland*, pp. 26–7; Barnard, *Cromwellian Ireland*, pp. 55–8
42 Smyth, 'Society and Settlement', p. 79
43 Gillespie, *Irish Economy 1550–1700*, p. 25
44 S. Rokkan, 'Territories, Centres and Peoples in Europe', in J. Gottman (ed.), *Centre and Periphery: Spatial Variations in Politics* (London: Sage Publications, 1980), pp. 161–80
45 S. G. Ellis, 'Economic Problems of the Church: Why the Reformation Failed in Ireland', *Journal of Ecclesiastical History*, vol. 41, no. 2, 1990, pp. 239–65
46 Ford, *Protestant Reformation*, especially pp. 1–18, 98–122 and 243–92. See also, N. Canny, 'Protestants, Planters and Apartheid in Early Modern Ireland', *Irish Historical Studies*, vol. 25, no. 98,

1986, pp. 105–15. The following analysis is dependent on Ellis's 'Economic Problems of the Church'.

47   Ford, *Protestant Reformation*, chapters 2 and 3

48   B. Millet, 'Irish Literature in Latin, 1550–1700', in Moody, Martin and Byrne (eds), *New History of Ireland, III*, pp. 564–67

49   Ford, *Protestant Reformation*, pp. 70–4; N. Canny, 'Why the Reformation Failed in Ireland: *Une question mal posée*', *Journal of Ecclesiastical History*, vol. 30, no. 4, 1979, pp. 423–41

50   Ford, *Protestant Reformation*, pp. 98–100, 111–12

51   Ellis, 'Economic Problems of the Church', pp. 258–63. In addition, Ellis argues that 'unsympathetic Catholic nobles and gentry on the commissions of the peace, on ecclesiastical commissions, acting as sheriffs or even simply by maintaining recusant priests for themselves and their tenants, could do much to hinder the progress of the Reformation', p. 258

52   Robinson, *The Plantation of Ulster*, pp. 69–72

53   This analysis is based on the appended tables in Ford, *Protestant Reformation*, pp. 81–9, 113–15, 137–42

54   K. Bottingheimer, 'The Failure of the Reformation in Ireland: *Une question bien posée*', *Journal of Ecclesiastical History*, vol. 6, no. 2, 1985, pp. 196–207

55   P. Corish, *The Catholic Community in the Seventeenth and Eighteenth Centuries* (Dublin: Helicon Press, 1981), pp. 21–2

56   ibid., p. 26

57   ibid., pp. 33–4

58   Many repressive legislative measures against the practice of Catholicism were then introduced, i.e. An Act for Convicting, Discovery and Repressing of Popish Recusants, An Act for the Better Observation of the Lord's Day.

59   Corish, *Catholic Community*, p. 49

60   'An account of the Roman clergy according to a return made April 1698', Mss Letter in the Royal Society Library, London

61   C. Lennon, *The Lords in Dublin in the Age of Reformation* (Dublin: Irish Academic Press, 1989), pp. 142–50, 184–7

62   Corish, *Catholic Community*, pp. 43–72

63   S. J. Connolly, *Religion, Law and Power: The Making of Protestant Ireland 1660–1770* (Oxford: Oxford University Press, 1992)

64   'Report on the State of Popery in Ireland', *Archivium Hibernicum*, vol. 1, pp. 10–27; vol. 2, pp. 108–56; vol. 3, pp. 124–58; vol. 4, pp. 131–77

65   ibid

66   Connolly, *Religion, Law and Power*, pp. 149–52

67   F. Ó Fearghail, 'The Catholic Church in County Kilkenny, 1600–1800', in Nolan and Whelan (eds), *Kilkenny*, p. 202

68   Corish, *Catholic Community*, pp. 100–3

69   K. Whelan, 'The Catholic Parish, the Catholic Chapel and Village Development in Ireland', *Irish Geography*, vol. 16, 1983, especially pp. 8–13

70   R. A. Gailey, 'The Scots Element in North Irish Popular Culture: Some Problems in the Interpretation of Historical Acculturation', *Ethnologia Europea*, vol. 8, 1975, pp. 2–21

71   ibid., pp. 3–4; see also, Connolly, *Religion, Law and Power*, pp. 167–8

72   P. Carr, *The Most Unpretending of Places – A History of Dundonald, County Down* (Belfast: White Row Press, 1987), p. 69

73   L. M. Cullen, 'Ireland and France 1600–1900', in L. M. Cullen and F. Furet (eds), *Ireland and France; 17th–20th Centuries – Towards a Comparative Study of Rural History* (Paris: Éditions de L'École des Hautes Études en Sciences Sociales, 1980), pp. 1–20; see also his, *Emergence of Modern Ireland*, pp. 109–10

74   Connolly, *Religion, Law and Power*, pp. 167–8

75   ibid., p. 168

76   Gailey, 'Scots Element' pp. 19–21

77   T. Jones Hughes, 'Village and Town in Nineteenth Century Ireland', *Irish Geography*, vol. 14, 1981, pp. 99–106. See also, his 'Administrative Divisions and the Development of Settlement in Nineteenth Century Ireland', *University Review*, vol. 3, no. 6, 1964, pp. 8–15

78   W. J. Smyth, 'Property, Patronage and Population: Reconstructing the Human Geography of Mid-Seventeenth Century Tipperary', in W. Nolan (ed.), *Tipperary: History and Society* (Dublin: Geography Publications, 1985), pp. 104–38, and 'Territorial, Social and Settlement

Hierarchies', pp. 125–58

79   L. M. Cullen, *Irish Towns and Villages*, Irish Heritage Series, no. 25 (Dublin: Irish Heritage, 1980)

80   Cullen, *Emergence of Modern Ireland*, p. 24; J. G. Simms, *The Williamite Confiscations in Ireland 1690–1703* (London: Faber and Faber, 1956). The first half of the eighteenth century saw a further whittling away both by voluntary and involuntary processes of the residual landed power of the old Catholic gentry.

81   T. W. Moody, Introduction in Moody, Martin and Byrne (eds), *New History of Ireland, III*, p. 1

82   R. Crotty, *Ireland in Crisis: A Study in Capitalist Colonial Underdevelopment* (Dingle: Brandon, 1986), pp. 30–40

83   See J. McMinn, *Jonathan's Travels: Swift and Ireland* (Belfast: Appletree Press; New York: St Martin's Press, 1994). This paragraph seeks to summarize the growth of current research on the 'diverse discourses' on the nature of 'conquest' in Ireland and elsewhere. See, for example, P. Coughlan, 'Cheap and Common Animals: The English Anatomy of Ireland', in T. Healy and J. Sawday (eds), *Literature and the English Civil War* (Cambridge: Cambridge University Press, 1990), pp. 205–23, and N. Canny 'The Ideology of Colonisation in England and America', *William and Mary Quarterly*, vol. 30, 1973, pp. 573–98. W. Petty, *Political Anatomy of Ireland* ([1672] 1691: repr. Shannon: Irish University Press, 1970).

84   W. J. Smyth, 'The Dynamic Quality of Irish "Village" Life – A Reassessment', in J. M. Dewailly and R. Dion (eds), *Campagnes et Littoraux d'Europe (Melanges Offert à Pierre Flatrès)* (Lille: Société de Géographie de Lille, Institut de Géographie de Lille, 1988), pp. 109–13

85   See chapters 7, 8, 9 this volume

86   See village descriptions in R. Loeber's 'New Light on Co. Wexford Architecture and Estates in the Seventeenth Century', *Journal of the Wexford Historical Society*, vol. 15, 1988–9, pp. 66–71

87   P. O'Connor, *Exploring Limerick's Past: An Historical Geography of Urban Development in County and City* (Limerick: Oireacht na Mumhan, 1987), pp. 21–7

88   F. H. A. Aalen, K. Whelan and M. Stout (eds), *Atlas of the Irish Rural Landscape* (Cork: Cork University Press, 1997) p. 150

89   W. J. Smyth, 'Making the Documents of Conquest Speak: The Transformation of Property, Society, and Settlement in Seventeenth Century Counties Kilkenny and Tipperary', in Silverman and Gulliver (eds), *Approaching the Past*, pp. 276–86

90   P. J. Duffy, 'The Territorial Organisation of Gaelic Landownership and Its Transformation in County Monaghan 1591–1640', *Irish Geography*, vol. 14, 1981, pp. 1–26

91   T. McErlean, 'The Irish Townland Scheme of Landscape Organisation', in T. Reeves Smyth and F. Hammond (eds), *Landscape Archaeology in Ireland*, BAR British Series, 116 (Oxford: British Archaeological Reports, 1983), pp. 315–39. My thanks to Dr Pat Nugent, Institute of Irish Studies, Liverpool University, for sharing his insights with regard to the territorial organization of life in seventeenth-century Co. Clare

92   P. J. Duffy, 'Farney in 1634: An Examination of Thomas Raven's Survey of the Essex Estate', *Clogher Record*, vol. 11, 1983, pp. 245–56

93   J. H. Andrews, 'Henry Pratt, Surveyor of Kerry Estates', *Journal of the Kerry Archaeological and Historical Society*, vol. 13, 1988, pp. 5–38

94   P. J. Duffy, 'The Evolution of Estate Properties in South Ulster 1600–1900', in Smyth and Whelan (eds), *Common Ground*, pp. 84–109; and in R. Gillespie, 'Ulster and the Outbreak of the 1641 Rising', in Brady and Gillespie (eds), *Natives and Newcomers*, pp. 193–6

95   See, for example, W. J. Smyth, 'Social, Economic and Landscape Transformations in County Cork from the Mid-Eighteenth to Mid-Nineteenth century', in P. O'Flanagan and C. G. Buttimer (eds), *Cork: History and Society* (Dublin: Geography Publications, 1993), pp. 655–98

96   Cullen, *Irish Towns and Villages*; Jones Hughes: 'Village and Town', pp. 99–106

97   See, for example, *Systema Agriculturae, Being the Mystery of Husbandry Discovered and Layd Open by J. W.* (London: Thomas Dring, 1675)

98   D. Dickson, 'An Economic History of the Cork Region in the Eighteenth Century', Ph.D. Thesis, Trinity College Dublin, 1977; also, Smyth, 'Social, Economic and Landscape Transformations in County Cork', pp. 655–98

99   D. Dickson, 'On Middlemen', in T. Bartlett and D. Hayton (eds), *Penal Era and Golden Age: Essays in Irish History 1690–1900* (Belfast: Ulster Historical Society, 1979), pp. 162–85. See also, K. Whelan, 'An Underground Gentry: Catholic Middlemen in the 18th Century', in J. Donnelly and K. Miller (eds), *Irish Popular Culture 1650–1850* (Dublin: Irish Academic Press, 1995)

100 I. Leister, *Das Werden der Agrarlandschaft in der Graftschaft Tipperary (Irland)* (Marburg: Marburger Geograpische Schriften, 1963), pp. 117–44

101 D. Dickson, *New Foundations: Ireland 1660–1800* (Dublin: Helicon Press, 1987), p. 114

11 Upheavals in Economy, Family Naming Patterns and Language, 1530–1750

1   J. Montague, 'The Grafted Tongue', *The Rough Field* (Oldcastle: Gallery Press, 1989), p. 39

2   J. Swift, letter of 1732, which description of Kilkenny county he sees as typical of the country as a whole, in J. McMinn, *Jonathan's Travels: Swift and Ireland* (Belfast: Appletree Press; New York: St Martin's Press, 1994), p. 135

3   D. Dickson, *New Foundations: Ireland 1660–1800* (Dublin: Helicon Press, 1987), pp. 83–5

4   See W. J. Smyth, 'Wresting with Petty's Ghost: The Origins, Nature and Relevance of the so-called "1659 Census"', new Introduction to S. Pender (ed.), *A Census of Ireland circa 1659* (Dublin: Irish Manuscripts Commission, 2002), pp. l–lxii

5   'Denizens in Ireland – a list of Protestants who, in pursuance of an Act of Parliament 13° Car. 2 for encouraging Protestant Strangers and others to inhabit and plant in the Kingdom of Ireland', Egerton Ms. 77, PRO, London, pp. 231–8. My thanks to Professor Kevin Whelan for drawing my attention to this material

6   'Incomplete abstract of 1732 census of Ireland barony by barony', Ms 1742, pp. 43–8, Lambeth Palace Library, London

7   T. P. O'Flanagan, 'Markets and Fairs in Ireland, 1600–1800: Index of Economic Development and Regional Growth', *Journal of Historical Geography*, vol. 11, no. 4, 1985, pp. 364–78

8   R. Gillespie, *The Transformation of the Irish Economy 1550–1700* (Dundalk: Economic and Social History Society of Ireland, 1991), pp. 26–7

9   P. J. O'Connor, *Fairs and Markets in Ireland: A Cultural Geography* (Midleton: Oireacht na Mumhan, 2003), pp. 34, 46, 50

10 R. A. Butlin (ed.), *The Development of the Irish Town* (London: Croom Helm, 1977), pp. 96–8

11 L. M. Cullen, *The Emergence of Modern Ireland 1600–1900* (London: Batsford, 1981); also, W. E. Crawford, *Domestic Industry in Ireland* (Dublin: Gill and Macmillan, 1972)

12 Dickson, *New Foundations*, p. 102

13 I. Leister, *Peasant Openfield Farming and Territorial Organisation in County Tipperary* (Marburg: Lahn, 1976)

14 S. J. Connolly, 'Law, Order and Popular Protest in Early Eighteenth-Century Ireland: The Case of the Houghers', in P. J. Corish (ed.), *Radicals, Rebels and Establishments* (Belfast: Appletree Press, 1985), pp. 51–68

15 Dickson, *New Foundations*, pp. 132–6

16 D. Dickson, C. Ó Gráda, and S. Daultrey, 'Hearth-tax, Household Size and Irish Population Change 1672–1821', *Proceedings of the Royal Irish Academy*, vol. 82C, no. 6, 1982, pp. 125–50

17 N. J. A. Williams (ed.), *Parliament Chloinne Tomáis* (Dublin: Dublin Institute of Advanced Studies, 1982). For more discussion on this poem, see subsection titled 'The Geography of Language Change' in this chapter

18 T. Ó Fiaich, 'Filíocht Uladh mar fhoinse don stair shóisialta san 18ú hAois', *Studia Hibernica*, vol. 11, no. 12, 1971–2, pp. 80–129

19 W. Petty, *Political Anatomy of Ireland* ([1672] 1691: repr. Shannon: Irish University Press, 1970), pp. 143–4

20 W. J. Smyth, 'Exploring the Social and Cultural Topographies of Sixteenth- and Seventeenth-Century Dublin', in F. H. A. Aalen and K. Whelan (eds), *Dublin City and County* (Dublin: Geography Publications, 1992), pp. 165–9

21 P. O'Connor, in his *Exploring Limerick's Past: An Historical Geography of Urban Development in County and City* (Limerick: Oireacht na Mumhan, 1987), p. 28, has also noted the rapid spread of tavern licences in the first decades of the seventeenth century

22 Petty, *Political Anatomy*, pp. 198–203

23 ibid., p. 199

24 A. Dobbs, *An Essay on Trade and Improvement in Ireland* (Dublin: Smith and Bruce, 1731), pp. 7–9; also, S. T. Carleton (ed.), *Heads and Hearths: The Hearth–Money Rolls and Poll-Tax Returns for County Antrim 1660–1669* (Belfast: Public Record Office of Northern Ireland, 1991), pp. 175–87

25 E. MacLysaght, *Irish Families: Their Names, Arms and Origins* (Dublin: Irish Academic Press, 1991), pp. 34–5; see also his 'Christian Names in Ireland', *North Munster Antiquarian Journal*, vol. 13, 1970, pp. 53–6

26   This analysis is based mainly on the typescript summaries of Trinity College Dublin MSS812–39, involving depositions concerning the Irish insurrection of 1641, with additional materials from the original manuscripts. My thanks to research assistant Ms Millie Glennon for assistance in this area. For a detailed analysis of this source, see N. Canny, 'The 1641 Depositions as a Source for the Writing of Social History: County Cork as a Case Study', in P. O'Flanagan and C. G. Buttimer (eds), *Cork: History and Society* (Dublin: Geography Publications 1993), pp. 249–308

27   R. M. Flatman (ed.), 'Some Inhabitants of the Baronies of Newcastle and Uppercross, Co. Dublin, c.1650', *Irish Genealogist*, vol. 7, 1989, pp. 496–503 and 3–14

28   E. MacLysaght, *More Irish Families* (Dublin: Irish Academic Press, 1996), p. 91

29   *The Irish Fiants of the Tudor Sovereigns – During the Reigns of Henry VIII, Edward VI, Philip and Mary, and Elizabeth I*, with a new Introduction by Kenneth Nicholls (Dublin: Edmund Burke, 1994), vols 1 and 2

30   MacLysaght, *Irish Families: Their Names, Arms and Origins*, pp. 199–210

31   Smyth, 'Wrestling with Petty's Ghost', pp. v–lxii

32   P. S. Robinson, *The Plantation of Ulster: A British Settlement in an Irish Landscape, 1600–1670* (Dublin: Gill and Macmillan, 1984)

33   W. Macafee, 'The Colonisation of the Maghera Region of South Derry during the Seventeenth and Eighteenth Centuries', *Ulster Folklife*, vol. 23, 1977, pp. 70–91. See also, W. Macafee and V. Morgan, 'Population in Ulster 1600–1700', in P. Roebuck (ed.), *Plantation to Partition: Essays on Ulster History in Honour of J. L. McCracken* (Belfast: Blackstaff Press, 1981)

34   See, for example, B. Adams, 'Surname Landscapes – Leitrim', *Bulletin of the Ulster Place-name Society*, vol. 1, no. 2, 1978, pp. 27–39; also in same journal his 'Surname Landscapes in Fermanagh', vol. 3, no 2, 1980, pp. 56–68. See also, B. S. Turner, 'An Observation on Settler Names in Fermanagh', *Clogher Record*, vol. 8, 1975, pp. 285–9

35   MacLysaght, *Irish Families: Their Names, Arms and Origins*, p. 21

36   ibid., p. 23

37   ibid., p. 31

38   ibid

39   National Archives, Ms 4921, Revd. B. O'Keeffe's manuscript returns (1904) of diocesan census of Cork, Cloyne and Ross (1766)

40   S. Ó Tuama and T. Kinsella (eds), *An Duanaire 1600–1900: Poems of the Dispossessed* (Mountrath/Portlaoise: Dolmen Press, 1981)

41   C. O'Rahilly (ed.), *Five Seventeenth-Century Political Poems* (Dublin: Dublin Institute for Advanced Studies, 1952). My thanks to Dr Brendán Ó Conchúir, University College Cork, for helpful discussions on these points, as well as for helpful insights on the nature and functions of Irish courts of poetry

42   T. Crowley's *The Politics of Language in Ireland 1366–1922: A Sourcebook* (London and New York: Routledge, 2000), pp. 12–25, provides a very helpful series of extracts of English Acts, ordinances and statutes relating to language behaviour in Ireland

43   ibid., pp. 2–3; B. Ó Cuív, 'The Irish Language in the Early Modern Period', in T. W. Moody, F. X. Martin and F. J. Byrne (eds), *A New History of Ireland, III: Early Modern Ireland 1534–1691* (Oxford: Clarendon Press, 1976), pp. 526–30

44   Crowley, *Politics of Language*, p. 19

45   A. Hadfield and W. Maley (eds), *J A View of the State of Ireland* (Oxford: Oxford University Press, 1997). Spenser states that 'therefore these two evil customs, of fostering and marrying with the Irish [by the Old English] most carefully to be restrained, for of them two, the third that is the evil custom of [bringing in the Irish] language . . . chiefly proceedeth'. See also, Crowley, *Politics of Language*, pp. 41–57

46   Sir John Davies (1612), *A Discovery of the True Causes Why Ireland was Never Entirely Subdued*, in A. B. Grosart (ed.), *The Works in Verse and Prose of Sir John Davies* (London: C. Tiplady, 1876)

47   ibid., pp. 525–6

48   N. Wachtel, *The Vision of the Vanquished: The Spanish Conquest of Peru through Indian Eyes, 1530–1570* (Brighton: Harvester Press, 1977); see Ó Cuív, 'Irish Language', p. 517

49   Ó Cuív, 'Irish Language', p. 526. See also, B. Ó Cuív (ed.), *A View of the Irish Language* (Dublin: Stationery Office, 1969), especially pp. 81–90 and 101–11.

50   S. Céitinn, *Foras Feasa ar Éirinn*, 4 vols, eds D. Comyn and P. Dineen (London: Irish Texts Society, 1901–8)

51   See, for example, J. Temple, *The Irish Rebellion* (London: R. White for Samuel Gellibrand, 1646),

which was reprinted on numerous occasions in the second half of the seventeenth century

52 Williams (ed.), *Pairlement Chloinne Tomáis*

53 See B. Ó Conchúir, 'Éigse Na Cúirteanna I gCúige Mumhan', in his *Saoi na hÉigse: Aistí in ómós do Sheán Ó Tuama* (Baile Átha Cliath: An Clóchomhar, 2000), pp. 55–81; L. M. Cullen, *The Hidden Ireland: Reassessment of a Concept* (Dublin: Lilliput Press, 1988); D. Corkery, *The Hidden Ireland: A Study of Gaelic Munster in the Eighteenth Century* ([1925] Dublin: Gill and Macmillan, 1967), see, in particular, S. Ó Tuama, *Repossessions: Selected Essays in the Irish Literary Heritage* (Cork: Cork University Press, 1995), especially pp. 101–33

54 In *A New Anatomy of Ireland: The Irish Protestants, 1649–1770* (New Haven and London: Yale University Press, 2003) historian Toby Barnard provides many new insights into the lives and lifestyles of this ruling caste, which included peers, the gentry, clergy, members of the professions, officeholders, army officers and landlord agents

55 E. Sapir, *Culture, Language and Personality* (Berkeley, CA: University of California Press, 1949), chapter 1

56 See L. M. Cullen, 'Patrons, Teachers and Literacy in Irish: 1700–1850', in M. Daly and D. Dickson (eds), *The Origins of Popular Literacy in Ireland: Language Change and Educational Development 1700–1920* (Dublin: UCD/TCD, 1990), pp. 15–44; P. J. Dowling, *The Hedge Schools of Ireland*, rev. edn (London: Longmans, Green, 1968)

57 K. Nicholls, *Gaelic and Gaelicised Ireland in the Middle Ages* (Dublin: Gill and Macmillan, 1972), pp. 44–6

58 See, for example, C. A. Empey and K. Simms, 'The Ordinances of the White Earl and the Problem of Coign in the Middle Ages', *Proceedings of the Royal Irish Academy*, vol. 75C, 1975, pp. 161–87

59 R. Stanihurst (1577), 'A Treatise Containing a Plain and Perfect Description of Ireland', in R. Holinshed, *The Chronicles of England, Scotland and Ireland*, 3 vols (1587)

60 ibid.; see also, Crowley, *Politics of Language*, pp. 35–6

61 N. Canny, *Making Ireland British 1580–1650* (Oxford: Oxford University Press, 2001), pp. 81–90, 415–17 and 450–5

62 M. MacCarthy-Morrogh, 'The English Presence in Early Seventeenth Century Munster', in C. Brady and R. Gillespie (eds), *Natives and Newcomers: Essays on the Making of Irish Colonial Society 1534–1641* (Dublin: Irish Academic Press, 1986), pp. 188–90

63 J. L. Kallan, 'Bilingualism and the genesis of Hiberno-English Syntax', *Teanga*, vol. 5, 1985, pp. 104–6

64 Lambeth Palace manuscript census, see note 6 above

65 Cullen, *The Emergence of Modern Ireland*, p. 89

66 ibid., pp. 89–90

67 J. P. Prendergast, *The Cromwellian Settlement of Ireland* (Dublin: McGlashan and Gill, 1875), pp. 117–18

68 L. Mac Mathúna, 'An Ghaeilge i mBaile Átha Cliath', in J. Kelly and U. MacGearailt (eds), *Dublin and Dubliners: Essays in the History and Literature of Dublin City* (Dublin: Helicon Press, 1990), pp. 147–73, especially 159–60

69 Cullen, 'Patrons, Teachers and Literacy in Irish', p. 29

70 Daly and Dickson (eds), *Popular Literacy in Ireland*, second page of preface

71 N. Ó Cíosáin, 'Printed Popular Literature in Irish 1750–1850', in Daly and Dickson (eds), *Popular Literacy in Ireland*, pp. 51–4

72 ibid., pp. 47–9

73 Cullen, 'Patrons, Teachers and Literacy in Irish', pp. 30–2

74 ibid., p. 31

75 This pattern is confirmed for the 1770s by G. Fitzgerald in 'The Decline of the Irish Language 1771–1881', in Daly and Dickson (eds.), *Popular Literacy in Ireland*, pp. 59–72

76 Based on an analysis of age cohorts per county in the introductory section of the 1841 Census which deals with literacy levels

77 G. Kirkham, 'Literacy in North-West Ulster 1680–1800', in Daly and Dickson (eds), *Popular Literacy in Ireland*, pp. 73–96

78 T. Ó Fiaich, 'Filíocht Uladh', pp. 80–129

79 J. H. Andrews, 'Road Planning in Ireland before the Railway Age', *Irish Geography*, vol. 15, no. 1, 1963, pp. 17–41

80 N. Ó Cíosáin, *Print and Popular Culture in Ireland, 1750–1850* (London and Basingstoke: Macmillan, 1997), pp. 52–64

81   ibid., especially Appendix, pp. 204–7
82   ibid., p. 56
83   B. Ó Conchúir, 'Na Cúirteanna Éigse', pp. 55–82. See also, the insightful analysis of Joep Leerssen in *Mere Irish and Fíor-Ghael: Studies in the Idea of Irish Nationality, Its Development and Literary Expression Prior to the Nineteenth Century*, 2nd edn (Cork: Cork University Press, 1996), vol. 3 in the Critical Conditions series, especially pp. 220–60.
84   Calculated from 1732 MSS Census, Lambeth Palace Library
85   Census of Ireland, 1841, introductory volume
86   Cornelius G. Buttimer, 'Gaelic Literature and Contemporary Life in Cork 1700–1840', in O'Flanagan and Buttimer (eds), *Cork: History and Society*
87   Andrews, 'Road Planning', pp. 17–41. See also, W. J. Smyth, 'Social, Economic and Landscape Transformations in County Cork from the Mid-Eighteenth to the Mid-Nineteenth Century', in O'Flanagan and Buttimer (eds), *Cork: History and Society*, pp. 680–4.
88   B. Ó Conchúir, *Scríobhaithe Chorcaí 1700–1850* (Baile Átha Cliath: An Clóchomhar, 1982); see also, Smyth, 'Social, Economic and Landscape Transformations', pp. 680–2
89   Ó Ciosáin, 'Printed Popular Literature', p. 54
90   Cullen, 'Patrons, Teachers and Literacy in Irish', p. 34
91   Based on analysis of 1841 Census, introductory volume
92   Cullen, *The Emergence of Modern Ireland*, pp. 11–24
93   MacCarthy-Morrogh, in 'English Presence', pp. 188–9, has documented the change in dress styles in Munster in the early seventeenth century.
94   A. Bliss, 'The Development of the English Language in Early Modern Ireland', in Moody, Martin and Byrne (eds), *A New History of Ireland*, III, pp. 554–8
95   Petty, *Political Anatomy*, pp. 214–17
96   H. F. Berry. *A History of the Royal Dublin Society* (New York, 1915); see also, Cullen, *The Emergence of Modern Ireland*, pp. 30–1; for earlier scientific endeavours, see, for example, J. H. Andrews, 'Science and Cartography in Ireland – William and Sameul Molyneux', *Proceedings of the Royal Irish Academy*, vol. 80C, 1980, pp. 231–50
97   K. Nicholls, unpublished paper on the Penal Laws
98   S. Ó Tuama, *Filí Faoi Scéimhle* (Cork: Cork University Press, 1979); also McMinn, *Jonathan's Travels*
99   E. Estyn Evans, 'The Scotch Irish in the New World', *Journal of the Royal Society of Antiquaries of Ireland*, vol. 95, 1965, pp. 39–49 also R. Fitzpatrick, *God's Frontiersmen – The Scots-Irish Epic* (London: Weidenfeld and Nicolson, 1989), pp. 52–77

12 Ireland and America – England's First Frontiers

1   TCD 1641 Depositions, Co. Cavan volume, George Crichtoun, folio 149(b)
2   Quoted in K. G. Davies, *The North Atlantic World in the Seventeenth Century* (Oxford: Oxford Univeristy Press, 1974), p. 27
3   D. B. Quinn, *The Elizabethans and the Irish* (Ithaca, NY: Cornell University Press, 1966), p. 58; see also chapter 6
4   Quinn, *The Elizabethans and the Irish*, p. 122
5   Noted by R. H. Brown, *Historical Geography of the United States* (New York: Harcourt Brace, 1948), p. 7
6   L. M. Cullen, *An Economic History of Ireland since 1660* (London: Batsford, 1972), p. 9. For America, see Brown, *Historical Geography*, chapter 2, and C. O. Paullin and J. K. Wright's *Atlas of the Historical Geography of the United States* (Washington: Carnegie Institution, 1932) p. 12
7   E. McCracken, *The Irish Woods since Tudor Times* (Newton Abbot: David and Charles, 1971)
8   K. H. Connell, 'The Colonisation of Waste Land in Ireland 1780–1845', *Economic History Review*, vol. 3, no. 1, 1950, pp. 44–71
9   Brown, *Historical Geography*, p. 2, estimates the number of Indians at 125,000, while, for example, H. Aptheker, *The Colonial Era* (New York: International Publishers, 1959), p. 18, suggests a figure of 200,000.
10   L. M. Cullen, 'Population Trends in Seventeenth-Century Ireland', *Economic and Social Review*, vol. 6, no. 2, 1975, pp. 149–65. See also, his 'Economic Trends, 1660–91', in T. W. Moody, F. X. Martin and F. J. Byrne (eds), *A New History of Ireland, III: Early Modern Ireland 1534–1691* (Oxford: Clarendon Press, 1976)
11   W. H. McNeill, *The Rise of the West* (Chicago: Mentor Paperback, 1965), p. 727
12   Practically all of the many writings of D. B. Quinn are illuminating in this respect – see especially *Raleigh and the British Empire* (London: Pelican Books, 1962); 'Sir Thomas Smith and the

Beginnings of English Colonial Theory', *Proceedings of the American Philosophical Society*, vol. 99, 1945, pp. 543–60, and 'Ireland and Seventeenth-Century European Expression', *Historical Studies*, vol. 1, 1958, pp. 318–44. See also, A. L. Rowse, *The Expansion of Elizabethan England* (London: Macmillan, 1957), especially on the role of the Hakluyts; also his *Elizabethans and America* (New York: Harper, 1959); C. Verlinden, *The Beginnings of Modern Colonisation* (New York: Cornell University Press, 1970); Davies, *North Atlantic World*. See also the stimulating review of Nicholas Canny, 'The British Atlantic World: Working Towards a Definition', *Historical Journal*, vol. 33, no. 2, 1990, pp. 479–97, and his *Kingdom and Colony: Ireland in the Atlantic World* (Baltimore and London: John Hopkins University Press, 1998)

13   D. W. Meinig, 'Outreach: The Creation of an Atlantic World', part 1 of *The Shaping of America: A Geographical Perspective of 500 Years of History, I:, Atlantic America 1492–1800* (New Haven and London: Yale University Press, 1986), pp. 24–55, especially 45–9 and Figure 7

14   D. B. Quinn, 'The Munster Plantation: Problems and Opportunities', *Journal of the Cork Historical and Archaeological Society*, vol. 71, 1966, pp. 19–41. See also, H. Mumford Jones, 'The Origins of the Colonial Idea in England', *Proceedings of the American Philosophical Society*, vol. 89, 1945, pp. 448–65, and Canny, *Kingdom and Colony*, pp. 1–29

15   *Calendar of State Papers, Colonial: America and the West Indies*, volume for 1583, p. 21

16   N. Canny, *The Elizabethan Conquest of Ireland* (Hassocks: Harvester Press, 1976). See also his 'The Ideology of English Colonisation: From Ireland to America', *William and Mary Quarterly*, vol. 30, 1973, pp. 575–98

17   Quinn, *Raleigh and the British Empire*, pp. 103–24. The argument that colonial involvement with Ireland deflected and retarded the English (and Scottish) engagement with the Americas (see Canny's Introduction to N. Canny (ed.), *The Oxford History of the British Empire, I: The Origins of Empire: British Overseas Enterprise to the Close of the Seventeenth Century* (Oxford: Oxford University Press, 1998)) could be qualified by the view that parallel British colonization in the Americas weakened its impact on, and capacity to anglicize, Ireland.

18   Quinn, 'Munster Plantation', pp. 22–31

19   *Calendar of State Papers, Colonial: America and the West Indies*, volume for 1583, p. 23

20   C. H. Andrews, *The Colonial Period of American History*, 2 vols (New Haven: Yale University Press, 1933), vol. 1, pp. 68–71

21   A. Lockhart, *Some Aspects of Emigration from Ireland to the North American Colonies between 1660 and 1775* (New York: Arno Press, 1976)

22   T. W. Moody, 'Introduction Early Modern Ireland', in Moody, Martin and Byrne (eds), *A New History of Ireland, III*, p. xi

23   This by way of some contrast to the French experience and in sharp contrast to the Latin-American colonies, where the immigration of settler families *in toto* was very rare

24   Quinn, 'Munster Plantation', pp. 25–8

25   T. K. Rabb, *Enterprise and Empire: Merchant and Gentry in the Expansion of England 1575–1630* (Cambridge, MA: Harvard University Press, 1967), pp. 25–30

26   Canny, *Elizabethan Conquest of Ireland*, pp. 86–7

27   Rabb, *Enterprise and Empire*, pp. 112–18 and 154–5

28   M. MacCurtain, *Tudor and Stuart Ireland* (Dublin: Gill and Macmillan, 1972), chapter 5

29   D. H. Akenson, *If the Irish Ran the World: Montserrat, 1630–1730* (Liverpool: Liverpool University Press, 1997), p. 18. See also, J. H. Andrews, 'Geography and Government in Elizabethan Ireland', in N. Stephens and R. Glasscock (eds), *Irish Geographical Studies* (Belfast: Geography Department, Queen's University Belfast, 1970), p. 182.

30   Based on a comparative analysis of settler population distribution and density per barony c.1659 in S. Pender (ed.), *A Census of Ireland circa 1659 with Supplementary Material from the Poll Money Ordinances 1660–1661* (Dublin: Irish Manuscripts Commission, 1939), and the distribution of Protestant denominations per barony, 'Census of population, Ireland', 1861

31   J. H. Andrews: 'Road Planning in Ireland before the Railway Age', *Irish Geography*, vol. 5, no. 1, 1964, pp. 17–41

32   See Quinn, *The Elizabethans and the Irish*, chapter 4; Canny, *Elizabethan Conquest of Ireland*, pp. 575–98, and *Kingdom and Colony*, pp. 2, 8, 18 and 35. See also, M. Hodgen, *Early Anthropology in the Sixteenth and Seventeenth Centuries* (Philadelphia: University of Pennsylvania Press, 1964), and H. Mumford Jones, *O Strange New World – American Culture: The Formative Years* (New York: Viking Press 1964), pp. 170–6. See also, W. J. Smyth, 'Semi-colonial Ireland?', in A. Baker (ed.) *Home and Colonial: Essays in Honour of Robin Butlin* (Cambridge: Cambridge University Historical Geography Research Series, 2004)

33   Quinn, *The Elizabethans and the Irish*

34   See T. W. Moody, *The Londonderry Plantation 1609–41* (Belfast: Wm McMullan, 1939); G. Camblin, *The Town in Ulster* (Belfast: Wm McMullan, 1951). For detailed local studies, see, for example, W. Macafee, 'The Colonisation of the Maghera Region of South Derry during the Seventeenth and Eighteenth Centuries', *Ulster Folklife*, vol. 23, 1977, pp. 70–91, and R. J. Hunter, 'Towns in the Ulster Plantation', *Studia Hibernica*, vol. 2, 1971, pp. 40–79

35   E. Estyn Evans, 'Old Ireland and New England', *Ulster Journal of Archaeology*, vol. 12, 1949, p. 109

36   J. Reps, *The Making of Urban America: A History of City Planning in the United States* (Princeton, NJ, Princeton University Press, 1965), pp. 174–7. See also, A. N. Garvan, *Architecture and Town Planning in Colonial Connecticut* (New Haven: Yale University Press, 1951)

37   Quinn, *The Elizabethans and the Irish* p. 121

38   Macafee, 'Colonisation of the Maghera Region'; see also, A. Gailey, 'The Scots Element in North Irish Popular Culture', *Ethnologia Europaea*, vol. 8, no. 1, 1975, pp. 2–22

39   R. J. Dickson, *Ulster Emigration to Colonial America 1718–1775* (London: Routledge and Kegan Paul, 1966). There is much controversy about the actual numbers migrating – the figure 100,000 may well be a conservative estimate. See also note 52 below

40   D. Boorstin, *The Americans – I: The Colonial Experience* (New York: Random House, 1958), part 2, 'The Inward Plantation'. See also, Evans, 'Old Ireland and New England', p. 108

41   E. Estyn Evans, 'The Scotch-Irish in the New World: An Atlantic Heritage', *Journal of the Royal Society of Antiquaries of Ireland*, vol. 95, 1965, 39–49. See also his 'Scotch-Irish – Their Cultural Adaptation in the American Old West', in E. R. R. Green (ed.), *Essays in Scotch-Irish History* (New York: Routledge and Kegan Paul, 1969), pp. 69–86, and D. McCourt, 'County Derry and New England – The Scotch-Irish Migration of 1718', in D. McCourt (ed.), *County Londonderry Handbook* (Belfast: Nicholson and Bass for Londonderry County Council, 1964), pp. 87–101

42   D. W. Meinig, 'The American Colonial Era: A Geographical Commentary', *Proceedings of the Royal Geographical Society, South Australian Branch*, 1957–8, pp. 1–22

43   J. Lemon, *The Best Poor Man's Country – A Geographical Study of Early South Eastern Pennsylvania* (Baltimore: John Hopkins University Press, 1972), pp. 30–1 and 171–82. See also, T. J. Wertenbaker, *The Founding of American Civilisation – The Middle Colonies* (New York: Cooper Square Publishers, 1938). I have to thank Professor T. Jones Hughes for first suggesting these ideas on the role of the family farm as an instrument of colonization on the raw frontier

44   Andrews, 'Geography and Government', pp. 186–8. See also, Moody, *Londonderry Plantation*, and Macafee, 'Colonisation of the Maghera Region'

45   Lemon, *Best Poorman's Country*, chapter 4

46   Andrews, 'Geography and Government', 186–99; Brown, *Historical Geography*, pp. 65–7

47   *Calendar of State Papers, Colonial: America and the West Indies*, volume for 1672, p. 404

48   R. V. Wells, *The Population of the British Colonies in America before 1776* (Princeton, NJ: Princeton University Press, 1975). See also, J. T. Adams, *The Epic of America* (New York: Blue Ribbon Books, 1941), chapter 1, and R. Hofstadter, *America at 1750* (London and New York: Vintage, 1972), chapter 1

49   Quinn, 'Munster Plantation', p. 39

50   Marquis of Lansdowne (ed.), *Petty Papers*, 2 vols (London and New York: Constable and Houghton Mifflin, 1927) vol. 2, pp. 109–10. As Bernard Bailyn points out in *The Peopling of British North America: An Introduction* (New York: Alfred A. Knopf, 1986), the sheer magnetism of economic betterment and religious toleration of the American colonies eventually created such a mighty flow that it reshaped patterns of European domestic mobility, to become one of the greatest events in recorded history

51   T. Bartlett, 'This Famous Island Set in a Virginian Sea: Ireland and the British Empire', in P. Marshall (ed.), *The Oxford History of the British Empire II: The Eighteenth Century* (Oxford: Oxford University Press, 1998), pp. 256–7

52   S. Smyth, 'Irish Emigration 1700–1920', in P. Emmer and M. Morner (eds), *European Expansion and Migration* (Oxford: Oxford University Press, 1992), p. 51

53   A. Bielenberg, 'Irish Emigration to the British Empire 1700–1914', in A. Bielenberg (ed.), *The Irish Diaspora* (London and New York: Longman, 2000), pp. 215–34

54   ibid., p. 216

55   ibid., pp. 215–17. See also, Akenson, *If the Irish Ran the World*, and his *The Irish Diaspora: A Primer* (Belfast: Institute of Irish Studies, Queen's University Belfast, 1996)

56   K. A. Miller, '"Scotch-Irish", "Black Irish" and "Real Irish": Emigrants and Identities in the Old

South', in Bielenberg (ed.), *The Irish Diaspora*, pp. 139–42. See also, David N. Doyle, *Ireland, Irishmen and Revolutionary America 1760–1820* (Dublin and Cork: Mercier Press, 1981), pp. 51–76. For a key Maryland planter family, see Ronald Hoffman, *Princes of Ireland, Planters of Maryland: A Carroll Saga, 1500–1782* (Chapel Hill and London: University of North Carolina Press, 2000)

57   J. H. Andrews, 'Land and People, c.1685', in Moody, Martin and Byrne (eds), *A New History of Ireland, III*, pp. 463–5

58   T. Jones Hughes, 'Society and Settlement in Nineteenth Century Ireland', *Irish Geography*, vol. 5, no. 2, 1965, pp. 80 and 86

59   Andrews, 'Land and People', 1976, pp. 464–5

60   Meinig, 'American Colonial Era', pp. 20–2. See also, Lemon, *Best Poor Man's Country*, pp. 98–117, and McNeill, *The Rise of the West* pp. 652–8

61   V. S. Pritchett, *Dublin: A Portrait* (New York: Harper Row, 1971), pp. 4–5

62   Meinig, *Shaping of America*, vol. 1, p. 378

63   ibid., p. 379

64   ibid., p. 377

65   ibid

66   F. G. James, *Ireland in the Empire 1688–1770* (Cambridge, MA: Harvard University Press, 1973), pp. 218–20; see also, pp. 241–2 and 251–312

67   Jones Hughes, 'Society and Settlement', pp. 80–7

68   E. Estyn Evans, *Irish Heritage* (Dundalk: Dundalgan Press, 1942). See also the numerous works by C. Ó Danachair (Irish Folklore Dept., University College Dublin) on regional variations in Irish material culture, and R. A. Breatnach, 'The End of a Tradition: A Survey of Eighteenth-Century Gaelic Literature', *Studica Hibernica*, vol. 1, 1961, pp. 128–38.

69   E. Estyn Evans, *The Personality of Ireland – Habitat, Heritage and History* (Cambridge: Cambridge University Press, 1973)

70   Canny, *Elizabethan Conquest of Ireland*, p. 1

71   D. B. Quinn and K. W. Nicholls, 'Ireland in 1534', in Moody, Martin and Byrne (eds), *A New History of Ireland, III*, p. 20

72   Andrews, 'Geography and Government', pp. 178–81, and also his 'Ireland in Maps: A Bibliographical Postscript', *Irish Geography*, vol. 4, no. 4, 1962, pp. 234–43

73   Quinn, 'Munster Plantation', pp. 27–8. See especially Meinig, *Shaping of America*, vol. 1, pp. 29–32, 38–40, 51, 240

74   Brown, *Historical Geography*, pp. 11–19. See also, J. Wreford Watson's section on 'The Indian Heritage' in his *North America: Its Countries and Regions* (New York: F. A. Praeger, 1967).

75   Meinig, 'American Colonial Era', pp. 9–11. See also, Francis Jennings, *The Invasion of America: Colonialism and the Cant of Conquest* (Chapel Hill and London: University of North Carolina Press, 1975) which notes that Jamestown, Plymouth and Salem, Boston, Providence, New Amsterdam and Philadelphia all grew up on sites previously occupied by Indian communities (p. 30).

76   Meinig, 'American Colonial Era', pp. 10–11

77   Boorstin, *The Americans*, pp. 96–8

78   Jones Hughes, 'Society and Settlement', pp. 79 and 83

79   Andrews, 'Geography and Government', pp. 184–5

80   Macafee, 'Colonisation of the Maghera Region', pp. 70–86

81   *Calendar of State Papers, Colonial: America and the West Indies*, volume for 1697–8, p. 241, and volume for 1698–9, p. 585

82   C. Rossiter, *The First American Revolution* (New York: Harcourt Brace, 1956), chapter 2. See also, C. R. Kein, 'Primogeniture and Entail in Virginia', *William and Mary Quarterly*, vol. 25, no. 1, 1968, pp. 580–5.

83   H. R. Merrens, *Colonial North Carolina in the Eighteenth Century* (Chapel Hill: University of North Carolina Press, 1964). See also his 'Settlement of the Colonial Atlantic Seaboard', in R. E. Ehrenberg (ed.), *Pattern and Process – Research in Historical Geography* (Washington: Harvard University Press, 1975), pp. 235–43

84   James, *Ireland in the Empire*, pp. 289–90. See also, R. B. McDowell, 'Ireland in the Eighteenth-Century British Empire', *Historical Studies*, 1974, pp. 49–63

85   James, *Ireland in the Empire*, chapter 2

86   See Meinig, 'American Colonial Era', pp. 1–5, and especially W. Zelinsky, *Cultural Geography of the United States* (New Jersey: Prentice Hall, 1973), pp. 10–33. See also, E. S. Gaustad, *Historical Atlas of Religion in America* (New York: Harper Row, 1962), pp. 1–29

87 See especially Boorstin, *The Americans*, part 3. See also, H. Mumford Jones, 'Victims of Philanthropy', in his *O Strange New World*, chapters 1, 6 and 7, especially pp. 71–98, and Zelinsky, *Cultural Geography*, pp. 61–4

88 James, *Ireland in the Empire*, pp. 1–3

89 R. A. Mohl and N. Betten (eds), *Urban America in Historical Perspective* (New York: Weybright and Talley, 1970), chapter 1, especially pp. 30–1

90 ibid., chapter 2, pp. 29–90

91 Cullen, *Economic History of Ireland*, pp. 84–5

92 L. M. Cullen, *Anglo–Irish Trade 1660–1800* (Manchester: Manchester University Press, 1968), pp. 7–24

93 C. L. Ver Steeg, *America – The Formative Years 1607–1763* (London: Macmillan, 1965), chapter 3, and especially chapter 2, pp. 177–86. See P. Goodman (ed.), *Essays in American Colonial History* (New York: Holt, Rinehart and Winston, 1967), pp. 383–90, and in particular T. M. Truxes, *Irish-American Trade 1660–1783* (Cambridge and New York: Cambridge University Press, 1988)

94 Cullen, *Anglo-Irish Trade*, pp. 17–18

95 Ver Steeg, *America – The Formative Years*, pp. 181–2

96 Wells, *Population of the British Colonies in America*, especially chapter 7

97 L. M. Cullen, 'Irish History without the Potato', *Past and Present*, vol. 40, 1968, and P. E. Razell, 'Population Growth and Economic Change in Eighteenth- and Nineteenth-Century England and Ireland', in E. Jones and G. Mingay (eds), *Land, Labour and Population in the Industrial Revolution* (London: Edward Arnold, 1967), pp. 268–75

98 Andrews, 'Road Planning in Ireland', pp. 17–25

99 D. R. McManis, *Colonial New England* (Oxford: Oxford University Press, 1975), pp. 139–43

100 Cullen, *Anglo-Irish Trade*, chapter 6, and Ver Steeg, *America – The Formative Years*, p. 181

101 Brown, *Historical Geography*, pp. 152–60. Also McManis, *Colonial New England*, pp. 122–36; Rossiter, *First American Revolution*, chapter 2; and E. Higbee 'The Three Earths of New England', *Geographical Review*, vol. 42, 1952, pp. 410–28

102 Cullen, *Economic History of Ireland*, 1972, pp. 84–5

103 W. H. Crawford, *Domestic Industry in Ireland* (Dublin: Gill and Macmillan, 1972). See also, Cullen, *Economic History of Ireland*, pp. 60–4

104 C. McLaughlin Green, *American Cities in the Growth of a Nation* (London: University of London, 1957), chapter 2, especially pp. 26–38. See also, C. L. Leyrman, *Commerce and Culture: The Maritime Communities of Colonial Massachusetts, 1690–1750* (New York and London: Norton, 1984)

105 R. H. Brown, *Mirror for Americans: Likeness of the Eastern Seaboard 1810* (New York: American Geographical Society, 1943). See also, L. B. Wright's *Everyday Life in Colonial America 1607–1763* (London: Hamish Hamilton, 1965) and his earlier *The Cultural Life of the American Colonies* (London: Hamish Hamilton, 1957)

106 Brown, *Historical Geography*, pp. 161–3, and Lemon, *Best Poor Man's Country*, chapter 8 and pp. 281–2 and 218–28

107 Lemon, *Best Poor Man's Country*, pp. 98–117

108 ibid., chapter 5, pp. 118–49, and Cullen *Anglo-Irish Trade*, chapter 5, 'The Organisation of Trade' and chapter 7, 'The Changing Structure of Trade'

109 F. G. James, 'Irish Colonial Trade in the Eighteenth Century', *William and Mary Quarterly*, vol. 20, 1963, pp. 574–84, and Truxes, *Irish-American Trade*, chapter 10

110 W. Cash, *The Mind of the South* (New York: Alfred A. Knopf, 1941),pp. 23–9. See J. P. Greene, *Interpreting Early America: Historiographical Essays* (Charlotteville and London: University Press of Virginia, 1996), pp. 475–81

111 C. Tunnard and H. H. Reed, *American Skyline: The Growth and Form of Our Cities and Towns* (New York: New American Library, 1956), pp. 43–8. See also, B. L. Dunnigan, *Frontier Metropolis: Picturing Early Detroit, 1701–1838* (Detroit: Wayne State University Press, 2001), and I. K. Steele, *The English Atlantic: An Exploration of Communications and Community* (New York and Oxford: Oxford University Press, 1986)

112 J. J. McCusker and R. R. Menard, *The Economy of British America* (Chapel Hill and London: University of North Carolina Press, 1985). See also, Canny 'The British Atlantic World', pp. 484–5

113 R. Gillespie, 'Explorers, Exploiters and Entrepreneurs: Early Modern Ireland and Its Context, 1500–1700', in B. J. Graham and L. J. Proudfoot (eds), *An Historical Geography of Ireland* (London and Toronto: Academic Press, 1993), p. 139

114 Greene, *Interpreting Early America*, p. 306
115 ibid., pp. 476–7. See also, K. Whelan, *The Tree of Liberty* (Cork: Cork University Press, 1996), vol. 1 in the Critical Conditions series
116 Doyle, *Ireland and Revolutionary America*, pp. xviii–xix

Conclusion

1 E. Bowen, *Bowen's Court* and *Seven Winters: Memories of a Dublin Childhood*, 3rd edn (London: Virago Press, 1984), with a new Introduction by Hermione Lee, p. xvi
2 See, for example, J. Barrington Moore, *The Social Origins of Dictatorship and Democracy* (Boston: Beacon Press, 1966), especially pp. 3–39 and pp. 111–15; D.W. Meinig, *The Shaping of America: A Geographical Perspective of 500 Years of History, I: Atlantic America, 1492–1800* (New Haven and London: Yale University Press, 1986), especially pp. 288–406
3 S. Deane, *Strange Country: Modernity and Nationhood in Irish Writing since 1790* (Oxford: Clarendon Press, 1997), p. 3
4 See, in particular in this Critical Conditions series, M. Caball, *Poets and Politics: Reaction and Continuity in Irish Poetry, 1558–1625* (Cork: Cork University Press, 1998), especially pp. 1–13 and pp. 144–52
5 ibid., p. 37
6 ibid., pp. 45–6
7 See, for example Ó hUiginn's:

> Mór an neamhchuid do neach éigin
> d'éigsibh an fhuinn ghealtholcaigh
> gan a rádh re fearaibh Fodla
> deabhaidh d'fhógra ar eachtronnchaibh

> Great unfriendliness – were it did
> None of the poets of the bright-knolled land
> Say to the men of Ireland that they should
> Declare war upon the foreigners.

My English translation is a slight modification of Caball's renderings (ibid., p. 49); see also J. Leerssen, *Mere Irish and Fíor-Ghael: Studies in the Idea of Irish Natonality, Its Development and Literary Expression Prior to the Nineteenth Century* (Cork: Cork University Press, 1996), especially pp. 177–89, who is less convinced of Tadhg Dall Ó hUiginn's position as a 'nationalizing' poet
8 See especially C. Brady's Introduction to *A Viceroy's Vindication? Sir Henry Sidney's Memoir of Service in Ireland, 1556–78* (Cork: Cork University Press, 2002), pp. 1–37, Irish Narratives series
9 For example, the countries of the Seven Septs of Leix had been confiscated and shired as King's County and Queen's County under Philip and Mary. Yet these counties 'presented a nearly continued scene of warfare between the colonists and the ancient inhabitants, the O' Mores and other septs having risen in insurrection and *had been suppressed no less than eighteen times'* [my italics] between 1556 and 1603 (R. C. Simington, *The Civil Survey A.D. 1654–1656*, viii, *County of Kildare* [Dublin: Irish Manuscripts Commission, 1952], p. xx). Sidney had been an early participant in this process of suppression. Risings/rebellions also erupted elsewhere in Sidney's time: amongst the Butlers and their allies in Leinster, the Desmond Fitzgeralds and their allies in Munster, even amongst the O'Briens of Thomond, the Clanricard Burkes of south Connacht, and, more particularly, the MacWilliam Burkes and their allies in north Connacht.
10 I refer to such narratives as the Desmond Survey, the Composition Book of Connacht, 'A book of the Kings lands found upon the last Generall Survey within the province of Ulster' (1608), the books of the Civil Survey, the terriers of the Down Survey, not to speak of the Books of Survey and Distribution, which are already impressive moves in the appropriation and colonization of Irish space
11 P. Palmer, *Language and Conquest in Early Modern Ireland* (Cambridge: Cambridge University Press, 2001), especially chapter 2, pp. 40–73; quotation is on p. 45
12 ibid., pp. 68–72
13 TCD Depositions, Co. Mayo volume, folio 190
14 This legal process is in sharp contrast to the exercise of Irish law by brehons. See N. Patterson, 'Brehon Law in Medieval Ireland: "Antiquarian and Obsolete" or "Traditional and Functional"?', *Cambridge Medieval Celtic Studies*, vol. 17, 1989, pp. 49–63, where she contrasts local community law to state law and argues that 'the brehons themselves were not socially distant from those whose disputes they adjudicated. The face-to-face quality of Irish law and the position of the

jurist as arbitrator in disputes, imparted an intimacy to the jural process that contrasted sharply with the kind of law which developed in England from the sixteenth century onward", p. 61. Nerys Patterson also comments on the specific implications of the Mayo mock-trial noted in reference 13 above. She sees this exercise of mock-justice as recapturing some characteristic features of Irish and pre-modern European legal customs, as well as demonstrating Irish country people's aversion to written law: 'here "the law" steps outside verbal expressions altogether, resorting to gestures to show that no communication is possible with those who break the basic bonds of society. In this Irish case the value underscored by the parody of the law should be intelligible to those who are subject to it', p. 62.

15   From the poem *Do frith, monuar, an uain si ar Éirinn* in *Five Seventeenth-Century Political Poems*, ed. C. O'Rahilly (Dublin: Dublin Institute for Advanced Studies, 1977), p. 8. The translation is a variation on that provided by Leerssen, *Mere Irish*, p. 210. Historian Robert Dunlop agrees that in the years after 1607: '. . . for the time the sword had done its work. Their chiefs slain, exiled or imprisoned, themselves decimated by the famine, the native Irish look on in impotent rage while the chicanery of the law stripped them one by one of lands to which they believed they possessed as an indefeasible right' (quoted O'Rahilly (ed.), *Political Poems*, p. 3).

16   C. Nash, 'Historical Geographies of Modernity', in (eds) Brian Graham and Catherine Nash, *Modern Historical Geographies* (Harlow: Prentice Hall, 2000), especially pp. 17–19, quotation on p. 18; see, in particular, W. D. Mignolo, *The Darker Side of the Renaissance: Literacy, Territoriality and Colonisation* (Ann Arbor: University of Michigan Press, 1995)

17   D. Dickson, *Arctic Ireland: The Extraordinary Story of the Great Frost and Forgotten Famine of 1740–41* (Belfast: White Row Press, 1997)

18   R. Cole Harris, paper on 'Old World/New World Comparisons', presented at the Conference of Historical Geographers, Oxford, summer 1983

19   Based on materials contained in Laurence Nowell's *General Description of England and Ireland*, Add Ms.62540, BL

20   T. Bartlett, *"The Academy of Warre": Military Affairs in Ireland, 1660 to 1800*, O'Donnell Lecture (Dublin: National University of Ireland, 2002), pp. 9–18; quotation is on p. 18.

21   ibid., pp. 9–18. It is striking also how a majority of Irish manuscript maps of the sixteenth and seventeenth centuries either incorporate or have the location and layout of military fortifications as their main focus.

22   Breandán Ó Buachalla, in *Aisling Ghéar: na Stíobhartaigh agus an t-Aos Léinn 1603–1788* (Dublin: An Clóchomhar, 1996), provides the most comprehensive interpretation for this period of the complex relationships between politics and poetry in the Irish language. See pp. 69–129 and especially pp. 117–26. Michelle O'Riordan in *The Gaelic Mind and the Collapse of the Gaelic World* (Cork: Cork University Press, 1990), and especially pp. 215–99, 'Old Themes in a "New" Order', takes a rather different view.

23   See also, N. Canny, *Making Ireland British 1580–1650* (Oxford: Oxford University Press, 2001), pp. 467–550

24   O'Rahilly (ed.), *Political Poems*, pp. vii–181. In particular, we might refer to the major themes developed in these poems: *Do frith monuar, an uain si ar Éirinn* (An opportunity arose, alas, to reduce Ireland) composed c.1640–1 by Donnchadh Mac an Chaoilfhiachlaig; *An Síogaí Rómhánach* (The Irish Vision at Rome) composed by a northern poet c.1650; *Aiste Dhaibhí Cúndún* (David Condon's poem c.1654–57); *Tuireamh na hÉireann* (The Lament for Ireland) composed c.1655–9 by Seán Ó Conaill; and *Mo lá leóin go deó go n-éagad* (My day of sadness, forever, until I die) written c.1658 by Éamonn Mac Donnchadh An Dúin. Four out of five of these poems were written by Munster poets – one of the great hearthlands of Irish literature in the Irish language.

25   ibid., p. viii. It was Seathrún Céitinn who laid the foundations for the mythico-historical outlook of the Catholic Irish, while the last of the great bardic poets, Dáithi Ó Bruadair, was one of the most eloquent spokespersons for the trauma that the Irish communities experienced during and after the Cromwellian conquest. My thanks to Tom Dunne for helpful discussions on all these matters.

26   ibid., pp. 44–8; 76–9 and 88–96. These five poets contrast Ireland's former prosperity with her present miserable condition. They contrast the fertility of the fields and the industry of its agriculturalists with the now devastated landscapes. They detail the sufferings of the people, the beheadings, hangings and executions; churches destroyed and desecrated; monasteries thrown down to furnish materials for the palaces and mansions of the new elite, whether lay or ecclesiastical; lands confiscated and the landowners transplanted to Connacht. Indeed, the most

frequent English words to appear in all the poems are 'transplantation' and 'transportation' – words that came to sound the death knell for the lives and lore of so many people

Like the Protestant Irish (and the Aztecs and Incas in Mexico and Peru), the Irish poets attribute the sufferings of their own people in religious terms to their own sinful ways and the vengeance of God. The great sins are those of internal disagreement and disunity within the Irish polity. Equally the poets condemn the waywardness, greed, and the neglect of Christian pieties amongst their own populations prior to the conquest.

27 ibid., p. 74. (Translation is from Leerssen's *Mere Irish*, p. 211.)

28 ibid., p. 58. At least 130 different manuscript versions of *Tuireamh na hÉireann* still survive

29 T. Jones Hughes, in 'Historical Geography of Ireland from circa 1700', in *Irish Geography Golden Jubilee 1934–1984* (Dublin: Geographical Society of Ireland, 1984), p. 156, notes: '. . . the typical planter farm and farmstead possessed carefully contrived and stylised layouts, perhaps as part of a conscious attempt to demonstrate superior tastes in what for him was a precarious situation. By contrast, the farmstead of the Gaelic tenant had remained, like the interior of his house, largely unadorned.'

30 Tom Dunne, in 'The Gaelic Response to Conquest and Colonisation: The Evidence of the Poetry', *Studia Hibernica*, vol. 20, 1980, pp. 7–30, may have a point in stressing the fatalistic and formulaic responses of many bardic poets, who chose not to see or speak of the chaotic socio-political situation developing in front of their eyes. Dunne also emphasizes the sophisticated adaptation of the bardic tradition by other poets in the face of the changing seventeenth century world. See his review article, 'Ireland, Irish and Colonialism' , *The Irish Review*, 30, spring–summer, 2003, pp. 95–104

31 K. Bottigheimer, 'The Failure of the Reformation in Ireland: *Une Question Bien Posée' Journal of Ecclesiastical History*, vol. 36, no. 2, 1985, p. 198

32 Jones Hughes, 'Historical Geography of Ireland', p. 158, notes that 'in an island where the soldiers' barrack was among the most conspicuous item in urban life, villages and towns came to act as overt battlegrounds between two traditions, and the more truculent features in the struggle had found landscape expression' as in the dichotomy of privileged market square at one end and the fairgreen at the other.

33 See, for example, B. McGrath, 'Ireland and the Third University: Attendance at the Inns of Court, 1603–1649', in D. Edwards (ed.), *Regions and Rulers in Ireland: Essays for Kenneth Nicholls* (Dublin: Four Courts Press, 2004) pp. 217–36

34 L. P. Ó Caithnia, *Scéal na hIománia: Ó Thosach Ama go 1884* (Baile Átha Cliath: An Clóchomhar, 1980), especially chapter 2, pp. 15–23, and chapter 3, pp. 24–52; see also, K. Whelan, 'The Bases of Regionalism', in P. Ó Drisceóil (ed.), *Culture in Ireland – Regions, Identity and Power* (Belfast: Institute of Irish Studies, Queen's University Belfast, 1993), pp. 13–18

35 See, for example, Kevin Whelan and T.P. Power (eds.), *Endurance and Emergence in Ireland in the Eighteenth Century* (Dublin: Irish Academic Press, 1990); see also, C. Chenevix Trench, *Grace's Card: Irish Catholic Landlords 1690–1800* (Cork: Mercier Press, 1997)

36 See, in particular, the section entitled 'The Parish and Its Settlement Centre' in Jones Hughes 'Historical Geography of Ireland', pp. 161–4

37 Toby Barnard provides rich insights as to the lifestyles and preoccupations of many members of this ruling elite in *A New Anatomy of Ireland: The Irish Protestants, 1649–1770* (New Haven and London: Yale University Press, 2003), as they sought to bolster and retain their precarious Ascendancy.

38 D. J. Butler, 'Contesting Hegemony: The Historical Geography of the Protestant and Roman Catholic Communities of South Tipperary *c.*1570–*c.*1841', Ph.D. dissertation, University College Cork, 2003, p. 303

39 J. Dunlop, *A Precarious Belonging: Presbyterians and the Conflict in Ireland* (Belfast: Blackstaff Press, 1995), p. 21

40 ibid., p. 24

41 ibid., p. 22

42 ibid., p. 25

43 T.C. Barnard, 'Historiographical Review: Farewell to Old Ireland', *Historical Journal*, vol. 36, no. 4, 1993, pp. 909–28

44 In addition to the iron grip established on urban governance, state-sponsored garrisons were augmented, while the landed estate – sometimes still focused on a fortified mansion – acted as the fulcrum of local Protestant settlement and later new settler 'colonies'. See, in particular, D. J. Butler, 'Defence from the Dispossessed: The State-Sponsored Garrisoning of the South

Tipperary Landscape *c.*1650–*c.*1730' *Irish Sword*, vol. 24, no. 95, summer 2004, pp. 45–56

45   The following comments owe much to T. Bartlett, 'Protestant Nationalism in Eighteenth-century Ireland' in *Studies on Voltaire and the Eighteenth Century*, 335, 1995, pp. 749–88; see also J.L. McCracken, 'Protestant Ascendancy and the Rise of Colonial Nationalism, 1714–60', Chapter 5 in T.W. Moody and W.E. Vaughan (eds), *A New History of Ireland IV: Eighteenth-Century Ireland 1691–1800*, (Oxford: Clarendon Press, 1986), pp. 105–22.

46   T. Bartlett, 'Protestant Nationalism', p. 81

47   See, for example, T. C. Barnard, 'Crises of Identity among Irish Protestants 1641–1685' *Past and Present*, vol. 127, May, 1990, p. 50, and his 'The Uses of 23 October 1641 and Irish Protestant Celebrations', *English Historical Review*, vol. 106, 1991, pp. 889–920. The first half of the eighteenth century – as the self-confidence of the Protestant nation expanded, boosted by the almost absolute reduction of Catholic Irish landed power and the ready availability of strategic use of the Penal Laws – may have been the darkest phase in Catholic Irish consciousness

48   See, for example, Stephen Daniels's review article 'Envisioning England', *Journal of Historical Geography*, vol. 17, no. 1, 1991, pp. 95–9, where he notes that after the weakening of monarchical rule in England, the great symbols of the walled garden and of enclosed property – so central to the iconography of the Tudor and Stuart states – were transferred to aristocratic definitions of English identity. Just as the landed estate and its representations provided a fertile metaphor for the English nation-state, so its equivalent in Ireland symbolized the new-found confidence and identity of the Protestant Anglo-Irish. So did the associated expressions of classical architecture, surrounding tree plantations whose species had been drawn from all over the empire, elaborate estate map-books, impressive paintings and often Irish-made silverware, appropriate furniture and dress styles and the culture of the stable and the breeding of thoroughbred horses (and hounds). See, in particular, Finola O'Kane, *Landscape Design in Eighteenth Century Ireland* (Cork: Cork University Press, 2004)

49   See, amongst others, J. A. Martin, 'The Social Geography of Mid Nineteenth Century Dublin City' in W. J. Smyth and K. Whelan (eds), *Common Ground: Essays on the Historical Geography of Ireland* (Cork: Cork University Press, 1988), especially pp. 173–7; M. Craig, *Dublin 1660–1860* (Dublin: Allen Figgis, 1969), pp. 3–70; also his *The Architecture of Ireland from the Earliest Times to 1880* (London and Dublin: Batsford and Eason, 1982), pp. 151–76, and Jones Hughes, 'Historical Geography', pp. 158–9

50   Van der Hagen's painting, *A Viceregal Ball in Dublin Castle in the time of the Duke of Dorset* (Private Collection)

51   Barnard, *Irish Protestants*, especially pp. 41–176

52   It is likely that for some the multiplicity of ruins and other sites in the landscape, the ruined abbeys, monasteries, churches, tower-houses, ancient battle sites and hill-top assembly points, the sites of so many institutions that had not survived the conquest, became important symbolic central places for story-telling, memory-making and stiffening resistance. See, in particular, L. Gibbons, *Transformations in Irish Culture*, Critical Conditions Series (Cork: Cork University Press, 1996), chapter 1, especially pp. 12–22.

53   Bartlett, 'Protestant Nationalism', p. 79

54   The groundswell of the French Revolution drove a further wedge into a now fractured and fragmenting colonial nationalism. Anglo-Irish claims that they were not a colony and not dependent on the military protection of the metropolitan power suddenly began to ring rather hollow. Its majority strand, consciously and formally reasserted the ideology of the Protestant Ascendancy, agreed to the Act of Union and abandoned, in Bartlett's apt phrase, 'the most potent symbol of a separate nationality, the parliament of Ireland' (ibid., p. 87). A minority strand helped to found the Society of United Irishmen (1791–8) with its dream of an all-Irish nation, inclusive of all religious traditions and none.

55   William Petty, 'A Treatise of Ireland, 1687', in C. H. Hull (ed.), *Economic Writings of Sir William Petty*, vol. 2 (London: Routledge/Thoemmes Press, 1898), pp. 546–621. Petty's overall objective in proposing this union of peoples is to 'cut up the Roots of those Evils in Ireland, which by Differences of Birth, Extractions, Manners, Languages, Customs and Religions have continually wasted the Blood and Treasure of both Nations for above 500 years'. Ireland is to be defended by a navy of 4,000 men and an army of 17,000 (2,000 of horse) and so establish a real *mare clausum*, to confirm England's supremacy over the adjacent seas. In effect, Petty is arguing that through the removal of most of the disaffected Irish people, England could be far more easily secured against foreign enemies

56   ibid., p. 577

57   ibid., p. 578. James II asked the diarist Pepys to assess Petty's plan to convert the country into a

cattlewalk, to make the island thus secure, while maximizing profit yields in the cattle trade for its new proprietors and providing urbanizing England with a more reliable and cheaper food supply. Petty died three months later. The plan was never heard of again, except to be mocked and satirised by Swift.

58   W. McNeill, *The Rise of the West: A History of the Human Community* (Chicago and London: University of Chicago Press, 1963), p. 664

59   ibid., p. 664

60   S. Deane, *Strange Country*, p. 17

Bibliography

Aalen, F. H. A., and Kevin Whelan (eds). *Dublin City and County: From Prehistory to Present* (Dublin: Geography Publications, 1992)
——, K. Whelan and M. Stout (eds). *Atlas of the Irish Rural Landscape* (Cork: Cork University Press, 1997)
Adams, Brendan G. 'Language in Ulster, 1820–1850', *Ulster Folklife*, vol. 19, 1973, pp. 50–5
——. 'Surname Landscapes – Leitrim', *Bulletin of the Ulster Place-Name Society*, vol. 1, no. 2, 1978, pp. 27–39
——. 'Surname Landscapes in Fermanagh', *Ulster Folklife*, vol. 3, no. 2, 1980, pp. 56–68
Adams, J. T. *The Epic of America* (New York: Blue Ribbon Books, 1941)
Adamson, John. 'The British Context of Viscount Lisle's Lieutenancy of Ireland', in Jane H. Ohlmeyer (ed.), *Ireland: From Independence to Occupation 1641–1660* (Cambridge: Cambridge University Press, 1995), ch. 7
Akenson, Donald H. *The Irish Diaspora: A Primer* (Belfast: Institute of Irish Studies, Queen's University Belfast, 1996)
——. *If the Irish Ran the World: Monserrat, 1630–1730* (Liverpool: Liverpool University Press, 1997)
Alpers, Svetlana. *The Art of Describing – Dutch Art in the Seventeenth Century* (Chicago: University of Chicago Press, 1983)
——. 'The Mapping Impulse in Dutch Art', in David Woodward (ed.), *Art and Cartography. Six Historical Essays* (Chicago: Chicago University Press, 1987), pp. 37–96
Andrews, C. H. *The Colonial Period of American History* (New Haven and London: Yale University Press, 1934), vol. 1
Andrews, J. H. 'Notes on the Historical Geography of the Irish Iron Industry', *Irish Geography*, vol. 3, no. 3, 1957, pp. 92–49
——. 'Road Planning in Ireland before the Railway Age', *Irish Geography*, vol.15, no. 1, 1963, pp. 17–41
——. 'The Irish Surveys of Robert Lythe', *Imago Mundi*, vol. 19, 1965, pp. 22–31
——. 'A Geographer's View of Irish History', in T. W. Moody and F. X Martin (eds), *The Course of Irish History* (Cork: Mercier Press, 1967), pp. 21–4
——. 'Robert Lythe's Petitions 1571', *Analecta Hibernica*, vol. 24, 1967, pp. 232–41
——. 'The French School of Irish Land Surveyors', *Irish Geography*, vol. 5, no. 4, 1967, pp. 285–92
——. 'Geography and Government in Elizabethan Ireland', in Nicholas Stephens and Robin Glasscock (eds), *Irish Geographical Studies in Honour of E. Estyn Evans* (Belfast: Queen's University Press, 1970), ch. 11
——. 'The Maps of the Escheated Counties of Ulster, 1609–10', *Proceedings of the Royal Irish Academy*, vol. 74C, no. 4, 1974, pp. 133–70
——. 'Land and People, c.1685', in T. W. Moody, F. X. Martin and F. J. Byrne (eds), *A New History of Ireland, III: Early Modern Ireland 1534–1691* (Oxford: Clarendon Press, 1976), pp. 458–65
——. *Plantation Acres: An Historical Study of the Irish Land Surveyor* (Belfast: Ulster Historical Foundation, 1985)

——. 'Colonial Cartography in a European Setting: The Case of Tudor Ireland', received by the author in manuscript form

——. 'Henry Pratt, Surveyor of Kerry Estates', *Journal of the Kerry Archaeological and Historical Society*, vol. 13, 1988, pp. 5–38

——. *Shapes of Ireland: Maps and Their Makers 1564–1839* (Dublin: Geography Publications, 1997)

——. 'The Mapping of Ireland's Cultural Landscape, 1550–1630', in Patrick Duffy, David Edwards and Elizabeth Fitzpatrick (eds), *Gaelic Ireland: Land Lordship and Settlement c.1250–c.1650* (Dublin and Portland: Four Courts Press, 2001), ch. 5

——. 'Sir Richard Bingham and the Mapping of Western Ireland', *Proceedings of the Royal Irish Academy*, vol. 103C, no. 3, 2003, pp. 61–95

——, and Rolf Loeber. 'An Elizabethan Map of Leix and Offaly: Cartography, Topography and Architecture', in William Nolan and Timothy P. O Neill (eds.), *Offaly: History and Society* (Dublin: Geography Publications, 1998), pp. 243–86

Andrews, K. R., N. P.Canny, P. E. H. and Hair (eds). *The Westward Enterprise: English Activities in Ireland, the Atlantic and America, 1480–1650* (Liverpool: Liverpool University Press, 1978)

Appadurai, Argun. 'Dead Certainty: Violence in the Era of Globalization', in Birgit Meyer and Peter Geschiere (eds), *Globalization and Identity* (Oxford and Malden, MA: Blackwell, 1999), pp. 305–24

Aptheker, H. *The Colonial Era* (New York: International Publishers, 1959)

Armitage, David. *The Ideological Origins of the British Empire* (Cambridge: Cambridge University Press, 2000)

——, and Michael J. Braddick (eds.), *The British Atlantic World 1500–1800* (Basingstoke: Palgrave Macmillan, 2002)

Arnold, Lawrence J. *The Restoration Land Settlement in County Dublin* (Dublin: Irish Academic Press, 1993)

Asch, Ronald G. *The Thirty Years War: The Holy Roman Empire and Europe 1618–1648* (London: Macmillan Press, 1997)

Bailyn, Bernard. *The Peopling of British North America: An Introduction* (New York: Alfred A. Knopf, 1988)

——, and Philip D. Morgan (eds), *Strangers within the Realm: Cultural Margins of the First British Empire* (Chapel Hill and London: University of North Carolina Press, 1991)

Baker, Alan (ed.), *Home and Colonial: Essays in Honour of Robin A. Butlin* (Cambridge: Cambridge University Press Historical Geography Research Series, No. 39, October 2004)

Baker, David. 'Off the Map: Charting Uncertainty in Renaissance Ireland', in Brendan Bradshaw, Andrew Hadfield and Willy Maley (eds), *Representing Ireland – Literature and the Origins of Conflict, 1534–1660* (Cambridge: Cambridge University Press, 1993), ch. 5

Ball, Francis E. *Southern Fingal* (Dublin: Gill and Macmillan, 1920)

——. *A History of the County of Dublin* (Dublin: Gill and Macmillan repr., 1979), vols 1–4

——. *Howth and Its environs* (Dublin: Gill and Macmillan repr., 1979)

Barber, Peter. 'England I: Pageantry, Defence and Government: Maps at Court to 1550', in David Buisseret (ed.), *Monarchs, Ministers and Maps* (Chicago and London: University of Chicago Press, 1992), ch. 2

——. 'England II: Monarchs, Ministers and Maps 1550–1625', in David Buisseret (ed.), *Monarchs, Ministers and Maps* (Chicago and London: University of Chicago Press, 1992), ch. 3.

Barnard, T. C. 'Planters and Policies in Cromwellian Ireland', *Past and Present*, vol. 61, 1973, pp. 31–69

——. *Cromwellian Ireland: English Government and Reform in Ireland 1649–1660* (Oxford: Oxford University Press, 1975)

——. 'Crisis of Identity among Irish Protestants, 1641–1685', *Past and Present*, vol. 127, May 1990, pp. 50–72

——. 'The Uses of 23 October 1641 and Irish Protestant Celebrations', *English Historical Review*, vol. 106, 1991, pp. 889–920

——. '1641: A Bibliographical Essay', in Brian MacCuarta (ed.), *Ulster 1641: Aspects of the Rising* (Belfast: Institute of Irish Studies, Queen's University Belfast, 1993), ch. 8

——. 'Farewell to Old Ireland', *Historical Journal*, vol. 36, no. 4, 1993, pp. 909–29

——. *A New Anatomy of Ireland: The Irish Protestants, 1649–1770* (New Haven and London: Yale University Press, 2003)

——, and Jane Fenlon (eds), *The Dukes of Ormonde 1640–1745* (Woodbridge: Boydell Press, 2000)

Barrington Moore, J. *The Social Origins of Dictatorship and Democracy* (Boston: Beacon Press, 1966)

Barth, Frederick (ed.). *Ethnic Groups and Boundaries: The Social Organisation of Cultural Difference* (Bergen-Oslo: Universitets Forlaget, and London: George Allen and Unwin, 1969)

Bartlett, Thomas. 'Protestant Nationalism in Eighteenth-Century Ireland', *Studies on Voltaire and the Eighteenth Century*, vol. 335, 1995, pp. 749–88

——. 'This Famous Island Set in a Virginian Sea: Ireland and the British Empire', in P. Marshall (ed.), *The Oxford History of the British Empire: The Eighteenth Century* (Oxford: Oxford University Press, 1998)

——. 'The Academy of Warre': Military Affairs in Ireland, 1660 to 1800. O'Donnell Lecture (National University of Ireland: Dublin, 2002)

——, and David Hayton (eds). *Penal Era and Golden Age: Essays in Irish History 1690–1900* (Belfast: Ulster Historical Foundation, 1979)

——, and Keith Jeffrey (eds). *A Military History of Ireland* (Cambridge: Cambridge University Press, 1996)

Beckett, J. C. *The Anglo-Irish Tradition* (London: Faber and Faber, 1976)

——, and R. E. Glasscock (eds), *Belfast: The Origin and Growth of an Industrial City* (Belfast: BBC, 1967)

Begley, D. F. (ed.). *Irish Genealogy: A Record Finder* (Dublin: Heraldic Artists, 1981)

Belmore, Earl of. *The History of Two Ulster Manors* (London: Longmans, Green, 1881)

Bielenberg, A. 'Irish Emigration to the British Empire 1700–1914', in A. Bielenberg (ed.), *The Irish Diaspora* (London and New York: Longman, 2000), pp. 215–34

Blake, Michael J. 'A Map of the County of Mayo in 1584', *Journal of the Galway Archaeological and Historical Society*, vol. 5, 1907, pp. 40–6

Bliss, A. 'The Development of the English language in Early Modern Ireland', in T. W. Moody, F. X. Martin and F. J. Byrne (eds), *A New History of Ireland, III: Early Modern Ireland 1534–1691* (Oxford: Clarendon Press, 1976), pp. 554–8

Blouet, Brian W., and Olivia W. Blouet (eds). *Latin America and the Caribbean* (New York: Wiley, 1997)

Boelhower, William. 'Inventing America: A Model of Cartographic Semiosis', *Word & Image*, vol. 4, no. 2, April–June 1988, pp. 475–97

Boland, Eavan. 'The Poets', *Selected Poems* (Manchester: Carcanet Press, 1989)

——. *In a Time of Violence* (Manchester: Carcanet Press, 1994)

Boorstin, D. *The Americas, I: The Colonial Experience* (New York: Random House, 1958), part 2, 'The Inward Plantation', and part 3 'Victims of Philantrophy'

Bossy, John. 'The Counter-Reformation and the People of Catholic Ireland, 1596–1641', *Past and Present*, vol. 47, 1970, pp. 51–70

Bottigheimer, Karl. S. *English Money and Irish Land: The 'Adventurers' in the Cromwellian Settlement of Ireland* (Oxford: Clarendon Press, 1971)

——. 'The Failure of the Reformation in Ireland: *Une Question Bien Posée*', *Journal of Ecclesiastical History*, vol. 6, no. 2, 1985, pp. 196–207

Bourke, Angela, *et al.* (eds). *The Field Day Anthology of Irish Writing, IV and V: Irish Women's Writings and Traditions* (Cork: Cork University Press in association with Field Day, 2002)

Bradshaw, Brendan. *The Dissolution of the Religious Orders in Ireland under Henry VIII* (Cambridge: Cambridge University Press, 1974)

——, Andrew Hadfield and Willy Maley (eds). *Representing Ireland: Literature and the Origins of Conflict, 1534–1660* (Cambridge: Cambridge University Press, 1993)

——, and John Morrill (eds). *The British Problem c.1534–1707: State Formation in the Atlantic Archipelago* (Basingstoke and London: Macmillan, 1996)

——, and Peter Roberts (eds). *British Consciousness and Identity: The Nationality of Britain, 1533–1707* (Cambridge: Cambridge University Press, 1998)

Brady, Ciaran. *The Chief Governors: The Rise and Fall of Reform Government in Tudor Ireland* (Cambridge: Cambridge University Press, 1994)

—— (ed.). *A Viceroy's Vindication? Sir Henry Sidney's Memoir of Service in Ireland, 1556–78*, Irish Narratives Series (Cork: Cork University Press, 2002)

——, and Raymond Gillespie (eds), *Natives and Newcomers: Essays in the Making of Irish Colonial Society 1534–1641* (Dublin: Irish Academic Press, 1986)

Brady, John, and Patrick J. Corish. 'The Church under the Penal Code' in Patrick J. Corish (ed.), *A History of Irish Catholicism*, 8 vols (Dublin and London: Gill and Macmillan, 1971), IV, pp. 1–88

Brady, Joseph, and Anngret Simms (eds), *Dublin Through Space and Time* (Dublin: Four Courts Press, 2001)

Breatnach, R. A. 'The End of a Tradition: A Survey of Eighteenth-Century Gaelic Literature', *Studia Hibernica*, vol. 1, 1961, pp. 128–38

Breen, John. 'Spenser's "Imaginative Groundplot: A View of the Present State of Ireland"', *Spenser Studies*, vol. 12, 1998), pp. 151–68

Brennan, Monica. 'The Making of the Protestant Ascendancy in County Kilkenny', unpublished Ph.D. thesis, State University of New York, 1985

——. 'The Changing Composition of Kilkenny's Landowners 1641–1700', W. Nolan, and K. Whelan (eds), *Kilkenny: History and Society* (Dublin: Geography Publications, 1990), ch. 8

Brooks, Eric St John. *Knights' Fees in Counties Wexford, Carlow and Kilkenny* (Dublin: Stationery Office, for the Irish Manuscripts Commission, 1950)

Brotton, Jeremy. *Trading Territories – Mapping the Early Modern World* (London: Reaktion Books, 1997)

Brown, R. H. *Mirror for Americans: Likeness of the Eastern Seaboard 1810* (New York: American Geographical Society, 1943)

——. *Historical Geography of the United States* (New York: Harcourt Brace, 1948)

Buchanan, R. H. 'Towns and Plantations, 1500–1700', in W. Nolan (ed.), *The Shaping of Ireland* (Cork: Mercier Press, 1986), pp. 84–98

——. 'Historical Geography of Ireland pre-1700', in *Irish Geography: Jubilee Volume 1934–1984* (Dublin: Geographical Society of Ireland, 1984), ch. 8

Buisseret, David (ed.). *Monarchs, Ministers and Maps* (Chicago and London: University of Chicago Press, 1992)

Burke, Nuala T. 'An Early Modern Dublin Suburb: The Estate of Francis Aungier, Earl of Longford', *Irish Geography*, vol. 6, no. 4, 1972, pp. 365–85

Burke, William P. *History of Clonmel* (Waterford: Harvey, 1907; new edn. Kilkenny: Roberts Books, 1983)

Burtchaell, Jack. 'The South Kilkenny Farm Villages', in William J. Smyth and Kevin Whelan (eds), *Common Ground: Essays on the Historical Geography of Ireland* (Cork: Cork University Press, 1988), pp. 110–23

Butler, David J. 'Contesting Hegemony: A Historical Geography of the Protestant and Roman Catholic Communities of South Tipperary c.1570–c.1841', Ph.D. thesis, National University of Ireland, University College Cork, 2003

——. 'Defence from the Dispossessed: The State-Sponsored Garrisoning of the South Tipperary Landscape c.1650–c.1730', *Irish Sword*, vol. 24, no. 95, summer 2004, pp. 45–56

——. *South Tipperary 1570–1841: Religion, Land and Rivalry* (Dublin: Four Courts Press, 2006)

Butlin, R.A. 'The Population of Dublin in the Late Seventeenth Century', *Irish Geography*, vol. 5, no. 2, 1965, pp. 51–66

——. 'Land and People c.1600', in T. W. Moody, F. X. Martin and F. J. Byrne (eds), *A New History of Ireland, III: Early Modern Ireland 1534–1691* (Oxford: Clarendon Press, 1976), pp. 142–67

——. 'Irish Towns in the Sixteenth and Seventeenth Centuries', R. A. Butlin (ed.), *The Development of the Irish Town* (London: Croom Helm, 1977), ch. 3

——. *The Development of the Irish Town* (London: Croom Helm, 1977)

——. *Historical Geography through the Gates of Space and Time* (London: Edward Arnold, 1993)

Buttimer, Cornelius G. 'Gaelic Literature and Contemporary Life in Cork 1700–1840', in Patrick O'Flanagan and Cornelius G. Buttimer (eds), *Cork: History and Society* (Dublin: Geography Publications, 1993), pp. 585–654

——. Review of *Gaelic Ireland: Land, Lordship and Settlement c.1250–c.1650* in *Journal of the Cork Historical and Archaeological Society*, vol. 108, 2002, pp. 217–28

Butzer, K. W. 'The Americas Before and After 1492: An Introduction to Current Geographic Research', *Annals of the Association of American Geographers*, vol. 82, 1992, pp. 345–68

Byrne, Aideen. 'Kilkenny City from the Civil Survey', unpublished BA dissertation, University College Dublin, 1985

Byrne, F. J. Reconstruction of Ptolemy's Map of Ireland *c.*150 A.D. Figure 14, in T. W. Moody, F. X. Martin and F. J. Byrne (eds), *A New History of Ireland, IX: Maps, Genealogies, Lists* (Oxford: Oxford University Press, 1984), p. 16

Caball, Marc. 'Faith, Culture and Sovereignty: Irish Nationality and Its Development, 1558–1625', in Brendan Bradshaw and Peter Roberts (eds), *British Consciousness and Identity: The Nationality of Britain, 1533–1707* (Cambridge: Cambridge University Press, 1998), pp. 112–39

——. *Poets and Politics: Reaction and Continuity in Irish Poetry, 1558–1625* (Cork: Cork University Press, 1998)

Camblin, G. *The Town in Ulster* (Belfast: Wm Mullan, 1951).

Camino, Mercedes Maroto. '"Methinks I See an Evil Lurk Unespied" – Visualising Conquest in Spenser's "A View of the State of Ireland"', *Spenser Studies*, vol. 12, 1998, pp. 169–94

Canny, Nicholas. 'The Ideology of English Colonisation: From Ireland to America', *William and Mary Quarterly*, vol. 30, 1973, pp. 575–98

——. *The Elizabethan Conquest of Ireland: A Pattern Established 1565–1576* (Hassocks: Harvester Press, 1976)

——. 'Why the Reformation Failed in Ireland: *Une Question Mal Posée*', *Journal of Ecclesiastical History*, vol. 30, no. 4, 1979, pp. 423–41

——. *The Upstart Earl: A study of the Social and Mental World of Richard Boyle, First Earl of Cork 1566–1643* (Cambridge: Cambridge University Press, 1982)

——. 'Migration and Opportunity: Britain, Ireland and the New World', *Irish Economic and Social History*, vol. 12, 1985, pp. 7–32

——. 'Protestants, Planters and Apartheid in Early Modern Ireland', *Irish Historical Studies*, vol. 25, no. 98, 1986, pp. 105–15

——. *From Reformation to Restoration: Ireland 1534–1660* (Dublin: Helicon Press, 1987)

——. 'Early Modern Ireland, *c.*1500– 1700', in R. Foster (ed.), *The Oxford Illustrated History of Ireland* (Oxford: Oxford University Press, 1989), pp. 104–60

——. 'The British Atlantic World: Working towards a Definition', *Historical Journal*, vol. 33, no. 2, 1990, pp. 479–97

——. 'The 1641 Depositions as a Source for the Writing of Social History: County Cork as a Case Study', in Patrick O'Flanagan and Cornelius G. Buttimer (eds), *Cork: History and Society* (Dublin: Geography Publications, 1993), ch. 8

——. 'English Migration into and across the Atlantic during the Seventeenth and Eighteenth Centuries', in Nicholas Canny (ed.), *Europeans on the Move: Studies in European Migration, 1500–1800* (Oxford: Clarendon Press, 1994), pp. 39–75

——. *Kingdom and Colony: Ireland in the Atlantic World* (Baltimore and London: John Hopkins University Press, 1998)

——. *Making Ireland British 1580–1650* (Oxford: Oxford University Press, 2001)

——. *et al.* (eds), *The Oxford History of the British Empire, I: The Origins of Empire* (Oxford: Oxford University Press, 1998)

Carey, Vincent. 'Neither Good English nor Good Irish: Bilingualism and Identity Formation in Sixteenth Century Ireland', in Hiram Morgan (ed.), *Political Ideology in Ireland 1541–1641* (Dublin: four Courts Press, 1001), pp. 45–61

Carleton, S. T. (ed.). *Heads and Hearths: The Hearth-Money Rolls and Poll-Tax Returns for County Antrim 1660–1669* (Belfast: Public Record Office of Northern Ireland, 1991)

Carpenter, Andrew. *Verse in English from Tudor and Stuart Ireland* (Cork: Cork University Press, 2003)

Carr, P. *The Most Unpretending of Places – A History of Dundonald, County Down* (Belfast: White Row Press, 1987)

Carrigan, William. *The History and Antiquities of the Diocese of Ossory*, new edn. (Kilkenny: Roberts Books, 2000)

Carroll, Clare. 'Barbarous Slaves and Civil Cannibals: Transplanting Civility in Early Modern Ireland', in Clare Carroll and Patricia King (eds), *Ireland and Postcolonial Theory* (Cork: Cork University Press, 2003), pp. 63–80

——, and Patricia King (eds). *Ireland and Postcolonial Theory* (Cork: Cork University Press, 2003)

Cary, G. S. 'Hearth-Money Roll for County Dublin', *Journal of the Kildare Archaeological and Historical Society*, vol. 11, 1940, pp. 245–466

Cash, W. *The Mind of the South* (New York: Alfred.A. Knopf, 1941)

Céitinn, Seathrún (Geoffrey Keating), *Foras Feasa ar Éirinn: The History of Ireland*, 4 vols, eds D. Comyn and P. Dineen (Dublin: Irish Texts Society, 1914)

Chart, D. A. (ed.). *Londonderry and the Companies 1609–1629, Being a Survey and Other Documents Submitted to King Charles I by Sir Thomas Phillips* (Belfast: HMSO, 1928)

Chevenix Trench, C. *Grace's Card: Irish Catholic Landowners 1690–1800* (Cork: Mercier Press, 1997)

Chubb, Thomas. *The Printed Maps in the Atlases of Great Britain and Ireland: A Bibliography 1579–1870* (London: Burrow, 1927)

Clarke, Aidan. *The Old English in Ireland 1625–1642* (London: Macgibbon and Kee, 1966)

——. 'The Irish Economy, 1600–60', in T. W. Moody, F. X. Martin, and F. J. Byrne, (eds), *A New History of Ireland, III: Early Modern Ireland, 1534–1691* (Oxford: Clarendon Press, 1976), pp. 168–86

——. 'The 1641 Depositions', in Peter Fox (ed.), *Treasures of the Library of Trinity College Dublin* (Dublin: Royal Irish Academy, 1986), pp. 111–22

——. 'The 1641 Rebellion and Anti-Popery in Ireland', in Brian MacCuarta (ed.), *Ulster 1641: Aspects of the Rising* (Belfast: Institute of Irish Studies, Queen's University Belfast, 1993), ch. 8

Clarke, Austin. *Collected Poems* (London, Oxford and New York: Dolmen and Oxford University Press, 1974)

Clarke, H., M. Hennessy and J. Prunty (eds). *Surveying Ireland's Past: Multidisciplinary Essays in Honour of Anngret Simms* (Dublin: Geography Publications, 2004)

Clarke, Howard B. (ed.). *Irish Cities* (Cork: Mercier Press, 1995)

Cleary, Joe. 'Misplaced Ideas? Colonialism, Location and Dislocation in Irish Studies', in Clare Carroll and Patricia King (eds), *Ireland and Postcolonial Theory* (Cork: Cork University Press, 2003), pp. 16–45

Commons Ireland, ii, 11 (1796)

Connell, K. H. 'The Colonisation of Waste Land in Ireland 1780–1845', *Economic History Review*, vol. 3, no. 1, 1950–1, pp. 44–71

Connolly, S. J. 'Law, Order and Popular Protest in Early Eighteenth-Century Ireland: The Case of the Houghers', in Patrick J. Corish and Ciaran Brady (eds), *Radicals, Rebels and Establishments* (Belfast: Appletree Press, 1985), pp. 51–68

——. *Religion, Law and Power: The Making of Protestant Ireland 1660–1770* (Oxford: Oxford University Press, 1992)

Corish, Patrick J. 'The Rising of 1641 and the Confederacy, 1641–5', 'The Cromwellian Conquest 1649–53', and 'The Cromwellian Regime', 1650–60', in T. W. F. X. Martin, and F. J. Byrne (eds), *A New History of Ireland, III: Early Modern Ireland 1534–1691* (Oxford: Clarendon Press, 1976), chs 11, 12, and 13

——. *The Catholic Community in the Seventeenth and Eighteenth Centuries* (Dublin: Helicon Press, 1981)

——, and Ciaran Brady (eds), *Radicals, Rebels and Establishments* (Belfast: Appletree Press, 1985), pp. 51–68.

Corkery, Daniel. *The Hidden Ireland – A Study of Gaelic Munster in the Eighteenth Century* (Dublin: Gill, 1924; new edn. Dublin: Gill and Macmillan, 1967)

Cormack, Lesley B. *Charting an Empire – Geography at the English Universities 1580–1620* (Chicago and London: University of Chicago Press, 1997)

Cortesao, Armando, and Avelino Teixeira da Mota (eds). *Portugaliae Monumenta Cartographica*, 5 vols (Lisboa: Republic of Portugal Government Publications, 1960)

Cosgrove, Denis. *Mappings* (London: Reaktion, 1999)

——, and Stephen Daniels (eds). *The Iconography of Landscape* (Cambridge: Cambridge University Press, 1988)

Coughlan, Patricia. "Cheap and Common Animals: The English Anatomy of Ireland in the Seventeenth Century', in Thomas Healy and Jonathan Sawday (eds), *Literature and the English Civil War* (Cambridge: Cambridge University Press, 1990), pp. 205–23
—— (ed.). *Spenser and Ireland: An Interdisciplinary Perspective* (Cork: Cork University Press, 1989)
Craig, Maurice. *Dublin 1660–1860* (Dublin: Allen Figgis, 1952; repr. 1968 and 1980)
——. *The Architecture of Ireland from the Earliest Times to 1880* (London and Dublin: Batsford and Eason, 1982)
Crane, Nicholas. *Mercator: The Man who Mapped the Planet* (London: Weidenfeld and Nicolson, 2002)
Crawford, W. H. *Domestic Industry in Ireland* (Dublin: Gill and Macmillan, 1972)
Cronin, Anthony. *Samuel Beckett: The Last Modernist* (London: Harper Collins, 1996)
Cronon, William. 'Modes of Prophecy and Production: Placing Nature in History', *Journal of American History*, vol. 76, 1990, pp. 22–31
Crookshank, Anne, and the Knight of Glin. *The Painters of Ireland c.1660–1920* (London: Barrie and Jenkins, 1978)
——. *Ireland's Painters 1600–1940* (New Haven and London: Yale University Press, 2002)
Crotty, R. *Irish Agricultural Production: Its Volume and Structure* (Cork: Cork University Press, 1966)
——. *Ireland in Crisis: A Study in Capitalist Colonial Underdevelopment* (Dingle: Brandon Press, 1986)
Crowley, Tony. *The Politics of Language in Ireland 1366–1922: A Sourcebook* (London and New York: Routledge, 2000)
Cullen, L. M. *Anglo-Irish trade 1660–1800* (Manchester: Manchester University Press, 1968)
——. *An Economic History of Ireland since 1660* (London: Batsford, 1972)
——. 'Population Trends in Seventeenth Century Ireland', *Economic and Social Review*, vol. 6, 1975, pp. 149–65
——. 'Economic Trends 1660–91', in T. W. Moody, F. X. Martin and F. J. Byrne (eds), *A New History of Ireland, III: Early Modern Ireland 1534–1691* (Oxford: Clarendon Press, 1976), ch. 15
——. 'Merchant Communities Overseas, the Navigation Acts and Irish and Scottish Responses', in L. M. Cullen and T. C. Smout (eds), *Comparative Aspects of Scottish and Irish Economic and Social History* (Edinburgh: John Donald, 1977), pp. 165–76
——. 'Ireland and France 1600–1900', in L. M. Cullen and F. Furet (eds), *Ireland and France; 17th–20th Centuries – Towards a Comparative Study of Rural History* (Paris: Éditions de l'École des Hautes Études en Sciences Sociales, 1980), pp. 9–20
——. *Irish Towns and Villages* (Dublin: Irish Heritage Series, no.25, 1980)
——. *The Emergence of Modern Ireland 1600–1900* (London: Batsford, 1981)
——. *The Hidden Ireland: Reassessment of a Concept* (Mullingar: Lilliput, 1988)
——. 'Patrons, Teachers and Literacy in Irish: 1700–1850', in Mary Daly and David Dickson (eds), *The Origins of Popular Literacy in Ireland: Language Change and Educational Development 1700–1920* (Dublin: University College Dublin and Trinity College Dublin, 1990), pp. 15–44
——. 'The Growth of Dublin 1600–1900', in F. H. A. Aalen, and Kevin Whelan (eds), *Dublin City and County: From Prehistory to Present* (Dublin: Geography Publications, 1992), pp. 251–78
——, and F. Furet (eds). *Ireland and France, 17th–20th Centuries – Towards a Comparative Study of Rural History* (Paris: Éditions de l'École des Hautes Études en Sciences Sociales, 1980)
——, and T.C. Smout (eds), *Comparative Aspects of Scottish and Irish Economic and Social History* (Edinburgh: John Donald, 1977)
Cunningham, Bernadette. 'The Composition of Connaught in the Lordships of Clanricard and Thomond 1577–1642', *Irish Historical Studies*, vol. 24, 1984, pp. 1–14
——. 'Native Culture and Political Change in Ireland, 1580–1640', in Ciaran Brady and Raymond Gillespie (eds), *Natives and Newcomers: The Making of Irish Colonial Society 1534–1641* (Dublin: Irish Academic Press, 1986), pp. 148–70
——. *The World of Geoffrey Keating: History, Myth and Religion in Seventeenth-Century Ireland* (Dublin: Four Courts Press, 2000)

Curtis, Edmund. 'The Court Book of Esker and Crumlin 1592–1600', *Journal of the Royal Society of Antiquaries of Ireland*, vol. 59, 1929, pp. 45–64 and 137–49, and vol. 60, 1930, pp. 38–51 and 137–49

—— (ed.). *Calendar of Ormond Deeds, 1172–1350*, vol.1 (Dublin: Irish Manuscripts Commission, 1932), and vol. 2 (1934)

Daly, Mary, and David Dickson (eds), *The Origins of Popular Literacy in Ireland: Language Change and Educational Development 1700–1920* (Dublin: University College Dublin and Trinity College Dublin, 1990)

Darby, H. C. (ed.). *An Historical Geography of England before AD 1800* (Cambridge: Cambridge University Press, 1963)

Davies, K. G. *The North Atlantic World in the Seventeenth Century* (Oxford: Oxford University Press, 1974)

Davies, Sir John (1612). *A Discovery of the True Causes why Ireland was Never Entirely Subdued*, in A. B. Grosart (ed.), *The Works in Verse and Prose of Sir John Davies*, (London and Blackburn: C. Tiplady, 1876)

de Paor, Liam. *The Peoples of Ireland: From Prehistory to Modern Times.* (London: Hutchinson, and Notre Dame: University of Notre Dame Press, 1986)

Deane, Seamus. *Strange Country: Modernity and Nationhood in Irish Writing since 1790* (Oxford: Clarendon Press, 1997)

—— (ed.). *The Field Day Anthology of Irish Writing*, vols 1–3 (Derry and London: Field Day Publications and Faber and Faber, 1991–2002)

Dee, John. *General and Rare Memorials Pertayning to the Perfect Art of Navigation* (London, 1577: facsimile, Amsterdam: Da Capo Press, 1968)

Delany, V. T. H. 'The Palatinate Court of the Liberty of Tipperary', *American Journal of Legal History*, vol. 5, 1961, pp. 95–117

Deleuze, Gilles. *Foucault*, trans. and ed. Seán Hand (Minneapolis and London: University of Minnesota Press, 1986)

Dickson, D. 'An Economic History of the Cork Region in the Eighteenth Century', Ph.D. thesis, Trinity College Dublin, 1977

——. 'On Middlemen', in Thomas Bartlett and David Hayton (eds), *Penal Era and Golden Age: Essays in Irish History 1690–1900* (Belfast: Ulster Historical Foundation, 1979), pp. 162–85

——. *New Foundations: Ireland 1660–1800* (Dublin: Helicon Press, 1987)

——. 'No Scythians Here; Women and Marriage in Seventeenth-Century Ireland', in Margaret MacCurtain and Mary O'Dowd (eds), *Women in Early Modern Ireland* (Dublin: Wolfhound Press, 1991), pp. 223–35

——. *Arctic Ireland: The Extraordinary Story of the Great Frost and Forgotten Famine of 1740–41* (Belfast: White Row Press, 1997)

——. *Old World Colony: Cork and South Munster 1630–1830* (Cork: Cork University Press, 2005)

——, C. Ó Gráda and S. Daultrey. 'Hearth-Tax, Household Size and Irish Population Change 1672–1821', *Proceedings of the Royal Irish Academy*, vol. 82C, no.6, 1982, pp. 125–50

Dickson, R. J. *Ulster Emigration to Colonial America 1718–1775* (London: Routledge and Kegan Paul, 1966)

Dillon, Charles, '*Cín Lae Uí Mhealláin*, Friar O Meallan Journal' in *Tyrone: History and Society*, 327–402

Dillon, Charles, and Henry A. Jeffries (eds). *Tyrone: History and Society* (Dublin: Geography Publications, 2000)

Dobbs, A. *An Essay on the Trade and Improvement in Ireland* (Dublin: Smith and Bruce, 1731)

Dodgshon, R. A. *The European Past: Societal Evolution and Spatial Order* (London: Macmillan, 1987)

——. *From Chiefs to Landlords: Social and Economic Change in the Western Highlands and Islands c.1493–1820* (Edinburgh: John Donald, 1998)

——, and R. A. Butlin (eds). *An Historical Geography of England and Wales* (London, New York and San Francisco: Academic Press, 1978)

Donnelly, J., and Kerby Miller (eds.). *Irish Popular Culture 1650–1850* (Dublin: Irish Academic Press, 1998)

Dorrian, Mark. 'On Some Spatial Aspects of the Colonial Discourse on Ireland', *Journal of Architecture*, vol. 6, spring 2001, pp. 27–51

Douglas, Mary. *Purity and Danger: An Analysis of the Concepts of Pollution and Taboo* (London and New York: Routledge, 1966)

Dowling, Patrick J. *The Hedge Schools of Ireland*, rev. edn. (London: Longmans, Green, 1968)

Doyle, David N. *Ireland, Irishmen and Revolutionary America 1760–1820* (Dublin and Cork:Mercier Press, 1981)

Duffy, Eamon. *The Stripping of the Altars: Traditional Religion in England 1400–1580* (New Haven and London: Yale University Press, 1992)

Duffy, Patrick J. 'The Territorial Organisation of Gaelic Landownership and Its Transformation in Co. Monaghan 1591–1640', *Irish Geography*, vol. 14, 1981, pp. 1–26

——. 'Farney in 1634: An Examination of Thomas Raven's Survey of the Essex Estate', *Clogher Record*, vol. 11, 1983, pp. 245–56

——. 'The Evolution of Estate Properties in South Ulster 1600– 1900', in W. Smyth and K. Whelan (eds), *Common Ground: Essays on the Historical Geography of Ireland* (Cork: Cork University Press, 1988), pp. 84–109

——. 'Social and Spatial Order in the MacMahon Lordship of Airghialla in the Late Sixteenth Century', in Patrick J. Duffy, David Edwards and Elizabeth Fitzpatrick (eds), *Gaelic Ireland: Land, Lordship and Settlement c.1250–c.1650* (Dublin and Portland: Four Courts Press, 2001), ch. 3

——, David Edwards and Elizabeth Fitzpatrick (eds). *Gaelic Ireland: Land, Lordship and Settlement c.1250–c.1650* (Dublin and Portland: Four Courts Press, 2001)

—— (ed.). *To and From Ireland: Planned Migration Schemes c.1600–2000* (Dublin: Geography Publications, 2004)

Duncan, James, and David Ley. *Place/Culture/Representation* (London and New York: Routledge, 1993)

Dunlop, John. *A Precarious Belonging: Presbyterians and the Conflict in Ireland* (Belfast, Blackstaff Press, 1995)

Dunlop, Robert. 'Sixteenth-Century Maps of Ireland', *English Historical Review*, vol. 20, 1905, pp. 309–37

——. *Ireland under the Commonwealth*, 2 vols (Manchester: Manchester University Press, 1913)

Dunne, Tom. 'The Gaelic Response to Conquest and Colonisation: The Evidence of the Poetry', *Studia Hibernica*, vol. 20, 1980, pp. 7–30

——. 'Ireland, Irish and Colonialism', *The Irish Review*, 30, 2003, pp. 95–104

Eckwall, Eilert. *Scandinavians and Celts in the North-West of England* (Lund: C. W. K. Gleerup, 1918)

Edwards, David. 'The Mac Giolla Padraigs (Fitzpatricks) of Upper Ossory, 1532–1641' in P. Lane and W. Nolan (eds), *Laois: History and Society* (Dublin: Geography Publications, 1999)

——. 'The Demographic Impact of the War in Elizabethan Ireland: A Case-Study of the Desmond Rebellion, 1579–83', paper given at the conference Age of Massacres: Violent Death in Ireland c.1547–1650 at Collins Barracks, Dublin, 20 April 2002

——. *The Ormond Lordship in County Kilkenny 1515–1642 – The Rise and Fall of Butler Feudal Power* (Dublin: Four Courts Press, 2003)

—— (ed.). *Regions and Rulers in Ireland 1100–1650: Essays for Kenneth Nicholls* (Dublin: Four Courts Press, 2004)

Ehrenberg, R. E. (ed.). *Pattern and Process: Research in Historical Geography* (Cambridge, MA: Harvard University Press, 1975)

Eisenstein, Elizabeth E. *The Printing Press as an Agent of Change: Communication and Cultural Transformations in Early Modern Europe* (Cambridge: Cambridge University Press, 1979)

Elliott, Bruce. 'Emigration from South Leinster to Eastern Upper Canada', in Kevin Whelan and William Nolan (eds), *Wexford: History and Society* (Dublin: Geography Publications, 1987), ch. 5

Elliott, Marianne. *The Catholics of Ulster: A History* (London and New York: Penguin Books, 2000)

Ellis, Steven G. 'Economic Problems of the Church: Why the Reformation failed in Ireland', *Journal of Ecclesiastical History*, vol. 41, no. 2, 1990, pp. 239–65

——. *Tudor Ireland: Crown and Community and the Conflict of Cultures, 1470–1603* (London and New York: Longman, 1985)

Empey, C. A. 'The Butler Lordship', *Journal of the Butler Society*, vols 1–3, 1970–1, pp. 174–87
——. 'Medieval Knocktopher', *Old Kilkenny Review*, vol.2, 1982, pp. 441–52
——, and Katharine Simms. 'The Ordinances of the White Earl and the Problem of Coign in the Middle Ages', *Proceedings of the Royal Irish Academy*, vol. 75C, 1975, pp. 161–87
Evans, E. Estyn. *Irish Heritage* (Dundalk: Dundalgan Press, 1942)
——. 'The Scotch-Irish in the New World: An Atlantic Heritage', *Journal of the Royal Society of Antiquaries of Ireland*, vol. 95, 1965, pp. 39–49
——. 'Scotch-Irish – Their Cultural Adaptation in the American Old West', in E. R. R. Green (ed.), *Essays in Scotch-Irish History* (New York: Humanities Press, 1969), pp. 69–86
——. *The Personality of Ireland – Habitat, Heritage and History* (Cambridge: Cambridge University Press, 1973; 2nd edn., Belfast: Blackstaff Press, 1981)
——. 'Old Ireland and New England', *Ulster Journal of Archaeology*, vol. 12, 1949, pp. 104–12
Fagan, Patricia. 'The Origin and Development of Villages in County Dublin', unpublished MA thesis, University College Dublin, 1987
Fellman, Allen. *Formations of Violence: The Narrative of the Body and Political Terror in Northern Ireland* (Chicago: University Chicago Press, 1991)
Fenlon, Jane. 'Restoring the Butler Heritage', *Irish Arts Review*, autumn 2002, pp. 95–103
Fennelly, Teddy. *Thomas Prior: His Life, Times and Legacy: The Story of the Founder of the Royal Dublin Society* (Naas: Leinster Leader, 2001)
Fewer, T. G. 'The Hearth Money Roll of 1665 for the City of Kilkenny', *Old Kilkenny Review*, vol. 53, 2001, pp. 89–102.
ffoliott, R. 'Irish Census Returns and Census Substitutes', in D. F. Begley (ed.), *Irish Genealogy: A Record Finder* (Dublin: Heraldic Artists, 1981)
Fiants of the Tudor Sovereigns – During the reigns of Henry VIII, Edward VI, Philip and Mary, and Elizabeth I, The Irish (Dublin, Edmund Burke, 1994), vols 1 and 2
Fishman, J. A. 'Language Maintenance and Language Shift as a Field of Enquiry', *Linguistics*, vol. 9, 1964, pp. 32–70
Fitzgerald, Garret. 'Estimates for Baronies of Minimum Level of Irish-speaking amongst Successful Decennial Cohorts 1771–1781 to 1861–1871', *Proceedings of the Royal Irish Academy*, vol. 84C, 1984, pp. 3–155
——. 'The Decline of the Irish Language 1771–1881', in Mary Daly and David Dickson (eds), *The Origins of Popular Literacy in Ireland: Language Change and Educational Development 1700–1920* (Dublin: University College Dublin and Trinity College Dublin), pp. 59–72
Fitzpatrick, Elizabeth. '*Leaca* and Gaelic Inauguration Ritual in Medieval Ireland', in R Welander, I. Breeze and T. Owen Clancy (eds), *The Stone of Destiny: Artefact and Icon* (Edinburgh: Historic Scotland, 2003), pp. 107–21
Flatman, R. 'Some Inhabitants of the Baronies of Uppercross and Newcastle, County Dublin, ca.1650', *Irish Genealogist*, vol. 7, 1989, pp. 496–504, vol. 8, 1990, pp. 3–14, vol. 9, 1991, pp. 162–74
Flatrès, Pierre. *Géographie Rurale de Quatre Contrées Celtiques* (Rennes: Librairie Universitaire J. Plihon, 1957)
Flinn, Michael (ed.). *Scottish Population History from the 17th Century to the 1930s* (Cambridge: Cambridge University Press, 1977)
Fogleman, Aaron. 'Migration to the Thirteen British North America Colonies, 1700–1775: New Estimates', *Journal of Interdisciplinary History*, vol. 22, no. 4, 1992, pp. 691–709
Ford, Alan. *The Protestant Reformation in Ireland 1590–1641* (Frankfurt am Main: Verlag Peter Lang, 1985; new edn. Dublin: Four Courts Press, 1997)
——. 'The Protestant Reformation in Ireland', in Ciaran Brady and Raymond Gillespie (eds.), *Natives and Newcomers: Essays in the Making of Irish Colonial Society 1534–1641* (Dublin: Irish Academic Press, 1986), pp. 50–74
Foster, R. F. *Modern Ireland 1600–1977* (London: Penguin Books, 1988)
—— (ed.). *The Oxford Illustrated History of Ireland* (Oxford: Oxford University Press, 1989)
Foster, Sally, Allan Macinnes and Ronald Macinnes (eds). *Scottish Power Centers* (Glasgow: Cruithne Press, 1988)
Foucault, Michel. *The Archaeology of Knowledge and the Discourse on Language* trans. Alan Sheridan (London and New York: Tavistock Publications, 1972)

——. *Surveiller et Punir: Naissance de la Prison* (Paris: Editions Gallimard, 1975), translated as *Discipline and Punish: The Birth of the Prison* by Alan Sheridan (London and New York: Allen Lane and Pantheon, 1977)

Fox, Peter (ed.). *Treasures of the Library of Trinity College Dublin* (Dublin: Royal Irish Academy, 1986)

Freeman, T. W. *Pre-Famine Ireland: A Study in Historical Geography* (Manchester: Manchester University Press, 1957)

——. *Ireland: A General and Regional Geography*, 2nd edn.(London: Methuen, 1960)

Friel, Brian. *Translations* (London: Faber and Faber, 1981)

Gailey, R. A. 'The Scots Element in North Irish Popular Culture: Some Problems in the Interpretation of Historical Acculturation', *Ethnologia Europea*, vol. 8, 1975, pp. 2–21

——, and D. Ó hÓgáin (eds). *Gold under the Furze: Studies in Folk Tradition* (Dublin: Glendale Press, 1982)

Gallwey, Hubert (ed.). 'The Dispossessed Landowners of Ireland, 1664 – Lists Given to the Duke of Ormonde to Select His Nominees for Restoration', *Irish Genealogist*,vol. 4, no.4, 1971, pp. 285–8

——. 'Tobin of Killaghy – The Line of Descent from 1514 to 1708', *Irish Genealogist*, vol. 5, no. 2, 1975, pp. 190–200

Garvan, A. N. *Architecture and Town Planning in Colonial Connecticut* (New Haven: Yale University Press, 1951)

Gaustad, E. S. *Historical Atlas of Religion in America* (New York: Harper and Row, 1962)

Gerald of Wales, *The History and Topography of Ireland*, trans. John J. O'Meara (London: Penguin, 1982)

Gernon, Luke. 'A Discourse of Ireland (1620)', reproduced in C. Litton Falkiner, *Illustrations of Irish History and Topography* (London, New York, Bombay: Longmans, Green, 1904)

Gibbons, Luke. *Transformations in Irish Culture* (Cork: Cork University Press, 1996)

Gillespie, Raymond. 'Thomas Raven and the Mapping of the Clandeboye Estates', *Journal of the Bangor Historical Society*, vol. 1, 1980, pp. 7–9

——. *Colonial Ulster – The Settlement of East Ulster 1600–1641* (Cork: Cork University Press, 1985)

——. 'The End of an Era: Ulster and the Outbreak of the 1641 Rising', in Ciaran Brady and Raymond Gillespie (eds), *Natives and Newcomers: Essays in the Making of Irish Colonial Society, 1534–1641* (Dublin: Irish Academic Press, 1986), pp. 191–214

——. *The Transformation of the Irish Economy 1550–1700* (Dundalk: Studies in Irish Economic and Social History 6, 1991)

——. 'Explorers, Exploiters and Entrepreneurs: Early Modern Ireland and Its Context, 1500–1700', in B. J. Graham and L. J. Proudfoot (eds), *An Historical Geography of Ireland* (London and Toronto: Academic Press, 1993), pp. 123–57

——. 'The Irish Economy at War, 1641–52', in Jane H. Ohlmeyer (ed.), *Ireland: From Independence to Occupation 1641–1660* (Cambridge: Cambridge University Press, 1995), pp. 160–80

——, and Gerard Moran (eds). *'A Various Country': Essays in Mayo History 1500–1900* (Westport: Foilseacháin Náisiúnta Teoranta, 1987)

Gleeson, Dermot F. *The Last Lords of Ormond*, new edn. (Nenagh: Relay Books 2001; 1st edn. London: Sheed and Ward, 1938)

Goblet, Y. M. *La Transformation de la Géographie Politique de l'Irlande au XVIIeme Siècle dans les Cartes et Essais Anthropogéographiques de Sir William Petty*, 3 vols (Paris: Berger-Levrault, 1930)

Goff, Henry. 'English Conquest of an Irish Barony: The Changing Patterns of Land Ownership in the Barony of Scarawalsh 1540–1640', in Kevin Whelan and William Nolan (eds), *Wexford: History and Society* (Dublin: Geography Publications, 1957), pp. 122–50

Goodman, P. (ed.). *Essays in American Colonial History* (New York: Holt, Rinehart and Winston, 1967)

Gordon, Colin (ed.). *Michel Foucault, Power/Knowledge: Selected Interviews and Other Writings 1972–1977* (Hassocks: Harvester Press, 1980)

Gottman, J. (ed.). *Centre and Periphery: Spatial Variation in Politics* (London and Beverly Hills: Sage Publications, 1980)

Graham, B. J. 'Anglo-Norman Settlement in County Meath', *Proceedings of the Royal Irish Academy*, vol. 75C, no. 11, 1975, pp. 223–48

——, and L. J. Proudfoot (eds). *An Historical Geography of Ireland* (London and Toronto: Academic Press, 1993)

Graham, Brian, and Catherine Nash (eds). *Modern Historical Geographies* (Harlow: Pearson Education, 2000)

Graham, J. M. 'South-West Donegal in the 17th century', *Irish Geography*, vol. 2, 1970, pp. 136–53

——. 'Rural Society in Connacht, 1600–1640', in Nicholas Stephens and Robin E. Glasscock (eds), *Irish Geographical Studies in Honour of E. Estyn Evans* (Belfast: Queen's University Belfast, 1970), ch. 12

Greaves, Richard L. *God's Other Children: Protestant Nonconformists and the Emergence of Denominational Churches in Ireland, 1660–1700* (Stanford: Stanford University Press, 1998)

Green, E. R. R. (ed.). *Essays in Scotch-Irish History* (New York: Humanities Press, 1969)

Greenblatt, Stephen. *Renaissance Self-Fashioning: From More to Shakespeare* (Chicago and London: University of Chicago Press, 1980)

Greene, Jack P. *Interpreting Early America: Historiographical Essays* (Charlotteville and London: University Press of Virginia, 1996)

Gregory, Derek. *The Colonial Present: Afghanistan: Palestine: Iraq.* (Maldon, Oxford and Carlton: Blackwell, 2004)

Grell, Ole Peter. *Calvinist Exiles in Tudor and Stuart England* (Aldershot: Scholar Press, 1996)

——. 'Godly Charity or Political Aid? – Irish Protestants and International Calvinism 1641–1645', *Historical Journal*, vol. 39, no. 3, 1996, pp. 743–53

Grosart, A. B. *The Works in Verse and Prose of Sir John Davies* (London and Blackburn: C. Tiplady, 1876)

Gurrin, Brian. *Pre-Census Sources for Irish Demography* (Dublin: Four Courts Press, 2002)

Gwynn, E. *The Metrical Dindshenchas*, Todd Lecture Series X (Dublin: Royal Irish Academy, 1913)

Hadfield, Andrew, and Willy Maley (eds). *Edmund Spenser: A View of the State of Ireland* (Oxford: Oxford University Press, 1997)

Hallinan, Michael. *Tipperary County: People and Places: An Anthology of the Evolution of County Tipperary* (Dublin: Kincora Press, 1993)

Hannigan, K., and W. Nolan (eds). *Wicklow: History and Society* (Dublin: Geography Publications, 1994)

Hardinge, W. H. 'Observations on the Earliest Known Manuscript Returns of the People in Ireland', *Transactions of the Royal Irish Academy*, vol. 24, 1864–5, pp. 317–28

——. 'List of Innocent Proprietors', *Transactions of the Royal Irish Academy*, vol. 24, no. 3, 1865, Appendix B, pp. 294–303

——. 'On Circumstances Attending the Outbreak of the Civil War in Ireland . . . The Numerical Extent and Manner of the Transplantation of Irish into Connaught and Clare', *Proceedings of the Royal Irish Academy*, vol. 24, 1866, pp. 379–417

——. 'The Civil War in Ireland 1641–1652', *Transactions of the Royal Irish Academy*, vol. 24, 1866, pp. 379–420

Harley, J. Brian. 'Deconstructing the Map', *Cartographica*, vol. 26, no. 2, 1989, pp. 1–20

——. 'Maps, Knowledge and Power', in Denis Cosgrove and Stephen Daniels (eds), *The Iconography of Landscape* (Cambridge: Cambridge University Press, 1988), pp. 277–312

——, and David Woodward (eds). *History of Cartography* (Chicago and London: University of Chicago Press, 1987)

Harvey, David. *The Condition of Postmodernity: An Enquiry into the Origins of Cultural Change* (Cambridge, MA: Blackwell, 1989)

Hayden, Robert. 'Imagined Communities and Real Victims: Self-Determination and Ethnic Cleansing in Yugoslavia', *American Ethnologist*, vol. 23, no. 4, 1996, pp. 783–801

Hayes-McCoy, G. A. (ed.). *Ulster and Other Irish Maps c.1600* (Dublin: Stationery Office, for the Irish Manuscripts Commission, 1964)

Healy, Thomas, and Jonathan Sawday (eds). *Literature and the English Civil War* (Cambridge: Cambridge University Press, 1990)

Healy, William. *History and Antiquities of Kilkenny (County and City)* (Kilkenny: Egan, 1893)
Heaney, Seamus. 'Markings', *Seeing Things* (London: Faber and Faber, 1991)
——. *Preoccupations: Selected Prose 1968–1978* (London: Faber and Faber, 1980)
Henry, Gráinne. *The Irish Military Community in Spanish Flanders, 1586–1621* (Dublin: Irish Academic Press, 1992)
Herries Davies, G. L (ed.). *Irish Geography: The Geographical Society of Ireland Golden Jubilee volume 1934–1984* (Dublin: Geography Society of Ireland, 1984)
Hickey, Kieran R. 'A Geographical Perspective on the Decline and Extermination of the Irish Wolf *Canis Lupus* – An Initial Assessment', *Irish Geography*, vol. 33, no. 2, 2000, pp. 185–98
Hickson, Mary. *Ireland in the Seventeenth Century or The Irish Massacres of 1641–42* (London: Longmans Green, 1884)
Higbee, E. 'The Three Earths of New England', *Geographical Review*, vol. 42, 1952, pp. 410–28
Hill, J. Michael. 'The Origins of the Scottish Plantations in Ulster in 1625: A Reinterpretation', *Journal of British Studies*, vol. 32, no. 1, 1993, pp. 24–43
Hodgen, Margaret T. *Early Anthropology in the Sixteenth and Seventeenth Centuries* (Philadelphia: University of Pennsylvania Press, 1964)
Hoffman, Ronald. *Princes of Ireland, Planters of Maryland: A Carroll Saga, 1500–1782* (Chapel Hill and London: University of North Carolina Press, 2000)
Hofstadter, R. *America at 1750: A Social Portrait* (London: Alfred A. Knopf, 1972)
Hooper, Glenn. 'Writings and Landscape in Early Modern Ireland', *Literature and History*, vol. 5, no. 2, autumn 1996, pp. 1–18
Hore, H. F. 'Woods and Fastnesses in Ancient Ireland', *Ulster Journal of Archaeology*, first series, vol.6, 1858, pp. 145–61
Horner, A. A. 'Carton, Co. Kildare – A Case Study in the Making of an Irish Demesne', *Quarterly Bulletin of Irish Georgian Society*, vol. 18, nos. 2 and 3, 1980, pp. 66–92
Howe, S. *Ireland and Empire: Colonial Legacies in Irish History and Culture* (Oxford: Oxford University Press, 2000)
Hulton, Paul. *America 1585 – The Complete Drawings of John White* (Chapel Hill: University of North Carolina Press, 1984)
Hunt, Lyn (ed.). *The New Cultural History* (Berkeley, Los Angeles, and London: University of California Press, 1989)
Hunter, R. J. 'Towns in the Ulster Plantation', *Studia Hibernica*, vol. 2, 1971, pp. 40–79
——. 'Ulster Plantation Towns 1609–41', in David Harkness and Mary O'Dowd (eds), *The Town in Ireland: Historical Studies XIII* (Belfast: Appletree Press, 1981), pp. 55–80
Ivins, William. *Prints and Visual Communication* (New York: Da Capo Press, 1969)
Jackson, Donald. *Intermarriage in Ireland 1550–1650* (Montreal and Minneapolis: Cultural and Educational Productions, 1970)
James, F. G. 'Irish Colonial Trade in the Eighteenth Century', *William and Mary Quarterly*, vol. 20, 1963, pp. 574–84
——. *Ireland in the Empire 1688–1770* (Cambridge, MA: Harvard University Press, 1973)
James, Preston E. *All Possible Worlds – A History of Geographical Ideas* (Indiana: Bobbs-Merrill, 1972)
Jennings, Francis. *The Invasion of America: Colonialism and the Cant of Conquest* (Chapel Hill and London: University of North Carolina Press, 1975)
Jones, E., and G. Mingay (eds). *Land, Labour and Population in the Industrial Revolution* (London: Edward Arnold, 1967)
Jones, H. M. 'The Origins of the Colonial Idea in England', *Proceedings of the American Philosophical Society*, vol. 89, 1945, pp. 448–65
Jones Hughes, T. 'Landlordism in the Mullet of Mayo', *Irish Geography*, vol. 4, no. 1, 1959, pp. 16–34
——. 'The Origin and Growth of Towns in Ireland', *University Review*, vol. 2, no. 7, 1960, pp. 8–15
——. 'Landholding and Settlement in the Cooley Peninsula of Louth', *Irish Geography*, vol. 4, no. 3, 1961, pp. 145–74
——. 'Society and Settlement in Nineteenth-Century Ireland', *Irish Geography*, vol. 5, no. 2, 1965, pp. 79–96

——. 'Town and Baile in Irish Place-Names', in R. Glasscock and N. Stephens (eds), *Irish Geographical Studies* (Belfast: Queen's University Belfast, 1971)

——. 'Village and Town in Nineteenth Century Ireland', *Irish Geography*, vol. 14, 1981, pp. 99–106

——. 'The Large Farm in Nineteenth Century Ireland', in R. A. Gailey and D. Ó hÓgáin (eds), *Gold under the Furze: Studies in Folk Tradition* (Dublin, Glendale Press, 1982), pp. 93–100

——. 'Historical Geography of Ireland from *circa* 1700', in G. L. Herries Davies (ed.), *Irish Geography: Tthe Geographical Society of Ireland Golden Jubilee Volume 1934–1984* (Dublin: Geographical Society of Ireland, 1984), pp. 149–66

——. 'Landholding and Settlement in County Tipperary in the Nineteenth Century', in William Nolan and Thomas G. McGrath (eds), *Tipperary: History and Society* (Dublin: Geography Publications, 1985), pp. 339–66

——. 'The Estate System of Landholding in Nineteenth-Century Ireland', in William Nolan (ed.), *The Shaping of Ireland – The Geographical Perspective* (Cork: Mercier Press, 1986), pp. 137–50

Joyce, Patrick W. *The Origin and History of Irish Names of Places*, 3 vols (repr. Dublin: Edmund Burke Publisher, 1995)

Kallan, Jeffrey L. 'Bilingualism and the Genesis of Hiberno-English Syntax', *Teanga*, vol. 5, 1985, pp. 104–6

Kearns, Gerry. 'Bare Life and the Territorial Structure of Britain and Ireland', unpublished paper, 2005

Kein, C. Ray. 'Primogeniture and Entail in Virginia', *William and Mary Quarterly*, vol. 25, no. 1, 1968, pp. 580–5

Kelly, Fergus. *Early Irish Farming* (Dublin: Dublin Institute for Advanced Studies, 1997)

Kelly, James, and Uaitear MacGearailt (eds). *Dublin and Dubliners: Essays in the History and Literature of Dublin City* (Dublin: Helicon Press, 1990)

Kelly, Mary. '"We do see the state of that kingdome principally with your eyes": Edmund Spenser, Fynes Moryson and William Petty and the Imaginative Geographies of Colonialism', unpublished M.Phil. thesis, University College Cork, 1999

Kennedy, Liam. *Colonialism, Religion and Nationalism in Ireland* (Belfast: Institute of Irish Studies, 1996)

Kennelly, Brendan (ed.). *The Penguin Book of Irish Verse* (Middlesex and Baltimore: Penguin Books, 1970)

Kerrigan, Paul M. *Castles and Fortifications in Ireland 1485–1945* (Cork: Collins Press, 1995)

Ketch, Catherine. 'County Waterford from the Civil Survey', in W. Nolan, T. P. Power and D. Cowman (eds), *Waterford: History and Society* (Dublin: Geography Publications, 1992), pp. 199–226

Kew, Graham. *The Irish Sections of Fynes Moryson's Unpublished Itinerary* (Dublin: Irish Manuscripts Commission, 1998)

Kiberd, Declan. *Irish Classics* (London: Granta Books, 2000)

King, Seamus J. *Tipperary's GAA Story 1935–1984* (Naas: Leinster Leader, 1988)

Kinsella, Thomas. *Collected Poems* (Manchester: Carcanet Press, 2001)

Kirkham, Graeme. 'Literacy in North-West Ulster 1680–1800', in Mary Daly and David Dickson (eds), *The Origins of Popular Literacy in Ireland: Language Change and Educational Development 1700–1920* (Dublin: University College Dublin and Trinity College Dublin), pp. 73–96

Klein, Bernhard. *Maps and the Writing of Space in Early Modern England and Ireland* (Basingstoke and New York: Palgrave, 2001)

Laffan, Thomas (ed.). *Tipperary Families: Being the Hearth Money Records for 1665–6–7* (Dublin: Duffy, 1911)

Lane, P., and W. Nolan (eds). *Laois: History and Society* (Dublin: Geography Publications, 1999)

Lansdowne, Marquis of (ed.). *Petty Papers*, 2 vols (London, Boston and New York: Constable and Houghton Mifflin, 1927)

Larcom, Thomas A (ed.). *A History of the Survey of Ireland commonly called the Down Survey by Doctor William Petty, A.D. 1655–6* (Dublin: Irish Archaeological Society, 1851)

Lavie, Smadar, and Ted Swedenburg. *Displacement, Diaspora and Geographies of Identity* (Durham and London: Duke University Press, 1996)

Leerssen, Joep. *Mere Irish and Fíor-Ghael: Studies in the Idea of Irish Nationality, Its Development and Literary Expression Prior to the Nineteenth Century*, 2nd edn. (Cork: Cork University Press, 1996), Critical Conditions series, vol. 3

Leigh Dunnigan, Brian. *Frontier Metropolis: Picturing Early Detroit, 1701–1838* (Detroit: Wayne State University Press, 2001)

Leister, Ingeborg. *Das Werden der Agrarlandschaft in der Graftschaft Tipperary (Irland)* (Marburg: Marburger Geographische Schriften, 1963)

——. *Peasant Open-Field Farming and Territorial Organisation in County Tipperary*, (Marburg: Lahn, 1976)

Lemon, J. *The Best Poor Man's Country – A Geographical Study of Early South Eastern Pennsylvania* (Baltimore: John Hopkins University Press, 1972)

Lenihan, Pádraig. 'War and Population, 1649–52', *Irish Economic and Social History*, vol. 24, 1997

——. *Confederate Catholics at War 1641–1649* (Cork: Cork University Press, 2001)

Lenman, Bruce. *England's Colonial Wars 1550–1688: Conflicts, Empire and National Identity* (London: Longman, 2001)

Lennon, Colm. 'Civil Life and Religion in Early Seventeenth-Century Dublin', *Archivium Hibernicum*, vol. 38, 1983, pp. 14–25

——. *The Lords of Dublin in the Age of Reformation* (Dublin: Irish Academic Press, 1989)

——. *Sixteenth-Century Ireland: The Incomplete Conquest* (Dublin: Gill and Macmillan, 1994)

Lepore, Jill. *The Name of War: King Philip's War and the Origins of American Identity* (New York: Alfred A. Knopf, 1998)

Leyrman, Christine L. *Commerce and Culture: The Maritime Communities of Colonial Massachusetts, 1690–1750* (New York and London: Norton, 1984)

Lindley, Keith. 'The Impact of the 1641 Rebellion upon England and Wales, 1641–5', *Irish Historical Studies*, vol. 18, no. 70, 1972, pp. 143–76

——. 'Irish Adventurers and Godly Militants in the 1640s', *Irish Historical Studies*, vol. 29, no. 113, May 1994, pp. 1–12

Litton Falkiner, C. *Illustrations of Irish History and Topography mainly of the Seventeenth Century* (London, New York and Bombay: Longmans, Green, 1904)

Livingstone, David N. *The Geographical Tradition* (Oxford: Blackwell, 1992)

——, and Charles W. J. Withers (eds). *Geography and Enlightenment* (Chicago and London: University of Chicago Press, 1999)

Lockhart, A. *Some Aspects of Emigration from Ireland to the North American Colonies between 1660 and 1775* (New York: Arno Press, 1976)

Loeber, Rolf. 'Irish Country Houses and Castles of the late Caroline Period: An Unremembered Past Recaptured', *Quarterly Bulletin of the Irish Georgian Society*, vol. 16, no. 102, 1973, pp. 1–60

——. 'New Light on Co. Wexford Architecture and Estates in the 17th Century', *Journal of the Wexford Historical Society*, vol. 12, 1988–9, pp. 66–71

——. *The Geography and Practice of English Colonisation in Ireland 1534 to 1609* (Athlone: Group for the Study of Irish Historic Settlement, 3, 1991)

——. 'Settlers' Utilisation of the Natural Resources'; in K. Hannigan and W. Nolan (eds), *Wicklow: History and Society* (Dublin: Geography Publications, 1994), ch. 8

Mac Mathúna, Liam. 'An Ghaeilge i mBaile Átha Cliath', in James Kelly and Uaiteur MacGearailt (eds), *Dublin and Dubliners: Essays in the History and Literature of Dublin City* (Dublin: Helicon Press, 1990), pp. 147–73

Macafee, William. 'The Colonisation of the Maghera Region of South Derry during the Seventeenth and Eighteenth centuries', *Ulster Folklife*, vol. 23, 1977, pp. 70–91

——, and Valerie Morgan. 'Population in Ulster 1660–1760', in P. Roebuck (ed.), *Plantation to Partition: Essays in Ulster History in Honour of J. L. McCracken* (Belfast: Blackstaff Press, 1981), pp. 46–63

Macalister, R. A. S. (ed.), *Lebar Gabála Érenn: The Book of the Taking of Ireland* (Dublin: Irish Texts Society, 1938)

McCabe, Richard A. 'The Fate of Irena: Spenser and Political Violence', in P. Coughlan (ed.),

Spenser and Ireland: An Interdisciplinary Perspective (Cork: Cork University Press, 1989), pp. 109–26

MacCana, Proinsias. 'The Rise of the Later Schools of Filidheacht', *Ériu*, vol. 25, 1974, pp. 126–46

McCarthy, Mark. 'The Forging of an Atlantic Port City: Socio-Economic and Physical Transformations in Cork 1600–1700; *Urban History*, vol. 28, no. 1, 2001, pp. 25-45

MacCarthy-Morrogh, Michael. *The Munster Plantation: English Migration to Southern Ireland 1583–1641* (Oxford: Oxford University Press, 1986)

——. 'The English Presence in Early Seventeenth Century Munster', in Ciaran Brady and Raymond Gillespie (eds), *Natives and Newcomers: Essays on the Making of Irish Colonial Society 1534–1641* (Dublin: Irish Academic Press, 1986), pp. 171–90

McCourt, Desmond. 'County Derry and New England – The Scotch-Irish Migration of 1718', in D. McCourt (ed.), *County Londonderry Handbook* (Belfast: Nicholson and Bass, for Londonderry County Council, 1964), pp. 87–101

McCracken, Eileen. *The Irish Woods since Tudor Times – Their Distribution and Exploitation* (Newton Abbot: David and Charles, 1971)

MacCuarta, Brian. 'A Planter's Interaction with Gaelic Culture: Sir Matthew de Renzi 1577–1634', *Irish Economic and Social History*, vol.1, no. 17, 1993, pp. 1–17

—— (ed.). *Ulster 1641: Aspects of the Rising* (Belfast: Institute of Irish Studies, Queen's University of Belfast, 1993

MacCurtain, Margaret. *Tudor and Stuart Ireland* (Dublin and London: Gill and Macmillan, 1972)

——, and Mary O'Dowd (eds). *Women in Early Modern Ireland* (Dublin: Wolfhound Press, 1991)

McCusker, John J., and Russell R. Menard. *The Economy of British America* (Chapel Hill and London: University of North Carolina Press, 1985)

McDowell, R.B. 'Ireland in the 18th Century British Empire', *Historical Studies*, vol. 11, 1974, pp. 49–63

MacEiteagaín, Darren. 'The Renaissance and the Late Medieval Lordship of Tír Chonaill 1461–1555', in W. Nolan, L. Ronayne, and M. Dunlevy (eds), *Donegal: History and Society* (Dublin: Geography Publications, 1992), pp. 203–28

McErlean, T. 'The Irish Townland Scheme of Landscape Organisation', in T. Reeves-Smyth and F. Hammond (eds), *Landscape Archaeology in Ireland* (Oxford: British Archaeological Reports, No. 116, 1983), pp. 315–39

MacGiolla Choille B., and R. C. Simington (eds). *Books of Survey and Distribution, Counties Roscommon, Mayo, Galway and Clare*, vols 1–4 (Dublin: Irish Manuscripts Commission, 1949–62)

Machiavelli, Niccolo. *The Prince*, rev. trans. Robert M. Adams (New York: Modern Library, 1940)

Macinnes, Allan I. *Clanship, Commerce and the House of Stuart; 1603–1758* (East Linton: Tuckwell Press, 1996)

McKenny, Kevin J. 'British Settler Society in Donegal c.1625–1685', in W. Nolan, L. Ronayne and M. Dunlevy (eds), *Donegal: History and Society* (Dublin: Geography Publications, 1995), ch. 11

MacLaughlin, Jim. *Reimagining the Nation-State: The Contested Terrains of Nation-Building* (London and Sterling, VA: Pluto Press, 2000)

McLaughlin Green, C. *American Cities in the Growth of a Nation* (London: University of London, 1957)

McLeod, Wilson. *Divided Gaels: Gaelic Cultural Identities in Scotland and Ireland c.1200–1650* (Oxford: Oxford University Press, 2004)

——, and Máire Ní Annracháin (eds). *Cruth na Tíre* (Coiscéim: Baile Átha Cliath, 2003)

MacLysaght, Edward. *Irish Life in the Seventeenth Century* (Cork: Cork University Press, 1969)

——. 'Christian Names in Ireland', *North Munster Antiquarian Journal*, vol. 13, 1970, pp. 53–6

——. *The Surnames of Ireland* (Dublin: Irish Academic Press, 1980)

——. *Irish Families: Their Names, Arms and Origins* (Dublin: Irish Academic Press, 1991_

——. *More Irish Families* (Dublin: Irish Academic Press, 1996)

McManis, D. R. *Colonial New England* (Oxford: Oxford University Press, 1975)

McMinn, Joseph (ed.). *Swift's Irish Pamphlets: An Introductory Selection* (Gerrards Cross: Colin Smythe, 1991)

——. *Jonathan's Travels: Swift and Ireland* (Belfast and New York: Appletree Press and St Martins Press, 1994)

McNeill, Charles. 'The Secular Jurisdiction of the Early Archbishops of Dublin', *Journal of the Royal Society of Antiquaries of Ireland*, vol. 45, 1915, pp. 81–108

McNeill, W. H. *The Rise of the West* (Chicago: University of Chicago Press, 1963, and Mentor Paperback, 1965)

MacNiocaill, Gearóid. *Irish Population before Petty*, O'Donnell Lecture (Dublin: National University of Ireland, 1981)

Maley, Willy. *Nation, State and Empire in English Renaissance Literature: Shakespeare to Milton* (Basingstoke and New York: Palgrave Macmillan, 2003)

Malkki, Liisa H. *Purity and Exile: Violence, Memory and National Cosmology among Hutu Refugees in Tanzania* (Chicago and London: University of Chicago Press, 1994)

Manning, Conleth (ed.). *Dublin and Beyond the Pale* (Bray: Wordwell, 1998)

Mannion, John J. *Irish Settlement in Eastern Canada – A study of Cultural Transfer and Adaptation* (Toronto: Toronto University Press, 1974)

Marshall, P. (ed.). *The Oxford History of the British Empire: The Eighteenth Century* (Oxford: Oxford University Press, 1998)

Martin, Geoffrey L., and Preston E. James. *All Possible Worlds: A History of Geographical Ideas* (New York: Wiley, 1993)

Martin, John H. 'The Social Geography of Mid Nineteenth Century Dublin City', in William J. Smyth and Kevin Whelan (eds), *Common Ground: Essays on the Historical Geography of Ireland* (Cork: Cork University Press, 1988), pp. 173–88

Maxwell, Constantia (ed.). *Irish History from Contemporary Sources 1509–1610* (London: Allen and Unwin, 1923)

Meigs, Samantha A. *The Reformations in Ireland: Tradition and Confessionalism, 1400–1690* (Dublin: Gill and Macmillan, 1997)

Meinig, D. W. 'The American Colonial Era: A Geographical Commentary', *Proceedings of the Royal Geographical Society, South Australian Branch*, 1957–8

——. 'Geographical Analysis of Imperial Expansion', in Alan Baker and Mark Billinge (eds), *Period and Place: Research Methods in Historical Geography* (Cambridge: Cambridge University Press, 1982), pp. 71–6

——. 'Outreach: The Creation of an Atlantic World', part 1 of *The Shaping of America: A Geographical Perspective of 500 years of History, I: Atlantic America 1492–1800* (New Haven and London: Yale University Press, 1986), pp. 3–78

Melville, Herman. *Moby-Dick; or, The Whale* (1851; repr. New York: Modern Library, 1992)

Merrens, H. R. *Colonial North Carolina in the Eighteenth Century* (Chapel Hill: University of North Carolina Press, 1964)

——. 'Settlement of the Colonial Atlantic Seaboard', in R. E. Ehrenberg (ed.), *Pattern and Process: Research in Historical Geography* (Cambridge, MA: Harvard University Press, 1975), pp. 235–43

Mervyn, Audely. *An Exact Relation of All Such Occurrences as have Happened in the Several Counties Donegall, London-Derry, in the North of Ireland since the Beginning of this Horrid, Bloody and Unparaleld Rebellion there, Begun in October last* (London: The Downes and William Bladen, 1642)

Mignolo, Walter D. *The Darker Side of the Renaissance: Literacy, Territoriality and Colonisation* (Ann Arbor: University of Michigan Press, 1995)

Miller, Kirby A. '"Scotch-Irish"; "Black Irish" and "Real Irish": Emigrants and Identities in the Old South', in A. Bielenberg (ed.), *The Irish Diaspora* (London and New York: Longman, 2000), pp. 139–42

Millet, B. 'Irish Literature in Latin, 1550–1700', in T. W. Moody, F. X. Martin and F. J. Byrne (eds), *New History of Ireland, III: Early Modern Ireland 1534–1691* (Oxford: Clarendon Press, 1976), pp. 561–86

Mitchell, Frank. *The Irish Landscape* (London: Collins, 1976)

Mitchison, Rosalind, and Peter Roebuck (eds). *Economy and Society in Scotland and Ireland 1500–1939* (Edinburgh: John Donald, 1998)

Mohl, R. A., and N. Betten (eds). *Urban America in Historical Perspective* (New York: Weybright and Talley, 1970)

Montague, John. 'The Grafted Tongue', *The Rough Field* (Oldcastle: Gallery Press, 1989).

Moody, T. W. *The Londonderry Plantation 1609–41* (Belfast: Wm Mullan, 1939)

——, and F. X. Martin (eds). *The Course of Irish History* (Cork: Mercier Press, 1967)

—— , F. X. Martin and F. J. Byrne (eds). *A New History of Ireland, III: Early Modern Ireland 1534–1691* (Oxford: Clarendon Press, 1976)

Moore, R. I. (ed.)., *The Hamlyn Historical Atlas* (London, New York, Sydney,Toronto: Hamlyn, 1981), map 47 'The Thirty Years War'

More, Thomas. *Utopia, IV, The Yale Edition of the Complete Works of Saint Thomas More*, eds E. Sartz and J. H. Hexter (New Haven: Yale University Press, 1965)

Morgan, Hiram. *Tyrone's Rebellion: The Outbreak of the Nine Years War in Ireland* (Woodbridge and Rochester: Boydell Press, for Royal Historical Society, 1993)

—— (ed.). *Political Ideology in Ireland 1541–1641* (Dublin: Four Courts Press, 1999)

Morrill, John. 'Historical Introduction and Overview: The Un-English Civil War', in John R. Young (ed.), *Celtic Dimensions of the British Civil Wars* (Edinburgh: John Donald, 1997), ch. 1

—— (ed.). *The Scottish National Covenant in Its British Context 1638–51* (Edinburgh: Edinburgh University Press, 1990)

Morrissey, John. *Negotiating Colonialism: Gaelic-Irish Resistance to English Expansion in Early Modern Tipperary* (Cambridge: Historical Geography Research Group, 2003)

Mumford Jones, Howard. *O Strange New World – American Culture: The Formative Years* (New York: Viking Press, 1964)

Murray, L. P. 'The County Armagh Hearth Money Rolls, A.D. 1664', *Archivium Hibernicum*, vol. 8, 1936, pp. 121–202

Nash, Catherine. 'Historical Geographies of Modernity', in Brian Graham and Catherine Nash (eds), *Modern Historical Geographies* (Harlow: Prentice Hall, 2000)

Neely, W. G. 'The Ormond Butlers of County Kilkenny 1575–1715', in W. Nolan, and K. Whelan (eds), *Kilkenny: History and Society* (Dublin: Geography Publications, 1990), ch. 6

Nicholls, Kenneth W. *Gaelic and Gaelicised Ireland in the Later Middle Ages* (Dublin: Gill and Macmillan, 1972)

——. Map of Irish lordships *c.*1534, in T. W. Moody, F. X. Martin and F. J. Byrne (eds), *A New History of Ireland, III*: *Early Modern Ireland 1534–1691* (Oxford: Clarendon Press, 1976)

——. 'Continuity and Decay of Late Medieval Urban Settlement in Ireland'. Paper read to conference on Villages and Towns in Ireland 1600–1900, Trinity College Dublin, February 1984

——. 'Woodland Cover in pre-Modern Ireland', in William Nolan (ed.), *The Shaping of Ireland – The Geographical Perspective* (Cork: Mercier Press, 1986), ch. 6

——. new Introduction, *The Irish Fiants of the Tudor Sovereigns*, 4 vols (Dublin: Edmund Burke, 1994)

Nolan, William. *Fassadinin and Settlement and Society in South-East Ireland* (Dublin: Geography Publications, 1979), pp. 65–148

——. 'Society and Settlement in the Valley of Glenasmole c.1750–c.1900', in F. H. A. Aalen and Kevin Whelan (eds), *Dublin: City and County: From Prehistory to Present* (Dublin: Geography Publications, 1992), pp. 181–228

——, and Thomas G. McGrath (eds). *Tipperary: History and Society* (Dublin: Geography Publications, 1985)

——, and Kevin Whelan (eds), *Kilkenny: History and Society* (Dublin: Geography Publications, 1990)

——, T. P. Power and Des Cowman (eds). *Waterford: History and Society*. (Dublin: Geography Publications, 1992), pp. 199–226

——, Liam Ronayne and Máiréad Dunlevy (eds). *Donegal: History and Society* (Dublin: Geography Publications, 1995)

——, and Timothy P. O'Neill (eds), *Offaly: History and Society* (Dublin: Geography Publications, 1998)

Noonan, K. '"The Cruell Pressure of an Enraged Barbarous People": Irish and English Identity in Seventeenth-Century Policy and Propaganda', *Historical Journal*, vol. 41, no. 1, 1998, pp. 151–78

Nora Pierre (ed). *Realms of Memory: The Construction of the French Past. Vol. 1. Conflicts and Divisions* (New York and Chichester, West Sussex: Columbia University Press, 1996) Vol. 2 *Traditions* (1997) and Vol. 3 *Symbols* (1998)

Nugent, Patrick. 'A Historical Geography of the Transformation in the Territorial Organisation of Gaelic Society in County Clare during the Early Modern Period', unpublished Ph.D. thesis, University College Cork, 2002

Ó Buachalla, Breandán. 'Annála Ríoghtachta Éireann is Foras Feasa ar Éirinn: An Comthéacs Comhaimseartha', *Studia Hibernica*, vols 22–3, 1982–3, pp. 59–105

——. *Aisling Ghéar: Na Stiobhartaigh agus an tAos Léinn* (Baile Átha Cliath: An Clóchomhar, 1996)

Ó Ceallaigh, Daltún (ed.). *New Perspectives on Ireland: Colonialism and Identity* (Dublin: Léirmheas, 1998)

Ó Ceallaigh, Seámus. *Gleanings from Ulster History – Punann ó Chois Bhanna* (Cork: Cork University Press, 1951)

Ó Ciardha, Éamonn. 'Tories and Moss-Troopers, Scotland and Ireland in the Interregnum: A Political Dimension', in John R. Young (ed.), *Celtic Dimensions of the British Civil Wars* (Edinburgh: John Donald, 1997), ch. 8

Ó Cíosáin, Niall. *Print and Popular Culture in Ireland, 1750–1850* (London and Basingstoke: Macmillan, 1997)

Ó Conbhuidhe, Colmcille. 'The Lands of St. Mary's Abbey, Dublin', *Proceedings of the Royal Irish Academy*, vol. 62C, 1962, pp. 21–84, and accompanying map

Ó Conchúir, Breandán. *Scríobhaithe Chorcaí 1700–1850* (Baile Átha Cliath: An Clóchomar, 1982)

——. 'Na Cúirteanna Éigse I gCúige Mumhan', in *Saoi na hÉigse: Aistí in ómós do Sheán Ó Tuama*, eds Pádraigín Riggs, Breandán Ó Conchúir and Seán Ó Coileán (Baile Átha Cliath: An Clóchomhar, 2000), pp. 55–81

Ó Corbuí, Máirtín. *Tipperary* (Dingle: Brandon, 1991)

Ó Crualaoich, Gearóid. 'Non-Sovereignty Queen: Aspects of the Otherworld Female in Irish Hag Legends: The Case of *Cailleach Bhéarra*', *Béaloideas*, 1994–5, pp. 147–62

——. *The Book of the Cailleach: Stories of the Wise-Woman Healer* (Cork: Cork University Press, 2003)

Ó Cuív, B. *A View of the Irish Language* (Dublin: Stationery Office, 1969)

——. 'The Irish Language in the Early Modern Period', in T. W. Moody, F. X. Martin and F. J. Byrne (eds), *A New History of Ireland, III: Early Modern Ireland 1534–1691* (Oxford: Clarendon Press, 1976), pp. 526–30

Ó Drisceóil, P. (ed.). *Culture in Ireland – Regions, Identity and Power* (Belfast: Institute of Irish Studies, Queen's University Belfast, 1993)

Ó Fearghail, Conchubhair. 'The Evolution of Catholic Parishes in Dublin City from the Sixteenth to the Nineteenth centuries', in F. H. A. Aalen and Kevin Whelan (eds), *Dublin City and County: From Prehistory to Present* (Dublin: Geography Publications, 1992), pp. 229–50

Ó Fiaich, Tomás. 'Filíocht Uladh mar fhoinse don stair shóisialta san 18ú hAois', *Studia Hibernica*, vols 11–12, 1971–2, pp. 80–129

Ó Laidhin, Tomás (ed.). *Sidney State Papers, 1565–70* (Dublin: Irish Manuscripts Commission, 1962)

Ó Muraíle, Nollaig. 'Settlement and Place-Names', in Patrick J. Duffy, David Edwards and Elizabeth Fitzpatrick (eds), *Gaelic Ireland: Land, Lordship and Settlement c.1250–c.1650* (Dublin and Portland: Four Courts Press, 2001), ch. 8

Ó Murchú, C. D. 'Land and Society in Seventeenth-Century Clare', unpublished Ph.D. thesis, University College Galway, 1982

Ó Siochrú, Micheál. *Confederate Ireland 1642–1649* (Dublin: Four Courts Press, 1999)

Ó Tuama, Seán. *Repossessions: Selected Essays in the Irish Literary Heritage* (Cork: Cork University Press, 1995)

——, and Thomas Kinsella. *An Duanaire 1600–1900: Poems of the Dispossessed* (Mountrath/Portlaoise: Dolmen Press, 1981)

O'Connor, Frank. *Leinster, Munster and Connaught* (London: R. Hale, 1950)

O'Connor, Patrick J. *Exploring Limerick's Past: An Historical Geography of Urban Development in County and City* (Limerick: Oireacht na Mumhan, 1987)

——. *Fairs and Markets in Ireland: A Cultural Geography* (Midleton: Oireacht na Mumhan, 2003)

O'Donovan, John (ed. and trans.). *Annála Rioghachta Éireann: Annals of the Kingdom of Ireland by the Four Masters from the Earliest Times to the Year 1616*, vols 1–7, 3rd edn. (Dublin: Edmund Burke, 1998)

O'Dowd, Mary. 'Gaelic Economy and Society', in Ciaran Brady and Raymond Gillespie (eds), *Natives and Newcomers: Essays in the Making of Irish Colonial Society 1534–1641* (Dublin: Irish Academic Press, 1986), ch. 5

——. *Power, Politics and Land: Early Modern Sligo 1568–1688* (Belfast: Institute of Irish Studies, Queen's Univeristy Belfast, 1991)

O'Dwyer, Sir Michael. *The O'Dwyers of Kilnamanagh: The History of an Irish Sept* (Herts: Oahspe, 1933)

O'Faolain, Sean. *The Irish* (1947: rev. edn. Middlesex: Penguin Books, 1969)

——. *The Great O'Neill – A Biography of Hugh O'Neill, Earl of Tyrone 1550–1616* (Cork and Chester Springs, PA: Mercier Press and Dufour Editions, 1997)

O'Flanagan, Patrick. 'Markets and Fairs in Ireland, 1600–1800: Index of Economic Development and Regional Growth', *Journal of Historical Geography*, vol. 2, no. 4, 1985, pp. 364–78

——. 'Placenames and Change in the Irish Landscape', in William Nolan (ed.), *The Shaping of Ireland – The Geographical Perspective* (Cork: Mercier Press, 1986), pp. 111–23

——, and Cornelius G. Buttimer (eds). *Cork: History and Society* (Dublin: Geography Publications, 1993)

Ogborn, Miles. 'Historical Geographies of Globalisation c.1500–1800', in Brian Graham and Catherine Nash (eds), *Modern Historical Geographies* (Harlow: Pearson Education, 2000), pp. 43–69

Ogilvie, Sheilagh G. 'Germany and the Seventeenth Century Crisis', *Historical Journal*, vol. 35, no. 2, 1992, pp. 417–41

O'Grady, Desmond. *Tipperary* (Galway: Salmon Publishing, 1991)

O'Hanlon, J. *History of the Queen's County* (Dublin: Sealy, Bryers and Walker, 1914), vols 1 and 2

Ohlmeyer, Jane H. *Ireland: From Independence to Occupation 1641–1660* (Cambridge: Cambridge University Press, 1995)

——. 'The Wars of Religion 1603–1660', in Thomas Bartlett and Keith Jeffrey (eds), *A Military History of Ireland* (Cambridge: Cambridge University Press, 1996), ch. 8

O'Kane, Finola. *Landscape Design in Eighteenth Century Ireland: Mixing Foreign Trees with the Natives* (Cork: Cork University Press, 2004)

O'Keefe, Tadgh. 'Medieval Frontiers and Fortifications: The Pale and Its Evolution', in F. H. A. Aalen and Kevin Whelan (eds), *Dublin City and County: From Prehistory to Present* (Dublin: Geography Publications, 1992), pp. 57–77

O'Kelly, Owen. *The Place-Names of County Kilkenny* (Kilkenny: Kilkenny Archaeological Society, 1985)

O'Mahony, S. C. 'Cromwellian Transplantation from Limerick, 1653', *North Munster Antiquarian Journal*, vol. 40, 2000, pp. 29–52

——. 'The Manor Courts of the Earl of Thomond 1666–1686', *Analecta Hibernica*, vol. 38, 2004, pp. 135–220

O'Meara, John. 'The O'Mearas of Lissinisky', *Tipperary Historical Journal*, vol. 9, 1996, pp. 117–35

O'Rahilly, Cecile (ed.). *Five Seventeenth-Century Political Poems* (Dublin: Dublin Institute for Advanced Studies, 1952)

O'Riordan, Michelle. *The Gaelic Mind and the Collapse of the Gaelic World* (Cork: Cork University Press, 1990)

Orme, A. R. *Ireland* (Chicago: Aldine Publishing, 1970)

——. 'Segregation as a Feature of Urban Development in Medieval and Plantation Ireland', *Geographical Viewpoint*, vol. 2, no. 3, 1971, pp. 193–206

Ortelius, Abraham. *Theatrum Orbis Terrarum* (London, 1606)

O'Sullivan, Paul (ed.). *Newcastle Lyons: A Parish of the Pale* (Dublin: CDVEC Curriculum Development Unit, 1986)

Otway-Ruthven, Jocelyn. 'The Medieval Church Lands of County Dublin', in John Watt, John Morrill and F. X. Martin (eds), *Medieval Studies Presented to Aubrey Gwynn, S.J.* (Dublin: C. Ó Lochlainn, 1961), pp. 54–73

Pagden, Anthony. *Lords of All the World: Ideologies of Empire in Spain, Britain and France c.1500–c.1800* (New Haven: Yale University Press, 1995)

Palmer, Patricia. *Language and Conquest in Early Modern Ireland* (Cambridge: Cambridge University Press, 2001)

Parker, Geoffrey. *The Military Revolution Revisited* (Cambridge: Cambridge University Press, 1988)

Patterson, Nerys. 'Brehon Law in Late Medieval Ireland: "Antiquarian and Obsolete" or "Traditional and Functional"?', *Cambridge Medieval Celtic Studies*, vol. 17, 1989, pp. 43–63

Paullin, C. O., and J. K. Wright. *Atlas of the Historical Geography of the United States* (New York: Carnegie Institution, 1932)

Pawlisch, Hans S. *Sir John Davies and the Conquest of Ireland – A Study in Legal Imperialism* (Cambridge: Cambridge University Press, 1985)

Pender, Seamus (ed.). *A Census of Ireland circa 1659 with supplementary material from the poll money ordinances 1660–1661* (Dublin: Irish Manuscripts Commission, 1939)

—— (ed.), *A Census of Ireland, c. 1659 with essential materials from the poll-money ordinances 1660–1661* (Dublin: Irish Manuscripts Commission, 2002), with a new Introduction by William J. Smyth

Perceval-Maxwell, M. *The Scottish Migration to Ulster in the Reign of James I* (London: Routledge and Kegan Paul, 1973)

——. *The Outbreak of the Irish Rebellion of 1641* (Dublin: Gill and Macmillan, 1994)

Petty, William. *Hiberniae Delineatio* (London: s.n., 1685)

——. *Political Anatomy of Ireland 1672* (London: Brown and Rogers, 1691; repr. Shannon: Irish University Press , 1970)

Philo, Chris. 'Foucault's Geography', *Environment and Planning D. Society and Space*, vol. 10, 1992, pp. 137–61

Pilsworth, N. J. 'Census or Poll-Tax', *Journal of the Royal Society of Antiquaries of Ireland*, 1943, pp. 22–4

Pine, Richard. *Brian Friel and Ireland's Drama* (London and New York: Routledge, 1990)

Pocock, J. G. A. 'The Atlantic Archipelago and the War of the Three Kingdoms', in John Morrill (ed.), *The British Problem 1534–1707* (Basingstoke and London: Macmillan Press, 1996), ch. 7

Poovey, Mary. *A History of the Modern Fact: Problems of Knowledge in the Sciences of Wealth and Society* (Chicago: University of Chicago Press, 1998)

Power, T. P. *Land, Politics and Society in Eighteenth-Century Tipperary* (Oxford: Clarendon Press, 1993)

Prendergast, John P. *The Cromwellian Settlement of Ireland* (Dublin: McGlashan and Gill, 1875)

Pritchett, V. S. *Dublin: A Portrait* (London and New York: Harper and Row, 1971)

Quinn, David B. 'Sir Thomas Smith and the Beginnings of English Colonial Theory,' *Proceedings of the American Philosophical Society*, vol. 99, 1945, pp. 543–60

——. 'Ireland and Seventeenth Century European Expansion,' *Historical Studies*, vol. 1, 1958, pp. 318–44

——. *Raleigh and the British Empire* (London: Pelican Books, 1962)

——. 'The Munster Plantation: Problems and Opportunities', *Journal of the Cork Historical and Archaeological Society*, vol. 71, 1966, pp. 19–41

——. *The Elizabethans and the Irish* (Ithaca, NY: Cornell University Press, 1966)

——, and Kenneth W. Nicholls. 'Ireland in 1534', in T. W. Moody, F. X. Martin and F. J. Byrne (eds), *A New History of Ireland, III: Early Modern Ireland 1534–1691* (Oxford: Clarendon Press, 1976), pp. 1–38

Rabb, T. K. *Enterprise and Empire: Merchant and Gentry in the Expansion of England 1575–1630* (Cambridge, MA: Harvard University Press, 1967)

Rackham, Oliver. *The History of the Countryside* (London: Dent, 1986)

Razell, P. E. 'Population Growth and Economic Change in Eighteenth- and Nineteenth-Century England and Ireland', in E. Jones and G. Mingay (eds), *Land, Labour and Population in the Industrial Revolution* (London: Edward Arnold, 1967), pp. 268–75

Read, Conyers. *Mr Secretary, Walsingham and the Policy of Queen Elizabeth* (Cambridge: Clarendon, 1925)

Rees, Alwyn, and Brinley Rees. *Celtic Heritage: Ancient Tradition in Ireland and Wales* (London: Thames and Hudson, 1961)

Reeves-Smyth, T., and F. Hammond (eds). *Landscape Archaeology in Ireland* (Oxford: British Archaeological Reports, No. 116, 1983)

Reinhard Lupton, Julia. '"Mapping Mutability" or Spenser's Irish Plot', in Brendan Bradshaw, Andrew Hadfield and Willy Maley (eds), *Representing Ireland: Literature and the Origins of Conflict, 1534–1660* (Cambridge: Cambridge University Press, 1993), ch. 6

Reps, J. *The Making of Urban America: A History of City Planning in the United States* (Princeton, NJ: Princeton University Press, 1965)

Reynolds, Henry. *The Other Side of the Frontier* (Harmondsworth and Ringwood, Victoria: Penguin, 1982)

Roberts, B. K., and R. E Glasscock (eds). *Village, Fields and Frontiers*, BAR International Series, 185 (Oxford:British Archaeological Reports, 1983)

Robinson, Philip S. *The Plantation of Ulster: A British settlement in an Irish Landscape 1600–1670* (Dublin: Gill and Macmillan, 1984; 2nd edn. Belfast: Ulster Historical Series, 1994)

——. 'The Ulster Plantation and Its Impact on the Settlement Pattern of Co. Tyrone', in Charles Dillon and Henry A. Jeffries (eds), *Tyrone: History and Society* (Dublin: Geography Publications, 2000), ch. 8

Roebuck, P. (ed.). *Plantation to Partition: Essays in Ulster History in Honour of John McCracken* (Belfast: Blackstaff Press, 1981)

Rokkan, S. 'Territories, Centres and Peoples in Europe', in J. Gottman (ed.), *Centre and Periphery* (London and Beverly Hills: Sage Publications, 1980), pp. 161–80

Ronan, Myles. *The Reformation in Dublin 1536–1558* (London: Longmans, Green, 1926)

——. 'Archbishop Bulkeley's Visitation of Dublin, 1630', in *Archivium Hibernicum*, vol. 8, 1941, pp. 56–98

——. 'Royal Visitation of Dublin, 1615' in *Archivium Hibernicum*, vol. 8, 1941, pp. 7–35

Ross, Kurt. *Codex Mendoza: Aztec Manuscript* (Fribourg: Liber, 1978–84)

Rossiter, C. *The First American Revolution* (New York: Harcourt Brace, 1956)

Rowse, A.L. *The England of Elizabeth* (London: Macmillan, 1950)

——. *The Expansion of Elizabethan England* (London: Macmillan, 1957)

——. *The Elizabethans and America* (New York: Harper, 1959)

Ruane, Joseph. 'Colonialism and the Interpretation of Irish Historical Development', in Marilyn Silverman and P. H. Gulliver (eds), *Approaching the Past: Historical Anthropology through Irish Case Studies* (New York: Columbia University Press, 1992), pp. 236–92

Russell, Conrad. *The Fall of the British Monarchies 1637–1642* (Oxford: Oxford University Press, 1991)

Ryan, Thomas. *Mooncoin – Landlords and Tenants 1650–1977* (Mooncoin: Thomas Ryan, 1977)

Sack, Robert D. *Human Territoriality: Its Theory and History* (Cambridge: Cambridge University Press, 1986)

Said, Edward W. *Culture and Imperialism* (London: Vintage Chatto and Windus, 1993)

——. *Nationalism, Colonialism and Literature: Yeats and Decolonisation* (Derry: Field Day, 1988)

Sapir, Edward. *Culture, Language and Personality* (Berkeley, CA: University of California Press, 1949)

Sauer, Carl. O. *The Early Spanish Main* (Berkeley, CA: University of California Press, 1966)

Schama, Simon. *Landscape and Memory* (London: HarperCollins, 1995)

Scheider, Louis, and Charles M. Bonjean (eds). *The Idea of Culture in the Social Sciences* (Cambridge: Cambridge University Press, 1970)

Seed, Patricia. *Ceremonies of Possession in Europe's Conquest of the New World* (Cambridge: Cambridge University Press, 1996)

Sheehan, Anthony. 'Irish Towns in a Period of Change 1558–1625', in Ciaran Brady and

Raymond Gillespie (eds), *Natives and Newcomers: Essays in the Making of Irish Colonial Society 1534–1641* (Dublin: Irish Academic Press, 1986), pp. 93–119

Sheridan, Alan. *Michel Foucault: The Will to Truth* (London and New York: Tavistock, 1980)

Sidney, Philip. *A Defence of Poetry*, ed. J. A. Van Dorstan (Oxford: Oxford University Press, 1966)

Silverman, Marilyn, and P. H. Gulliver (eds). *Approaching the Past: Historical Anthropology through Irish Case Studies* (New York: Columbia University Press, 1992

Simington, R. C. (ed.). *The Civil Survey A.D. 1654–1656, I and II, County of Tipperary* (Dublin: Irish Manuscripts Commission, 1931–4)

—— (ed.). *The Civil Survey A.D. 1654–1656; III, Counties Donegal, Derry and Tyrone* (Dublin, Irish Manuscripts Commission, 1937)

—— (ed.). *The Civil Survey A.D. 1654–1656, IV, County Limerick* (Dublin, Irish Manuscripts Commission, 1938)

—— (ed.). *The Civil Survey A.D. 1654–1656, V, County Meath* (Dublin, Irish Manuscripts Commission, 1940)

—— (ed.). *The Civil Survey A.D. 1654–1656, VI, Co. Waterford, Muskerry Barony (Co. Cork) and Kilkenny City* (Dublin, Irish Manuscripts Commission, 1942)

—— (ed.). *The Civil Survey A.D. 1654–1656, VII, County of Dublin* (Dublin, Irish Manuscripts Commission, 1945)

—— (ed). *The Civil Survey A.D. 1654–1656, VIII, County of Kildare* (Dublin: Irish Manuscripts Commission, 1952)

—— (ed.). *The Civil Survey, A.D. 1654–1656, IX, County Wexford* (Dublin, Irish Manuscripts Commission, 1953)

——. 'A "Census" of Ireland, c.1659 – The Term "Titulado"', *Analecta Hibernica*, vol. 12, 1943, pp. 177–8

——. *The Transplantation to Connacht 1654–58* (Dublin: Irish University Press, 1970)

Simms, Anngret. 'Rural Settlement in Medieval Ireland: The example of the Royal Manors of Newcastle Lyons and Esker in South County Dublin', in B. K. Roberts and R. E. Glasscock (eds), *Village, Fields and Frontiers* (Oxford: BAR International Series, 185, 1983), pp. 135–52

——. 'Core and Periphery in Medieval Europe: The Irish Experience in a Wider Context', in William J. Smyth and Kevin Whelan (eds), *Common Ground: Essays on the Historical Geography of Ireland* (Cork: Cork University Press, 1988), pp. 22–40

——, and J. H. Andrews (eds), *Irish Country Towns*, RTE Thomas Davis Lectures (Cork: Mercier Press, 1994)

——, and Patricia Fagan. 'Villages in County Dublin: Their Origins and Inheritance', in F. H. A Aalen and KevinWhelan (eds), *Dublin City and County: From Prehistory to Present* (Dublin: Geography Publications, 1992), ch. 5

Simms, Hilary. 'Violence in County Armagh, 1641', in Brian MacCurta (ed.), *Ulster 1641: Aspects of the Rising* (Belfast: Institute of Irish Studies, Queen's University Belfast, 1993), pp. 123–38

Simms, J. G. 'The Civil Survey, 1654–1656', *Irish Historical Studies*, vol. 9, no. 35, 1955, pp. 253–63

——. *The Williamite Confiscations in Ireland 1690–1703* (London: Faber and Faber, 1956)

Simms, Katharine. *From Kings to Warlords: The Changing Political Structure of Gaelic Ireland in the Later Middle Ages* (Woodbridge: Boyell Press, 1987)

Skelton, R. A. (ed.). *Saxton's Survey of England and Wales* (Amsterdam: Nico Israel, 1974)

——, and J. Summerson. *A Description of the Maps and Architectural Drawings in the Collection Made by William Cecil, Baron Burghley now at Hatfield House* (Oxford: Roxburghe Club, 1971)

Smyth, Gerry. *Space and the Irish Cultural Imagination* (Basingstoke: Palgrave, 2001)

Smyth, Seamus. 'Irish Emigration 1700–1920', in P. Emmer and M. Morner (eds), *European Expansion and Migration* (Oxford: Oxford University Press, 1992), pp. 49–78

Smyth, William J. 'Estate Records and the Making of the Irish Landscape', *Irish Geography*, vol. 9, 1976, pp. 26–49

——. 'The Western Isle of Ireland and the Eastern Seaboard of America: England's First Frontiers', *Irish Geography*, vol. 11, 1978, pp. 1–22

——. 'Land Values, Landownership and Population Patterns in County Tipperary for 1641–60 and 1841–50; Some Comparisons', in L. M. Cullen and F. Furet (eds), *Ireland*

and France, 17th–20th Centuries – Towards a Comparative Study of Rural History (Paris: Éditions de l'École des Hautes Études en Sciences Sociales, 1980), pp. 159–94

——. 'The Long-Term Cultural Impact of the Normans in Ireland', unpublished lecture, Cumann Merriman, Lahinch, August 1982

——. 'Property, Patronage and Population: Reconstructing the Human Geography of Mid-Seventeenth Century Tipperary', in W. Nolan (ed.), Tipperary: History and Society, (Dublin, Geography Publications, 1985), pp. 104–38

——. 'Society and Settlement in Seventeenth Century Ireland: The Evidence of the "1659 Census"', in W. J. Smyth and K. Whelan (eds), Common Ground: Essays on the Historical Geography of Ireland (Cork: Cork University Press, 1988), pp. 55–83

——. 'The Dynamic Quality of Irish "Village" Life – A Reassessment', in J. M. Dewailly and R. Dion (eds), Campagnes et Littoraux d'Europe (Melanges Offert à Pierre Flatrès) (Lille, Société de Géographie de Lille, Institut de Géographie de Lille, 1988)

——. 'Territorial, Social and Settlement Hierarchies in Seventeenth Century Kilkenny', in W. Nolan and K. Whelan (eds), Kilkenny: History and Society (Dublin, Geography Publications, 1990), pp. 125–58

——. 'Towns and Townlife in Mid-17th-Century Co. Tipperary', Tipperary Historical Journal, vol. 4, 1991, pp. 163–70

——. 'Exploring the Social and Cultural Topographies of Sixteenth- and Seventeenth-Century County Dublin', in F. H. A. Aalen and Kevin Whelan (eds), Dubin City and County: From Prehisory to Present (Dublin, Geography Publications, 1992), ch. 6

——. 'Making the Documents of Conquest Speak: The Transformation of Property, Society, and Settlement in Seventeenth Century Counties Kilkenny and Tipperary', in Marilyn Silverman and P. H. Gulliver (eds), Approaching the Past: Historical Anthropology through Irish Case Studies (New York: Columbia University Press, 1992), pp. 276–86

——. 'Social, Economic and Landscape Transformations in County Cork from the Mid-Eighteenth to the Mid-Nineteenth Century', in Patrick O'Flanagan and Cornelius G. Buttimer (eds), Cork: History and Society (Dublin: Geography Publications, 1993), pp. 655–98

——. 'Wrestling with Petty's Ghost: The Origins, Nature and Relevance of the so-called "1659 Census"', new Introduction in Seamus Pender (ed.), A Census of Ireland circa 1659 (Dublin: Irish Manuscripts Commission, 2002), pp. v–lxii

——. Atlas of Family Names in Ireland: Part I, CD on Documents of Ireland, University College Cork, 2002

——. 'Excavating, Mapping and Interrogating Ancestral Terrains: Towards a Cultural Geography of First and Second Names in Ireland', in H. Clarke, M. Hennessy and J. Prunty (eds), Surveying Ireland's Past: Multidisciplinary Essays in Honour of Anngret Simms (Dublin: Geography Publications, 2004), pp. 243–80

——. 'Semi-Colonial Ireland?', in Alan Baker (ed.), Home and Colonial: Essays in Honour of Robin A. Butlin (Cambridge: Cambridge University Press Historical Geography Research Series, No. 39, October 2004), pp. 53–65

Sopher, David. 'Notes on the Spatial Patterning of Culture', in Louis Scheider and Charles M. Bonjean (eds), The Idea of Culture in the Social Sciences (Cambridge: Cambridge University Press, 1970), ch. 6

Speed, John. The Theatre of the Empire of Great Britaine (London: Dudbury and Humble, 1611)

Spenser, Edmund. A View of the State of Ireland, ed. W. L. Renwick (Oxford: Clarendon Press, 1970)

Stanihurst, Richard. 'A Treatise Containing a Plain and Perfect Description of Ireland' (1577), in R. Holinshed, The Chronicles of England, Scotland and Ireland (1587), 3 vols

Starkey, Armstrong. European and Native American Warfare 1675–1810 (London: University College London Press, 1988)

Steele, Ian K. The English Atlantic: An Exploration of Communications and Community (New York and Oxford: Oxford University Press, 1986)

Stephens, Nicholas, and Robin Glasscock (eds), Irish Geographical Studies in Honour of E. Estyn Evans (Belfast: Department of Geography, Queen's University Belfast, 1970)

Stevenson, David. The Scottish Revolution 1637–1644: The Triumph of the Covenanters (Newton Abbot: Saltire, 1973)

———. *Scottish Covenanters and Irish Confederates. Scottish-Irish Relations in the Mid-Seventeenth Century* (Belfast: Ulster Historical Foundation, 1981)

Stewart, Alan. *Philip Sidney: A Double Life* (London: Chatto and Windus, 2001)

Swift, Jonathan. 'A Letter from a Member of the House of Commons of Ireland', in Joseph McMinn (ed.), *Swift's Irish Pamphlets: An Introductory Selection* (Gerrards Cross: Colin Smythe, 1991)

Swift, Michael. *Historical Maps of Ireland* (London: Parkgate Books, 1999)

Systema Agriculturae, Being the Mystery of Husbandry Discovered and Layd Open by J. W. (London: Thomas Dring, 1675)

Taussig, Michael. *The Nervous System* (New York: Routledge, 1991)

Temple, J. *The Irish Rebellion* (London: R. White, for Samuel Gellibrand, 1646)

Theibault, John. 'The Rhetoric of Death and Destruction in the Thirty Years War', *Journal of Social History*, vol. 27, no. 2, 1993, pp. 271–98

Thirst, Joan. *Tudor Enclosures* (London: Routledge and Kegan Paul, 1959)

Tilly, Charles. *Coercion, Capital and European States, AD 900–1990* (Cambridge, MA: Harvard University Press, 1990)

Treadwell, V. W. 'The Establishment of the Farm in the Irish Customs, 1603–10', *English Historical Review*, vol. 93, 1978, pp. 580–616

———. *Buckingham and Ireland 1616–1628 – A Study in Anglo-Irish Politics* (Dublin: Four Courts Press, 1998)

Truxes, Thomas M. *Irish-American Trade 1660–1783* (Cambridge and New York: Cambridge University Press, 1988)

Tunnard, C., and H. H. Reed. *American Skyline: The Growth and Form of Our Cities and Towns* (New York: New American Library, 1956)

Turner, Brian S. 'An Observation on Settler Names in Fermanagh', *Clogher Record*, vol. 8, 1975, pp. 285–9

Tynan, Michael. *Catholic Instruction in Ireland 1720–1980* (Dublin: Four Courts Press, 1985)

Ver Steeg, C. L. *America – The Formative Years 1607–1763* (London: Macmillan, 1965)

Verlinden, Charles. *The Beginnings of Modern Colonisation* (Ithaca, NY: Cornell University Press, 1970)

Wachtel, N. *The Vision of the Vanquished: The Spanish Conquest of Peru through Indian Eyes, 1530–1570* (Hassocks: Harvester Press, 1977)

Walsh, Robert. *Fingal and Its Churches* (Dublin: McGee, 1888)

Walton, Julian. 'The Subsidy Roll of Co. Waterford, 1662', *Analecta Hibernica*, vol. 30, 1982, pp. 49–95

———. 'The Hearth Money Rolls of County Kilkenny – Extracted from the Carrigan MSS', *Irish Genealogist*, vol. 5, no. 1, 1985, and no. 2, 1985

Wells, R. V. *The Population of the British Colonies in America before 1776* (Princeton, NJ: Princeton University Press, 1975)

Wertenbaker, T. J. *The Founding of American Civilisation – The Middle Colonies* (New York: Cooper Square Publishers, 1938)

West, Robert C. 'Aboriginal and Colonial Geography of Latin America', in Brian W. Blouet and Olivia W. Blouet (eds), *Latin America and the Caribbean* (New York: Wiley, 1997), pp. 45–88

Wheeler, James S. *Cromwell in Ireland* (Dublin: Gill and Macmillan, 1999)

Whelan, Kevin. 'The Catholic Parish, the Catholic Chapel and Village Development in Ireland', *Irish Geography*, vol. 16, 1983, pp. 1–15

———. 'The Bases of Regionalism', in P. Ó Drisceóil (ed.), *Culture in Ireland – Regions, Identity and Power* (Belfast: Institute of Irish Studies, Queen's University Belfast, 1993), pp. 5–62

———. 'The Geography of Hurling', *History Ireland*, vol.1, 1993, pp. 27–31

———. *The Tree of Liberty: Radicalism, Catholicism and the Constitution of Irish Identity* (Cork: Cork University Press, 1996)

———. 'An Underground Gentry: Catholic Middlemen in the 18th Century', in J. S. Donnelly and Kerby Miller (eds), *Irish Popular Culture 1650–1850* (Dublin: Irish Academic Press, 1998), pp. 118–72

———, and T. P. Power (eds). *Endurance and Emergence in Ireland in the Eighteenth Century* (Dublin: Irish Academic Press, 1990)

——, and William Nolan (eds). *Wexford: History and Society* (Dublin: Geography Publications, 1987)

Williams, N. J. A. (ed.). *Pairlement Chloinne Tomáis* (Dublin: Dublin Institute for Advanced Studies, 1982)

Wolf, E. R. *Sons of the Shaking Earth: The People of Mexico and Guatemala and Their Lands, History and Culture* (Chicago and London : University of Chicago Press, 1959)

Wood, Herbert (ed.). *Sir James Perrott's The Chronicle of Ireland 1584–1608* (Dublin: Irish Manuscripts Commission, 1933)

Woodward, David (ed.). *Art and Cartography. Six Historical Essays* (Chicago: University of Chicago Press, 1987)

Woodward, Donald. 'The Anglo-Irish Livestock Trade in the Seventeenth Century', *Irish Historical Studies*, vol. 17, 1973, pp. 489–523

——. 'A Comparative Study of the Irish and Scottish Livestock Trades in the Seventeenth Century', in L. M Cullen and T. C. Smout (eds), *Comparative Aspects of Scottish and Irish Economic and Social History* (Edinburgh: John Donald, 1977), pp. 147–64

Woolway, Joanne. 'Significant Spaces in Spencer's *Vewe of the Present State of Ireland*', *Early Modern Literary Studies*, vol. 4, no. 2, Special Issue 3. 1998, pp. 1–21

Wreford Watson, J. 'The Indian Heritage', in J Wreford Watson, *North America: Its Countries and Regions* (New York: Praeger, 1967), pp. 77–109

Wright, L. B. *The Cultural Life of the American Colonies 1607–1763* (London: Hamish Hamilton, 1957)

——. *Everyday Life in Colonial America* (London: Hamish Hamilton, 1965)

Yates, Francis A. *Astraea: The Imperial Theme in the Sixteenth Century* (London and Boston: Ark, 1985)

Yelling, J. A. 'Agriculture 1500–1730', in R. A. Dodgshon and R. A. Butlin (eds), *An Historical Geography of England and Wales* (London: Academic Press, 1978), pp. 151–72

Young, John R. (ed.). *Celtic Dimensions of the British Civil Wars* (Edinburgh: John Donald, 1997)

Zelinsky, Wilbur. *Cultural Geography of the United States* (New Jersey: Prentice-Hall, 1973)

Manuscript Sources

Bibliothèque Nationale, Paris

Cartes des baronies d'Irlande – Hiberniae Regnum – Sir William Petty's manuscript map collection of 214 barony maps of Ireland (1 and 2 Fonds Anglais)

Bodleian Library, Oxford

A booke of the King's lands … Ulster, 1608 (Ms Rawlinson A.237)

Sir William Petty's full manuscript collection (on microfilm: Mss film 935-950)

Bolton Library, Cashel

O'Callaghan/Viscount Lismore estate papers (Looney Collection)

British Library

Original letters and papers, including 'A Discourse on Ireland', in the time of Queen Elizabeth I, Cotton Collection (Titus B XI–XII)

Map showing distributions of barracks, 1700, Kings Collection (2f. 41)

'Cotton' Ireland map *c*.1526, Cotton Collection (Ms. Augustus I, ii, 21)

Leix and Offaly map *c*.1561, Cotton Collection (Ms. Augustus, 1, ii, 40)

Co. Longford plantation maps *c*.1618, Cotton Collection (Ms. Augustus, 1, ii, 25)

Norden's (or Bodley's) maps of the Escheated Counties in Ulster *c*.1610, Cotton Collection (Ms. Augustus, I, ii, 44)

Nowell, Laurence, Ireland map 1564–5 (Add Ms. 62540)

Sir William Petty's full manuscript collections (originally held by the Earl of Shelburne, including Literary MSS, Writings and Official Papers on Ireland, Letters, '1659 Census' and Down Survey Mss. Maps)

Revenue of England and Ireland, Anno 1659, and the charges of the Army and Navy (Add. Ms. 32, 471)

Rocque, J., Map of County of Dublin, Kings Collection (Map Library)

Saxton, Christopher, Atlas of England and Wales (Sp. Collection, Hunterian, Di.1.12)

Survey of the lands belonging to Edward Roberts Esq by Thos. Taylor (Harley Ms. 4784)

Trustees Survey maps (1701) counties Leitrim, Mayo and Sligo (Add. Mss.14405)

Lambert Palace Library

Incomplete abstract of 1732 Census of Ireland, barony by barony (Ms. 1742)

Marsh's Library Dublin

Allocation of lots to the 'Adventurers' per barony (Ms. Z.2.[1.5])

National Archives of Ireland

Abstract of grants of fairs and markets in Ireland in the Chancery Rolls 1293–1773

Books of Survey and Distribution (for counties Cavan, Cork, Dublin, Kilkenny, Meath, Tipperary)

Census of South Co. Dublin *c.*1650–52 for baronies of Uppercross and Newcastle (Ms. 2467)

O'Keefe (1904) manuscript copy of 1766 diocesan census of Cork, Cloyne and Ross (Ms. 4921)

Poll-money book for parish of Urney, Co. Tyrone (Ms. 469)

National Library of Ireland

Bartlett, Richard, Ulster Manuscript Maps (Ms. 2656)

Down Survey parish maps for Crannagh barony, Co. Kilkenny (Ms. 720)

Down Survey parish maps for Co. (East) Meath (Ms. 715)

Down Survey parish maps for Co. Waterford (Ms. 722)

Hearth Money Roll, Co. Tyrone (Ms. 9583)

Johnston, R./Simington, R. C. Composite Down Survey/OS six-inch maps (20D)

Raleigh, Sir Walter, manuscript map of his lands in Co. Cork (Ms. 16.L.33[18])

Presentments at the Sherriff's Court, Co. Kilkenny, 1637 (D.4052)

Tythes of Earl of Ormond for Co. Kilkenny in 1619 (D.3633)

National Maritime Museum, Greenwich

Map of Dublin harbour and Howth Head (B 8956/I)

Jobson, Francis, maps of the Province of Munster *c.* 1591 (Ms. P.49, 20 and Ms. P.49.27)

Map of Smerwick and the Dingle peninsula (Ms. P.49.31)

National Museum of Ireland

St Joseph's Aerial Photographic Collection for Ireland

Private Collection

Earl of Shelburne (Bowood House, Calne, Wiltshire)

Original Mss. volumes of so-called '1659 Census' compiled by William Petty (now in British Library)

Public Record Office, London

Bartlett, Richard, Map, *A Generalle Description of Ulster* (MPF 1/35)

Bartlett, Richard, *Map of South Ulster* (MPF 1/36)

Bodley Ulster plantation barony maps (MPF 1/35 and MPF 1/36)

Denizens in Ireland . . . encouraging Protestant strangers to plant in the kingdom of Ireland (Egerton Ms. 77)

Goghe, John, Ireland map, 1567 (MPF 1/68)

Grafton map of counties Mayo and Sligo, 1587 (MPF 1/71)

Lythe, Robert, Corkbeg fort map (MPF 1/36)

Lythe, Robert, *A Single Draght of Mounster* (MPF 1/73)
Mid-sixteenth-century Ireland map (MPF 1/72)
Norden, John, Ireland map *c.* 1610 (MPF 1/117)
North-east Ulster coastal map *c.*1580 (MPF 1/88)
Jobson, Francis, 1598 map of Ulster (MPF 1/312)
Rough map of Munster, *c.*1585–6 (MPF 1/273)
Wicklow and Ferns, proposed counties map (MPF 1/69)

Public Record Office of Northern Ireland
Down Survey barony and parish maps for counties Armagh, Down and Tyrone (D. 597)
Hearth Money Roll, Co. Tyrone (T. 283 D/2)
Poll-tax Return, Aghlow parish (T. 1365/3)
Raven, Thomas, Hamilton Estate Maps of 1625 (copies of the originals at Council Office, Bangor)

Registry of Deeds, Kings Inns
Deeds relating to Co. Tipperary townlands from 1708 (with particular reference to the parishes of Shanrahan, Templetenny, Tullaghhorton and Whitechurch)

Religious Society of Friends Library, Dublin
Records and papers relating to the Grubb and Fennell families

Royal Irish Academy, Dublin
Ordnance Survey Letters for Co. Kilkenny, 2 vols (14.D.9; 14.D.10)
Ordnance Survey Letters for Co. Tipperary, 3 vols (14.F.18; 14.F.19; 14.F.20)
Tracts and Pamphlets (1578-1642)

Royal Society, London
An account of Popish clergy according to the return made April 1698 (Pepys Ms. Vii(1) and vii(2))
The Improvement of Ireland (14pp) (Cl.P.XXII.18)
List of all seamen, fishermen . . . in kingdom of Ireland, 1697 (Cl.P.19.3)
Letters of Sir William Petty (3160-3182)

Tipperary South County Museum
Poll-money book for Clonmel, 1661

Trinity College Dublin Department of Manuscripts
Browne, John, I and II, Map of Connacht and Clare (Ms. 1209/68)
Early seventeenth-century map (*c.*1601) of Ulster (Ms. 1209/14)
Jobson, Francis, map of Co. Cork (Ms. 1209/43)
Sea-chart of coastlands north from Co. Mayo around to Co. Dublin (Ms. 1209/18)
TCD 1641 Depositions, Mss 812-839 (including typescript summary volumes for all counties)
The Plat of Coleraine, *c.*1611 (Ms. 1209/24)
River Foyle and City of Londonderry 1625 (Ms. 1209/24)
The Towne and Castell of Monoghan, *c.*1611 (Ms. 1209/32)

Index